(ex·ploring)

SERIES

1. Investigating in a systematic way: examining. 2. Searching into or ranging over for the purpose of discovery.

Microsoft®

Access 2016

Comprehensive

Series Editor **Mary Anne Poatsy**

Cameron | Williams

Series Created by Dr. Robert T. Grauer

PEARSON

Boston   Columbus   Indianapolis   New York   San Francisco   Hoboken
Amsterdam   Cape Town   Dubai   London   Madrid   Milan   Munich   Paris   Montréal   Toronto
Delhi   Mexico City   São Paulo   Sydney   Hong Kong   Seoul   Singapore   Taipei   Tokyo

Vice President of Career Skills: Andrew Gilfillan
Senior Editor: Samantha Lewis
Team Lead, Project Management: Laura Burgess
Project Manager: Laura Karahalis
Program Manager: Emily Biberger
Development Editor: Barbara Stover
Editorial Assistant: Michael Campbell
Director of Product Marketing: Maggie Waples
Director of Field Marketing: Leigh Ann Sims
Product Marketing Manager: Kaylee Carlson
Field Marketing Managers: Molly Schmidt & Joanna Sabella
Marketing Coordinator: Susan Osterlitz
Senior Operations Specialist: Diane Peirano
Senior Art Director: Diane Ernsberger
Interior and Cover Design: Diane Ernsberger
Cover Photo: Courtesy of Shutterstock® Images
Associate Director of Design: Blair Brown
Senior Product Strategy Manager: Eric Hakanson
Product Manager, MyITLab: Zachary Alexander
Media Producer, MyITLab: Jaimie Noy
Digital Project Manager, MyITLab: Becca Lowe
Media Project Manager, Production: John Cassar
Full-Service Project Management: Jenna Vittorioso, Lumina Datamatics, Inc.
Composition: Lumina Datamatics, Inc.
Efficacy Curriculum Manager: Jessica Sieminski

Credits and acknowledgments borrowed from other sources and reproduced, with permission, in this textbook appear on the appropriate page within text.

Library of Congress Control Number: 2015956946

ISBN 10:   0-13-447945-9
ISBN 13: 978-0-13-447945-3

Dedications

For my husband, Ted, who unselfishly continues to take on more than his share to support me throughout the process; and for my children, Laura, Carolyn, and Teddy, whose encouragement and love have been inspiring.

Mary Anne Poatsy

I dedicate this book to my wife Anny, for supporting me through the writing process, to my nieces Daniela and Gabriela, who someday will be old enough to think it is cool their names are in a book, and to my students, who make a career in teaching fulfilling. May you all go forward, change the world and inspire others.

Eric Cameron

I offer thanks to my family and colleagues who have supported me on this journey. I would like to dedicate the work I have performed toward this undertaking to my little grandson, Yonason Meir (known for now as Mei-Mei), who as his name suggests, is the illumination in my life.

Jerri Williams

To my husband Dan, whose encouragement, patience, and love helped make this endeavor possible. Thank you for taking on the many additional tasks at home so that I could focus on writing.

Amy Rutledge

About the Authors

Mary Anne Poatsy, Series Editor, Windows 10 Author

Mary Anne is a senior faculty member at Montgomery County Community College, teaching various computer application and concepts courses in face-to-face and online environments. She holds a B.A. in Psychology and Education from Mount Holyoke College and an M.B.A. in Finance from Northwestern University's Kellogg Graduate School of Management.

Mary Anne has more than 12 years of educational experience. She is currently adjunct faculty at Gwynedd-Mercy College and Montgomery County Community College. She has also taught at Bucks County Community College and Muhlenberg College, as well as conducted personal training. Before teaching, she was Vice President at Shearson Lehman in the Municipal Bond Investment Banking Department.

Eric Cameron, Access Author

Eric Cameron is a tenured Associate Professor at Passaic County Community College, where he has taught in the Computer and Information Sciences department since 2001. He holds an M.S. in Computer Science and a B.S. degree in Computer Science with minors in Mathematics and Physics, both from Montclair State University. He currently co-chairs the College's General Education committee and served as a member of the College's Academic Assessment, College Writing, and Educational Technology committees at various points. Eric has also developed degrees in Graphic Design and Medical Informatics for the College. Eric previously worked as a software engineer both as a full-time employee and contractor, most recently for ITT/Exelis (now part of Harris Corporation).

This is Eric's fourth publication for Pearson, after authoring Web 2.0 and Windows 8 books in the Your Office series and co-authoring the Exploring Access 2013 text.

Jerri Williams, Access Author

Jerri Williams is a Senior Instructor at Montgomery County Community College in Pennsylvania. Jerri also works as an independent corporate trainer, technical editor, and content developer. She is interested in travel, cooking, movies, and tending to her colonial farmhouse. Jerri is married, and is the mother of two daughters, Holly (an Accounting graduate and full-time mother to an adorable son, Meir) and Gwyneth (a corporate defense attorney). Jerri and Gareth live in the suburbs of Philadelphia. They enjoy their home and garden, and spending time with family and good friends.

Amy Rutledge, Common Features Author

Amy Rutledge is a Special Instructor of Management Information Systems at Oakland University in Rochester, Michigan. She coordinates academic programs in Microsoft Office applications and introductory management information systems courses for the School of Business Administration. Before joining Oakland University as an instructor, Amy spent several years working for a music distribution company and automotive manufacturer in various corporate roles including IT project management. She holds a B.S. in Business Administration specializing in Management Information Systems, and a B.A. in French Modern Language and Literature. She holds an M.B.A from Oakland University. She resides in Michigan with her husband, Dan and daughters Emma and Jane.

Dr. Robert T. Grauer, Creator of the Exploring Series

Bob Grauer is an Associate Professor in the Department of Computer Information Systems at the University of Miami, where he is a multiple winner of the Outstanding Teaching Award in the School of Business, most recently in 2009. He has written numerous COBOL texts and is the vision behind the Exploring Office series, with more than three million books in print. His work has been translated into three foreign languages and is used in all aspects of higher education at both national and international levels. Bob Grauer has consulted for several major corporations including IBM and American Express. He received his Ph.D. in Operations Research in 1972 from the Polytechnic Institute of Brooklyn.

Brief Contents

Contents

Application Capstone Exercises

Acknowledgments

The Exploring team would like to acknowledge and thank all the reviewers who helped us throughout the years by providing us with their invaluable comments, suggestions, and constructive criticism.

Adriana Lumpkin
Midland College

Alan S. Abrahams
Virginia Tech

Alexandre C. Probst
Colorado Christian University

Ali Berrached
University of Houston–Downtown

Allen Alexander
Delaware Technical & Community College

Andrea Marchese
Maritime College, State University of
New York

Andrew Blitz
Broward College; Edison State College

Angel Norman
University of Tennessee, Knoxville

Angela Clark
University of South Alabama

Ann Rovetto
Horry-Georgetown Technical College

Astrid Todd
Guilford Technical Community College

Audrey Gillant
Maritime College, State University of
New York

Barbara Stover
Marion Technical College

Barbara Tollinger
Sinclair Community College

Ben Brahim Taha
Auburn University

Beverly Amer
Northern Arizona University

Beverly Fite
Amarillo College

Biswadip Ghosh
Metropolitan State University of Denver

Bonita Volker
Tidewater Community College

Bonnie Homan
San Francisco State University

Brad West
Sinclair Community College

Brian Powell
West Virginia University

Carol Buser
Owens Community College

Carol Roberts
University of Maine

Carolyn Barren
Macomb Community College

Carolyn Borne
Louisiana State University

Cathy Poyner
Truman State University

Charles Hodgson
Delgado Community College

Chen Zhang
Bryant University

Cheri Higgins
Illinois State University

Cheryl Brown
Delgado Community College

Cheryl Hinds
Norfolk State University

Cheryl Sypniewski
Macomb Community College

Chris Robinson
Northwest State Community College

Cindy Herbert
Metropolitan Community College–Longview

Craig J. Peterson
American InterContinental University

Dana Hooper
University of Alabama

Dana Johnson
North Dakota State University

Daniela Marghitu
Auburn University

David Noel
University of Central Oklahoma

David Pulis
Maritime College, State University of
New York

David Thornton
Jacksonville State University

Dawn Medlin
Appalachian State University

Debby Keen
University of Kentucky

Debra Chapman
University of South Alabama

Debra Hoffman
Southeast Missouri State
University

Derrick Huang
Florida Atlantic University

Diana Baran
Henry Ford Community College

Diane Cassidy
The University of North Carolina at
Charlotte

Diane L. Smith
Henry Ford Community College

Dick Hewer
Ferris State College

Don Danner
San Francisco State University

Don Hoggan
Solano College

Don Riggs
SUNY Schenectady County Community
College

Doncho Petkov
Eastern Connecticut State University

Donna Ehrhart
State University of New York at
Brockport

Elaine Crable
Xavier University

Elizabeth Duett
Delgado Community College

Erhan Uskup
Houston Community College–Northwest

Eric Martin
University of Tennessee

Erika Nadas
Wilbur Wright College

Floyd Winters
Manatee Community College

Frank Lucente
Westmoreland County Community College

G. Jan Wilms
Union University

Gail Cope
Sinclair Community College

Gary DeLorenzo
California University of Pennsylvania

Gary Garrison
Belmont University

Gary McFall
Purdue University

George Cassidy
Sussex County Community College

Gerald Braun
Xavier University

Gerald Burgess
Western New Mexico University

Gladys Swindler
Fort Hays State University

Hector Frausto
California State University
Los Angeles

Heith Hennel
Valencia Community College

Henry Rudzinski
Central Connecticut State University

Irene Joos
La Roche College

Iwona Rusin
Baker College; Davenport University

J. Roberto Guzman
San Diego Mesa College

Jacqueline D. Lawson
Henry Ford Community College

Jakie Brown Jr.
Stevenson University

James Brown
Central Washington University

James Powers
University of Southern Indiana

Jane Stam
Onondaga Community College

Janet Bringhurst
Utah State University

Jean Welsh
Lansing Community College

Jeanette Dix
Ivy Tech Community College

Jennifer Day
Sinclair Community College

Jill Canine
Ivy Tech Community College

Jill Young
Southeast Missouri State University

Jim Chaffee
The University of Iowa Tippie College of
Business

Joanne Lazirko
University of Wisconsin–Milwaukee

Jodi Milliner
Kansas State University

John Hollenbeck
Blue Ridge Community College

John Seydel
Arkansas State University

Judith A. Scheeren
Westmoreland County Community College

Judith Brown
The University of Memphis

Juliana Cypert
Tarrant County College

Kamaljeet Sanghera
George Mason University

Karen Priestly
Northern Virginia Community College

Karen Ravan
Spartanburg Community College

Karen Tracey
Central Connecticut State University

Kathleen Brenan
Ashland University

Ken Busbee
Houston Community College

Kent Foster
Winthrop University

Kevin Anderson
Solano Community College

Kim Wright
The University of Alabama

Kristen Hockman
University of Missouri–Columbia

Kristi Smith
Allegany College of Maryland

Laura Marcoulides
Fullerton College

Laura McManamon
University of Dayton

Laurence Boxer
Niagara University

Leanne Chun
Leeward Community College

Lee McClain
Western Washington University

Linda D. Collins
Mesa Community College

Linda Johnsonius
Murray State University

Linda Lau
Longwood University

Linda Theus
Jackson State Community College

Linda Williams
Marion Technical College

Lisa Miller
University of Central Oklahoma

Lister Horn
Pensacola Junior College

Lixin Tao
Pace University

Loraine Miller
Cayuga Community College

Lori Kielty
Central Florida Community College

Lorna Wells
Salt Lake Community College

Lorraine Sauchin
Duquesne University

Lucy Parakhovnik
California State University, Northridge

Lynn Keane
University of South Carolina

Lynn Mancini
Delaware Technical Community College

Mackinzee Escamilla
South Plains College

Marcia Welch
Highline Community College

Margaret McManus
Northwest Florida State College

Margaret Warrick
Allan Hancock College

Marilyn Hibbert
Salt Lake Community College

Mark Choman
Luzerne County Community College

Maryann Clark
University of New Hampshire

Mary Beth Tarver
Northwestern State University

Mary Duncan
University of Missouri–St. Louis

Melissa Nemeth
Indiana University-Purdue University
Indianapolis

Melody Alexander
Ball State University

Michael Douglas
University of Arkansas at Little Rock

Michael Dunklebarger
Alamance Community College

Michael G. Skaff
College of the Sequoias

Michele Budnovitch
Pennsylvania College of Technology

Mike Jochen
East Stroudsburg University

Mike Michaelson
Palomar College

Mike Scroggins
Missouri State University

Mimi Spain
Southern Maine Community College

Muhammed Badamas
Morgan State University

NaLisa Brown
University of the Ozarks

Nancy Grant
Community College of Allegheny County–
South Campus

Nanette Lareau
University of Arkansas Community
College–Morrilton

Nikia Robinson
Indian River State University

Pam Brune
Chattanooga State Community College

Pam Uhlenkamp
Iowa Central Community College

Patrick Smith
Marshall Community and Technical College

Paul Addison
Ivy Tech Community College

Paula Ruby
Arkansas State University

Peggy Burrus
Red Rocks Community College

Peter Ross
SUNY Albany

Philip H. Nielson
Salt Lake Community College

Philip Valvalides
Guilford Technical Community College

Ralph Hooper
University of Alabama

Ranette Halverson
Midwestern State University

Richard Blamer
John Carroll University

Richard Cacace
Pensacola Junior College

Richard Hewer
Ferris State University

Richard Sellers
Hill College

Rob Murray
Ivy Tech Community College

Robert Banta
Macomb Community College

Robert Dušek
Northern Virginia Community College

Robert G. Phipps Jr.
West Virginia University

Robert Sindt
Johnson County Community College

Robert Warren
Delgado Community College

Rocky Belcher
Sinclair Community College

Roger Pick
University of Missouri at Kansas City

Ronnie Creel
Troy University

Rosalie Westerberg
Clover Park Technical College

Ruth Neal
Navarro College

Sandra Thomas
Troy University

Sheila Gionfriddo
Luzerne County Community College

Sherrie Geitgey
Northwest State Community College

Sherry Lenhart
Terra Community College

Sophia Wilberscheid
Indian River State College

Sophie Lee
California State University,
Long Beach

Stacy Johnson
Iowa Central Community College

Stephanie Kramer
Northwest State Community College

Stephen Z. Jourdan
Auburn University at Montgomery

Steven Schwarz
Raritan Valley Community College

Sue A. McCrory
Missouri State University

Sumathy Chandrashekar
Salisbury University

Susan Fuschetto
Cerritos College

Susan Medlin
UNC Charlotte

Susan N. Dozier
Tidewater Community College

Suzan Spitzberg
Oakton Community College

Suzanne M. Jeska
County College of Morris

Sven Aelterman
Troy University

Sy Hirsch
Sacred Heart University

Sylvia Brown
Midland College

Tanya Patrick
Clackamas Community College

Terri Holly
Indian River State College

Terry Ray Rigsby
Hill College

Thomas Rienzo
Western Michigan University

Tina Johnson
Midwestern State University

Tommy Lu
Delaware Technical Community College

Troy S. Cash
Northwest Arkansas Community College

Vicki Robertson
Southwest Tennessee Community

Vickie Pickett
Midland College

Weifeng Chen
California University of Pennsylvania

Wes Anthony
Houston Community College

William Ayen
University of Colorado at Colorado Springs

Wilma Andrews
Virginia Commonwealth University

Yvonne Galusha
University of Iowa

Special thanks to our content development and technical team:

Barbara Stover	Joyce Nielsen
Julie Boyles	Linda Pogue
Lori Damanti	Sean Portnoy
Elizabeth Lockley	Steven Rubin

Preface

The Exploring Series and You

Exploring is Pearson's Office Application series that requires students like you to think "beyond the point and click." In this edition, we have worked to restructure the Exploring experience around the way you, today's modern student, actually use your resources.

The goal of Exploring is, as it has always been, to go farther than teaching just the steps to accomplish a task—the series provides the theoretical foundation for you to understand when and why to apply a skill. As a result, you achieve a deeper understanding of each application and can apply this critical thinking beyond Office and the classroom.

The How & Why of This Revision

Outcomes matter. Whether it's getting a good grade in this course, learning how to use Excel so students can be successful in other courses, or learning a specific skill that will make learners successful in a future job, everyone has an outcome in mind. And outcomes matter. That is why we revised our chapter opener to focus on the outcomes students will achieve by working through each Exploring chapter. These are coupled with objectives and skills, providing a map students can follow to get everything they need from each chapter.

Critical Thinking and Collaboration are essential 21st century skills. Students want and need to be successful in their future careers—so we used motivating case studies to show relevance of these skills to future careers and incorporated Soft Skills, Collaboration, and Analysis Cases with Critical Thinking steps in this edition to set students up for success in the future.

Students today read, prepare, and study differently than students used to. Students use textbooks like a tool—they want to easily identify what they need to know and learn it efficiently. We have added key features such as Tasks Lists (in purple), Step Icons, Hands-On Exercise Videos, and tracked everything via page numbers that allow efficient navigation, creating a map students can easily follow.

Students are exposed to technology. The new edition of Exploring moves beyond the basics of the software at a faster pace, without sacrificing coverage of the fundamental skills that students need to know.

Students are diverse. Students can be any age, any gender, any race, with any level of ability or learning style. With this in mind, we broadened our definition of "student resources" to include physical Student Reference cards, Hands-On Exercise videos to provide a secondary lecture-like option of review; and MyITLab, the most powerful and most ADA-compliant online homework and assessment tool around with a direct 1:1 content match with the Exploring Series. Exploring will be accessible to all students, regardless of learning style.

Providing You with a Map to Success to Move Beyond the Point and Click

All of these changes and additions will provide students an easy and efficient path to follow to be successful in this course, regardless of where they start at the beginning of this course. Our goal is to keep students engaged in both the hands-on and conceptual sides, helping achieve a higher level of understanding that will guarantee success in this course and in a future career.

In addition to the vision and experience of the series creator, Robert T. Grauer, we have assembled a tremendously talented team of Office Applications authors who have devoted themselves to teaching the ins and outs of Microsoft Word, Excel, Access, and PowerPoint. Led in this edition by series editor Mary Anne Poatsy, the whole team is dedicated to the Exploring mission of moving students **beyond the point and click**.

Key Features

The **How/Why Approach** helps students move beyond the point and click to a true understanding of how to apply Microsoft Office skills.

- **White Pages/Yellow Pages** clearly distinguish the theory (white pages) from the skills covered in the Hands-On Exercises (yellow pages) so students always know what they are supposed to be doing and why.

- **Case Study** presents a scenario for the chapter, creating a story that ties the Hands-On Exercises together.

- **Hands-On Exercise Videos** are tied to each Hands-On Exercise and walk students through the steps of the exercise while weaving in conceptual information related to the Case Study and the objectives as a whole.

The **Outcomes focus** allows students and instructors to know the higher-level learning goals and how those are achieved through discreet objectives and skills.

- **Outcomes** presented at the beginning of each chapter identify the learning goals for students and instructors.

- **Enhanced Objective Mapping** enables students to follow a directed path through each chapter, from the objectives list at the chapter opener through the exercises at the end of the chapter.
  - **Objectives List:** This provides a simple list of key objectives covered in the chapter. This includes page numbers so students can skip between objectives where they feel they need the most help.
  - **Step Icons:** These icons appear in the white pages and reference the step numbers in the Hands-On Exercises, providing a correlation between the two so students can easily find conceptual help when they are working hands-on and need a refresher.
  - **Quick Concepts Check:** A series of questions that appear briefly at the end of each white page section. These questions cover the most essential concepts in the white pages required for students to be successful in working the Hands-On Exercises. Page numbers are included for easy reference to help students locate the answers.
  - **Chapter Objectives Review:** Appears toward the end of the chapter and reviews all important concepts throughout the chapter. Newly designed in an easy-to-read bulleted format.

Watch the Video for this Hands-On Exercise!

- **MOS Certification Guide** for instructors and students to direct anyone interested in prepping for the MOS exam to the specific locations to find all content required for the test.

End-of-Chapter Exercises offer instructors several options for assessment. Each chapter has approximately 11–12 exercises ranging from multiple choice questions to open-ended projects.

ANALYSIS CASE

CREATIVE CASE

MyITLab® HOE1 Training   MyITLab® Grader

- **Multiple Choice, Key Terms Matching, Practice Exercises, Mid-Level Exercises, Beyond the Classroom Exercises, and Capstone Exercises** appear at the end of all chapters.
  - **Enhanced Mid-Level Exercises** include a **Creative Case** (for PowerPoint and Word), which allows students some flexibility and creativity, not being bound by a definitive solution, and an **Analysis Case** (for Excel and Access), which requires students to interpret the data they are using to answer an analytic question, as well as **Discover Steps**, which encourage students to use Help or to problem-solve to accomplish a task.

- **Application Capstone** exercises are included in the book to allow instructors to test students on the entire contents of a single application.

Resources

Instructor Resources

The Instructor's Resource Center, available at **www.pearsonhighered.com**, includes the following:

- **Instructor Manual** provides one-stop-shop for instructors, including an overview of all available resources, teaching tips, as well as student data and solution files for every exercise.

- **Solution Files with Scorecards** assist with grading the Hands-On Exercises and end-of-chapter exercises.

- **Prepared Exams** allow instructors to assess all skills covered in a chapter with a single project.

- **Rubrics** for Mid-Level Creative Cases and Beyond the Classroom Cases in Microsoft Word format enable instructors to customize the assignments for their classes.

- **PowerPoint Presentations** with notes for each chapter are included for out-of-class study or review.

- **Multiple Choice, Key Term Matching, and Quick Concepts Check Answer Keys**

- **Test Bank** provides objective-based questions for every chapter.

- **Scripted Lectures** offer an in-class lecture guide for instructors to mirror the Hands-On Exercises.

- **Syllabus Templates**
  - Outcomes, Objectives, and Skills List
  - Assignment Sheet
  - File Guide

Student Resources

Student Data Files

Access your student data files needed to complete the exercises in this textbook at **www.pearsonhighered.com/exploring.**

Available in MyITLab

- **Hands-On Exercise Videos** allow students to review and study the concepts taught in the Hands-On Exercises.
- **Audio PowerPoints** provide a lecture review of the chapter content, and include narration.
- **Multiple Choice quizzes** enable you to test concepts you have learned by answering auto-graded questions.
- **Book-specific 1:1 Simulations** allow students to practice in the simulated Microsoft Office 2016 environment using hi-fidelity, HTML5 simulations that directly match the content in the Hands-On Exercises.
- **eText** available in some MyITLab courses and includes links to videos, student data files, and other learning aids.
- **Book-specific 1:1 Grader Projects** allow students to complete end of chapter Capstone Exercises live in Microsoft Office 2016 and receive immediate feedback on their performance through various reports.

(ex·ploring)

SERIES

1. Investigating in a systematic way: examining. 2. Searching into or ranging over for the purpose of discovery.

Microsoft®

Access 2016

Comprehensive

Office 2016 Common Features

LEARNING OUTCOME You will apply skills common across the Microsoft Office suite to create and format documents and edit content in Office 2016 applications.

OBJECTIVES & SKILLS: After you read this chapter, you will be able to:

CASE STUDY | Spotted Begonia Art Gallery

You are an administrative assistant for Spotted Begonia, a local art gallery. The gallery does a lot of community outreach and tries to help local artists develop a network of clients and supporters. Local schools are invited to bring students to the gallery for enrichment programs.

As the administrative assistant for Spotted Begonia, you are responsible for overseeing the production of documents, spreadsheets, newspaper articles, and presentations that will be used to increase public awareness of the gallery. Other clerical assistants who are familiar with Microsoft Office will prepare the promotional materials, and you will proofread, make necessary corrections, adjust page layouts, save and print documents, and identify appropriate templates to simplify tasks. Your experience with Microsoft Office 2016 is limited, but you know that certain fundamental tasks that are common to Word, Excel, and PowerPoint will help you accomplish your oversight task. You are excited to get started with your work!

Taking the First Step

FIGURE 1.1 Spotted Begonia Art Gallery Memo and Flyer

CASE STUDY | Spotted Begonia Art Gallery

Starting Files	Files to be Submitted
f01h1Letter	f01h2Flyer_LastFirst
f01h2Flyer	f01h3Letter_LastFirst
Blank document	

Getting Started with Office Applications

Organizations around the world rely heavily on Microsoft Office software to produce documents, spreadsheets, presentations, and databases. *Microsoft Office* is a productivity software suite including a set of software applications, each one specializing in a particular type of output. You can use *Word* to produce all sorts of documents, including memos, newsletters, forms, tables, and brochures. *Excel* makes it easy to organize records, financial transactions, and business information in the form of worksheets. With *PowerPoint*, you can create dynamic presentations to inform and persuade audiences. *Access* is a relational database software application that enables you to record and link data, query databases, and create forms and reports.

You will sometimes find that you need to use two or more Office applications to produce your intended output. You might, for example, find that an annual report document you are preparing in Word for an art gallery should also include a chart of recent sales stored in Excel. You can use Excel to prepare the summary and then incorporate the worksheet in the Word document. Similarly, you can integrate Word tables and Excel charts into a PowerPoint presentation. The choice of which software applications to use really depends on what type of output you are producing. Table 1.1 describes the major tasks of the four primary applications in Microsoft Office.

TABLE 1.1 Microsoft Office Software	
Office 2016 Product	**Application Characteristics**
Word	Word processing software used with text to create, edit, and format documents such as letters, memos, reports, brochures, resumes, and flyers.
Excel	Spreadsheet software used to store quantitative data and to perform accurate and rapid calculations with results ranging from simple budgets to financial and statistical analyses.
PowerPoint	Presentation graphics software used to create slide shows for presentation by a speaker, to be published as part of a website, or to run as a stand-alone application on a computer kiosk.
Access	Relational database software used to store data and convert it into information. Database software is used primarily for decision making by businesses that compile data from multiple records stored in tables to produce informative reports.

Pearson Education, Inc.

As you become familiar with Microsoft Office, you will find that although each software application produces a specific type of output, all applications share common features. Such commonality gives a similar feel to each software application so that learning and working with Office software products is easy.

In this section, you will learn how to open an application, log in with your Microsoft account, and open and save a file. You will also learn to identify features common to Office software applications, including interface components such as the Ribbon, Backstage view, and the Quick Access Toolbar. You will experience Live Preview. You will learn how to get help with an application. You will also learn how to search for and install Office add-ins.

Starting an Office Application

STEP 1 ▶▶ Microsoft Office applications are launched from the Start menu. Click the Start button, and then click the app tile for the application in which you want to work. If the application tile is not on the Start menu, you can open the program from All apps, or alternatively, you can click in the search box on the task bar, type the name of the program, and press Enter. The program will open automatically.

Change Your Microsoft Account

Although you can log in to Windows as a local network user, you can also log in using a Microsoft account. When you have a Microsoft account, you can sign in to any Windows computer and you will be able to access the saved settings associated with your Microsoft account. That means the computer will have the same familiar look that you are used to seeing on other computers and devices. Your Microsoft account will automatically sign in to all of the apps and services that use a Microsoft account as the authentication. You can also save your sign-in credentials for other websites that you frequently visit. If you share your computer with another user, each user can have access to his own Microsoft account; you can easily switch between accounts so you can access your own files.

To switch between accounts in an application such as Word, complete the following steps:

1. Click the profile name at the top-right of the application.
2. Select Switch account. Select an account from the list, if the account has already been added to the computer, or add a new account.

Logging in with your Microsoft account also provides additional benefits such as being connected to all of Microsoft's resources on the Internet. These resources include a free Outlook email account and access to OneDrive cloud storage. *Cloud storage* is a technology used to store files and to work with programs that are stored in a central location on the Internet. *OneDrive* is an app used to store, access, and share files and folders. It is accessible using an installed desktop app or as cloud storage using a Web address. For Office applications, OneDrive is the default location for saving files. Documents saved in OneDrive are accessible from any computer that has an Internet connection. As long as the document has been saved in OneDrive, the most recent version of the document will be accessible when you log in from any computer connected to the Internet. Moreover, files and folders stored on the computer's hard drive or saved on a portable storage device can be synced with those on the OneDrive account.

OneDrive enables you to collaborate with others. You can easily share your documents with others or edit a document on which you are collaborating. You can even work with others simultaneously on the same document.

Working with Files

When working with an Office application, you can begin by opening an existing file that has already been saved to a storage medium, or you can begin work on a new file. When you open an application within Office, you can select a template to use as you begin working on a new file.

Create a New File

After opening an Office application, such as Word, Excel, or PowerPoint, you will be presented with template choices. Click Blank document (workbook, presentation, etc.) to start a new blank file. Perhaps you are already working with a document in an Office application but want to create a new file.

To create a new Office file, complete the following steps:

1. Click the File tab and click New.
2. Click Blank.

Open a File

 You will often work with a file, save it, and then continue the project at a later time. To open an existing file, you can click a location such as This PC or OneDrive and navigate to the folder or drive where your document is stored. Once you make your way to the file to be opened, double-click the file name to open the file (see Figure 1.2).

To open a file, complete the following steps:

1. Open the application.
2. Click Open Other Documents (Workbooks, etc.).
3. Click the location for your file (such as This PC or OneDrive).
4. Navigate to the folder or drive and double-click the file to open it.

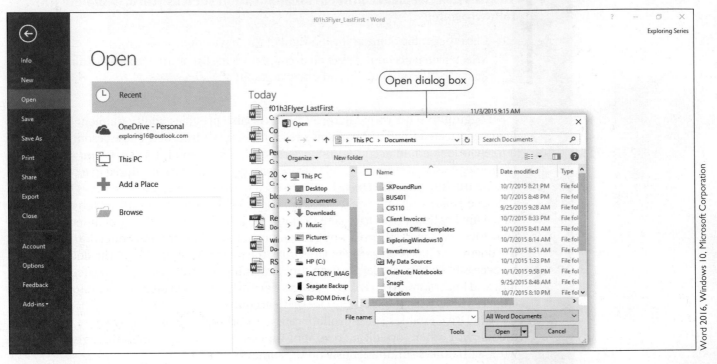

FIGURE 1.2 The Open Dialog Box

Office simplifies the task of reopening the file by providing a Recent documents list with links to your most recently opened files. Previously saved files, such as the data files for this book, are available in the Recent documents list, shown in Figure 1.3. If you just opened the application, the recent list displays at the left. If you do not see your file listed, you can click the link to Open Other Documents (or Workbooks, Presentations, etc.)

To access the Recent documents list, complete the following steps:

1. Open the application.
2. Click any file listed in the Recent documents list to open that document.

The list constantly changes to reflect only the most recently opened files, so if it has been quite some time since you worked with a particular file, you might have to browse for your file instead of using the Recent documents list to open the file.

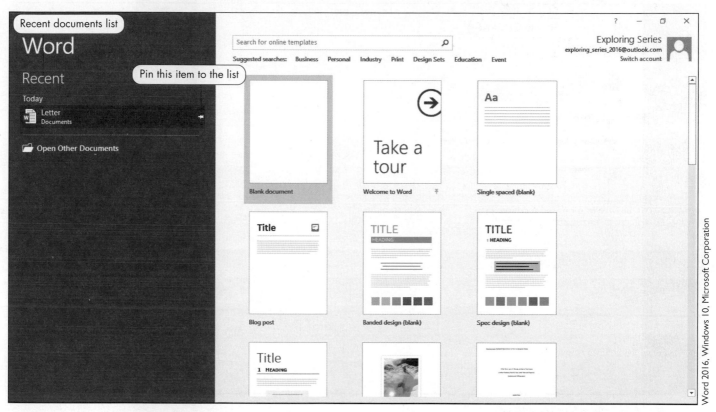

FIGURE 1.3 Recent Documents List

Save a File

STEP 3 ❯❯ Saving a file enables you to later open it for additional updates or reference. Files are saved to a storage medium such as a hard drive, CD, flash drive, or to the cloud on OneDrive.

The first time that you save a file, you should indicate where the file will be saved and assign a file name. Of course, you will want to save the file in an appropriately named folder so that you can find it easily later. Thereafter, you can quickly save the file with the same settings, or you can change one or more of those settings, perhaps saving the file to a different storage device as a backup copy. Figure 1.4 shows a typical Save As pane for Office that enables you to select a location before saving the file.

It is easy to save a previously saved file with its current name and file location; click the Save icon on Quick Access Toolbar. There are instances where you may want to rename the file or save it to a different location. For example, you might reuse an event flyer for another event and simply update some of the details for the new event.

To save a file with a different name and/or file location, complete the following steps:

1. Click the File tab.
2. Click Save As.
3. Select a location or click Browse to navigate to the desired file storage location.
4. Type the file name.
5. Click Save.

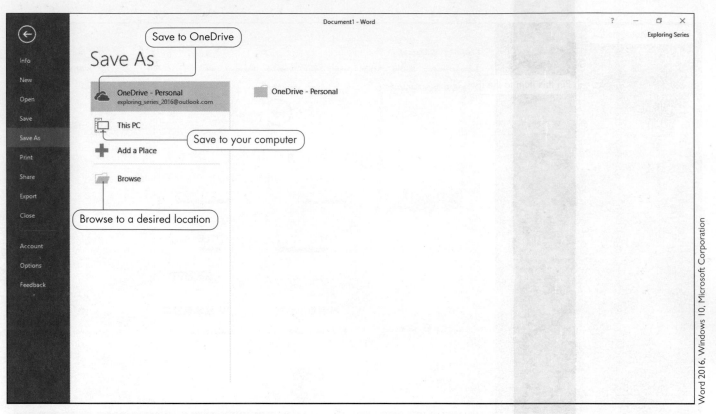

FIGURE 1.4 Save As in Backstage View

As previously mentioned, signing in to your Microsoft account enables you to save files to OneDrive and access them from virtually anywhere. To save a file to your OneDrive account follow the same steps as saving a file to your hard drive but select OneDrive and then the desired storage location on your OneDrive. You must be connected to the Internet in order to complete this action.

Using Common Interface Components

When you open any Office application you will first notice the title bar and Ribbon. The *title bar* identifies the current file name and the application in which you are working. It also includes Ribbon display options and control buttons that enable you to minimize, restore down, or close the application window (see Figure 1.5). The Quick Access Toolbar, on the left side of the title bar, enables you to save the file, and undo or redo editing. Located just below the title bar is the Ribbon. The *Ribbon* is the command center of Office applications. It is the long bar located just beneath the title bar, containing tabs, groups, and commands.

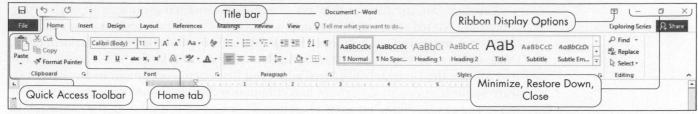

FIGURE 1.5 The Title Bar and Quick Access Toolbar

Use the Ribbon

The Ribbon is composed of tabs. Each *tab* is designed to appear much like a tab on a file folder, with the active tab highlighted. The File tab is located at the far left of the Ribbon. The File tab provides access to Backstage view which contains Save and Print, as well as additional functions. Other tabs on the Ribbon enable you to modify a file. The active tab in Figure 1.6 is the Home tab.

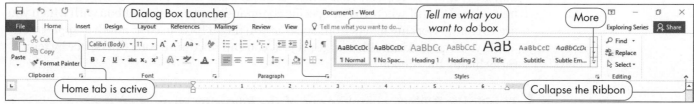

FIGURE 1.6 The Ribbon

Office applications enable you to work with objects such as images, shapes, charts, and tables. When you include such objects in a project, they are considered separate components that you can manage independently. To work with an object, you must select it. When you select an object, the Ribbon is modified to include one or more *contextual tabs* that contain groups of commands related to the selected object. Figure 1.7 shows a contextual tab related to a selected picture in a Word document. When you click away from the selected object, the contextual tab disappears.

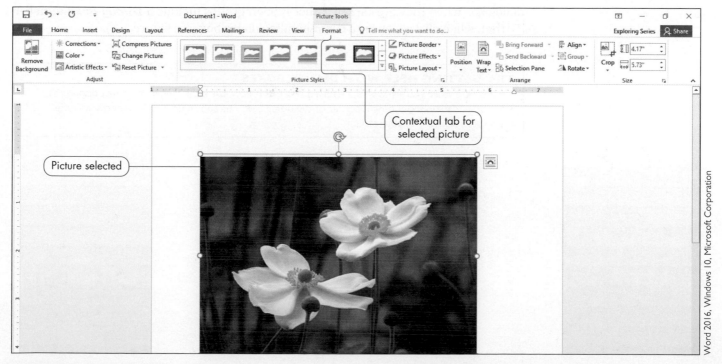

FIGURE 1.7 A Contextual Tab

On each tab, the Ribbon displays several task-oriented groups, with each group containing related commands. A *group* is a subset of a tab that organizes similar tasks together. A *command* is a button or area within a group that you click to perform tasks. Office is designed to provide the most functionality possible with the fewest clicks. For that reason, the Home tab, displayed when you first open a document in an Office software application, contains groups and commands that are most commonly used. For example, because you often want to change the way text is displayed, the Home tab in each Office application includes a Font group with commands related to modifying text. Similarly, other tabs contain groups of related actions, or commands, many of which are unique to the particular Office application.

Word, PowerPoint, Excel, and Access all share a similar Ribbon structure. Although the specific tabs, groups, and commands vary among the Office programs, the way in which you use the Ribbon and the descriptive nature of tab titles is the same regardless of which program you are using. For example, if you want to insert a chart in Excel, a header in Word, or a shape in PowerPoint, you will click the Insert tab in any of those programs. The first thing that you should do as you begin to work with an Office application is to study the Ribbon. Take a look at all tabs and their contents. That way, you will have a good idea of where to find specific commands and how the Ribbon with which you are currently working differs from one that you might have used in another application.

If you are working with a large project, you can maximize your workspace by temporarily hiding the Ribbon.

To hide the Ribbon, complete one of the following steps:

- Double-click the active tab to hide the Ribbon.
- Click Collapse the Ribbon (refer to Figure 1.6), located at the right side of the Ribbon.

To unhide the Ribbon, double-click any tab to redisplay the Ribbon.

Some actions do not display on the Ribbon because they are not as commonly used, but are related to commands displayed on the Ribbon. For example, you might want to change the background of a PowerPoint slide to include a picture. In that case, you will work with a *dialog box* that provides access to more precise, but less frequently used, commands. Figure 1.8 shows the Font dialog box in Word. Some commands display a dialog box when they are clicked. Other Ribbon groups include a *Dialog Box Launcher* that, when clicked, opens a corresponding dialog box (see Figure 1.8).

> **TIP: GETTING HELP WITH DIALOG BOXES**
> Getting help while you are working with a dialog box is easy. Click the Help button that displays as a question mark in the top-right corner of the dialog box. The subsequent Help window will offer suggestions relevant to your task.

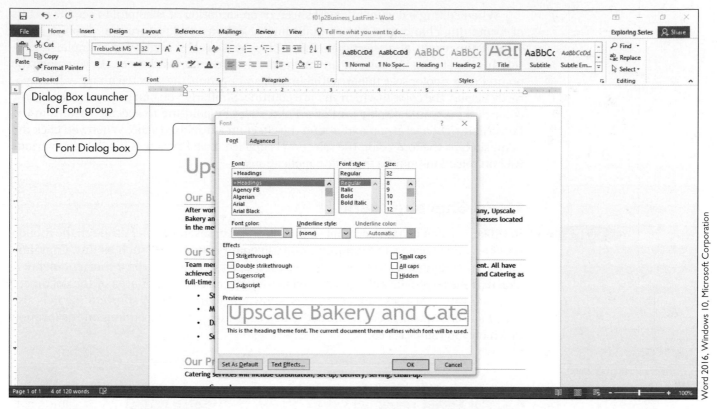

FIGURE 1.8 The Font Dialog Box

The Ribbon contains many selections and commands, but some selections are too numerous to include in the Ribbon's limited space. For example, Word provides far more text styles than it can easily display at once, so additional styles are available in a ***gallery***. A gallery also provides a choice of Excel chart styles and PowerPoint transitions. Figure 1.9 shows an example of a PowerPoint Themes gallery. Most often, you can display a gallery of additional choices by clicking the More button ⬇ (refer to Figure 1.6) that is found in some Ribbon selections.

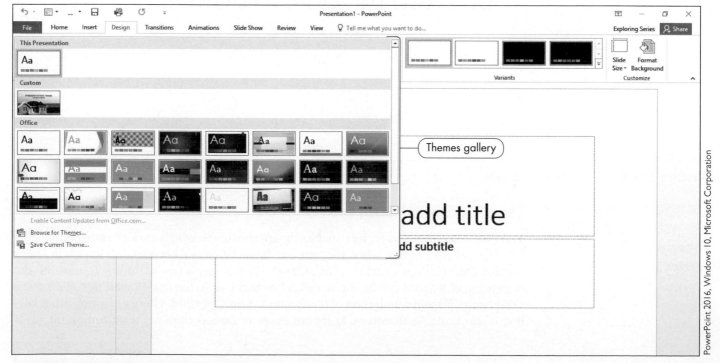

FIGURE 1.9 The Themes Gallery in PowerPoint

When editing a document, worksheet, or presentation, it is helpful to see the results of formatting changes before you make final selections. The feature that displays a preview of the results of a selection is called **Live Preview**. You might, for example, be considering modifying the color of an image in a document or worksheet. As you place the pointer over a color selection in a Ribbon gallery or group, the selected image will temporarily display the color to which you are pointing. Similarly, you can get a preview of how color designs would display on PowerPoint slides by pointing to specific themes in the PowerPoint Themes group and noting the effect on a displayed slide. When you click the item, such as the font color, the selection is applied. Live Preview is available in various Ribbon selections among the Office applications.

Use a Shortcut Menu

 In Office, you can usually accomplish the same task in several ways. Although the Ribbon provides ample access to formatting and Clipboard commands (such as Cut, Copy, and Paste), you might find it convenient to access the same commands on a shortcut menu. A **shortcut menu** provides choices related to the object, selection, or area of the document at which you right-click, such as the one shown in Figure 1.10. A shortcut menu is also called a *context menu* because the contents of the menu vary depending on the location at which you right-clicked.

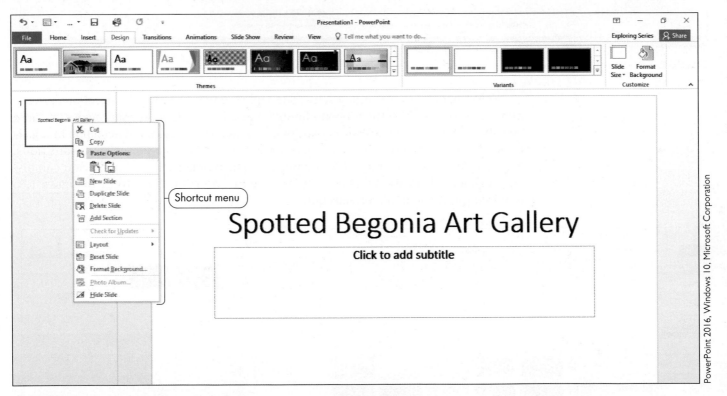

FIGURE 1.10 A Shortcut Menu in PowerPoint

Use Keyboard Shortcuts

You might find that you prefer to use keyboard shortcuts, which are keyboard equivalents for software commands, when they are available. Universal keyboard shortcuts in Office include Ctrl+C (Copy), Ctrl+X (Cut), Ctrl+V (Paste), and Ctrl+Z (Undo). To move to the beginning of a Word document, to cell A1 in Excel, or to the first PowerPoint slide, press Ctrl+Home. To move to the end of those items, press Ctrl+End. There are many other keyboard shortcuts. To discover a keyboard shortcut for a commonly used command, press

Alt to display Key Tips for commands available on the Ribbon and Quick Access Toolbar. You can press the letter or number corresponding to Ribbon commands to invoke the action from the keyboard. Press Alt again to remove the Key Tips.

TIP: USING RIBBON COMMANDS WITH ARROWS
Some commands, such as Paste in the Clipboard group, contain two parts: the main command and an arrow. The arrow may be below or to the right of the command, depending on the command, window size, or screen resolution. Instructions in the *Exploring* series use the command name to instruct you to click the main command to perform the default action (e.g., Click Paste). Instructions include the word *arrow* when you need to select the arrow to access an additional option (e.g., Click the Paste arrow).

Customize the Ribbon

The Ribbon provides access to commands to develop, edit, save, share, and print documents. Office applications enable users to personalize the Ribbon, giving them easier access to a frequently used set of commands that are unique to them or their business. You can create and name custom tabs on the Ribbon, add groups of commands to custom or existing tabs, and alter the positioning of tabs on the Ribbon (see Figure 1.11). By default, the command list displays popular commands associated with other tabs (e.g. Paste, Delete, Save As), but all available commands can be displayed in the list's respective menu. The custom tabs are unique to the Office program in which they are created. You can add and remove Ribbon tabs, as well as rename them.

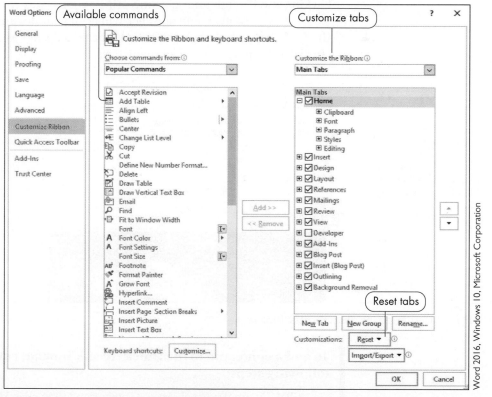

FIGURE 1.11 Customize the Ribbon in Word

Word 2016, Windows 10, Microsoft Corporation

To customize the Ribbon, complete the following steps:

1. Click the File tab and click Options.
2. Click Customize Ribbon. By deselecting a tab name, you can remove it from the Ribbon. Later, you can select it again to redisplay it.
3. Click a tab name and click Rename to change the name of the tab.
4. Type a new name and press Enter.

To return to showing all of the original tabs, click Reset and click Reset all customizations (refer to Figure 1.11).

Use the Quick Access Toolbar

The **Quick Access Toolbar**, located at the top-left corner of any Office application window (refer to Figure 1.5), provides one-click access to commonly executed tasks such as saving a file or undoing recent actions. By default, the Quick Access Toolbar includes buttons for saving a file and for undoing or redoing recent actions. You can recover from a mistake by clicking Undo on the Quick Access Toolbar. If you click the arrow beside Undo—known as the Undo arrow—you can select from a list of previous actions in order of occurrence. The Undo list is not maintained when you close a file or exit the application, so you can only erase an action that took place during the current Office session. Similar to Undo, you can also Redo (or Replace) an action that you have just undone. You can also customize the Quick Access Toolbar to include buttons you frequently use for commands such as printing or opening files. Because the Quick Access Toolbar is onscreen at all times, the most commonly accessed tasks are just a click away.

Customize the Quick Access Toolbar

There are certain actions in an Office application that you use often, and for more convenient access, you can add a button for each action to the Quick Access Toolbar (see Figure 1.12). One such action you may want to add is a Quick Print button. Rather than clicking the File tab and selecting print options, you can add a Quick Print icon to the Quick Access Toolbar, and one click will print your document with the default settings of the Print area. Other buttons can also be added such as Spelling & Grammar to quickly check the spelling of the document.

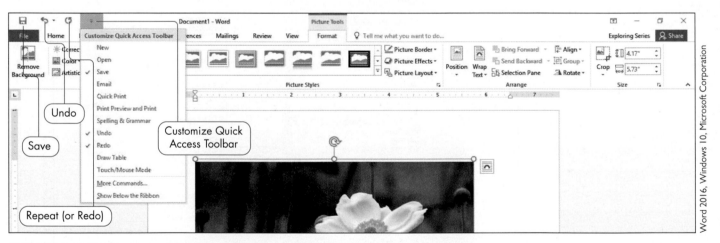

FIGURE 1.12 Customize the Quick Access Toolbar

> **To add a command to the Quick Access Toolbar, complete one of the following steps:**
>
> - Click Customize Quick Access Toolbar and then click More Commands near the bottom of the menu options. Then, select commands from a list and click Add.
> - Right-click the command on the Ribbon and click Add to Quick Access Toolbar.

Similarly, remove a command from the Quick Access Toolbar by right-clicking the icon on the Quick Access Toolbar and clicking *Remove from Quick Access Toolbar*. If you want to display the Quick Access Toolbar beneath the Ribbon, click *Customize Quick Access Toolbar* and click *Show Below the Ribbon*.

Getting Help

One of the most frustrating things about learning new software is determining how to complete a task. Microsoft includes comprehensive help with Office so that you are less likely to feel such frustration. As you work with any Office application, you can access help online as well as within the current software installation.

Use the *Tell me what you want to do* Box

STEP 5 ›› New to Office 2016 is the *Tell me what you want to do* box. The ***Tell me what you want to do box***, located to the right of the last tab (see Figure 1.13), not only enables you to search for help and information about a command or task you want to perform, but it will also present you with a shortcut directly to that command and in some instances (like Bold) it will complete the action for you. Perhaps you want to find an instance of a word in your document and replace it with another word but cannot locate the command on the Ribbon. You can type *find and replace* in the *Tell me what you want to do* box and a list of commands related to the skill will display. For example, in Figure 1.13, you see that Replace displays as an option in the list. If you click this option, the Find and Replace dialog box opens without you having to locate the button to do so.

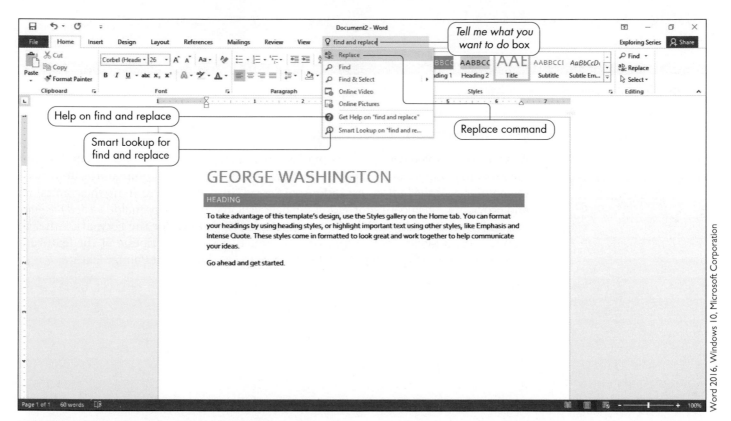

FIGURE 1.13 The *Tell me what you want to do* Box

Should you want to read about the feature instead of apply it, you can click *Get Help on "find and replace"* option, which will open Office Help for the feature. Another new feature is Smart Lookup. This feature opens the Insights pane that shows results from a Bing search on the task description typed in the box (see Figure 1.14). **Smart Lookup** provides information about tasks or commands in Office, and can also be used to search for general information on a topic such as *President George Washington*. Smart Lookup is also available on the shortcut menu when you right-click text.

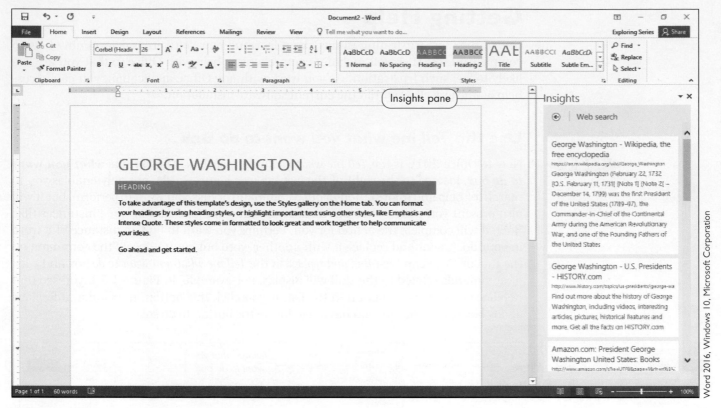

FIGURE 1.14 Smart Lookup

Use Enhanced ScreenTips

As you work on your projects you may wonder about the purpose of a specific icon on the Ribbon. For quick summary information on the purpose of a command button, place the pointer over the button. An ***Enhanced ScreenTip*** displays, describing the command, and providing a keyboard shortcut, if applicable. Some ScreenTips include a *Tell me more* option for additional help. The Enhanced ScreenTip, shown for the Format Painter in Figure 1.15, provides context-sensitive assistance. A short description of the feature is shown in addition to the steps that discuss how to use the Format Painter feature.

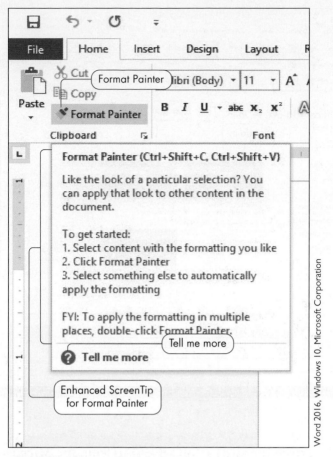

FIGURE 1.15 Enhanced ScreenTip

Installing Add-ins

Sometimes it is helpful to extend the functionality of Office programs by adding a Microsoft or third-party add-in to the program. An **add-in** is a custom program or additional command that extends the functionality of a Microsoft Office program (see Figure 1.16). Some add-ins are available for free while others may have a cost associated with them. For example, in PowerPoint you could add a Poll Everywhere poll that enables you to interact with your audience by having them respond to a question you have asked. The audience's electronic responses will appear on a slide as a real-time graph or word cloud. In Excel, add-ins provide additional functionality that can help with statistics and data mining.

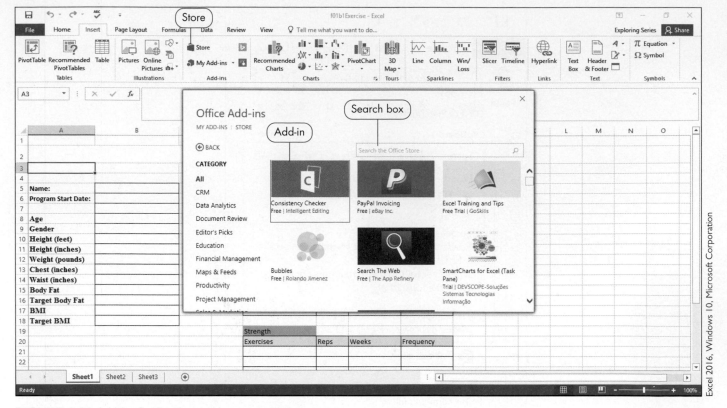

FIGURE 1.16 Add-Ins for Excel

To search for and install an add-in from the Microsoft Store, complete the following steps:

1. Click the Insert tab.

2. Click Store (refer to Figure 1.16). Browse the list of add-ins or use the search box.

3. Click the add-in. A box will display with information about the add-in such as its purpose, the cost (if any), and information it may access.

4. Click Trust It to add the add-in to your application. The newly added add-in will be available for future use in the My Add-ins list located on the Insert tab.

Quick Concepts

1. What are the benefits of logging in with your Microsoft account? *p. 5*

2. What is the purpose of the Quick Access Toolbar? *p. 14*

3. You are having trouble completing a task in Microsoft Word. What are some of the Office application features you could use to assist you in getting help with that task? *pp. 15–17*

Hands-On Exercises

Skills covered: Open a Microsoft Office Application • Open a File • Save a File • Use a Shortcut Menu • Use the *Tell me what you want to do* Box

1 Getting Started with Office Applications

The Spotted Begonia Art Gallery just hired several new clerical assistants to help you develop materials for the various activities coming up throughout the year. A coworker sent you a letter and asked for your assistance in making a few minor formatting changes. The letter is to thank the ABC Arts Foundation for its generous donation to the *Discover the Artist in You!* program and to invite them to the program's kickoff party. To begin, you will open Word and then open an existing document. You will use the Shortcut menu to make simple changes to the document. Finally, you will use the *Tell me what you want to do* box to apply a style to the first line of text.

STEP 1 ›› OPEN A MICROSOFT OFFICE APPLICATION

You start Microsoft Word from the Windows Start menu. Refer to Figure 1.17 as you complete Step 1.

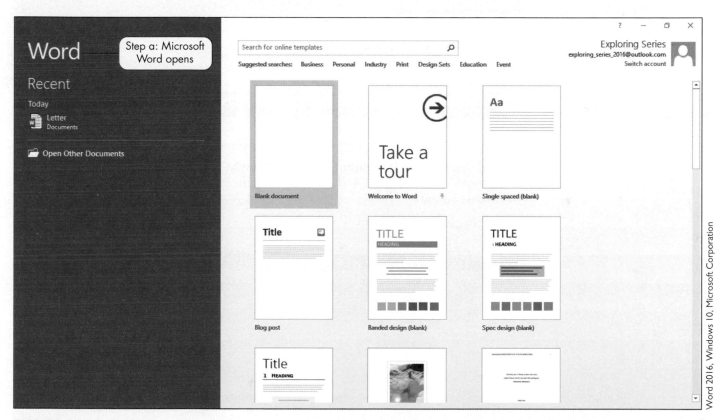

FIGURE 1.17 Open Word

a. Start your computer and log into your Microsoft account. On the Start menu, click **All apps** and click **Word 2016**.

Microsoft Word displays.

You open a thank-you letter that you will later modify. Refer to Figure 1.18 as you complete Step 2.

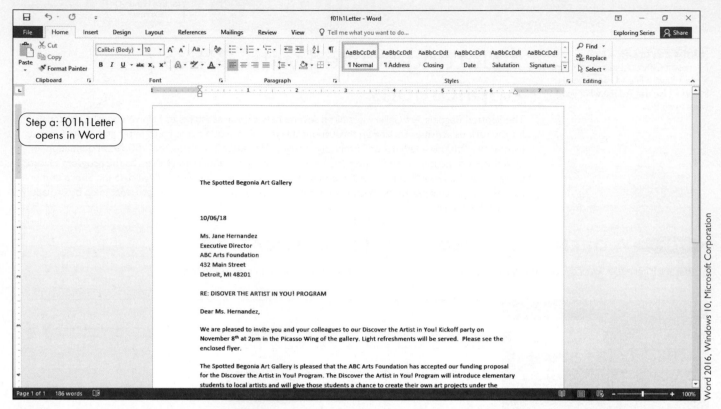

FIGURE 1.18 Open the Letter

> **a.** Click **Open Other Documents** and click **Browse**. Navigate to the location of your student files. Double-click *f01h1Letter* to open the file shown in Figure 1.18. Click Enable Content.
>
> The thank-you letter opens.

> **TROUBLESHOOTING:** When you open an file from the student files associated with this book, you will need to enable the content. You may be confident of the trustworthiness of the files for this book.

You save the document with a different name, to preserve the original file. Refer to Figure 1.19 as you complete Step 3.

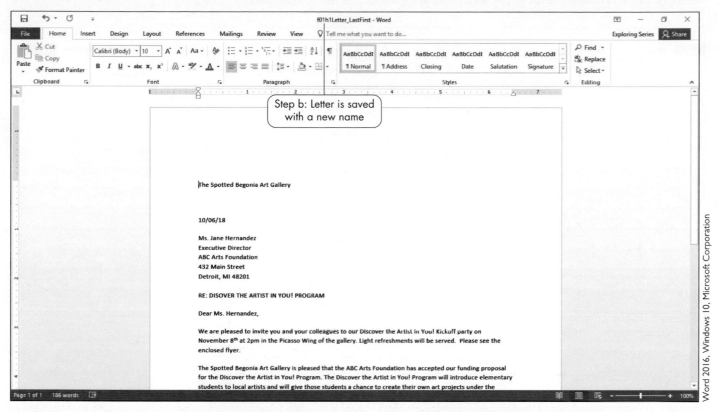

FIGURE 1.19 Save the Letter with a New Name

a. Click the **File tab**, click **Save As**, and then click **Browse** to display the Save As dialog box. Click **This PC** or click the location where you are saving your files.

b. Click in the **File name box** and type **f01h1Letter_LastFirst**.

When you save files, use your last and first names. For example, as the Common Features author, I would name my document "f01h1Letter_RutledgeAmy".

> **TROUBLESHOOTING:** If you make any major mistakes in this exercise, you can close the file, open *f01h1Letter* again, and then start this exercise over.

c. Click **Save**.

The file is now saved as f01h1Letter_LastFirst. You can check the title bar of the workbook to confirm that the file has been saved with the correct name.

You would like to apply italics to the *Discover the Artist in You!* text in the first sentence of the letter. You will select the text and use the shortcut menu to apply italics to the text. Refer to Figure 1.20 as you complete Step 4.

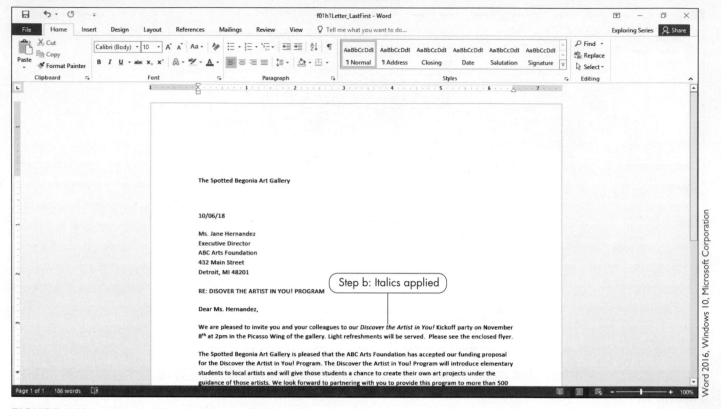

FIGURE 1.20 Apply Italics Using the Shortcut Menu

a. Select the text **Discover the Artist in You!** in the first sentence of the letter that starts with *We are pleased*.

The text is selected.

b. Right-click the selected text. Click **Font** on the Shortcut menu. Click **Italic** under Font style, and click **OK**.

Italics is applied to the text.

c. Click **Save** on the Quick Access Toolbar.

You would like to apply a style to the first line in the letter. Since you do not know how to complete the task, you use the *Tell me what you want to do* box to search for and apply the change. Refer to Figure 1.21 as you complete Step 5.

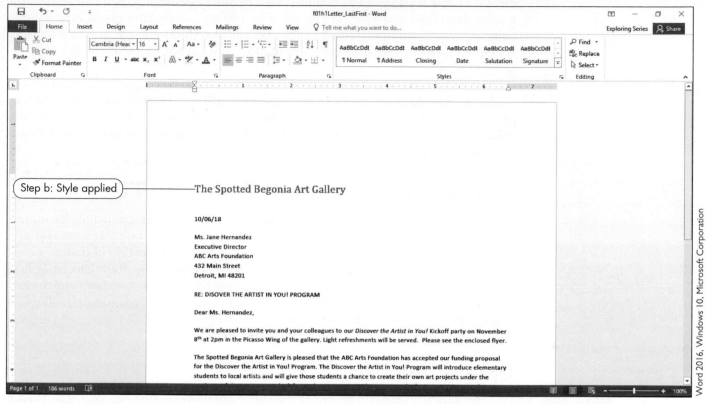

FIGURE 1.21 Change the Text Style Using the *Tell me what you want to do* Box

a. Triple-click the entire first line of the letter that starts with *The Spotted Begonia Art Gallery* to select it. Click the ***Tell me what you want to do* box**, and type **heading 1**.

A list of options appears below the box.

b. Click **Promote to Heading1** to apply the style to the selected text.

The Heading 1 style is applied to the text.

c. Save the document. Keep the document open if you plan to continue with the next Hands-On Exercise. If not, save and close the workbook, and exit Word.

Format Document Content

After creating a document, worksheet, or presentation, you will probably want to make some formatting changes. You might prefer to center a title, or maybe you think that certain budget worksheet totals should be formatted as currency. You can change the font so that typed characters are larger or in a different style. You might even want to bold text to add emphasis. In all Office applications, the Home tab provides tools for selecting and editing text. You can also use the Mini toolbar for making quick changes to selected text.

In this section you will explore themes and templates. You will learn to use the Mini toolbar to quickly make formatting changes. You will learn how to select and edit text, as well as check your grammar and spelling. You will learn how to move, copy, and paste text, as well as insert pictures. And, finally, you will learn how to resize and format pictures and graphics.

Using Templates and Applying Themes

You can enhance your documents by using a template or applying a theme. A ***template*** is a predesigned file that incorporates formatting elements, such as a theme and layouts, and may include content that can be modified. A ***theme*** is a collection of design choices that includes colors, fonts, and special effects used to give a consistent look to a document, workbook, or presentation. Microsoft provides high quality templates and themes, designed by professional designers to make it faster and easier to create high-quality documents. Even if you use a theme to apply colors, fonts, and special effects, they can later be changed individually or to a completely different theme.

Open a Template

STEP 1 ➤➤ You can access a template in any of the Office applications (see Figure 1.22). Even if you know only a little bit about the software, you could then make a few changes so that the file would accurately represent your specific needs. The document also would be prepared much more quickly than if you designed it yourself from a blank file. For example, you might want to prepare a home budget using an Excel template, such as the Family monthly budget planner template, that is available by typing *Budget* in the *Suggested searches* template list.

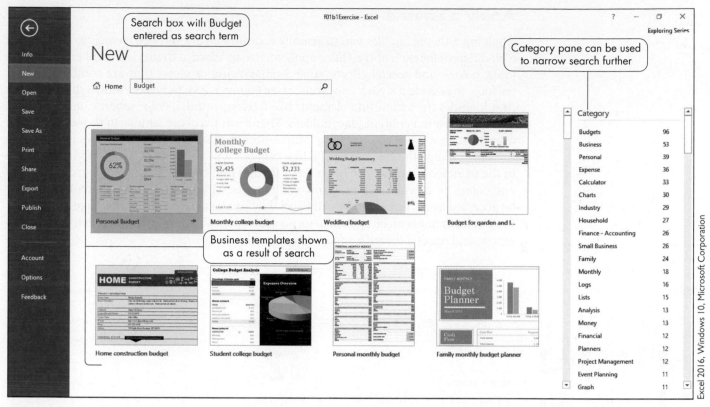

Search box with Budget entered as search term

Category pane can be used to narrow search further

Business templates shown as a result of search

Excel 2016, Windows 10, Microsoft Corporation

FIGURE 1.22 Templates in Excel

The Templates list is comprised of template groups available within each Office application. The search box enables you to locate other templates that are available online. When you click one of the Suggested searches, additional choices are displayed. Once you select a template, you can view more information about the template including author information, a general overview about the template, and additional views (if applicable).

To search for and use a template, complete the following steps:

1. Open the Microsoft application with which you will be working.
2. Type a search term in the *Search for online templates box*, or click one of the Suggested search terms.
3. Scroll through the template options or use the pane at the right to narrow your search further.
4. Select a template, and review its information in the window that opens.
5. Click Create to open the template in the application.

A Help window may display along with the worksheet template. Read it for more information about the template, or close it to continue working.

Apply a Theme

Applying a theme enables you to visually coordinate various page elements. Themes are a bit different for each of the Office applications. In Word, a theme is a set of coordinating fonts, colors, and special effects, such as shadowing or glows that are combined into a package to provide a stylish appearance (see Figure 1.23). In PowerPoint, a theme is a file that includes the formatting elements like a background, a color scheme, and slide layouts that position content placeholders. Themes in Excel are similar to those in Word in that they are a set of coordinating fonts, colors, and special effects. Themes in Excel will not only change the color of the fill in a cell, but will also affect any SmartArt or charts in the workbook. Access also has a set of themes that coordinate the appearance of fonts and colors for objects such as Forms and Reports. In Word and PowerPoint, themes can be accessed from the Design tab. In Excel they can be accessed from the Page Layout tab. In Access, themes can be applied to forms and reports. To apply a theme, click the Themes arrow, and select a theme from the Themes gallery.

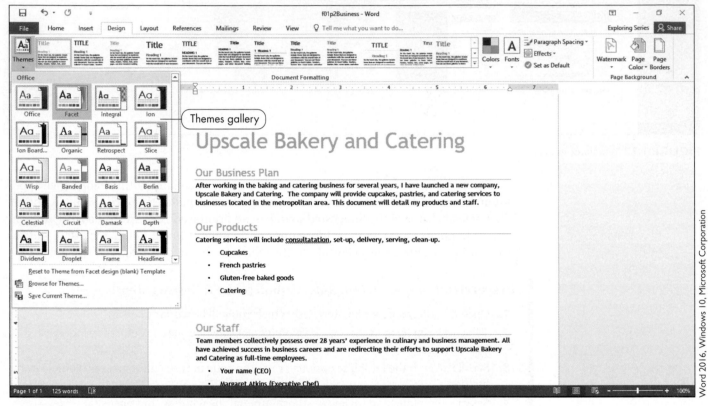

FIGURE 1.23 Themes in Word

Modifying Text

Formatting and modifying text in documents, worksheets, or presentations is an essential function when using Office applications. Centering a title, formatting cells, or changing the font color or size are tasks that occur frequently. In all Office applications, the Home tab provides tools for editing selected text. You can also use the Mini toolbar for making quick changes to selected text.

Select Text

STEP 2 ⟫ Before making any changes to existing text or numbers, you must first select the characters. A general rule that you should commit to memory is "Select, then do." A foolproof way to select text or numbers is to place the pointer before the first character of the text you want to select, and then drag to highlight the intended selection. Before you drag, be sure that the pointer takes on the shape of the letter *I*, called the *I-beam* $\boxed{\text{I}}$. Although other methods for selecting exist, if you remember only one way, it should be the click-and-drag method. If your attempted selection falls short of highlighting the intended area, or perhaps highlights too much, click outside the selection and try again.

Sometimes it can be difficult to precisely select a small amount of text, such as a single word or sentence. Other times, the task can be overwhelming large, such as when selecting an entire 550-page document. In either case there are shortcuts to selecting text. The shortcuts shown in Table 1.2 are primarily applicable to text in Word and PowerPoint. When working with Excel, you will more often need to select multiple cells. To select multiple cells, drag the intended selection when the pointer displays as a large white plus sign $\boxed{\oplus}$.

TABLE 1.2 Shortcut Selection in Word and PowerPoint	
Item Selected	**Action**
One word	Double-click the word.
One line of text	Place the pointer at the left of the line, in the margin area. When the pointer changes to a right-pointing arrow, click to select the line.
One sentence	Press and hold Ctrl, and click in the sentence to select it.
One paragraph	Triple-click in the paragraph.
One character to the left of the insertion point	Press and hold Shift, and press the left arrow on the keyboard.
One character to the right of the insertion point	Press and hold Shift, and press the right arrow on the keyboard.
Entire document	Press and hold Ctrl, and press A on the keyboard.

Pearson Education, Inc.

Once you have selected the desired text, besides applying formatting, you can delete or simply type over to replace the text.

Edit Text

At times, you will want to make the font size larger or smaller, change the font color, or apply other font attributes. For example, if you are creating a handout for a gallery show opening, you may want to apply a different font to emphasize key information such as dates and times. Because such changes are commonplace, Office places those formatting commands in many convenient places within each Office application.

You can find the most common formatting commands in the Font group on the Home tab. As noted earlier, Word, Excel, and PowerPoint all share very similar Font groups that provide access to tasks related to changing the character font. Remember that you can place the pointer over any command icon to view a summary of the icon's purpose, so although the icons might at first appear cryptic, you can use the pointer to quickly determine the purpose and applicability to your desired text change.

The way characters display onscreen or print in documents, including qualities such as size, spacing, and shape, is determined by the font. Office applications have a default font, Calibri, which is the font that will be in effect unless you change it. Other font attributes include bold, italic, and font color, all of which can be applied to selected text. Some formatting commands, such as Bold and Italic, are called **toggle commands**. They act somewhat like light switches that you can turn on and off. Once you have applied bold formatting to text, the Bold command is highlighted on the Ribbon when that text is selected again. To undo bold formatting, click Bold again.

If you want to apply a different font to a section of your project for added emphasis or interest, you can make the change by selecting a font from within the Font group on the Home tab. You can also change the font by selecting from the Mini toolbar.

If the font change that you plan to make is not included as a choice on either the Home tab or the Mini toolbar, you can find what you are looking for in the Font dialog box. Click the Dialog Box Launcher in the bottom-right corner of the Font group. Figure 1.24 shows a sample Font dialog box. Because the Font dialog box provides many formatting choices in one window, you can make several changes at once. Depending on the application, the contents of the Font dialog box vary slightly, but the purpose is consistent—providing access to choices related to modifying characters.

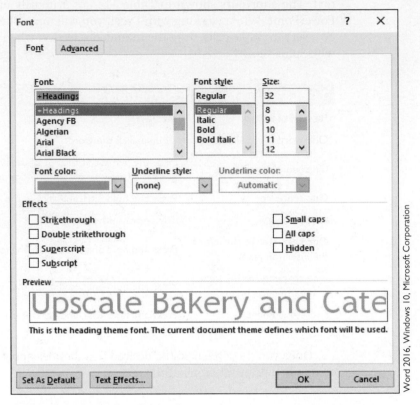

FIGURE 1.24 The Font Dialog Box

Use the Mini Toolbar

You have learned that you can always use commands on the Home tab of the Ribbon to change selected text within a document, worksheet, or presentation. Although using the Ribbon to select commands is simple enough, the **Mini toolbar** provides an even faster way to accomplish some of the same formatting changes. When you select any amount of text within a worksheet, document, or presentation, move the pointer slightly within the selection to display the Mini toolbar (see Figure 1.25). The Mini toolbar provides access to the most common formatting selections, such as bold or italic, or font type or color. Unlike the Quick Access Toolbar, the Mini toolbar is not customizable, which means that you cannot add or remove options from the toolbar.

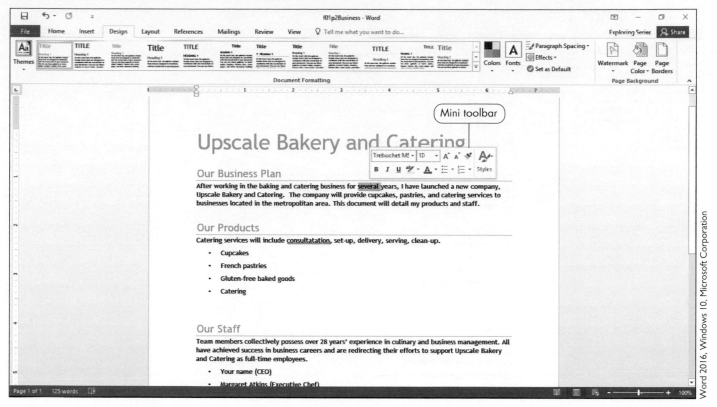

FIGURE 1.25 The Mini Toolbar

The Mini toolbar is displayed only when text is selected. The closer the pointer is to the Mini toolbar, the darker the toolbar becomes. As you move the pointer away from the selected text, the Mini toolbar eventually fades away. If the Mini toolbar is no longer displayed, you can right-click the selection to make the Mini toolbar appear again. To make selections from the Mini toolbar, click a command on the toolbar. To temporarily remove the Mini toolbar from view, press Esc.

> **To permanently disable the Mini toolbar so that it does not display in any open file when text is selected, complete the following steps:**
>
> 1. Click the File tab and click Options.
> 2. Click General.
> 3. Click the *Show Mini toolbar on selection* check box to deselect it.
> 4. Click OK.

Copy Formats with Format Painter

STEP 3 Using **Format Painter**, you can copy all formatting from one area to another in Word, PowerPoint, and Excel (see Figure 1.26). If, for example, a heading in Word includes multiple formatting features, you will save time by copying the entire set of formatting options to the other headings. In so doing, you will ensure the consistency of formatting for all headings because they will appear exactly alike.

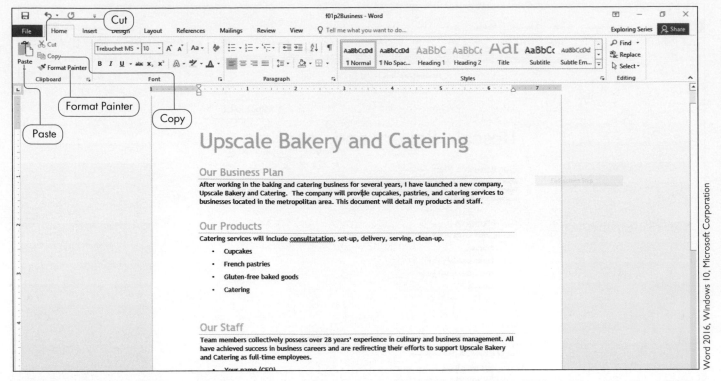

FIGURE 1.26 Format Painter

> **To copy a format, complete the following steps:**
>
> 1. Select the text containing the desired format.
> 2. Single-click Format Painter if you want to copy the format to only one other selection. If, however, you plan to copy the same format to multiple areas, double-click Format Painter.
> 3. Select the area to which the copied format should be applied.

If you single-clicked Format Painter to copy the format to one other selection, Format Painter turns off once the formatting has been applied. If you double-clicked Format Painter to copy the format to multiple locations, continue selecting text in various locations to apply the format. Then, to turn off Format Painter, click Format Painter again or press Esc.

Relocating Text

On occasion, you will want to relocate a section of text from one area to another. Suppose that you have included text on a PowerPoint slide that you believe would be more appropriate on a different slide. Or perhaps an Excel formula should be copied from one cell to another because both cells should be totaled in the same manner. You can move the slide text or copy the Excel formula by using the cut, copy, and paste features found in the Clipboard group on the Home tab. The Office ***Clipboard*** is an area of memory reserved to temporarily hold selections that have been cut or copied and allows you to paste the selections. When the computer is shut down or loses power, the contents of the Clipboard are erased, so it is important to finalize the paste procedure during the current session.

Cut, Copy, and Paste Text

STEP 4 ⟩⟩ To *cut* means to remove a selection from the original location and place it in the Office Clipboard. To *copy* means to duplicate a selection from the original location and place a copy in the Office Clipboard. Although the Clipboard can hold up to 24 items at one time, the usual procedure is to paste the cut or copied selection to its final destination fairly quickly. To *paste* means to place a cut or copied selection into another location. In addition to using the Clipboard group icons, you can also cut, copy, and paste in any of the ways listed in Table 1.3.

TABLE 1.3	Cut, Copy, and Paste Options
Command	**Actions**
Cut	• Click Cut in Clipboard group. • Right-click selection and select Cut. • Press Ctrl+X.
Copy	• Click Copy in Clipboard group. • Right-click selection and select Copy. • Press Ctrl+C.
Paste	• Click in destination location and select Paste in Clipboard group. • Click in destination location and press Ctrl+V. • Click Clipboard Dialog Box Launcher to open Clipboard pane. Click in destination location. With Clipboard pane open, click arrow beside intended selection and select Paste.

Pearson Education, Inc.

To cut or copy text, complete the following steps:

1. Select the text you want to cut or copy.
2. Click the appropriate icon in the Clipboard group either to cut or copy the selection. Remember that cut or copied text is actually placed in the Clipboard, remaining there even after you paste it to another location. It is important to note that you can paste the same item multiple times, because it will remain in the Clipboard until you power down your computer or until the Clipboard exceeds 24 items.
3. Click the location where you want the cut or copied text to be placed. The location can be in the current file or in another open file within any Office application.
4. Click Paste in the Clipboard group on the Home tab.

When you paste text you may not want to paste the text with all of its formatting. In some instances, you may want to paste only the text, unformatted, so that it fits in with the formatting of its new location. When pasting text, there are several options available and those options will depend on the program you are using.

Use the Office Clipboard

When you cut or copy selections, they are placed in the Office Clipboard. Regardless of which Office application you are using, you can view the Clipboard by clicking the Clipboard Dialog Box Launcher, as shown in Figure 1.27.

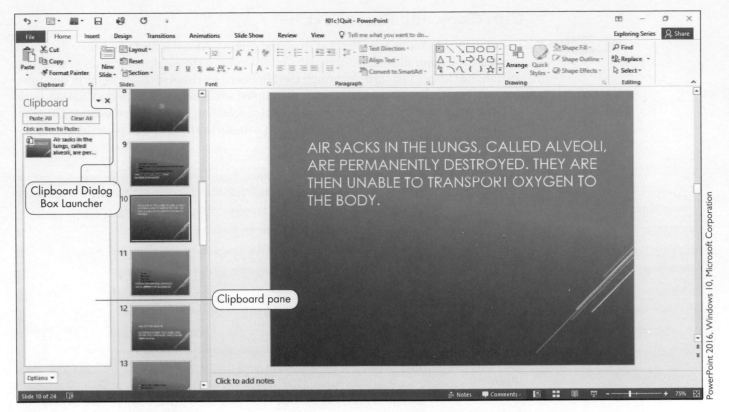

FIGURE 1.27 The Office Clipboard

Unless you specify otherwise when beginning a paste operation, the most recently added Clipboard item is pasted. You can, however, select an item from the Clipboard pane to paste. Click the item in the list to add it to the document. You can also delete items from the Clipboard by clicking the arrow next to the selection in the Clipboard pane and then clicking Delete. You can remove all items from the Clipboard by clicking Clear All. The Options button in the Clipboard pane enables you to control when and where the Clipboard is displayed. Close the Clipboard pane by clicking the Close ☒ button in the top-right corner of the pane or by clicking the arrow in the title bar of the Clipboard pane and selecting Close.

Checking Spelling and Grammar

 As you create or edit a file you will want to make sure no spelling or grammatical errors exist. You will also be concerned with wording, being sure to select words or phrases that best represent the purpose of the document, worksheet, or presentation. On occasion, you might even find yourself at a loss for an appropriate word. Word, Excel, and PowerPoint all provide standard tools for proofreading, including a spelling and grammar checker and thesaurus.

Word and PowerPoint check your spelling and grammar as you type. If a word is unrecognized, it is flagged as misspelled or grammatically incorrect. Even though Excel does not check your spelling as you type, it is important to run the spelling checker in Excel. Excel's spelling checker will review charts, pivot tables, and other reports that all need to be spelled correctly. Misspellings are identified with a red wavy underline, grammatical problems are underlined in green, and word usage errors (such as using bear instead of bare) have a blue underline.

To check the spelling for an entire file, complete the following steps:

1. Click the Review tab.
2. Click Spelling and Grammar.

Beginning at the top of the document, each identified error is highlighted in a pane similar to Figure 1.28. You can then choose how to address the problem by making a selection from the options in the pane.

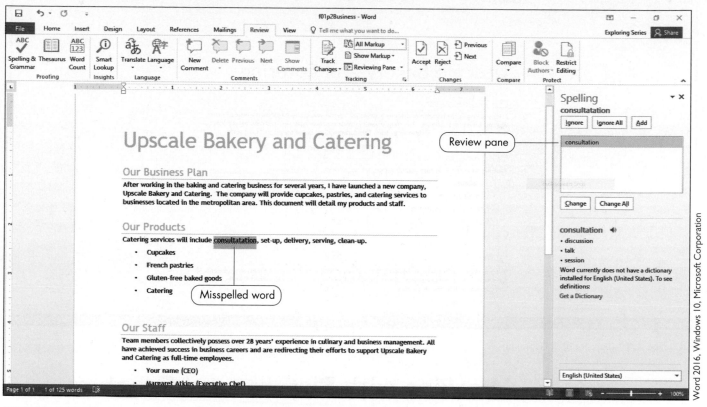

FIGURE 1.28 Checking for Spelling and Grammatical Errors

If the word or phrase is truly in error—that is, it is not a person's name or an unusual term that is not in the application's dictionary—you can correct it manually, or you can let the software correct it for you. If you right-click a word or phrase that is identified as a mistake, you will see a shortcut menu similar to that shown in Figure 1.29. If the Office dictionary makes a suggestion with the correct spelling, you can click to accept the suggestion and make the change. If a grammatical rule is violated, you will have an opportunity to select a correction. However, if the text is actually correct, you can click Ignore or Ignore All (to bypass all occurrences of the flagged error in the current document). Click *Add to Dictionary* if you want the word to be considered correct whenever it appears in any document. Similar selections on a shortcut menu enable you to ignore grammatical mistakes if they are not errors.

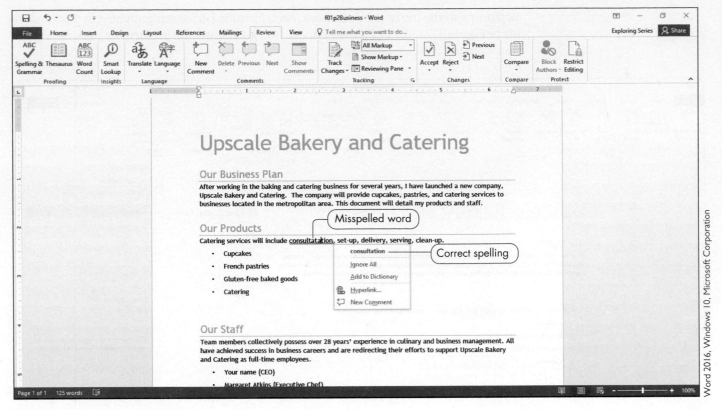

FIGURE 1.29 Correcting Misspelling

Working with Pictures and Graphics

Documents, worksheets, and presentations can include much more than just words and numbers. You can add energy and additional description to a project by including pictures and other graphic elements. Although a ***picture*** is usually just that—a digital photo—it is actually defined as a graphic element.

Insert Pictures and Graphics

 You can insert pictures from your own library of digital photos you have saved on your hard drive, OneDrive, or another storage medium, or you can initiate a Bing Image Search for online pictures directly inside the Office program you are using. The Bing search filters are set to use the Creative Commons license system. These are images and drawings that can be used more freely than images from websites. You should read the Creative Commons license for each image you use to avoid copyright infringement. You can also insert a picture from social media sites, such as Facebook, by clicking the Facebook icon at the bottom of the Online Pictures dialog box.

> **To insert an online picture from a Bing Image Search, complete the following steps:**
>
> 1. Click in the file where you want the picture to be placed.
> 2. Click the Insert tab.
> 3. Click Online Pictures in the Illustrations group.
> 4. Type a search term in the Bing Image Search box and press Enter.
> 5. Select your desired image and click Insert (see Figure 1.30).

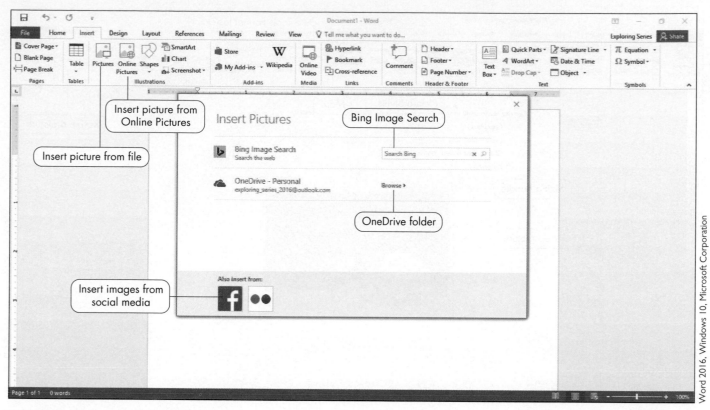

FIGURE 1.30 Inserting Online Pictures

To insert a picture from a file stored on your computer, complete the following steps:

1. Click in the file where you want the picture to be placed.
2. Click the Insert tab.
3. Click Pictures in the Illustrations group to search for a file located on your computer.
4. Locate the file and select it. Click Insert at the bottom of the dialog box to insert the file into your document.

Resize and Format Pictures and Graphics

You have learned how to add a picture to your document, but quite often, a picture is inserted in a size that is too large or too small for your purposes. To resize a picture, you can drag a corner sizing handle. You should never resize a picture by dragging a center sizing handle, as doing so would skew the picture. You can also resize a picture by adjusting settings in the Size group of the Picture Tools Format tab. When a picture is selected, the Picture Tools Format tab includes options for modifying a picture (see Figure 1.31). You can apply a picture style or effect, as well as add a picture border, from selections in the Picture Styles group. Click More (see Figure 1.31) to view a gallery of picture styles. As you point to a style, the style is shown in Live Preview, but the style is not applied until you click it. Options in the Adjust group simplify changing a color scheme, applying creative artistic effects, and even adjusting the brightness, contrast, and sharpness of an image.

Word 2016, Windows 10, Microsoft Corporation

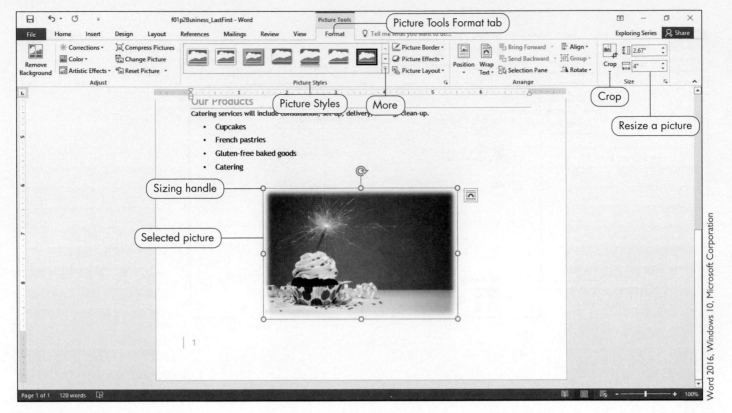

FIGURE 1.31 Formatting a Picture

If a picture contains more detail than is necessary, you can crop it, which is the process of trimming edges that you do not want to display. The Crop tool is located on the Picture Tools Format tab (refer to Figure 1.31). Even though cropping enables you to adjust the amount of a picture that displays, it does not actually delete the portions that are cropped out unless you actually compress the picture. Therefore, you can later recover parts of the picture, if necessary. Cropping a picture does not reduce the file size of the picture or the document in which it displays.

Quick Concepts

4. What is the difference between a theme and a template? *p. 24*

5. Give an example of when Format Painter could be used. *p. 29*

6. When will an Office application identify a word as misspelled that is not actually misspelled? *p. 33*

Hands-On Exercises

Skills covered: Open a Template • Select Text • Edit Text • Use the Mini Toolbar • Format Painter • Cut, Copy, and Paste Text • Check Spelling and Grammar • Insert a Picture

2 Format Document Content

As the administrative assistant for the Spotted Begonia Art Gallery, you want to create a flyer to announce the *Discover the Artist in You!* kickoff event. You decide to use a template to help you get started more quickly. You will modify the flyer created with the template by adding and editing text and a photo.

STEP 1 ›› OPEN A TEMPLATE

To expedite the process of creating a flyer, you will review the templates that are available in Microsoft Word. You search for flyers and finally choose one that is appropriate for the gallery, knowing that you will be able to replace the photos with your own. Refer to Figure 1.32 as you complete Step 1.

Step b: Flyer template opened

[Add Key Event Info Here!]

[Don't Be Shy— Tell Them Why

[One More Point Here!]

[Add More Great Info Here!]

[You Have Room for Another One Here!]

[DATE] [EVENT TITLE HERE]

Word 2016, Windows 10, Microsoft Corporation

FIGURE 1.32 Use a Template

a. Start Word. In the *Search for online templates* box type the search term **event flyer** to search for event flyer templates Click **Search**.

Your search results in a selection of event flyer templates.

b. Locate the event flyer template in Figure 1.32 and click to select it. The template appears in a preview. Click **Create** to open the flyer template.

The flyer template that you selected opens in Word.

TROUBLESHOOTING: If you do not find the template in the figure, you may access the template from the student data files – *f01h2Flyer*.

c. Click **Save** on the Quick Access Toolbar. Save the document as **f01h2Flyer_LastFirst**. Because this is the first time to save the flyer file, the Save button on the Quick Access Toolbar opens a dialog box in which you must indicate the location of the file and the file name.

You will replace the template text to create the flyer, adding information such as a title, date, and description. After adding the text to the document, you will modify the organization name in the flyer so it is more like the logo text. Refer to Figure 1.33 as you complete Step 2.

FIGURE 1.33 Select and Edit Text

a. Click the [Date] **placeholder** in the main body of the text and type **May 31, 2018** in the placeholder. Click the [Event Title Here] **placeholder** and type **Discover the Artist in You!** in the placeholder. Press **Enter** and continue typing **Spotted Begonia Art Gallery**. Click the [Event Description Heading] **placeholder** and type **A Special Childrens Event**. (Ignore the misspelling at this time.)

You modify the placeholders to customize the flyer for your purposes.

b. Point to the text **Discover the Artist in You!** until the pointer becomes an I-beam. Click and drag to select the text. Click the **Font arrow** on the Mini toolbar. Select **Eras Bold ITC**.

The font is changed.

c. Select the text, **May 31, 2018**. Click the **Font Size arrow** on the Mini toolbar. Select **26** on the Font Size menu.

The font size is changed to 26 pt.

d. Click Save on the Quick Access Toolbar to save the document.

STEP 3)) USE FORMAT PAINTER

You want the gallery name font to match that of the event description heading in the flyer. You recently learned about using the Format Painter tool to quickly apply font attributes to text. Refer to Figure 1.34 as you complete Step 3.

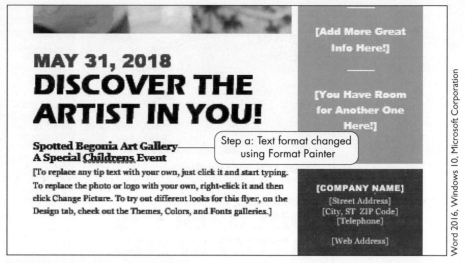

FIGURE 1.34 Use Format Painter

a. Click the **Home tab**. Select the text **A Special Childrens Event**, and click **Format Painter** in the Clipboard group. Drag to select the text **Spotted Begonia Art Gallery**.

The text is now modified to match the font and size of the event description heading.

b. Save the document.

STEP 4)) CUT, COPY, AND PASTE TEXT

You decide that one of the paragraphs in the flyer would be best near the end of the document. You cut the paragraph and paste it in the new location. Refer to Figure 1.35 as you complete Step 4.

FIGURE 1.35 Move Text

a. Point to the text **Spotted Begonia Art Gallery** until the pointer becomes an I-beam. Click and drag to select the text. Press **Ctrl+X**.

The paragraph text is cut from the document and placed in the Office Clipboard.

b. Click before the word *May*. Press **Ctrl+V** to paste the previously cut text.

The text is now moved above the event date.

c. Save the document.

Because this flyer will be seen by the public, it is important to check the spelling and grammar for your document. Refer to Figure 1.36 as you complete Step 5.

FIGURE 1.36 Check Spelling and Grammar

a. Press **Ctrl+Home**. Click the **Review tab**, and click **Spelling & Grammar**. in the Proofing group Click **Change** to accept the suggested change to *Children's* in the Spelling pane. Click **OK** to close the dialog box.

   The spelling and grammar check is complete.

b. Save the document.

You want to add an image saved on your computer that was taken at a previous children's event held at the gallery. Refer to Figure 1.37 as you complete Step 6.

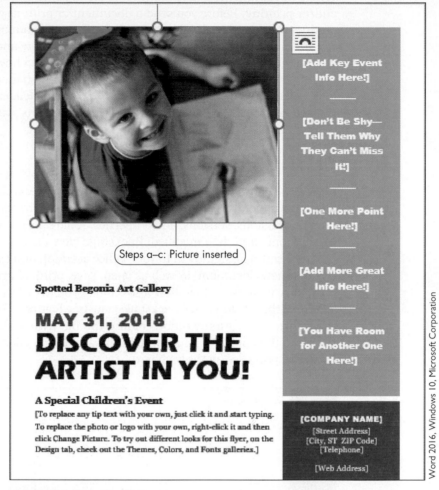

FIGURE 1.37 Insert Picture

a. Click the **image** to select it. Click the **Insert tab** and then click **Pictures**. Browse to your student data files and locate the *f01h2Art* picture file. Click **Insert**.

The child's image is inserted into the flyer and replaces the template image of the children with ice cream.

b. Save and close the document. You will submit this file to your instructor at the end of the last Hands-On Exercise.

Modify Document Layout and Properties

When working with a document, at some point you must get it ready for distribution and/or printing. Before you send a document or print it, you will want to view the final product to make sure that your margins and page layout are as they should be.

In this section you will learn about Backstage view and explore how to view and edit document properties. You will learn about views and how to change a document view to suit your needs. Additionally, you will learn how to modify the page layout including page orientation and margins as well as how to add headers and footers. Finally, you will explore Print Preview and the various printing options available to you.

Using Backstage View

Backstage view is a component of Office that provides a concise collection of commands related to a file. Using Backstage view, you can view or specify settings related to protection, permissions, versions, and properties. A file's properties include the author, file size, permissions, and date modified. Backstage view also includes options for customizing program settings, signing in to your Office account, and exiting the application. You can create a new document, as well as open, save, print, share, export, and close files using Backstage view. Backstage view also enables you to exit the application.

Click the File tab to see Backstage view (see Figure 1.38). Backstage view will occupy the entire application window, hiding the file with which you are working. You can return to the application in a couple of ways. Either click the Back arrow in the top-left corner or press Esc on the keyboard.

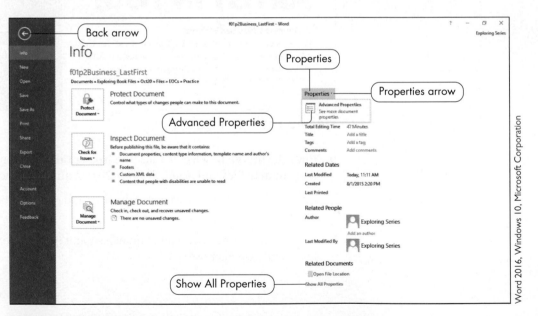

FIGURE 1.38 Backstage View and Document Properties

Customize Application Options

General settings in the Office application in which you are working can also be customized (see Figure 1.39). For example, you can change the AutoRecover settings, a feature that enables Word to recover a previous version of a document, such as the location and save frequency. You can alter how formatting, spelling, and grammar are checked by the application such as ignoring words in all uppercase letters. You can also modify the AutoCorrect feature. Additionally, you can change the language in which the application is displayed or the language for spelling and grammar checking, which may be helpful for a language course.

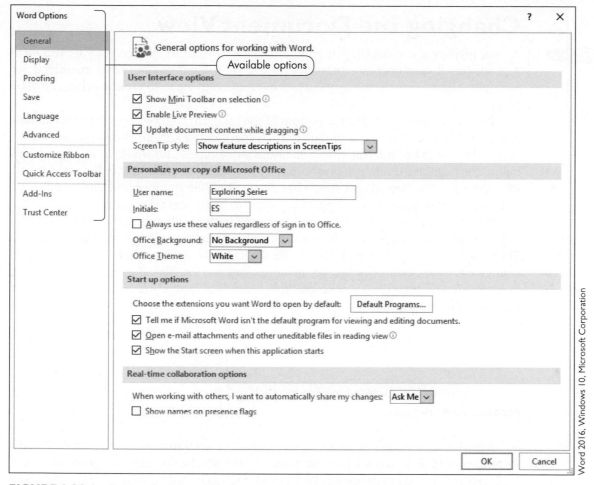

FIGURE 1.39 Application Options in Word

To customize an Office application, complete the following steps:

1. Click the File tab.
2. Click Options and select the option of your choice.
3. Click OK.

View and Edit Document Properties

STEP 1 ⟩⟩ It is good to include information that identifies a document, such as the author, document purpose, intended audience, or general comments. Those data elements, or metadata, are saved with the document, but do not appear in the document as it displays onscreen or is printed. You can use the Document Properties, located in Backstage view, to display descriptive information. You can even search for a file based on metadata you assign a document. For example, suppose you apply a tag of *Picasso* to all documents you create that are associated with that particular artist. Later, you can use that keyword as a search term, locating all associated documents. Statistical information related to the current document such as file size, number of pages, and total words are located on the Info page of Backstage view. You can modify some document information, such as adding a title or comments, but for more possibilities, display the Advanced Properties (refer to Figure 1.38).

To display the Advanced Properties, complete the following steps:

1. Click the File tab.
2. Click the Properties arrow on the Info page.

Changing the Document View

STEP 2 »» As you prepare a document, you may find that you want to change the way you view it. A section of your document may be easier to view when you can see it magnified, for example. Alternatively, some applications have different views to make working on your project easier.

The *status bar*, located at the bottom of the program window, contains information relative to the open file and is unique to each specific application. When you work with Word, the status bar informs you of the number of pages and words in an open document. The Excel status bar displays summary information, such as average and sum, of selected cells. The PowerPoint status bar shows the slide number and total number of slides in the presentation. It also provides access to Notes and Comments.

The status bar also includes commonly used tools for changing the *view*—the way a file appears onscreen—and for changing the zoom size of onscreen file contents. The view buttons (see Figure 1.40) on the status bar of each application enable you to change the view of the open file. For instance, you can use Slide Sorter view to look at a PowerPoint slide presentation with multiple slides displayed or use Normal view to show only one slide in large size.

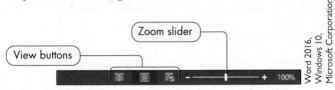

FIGURE 1.40 The Status Bar

Additional views for all Office applications are available on the View tab. Word's Print Layout view is useful when you want to see both the document text and such features as margins and page breaks. Web Layout view is useful to see what the page would look like on the Internet. Read Mode view provides a clean look that displays just the content without the Ribbon or margins. It is ideal for use on a tablet where the screen may be smaller than on a laptop or computer. PowerPoint, Excel, and Access also provide other unique view options. As you learn more about Office applications, you will become aware of the views that are specific to each application.

The *Zoom slider* is a horizontal bar on the bottom-right side of the status bar that enables you to increase or decrease the size of the document onscreen. You can drag the tab along the slider in either direction to increase or decrease the magnification of the file (refer to Figure 1.40). Be aware, however, that changing the size of text onscreen does not change the font size when the file is printed or saved.

Changing the Page Layout

When you prepare a document or worksheet, you are concerned with the way the project appears onscreen and possibly in print. The Layout tab in Word and the Page Layout tab in Excel provide access to a full range of options such as margin settings and page orientation. PowerPoint does not have a Page Layout tab, since its primary purpose is displaying contents onscreen rather than in print.

Because a document or workbook is most often designed to be printed, you may need to adjust margins and change the page orientation for the best display. In addition, perhaps the document or spreadsheet should be centered on the page vertically or the text should be aligned in columns. You will find these and other common page settings in the Page Setup group on the Layout (or Page Layout) tab. For less common settings, such as determining whether headers should print on odd or even pages, you use the Page Setup dialog box.

Change Margins

STEP 3 ►► A *margin* is the area of blank space that displays to the left, right, top, and bottom of a document or worksheet. Margins display when you are in Print Layout or Page Layout view, or in Backstage view previewing a document to print. As shown in Figure 1.41, you can change the margins by clicking Margins in the Page Setup group. You can also change margins in the Print area on Backstage view.

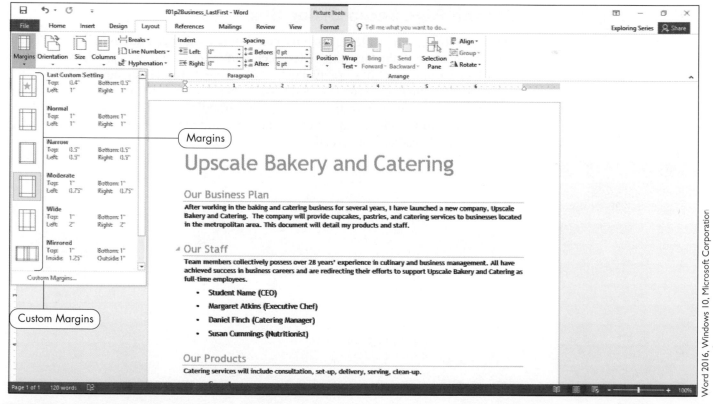

FIGURE 1.41 Page Margins in Word

To change margins in Word and Excel, complete the following steps:

1. Click the Layout (or Page Layout) tab.
2. Click Margins in the Page Setup group.
3. Select a preset margin option or click Custom Margins (refer to Figure 1.41) to display the Page Setup dialog box where you can apply custom margin settings.
4. Click OK to accept the settings and close the dialog box.

Change Page Orientation

Documents and worksheets can be displayed in different page orientations. A page displayed or printed in *portrait orientation* is taller than it is wide. A page in *landscape orientation* is wider than it is tall. Word documents are usually more attractive displayed in portrait orientation, whereas Excel worksheets are often more suited to landscape orientation.

To change the page orientation, complete the following steps:

1. Click the Layout (or Page Layout) tab.
2. Click Orientation in the Page Setup group.
3. Select Portrait or Landscape.

Orientation is also an option in the Print area of Backstage view.

Use the Page Setup Dialog Box

The Page Setup group contains the most commonly used page options in the particular Office application. Some are unique to Excel, and others are more applicable to Word. Other less common settings are available in the Page Setup dialog box only, displayed when you click the Page Setup Dialog Box Launcher. The Page Setup dialog box includes options for customizing margins, selecting page orientation, centering horizontally or vertically, printing gridlines, and creating headers and footers. Figure 1.42 shows both the Excel and Word Page Setup dialog boxes.

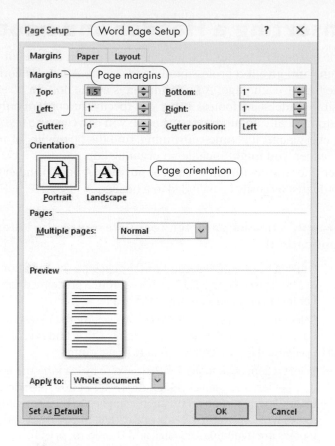

FIGURE 1.42 Page Setup Dialog Boxes in Word and Excel

Word 2016, Windows 10, Microsoft Corporation

Inserting a Header and Footer

 STEP 4 ▶▶ The purpose of including a header or footer in a document is to better identify the document and give it a professional appearance. A ***header*** consists of one or more lines at the top of each page. A ***footer*** displays at the bottom of each page. One advantage of using headers and footers is that you specify the content only once, after which it displays automatically on all pages. Although you can type the text yourself at the top or bottom of every page, it is time-consuming, and the possibility of making a mistake is great. As a header, you might include an organization name or a class number so that each page identifies the document's origin or purpose. A page number is a typical footer, although it could just as easily be included in a header.

> **To apply a header or footer, complete one of the following steps (based on the application):**
>
> - Select a header or footer in Word by clicking the Insert tab and then clicking Header or Footer (see Figure 1.43). Choose from a predefined list, or click Edit Header (or Edit Footer) to create an unformatted header or footer.
>
> - Select a header or footer in Excel by clicking the Insert tab and clicking Header and Footer. Select the left, center, or right section and type your own footer or use a predefined field code such as date or file name.
>
> - Select a header or footer for PowerPoint by clicking the Insert tab, clicking Header and Footer, and then checking the footer option for slides. In PowerPoint, a footer's location will depend on the theme applied to the presentation. For some themes, the footer will appear on the side of the slide rather than at the bottom. Headers and footers are available for Notes and Handouts as well.

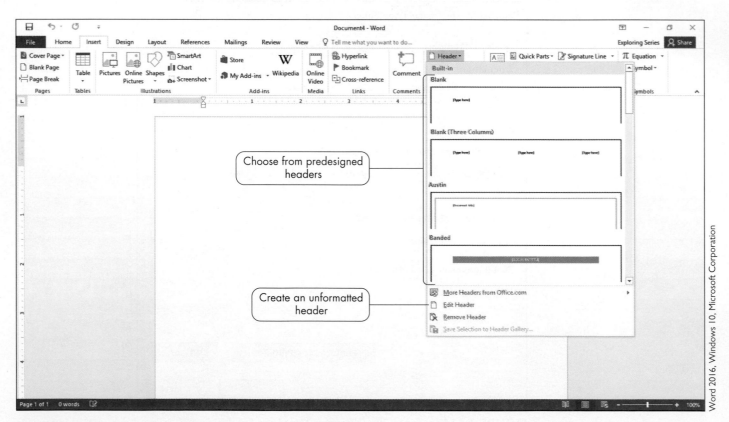

FIGURE 1.43 Insert Header in Word

After typing a header or footer, it can be formatted like any other text. It can be formatted in any font or font size. In Word or Excel, when you want to leave the header and footer area and return to the document, click Close Header and Footer (see Figure 1.44).

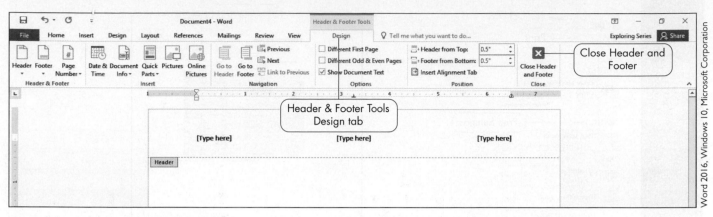

FIGURE 1.44 Close Header and Footer

Previewing and Printing a File

STEP 5 ▶▶ When you want to print an Office file, you can select from various print options, including the number of copies and the specific pages to print. It is a good idea to take a look at how your document or worksheet will appear before you print it. The Print Preview feature of Office enables you to do just that. In the Print Preview pane, you will see all items, including any headers, footers, graphics, and special formatting.

To view a file before printing, complete the following steps:

1. Click the File tab.
2. Click Print.

The subsequent Backstage view shows the file preview on the right, with print settings located in the center of the Backstage screen. Figure 1.45 shows a typical Backstage Print view. If you know that the page setup is correct and that there are no unique print settings to select, you can simply print without adjusting any print settings.

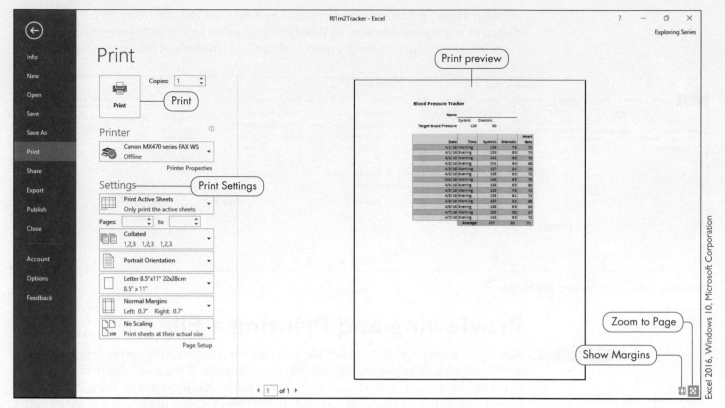

FIGURE 1.45 Backstage Print View in Excel

Options to show the margins (*Show Margins*) and to increase the size of the print preview (*Zoom to Page*) are found on the bottom-right corner of the preview (refer to Figure 1.45). Remember that increasing the font size by adjusting the zoom applies to the current display only; it does not actually increase the font size when the file is printed or saved. To return the preview to its original view, click *Zoom to Page* once more.

Other options in the Backstage Print view vary depending on the application in which you are working. For example, PowerPoint's Backstage Print view includes options for printing slides and handouts in various configurations and colors, whereas Excel's focuses on worksheet selections and Word's includes document options. Regardless of the Office application, you will be able to access Settings options from Backstage view, including page orientation (landscape or portrait), margins, and paper size. To print a file, click the Print button (refer to Figure 1.45).

Quick Concepts

7. What functions and features are included in Backstage view? *p. 42*

8. Why would you need to change the view of a document? *p. 44*

9. What is the purpose of a header or footer? *p. 48*

Hands-On Exercises

Skills covered: Enter Document Properties • Change the Document View • Change Margins • Insert a Footer • Preview a File • Change Page Orientation

3 Modify Document Layout and Properties

You continue to work on the thank-you letter you previously started. As the administrative assistant for the Spotted Begonia Art Gallery, you must be able to search for and find documents previously created. You know that by adding tags to your letter you will more easily be able to find it at a later time. You will review and add document properties, and prepare the document to print and distribute by changing the page setup. Additionally, you will add a footer with Spotted Begonia's information. Finally, you will explore printing options, and save the letter.

STEP 1 ❯❯ ENTER DOCUMENT PROPERTIES

You will add document properties, which will help you locate the file when performing a search of your hard drive. Refer to Figure 1.46 as you complete Step 1.

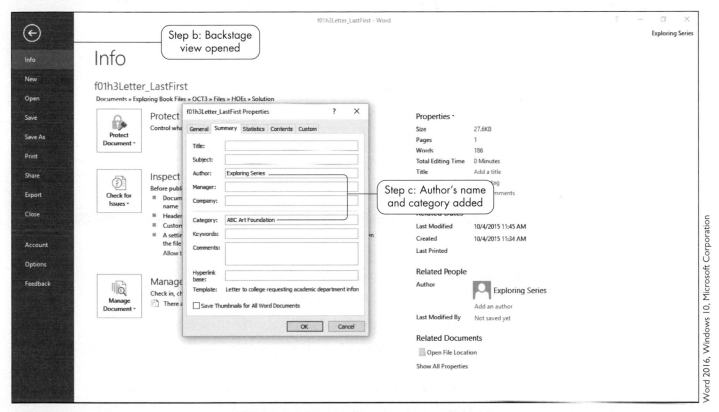

FIGURE 1.46 Backstage View

a. Open *f01h1Letter_LastFirst* if you closed it at the end of Hands-On Exercise 1, and save it as **f01h3Letter_LastFirst**, changing h1 to h3.

The letter is now open in Word.

b. Click the **File tab** and click **Properties** at the top-right of Backstage view. Click **Advanced Properties**.

The Properties dialog box opens so you can make changes.

c. Select the **Author box** and type your first and last name. Select the **Category box** and type **ABC Art Foundation**. Click **OK**.

You added the Author and Category properties to your document.

d. Save the document.

STEP 2 ﹥﹥ CHANGE THE DOCUMENT VIEW

To get a better perspective on your letter, you want to explore the various document views available in Word. Refer to Figure 1.47 as you complete Step 2.

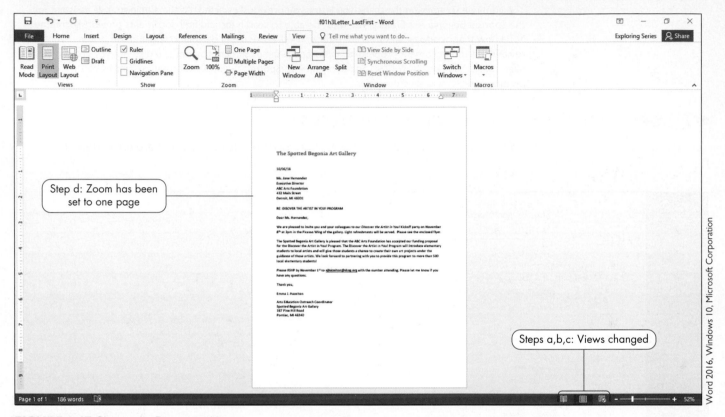

FIGURE 1.47 Change the Document View

a. Click **Read Mode** on the status bar. Observe the changes to the Ribbon.

The view is changed to Read Mode, which is a full-screen view.

b. Click **Web Layout** on the status bar. Observe the changes to the view.

The view is changed to Web Layout and simulates how the document would appear on the Web.

c. Click **Print Layout** on the status bar. Observe the changes to the view.

The document has returned to Print Layout view.

d. Click the **View tab** and click **Zoom** in the Zoom group. Click the **One Page option**. Click **OK**.

The entire letter is displayed.

While the letter was displayed in One Page zoom, you observed that the margins were too large. You will change the margins so they are narrower. Refer to Figure 1.48 as you complete Step 3.

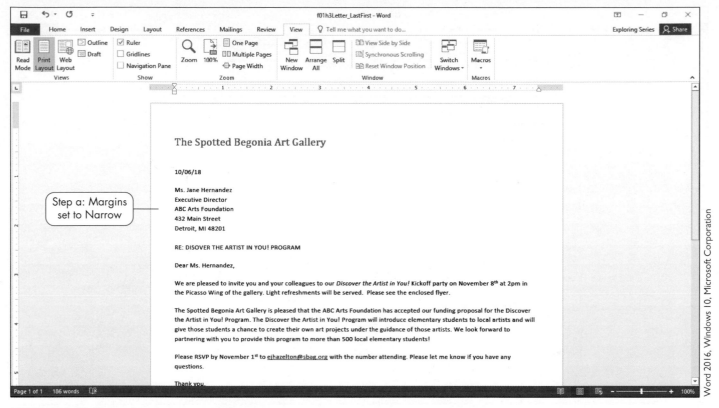

FIGURE 1.48 Change Margins

a. Click the **Layout tab** and click **Margins** in the Page Setup group. Select **Narrow**. Observe the changes.

The document margins were changed to Narrow.

b. Click the **View tab** and click **100%** in the Zoom group.

The document returns to its previous view.

c. Save the document.

Additional information such as a phone number and website need to be added to the letter. You decide to add these to the letter as a footer. Refer to Figure 1.49 as you complete Step 4.

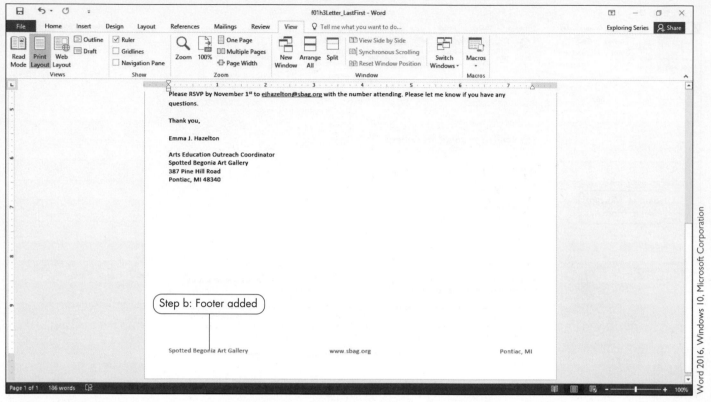

FIGURE 1.49 Footer

a. Click the **Insert tab** and click **Footer** in the Header & Footer group. Click the **Blank (three columns)** footer.

The document opens in Header and Footer view. You select a footer with little formatting.

b. Click **[Type here]** on the far left of the footer. Type **Spotted Begonia Art Gallery** in that placeholder. Click **[Type here]** in the center of the footer. Type **www.sbag.org** in that placeholder. Click **[Type here]** on the far right of the footer. Type **Pontiac, MI** in that placeholder. On the Header & Footer Tools Design tab, click **Close Header and Footer** in the Close group.

The footer information is entered.

c. Save the document.

You have reviewed and finalized the letter, so you will print the document so it can be sent to its recipient. You will first preview the document as it will appear when printed. Refer to Figure 1.50 as you complete Step 5.

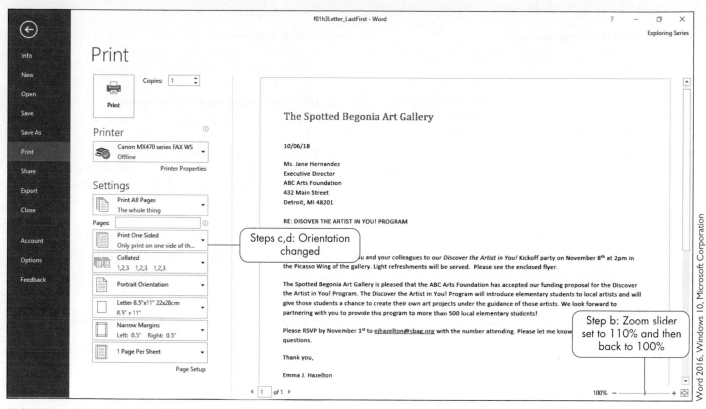

FIGURE 1.50 Backstage Print View

a. Click the **File tab** and click **Print**.

It is always a good idea to check the way a file will look when printed before actually printing it.

b. Drag the **Zoom slider on the status bar** to increase the document view to 110%. Click **Zoom to Page** 🔲 (located at the far right of the status bar).

Your print preview returns to the original size.

c. Click **Portrait Orientation** in the Settings area. Click **Landscape Orientation**.

The letter appears in a wider and shorter view.

d. Return to Portrait Orientation to see the original view.

You decide that the flyer is more attractive in portrait orientation, so you return to that setting.

e. Save and close the file. Based on your instructor's directions, submit the following:

f01h2Flyer_LastFirst

f01h3Letter_LastFirst

Chapter Objectives Review

After reading this chapter, you have accomplished the following objectives:

1. Start an Office application.
- Your Microsoft account connects you to all of Microsoft's Internet-based resources.
- Change a Microsoft account: If you share your computer with another user, each user can have access to his own Microsoft account; you can easily switch between accounts so you can access your own files.

2. Work with files.
- Create a new file: You can create a document as a blank document or with a template.
- Open a file: You can open an existing file using the Open dialog box. Previously saved files can be accessed using the Recent documents list.
- Save a file: Saving a file enables you to open it later for additional updates or reference. Files are saved to a storage medium such as a hard drive, CD, flash drive, or to the cloud on OneDrive.

3. Use common interface components.
- Use the Ribbon: The Ribbon, the long bar located just beneath the title bar containing tabs, groups, and commands, is the command center of Office applications.
- Use a shortcut menu: A shortcut menu provides choices related to the object, selection, or area of the document on which you right-click.
- Use keyboard shortcuts: Keyboard shortcuts are keyboard equivalents for software commands. Universal keyboard shortcuts in Office include Ctrl+C (Copy), Ctrl+X (Cut), Ctrl+V (Paste), and Ctrl+Z (Undo).
- Customize the Ribbon: You can personalize the Ribbon in your Office applications, giving you easier access to a frequently used set of commands that are unique to you or your business.
- Use the Quick Access Toolbar: The Quick Access Toolbar, located at the top-left corner of any Office application window, provides one-click access to commonly executed tasks such as saving a file or undoing recent actions.
- Customize the Quick Access Toolbar: You use certain actions in an Office application often, and for more convenient access, you can add a button for each action to the Quick Access Toolbar.

4. Get help.
- Use the *Tell me what you want to do* box: The *Tell me what you want to do* box not only links to online resources and technical support but also provides quick access to functions.
- Use Enhanced ScreenTips: An Enhanced ScreenTip describes a command and provides a keyboard shortcut, if applicable.

5. Install add-ins.
- Add-ins are custom programs or additional commands that extend the functionality of a Microsoft Office program.

6. Use templates and apply themes.
- Open a template: Templates are a convenient way to save time when designing a document.
- Apply a theme: Themes are a collection of design choices that include colors, fonts, and special effects used to give a consistent look to a document, workbook, or presentation.

7. Modify text.
- Select text: To select text or numbers, place the pointer before the first character or digit you want to select, and then drag to highlight the intended selection. Before you drag, be sure that the pointer takes on the shape of the letter *I*, called the I-beam.
- Edit text: You can edit the font, font color, size, and many other attributes.
- Use the Mini toolbar: The Mini toolbar provides instant access to common formatting commands after text is selected.
- Copy formats with the Format Painter: Easily apply formatting from one selection to another by using Format Painter.

8. Relocate text.
- Cut, copy, and paste text: To cut means to remove a selection from the original location and place it in the Office Clipboard. To copy means to duplicate a selection from the original location and place a copy in the Office Clipboard. To paste means to place a cut or copied selection into another location.
- Use the Office Clipboard: When you cut or copy selections, they are placed in the Office Clipboard. You can paste the same item multiple times; it will remain in the Clipboard until you power down your computer or until the Clipboard exceeds 24 items.

9. Check spelling and grammar.
- Office applications check and mark spelling and grammar errors as you type for later correction. The Thesaurus enables you to search for synonyms.

10. Work with pictures and Graphics.
- Insert pictures and graphics: You can insert pictures from your own library of digital photos you have saved on your hard drive, OneDrive, or another storage medium, or you can initiate a Bing search for online pictures directly inside the Office program you are using.
- Resize and format pictures and graphics: To resize a picture, drag a corner sizing handle; never resize a picture by dragging a center sizing handle. You can apply

a picture style or effect, as well as add a picture border, from selections in the Picture Styles group.

11. Use Backstage view.

- Customize application options: You can customize general settings in the Office application in which you are working, such as AutoRecover settings and location and save frequency.
- View and edit document properties: Information that identifies a document, such as the author, document purpose, intended audience, or general comments can be added to the document's properties. Those data elements are saved with the document, but do not appear in the document as it displays onscreen or is printed.

12. Change the document view.

- The status bar provides information relative to the open file and quick access to View and Zoom level options. Each application has a set of views specific to the application.

13. Change the page layout.

- Change margins: A margin is the area of blank space that displays to the left, right, top, and bottom of a document or worksheet.

- Change page orientation: Documents and worksheets can be displayed in different page orientations. Portrait orientation is taller than it is wide; landscape orientation is wider than it is tall.
- Use the Page Setup dialog box: The Page Setup dialog box includes options for customizing margins, selecting page orientation, centering horizontally or vertically, printing gridlines, and creating headers and footers.

14. Insert a header and footer.

- A footer displays at the bottom of each page.
- A header consists of one or more lines at the top of each page.

15. Preview and print a file.

- It is important to review your file before printing.
- Print options can be set in Backstage view and include page orientation, the number of copies, and the specific pages to print.

Key Terms Matching

Match the key terms with their definitions. Write the key term letter by the appropriate numbered definition.

a. Access
b. Add-in
c. Clipboard
d. Backstage view
e. Cloud storage
f. Format Painter
g. Footer
h. Group
i. Header
j. Margin

k. Microsoft Office
l. Mini toolbar
m. OneDrive
n. Quick Access Toolbar
o. Ribbon
p. Status bar
q. Tab
r. *Tell me what you want to do* box
s. Template
t. Theme

1. _____ A tool that copies all formatting from one area to another. **p. 29**

2. _____ Stores up to 24 cut or copied selections for use later on in your computing session. **p. 30**

3. _____ A task-oriented section of the Ribbon that contains related commands. **p. 10**

4. _____ An online app used to store, access, and share files and folders. **p. 5**

5. _____ Custom programs or additional commands that extend the functionality of a Microsoft Office program. **p. 17**

6. _____ A component of Office that provides a concise collection of commands related to an open file and includes save and print options. **p. 42**

7. _____ A tool that displays near selected text that contains formatting commands. **p. 28**

8. _____ Relational database software used to store data and convert it into information. **p. 4**

9. _____ Consists of one or more lines at the bottom of each page. **p. 48**

10. _____ A predesigned file that incorporates formatting elements, such as a theme and layouts, and may include content that can be modified. **p. 24**

11. _____ A collection of design choices that includes colors, fonts, and special effects used to give a consistent look to a document, workbook, or presentation. **p. 24**

12. _____ A component of the Ribbon that is designed to appear much like a tab on a file folder. **p. 9**

13. _____ Provides handy access to commonly executed tasks such as saving a file and undoing recent actions. **p. 14**

14. _____ The long bar at the bottom of the screen that houses the Zoom slider and various View buttons. **p. 44**

15. _____ A productivity software suite including a set of software applications, each one specializing in a particular type of output. **p. 4**

16. _____ Allows you to search for help and information about a command or task you want to perform, and will also present you with a shortcut directly to that command. **p. 15**

17. _____ The long bar located just beneath the title bar containing tabs, groups, and commands. **p. 8**

18. _____ The area of blank space that displays to the left, right, top, and bottom of a document or worksheet **p. 45**

19. _____ A technology used to store files and to work with programs that are stored in a central location on the Internet. **p. 5**

20. _____ Consists of one or more lines at the top of each page. **p. 48**

Multiple Choice

1. The Recent documents list shows documents that have been previously:
   - (a) Printed.
   - (b) Opened.
   - (c) Saved in an earlier software version.
   - (d) Deleted.

2. In Word or PowerPoint a quick way to select an entire paragraph is to:
   - (a) Place the pointer at the left of the line, in the margin area, and click.
   - (b) Triple-click inside the paragraph.
   - (c) Double-click at the beginning of the paragraph.
   - (d) Press Ctrl+C inside the paragraph.

3. When you want to copy the format of a selection but not the content, you should:
   - (a) Double-click Copy in the Clipboard group.
   - (b) Right-click the selection and click Copy.
   - (c) Click Copy Format in the Clipboard group.
   - (d) Click Format Painter in the Clipboard group.

4. Which of the following is *not* a benefit of using OneDrive?
   - (a) Save your folders and files to the cloud.
   - (b) Share your files and folders with others.
   - (c) Hold video conferences with others.
   - (d) Simultaneously work on the same document with others.

5. What does a red wavy underline in a document, spreadsheet, or presentation mean?
   - (a) A word is misspelled or not recognized by the Office dictionary.
   - (b) A grammatical mistake exists.
   - (c) An apparent word usage mistake exists.
   - (d) A word has been replaced with a synonym.

6. Which of the following is *true* about headers and footers?
   - (a) They can be inserted from the Layout tab.
   - (b) Headers and footers only appear on the last page of a document.
   - (c) Headers appear at the top of every page in a document.
   - (d) Only page numbers can be included in a header or footer.

7. Live Preview:
   - (a) Opens a predesigned document or spreadsheet that is relevant to your task.
   - (b) Provides a preview of the results of a choice you are considering before you make a final selection.
   - (c) Provides a preview of an upcoming Office version.
   - (d) Enlarges the font onscreen.

8. You can get help when working with an Office application in which one of the following areas?
   - (a) The *Tell me what you want to do* box
   - (b) Status bar
   - (c) Backstage view
   - (d) Quick Access Toolbar

9. In PowerPoint, a file that includes formatting elements such as a background, a color scheme, and slide layout is a:
   - (a) Theme.
   - (b) Template.
   - (c) Scheme.
   - (d) Variant.

10. A document or worksheet printed in landscape orientation is:
    - (a) Taller than it is wide.
    - (b) Wider than it is tall.
    - (c) A document with 2" left and right margins.
    - (d) A document with 2" top and bottom margins.

Practice Exercises

1 Designing Webpages

You have been asked to make a presentation to the local business association. With the mayor's renewed emphasis on growing the local economy, many businesses are interested in establishing a Web presence. The business owners would like to know a little bit more about how webpages are designed. In preparation for the presentation, you will proofread and edit your PowerPoint file. You decide to insert an image to enhance your presentation. Refer to Figure 1.51 as you complete this exercise.

FIGURE 1.51 Designing Webpages Presentation

a. Open *f01p1Design*. Click the **File tab**, click **Save As**, and save the file as **f01p1Design_LastFirst**.

b. Ensure that Slide 1 is visible, select the text *Firstname Lastname*, and type your own first and last names. Click an empty area of the slide to cancel the selection.

c. Click the **Design tab**, then click the **Celestial theme** in the Themes group to apply it to all slides.

d. Click the **Review tab** and click **Spelling** in the Proofing group. In the Spelling pane, click **Change** or **Ignore** to make changes as needed. Most identified misspellings should be changed. The words *KompoZer* and *Nvu* are not misspelled, so you should ignore them when they are flagged. Click **OK** when you have finished checking spelling.

e. Click the **Slide Show tab**. Click **From Beginning** in the Start Slide Show group. Click each slide to view the show and press **Esc** when you reach the last slide, slide 6.

f. Click **Slide 2** in the Slides pane on the left. Triple-click to select the **Other tools** text on the slide and press **Backspace** on the keyboard to delete the text.

g. Click **Slide 4** in the Slides pane. Triple-click to select the **FrontPage**, **Nvu** text and press **Backspace** to delete the text.

h. Click the **Insert tab**. Click **Header & Footer** in the Text group. Click the **Slide number check box** to select it and click **Apply to All**.

i. Press **Ctrl+End** to place the insertion point at the end of *Templates* on Slide 4 and press **Enter**. Type **Database Connectivity** to create a new bulleted item.

j. Click **Slide 3** in the Slides pane. Click the **Insert tab** and click **Pictures** in the Images group. Browse to the student data files, locate and select *f01p1website*, and then click **Insert**.

k. Click the **Shape height box** in the Size group on the Picture Tools Format tab. Type **4** and then press Enter.

l. Click **Slide 6** in the Slides pane. Click the **Insert tab**, and then click **Store** in the Add-ins group. In the search box, type **multiple response poll**. Press **Enter**. The add-in will resize if the window or resolution is small.

m. Click the **Multiple Response Poll** and then click **Trust It** to insert it into the slide.

n. Click the **Insert question here text box** in the poll window, and type **Do you have a website?**

o. Click the first **Insert option here text box** and type **Yes**. Click the second **Insert option here text box** and type **No**. Click **Preview** in the poll window.

p. Click the **File tab** and click **Print**. Click the **Full Page Slides arrow** and click **6 Slides Horizontal** to see a preview of all of the slides as a handout. Click the **Back arrow**.

q. Click **Slide 1** in the Slides pane to move to the beginning of the presentation.

r. Drag the **Zoom slider** on the status bar to the right to **130%** to magnify the text. Use the **Zoom slider** to move to **60%**.

s. Save and close the file. Based on your instructor's directions, submit f01p1Design_LastFirst.

You have always been interested in baking and have worked in the field for several years. You now have an opportunity to devote yourself full time to your career as the CEO of a company dedicated to baking cupcakes and pastries, and to catering. One of the first steps in getting the business off the ground is developing a business plan so that you can request financial support. You will use Word to develop your business plan. Refer to Figure 1.52 as you complete this exercise.

a. Open *f01p2Business.* Click the **File tab**, click **Save As**, and save the file as **f01p2Business_LastFirst**.

b. Click the **Review tab** and click **Spelling & Grammar** in the Proofing group. Click **Change** for all suggestions and then click OK.

c. Select the paragraphs beginning with *Our Staff* and ending with *(Nutritionist)*. Click the **Home tab** and click **Cut** in the Clipboard group. Click to the left of *Our Products* and click **Paste**.

Upscale Bakery and Catering

Our Business Plan

After working in the baking and catering business for several years, I have launched a new company, Upscale Bakery and Catering. The company will provide cupcakes, pastries, and catering services to businesses located in the metropolitan area. This document will detail my products and staff.

Our Staff

Team members collectively possess over 28 years' experience in culinary and business management. All have achieved success in business careers and are redirecting their efforts to support Upscale Bakery and Catering as full-time employees.

- Student Name (CEO)
- Margaret Atkins (Executive Chef)
- Daniel Finch (Catering Manager)
- Susan Cummings (Nutritionist)

Our Products

Catering services will include consultation, set-up, delivery, serving, clean-up.

- Cupcakes
- French pastries
- Gluten-free baked goods
- Catering

1

Word 2016, Windows 10, Microsoft Corporation

FIGURE 1.52 Upscale Bakery Business Plan

d. Select the text **Your name** in the first bullet in the *Our Staff* section and replace it with your first and last names. Select the entire bullet list, click the **Font Size arrow** and then click **11**.

e. Double-click **Format Painter** in the Clipboard group on the Home tab. Drag the Format Painter pointer to change the other *Our Staff* bullets' font size to **11 pt**. Drag across all four *Our Products* bullets. Click Format Painter to deselect it.

f. Click the ***Tell me what you want to do* box**, and type **Footer**. Click **Add a Footer** scroll to locate the **Sideline footer**, click to add it to the page. Click **Close Header and Footer** on the Header & Footer Tools Design tab.

g. Select the last line in the document, which says *Insert and position picture here*, and press **Delete**. Click the **Insert tab** and click **Online Pictures** in the Illustrations group.

- Click in the **Bing Image Search box**, type **Cupcakes**, and then press **Enter**.
- Select any cupcake image and click **Insert**. Do not deselect the image.

TROUBLESHOOTING: If you are unable to find a cupcake image in the Bing Image Search then you can use f01p2Cupcake from the student data files.

- Ensure the **Picture Tools Format tab** is active, and in the Picture Styles group, click the **Soft Edge Rectangle**.
- Click the **Shape width box** in the Size group and change the width to **4**.
- Click outside the picture.

h. Click the **File tab**. In the Properties section, add the tag **Business Plan**. Add your first and last name to the Author property.

i. Click **Print** in Backstage view. Change Normal Margins to **Moderate Margins**. Click the **Back arrow**.

j. Click the **picture** and click **Center** in the Paragraph group on the Home tab.

k. Save and close the file. Based on your instructor's directions, submit f01p2Business_LastFirst.

Mid-Level Exercises

1 Reference Letter

You are an instructor at a local community college. A student asked you to provide her with a letter of reference for a job application. You have used Word to prepare the letter, but now you want to make a few changes before it is finalized.

a. Open *f01m1RefLetter* and save it as **f01m1RefLetter_LastFirst**.

b. Select the date and point to several font sizes on the Mini toolbar. Use Live Preview to compare them. Click **11**.

c. Change the rest of the letter (below the date) to font size 11.

d. Apply bold to the student's name, *Stacy VanPatten*, in the first sentence.

e. Customize the Quick Access Toolbar so that a Spelling and Grammar button is added.

f. Use the button you just added to correct all errors using Spelling & Grammar. Stacy's last name is spelled correctly.

g. Select the word *intelligent* in the second paragraph, and use the Thesaurus to find a synonym. Replace *intelligent* with **gifted**. Change the word *an* to **a** just before the new word. Close the Thesaurus.

h. Add the tag **reference letter** to the Properties for the file in Backstage view.

i. Move the last paragraph—beginning with *In my opinion*—to position it before the second paragraph—beginning with *Stacy is a gifted*.

j. Move the insertion point to the beginning of the document.

k. Change the margins to **Narrow**.

l. Preview the document as it will appear when printed.

m. Save and close the file. Based on your instructor's directions, submit f01m1RefLetter_LastFirst.

2 Medical Monitoring

You are enrolled in a Health Informatics program of study in which you learn to manage databases related to health fields. For a class project, your instructor requires that you monitor your blood pressure, recording your findings in an Excel worksheet. You have recorded the week's data and will now make a few changes before printing the worksheet for submission.

a. Open *f01m2Tracker* and save it as **f01m2Tracker_LastFirst**.

b. Preview the worksheet as it will appear when printed. Change the orientation of the worksheet to **Landscape**. Close the Preview.

c. Click in the cell to the right of *Name* and type your first and last names. Press **Enter**.

d. Change the font of the text in **cell C1** to **Verdana**. Use Live Preview to try some font sizes. Change the font size to **20**.

e. Add the Spelling and Grammar feature to the Quick Access Toolbar, and then check the spelling for the worksheet to ensure that there are no errors.

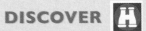 f. Get help on showing decimal places. You want to increase the decimal places for the values in **cells E22**, **F22**, and **G22** so that each value shows one place to the right of the decimal. Select the cells and then use the *Tell me what you want to do* box to immediately apply the changes. You might use **Increase Decimals** as a search term. When you find the answer, increase the decimal places to **1**.

 g. Click **cell A1** and insert an Online Picture of your choice related to blood pressure. Resize and position the picture so that it displays in an attractive manner. Apply the **Soft Edges** picture effect to the image and set to **5 pt**.

h. Change the page margins to **Wide**.

i. Insert a footer with the page number in the center of the spreadsheet footer area. Click on any cell in the worksheet.

j. Change the View to **Normal**.

k. Open Backstage view and adjust print settings to print two copies. You will not actually print two copies unless directed by your instructor.

l. Save and close the file. Based on your instructor's directions, submit f01m2Tracker_LastFirst.

3 Today's Musical Artists

CREATIVE CASE

COLLABORATION CASE

With a few of your classmates, you will use PowerPoint to create a single presentation on your favorite musical artists. Each student must create at least one slide and then all of the slides will be added to the presentation. Because everyone's schedule is varied, you will use your OneDrive to pass the presentation file among the group.

a. Designate one student to create a new presentation and save it as **f01m3Music_GroupName**.

b. Add your group member names to the Author Properties in Backstage view.

c. Add a theme to the presentation.

d. Add one slide that contains the name of an artist, the genre, and two or three interesting facts about the artist.

e. Insert a picture of the artist or clip art that represents the artist.

f. Put your name on the slide that you created. Save the presentation.

g. Pass the presentation to the next student so that he or she can perform the same tasks in Steps d–f and save the presentation before passing it on to the next student. Continue until all group members have created a slide in the presentation.

h. Save and close the file. Based on your instructor's directions, submit f01m3Music_GroupName.

Beyond the Classroom

Fitness Planner
GENERAL CASE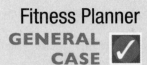

You will use Microsoft Excel to develop a fitness planner. Open *f01b1Exercise* and save it as **f01b1Exercise_LastFirst**. Because the fitness planner is a template, the exercise categories are listed, but without actual data. You will personalize the planner. Change the orientation to **Landscape**. Move the contents of **cell A2** (*Exercise Planner*) to **cell A1**. Click **cell A8** and use Format Painter to copy the format of that selection to **cells A5** and **A6**. Increase the font size of **cell A1** to **18**. Use the *Tell me what you want to do* box to learn how to insert a header and put your name in the header. Begin the fitness planner, entering at least one activity in each category (warm-up, aerobics, strength, and cooldown). Insert a picture from a Bing Image Search that is appropriate for the planner. You may want to use **exercise** as your search term. Check the spelling in the workbook. Add the tag **Exercise Planner** to the Properties in Backstage view. Review the document in Print Preview. Ensure that the tracker fits on a single sheet of paper when printed. Resize the image if necessary to fit on the page. Save and close the file. Based on your instructor's directions, submit f01b1Exercise_LastFirst.

Household Records
DISASTER RECOVERY

FROM SCRATCH

Use Microsoft Excel to create a detailed (fictional) record of valuables in your household. In case of burglary or disaster, an insurance claim is expedited if you are able to itemize what was lost along with identifying information such as serial numbers. You will then make a copy of the record on another storage device for safekeeping outside your home (in case your home is destroyed by a fire or weather-related catastrophe). Design a worksheet listing at least five fictional appliances and pieces of electronic equipment along with the serial number of each. Change the orientation to **Landscape**. Use the *Tell me what you want to do* box to learn how to insert a header and put your name in the header. Return to Normal view. Insert a picture from a Bing Image Search that is appropriate for the record. You may want to use **appliances** as your search term. Review the document in Print Preview. Ensure that the records fit on a single sheet of paper when printed. Move and resize the image as necessary so that it fits on the page when printed. Check the spelling in the workbook. Add the tag **Disaster Recovery** to the Properties in Backstage view. Save the workbook as **f01b2Household_LastFirst**. Save and close the file. Based on your instructor's directions, submit f01b2Household_LastFirst.

Capstone Exercise

You are a member of the Student Government Association (SGA) at your college. As a community project, the SGA is sponsoring a Stop Smoking drive designed to provide information on the health risks posed by smoking cigarettes and to offer solutions to those who want to quit. The SGA has partnered with the local branch of the American Cancer Society as well as the outreach program of the local hospital to sponsor free educational awareness seminars. As the secretary for the SGA, you will help prepare a PowerPoint presentation that will be displayed on screens around campus and used in student seminars. The PowerPoint presentation has come back from the reviewers with only one comment: A reviewer suggested that you spell out Centers for Disease Control and Prevention, instead of abbreviating it. You will use Microsoft Office to help with those tasks.

Open and Save Files

You will open, review, and save a PowerPoint presentation.

a. Open *f01c1Quit* and save it as **f01c1Quit_LastFirst**.

Select Text, Move Text, and Format Text

A reviewer commented that you should modify the text on slide 12. The last sentence in the paragraph should be first since it is the answer to the question on the previous slide. You also add emphasis to the sentence.

a. Click **Slide 12**, and select the text **Just one cigarette – for some people**.

b. Cut the selected text and then paste it at the beginning of the paragraph.

c. Use the Mini toolbar to apply **Italics** to the text *Just one cigarette – for some people*.

Apply a Theme and Change the View

There is a blank theme for the slides, so you apply a different theme to the presentation.

a. Apply the **Metropolitan** theme to the presentation.

b. Change the View to Slide Sorter. Click **Slide 2** and drag to move Slide 2 to the end of the presentation. It will become the last slide (Slide 22).

c. Return to Normal view.

Insert and Modify a Picture

You will add a picture to the first slide and then resize it and position it.

a. Click **Slide 1**, and insert an online picture appropriate for the topic of **smoking**.

b. Resize the picture and reposition it.

c. Click outside the picture to deselect it.

Use the *Tell me what you want to do* Box

A reviewer suggested that you spell out Centers for Disease Control and Prevention, instead of abbreviating it. You know that there is a find and replace option to do this but you cannot remember where it is. You use the *Tell me what you want to do* box to help you with this function. You then replace the text.

a. Use the *Tell me what you want to do* box to search **replace**.

b. Use the results from your search to find a function that will find and then replace the single occurrence of *CDC* with **Centers for Disease Control and Prevention**.

Customize the Quick Access Toolbar

You often preview and print your presentations and find it would be easier to have a button on the Quick Access Toolbar to do so. You customize the toolbar by adding this shortcut.

a. Add the Print Preview button to the Quick Access Toolbar.

b. Add the Print button to the Quick Access Toolbar.

Use Print Preview, Change Print Layout, and Print

To get an idea of how the presentation will look when printed, you will preview the presentation. You decide to print the slides so that two slides will appear on one page.

a. Preview the document as it will appear when printed.

b. Change the Print Layout to **2 Slides** (under the Handouts section).

c. Preview the document as it will appear when printed.

d. Adjust the print settings to print two copies. You will not actually print two copies unless directed by your instructor.

Check Spelling and Change View

Before you call the presentation complete, you will correct any spelling errors and view the presentation as a slide show.

a. Check the spelling. The word *hairlike* is not misspelled, so it should not be corrected.

b. View the slide show. Click after reviewing the last slide to return to the presentation.

c. Save and close the file. Based on your instructor's directions, submit f01c1Quit_LastFirst.

LEARNING OUTCOME You will demonstrate understanding of relational database concepts.

OBJECTIVES & SKILLS: After you read this chapter, you will be able to:

CASE STUDY | Managing a Business in the Global Economy

Northwind Traders is an international gourmet food distributor that imports and exports specialty foods from around the world. Keeping track of customers, vendors, orders, and inventory is a critical task. The owners of Northwind have just purchased an order-processing database created with Microsoft Access 2016 to help manage their customers, suppliers, products, and orders.

You have been hired to learn, use, and manage the database. Northwind's owners are willing to provide training about their business and Access. They expect the learning process to take about three months. After three months, your job will be to support the order-processing team as well as to provide detail and summary reports to the sales force as needed. Your new job at Northwind Traders will be a challenge, but it is also a good opportunity to make a great contribution to a global company. Are you up to the task?

Finding Your Way Through
an Access Database

FIGURE 1.1 Northwind Traders Database

FIGURE 1.2 Northwind Traders Contacts Database

CASE STUDY | Managing a Business in the Global Economy

Starting File	Files to be Submitted
a01h1Traders	a01h1Traders_LastFirst_*CurrentDate*
	a01h2Traders_LastFirst
	a01h3Contacts_LastFirst

Databases Are Everywhere!

A *database* is a collection of data organized as meaningful information that can be accessed, managed, stored, queried, sorted, and reported. You probably participate in data collection and are exposed to databases on a regular basis. Your college or university stores your personal and registration data. When you registered for this course, your data was entered into a database. If you have a bank account, have a Social Security card, have a medical history, or have booked a flight with an airline, your information is stored in a database.

You use databases online without realizing it, such as when you shop or check your bank statement. Even when you type a search phrase into Google and click Search, you are using Google's massive database with all of its stored webpage references and keywords. Look for something on Amazon, and you are searching Amazon's database to find a product that you might want to buy. Figure 1.3 shows the results of searching for a term on Pearson's website. The search has accessed the Pearson database, and the results are displayed in a webpage.

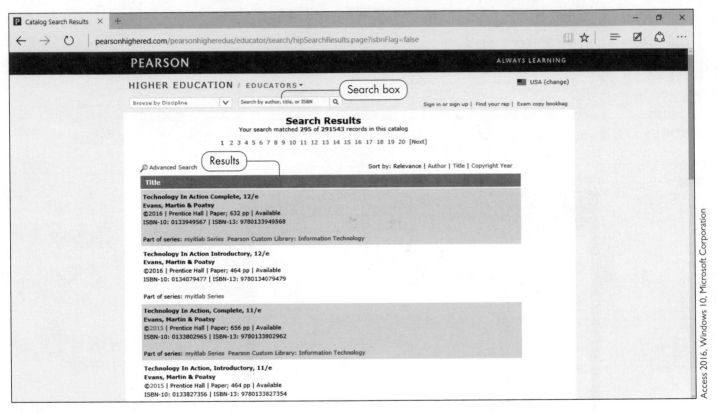

FIGURE 1.3 Pearson Website Search

A *database management system (DBMS)* is a software system that provides the tools needed to create, maintain, and use a database. Database management systems make it possible to access and control data and display the information in a variety of formats. *Access* is the database management system included in professional editions of the Office 2016 suite. Access is a valuable decision-making tool used by many organizations. More advanced DBMS packages include Microsoft SQL Server, MySQL, and Oracle.

Organizations from all industries rely on data to conduct daily operations. Businesses maintain and analyze data about their students, customers, employees, orders, volunteers, activities, and facilities. Data and information are two terms that are often used interchangeably. However, when it comes to databases, the two terms mean different things. Data is what is entered into a database. Information is the finished product that is produced by the database. Data is converted to information by selecting, performing calculations, and sorting. Decisions in an organization are usually based on information produced by a database, rather than raw data. For example, the number 55 is just data, because it could mean anything. Only when a label is attached to it (for example, as someone's age) does it take on meaning and become information.

In this section, you will learn the fundamentals of organizing data in a database, explore Access database objects and the purpose of each object, and examine the Access interface.

Opening, Saving, and Enabling Content in a Database

STEP 1 ❱❱ As you work through the material in this book, you will frequently be asked to open a database, save it with a new name, and enable content. You can also start by creating a new database if appropriate.

If you have been provided a database, open the file to get started. When you open any database for the first time, you will be presented with a warning that it might contain harmful code. By enabling the content, the database file will be trusted on the computer you are working on. All content from this publisher and associated with this book can be trusted.

To open an existing Access database and enable content, complete the following steps:

1. Start Access 2016. Backstage view displays. (Note: If Access is already open, click the File tab to display Backstage view).
2. Click Open Other Files.
3. Click Browse ▭ to open the Open dialog box.
4. Locate and select the database and click Open.
5. Click Enable Content on the message bar (see Figure 1.4). Access will close and reopen the database, and the security warning disappears and will not appear again for this database.

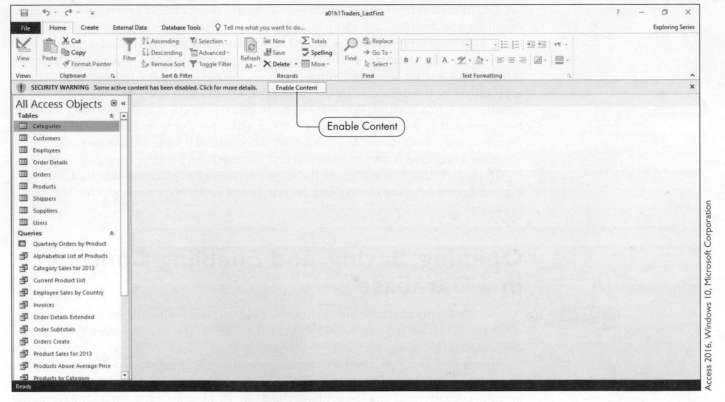

FIGURE 1.4 Access Security Warning

Backstage view gives you access to the Save As command. Most assignments will have you save the starting database file with a new name.

> **To save the database with a new name, complete the following steps:**
> 1. Click the File tab.
> 2. Select Save As.
> 3. Ensure Save Database As is selected (see Figure 1.5).
> 4. Click Save As.
> 5. Type the new name for your database, and click Save.

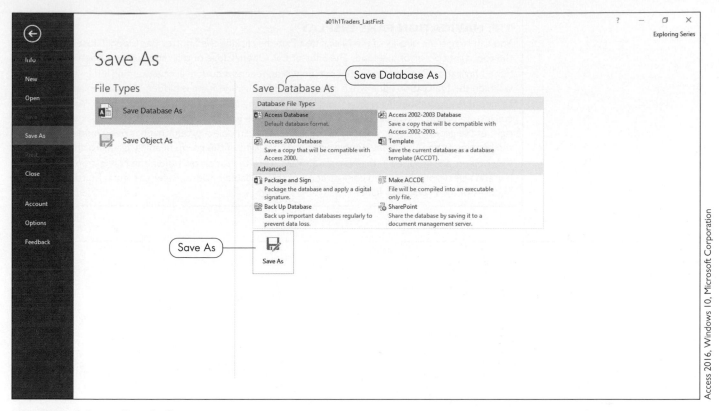

FIGURE 1.5 Access Save As Options

TIP: ALTERNATIVE SAVE FORMAT: ACCESS DATABASE EXECUTABLE

Creating an Access Database Executable (ACCDE) file allows users to enter data, but not add, modify, or delete objects. In other words, the only task they can do is data entry. This file format protects against users changing designs or deleting objects.

To create an Access Database Executable, click the File tab, click Save As, and double-click Make ACCDE. Click Save to save as an Access Database Executable.

Recognizing Database Object Types

 Databases must be carefully managed to keep information accurate. Data need to be changed, added, and deleted. Managing a database also requires that you understand when data is saved and when you need to use the Save commands.

In Access, each component created and used to make the database function is known as an *object*. Objects include tables, queries, forms, and reports, and can be found in the *Navigation Pane*. The Navigation Pane is an Access interface element that organizes and lists the objects in an Access database. The Navigation Pane appears on the left side of the screen, and displays all objects. You can open any object by double-clicking the object's name in the list.

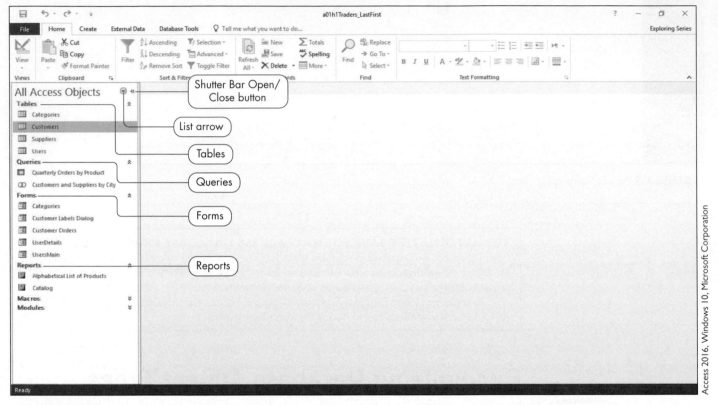

FIGURE 1.6 Navigation Pane Features

Access 2016, Windows 10, Microsoft Corporation

Most databases contain multiple tables. By default, the objects display in groups by object type in the Navigation Pane. In other words, you will see a list of tables, followed by queries, followed by forms, followed by reports. The purpose of each of these objects is described below.

- A *table* is where all data is stored in your database, and thus can be said to be the foundation of each database. Tables organize data into columns and rows. Each column represents a *field*, a category of information we store in a table. For example, in the Northwind database, a table containing customer information would include fields such as Customer ID, Company Name, and City. Each row in a table contains a *record*, a complete set of all the fields about one person, place, event, or concept. A customer record, for example, would contain all of the fields about a single customer, including the Customer ID, the Company Name, Contact Name, Contact Title, Address, City, etc. Figure 1.7 shows both fields and records. The *primary key* is a field (or combination of fields) that uniquely identifies each record in a table. Common primary keys are driver's license number, government

ID number (such as a Social Security number), passport number, and student ID. Many of these primary keys are generated by a database. Your college or university's database likely assigns a unique identifier to a student as soon as they apply, for example.

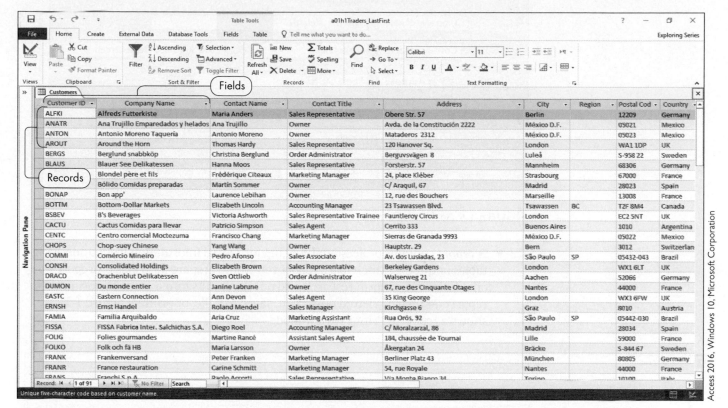

FIGURE 1.7 An Access Table

- A *query* (or queries, plural) is a question you ask about the data in your database. Notice the word query is similar to the word inquiry, which means question. It produces a subset of data that provides information about the question you have asked. For example, a query may display a list of which customers live in a specific town, or a list of children registered for a specific after-school program. You can double-click a query in the Navigation Pane and you will notice the interface is similar to that of a table, as shown in Figure 1.8.

Company Name		Contact Name	Country	City	Region	Phone
Bólido Comidas preparadas		Martín Sommer	Spain	Madrid		(91) 555 22 82
FISSA Fabrica Inter. Salchichas S.A.		Diego Roel	Spain	Madrid		(91) 555 94 44
Romero y tomillo		Alejandra Camino	Spain	Madrid		(91) 745 6200

Customers in Madrid

FIGURE 1.8 An Access Query

- A *form* allows simplified entry and modification of data. Much like entering data on a paper form, a database form enables you to add, modify, and delete table data. Most forms display one record at a time, which helps prevent data entry errors. Forms are typically utilized by the users of the database, while the database designer creates and edits the form structure. Figure 1.9 shows a form. Notice a single record is displayed.

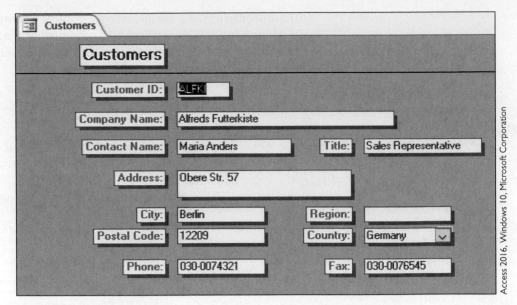

FIGURE 1.9 An Access Form

- A *report* contains professional-looking formatted information from underlying tables or queries. Much like a report you would prepare for a class, a report enables you to perform research and put the results into a readable format. The report can then be viewed on-screen, saved to a file, or printed. Figure 1.10 shows a report in Print Preview mode.

Customer Contacts

Customer Contacts

Contact Name	Company Name	Contact Title	Phone	City	Region	Country
Alejandra Camino	Romero y tomillo	Accounting Manager	(91) 745 6200	Madrid		Spain
Alexander Feuer	Morgenstern Gesundkost	Marketing Assistant	0342-023176	Leipzig		Germany
Ana Trujillo	Ana Trujillo Emparedados y helados	Owner	(5) 555-4729	México D.F.		Mexico
Anabela Domingues	Tradição Hipermercados	Sales Representative	(11) 555-2167	São Paulo	SP	Brazil
André Fonseca	Gourmet Lanchonetes	Sales Associate	(11) 555-9482	Campinas	SP	Brazil
Ann Devon	Eastern Connection	Sales Agent	(171) 555-0297	London		UK
Annette Roulet	La maison d'Asie	Sales Manager	61.77.61.10	Toulouse		France
Antonio Moreno	Antonio Moreno Taquería	Owner	(5) 555-3932	México D.F.		Mexico
Aria Cruz	Familia Arquibaldo	Marketing Assistant	(11) 555-9857	São Paulo	SP	Brazil
Art Braunschweiger	Split Rail Beer & Ale	Sales Manager	(307) 555-4680	Lander	WY	USA
Bernardo Batista	Que Delícia	Accounting Manager	(21) 555-4252	Rio de Janeiro	RJ	Brazil
Carine Schmitt	France restauration	Marketing Manager	40.32.21.21	Nantes		France
Carlos González	LILA-Supermercado	Accounting Manager	(9) 331-6954	Barquisimeto	Lara	Venezuela
Carlos Hernández	HILARIÓN-Abastos	Sales Representative	(5) 555-1340	San Cristóbal	Táchira	Venezuela
Catherine Dewey	Maison Dewey	Sales Agent	(02) 201 24 67	Bruxelles		Belgium
Christina Berglund	Berglund snabbköp	Order Administrator	0921-12 34 65	Luleå		Sweden
Daniel Tonini	La corne d'abondance	Sales Representative	30.59.84.10	Versailles		France

Page: 1   No Filter

FIGURE 1.10 An Access Report

Access 2016, Windows 10, Microsoft Corporation

Figure 1.11 displays the different object types in Access with the foundation object—the table—in the center of the illustration. The purpose each object serves is explained underneath the object name. The flow of information between objects is indicated by single-arrowhead arrows if the flow is one direction only. Two-arrowhead arrows indicate that the flow goes both directions. For example, you can use forms to view, add, delete, or modify data from tables.

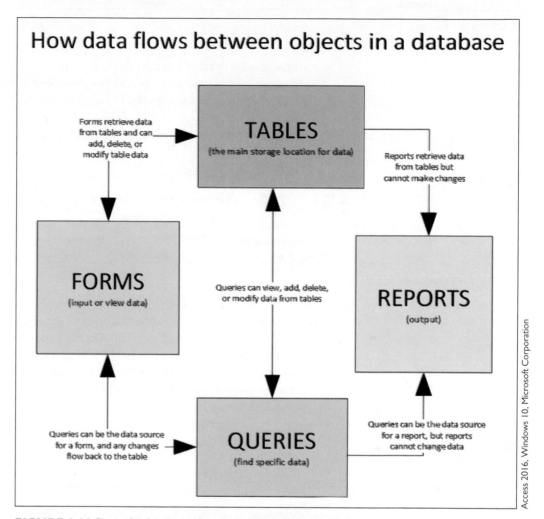

How data flows between objects in a database

Forms retrieve data from tables and can add, delete, or modify table data

TABLES
(the main storage location for data)

Reports retrieve data from tables but cannot make changes

FORMS
(input or view data)

Queries can view, add, delete, or modify data from tables

REPORTS
(output)

Queries can be the data source for a form, and any changes flow back to the table

QUERIES
(find specific data)

Queries can be the data source for a report, but reports cannot change data

Access 2016, Windows 10, Microsoft Corporation

FIGURE 1.11 Flow of Information Between Object Types

Two other object types, macros and modules, are rarely used by beginning Access users. A ***macro*** object is a stored series of commands that carry out an action. Macros are often used to automate tasks. A ***module*** is an advanced object written using the VBA (Visual Basic® for Applications) programming language. Modules provide more functionality than macros, but are not generally required for even intermediate users.

Examine the Access Interface

While Access includes the standard elements of the Microsoft Office applications interface such as the title bar, the Ribbon, the Home tab, Backstage view, and scroll bars, it also includes elements unique to Access.

The Access Ribbon has five tabs that always display, as well as tabs that appear only when particular objects are open. The two tabs that are unique to Access are:

- External Data tab: Contains all of the operations used to facilitate data import and export. See Figure 1.12.

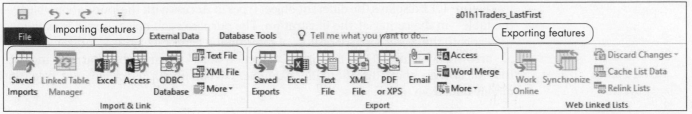

FIGURE 1.12 External Data Tab

Access 2016, Windows 10, Microsoft Corporation

- Database Tools tab: Contains the feature that enables users to create relationships between tables and enables use of more advanced features of Access. Figure 1.13 shows the Database Tools tab.

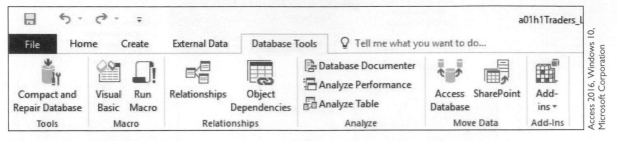

FIGURE 1.13 Database Tools Tab

Access 2016, Windows 10, Microsoft Corporation

By default, Access uses a Tabbed Documents interface. That means that each object that is open has its own tab beneath the Ribbon and to the right of the Navigation Pane. You can switch between open objects by clicking a tab to make that object active, similar to the way an Excel worksheet has tabs at the bottom of the screen. Figure 1.14 shows the Access interface with multiple objects open.

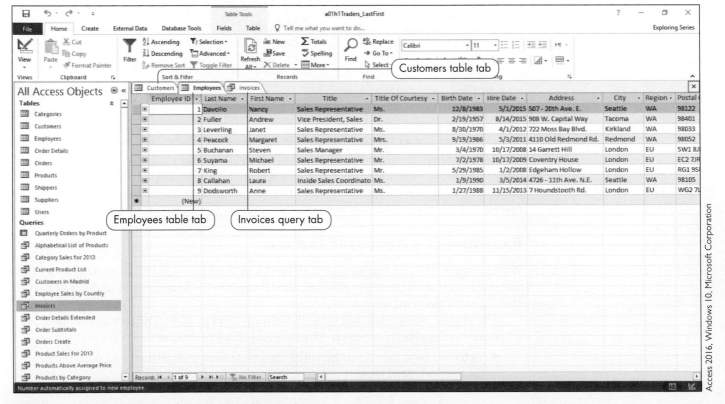

FIGURE 1.14 Access Database with Multiple Objects Open

Access 2016, Windows 10, Microsoft Corporation

Explore Table Datasheet View

Access provides two different ways to view a table: Datasheet view and Design view. When you double-click a table, Datasheet view displays by default. **Datasheet view** is a grid containing fields (columns) and records (rows). You can view, add, edit, and delete records in Datasheet view. Figure 1.15 shows the Customers table in Datasheet view. Each row contains a record for a specific customer. Click the record selector, or row heading, at the beginning of a row to select the record. Each column represents a field, or one attribute about a customer. Click the field selector, or column heading, to select a field.

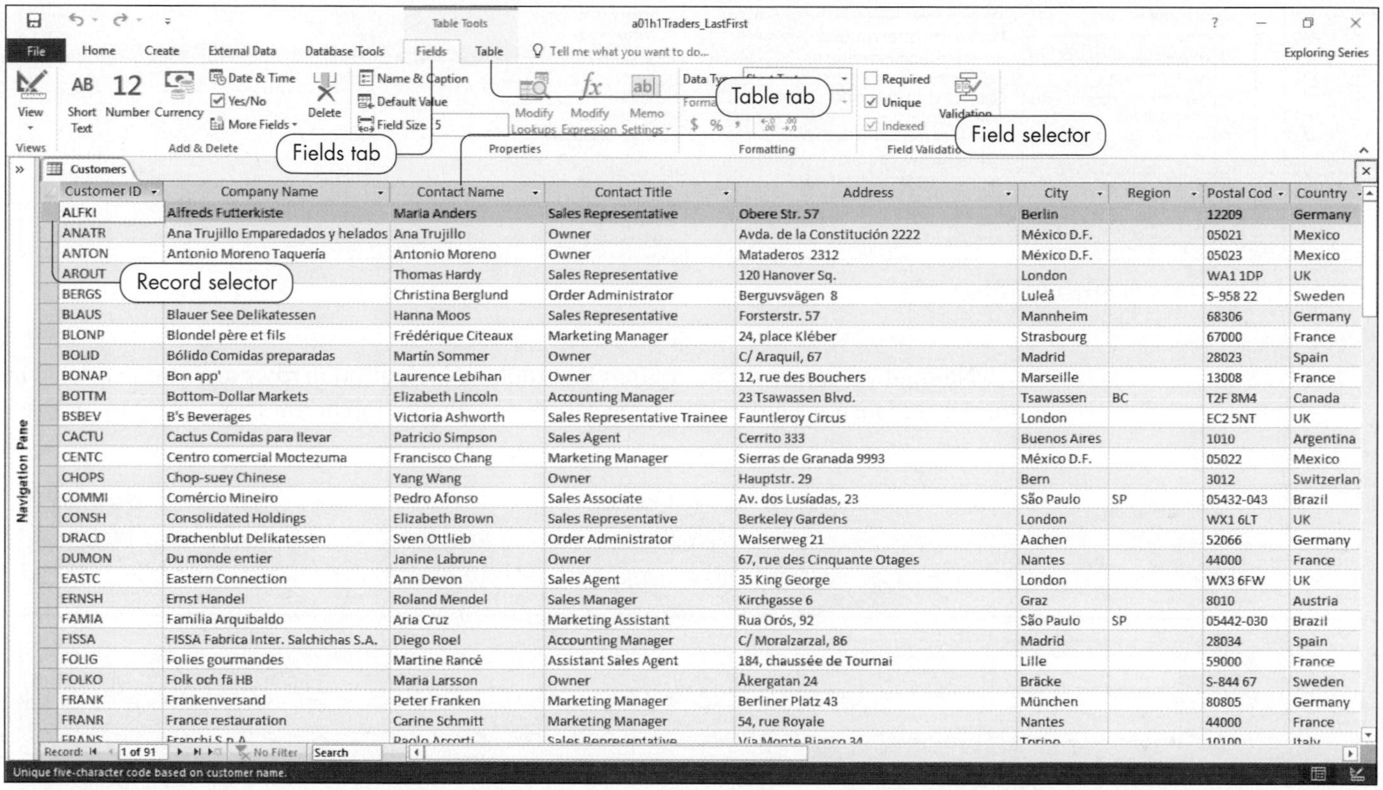

FIGURE 1.15 Datasheet View for Customers Table

Notice the Customers table shows records for 91 employees. The customer records contain multiple fields about each customer, including the Company Name, Contact Name, and so on. Occasionally a field does not contain a value for a particular record. For example, many customers do not have a Region assigned. Access shows a blank cell when data is missing.

Navigate Through Records

The navigation bar at the bottom of Figure 1.16 shows that the Customers table has 91 records and that record number 18 is the current record. The pencil symbol to the left of record 18 indicates that the data in that record is being edited and that changes have not yet been saved. The pencil icon disappears when you move to another record. Access saves data automatically as soon as you move from one record to another. This may seem counterintuitive at first because other Office applications, such as Word and Excel, do not save changes and additions automatically. The navigation arrows enable you to go to the first record, the previous record, the next record, or the last record. Click the right arrow with a yellow asterisk to add a new (blank) record.

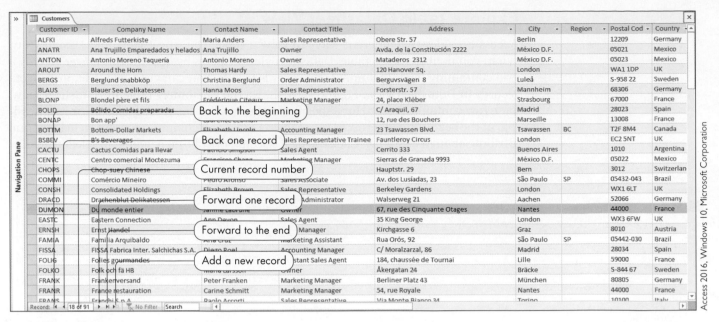

FIGURE 1.16 Navigation Arrows in a Table

Navigation works for more than just tables. Navigation arrows are also available in queries and forms. Figure 1.17 shows the same navigation arrows appearing in forms.

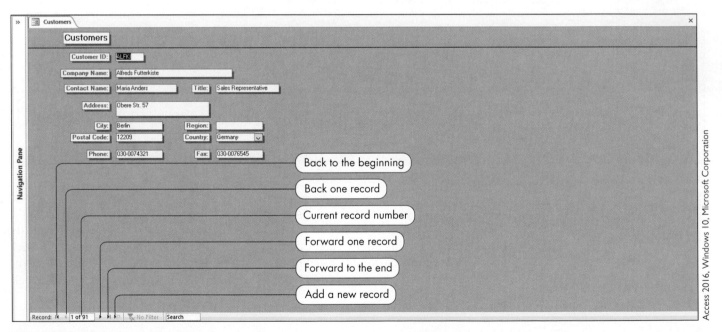

FIGURE 1.17 Navigation Arrows in a Form

In addition to navigating, you also have access to the Find command. The Find command is located in the Find group on the Home tab, and can be used to locate specific records. You can search for a single field or the entire record, match all or part of the selected field(s), move forward or back in a table, or specify a case-sensitive search.

To find a record using the Find command, complete the following steps:

1. Open the table that contains the data you are searching for. Note that if you want to search a query, form, or report, you can follow the same steps, except open the appropriate object instead of the table.
2. Click any cell within the field you want to search. For example, if you want to search the City field in the Customers table, as shown in Figure 1.18, click any City value.
3. Ensure the Home tab is selected.
4. Click Find in the Find group.
5. Type the value you are searching for in the Find What box. Note that the entry is not case sensitive.
6. Click Find Next to find the next matching value.

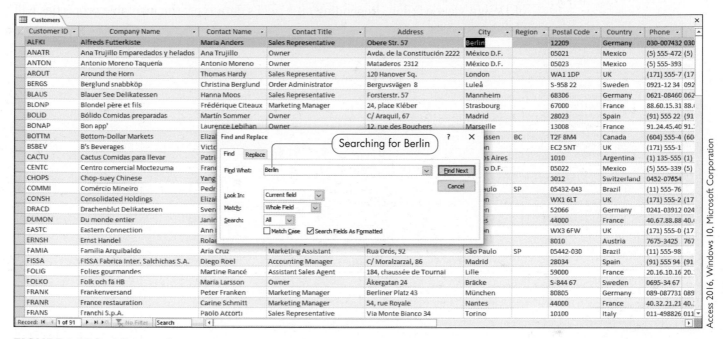

FIGURE 1.18 Find Command

Explore Table Design View

Design view gives you a detailed view of the table's structure and is used to create and modify a table's design by specifying the fields it will contain, the fields' data types, and their associated properties. When you double-click a table in the Navigation Pane, it will open in Datasheet view, as the design of a table typically does not change frequently.

To switch between Datasheet and Design view, complete the following steps:

1. Click the Home tab.
2. Click View in the Views group to toggle between the current view and the previous view. See Figure 1.19.

FIGURE 1.19 View Button

Also notice the arrow that allows you to select either Design or Datasheet view. Either way of performing this task is correct.

Data types define the type of data that will be stored in a field, such as short text, numeric, currency, date/time, etc. For example, if you need to store the hire date of an employee, you would input a field name and select the Date/Time data type. A **_field property_** defines the characteristics of a field in more detail. For example, for the field OrderDate, you could set add validation (the OrderDate must be today's date or later), or choose whether the field is required or not. Though some changes can be made to the field properties in Datasheet view, Design view gives you access to more properties.

Figure 1.20 shows Design view for the Orders table. In the top portion, each row contains the field name the data type, and an optional description for each field in the table. In the bottom portion, the Field Properties pane contains the properties (details) for a field. Click a field, and the properties for that field display in the Field Properties section of Design view window. Depending on a field's data type, the available properties will change.

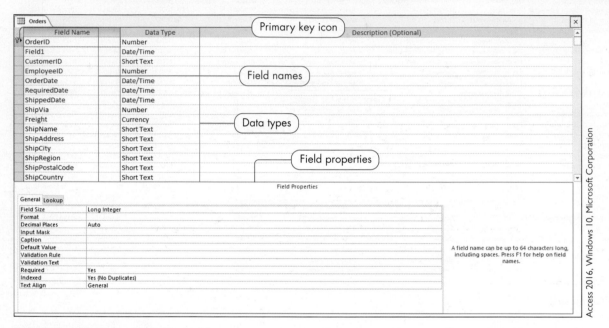

FIGURE 1.20 Orders Table Design View

Notice the key icon next to the OrderID field; this denotes this field is the primary key in the Orders table; it ensures that each record in the table is unique and can be distinguished from every other record. You may have multiple orders from the same customer, but you can tell they are different because there are two separate OrderIDs. This is why many companies ask for you to include your account number when you pay a bill. The account number, similar to an OrderID, uniquely identifies you and helps ensure that the payment is not applied to the wrong customer.

In Figure 1.20, the OrderID field has an AutoNumber data type—a number that is generated by Access and is automatically incremented each time a record is added. Each field's data type determines the type of input accepted. Data types will be discussed further in a later chapter.

Rename and Describe Tables

To make a table easy to use, Access includes a few properties you can modify. Tables default to a name of Table1 (or Table2, etc.) if you do not specify otherwise. As you can imagine, this would be very difficult to navigate.

> **To rename a table, complete the following steps:**
>
> 1. Verify that the table is closed. If it is not closed, right-click the table tab and select Close. A table cannot be renamed while it is open.
> 2. Right-click the table name in the Navigation Pane.
> 3. Select Rename on the shortcut menu.
> 4. Type the new name over the selected text and press Enter.

Tables also include a description, which can be useful to provide documentation about the contents of a table. For example, most tables in the Northwind database are straightforward. However, just in case, the database comes with predefined descriptions for most tables. This can provide a user with additional clarification regarding the purpose of a table if they know where to look. By default, descriptions are not shown unless you right-click the table and select Table Properties. If you are working with a complex database, adding descriptions can be extremely helpful for new users. Figure 1.21 shows a table description.

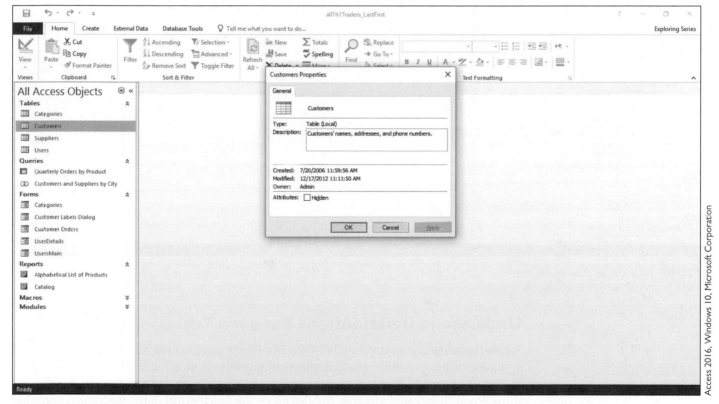

Access 2016, Windows 10, Microsoft Corporation

FIGURE 1.21 Previewing a Table Description

> **To enter a table description, complete the following steps:**
>
> 1. Right-click the table name in the Navigation Pane.
> 2. Select Table Properties on the shortcut menu.
> 3. Type the description in the Table Properties dialog box and click OK.

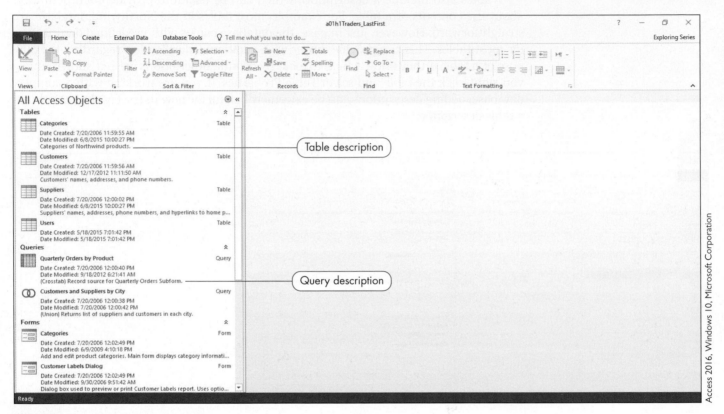

FIGURE 1.22 Detail View of Objects

Understand Relationships Between Tables

A *relationship* is a connection between two tables using a common field. The benefit of a relationship is the ability to efficiently combine data from related tables for the purpose of creating queries, forms, and reports. If you are using an existing database, relationships are likely created already. The design of the Northwind database, which contains multiple tables, is illustrated in Figure 1.23. The tables have been created, the field names have been added, and the data types have been set. The diagram shows the relationships that were created between tables using join lines. Join lines enable you to create a relationship between two tables using a common field. For example, the Suppliers table is joined to the Products table using the common field SupplierID. These table connections enable you to query the database for information stored in multiple tables. This feature gives the manager the ability to ask questions like "What products are produced by the supplier Exotic Liquids?" In this case, the name of the supplier (Exotic Liquids) is stored in the Supplier table, but the products are stored in the Products table. Notice in Figure 1.24, you can tell there is a table related to the Supplier table, because a plus sign ⊞ appears to the left of each Supplier. If you click the plus sign, you will see a list of products produced by this company.

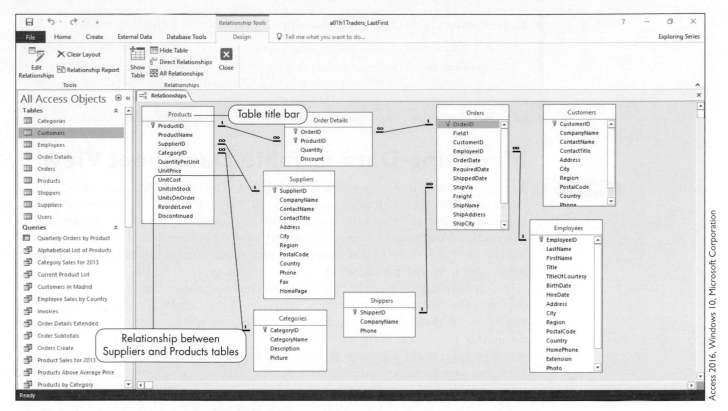

FIGURE 1.23 Northwind Database Relationships

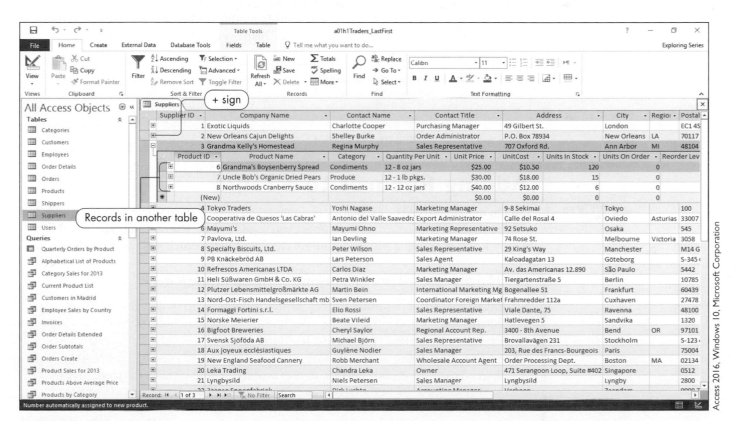

FIGURE 1.24 Related Tables

Relationships will be discussed further in a later chapter. However, you can view the existing relationships in any database to familiarize yourself with the way tables work together.

Modifying Data in Table Datasheet View

The Save function in Access works differently than the other Office applications. Word, Excel, and PowerPoint all work primarily from memory (RAM). In those applications, your work is not automatically saved to your storage location. Office may perform an automatic recovery and save every specified amount of minutes; however, you should not rely on that feature, so you should save your work. If the computer crashes or power is lost, you may lose part or all of your document. Access, on the other hand, works primarily from storage (i.e., the hard drive). As you enter and update the data in an Access database, the changes are automatically saved to the storage location you specified when you saved the database. If a power failure occurs, you will lose only the changes to the record that you are currently editing.

When you make a change to a record's content in an Access table (for example, changing a customer's phone number), Access saves your changes as soon as you move the insertion point to a different record. You will only be prompted to save if you make changes to the design of the table (such as changing the font or background color). Editing data is done similarly in queries and forms. Recall that reports cannot change data, so changes to data cannot be done there.

To edit a record, tab to the field you want to modify and type the new data. When you start typing, you erase all existing data in the field because the entire field is selected.

> **TIP: UNDO WORKS DIFFERENTLY**
> You can click Undo to reverse the most recent change (the phone number you just modified, for example) to a single record immediately after making changes to that record. However, unlike other Office programs that enable multiple Undo steps, you cannot use Undo to reverse multiple edits in Access. Undo (and Redo) are found on the Quick Access Toolbar.

Adding Records to a Table

Data in a database will be constantly changing. You should expect new data to be added. If you are working with a Customer database, you would expect new customers to be added constantly. If you are dealing with a Restaurant database, new menu items could be added daily.

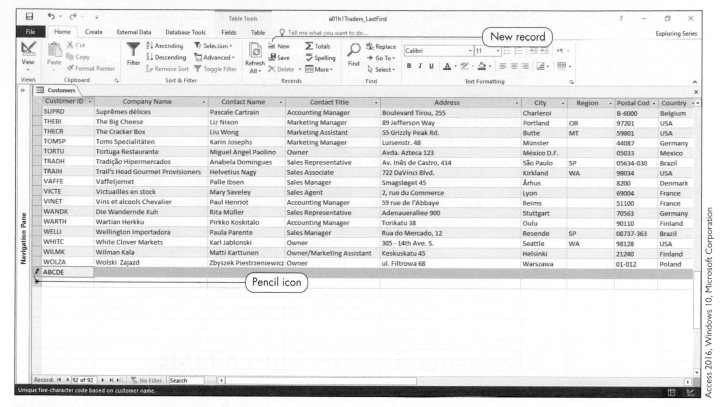

FIGURE 1.25 Adding a Record Using a Table

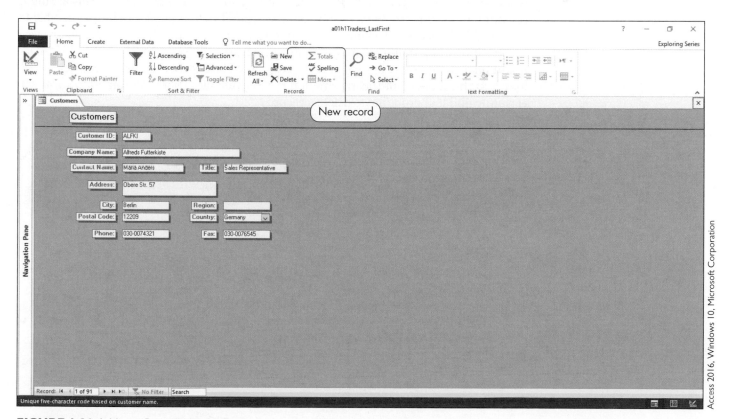

FIGURE 1.26 Adding a Record Using a Form

As with most of Office, there are a number of ways to perform the same task. Data entry is the same. See Table 1.1 for a list of some shortcuts you can use when performing data entry.

TABLE 1.1	Keyboard Shortcuts for Entering Data
Keystroke	**Result**
Up arrow (↑)	Moves insertion point up one row.
Down arrow (↓)	Moves insertion point down one row.
Left arrow (←)	Moves insertion point left one field in the same row.
Right arrow (→)	Moves insertion point right one field in the same row.
Tab or Enter	Moves insertion point right one field in the same row.
Shift+Tab	Moves insertion point left one field in the same row.
Home	Moves insertion point to the first field in the current row.
End	Moves insertion point to the last field in the current row.
Esc	Cancels any changes made in the current field while in Edit mode.
Ctrl+Z	Reverses the last unsaved edit.

Pearson Education, Inc.

Deleting Records from a Table

STEP 5 ▸▸ Deciding to delete records is not a simple decision. Many times, deleting records is a bad idea. Say you are working in the database for an animal shelter. Once an animal has been adopted, you may be tempted to delete the animal from the database. However, you would then lose any record of the animal ever existing, and if the owner calls asking if the animal has had its shots, or how old the animal is, you would no longer be able to provide that information. Often, instead of deleting information, you would create a yes/no field indicating that a record is no longer relevant. For example, the shelter database might have a check box for adopted. If the adopted box is checked yes, the animal is no longer at the shelter, but the information is still available. That said, sometimes you will certainly find it appropriate to delete a record.

To delete a record from a table, complete the following steps:

1. Click the record selector for the record you want to delete (see Figure 1.27).
2. Click Delete in the Records group on the Home tab. Click Yes in the warning dialog box. Note that you can take similar steps in queries and forms.

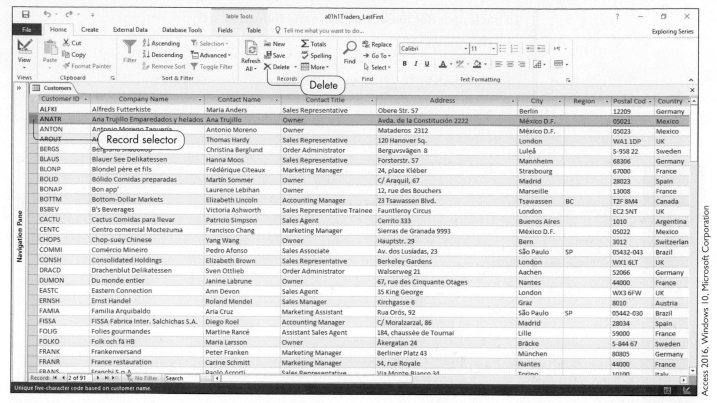

FIGURE 1.27 Deleting a Record

If you attempt to delete a record, you may get an error message. For example, if you try to delete a customer who has adopted pets, you may get a message stating *You cannot delete this record because another table has related records*. Even though the customer may have moved, they cannot be deleted because related records exist in another table, in this case, animals the customer has adopted.

Using Database Utilities

Database administrators spend a lot of time maintaining databases. Software utility programs make this process simpler. As Access is a database management utility, there are a number of tools that can be used to protect, maintain, and improve performance of a database.

Back Up a Database

STEP 6 **Back Up Database** is a utility that creates a duplicate copy of the entire database to protect from loss or damage. Imagine what would happen to a firm that loses track of orders placed, a charity that loses the list of donor contributions, or a hospital that loses the digital records of its patients. Making backups is especially important when you have multiple users working with the database. When you use the Back Up Database utility, Access provides a file name for the backup that uses the same file name as the database you are backing up, an underscore, and the current date. This makes it easy for you to keep track of databases by the date they were created.

Keep in mind, backing up a database on the same storage device as the original database can leave you with no protection in the event of hardware failure. Backups are typically stored on a separate device, such as an external hard drive or network drive.

To back up a database, complete the following steps:

1. Click the File tab.
2. Click Save As.
3. Click Back Up Database under the Advanced group (see Figure 1.28).
4. Click Save As. Revise the location and file name if you want to change either and click Save.

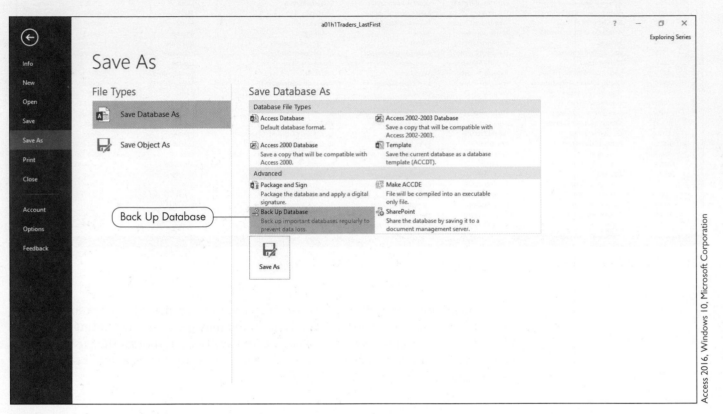

FIGURE 1.28 Back Up Database Option

Compact and Repair a Database

Databases have a tendency to expand with everyday use and may become corrupt, so Access provides the ***Compact and Repair Database*** utility. Compact and Repair Database reduces the size of a database and fixes any errors that may exist in the file.

To compact and repair an open database, complete the following steps:

1. Click the File tab.
2. Click Compact and Repair Database in the Info options. If you have any unsaved design changes, you will be prompted to save before the compact and repair can complete.

Alternately, you can have Access perform a Compact and Repair automatically.

To have Access compact and repair a database each time you close the database, complete the following steps:

1. Click the File tab.
2. Click Options.
3. Click Current Database.
4. Click the Compact on Close check box under Application Options in the Options for the current database pane.
5. Click OK.

TIP: SPLIT DATABASES

Another utility built into Access is the *Database Splitter* tool, which puts the tables in one file (the back-end database), and the queries, forms, and reports in a second file (the front-end database). This way, each user can create their own queries, forms, and reports without potentially changing an object someone else needs.

To split a database, click the Database Tools tab and click Access Database in the Move Data group. Click Split Database and click OK.

Encrypt a Database

To protect a database from unauthorized access, you can encrypt the database, which enables you to password-protect the stored information. Adding a password requires that the database be opened in exclusive mode. Open Exclusive mode guarantees that you are the only one currently using the database.

To open a database in exclusive mode, complete the following steps:

1. Ensure that the database is closed. You cannot open a database with exclusive access unless it is currently closed.
2. Click the File tab.
3. Click Open.
4. Click Browse to display the Open dialog box.
5. Locate and click the database you want to open, and click the Open arrow at the bottom of the dialog box. Make sure you click the arrow next to the word Open, and not the Open button.
6. Select Open Exclusive from the list. The database opens in exclusive mode.

To add a password once the database has been opened in exclusive mode, complete the following steps:

1. Click the File tab.
2. Click Encrypt with Password. The Set Database Password dialog box opens.
3. Type a password, and re-enter the password in the Verify box. Click OK.

Print Information

Though Access is primarily designed to store data electronically, you may want to produce a print copy of your data.

> **To print information from any object (table, query, form, report) in your database, complete the following steps:**
>
> 1. Click the File tab.
> 2. Click Print. The right panel display changes to enable you to choose a print option.
> 3. Click Print.
> 4. Change any settings that may need changing (for example, the print range or number of copies).
> 5. Click OK.

It is good practice to preview your work before printing a document. This way, if you notice an error, you can fix it and not waste paper.

> **To preview your work before printing, complete the following steps:**
>
> 1. Click the File tab.
> 2. Click Print.
> 3. Click Print Preview.
> 4. Click Close Print Preview on the Print Preview tab to exit without printing, or click Print to open the Print dialog box (see Figure 1.29).

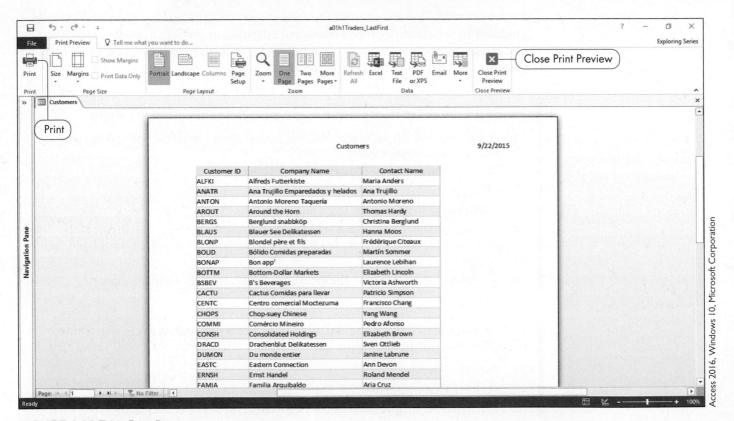

FIGURE 1.29 Table Print Preview

Quick Concepts

1. Name the four main types of objects in an Access database and briefly describe the purpose of each. **pp. 74–76**

2. What is the difference between Datasheet view and Design view in a table? **pp. 79, 81**

3. How does Access handle saving differently than other Office programs such as Excel? **p. 86**

4. How do relationships benefit a database user? **p. 84**

Hands-On Exercises

Skills covered: Open a Database • Save a Database with a New Name • Enable Content in a Database • Examine the Access Interface • Explore Table Datasheet View • Navigate Through Records • Explore Table Design View • Rename and Describe Tables • Understand Relationships Between Tables • Understand the Difference Between Working in Storage And Memory • Change Data in Table Datasheet View • Add Records to a Table • Delete Records from A Table • Back Up a Database • Compact and Repair a Database • Encrypt a Database • Print Information

1 Databases Are Everywhere!

Northwind purchases food items from suppliers around the world and sells them to restaurants and specialty food shops. Northwind depends on the data stored in its Access database to process orders and make daily decisions. You will open the Northwind database, examine the Access interface, review the existing objects in the database, and explore Access views. You will add, edit, and delete records using both tables and forms. Finally, you will back up the database.

STEP 1 » **OPEN, SAVE, AND ENABLE CONTENT IN A DATABASE**

As you begin your job, you first will become familiar with the Northwind database. This database will help you learn the fundamentals of working with database files. Refer to Figure 1.30 as you complete Step 1.

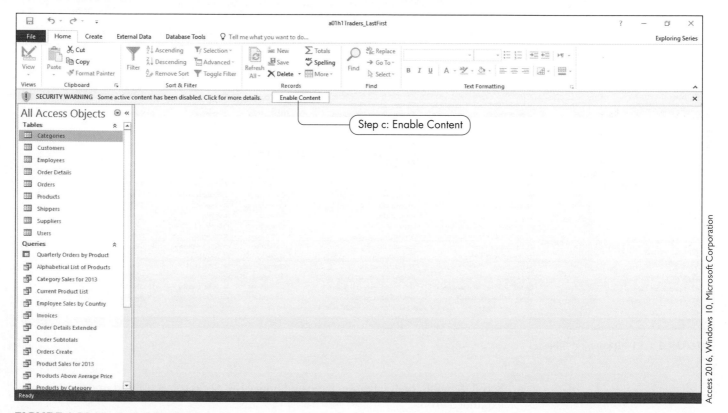

FIGURE 1.30 Northwind Database

a. Open Access, click **Open Other Files**, and click **Browse** 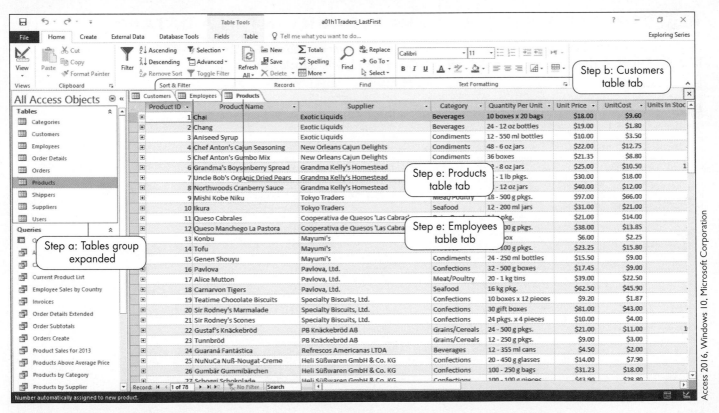. Navigate to the folder location designated by your instructor. Click *a01h1Traders* and click **Open**.

> **TROUBLESHOOTING:** If you make any major mistakes in this exercise, you can close the file, open *a01h1Traders* again, and then start this exercise over.

b. Click the **File tab** and click **Save As**. Click **Save As** and save the file as **a01h1Traders_LastFirst**.

When you save files, use your last and first names. For example, as the Access author, I would save my database as "a01h1Traders_CameronEric."

The Security Warning message bar appears below the Ribbon, indicating that some database content is disabled.

c. Click **Enable Content** on the Security Warning message bar.

When you open an Access file, you should enable the content.

STEP 2 ›› RECOGNIZE DATABASE OBJECT TYPES

Now that you have opened the Northwind database, you examine the Navigation Pane, objects, and views to become familiar with these fundamental Access features. Refer to Figure 1.31 as you complete Step 2.

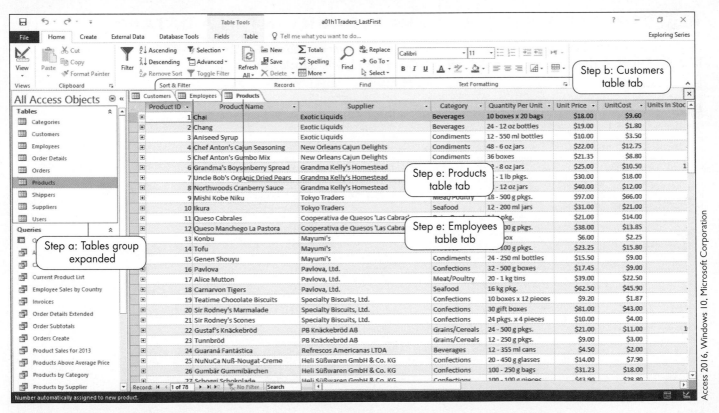

FIGURE 1.31 Northwind Objects

a. Scroll through the Navigation Pane and notice the Access objects listed under each expanded group.

The Tables group and the Forms group are expanded, displaying all of the table and form objects. The Queries, Reports, Macros, and Modules groups are collapsed so that the objects in those groups are not displayed.

b. Double-click the **Customers table** in the Navigation Pane.

The Customers table opens in Datasheet view, showing the data contained in the table. The Customers tab displays below the Ribbon indicating the table object is open. Each customer's record displays on a table row. The columns of the table display the fields that comprise the records.

c. Click **View** in the Views group on the Home tab.

The view of the Customers table switches to Design view. The top portion of Design view displays each field that comprises a customer record, the field's data type, and an optional description of what the field should contain. The bottom portion of Design view displays the field properties (details) for the selected field.

d. Click **View** in the Views group on the Home tab again.

Because the View button is a toggle, your view returns to Datasheet view, which shows the data stored in the table.

e. Double-click **Employees** in the Tables group of the Navigation Pane. Double-click **Products** in the same location.

The Employees and Products tables open. The tabs for three table objects display below the Ribbon: Customers, Employees, and Products.

f. Click **Shutter Bar Open/Close** [«] on the title bar of the Navigation Pane to hide the Navigation Pane. Click again to [»] show the Navigation Pane.

Shutter Bar Open/Close toggles to allow you to view more in the open object window, or to enable you to view your database objects.

g. Scroll down in the Navigation Pane and click **Reports**.

The Reports group expands, and all report objects display.

h. Scroll up until you can see Forms. Click **Forms** in the Navigation Pane.

The Forms group collapses and individual form objects no longer display.

You want to learn to edit the data in the Northwind database, because data can change. For example, employees will change their address and phone numbers when they move, and customers will change their order data from time to time. Refer to Figure 1.32 as you complete Step 3.

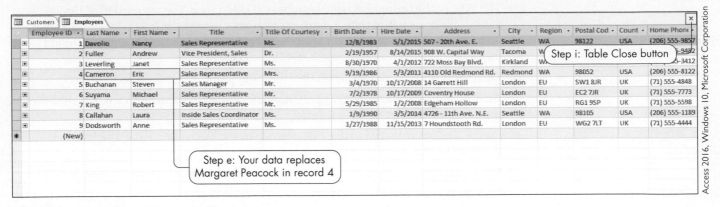

FIGURE 1.32 Northwind Employees Table

a. Click the **Employees tab** to view the Employees table.

b. Double-click **Peacock** (the value of the Last Name field in the fourth row); the entire name highlights. Type your last name to replace Peacock.

    The pencil symbol in the record selector box indicates that the record is being edited but has not yet been saved.

c. Press **Tab** to move to the next field in the fourth row. Replace Margaret with your first name and press **Tab**.

    You have made changes to two fields in the same record.

d. Click **Undo** on the Quick Access Toolbar.

    Your first and last names revert back to Margaret Peacock because you have not yet left the record.

e. Type your first and last names again to replace Margaret Peacock. Press **Tab**.

    You should now be in the title field and the title, Sales Representative, is selected. The record has not been saved, as indicated by the pencil symbol in the record selector box.

f. Click anywhere in the third row where Janet Leverling's data is stored.

    The pencil symbol disappears, indicating that your changes have been saved.

g. Click the **Address field** in the first row, Nancy Davolio's record. Select the entire address and then type **4004 East Morningside Dr.** Click anywhere on the second record, Andrew Fuller's record.

h. Click **Undo**.

    Nancy Davolio's address reverts back to 507 - 20th Ave. E. However, the Undo command is now faded. You can no longer undo the change that you made replacing Margaret Peacock's name with your own.

i. Click **Close** ☒ at the top of the table to close the Employees table.

    The Employees table closes. You are not prompted to save your changes; they have already been saved for you because Access works in storage, not memory. If you reopen the Employees table, you will see your name in place of Margaret Peacock's name.

You have been asked to add new information about a new line of products to the Northwind database. Refer to Figure 1.33 as you complete Step 4.

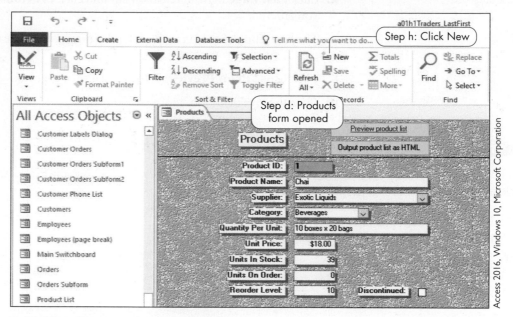

FIGURE 1.33 Adding Data Using Products Form

a. Right-click the **Customers tab** and click **Close All**.

b. Click the **Tables group** in the Navigation Pane to collapse it. Click the **Reports group** in the Navigation Pane to collapse it as well.

c. Click the **Forms group** in the Navigation Pane to expand the list of available forms.

d. Double-click the **Products form** to open it.

e. Click the **Next record** arrow. Click **Last record**, click **Previous record**, and then click **First record**.

f. Click **Find** in the Find group on the Home tab, type **Grandma** in the **Find box**, click the **Match arrow**, and then select **Any Part of Field**. Click **Find Next**.

   You should see the data for Grandma's Boysenberry Spread. Selecting the Any Part of Field option will return a match even if it is contained in the middle of a word.

g. Close the Find dialog box.

h. Click **New** in the Records group of the Home tab.

i. Type the following information for a new product. Click, or press **Tab**, to move into the next cell. Notice as soon as you begin typing, Access will assign a ProductID to this product.

Field Name	Value to Type
Product Name	*Your name*s Pecan Pie (replacing Your name with your last name)
Supplier	**Grandma Kelly's Homestead** (click the arrow to select from the list of Suppliers)
Category	**Confections** (click the arrow to select from the list of Categories)
Quantity Per Unit	1
Unit Price	15.00
Units in Stock	18
Units on Order	50
Reorder Level	20
Discontinued	**No** (leave the check box unchecked)

j. Click anywhere on the Pecan Pie record you just typed. Click the **File tab**, click **Print**, and then click **Print Preview**.

The first four records display in the Print Preview.

k. Click **Last Page** in the navigation bar and click **Previous Page** to show the new record you entered.

The beginning of the Pecan Pie record is now visible. The record continues on the next page.

l. Click **Close Print Preview** in the Close Preview group.

m. Close the Products form.

STEP 5 ›› **DELETE RECORDS FROM A TABLE**

To help you understand how Access stores data, you verify that the new product is in the Products table. You also attempt to delete a record. Refer to Figure 1.34 as you complete Step 5.

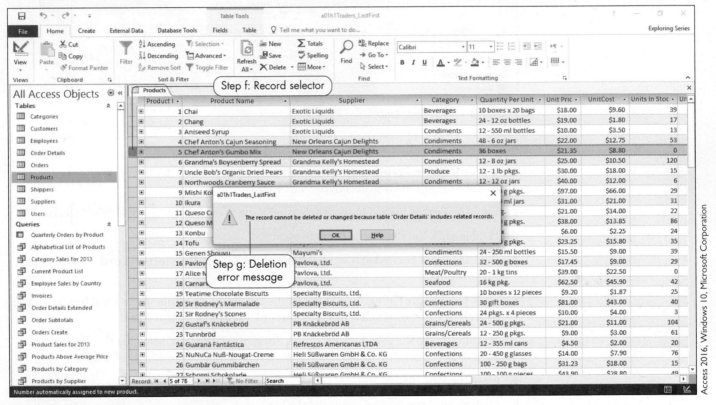

FIGURE 1.34 Deleting Data

a. Click the **Forms group** in the Navigation Pane to collapse it. Expand the **Tables group**.

b. Double-click the **Products table** to open it.

c. Click **Last record** in the navigation bar.

The Pecan Pie record you entered in the Products form is listed as the last record in the Products table. The Products form was created from the Products table. Your newly created record, Pecan Pie, is stored in the Products table even though you added it using the form.

d. Navigate to the fifth record in the table, Chef Anton's Gumbo Mix.

e. Use the horizontal scroll bar to scroll right until you see the Discontinued field.

The check mark in the Discontinued check box tells you that this product has been discontinued.

f. Click the **record selector** to the left of the fifth record.

A border surrounds the record and the record is shaded, indicating it is selected.

g. Click **Delete** in the Records group and read the error message.

The error message that displays tells you that you cannot delete this record because the table 'Order Details' has related records. (Customers ordered this product in the past.) Even though the product is now discontinued and no stock remains, it cannot be deleted from the Products table because related records exist in the Order Details table.

h. Click **OK**.

i. Navigate to the last record and click the **record selector** to highlight the entire row.

The Pecan Pie record you added earlier is displayed.

j. Click **Delete** in the Records group. Read the warning.

The warning box that displays tells you that this action cannot be undone. Although this product can be deleted because it was just entered and no orders were created for it, you do not want to delete the record.

k. Click **No**. You do not want to delete this record. Close the Products table.

> **TROUBLESHOOTING:** If you clicked Yes and deleted the record, return to Step 4d. Re-open the form and re-enter the information for this record. This will be important later in this lesson.

STEP 6 ›› USE DATABASE UTILITIES

You will protect the Northwind database by using the Back Up Database utility. Refer to Figure 1.35 as you complete Step 6.

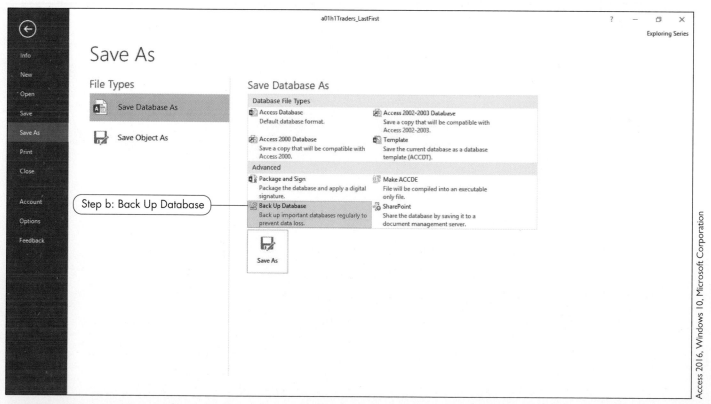

FIGURE 1.35 Backing Up a Database

Access 2016, Windows 10, Microsoft Corporation

a. Click the **File tab** and click **Save As**.

b. Double-click **Back Up Database** under the Advanced section to open the Save As dialog box.

The backup utility assigns the default name by adding a date to your file name.

c. Verify that the Save in folder displays the location where you want your file saved and click **Save**.

You just created a backup of the database after completing Hands-On Exercise 1. The original database file remains onscreen.

d. Keep the database open if you plan to continue with Hands-On Exercise 2. If not, close the database and exit Access.

Filters and Sorts

Access provides you with many tools that you can use to change the order of information and to identify and extract only the data needed at the moment. You may want to find specific information, such as which suppliers are located in Denton, TX, or which customers have placed orders in the last seven days. There may be other times you simply want to sort information rather than extract information.

In this section, you will learn how to sort information and to isolate records in a table based on criteria.

Working with Filters

Suppose you wanted to see a list of the products in the Confections category in the Northwind database. To obtain this list, you would open the Products table in Datasheet view and create a filter. A *filter* allows you to specify conditions to display only those records that meet those conditions. These conditions are known as criteria (or criterion, singular), and are a number, a text phrase, or an expression (such as >50) used to select records from a table. Therefore, to view a list of all Confections, you would filter the Products table, displaying only records with a Category value of Confections. In this case, Category being equal to Confections is the criterion.

You can use filters to analyze data quickly. Applying a filter does not delete any records; filters only hide records that do not match the criteria. Two types of filters are discussed in this section: Selection filter and Filter By Form.

Use a Selection Filter to Find Exact Matches

STEP 1 ›› A *Selection filter* displays only the records that match a criterion you select. You can use a Selection filter to find records that equal a criterion. For example, if you filter a name field and you select "equals Eric", you would only find customers who have a name of Eric (but not any other variation). Selection filters are not case sensitive, so any variation of capitalization (ERIC, eric) would also appear in the search results.

> **To use a Selection filter to find an exact match, complete the following steps:**
>
> 1. Click in any field that contains the criterion on which you want to filter.
> 2. Click Selection in the Sort & Filter group on the Home tab.
> 3. Select Equals "criterion" from the list of options (*criterion* will be replaced by the value of the field).

Figure 1.36 displays a Customers table with 91 records. The records in the table are displayed in sequence according to the CustomerID. The navigation bar at the bottom indicates that the active record is the second row in the table. Owner in the Job Title field is selected.

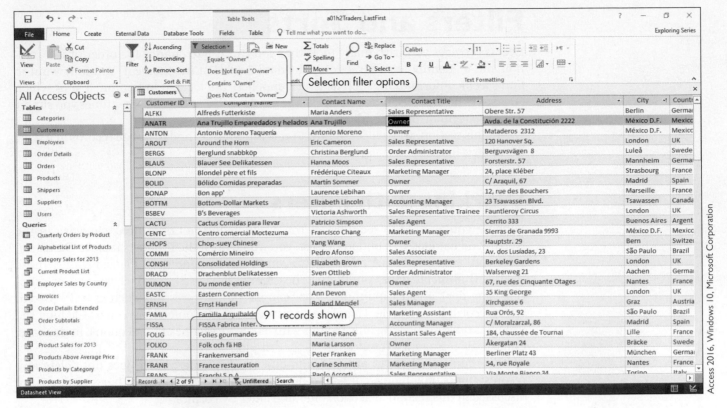

FIGURE 1.36 Unfiltered Customers Table

Figure 1.37 displays a filtered view of the Customers table, showing records with the job title Owner. The navigation bar shows that this is a filtered list containing 17 records matching the criterion. The Customers table still contains the original 91 records, but only 17 records are visible with the filter applied.

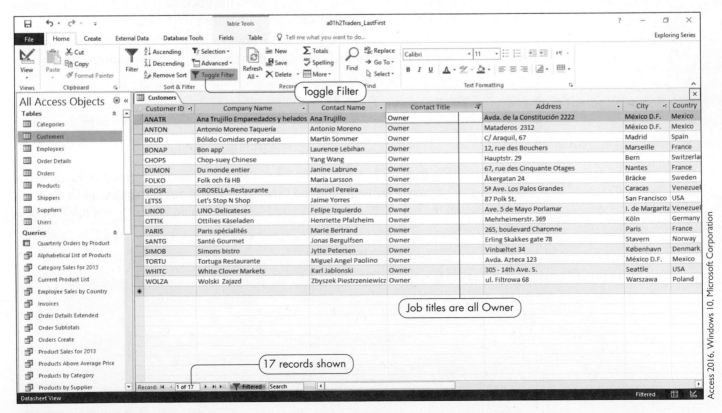

FIGURE 1.37 Filtered Customers Table

You can click Toggle Filter (refer to Figure 1.37) at any time to remove all filters and display all the records in the table. Filters are a temporary method for examining table data. If you close the filtered table and reopen it, the filter will be removed and all of the records will be visible again. You can at any point click Toggle Filter to display the results of the last saved filter.

Use a Selection Filter to Find Records Containing a Value

STEP 2 ›› You can also use a Selection filter to find records that contain a criterion. For example, if you filter a name field and you select "contains Eric", it would find Eric, as well as names containing Eric (such as Erica, Erich, Erick, and even Broderick, Frederick, and Frederica). As with the exact match, this is not case sensitive, as shown in the results in Figure 1.38.

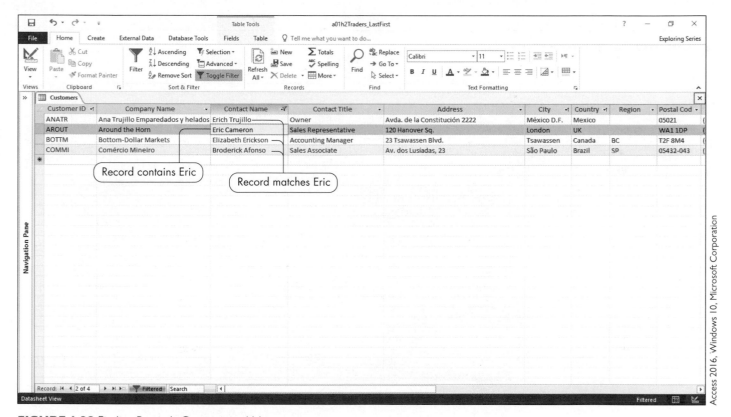

FIGURE 1.38 Finding Records Containing a Value

> **To use a Selection filter to find all values containing certain text, complete the following steps:**
>
> 1. Click in any field that contains the criterion on which you want to filter.
> 2. Click Selection in the Sort & Filter group on the Home tab.
> 3. Select Contains "criterion" from the list of options (*criterion* will be replaced by the value of the field).

Your results will show all records containing a partial or full match.

Use Filter By Form

STEP 3 ›› *Filter By Form* is a more versatile method of selecting data because it enables you to display records based on multiple criteria. When you use Filter By Form, all of the records are hidden and Access creates a blank form in a design grid. You see only field names with an arrow in the first field. Figure 1.39 shows Filter By Form in Datasheet view, and Figure 1.40 shows Filter By Form in a form view.

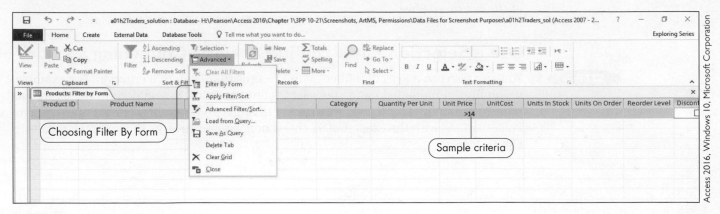

FIGURE 1.39 Filter By Form in a Table

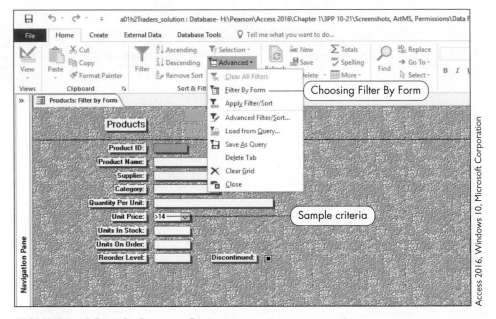

FIGURE 1.40 Filter By Form in a Form

An advantage of using this filter method is that you can specify AND and OR logical operators. If you use the AND operator, a record is included in the results if all the criteria are true. If you use the OR operator, a record is included if at least one criterion is true. Another advantage of Filter By Form is that you can use a comparison operator such as equal (=), not equal (<>), greater than (>), less than (<), greater than or equal to (>=), and less than or equal to (<=).

To use Filter By Form, complete the following steps:

1. Click Advanced in the Sort & Filter group on the Home tab.
2. Click Filter By Form.
3. Click in the field you want to use as a criterion. Click the arrow to select the criterion from existing data.
4. Add additional criterion and comparison operators as required.
5. Click Toggle Filter in the Sort & Filter group on the Home tab to apply the filter.

Performing Sorts

You can change the order of information by sorting one or more fields. A *sort* lists records in a specific sequence, such as alphabetically by last name or by ascending EmployeeID.

Sort Table Data

STEP 4 ▸▸ Ascending sorts a list of text data in alphabetical order or a numeric list in lowest to highest order. Descending sorts a list of text data in reverse alphabetical order or a numeric list in highest to lowest order. You can equate this to these terms outside of a database. When you are coming down from a high place (such as the top of a ladder), you are said to be descending, and when you are climbing a ladder, you are ascending. Figure 1.41 shows the Customers table sorted in ascending order by city name.

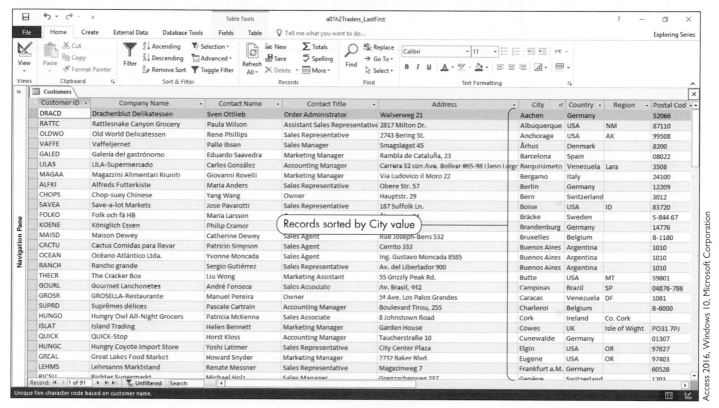

FIGURE 1.41 Sorted Customers Table

> **To sort a table on one criterion, complete the following steps:**
> 1. Click in the field that you want to use to sort the records.
> 2. Click Ascending or Descending in the Sort & Filter group on the Home tab.

Access can sort records by more than one field. When sorting by multiple criteria, Access first sorts by the field located on the left. It is important to understand that in order to sort by multiple fields, you must arrange your columns in this order. This may lead to moving a field to the left so it is sorted first.

To move a field, complete the following steps:

1. Click the column heading and hold down the left mouse button. A thick line appears to the left of the column.
2. Drag the field to the appropriate position.

Once the column has been moved, you can perform a sort by selecting the field to the left, sorting, and then doing the same for the secondary sort column.

Quick Concepts

5. What is the purpose of creating a filter? *p. 101*

6. What is the difference between a Selection filter and a Filter By Form? *pp. 101, 103*

7. What is a comparison operator and how is it used in a filter? *p. 104*

8. What are the benefits of sorting records in a table? *p. 105*

Hands-On Exercises

Watch the Video for this Hands-On Exercise!

MyITLab®
HOE2 Training

Skills covered: Use a Selection Filter to Find Exact Matches • Use a Selection Filter to Find Records Containing a Value • Use Filter By Form • Sort Table Data

2 Filters and Sorts

The sales manager at Northwind Traders wants quick answers to her questions about customer orders. You use the Access database to filter tables to answer these questions, then sort the records based on the manager's requirements.

STEP 1 » USE A SELECTION FILTER TO FIND EXACT MATCHES

The sales manager asks for a list of customers who live in London. You use a Selection filter with an equal condition to locate these customers. Refer to Figure 1.42 as you complete Step 1.

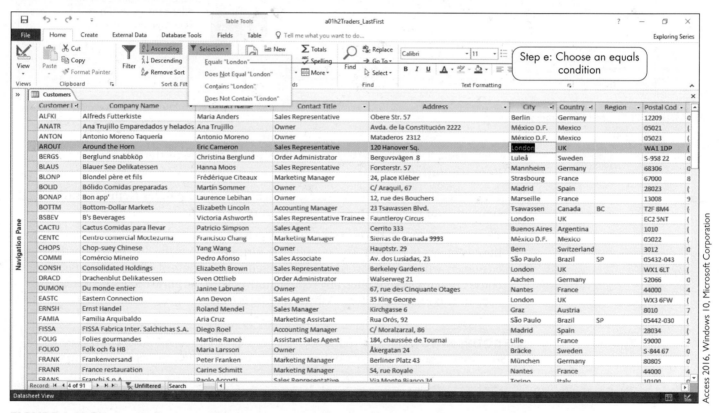

FIGURE 1.42 Filtering the Customers Table

a. Open the *a01h1Traders_LastFirst* database if you closed it after the last Hands-On Exercise and save it as **a01h2Traders_LastFirst**, changing h1 to h2. Click **Enable Content**.

b. Double-click the **Customers table** in the Navigation Pane, navigate to record 4, and then replace Thomas Hardy with your name in the Contact Name field.

c. Scroll right until the City field is visible. The fourth record has a value of London in the City field. Click the field to select it.

d. Click **Selection** in the Sort & Filter group on the Home tab.

e. Select **Equals "London"** from the menu. Six records are displayed.

Access 2016, Windows 10, Microsoft Corporation

Hands-On Exercise 2

107

The navigation bar display shows that six records that meet the London criterion are available. The other records in the Customers table are hidden. The Filtered icon also displays on the navigation bar and column heading, indicating that the Customers table has been filtered.

f. Click **Toggle Filter** in the Sort & Filter group to remove the filter.

g. Click **Toggle Filter** again to reset the filter.

STEP 2 ⟩⟩ **USE A SELECTION FILTER TO FIND RECORDS CONTAINING A VALUE**

The sales manager asks you to narrow the list of London customers so that it displays only Sales Representatives. To accomplish this task, you add a second layer of filtering using a Selection filter. Refer to Figure 1.43 as you complete Step 2.

Access 2016, Windows 10, Microsoft Corporation

FIGURE 1.43 Filtered Customers

a. Click in any field value in the Contact Title field that contains the value **Sales Representative**.

b. Click **Selection** in the Sort & Filter group, click **Contains "Sales Representative"**, and compare your results to those shown in Figure 1.43.

Three records match the criteria you set. You have applied a second layer of filtering to the customers in London. The second layer further restricts the display to only those customers who have the words Sales Representative contained in their titles. Because you chose Contains as your filter, any representatives with the phrase Sales Representative appear. This includes Victoria Ashworth, who is a Sales Representative Trainee.

> **TROUBLESHOOTING:** If you do not see the record for Victoria Ashworth, you selected Equals "Sales Representative" instead of Contains "Sales Representative". Repeat Steps a and b, making sure you select Contains "Sales Representative".

c. Close the Customers table. Click **Yes** when prompted to save the design changes to the Customers table.

You are asked to provide a list of records that do not match just one set of criteria. You will provide a list of all extended prices less than $50 for a specific sales representative. Use Filter By Form to provide the information when two or more criteria are necessary. You also preview the results in Print Preview to see how the list would print. Refer to Figure 1.44 as you complete Step 3.

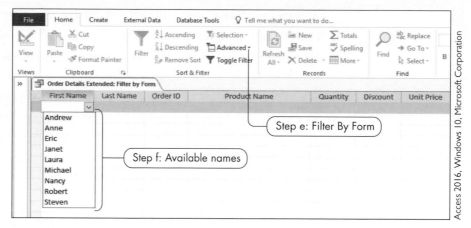

FIGURE 1.44 Using Filter By Form

a. Click the **Tables group** in the Navigation Pane to collapse the listed tables.

b. Click the **Queries group** in the Navigation Pane to expand the list of available queries.

c. Locate and double-click **Order Details Extended** to open it.

This query contains information about orders. It has fields containing information about the sales person, the Order ID, the product name, the unit price, quantity ordered, the discount given, and an extended price. The extended price is a field used to total order information.

d. Click **Advanced** in the Sort & Filter group and select **Filter By Form** from the list. The first field, First Name, is active by default.

All of the records are now hidden, and you see only field names and an arrow in the first field. Although you are applying Filter By Form to a query, you can use the same process as applying Filter By Form to a table. You are able to input more than one criterion using Filter By Form.

e. Click the **First Name arrow**.

A list of all available first names appears. Your name should be on the list. Figure 1.44 shows *Eric Cameron*, which replaced Margaret Peacock in Hands-On Exercise 1.

> **TROUBLESHOOTING:** If you do not see your name and you do see Margaret on the list, you probably skipped steps in Hands-On Exercise 1. Close the query without saving changes, return to the first Hands-On Exercise, and then rework it, making sure not to omit any steps. Then you can return to this location and work the remainder of this Hands-On Exercise.

f. Select your first name from the list.

g. Click in the first row under the Last Name field to reveal the arrow. Locate and select your last name by clicking it.

h. Scroll right until you see the Extended Price field. Click in the first row under the Extended Price field and type **<50**.

> This will select all of the items that you ordered where the total was less than 50.

i. Click **Toggle Filter** in the Sort & Filter group.

> You have specified which records to include and have executed the filtering by clicking Toggle Filter.

j. Click the **File tab**, click **Print**, and then click **Print Preview**.

> You instructed Access to preview the filtered query results. The preview displays the query title as a heading. The current filter is applied, as well as page numbers.

k. Click **Close Print Preview** in the Close Preview group.

l. Close the Order Details Extended query. Click **Yes** when prompted to save your changes.

STEP 4 ›› **SORT TABLE DATA**

The Sales Manager is pleased with your work; however, she would like some of the information to appear in a different order. You will now sort the records in the Customers table using the manager's new criteria. Refer to Figure 1.45 as you complete Step 4.

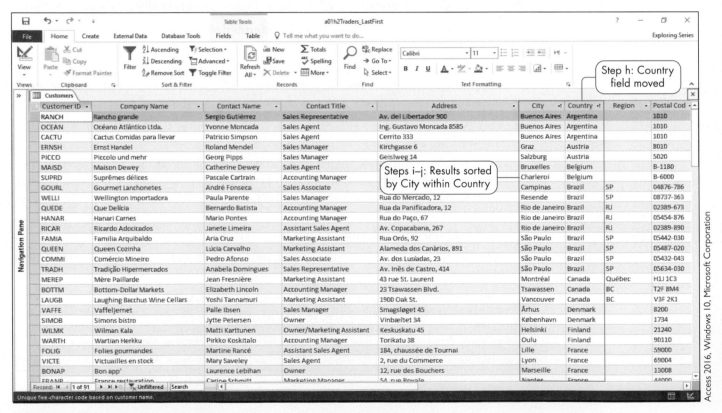

FIGURE 1.45 Updated Customers Table

a. Click the **Queries group** in the Navigation Pane to collapse the listed queries.

b. Click the **Tables group** in the Navigation Pane to expand the list of available tables and double-click the **Customers table** to open it.

> This table contains information about customers. The table is sorted in alphabetical order by Company Name.

c. Click **Shutter Bar Open/Close** in the Navigation Pane to hide the Navigation Pane.

It will be easier to locate fields in the Customer table if the Navigation Pane is hidden.

d. Click any entry in the Customer ID field. Click **Descending** in the Sort & Filter group on the Home tab.

Sorting in descending order on a text field produces a reverse alphabetical order.

e. Scroll right until you can see both the Country and City fields.

f. Click the **Country column heading**.

The entire field is selected.

g. Click the **Country column heading** again and hold down the **left mouse button**.

A thick line displays on the left edge of the Country field.

h. Check to make sure that you see the thick line. Drag the **Country field** to the left until the thick line moves between the City and Region fields. Release the mouse button and the Country field position moves to the right of the City field.

You moved the Country field next to the City field so that you can easily sort the table based on both fields.

i. Click any city name in the City field and click **Ascending** in the Sort & Filter group.

The City field displays the cities in alphabetical order.

j. Click any country name in the Country field and click **Ascending**.

The countries are sorted in alphabetical order. The cities within each country also are sorted alphabetically. For example, the customer in Graz, Austria, is listed before the customer in Salzburg, Austria.

k. Close the Customers table. Click **Yes** to save the changes to the design of the table.

l. Click **Shutter Bar Open/Close** in the Navigation Pane to show the Navigation Pane.

STEP 5 ►► VIEW RELATIONSHIPS

To further familiarize yourself with the database, you examine the connections between the tables in the Northwind database. Refer to Figure 1.46 as you complete Step 5.

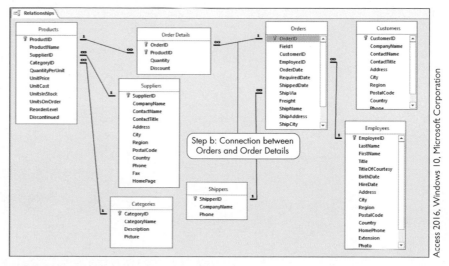

FIGURE 1.46 Northwind Relationships

a. Click the **Database Tools tab** and click **Relationships** in the Relationships group.

b. Examine the join lines showing the relationships that connect the various tables. For example, the Orders table is connected to the Order Details table using the OrderID field as the common field.

c. Close the Relationships.

d. Close the database. You will submit this file to your instructor at the end of the last Hands-On Exercise.

Access Database Creation

Now that you have examined the fundamentals of an Access database and explored the power of databases, it is time to create one! In this section, you explore the benefits of creating a database using each of the methods discussed in the next section.

Creating a Database

When you first start Access, Backstage view opens and provides you with three methods for creating a new database. These methods are:

- Create a blank desktop database
- Create a database from a template (note: there will be many templates shown)
- Create a custom web app

Creating a blank desktop database lets you create a database specific to your requirements. Rather than starting from scratch by creating a blank desktop database, you may want to use a template to create a new database. An Access *template* is a predefined database that includes professionally designed tables, forms, reports, and other objects that you can use to jumpstart the creation of your database. Creating a *custom web app* enables you to create a database that you can build and then use and share with others through the Web.

Figure 1.47 shows the options for creating a custom web app, a blank desktop database, and multiple templates from which you can select the method for which you want to create a database.

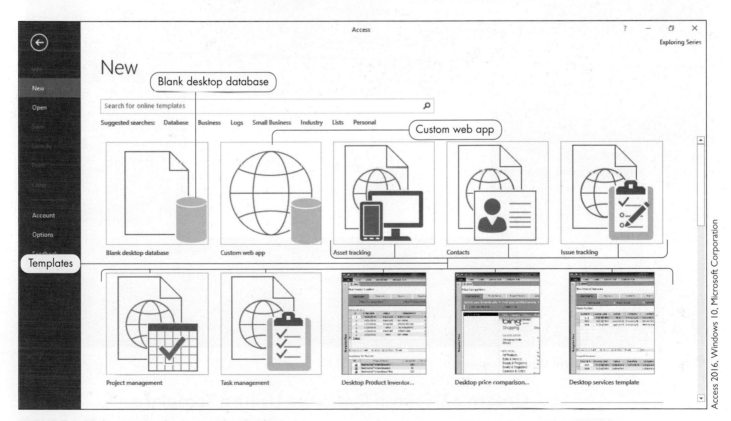

FIGURE 1.47 Options for Creating a New Database

Create a Blank Desktop Database

Often, if you are migrating from Excel to Access, you would start by creating a blank desktop database. At that point, you could import your existing structure and data into a new table. Another time you might use a blank desktop database is when you are starting a project and want to design your own tables.

When you create a blank desktop database, Access opens to a blank table in Datasheet view where you can add fields or data. You can also refine the table in Design view. You would then create additional tables and objects as necessary. Obviously, this task requires some level of Access knowledge, so unless you have requirements to follow, you may be better served using a template.

To create a blank desktop database, complete the following steps:

1. Open Access. (If Access is already open, click the File tab to open Backstage view and click New.)
2. Click the Blank desktop database tile.
3. Type the file name for the file in the text box, click Browse to navigate to the folder where you want to store the database file, and then click OK.
4. Click Create (see Figure 1.48).
5. Type data in the empty table that displays.

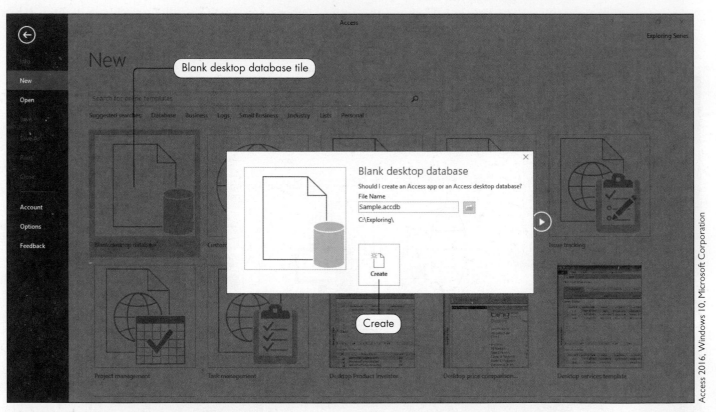

FIGURE 1.48 Creating a Blank Desktop Database

Create a Desktop Database Using a Template

 Using a template to start a database saves you a great deal of creation time. Working with a template can also help a new Access user become familiar with database design. Templates are available from Backstage view, where you can select from a variety of templates or search online for more templates.

Access also provides templates for desktop use.

To create a desktop database from a template, complete the following steps:

1. Open Access. (If Access is already open, click the File tab to open Backstage view and click New.)
2. Click the desktop database template you want to use, or use the search box at the top of the page. Figure 1.49 shows some examples of templates.
3. Type the file name for the file in the text box, click Browse to navigate to the folder where you want to store the database file, and then click OK.
4. Click Create to download the template.

   The database will be created and will open.
5. Click Enable Content in the Security Warning message bar.

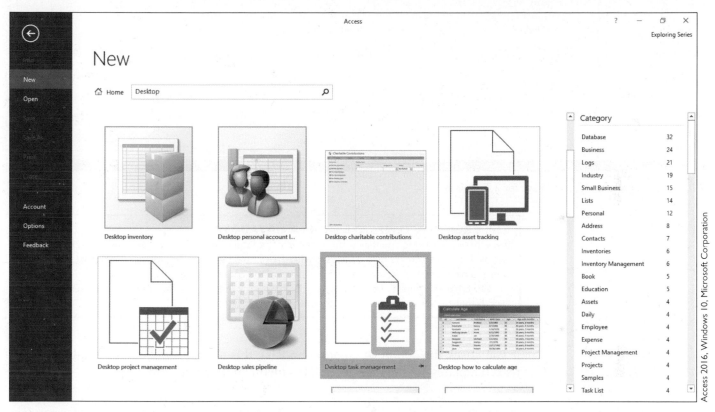

FIGURE 1.49 Database Templates

Once the database is open, you may see a Getting Started page that includes links you can use to learn more about the database. When finished reviewing the learning materials, close the Getting Started page to view the database. Figure 1.50 displays the Getting Started page included with the Desktop task management template. Notice the hyperlink to import contacts from Microsoft Outlook. If you use Outlook, this is a nice feature. Close the Getting Started page to return to the database. Because you downloaded a template, some objects will have already been created. You can work with these objects just as you did in the first three sections of this chapter. Edit any object to meet your requirements.

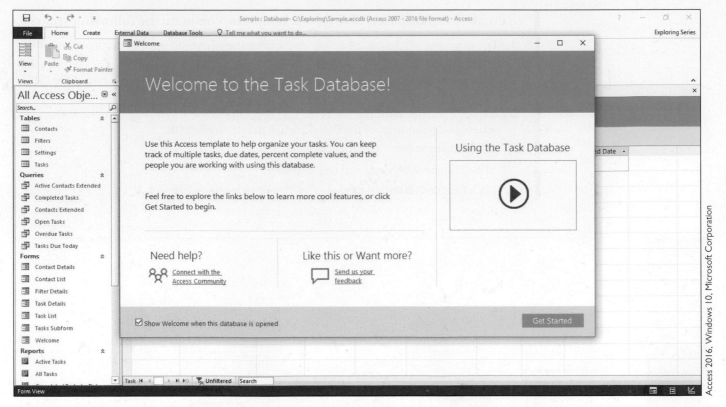

FIGURE 1.50 Getting Started Page for a Template

> **TIP: CREATE A TEMPLATE FROM A DATABASE**
> If you have a database you may want to reuse in the future, you can save it as a template. Doing so will enable you to create new databases with the same tables, queries, forms, and reports as the one you have created. You can also reuse parts of the database as application parts.
>   To create a template from an existing database, click the File tab, click Save As, and then double-click Template. Set options such as the name and description and click OK.

If you check the option for Application Part, this template will also be available under User Templates on the Application Parts menu on the Create tab.

Add Records to a Downloaded Desktop Database

STEP 2 >> Once a desktop database template has been downloaded, you can use it as you would use any Access database. Figure 1.51 shows the Desktop Task Management template. Review the objects listed in the Navigation Pane. Once you are familiar with the database design, you can enter your data using a table or form.

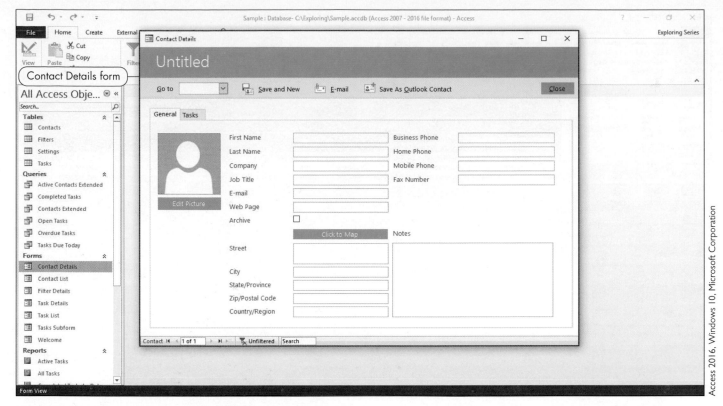

FIGURE 1.51 Desktop Task Management Database

Explore the Database Objects in a Downloaded Desktop Database Template

STEP 3 ⟩⟩ One of the reasons to use a template is so you do not have to create any of the objects. Therefore, you will notice each template comes with a varying amount of predefined queries, forms, and reports. Familiarize yourself with the unique features of a template; as they are professionally designed, they are typically well thought out.

Create a Table Using an Application Part

An *application part* enables you to add a set of common Access components to an existing database, such as a table, a form, and a report for a related task. These are provided by Microsoft and offer components (for example, a Contacts table) you can add to an existing database, rather than creating an entirely new database, as shown in Figure 1.52.

> **To add an application part to a database, complete the following steps:**
>
> 1. Click Application Parts in the Templates group on the Create tab.
> 2. Select one of the options from the list.
> 3. Respond to the dialog boxes. For example, if you insert an Issues application part, you may be prompted to create a relationship between Issues and an existing table (such as Customers). Setting up a relationship is not required, but may be appropriate.
> 4. Check the Navigation Pane to verify that the new components were created.

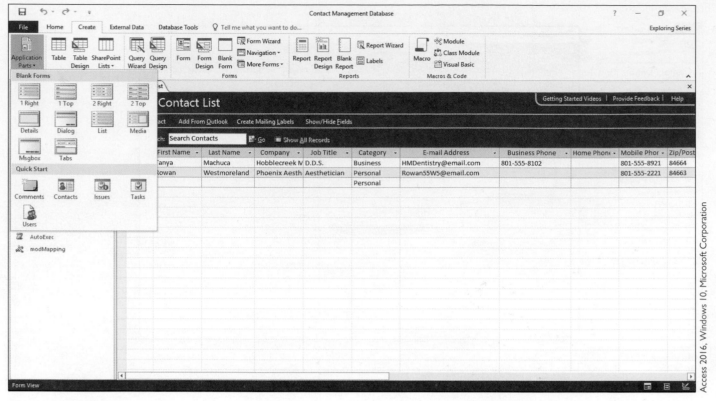

FIGURE 1.52 Adding an Application Part

Create a Web App Using a Template

An Access Web app (or application) is a type of database that lets you build a browser-based database app. You can create a database in the cloud that you and others can access and use simultaneously. This requires that you use a host server such as SharePoint (a Web app platform developed by Microsoft) or Office 365 (a cloud service edition of SharePoint).

Before creating a Web app, ensure that you have access to a host server. In a business environment, this would likely be set up and maintained by your Information Technology department. Your college or university may not give students access to this server. If they do, your professor can give you the information you will need.

> **To create a Web app using SharePoint, complete the following steps:**
>
> 1. Click the File tab.
> 2. Click New.
> 3. Click Custom web app.
> 4. Type an App Name.
> 5. Input the web location (which will be provided by your company's technology professionals or by your professor, if available).
> 6. Click Create.
> 7. Create tables. This can be done manually, from a template, or from an existing data source.

In a business environment (and on the Microsoft Office Specialist examination for Access) you may need to migrate the database you have created to a SharePoint server. Doing so is similar to the Save operation covered earlier in the chapter.

To migrate an existing database to a SharePoint server, complete the following steps:

1. Click the File tab.
2. Click Save As.
3. Click SharePoint.
4. Click Save As.
5. Select the location on the SharePoint server where you wish to save your database, and click Save.

As mentioned earlier, SharePoint is typically used more in a corporate environment, so you may not have a SharePoint server available at your college or university.

Quick Concepts

9. What is a custom web app, and what is required to build a custom web app? *p. 113*

10. What are two benefits of using a template to create a database? *p. 114*

11. If you want to add a component to an existing database (such as a Contacts table), what would you use? *p. 117*

Watch the Video for this Hands-On Exercise!

MyITLab®
HOE3 Training

3 Access Database Creation

After working with the Northwind database on the job, you decide to use Access to create a personal contact database. Rather than start from a blank table, you use an Access Contact Manager desktop template to make your database creation simpler.

STEP 1 ›› CREATE A DATABASE USING A TEMPLATE

You locate an Access desktop template that you can use to create your personal contact database. This template not only allows you to store names, addresses, telephone numbers, and other information, but also lets you categorize your contacts, send email messages, and create maps of addresses. You download and save the template. Refer to Figure 1.53 as you complete Step 1.

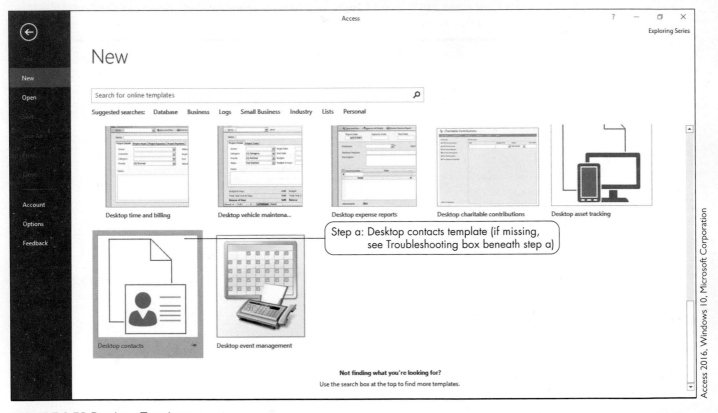

Step a: Desktop contacts template (if missing, see Troubleshooting box beneath step a)

FIGURE 1.53 Database Templates

a. Open Access. Scroll down and click the **Desktop contacts** template tile.

> **TROUBLESHOOTING:** If the Desktop contacts template is not visible, type **contacts** in the search box at the top of the screen and click the magnifying glass. Note there may be slight differences to the name, so look for the template matching the icon above.

b. Click **Browse** to navigate to the folder where you are saving your files, type **a01h3Contacts_LastFirst** as the file name, and then click **OK**.

c. Click **Create** to download the template.

d. Click the *Show Getting Started when this database is opened* check box to deselect it, and close the Getting Started with Contacts page.

The database displays the Contact List form.

e. Click **Enable Content** on the Security Warning message bar.

STEP 2 ›› ADD RECORDS TO A DOWNLOADED DESKTOP DATABASE

Because the database opens in the Contact List form, you decide to begin by entering a contact in the form. Refer to Figure 1.54 as you complete Step 2.

FIGURE 1.54 Contact Details for Tanya Machuca

a. Click in the First Name field of the first record. Type the following information, pressing **Tab** between each entry. Do not press Tab after entering the ZIP/Postal Code.

Field Name	Value to Type
First Name	**Tanya**
Last Name	**Machuca**
Company	**Hobblecreek Mountain Dentistry**
Job Title	**D.D.S.**
Category	**Business** (select from list)
E-mail	**HMDentistry@email.com**
Business Phone	**801-555-8102**
Home Phone	(leave blank)
Mobile Phone	**801-555-8921**
Zip/Postal Code	**84664**

b. Click **Open** in the first field of Dr. Machuca's record.

Open is a hyperlink to a different form in the database. The Contact Details form opens, displaying Dr. Machuca's information. More fields are available for you to use to store information. (Note that this form could also be opened from the Navigation Pane.)

c. Type the following additional information to the record:

Field Name	Value to Type
Street	**56 West 200 North**
City	**Mapleton**
State/Province	**UT**
Country/Region	**USA**
Notes	**Available Tuesday - Friday 7 a.m. to 4 p.m.**

d. Click the **Click to Map** hyperlink to view a map to Dr. Machuca's office.

Bing displays a map to the address in the record. You can get directions, locate nearby businesses, and use many other options.

> **TROUBLESHOOTING:** You may be prompted to choose an application. Select any Web browser such as Microsoft Edge from the list.

e. Close the map. Click **Save and Close** in the top center of the form to close the Contact Details form.

The record is saved.

f. Click **New Contact** beneath the Contact List title bar.

The Contact Details form opens to a blank record.

g. Type the following information for a new record, pressing **Tab** to move between fields. Some fields will be blank.

Field Name	Value to Type
First Name	**Rowan**
Last Name	**Westmoreland**
Company	**Phoenix Aesthetics**
Job Title	**Aesthetician**
Mobile Phone	**801-555-2221**
Street	**425 North Main Street**
City	**Springville**
State/Province	**UT**
Zip/Postal Code	**84663**
Category	**Personal**
E-mail	**Rowan55W5@email.com**
Notes	**Recommended by Michelle**

h. Click **Save and Close**.

You explore the objects created by the template so that you understand the organization of the database. Refer to Figure 1.55 as you complete Step 3.

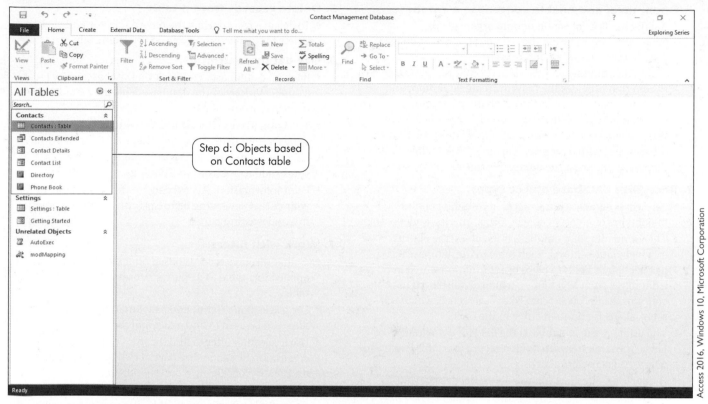

FIGURE 1.55 Tables and Related Views

a. Double-click the **Contacts table** in the Navigation Pane.

   The information you entered using the Contact List form and the Contact Details form displays in the Contacts table.

b. Double-click the **Phone Book report** in the Navigation Pane.

   The Phone Book report opens displaying the contact name and phone information organized by category.

c. Double-click the **Directory report** in the Navigation Pane.

   The Directory report opens, displaying a full alphabetical contact list. The Directory report was designed to display more fields than the Phone Book, but it is not organized by category.

d. Click **All Access Objects** on the Navigation Pane and select **Tables and Related Views**.

   You can now see the objects that are based on the Contacts table.

e. Right-click the **Directory report tab** and select **Close All**.

f. Close the database and exit Access. Based on your instructor's directions, submit the following:

   a01h1Traders_LastFirst_*CurrentDate*

   a01h2Traders_LastFirst

   a01h3Contacts_LastFirst

Chapter Objectives Review

After reading this chapter, you have accomplished the following objectives:

1. Open, save, and enable content in a database.

- A database is a collection of data organized as meaningful information that can be accessed, managed, stored, queried, sorted, and reported.
- A database management system (DBMS) is a software system that provides the tools to create, maintain, and use a database. Access is the database management system found in business versions of Microsoft Office.
- When a database is first opened, Access displays a message bar with a security warning. Click Enable Content if you trust the database's source.

2. Recognize database object types.

- An Access database is a structured collection of four major types of objects—tables, forms, queries, and reports.
- The foundation of a database is its tables, the objects in which data is stored. Each table in the database has a collection of fields (a piece of information stored in a database, such as a name), which are displayed as columns. Each row is referred to as a record, which is a set of all fields about an entry in the table.
- The primary key in a table is the field (or combination of fields) that uniquely identifies a record in a table (such as a driver's license number).
- A query is a question you ask about the data in your database.
- A form enables simplified entry and modification of data.
- A report contains professional-looking formatted information from underlying tables or queries.
- Examine the Access interface: Objects are organized and listed in the Navigation Pane. Access also uses a Tabbed Documents interface in which each object that is open has its own tab.
- Explore table Datasheet view: Datasheet view is a grid containing fields (columns) and records (rows).
- Navigate through records: Navigation arrows enable you to move through records, with arrows for the first, previous, next, and last records, as well as one to add a new record.
- Explore table Design view: Design view gives you a detailed view of the table's structure and is used to create and modify a table's design by specifying the fields it will contain, the fields' data types, and their associated properties.
- Rename and describe tables: Tables can be renamed as necessary and a description can be added. The description gives the user more information about what an object does.

3. Modify data in table Datasheet view.

- Access works primarily from storage. Records can be added, modified, or deleted in the database, and as the information is entered, it is automatically saved. Undo cannot reverse edits made to multiple records.

4. Add records to a table.

- A pencil symbol displays in the record selector box to indicate when you are in editing mode. Moving to another record saves the changes.

5. Delete records from a table.

- To delete a record, click the record selector and click Delete in the Records group on the Home tab.

6. Use database utilities.

- Back up a database: The Back Up Database utility creates a duplicate copy of the database. This may enable users to recover from failure.
- The Compact and Repair utility reduces the size of a database and fixes any errors that may exist in the file.
- Encrypt a database: Encrypting databases enables you to add a password to a database.
- Print information: Access can create a print copy of your data. Previewing before printing is a good practice to avoid wasting paper.

7. Work with filters.

- A filter displays records based on a set of criteria that is applied to a table to display a subset of records in that table.
- Use a selection filter to find exact matches: A selection filter can be used to find exact matches.
- Use a selection filter to find records containing a value: A selection filter can find partial matches, for example, find values containing a certain phrase.
- Use filter by form: Filter By Form displays records based on multiple criteria and enables the user to apply logical operators and use comparison operators.

8. Perform sorts.

- Sort table data: Sorting changes the order of information, and information may be sorted by one or more fields.
- Data can be sorted ascending (low to high) or descending (high to low).

9. Create a database.

- Creating a blank desktop database: Creating a blank desktop database enables you to create a database specific to your requirements.
- Create a desktop database using a template: A template is a predefined database that includes professionally designed tables, forms, reports, and other objects that you can use to jumpstart the creation of your database.
- Add records to a downloaded desktop database: Once a database has been created, it can be used as any other database is.
- Explore the database objects in a downloaded database template: Once you create a database using a template, explore it and become familiar with the contents.
- Create a table using an application part: If you require a certain type of table (such as Contacts) you can add them using an application part.
- Create a Web app using a template: Creating a custom web app enables you to create a database that you can build and use and share with others through the Web.

Key Terms Matching

Match the key terms with their definitions. Write the key term letter by the appropriate numbered definition.

a. Application part
b. Database
c. Database Management System (DBMS)
d. Datasheet view
e. Design view
f. Field
g. Filter
h. Filter By Form
i. Form
j. Navigation Pane
k. Object
l. Primary key
m. Query
n. Record
o. Relationship
p. Report
q. Selection filter
r. Sort
s. Table
t. Template

1. _____ A filtering method that displays only records that match selected criteria. **p. 101**

2. _____ A filtering method that displays records based on multiple criteria. **p. 103**

3. _____ A main component that is created and used to make a database function, such as a table or form. **p. 73**

4. _____ A method of listing records in a specific sequence (such as alphabetically). **p. 105**

5. _____ A predefined database that includes professionally designed tables, forms, reports, and other objects. **p. 113**

6. _____ A question you ask about the data in your database. **p. 75**

7. _____ An Access interface element that organizes and lists database objects in a database. **p. 73**

8. _____ An Access object that simplifies entering, modifying, and deleting table data. **p. 75**

9. _____ A set of common Access components that can be added to an existing database. **p. 117**

10. _____ An object that contains professional-looking formatted information from underlying tables or queries. **p. 76**

11. _____ An object used to store data, organizing data into columns and rows. **p. 74**

12. _____ Complete set of all the fields about one person, place, event, or concept. **p. 74**

13. _____ The field (or combination of fields) that uniquely identifies each record in a table. **p. 74**

14. _____ View that enables you to create and modify a table design. **p. 81**

15. _____ A collection of data organized as meaningful information that can be accessed, managed, stored, queried, sorted, and reported. **p. 70**

16. _____ A connection between two tables using a common field. **p. 84**

17. _____ A grid that enables you to add, edit, and delete the records of a table. **p. 79**

18. _____ A piece of information stored in a table, such as a company name or city. **p. 74**

19. _____ A software system that provides the tools needed to create, maintain, and use a database. **p. 70**

20. _____ Enables you to specify conditions to display only those records that meet certain conditions. **p. 101**

Multiple Choice

1. Which of the following is an example of an Access object?

    (a) Database

    (b) Field

    (c) Form

    (d) Record

2. Where is data in a database stored?

    (a) Form

    (b) Query

    (c) Report

    (d) Table

3. You edit several records in an Access table. When should you execute the Save command?

    (a) Immediately after you edit a record

    (b) Once at the end of the session

    (c) Records are saved automatically; the save command is not required

    (d) When you close the table

4. Which of the following is *not* true of an Access database?

    (a) Each field has a data type that establishes the kind of data that can be entered.

    (b) Every record in a table has the same fields as every other record.

    (c) Every table in a database contains the same number of records as every other table.

    (d) A primary key uniquely identifies a record.

5. Which of the following is true regarding table views?

    (a) You can add, edit, and delete records using Design view.

    (b) Datasheet view shows a detailed view of the table design.

    (c) Datasheet view provides access to more field properties than Design view.

    (d) Changes made in Datasheet view are automatically saved when you move the insertion point to a different record.

6. Which of the following utilities is used to recover in the event of loss or damage?

    (a) Back Up Database

    (b) Compact and Repair Database

    (c) Database Splitter

    (d) Encrypt Database

7. Which of the following would be matched if you use a Selection filter's exact match option for the name Ann?

    (a) Ann, ANN, and ann

    (b) Danny, Ann, and Anny

    (c) Ann (but not ANN)

    (d) Both a and b

8. Which of the following conditions is available through a Selection filter?

    (a) Equal condition

    (b) Delete condition

    (c) AND condition

    (d) OR condition

9. All of the following statements are true about creating a database *except*:

    (a) Creating a custom web app requires that you use a server (such as SharePoint).

    (b) When creating a blank desktop database, Access opens to a blank table in Datasheet view.

    (c) Using a template to create a database saves time because it includes predefined objects.

    (d) The objects provided in a template cannot be modified.

10. To add a predefined table to an existing database, you should use which of the following?

    (a) Application part

    (b) Blank desktop database

    (c) Custom web app

    (d) Database template

Practice Exercises

1 Replacement Parts

As a recent hire at Replacement Parts, you are tasked with performing updates to the customer database. You have been asked to open the company's database, save it with a new name, and then modify, add, and delete records. You will then back up the database, apply filters and sorts, and use an application part to add a new table that will be used to track customer shipping and receiving complaints. Refer to Figure 1.56 as you complete the exercise.

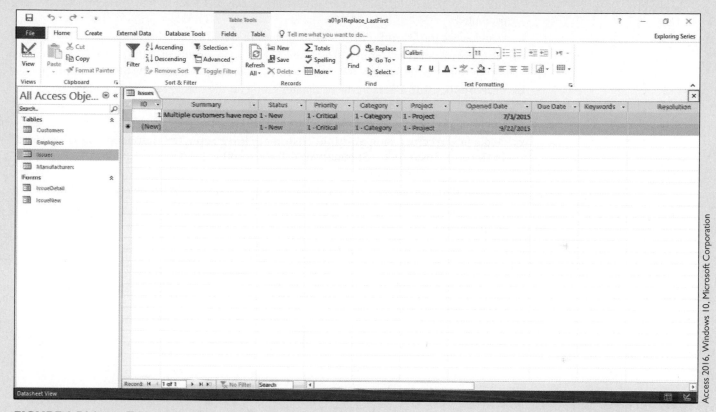

FIGURE 1.56 Issues Table Added to Replacement Parts Database

a. Open the *a01p1Replace* file. Save the database as **a01p1Replace_LastFirst**. Click **Enable Content** on the message bar.

b. Double-click the **Manufacturers table** to open the table in Datasheet view. Locate record 800552 (Haas). Change the name to **Haas International** and the CountryOfOrigin to **Austria**.

c. Type the following new records:

MfgID	ManufacturerName	CountryOfOrigin	EmployeeID
801411	Bolshoy Fine China	Russia	817080
801422	Tejada and Sons	Dominican Republic	816680
801433	Lubitz UK	England	817580

d. Delete record **800661** (John Bradshaw).

e. Close the Manufacturers table.

f. Click the **File tab**, click **Save As**, and then double-click **Back Up Database**. Accept the default backup file name and click **Save**.

g. Double-click the **Customers table** to open the table in Datasheet view.

h. Click the **State field** for the first record (Diego Martinez). Click **Selection** in the Sort & Filter group, and then click **Equals "OR"** to display the two customers in Oregon. Close the table, selecting **Save** when prompted.

i. Double-click the **Employees table** to open the table in Datasheet view.

j. Click the **plus sign** ⊞ next to Alfonso Torres. Notice he is assigned as the representative for the manufacturer Antarah.

This information is available due to the relationship already created in the database between Employees and Manufacturers.

k. Click **Advanced** in the Sort & Filter group on the Home tab, and select **Filter By Form.** Click in the Salary field. Type **>60000** and click **Toggle Filter** in the Sort & Filter group on the Home tab to apply the filter. Six employees are displayed. Close the table, selecting **Save** when prompted.

l. Double-click the **Manufacturers table** to open the table in Datasheet view.

m. Click any value in the Manufacturer Name field. Click **Ascending** in the Sort & Filter group to sort the table by the name of the manufacturer. Close the table, selecting **Save** when prompted.

n. Click **Application Parts** in the Templates group on the Create tab. Select **Issues**. Select the option for "There is no relationship." Click **Create**.

o. Double-click the **Issues table** to open the table in Datasheet view.

p. Add a new record, typing **Multiple customers have reported damaged goods received in Denton, Texas.** in the Summary field. Leave all other fields as the default values. Compare your results to Figure 1.56.

q. Close the database and exit Access. Based on your instructor's directions, submit the following:

a01p1Replace_LastFirst

a01p1Replace_LastFirst_*CurrentDate*

2 Custom Coffee

The Custom Coffee Company provides coffee, tea, and snacks to offices in Miami. Custom Coffee also provides and maintains the equipment for brewing the beverages. To improve customer service, the owner recently had an Access database created to keep track of customers, orders, and products. This database will replace the Excel spreadsheets currently maintained by the office manager. The company hired you to verify and input all the Excel data into the Access database. Refer to Figure 1.57 as you complete the exercise.

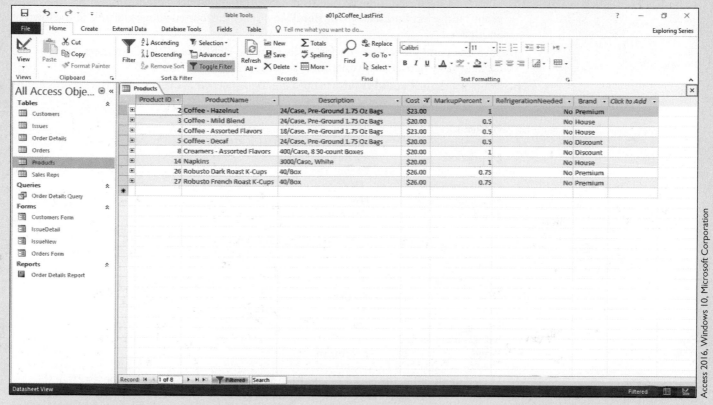

FIGURE 1.57 Filtered Products Table

a. Open the *a01p2Coffee* file and save the database as **a01p2Coffee_LastFirst**. Click **Enable Content** on the message bar.

b. Click the **Database Tools tab** and click **Relationships** in the Relationships group. Review the table relationships. Notice the join line between the Customers and Orders tables.

c. Click **Close** in the Relationships group.

d. Double-click the **Sales Reps table** to open it in Datasheet view. For rep number 2, replace **YourFirstName** and **YourLastName** with your first and last names. For example, as the Access author, I would type *Eric* in place of YourFirstName and *Cameron* in place of YourLastName. Close the table by clicking **Close** on the right side of the Sales Reps window.

e. Double-click the **Customers table** to open it in Datasheet view. Click **New** in the Records group. Add a new record by typing the following information; press **Tab** after each field:

Customer Name:	**Bavaro Driving School**
Contact:	**Ricky Watters**
Address1:	**1 Clausen Way**
Address2:	**Floor 2**
City:	**South Bend**

State:	IN
Zip Code:	46614
Phone:	(857) 519-6661
Credit Rating:	A
Sales Rep ID:	2

Notice the pencil symbol in the record selector for the new row. This symbol indicates the new record has not been saved. Press **Tab**. The pencil symbol disappears, and the new customer is automatically saved to the table.

f. Click the **City field** for the second record (South Bend). Click **Selection** in the Sort & Filter group, and select **Equals "South Bend"** to display the four customers located in the town of South Bend.

g. Save and close the table by clicking **Close** on the right side of the Customers window, and clicking **Yes** when asked if you want to save the changes.

h. Double-click the **Products** table to open it in Datasheet view. Click **New** in the Records group. Add a new record by typing the following information:

Product ID:	26
ProductName:	**Robusto Dark Roast K-Cups**
Description:	**40/Box**
Cost:	26
MarkupPercent:	.75
RefrigerationNeeded	**No**
Brand	**Premium**

i. Add a second product using the following information:

Product ID:	27
ProductName:	**Robusto French Roast K-Cups**
Description:	**40/Box**
Cost:	26
MarkupPercent:	.75
RefrigerationNeeded	**No**
Brand	**Premium**

j. Click **Advanced** in the Sort & Filter group and select **Filter By Form**. Type **>=20** in the Cost field and click **Toggle Filter** in the Sort & Filter group.

All products costing $20 or more (there will be 8) display. See Figure 1.57.

k. Save and close the table by clicking **Close** on the right side of the Products window, and clicking Yes when asked if you want to save the changes.

l. Click the **File tab**, click **Save As**, and then double-click **Back Up Database**. Accept the default backup file name and click **Save**.

m. Click **Application Parts** in the Templates group of the Create tab. Select **Issues**. Click **Next** to accept the default relationship. Select **CustomerName** as the Field from 'Customers', select **Sort Ascending** from Sort this field, and then type **Customer** as the name for the lookup column. Click Create.

n. Double-click the **Issues table** to open it in Datasheet view.

o. Select **Advantage Sales** for the Customer and type **Customer reports hazelnut coffee delivered instead of decaf.** in the Summary field. Leave all other fields as the default values.

p. Close the database and exit Access. Based on your instructor's directions, submit the following:

a01p2Coffee_LastFirst

a01p2Coffee_LastFirst_*CurrentDate*

3 Healthy Living

You and two friends from your gym have decided to use Access to help you reach your weight goals. You decide to use the Access Nutrition template to help you get organized. Refer to Figure 1.58 as you complete this exercise.

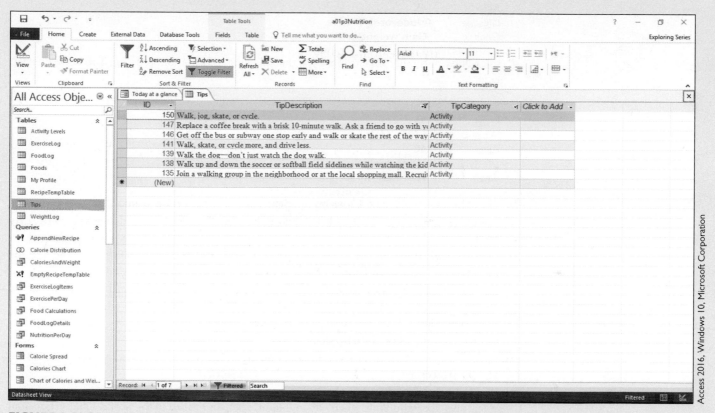

FIGURE 1.58 Filtered Tips Table

a. Open Access and click the **Nutrition tracking** template in Backstage view.

b. Type **a01p3Nutrition_LastFirst** in the File name box. Click **Browse**. Navigate to the location where you are saving your files in the File New Database dialog box, click **OK** to close the dialog box, and then click **Create** to create the new database.

c. Click **Enable Content** on the message bar. Double-click the **My Profile** table in the Navigation Pane to open it in Datasheet view.

d. Delete the existing record.

e. Type the following information in as a new record, pressing **Tab** between each field:

Sex:	**Male**
Height:	**64**
Weight:	**190**
Age:	**48**
Lifestyle:	**Lightly Active**
Goal:	**Lose weight**

f. Click **New** in the Records group. Type the following information, pressing **Tab** between each field:

Sex:	**Male**
Height:	**69**
Weight:	**140**
Age:	**45**
Lifestyle:	**Moderately Active**
Goal:	**Gain weight**

g. Click **New** in the Records group. Type the following information, pressing **Tab** between each field:

Sex:	**Female**
Height:	**66**
Weight:	**140**
Age:	**40**
Lifestyle:	**Moderately Active**
Goal:	**Maintain my weight**

h. Close the table by clicking **Close** on the right side of the My Profile window.

i. Double-click the **Foods table**. Click **Advanced** in the Records group and then select **Filter By Form**.

j. Click the **Calories field** for the first record. Type **<200** in the Calories field and **>=15** in the Fiber [grams] field. Click **Toggle Filter** in the Sort & Filter group.

You will have a list of all high = fiber, low = calorie foods in the database (there are three).

k. Save and close the table by clicking **Close** on the right side of the Foods window, and clicking **Yes** when asked if you want to save the changes.

l. Double-click the **Tips table** to open it in Datasheet view.

m. Click in the first **TipCategory**. Click **Ascending** in the Sort & Filter group to sort the tips in alphabetical order.

n. Highlight the word **Walk** in the fifth record (ID #138). Make sure you do not highlight the space after the word Walk when you highlight. Click **Selection** in the Sort & Filter group, and select **Contains "Walk"**.

Seven tips appear that contain the word walk. See Figure 1.58.

o. Save and close the table by clicking **Close** on the right side of the Tips window, and clicking **Yes** when asked if you want to save the changes.

p. Click the **File tab**, click **Save As**, and then double-click **Back Up Database**. Use the default backup file name.

q. Close the database and exit Access. Based on your instructor's directions, submit the following:

a01p3Nutrition_LastFirst

a01p3Nutrition _LastFirst_*CurrentDate*

Mid-Level Exercises

1 Sunshine Mental Health Services

Sunshine Mental Health Services provides counseling and medication services. They have recently expanded their database to include patients in addition to the staff. You were hired to replace their former Information Technology support staff member. You will work to update the data in the database, familiarize yourself with the table relationships, filter and sort a table, and add a table to keep track of user accounts.

a. Open the *a01m1Sunshine* file and save the database as **a01m1Sunshine_LastFirst**. Click **Enable Content** on the Security Warning message bar.

b. Open the **Staff table** in Datasheet view.

c. Locate the record for Kovit Ang (StaffID 80073). Replace his Address with **11 Market Street**, replace his City with **Harrison**, and his ZIPCode with **04040**. Leave all other fields with their current values.

d. Add yourself as a new staff member. Type a StaffID of **99999** and type your name in the FullName field. Type **1 Clinton Terrace** for your Address, **Harrison** as your City, **ME** as your State, and **04040** as your ZIP. Type a JobCode of **300**, a Salary of **48500**, and a 401k contribution of **0.02**. Click the box in the Active field so a check box appears in the box.

e. Delete record **80399** (Stan Marsh).

f. Sort the table by Salary in descending order. Save and close the table.

g. Click **Relationships** in the Relationships group on the Database Tools tab and notice the relationship between the Position table and the Staff table, and the relationship between the Staff table and Patients table. Each position has staff associated with it, and staff members have patients associated with them. Close the Relationships window.

h. Rename the **Pos table** to **Position**. Add a description to the table stating **This table contains a list of all available job titles at the company**. Click **OK**.

i. Open the **Position table** in Datasheet view. Click the **plus sign** next to JobCode 100 (Social Worker). Notice seven social workers are employed by the company. Click the **plus sign** next to JobCode 300 (IT Support). Only your name should appear. Close the table.

j. Open the **Patients table** in Datasheet view. Use a Selection filter to show all patients associated with StaffID **80073**. Save and close the table.

k. Open the **Staff table** in Datasheet view. Use Filter By Form to display all staff members who earn a salary of more than **80000**. Toggle the filter to verify the results. Save and close the table.

l. Back up the database. Accept the default file name.

m. Add a **Users application part** to the database. Change the relationship so there is One 'Staff' to many 'Users' by clicking the arrow next to Patients and selecting **Staff**. Click **Next**. Select the **FullName** field from 'Staff', choose the **Sort Ascending** option, and name the lookup column **User**. Click **Create**.

n. Open the **Users table** in Datasheet view.

o. Select **Adolfo Ortiz** in the User field. Type **aortiz@sunshinementalhealth.org** for Email and **aortiz** for Login. Leave the FullName blank. Close the table.

p. Create a form based on the Patients table using the Form button in the Forms group of the Create tab. Save the form as **Patient Data Entry.**

q. Switch to Form view of the form. Delete the phone number for PatientID **1** (Minoru Kobayashi). Close the form.

r. Close the database and exit Access. Based on your instructor's directions, submit the following:
a01m1Sunshine_LastFirst
a01m1Sunshine_LastFirst_*CurrentDate*

2 National Conference

ANALYSIS CASE

The Association of Higher Education will host its National Conference on your campus next year. To facilitate the conference, the Information Technology department has replaced last year's Excel spreadsheets with an Access database containing information on the rooms, speakers, and sessions. Your assignment is to create a room itinerary that will list all of the sessions, dates, and times for each room. The list will be posted on the door of each room for the duration of the conference.

a. Open the *a01m2NatConf* file and save the database as **a01m2NatConf_LastFirst**. Click **Enable Content** on the Security Warning message bar.

b. Open **Relationships**.

c. Review the objects and relationships in the database. Notice that there is a relationship between Speakers and SessionSpeaker. Close the relationships.

d. Open the **SessionSpeaker table**. Scroll to the first blank record at the bottom of the table and type a new record using SpeakerID **99** and SessionID **09**. (Note: Speaker 99 does not exist.) How does Access respond? Press **Escape** twice to cancel your change.

e. Open the **Speakers table**. Replace *YourFirstName* with your first name and *YourLastName* with your last name. Close the Speakers table.

f. Open the **Sessions table** and use a Selection filter to identify the sessions that take place in room 101.

g. Sort the filtered results in ascending order by the **SessionTitle** field. Save and close the table.

h. Open the **Master List - Sessions and Speakers** report. Right-click the **Master List - Sessions and Speakers** tab and select **Report View**.

DISCOVER

i. Apply a filter that limits the report to sessions in **Room 101** only. The process will be similar to applying a filter to a table.

j. View the report in Print Preview. Close Print Preview and close the report.

k. Back up the database. Use the default backup file name.

★ l. Open the *a01m2Analysis* document in Word and save as **a01m2Analysis_LastFirst**. Use the database objects you created to answer the questions. Save and close the document.

m. Close the database and exit Access. Based on your instructor's directions, submit the following:
a01m2NatConf_LastFirst
a01m2NatConf_LastFirst_*CurrentDate*
a01m2Analysis_LastFirst

3 New Castle County Technical Services

RUNNING CASE

New Castle County Technical Services (NCCTS) provides technical support for a number of companies in the greater New Castle County, Delaware, area. They are working to move their record keeping to an Access database. You will add, update, and delete some records, add filters, and create a backup.

This project is a running case. You will use the same database file across Chapters 1 through 4.

a. Open the database *a01m3NCCTS* and save the database as **a01m3NCCTS_LastFirst**. Click **Enable Content** on the Security Warning message bar.

b. Open the **Call Types table** in Datasheet view. Type the following rates for the HourlyRate field and then close the table:

Description	HourlyRate
Hardware Support	30
Software Support	25
Network Troubleshooting	40
Network Installation	40
Training	50

Description	HourlyRate
Security Camera Maintenance	40
Virus Removal	25
Disaster Recovery	60
VoIP Service	45
Other	35

c. Open the **Reps table** in Datasheet view. Add a new record, filling in the value **8** for the RepID field, your last name as the rep's last name, and your first name as the rep's first name.

d. Sort the Reps table by **LastName** in ascending order. Close the table.

e. Open the **Customers table** in Datasheet view. Locate the record for **Edwin VanCleef** (PC030). Delete the entire record.

f. Click in the **City field** for SVC Pharmacy. Use the Selection filter to only show customers who are located in the city of **Newark**. Save and close the table.

g. Open the **Calls table** in Datasheet view. Use **Filter By Form** to filter the HoursLogged field so only calls with 10 or more hours logged on the call (**>=10**) are displayed. Save and close the table.

h. Back up the database, using the default name.

i. Close the database and exit Access. Based on your instructor's directions, submit the following:
a01m3NCCTS_LastFirst
a01m3NCCTS_LastFirst_*CurrentDate*

Beyond the Classroom

Creating a Student Database

GENERAL CASE

FROM SCRATCH

Create a new blank desktop database, name the file **a01b1Students_LastFirst**, and then save the database in the location where you are saving your files. Create a new table using the Contacts application part. Delete the Company, JobTitle, BusinessPhone, HomePhone, FaxNumber, Country/Region, WebPage, Attachments, ContactName, and FileAs fields from the Company table. Save the table, then switch to Datasheet view. Enter the information about at least five students, fictional or real, including your own information. Enter their major in the Notes field. Sort the table by last name in ascending order. Create a filter to display students with your major. Delete all queries, forms, and reports. Close the database and exit Access. Based on your instructor's directions, submit a01b1Students_LastFirst.

Lugo Web Hosting

DISASTER RECOVERY ✚

Your Access database has become corrupted and you are in the process of restoring it from a backup from two weeks ago. In the last two weeks, there have been only a few changes. All users who previously had a 900 GB quota have had their quotas increased to 1 TB. In addition, all users who were previously on the server named Aerelon have been moved to another server, Caprica. You have determined you can use filters to help fix the data in the Users table. Open the *a01b2Lugo_Backup* file and save the database as **a01b2Lugo_LastFirst**. Apply filters to show users who meet the conditions above and then manually change the data for each user. Sort the table by the server in ascending order. Close the database and exit Access. Based on your instructor's directions, submit a01b2Lugo_LastFirst.

Capstone Exercise

You are employed as a technical supervisor at a chain of bookstores. One of the store managers has expressed confusion about Access. You have offered to train her on the basics of Access. To avoid mistakes in the main database, you will save the file with a new name. You will then train her on the basics of the database system, including making data modifications, sorting and filtering, adding a table using an application part, and creating a backup.

Modify Data in a Table

You will open an original database file and save the database with a new name. You will then demonstrate adding, updating, and deleting information.

a. Open the *a01c1Books* file and save the database as **a01c1Books_LastFirst**.

b. Open the **Publishers table** in Datasheet view. Notice that some of the publisher city and state information is missing. Update the database with the information below and close the table.

PubID	PubName	PubCity	PubState
DC	DC Comics	New York	NY
SM	St. Martin	Boston	MA
TB	Triumph Books	Chicago	IL
TL	Time Life	Pueblo	CO

c. Change the PubCity for Pearson to **Hoboken**.

d. Close the Publishers table.

e. Open the **Author table** in Datasheet view.

f. Navigate to the last record (Author ID of XXXX01) and replace **YourFirstName** with your first name and **YourLastName** with your last name. Close the table.

g. Open the **Author table** again and notice the changes you made have been stored.

h. Click the **plus sign** next to your name. Notice the book Social Media: A Student's View is listed. Close the table again.

i. Open the **Books table** in Datasheet view. Notice the book with ISBN 9780809400775 (American Cooking: The Northwest) has no items in stock. Delete this record.

j. Close the table.

Sort a Table and Apply a Selection Filter

You will sort the publisher's table by name and then apply a filter to display only publishers located in New York.

a. Open the **Publishers table** in Datasheet view. Notice Time Life appears after Triumph Books. This is because the table is sorted by the PubID field.

b. Click in any record in the PubName field and sort the field in ascending order.

c. Apply a Selection filter to display only publishers with a PubCity equal to **New York**.

d. Close the table and save the changes.

Use Filter By Form

You will obtain a list of all books with more than 50 units in stock. This will help the management decide on what books to put on sale. You will use Filter By Form to accomplish this. You will also demonstrate how filters are saved.

a. Open the **Books table** in Datasheet view.

b. Use Filter By Form to display books with more than **50** units in stock. Save and close the table.

c. Open the **Books table** in Datasheet view. Click **Toggle Filter** in the Sort & Filter group to demonstrate that the filter is saved.

Back Up a Database and Add an Application Part

You will demonstrate adding an application part to the manager to show how tables are created. You will first back the database up to reinforce the importance of backing up the data.

a. Create a backup copy of your database, accepting the default file name.

b. Add a Comments application part, selecting the option **One 'Books' to many 'Comments'**. Select the **Title field** for the Field from Books and **Sort Ascending** for Sort this field. Name the lookup column **Book**.

c. Open the **Comments table** in Datasheet view. Add a new comment. Select **Social Media: A Student's View** for the Book. Use the current date and add **A fun and insightful book!** for the Comment field.

d. Close the database and exit Access. Based on your instructor's directions, submit the following:

a01c1Books_LastFirst

a01c1Books_LastFirst_*CurrentDate*

Tables and Queries in Relational Databases

LEARNING OUTCOMES

- You will create and modify tables for data input and organization.
- You will develop queries to extract and present data.

OBJECTIVES & SKILLS: After you read this chapter, you will be able to:

CASE STUDY | Bank Audit

During a year-end review, a bank auditor uncovers mishandled funds at Commonwealth Federal Bank in Wilmington, Delaware. In order to analyze the data in more detail, the auditor asks you to create an Access database so he can review the affected customers, the compromised accounts, and the branches involved.

As you begin, you realize that some of the data are contained in external Excel and Access files that you decide to import directly into the new database. Importing from Excel and Access is fairly common, and will help to avoid errors that are associated with data entry. Once the data have been imported, you will use queries to determine exactly which records are relevant to the investigation.

This chapter introduces the Bank database case study to present the basic principles of table and query design. Once the new database is created and all the data are entered, you will help the auditor answer questions by creating and running queries. The value of that information depends entirely on the quality of the underlying data—the tables.

Designing Databases and Extracting Data

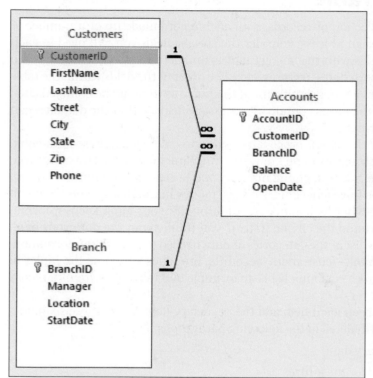

Number of Customer Accounts	
Customer ID ▾	Number of Accounts ▾
30001	5
30002	1
30003	4
30004	4
30005	4
30006	1
30007	2
30009	2
30010	2
30011	3

Access 2016, Windows 10, Microsoft Corporation

FIGURE 2.1 Bank Audit Database

CASE STUDY | Bank Audit

Starting Files	File to be Submitted
Blank desktop database a02h2Accounts a02h2Customers	a02h4Bank_LastFirst

Table Design, Creation, and Modification

Good database design begins with the tables. Tables provide the framework for all of the activities you perform in a database. If the framework is poorly designed, the database will not function as expected. Whether you are experienced in designing tables or are a new database designer, the process should not be done haphazardly. You should follow a systematic approach when creating tables for a database.

In this section, you will learn the essentials of good table design. After developing and analyzing the table design on paper, you will implement that design in Access. While you learned to create tables in the previous chapter, in this chapter you will learn to refine them by changing the properties of various fields.

Designing a Table

Recall that a table is a collection of records, with each record made up of a number of fields. During the table design process, consider the specific fields you will need in each table; list the proposed fields with the correct tables, and determine what type of data each field will store (numbers, dates, pictures, etc.) The order of the fields within the table and the specific field names are not significant at this stage as they can be changed later. What is important is that the tables contain all necessary fields so that the database can produce the required information later.

For example, consider the design process necessary to create a database for a bank. Most likely you have a bank account and know that the bank maintains data about you. Your bank has your name, address, phone number, and Social Security number. It also knows which accounts you have (checking, savings, money market), if you have a credit card with that bank, and what its balance is. Additionally, your bank keeps information about its branches around the city or state. If you think about the data your bank maintains, you can make a list of the categories of data needed to store that information. These categories for the bank—customers, accounts, branches—become the tables in the bank's database. A bank's customer list is an example of a table; it contains a record for each bank customer.

After the tables have been identified, add the necessary fields using these six guidelines, which are discussed in detail in the following paragraphs:

- Include the necessary data.
- Design for now and for the future.
- Store data in their smallest parts.
- Determine primary keys.
- Link tables using common fields.
- Design to accommodate calculations.

Figure 2.2 shows a customer table and two other tables found in a sample Bank database. It also lists fields that would be needed in each table.

Customers Table	Accounts Table	Branch Table
CustomerID	AccountID	BranchID
FirstName	CustomerID	Manager
LastName	BranchID	Location
Street	OpenDate	StartDate
City		
State		
Zip		
Phone		

FIGURE 2.2 Rough Draft of Tables and Fields in a Sample Bank Database

Include Necessary Data

A good way to determine what data are necessary in tables is to consider the output you will need from your database. You will probably need to create professional-looking reports for others, so begin by creating a rough draft of the reports you will need. Then design tables that contain the fields necessary to create those reports. In other words, ask yourself what information will be expected from the database (output) and determine the data required (input) to produce that information. Consider, for example, the tables and fields in Figure 2.2. Is there required information that could not be generated from those tables?

- You will be able to determine how long a customer has banked with the branch because the date he or she opened the account is stored in the Accounts table, which will connect to the Customers and Branch tables.

- You will be able to determine which branch a customer uses because the Accounts table includes both the CustomerID and the BranchID. The Accounts table will eventually connect to both the Customers and Branch tables, making it possible to gather this information.

- You will not be able to generate the monthly bank statement. In order to generate a customer bank statement (showing all deposits and withdrawals for the month), you would need to add an additional table—to track activity for each account.

- You will not be able to email a customer because the Customers table does not contain an email field at this time.

If you discover a missing field, such as the email field, you can add it during the initial design process or later.

Design for Now and for the Future

As the information requirements of an organization evolve over time, the database systems that hold the data must change as well. When designing a database, try to anticipate the future needs of the system and build in the flexibility to satisfy those demands. For example, you may also decide to create additional fields for future use (such as an email or customer photo field). However, additional fields will also require more storage space, which you will need to calculate, especially when working with larger databases. Good database design must balance the data collection needs of the company with the cost associated with collection and storage. Plans must also include the frequency and cost necessary to modify and update the database.

In the Bank database, for example, you would store each customer's name, address, and home phone number. You would also want to store additional phone numbers for many customers—a cell phone number, and perhaps a work number. As a database designer, you will design the tables to accommodate multiple entries for similar data.

Store Data in Their Smallest Parts

The table design in Figure 2.2 divides a customer's name into two fields (FirstName and LastName) to store each value individually. You might think it easier to use a single field consisting of both the first and last name, but that approach is too limiting. Consider a list of customer names stored as a single field:

- Sue Grater
- Rick Grater
- Nancy Gallagher
- Harry Weigner
- Barb Shank
- Pete Shank

The first problem in this approach is the lack of flexibility: You could not easily create a salutation for a letter using the form *Dear Sue* or *Dear Ms. Gallagher* because the first and last names are not accessible individually.

A second difficulty is that the list of customers cannot be easily displayed in alphabetical order by last name because the last name begins in the middle of the field. The most common way to sort names is by the last name, which you can do more efficiently if the last name is stored as a separate field.

Think of how an address might be used. The city, state, and postal code should always be stored as separate fields. You may need to select records from a particular state or postal code, which will be easier if you store the data as separate fields.

Determine Primary Keys

When designing your database tables, it is important to determine the primary key, the field that will uniquely identify each record in a table. For example, in Figure 2.2, the CustomerID field will uniquely identify each customer in the database.

Plan for Common Fields Between Tables

As you create the tables and fields for the database, keep in mind that some tables will be joined in relationships using common fields. Creating relationships will help you to extract data from more than one table when creating queries, forms, and reports. For example, you will be able to determine which customers have which accounts by joining the Customers and Accounts tables. For now, you should name the common fields the same (although that is not a firm requirement in Access). For example, CustomerID in the Customers table will join to the CustomerID field in the Accounts table. Draw a line between common fields to indicate the joins, as shown in Figure 2.3. These join lines will be created in Access when you learn to create table relationships later in the chapter.

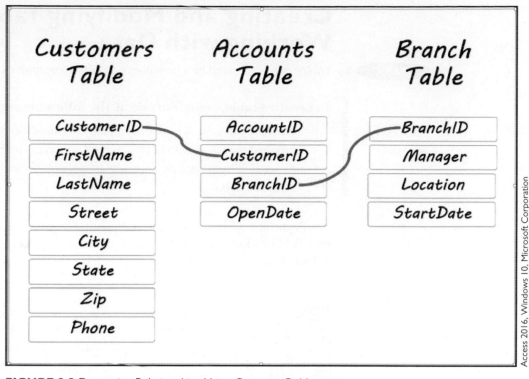

Customers Table — CustomerID, FirstName, LastName, Street, City, State, Zip, Phone

Accounts Table — AccountID, CustomerID, BranchID, OpenDate

Branch Table — BranchID, Manager, Location, StartDate

FIGURE 2.3 Determine Relationships Using Common Fields

Avoid **data redundancy**, which is the unnecessary storing of duplicate data in two or more tables. Having redundant or duplicate data in multiple tables can lead to serious errors. Suppose the customer address data were stored in both the Customers and Accounts tables. If a customer moved to a new address, it is possible that the address would be updated in only one of the two tables. The result would be inconsistent and unreliable information. Depending on which table you would use to check an address, either the new or the old one might be given to someone requesting the information. Storing the address in only one table is more reliable; if it changes, it only needs to be updated one time (in the Customers table) and can be referenced again and again from that table.

TIP: ADD CALCULATED FIELDS TO A TABLE

A calculated field produces a value from an expression or function that references one or more existing fields. Access enables you to store calculated fields in a table using the calculated data type, and to include those fields in queries, forms, and reports. However, many Access users prefer to create calculated fields in their query designs rather than in the tables themselves.

Design to Accommodate Calculations

Calculated fields are frequently created in database objects with numeric data, such as a monthly interest field that multiplies the balance in a customer's account by 1% each month (Balance*.01). You can also create calculated fields using date/time data. For example, if you want to store the length of time a customer has had an account, you can create a calculated field that subtracts the opening date from today's date. The result will be the number of days each customer has been an account holder.

A person's age is another example of a calculated field using date arithmetic—the date of birth is subtracted from today's date and the result is divided by 365 (or 365.25 to account for leap years). It might seem easier to store a person's age as a number rather than the birth date and avoid the calculated field, but that would be a mistake because age changes over time and the field would need to be updated each time it changes. You can use date arithmetic to subtract one date from another to find out the number of days, months, or years that have elapsed between them.

Creating and Modifying Tables and Working with Data

STEP 1 ⟫ Tables can be created in a new blank database or in an existing database.

> **To create a table, complete one of the following steps:**
>
> - Enter field names and table data directly in Datasheet view.
> - Type field names in rows in Design view and then enter the data in Datasheet view.
> - Import data from another database or application, such as Excel.
> - Use a template.

Regardless of how a table is first created, you can always modify it later to include a new field or modify an existing field. Figure 2.4 shows a table created by entering fields in Design view.

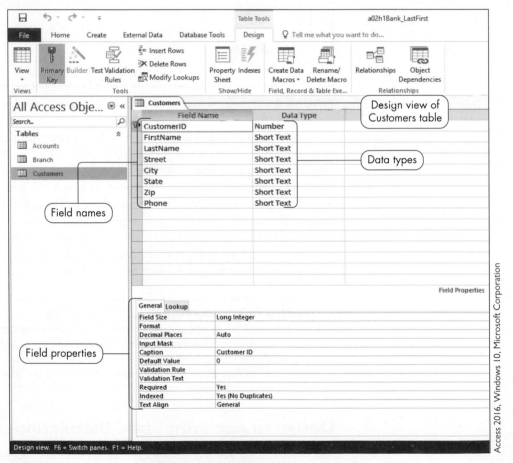

FIGURE 2.4 Customers Table Created in Design View

When you add a new field to a table, the field must be given an appropriate name to identify the data it holds. The field name should be descriptive of the data and can be up to 64 characters in length, including letters, numbers, and spaces. Field names cannot begin with a leading blank space. Database developers sometimes use Pascal Case notation for field names. Instead of spaces in multiword field names, you can use uppercase letters to distinguish the first letter of each new word, for example, ProductCost or LastName (sometimes developers use Camel Case, which is similar to Pascal Case, where the first letter of the first word is lowercase). It is sometimes preferable to avoid spaces in field names, because spaces can cause naming conflicts with other applications that may use these fields, such as Microsoft Visual Basic for Applications.

Fields can be added, deleted, or renamed either in Design view or Datasheet view. To delete a field in Datasheet view, select the field and press Delete. Click Yes in the message box.

To delete a field in Design view, complete the following steps:

1. Click the record selector of the field you want to delete to select it.
2. Click Delete Rows in the Tools group on the Design tab.
3. Click Yes in the message box that displays to confirm that you want to permanently delete the field and the data in it. Click No if you do not want to delete the field.
4. Click Yes in the second message box that displays if the selected field you are deleting is a primary key. Click No if you do not want to delete the primary key.

To rename a field, double-click the field name you want to change, type the new field name, press Enter, and then save the table.

> **TIP: HIDE FIELDS IN AN ACCESS DATASHEET**
> To hide a field in a datasheet, right-click the column selector that displays the field name and from the shortcut menu, select Hide Fields. To make the field visible again, right-click any column selector, select Unhide Fields, and select the appropriate column's check box.

Determine Data Type

Every field has an assigned ***data type*** that determines the type of data that can be entered and the operations that can be performed on that data. Access recognizes 12 data types. Table 2.1 lists these data types, their uses, and examples of each. You can change a data type after you have entered data into your table, but do so with caution. Be aware of messages from Access indicating that you may lose data when you save your changes. In some cases, changing data types is inconsequential; for example, you may want to convert a number to a currency value. This type of change would only affect the formatting displayed with the values, but not the underlying values themselves. In any case, when designing tables, choose the initial data type carefully, and be sure to back up your database before changing data types.

TABLE 2.1	Data Types and Uses	
Data Type	**Description**	**Example**
Short Text	Stores alphanumeric data, such as a customer's name or address. It can contain alphabetic characters, numbers, and/or special characters (e.g., an apostrophe in O'Malley). Social Security numbers, telephone numbers, and postal codes should be designated as text fields because they are not used in calculations and often contain special characters such as hyphens and parentheses. A short text field can hold up to 255 characters.	2184 Walnut Street
Long Text	Lengthy text or combinations of text and numbers, such as several sentences or paragraphs; used to hold descriptive data. Long text controls can display up to 64,000 characters.	A description of product packaging
Number	Contains a value that can be used in a calculation, such as the number of credits a course is worth. The contents are restricted to numbers, a decimal point, and a plus or minus sign.	12
Date/Time	Stores dates or times that can be used in date or time arithmetic.	10/31/2018 1:30:00 AM
Currency	Used for fields that contain monetary values.	$1,200

TABLE 2.1 Continued

Data Type	Description	Example
AutoNumber	A special data type used to assign the next consecutive number each time you add a record. The value of an AutoNumber field is unique for each record in the table.	1, 2, 3
Yes/No	Only one of two values can be stored, such as Yes or No, True or False, or On or Off (also known as a Boolean). For example, is a student on the Dean's list: Yes or No.	Yes
OLE Object	Contains an object created by another application. OLE objects include pictures and sounds.	JPG image
Hyperlink	Stores a Web address (URL) or the path to a folder or file. Hyperlink fields can be clicked to retrieve a webpage or to launch a file stored locally.	http://www.irs.gov
Attachment	Used to store multiple images, spreadsheet files, Word documents, and other types of supported files.	An Excel workbook
Calculated	The results of an expression that references one or more existing fields.	[Price]*.05
Lookup Wizard	Creates a field that enables you to choose a value from another table or from a list of values by using a list box or a combo box.	Accounts table with a CustomerID field that looks up the customer from the records in the Customers table

Pearson Education, Inc.

Set a Table's Primary Key

STEP 2 »» The primary key is the field (or possibly a combination of fields) that uniquely identifies each record in a table. Access does not require that each table have a primary key. However, a good database design usually includes a primary key in each table. You should select unique and infrequently changing data for the primary key. For example, a credit card number may seem to be unique, but would not make a good primary key because it is subject to change when a new card is issued due to fraudulent activity.

You probably would not use a person's name as the primary key, because several people could have the same name. A value like CustomerID, as shown in the Customers table in Figure 2.5, is unique and is a better choice for the primary key. When no field seems to stand out as a primary key naturally, you can create a primary key field with the AutoNumber data type. The **AutoNumber** data type is a number that automatically increments each time a record is added.

Figure 2.6 depicts a Speakers table, where no unique field can be identified from the data itself. In this case, you can identify the SpeakerID field with an AutoNumber data type. Access automatically numbers each speaker record sequentially with a unique ID as each record is added.

Customers

Customer ID	FirstName	LastName	Street	City	State	Zip	Phone	Click to Add
30001	Allison	Millward	2732 Baker Blvd.	Greensboro	NC	27492	(555) 334-5678	
30002	Bernett	Fox	12 Orchestra Terrace	High Point	NC	27494	(555) 358-5554	
30003	Clay	Hayes	P.O. Box 555	Greensboro	NC	27492	(555) 998-4457	
30004	Cordle	Collins	2743 Bering St.	Winston-Salem	NC	27492	(555) 447-2283	
30005	Eaton	Wagner	2743 Bering St.	Greensboro	NC	27492	(555) 988-3346	
30006	Kwasi	Williams	89 Jefferson Way	High Point	NC	27494	(555) 447-5565	
30007	Natasha	Simpson	187 Suffolk Ln.	Greensboro	NC	27493	(555) 775-3389	
30008	Joy	Jones	305 - 14th Ave. S.	Winston-Salem	NC	27493	(555) 258-7655	
30009	John	Nunn	89 Chiaroscuro Rd.	Greensboro	NC	27494	(555) 998-5557	
30010	Laura	Peterson	120 Hanover Sq.	Winston-Salem	NC	27492	(555) 334-6654	
30011	YourName	YourName	800 University Ave.	High Point	NC	27494	(555) 447-1235	
* 0								

Access 2016, Windows 10, Microsoft Corporation

FIGURE 2.5 Customers Table with a Natural Primary Key

FIGURE 2.6 Speakers Table with an AutoNumber Primary Key

Explore a Foreign Key

In order to share data between two tables, the tables must share a common field. The common field will generally be the primary key in one table; the same field in the adjoining table is denoted as the *foreign key*. The CustomerID is the primary key (identified with a primary key icon) in the Customers table and uniquely identifies each customer in the database. It also displays as a foreign key in the related Accounts table. The Accounts table contains the CustomerID field to establish which customer owns the account. A CustomerID can be entered only one time in the Customers table, but it may be entered multiple times in the Accounts table because one customer may own several accounts (checking, savings, credit card, etc.). Therefore, the CustomerID is the primary key in the Customers table and a foreign key in the Accounts table, as shown in Figure 2.7.

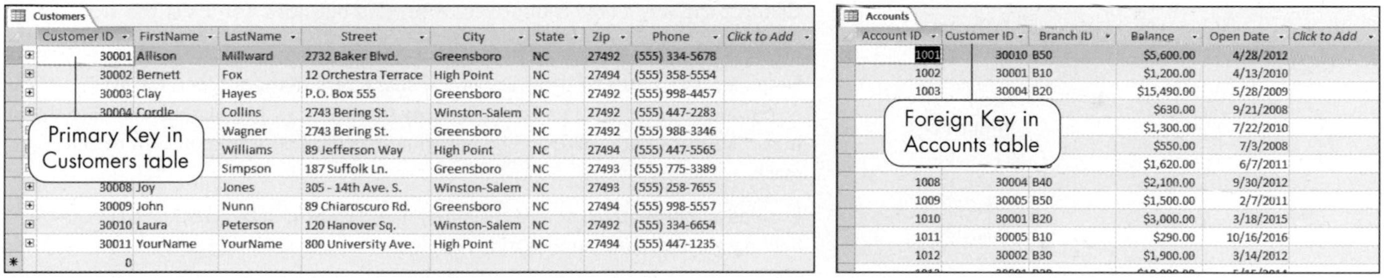

FIGURE 2.7 Two Tables Illustrating Primary and Foreign Keys

> **TIP: BEST FIT COLUMNS**
> If a field name is cut off in Datasheet view, you can adjust the column width by positioning the pointer on the vertical border on the right side of the column. When the pointer displays as a two-headed arrow, double-click the border. You can also click More in the Records group on the Home tab, select Field Width, and then click Best Fit in the Column Width dialog box.

Work with Field Properties

STEP 3 »» While a field's data type determines the type of data that can be entered and the operations that can be performed on that data, its *field properties* determine how the field looks and behaves. The field properties are set to default values according to the data type, but you can modify them if necessary. Field properties are commonly set in Design view, as shown in Figure 2.4; however, certain properties can be set in Datasheet view, on the Table Tools Fields tab. Common property types are defined in Table 2.2.

Field Size is a commonly changed field property. The field size determines the amount of space a field uses in the database. A field with a Short Text data type can store up to 255 characters; however, you can limit the characters by reducing the field size property. For example, you might limit the State field to only two characters because all state abbreviations are two letters. When setting field sizes, you may want to anticipate any future requirements of the database that might necessitate larger values to be stored.

You can set the **Caption property** to create a label that is more understandable than a field name. While Pascal Case is often preferred for field names, adding a space between words is often more readable. When a caption is set, it displays at the top of a table or query column in Datasheet view (instead of the field name), and when the field is used in a report or form. For example, a field named CustomerID could have the caption *Customer Number*.

Set the Validation Rule property to restrict data entry in a field to ensure that correct data are entered. The validation rule checks the data entered when the user exits the field. If the data entered violate the validation rule, an error message displays and prevents the invalid data from being entered into the field. For example, if you have set a rule on a date field that the date entered must be on or after today, and a date in the past is entered in the field, an error message will display. You can customize the error message (validation text) when you set the validation rule.

The Input Mask property simplifies data entry by providing literal characters that are typed for every entry, such as hyphens in a Social Security number (- -), or dashes in a phone number. Input masks ensure that data in fields such as these are consistently entered and formatted.

TABLE 2.2 Common Access Table Property Types and Descriptions

Property Type	Description
Field Size	Determines the maximum number of characters of a text field or the format of a number field.
Format	Changes the way a field is displayed or printed but does not affect the stored value.
Input Mask	Simplifies data entry by providing literal characters that are typed for every entry, such as hyphens in a Social Security number (- -) or slashes in a date. It also imposes data validation by ensuring that data entered conform to the mask.
Caption	Enables an alternate (or more readable) name to be displayed other than the field name; alternate name displays in datasheets, forms, and reports.
Default Value	Enters automatically a predetermined value for a field each time a new record is added to the table. For example, if most customers live in Los Angeles, the default value for the City field could be set to Los Angeles to save data entry time and promote accurate data entry.
Validation Rule	Requires data entered to conform to a specified rule.
Validation Text	Specifies the error message that is displayed when the validation rule is violated.
Required	Indicates that a value for this field must be entered. Primary key fields always require data entry.
Allow Zero Length	Allows entry of zero length text strings ("") in a Hyperlink, or Short or Long Text fields.
Indexed	Increases the efficiency of a search on the designated field.
Expression	Used for calculated fields only. Specifies the expression you want Access to evaluate and store.
Result Type	Used for calculated fields only. Specifies the format for the calculated field results.

Pearson Education, Inc.

Create a New Field in Design View

STEP 4 ❯❯ At times, it may be necessary to add table fields that were not included in the original design process. While it is possible to add fields in Datasheet view (using the Click to Add arrow at the top of an empty column), Design view, as shown in Figure 2.4, offers more flexibility in setting field properties.

To add a new field in Design view, complete the following steps:

1. Click in the first empty field row in the top pane of the table's Design view.
2. Enter the Field Name, Data Type, and Description (optional), and then set the Field Properties.
3. Click the row selector, and then click and drag the new field to place it in a different position in the table.
4. Click Save on the Quick Access Toolbar, and then switch to Datasheet view to enter or modify data.

Modify the Table in Datasheet View

STEP 5 ❯❯ Whereas Design view is commonly used to create and modify the table structure by enabling you to add and edit fields and set field properties, Datasheet view is used to add, edit, and delete records. Datasheet view of an Access table displays data in a grid format—rows represent records and columns represent fields. You can select a record by clicking the record selector on the left side of each record. Use the new blank record (marked with an asterisk) at the end of the table to add a new record, or click the New (blank) record button on the navigation bar at the bottom of the table.

Quick Concepts

1. What is meant by "Store data in its smallest parts" when designing database tables? **p. 142**
2. What is the difference between a primary key and a foreign key? **p. 147**
3. Which field property creates a more readable label that displays in the top row in Datasheet view and in forms and reports? **p. 148**

Hands-On Exercises

Watch the Video
for this Hands-On
Exercise!

MyITLab®
HOE1 Training

1 Table Design, Creation, and Modification

Creating a database for the bank auditor at Commonwealth Federal Bank as he investigates the mishandled funds will be a great opportunity for you to showcase your database design and Access skills.

STEP 1 ›› CREATE A TABLE IN DATASHEET VIEW

You create a new desktop database to store information about the mishandled funds. You enter the data for the first record (BranchID, Manager, and Location). Refer to Figure 2.8 as you complete Step 1.

ID	BranchID	Manager	Location	Click to Add
1	B10	Krebs	Uptown	
2	B20	Esposito	Eastern	
3	B30	Amoako	Western	
4	B40	Singh	Southern	
5	B50	YourLastName	Campus	
*	(New)			

Step i: Save the table as Branch

Step h: Type the data directly into the datasheet

Access 2016, Windows 10, Microsoft Corporation

FIGURE 2.8 Create the Branch Table in Datasheet View

a. Start Microsoft Office Access 2016 and click **Blank desktop database**.

b. Type **a02h1Bank_LastFirst** into the File Name box.

c. Click **Browse** to find the folder location where you will store the database and click **OK**. Click **Create** to create the new database.

Access will create the new database named a02h1Bank_LastFirst and a new table will automatically open in Datasheet view. There is already an ID field in the table by default.

d. Click **Click to Add** and select **Short Text** as the Data type.

Click to Add changes to Field1. Field1 is selected to make it easier to change the field name.

e. Type **BranchID** and press **Tab**.

A list of data types for the third column opens so that you can select the data type for the third column.

f. Select Short Text in the Click to Add window, type **Manager**, and then press **Tab**.

g. Select Short Text in the Click to Add window, and then type **Location**.

h. Click in the first column (the ID field) next to the New Record asterisk, press **Tab**, and then type the data for the new table as shown in Figure 2.8, letting Access assign the ID field for each new record (using the AutoNumber data type). Replace *YourLastName* with your own last name.

i. Click **Save** on the Quick Access Toolbar. Type **Branch** in the Save As dialog box and click **OK**.

Entering field names, data types, and data directly in Datasheet view provides a simplified way to create the table initially.

It is possible to modify tables even after data have been entered; however, be alert to potential messages from Access after you make design changes that may affect your data. In this step, you will modify the Branch table. You examine the design of the table and realize that the BranchID field is a unique identifier, making the ID field redundant. You delete the ID field and make the BranchID field the primary key field. Refer to Figure 2.9 as you complete Step 2.

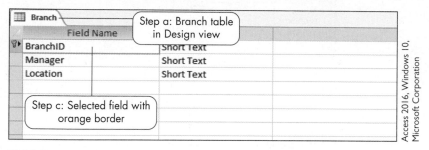

FIGURE 2.9 Branch Table in Design View

a. Click **View** in the Views group on the Home tab to switch to Design view of the Branch table.

The field name for each of the four fields displays along with the data type.

b. Ensure that the ID field selected, click **Delete Rows** in the Tools group on the Design tab. Click **Yes** to both warning messages.

Access responds with a warning that you are about to permanently delete a field and a second warning that the field is the primary key. You delete the field because you will set the BranchID field as the primary key.

c. Ensure that the BranchID field is selected, as shown in Figure 2.9.

d. Click **Primary Key** in the Tools group on the Design tab.

You set BranchID as the primary key. The Indexed property in the Field Properties section at the bottom of the design window displays Yes (No Duplicates).

e. Click **Save** on the Quick Access Toolbar to save the table.

TIP: SHORTCUT MENU

You can right-click a row selector to display a shortcut menu to copy a field, set the primary key, insert or delete rows, or access table properties. Use the shortcut menu to make these specific changes to the design of a table.

You will modify the table design further to comply with the bank auditor's specifications. Refer to Figure 2.10 as you complete Step 3.

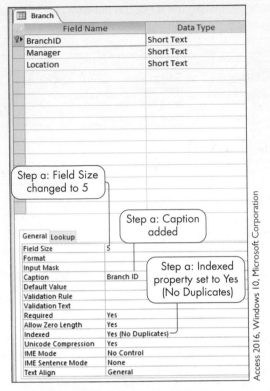

FIGURE 2.10 Changes to the Field Properties of the Branch Table in Design View

a. Click in the **BranchID field name**; modify the BranchID field properties by completing the following steps:

- Click in the **Field Size box** and change 255 to **5**.
- Click in the **Caption box** and type **Branch ID**. Make sure Branch and ID have a space between them.
  A caption provides a more descriptive field name. It will display as the column heading in Datasheet view.
- Check the Indexed property; confirm it is Yes (No Duplicates).

b. Click the **Manager field name**; modify the Manager field properties by completing the following steps:

- Click in the **Field Size box** in the Field Properties pane, and change 255 to **30**.
- Click in the **Caption box** in the Field Properties pane, and type **Manager's Name**.

c. Click the **Location field name** and modify the following Location field properties by completing the following steps:

- Click in the **Field Size box** and change 255 to **30**.
- Click in the **Caption box** and type **Branch Location**.

TIP: F6 FUNCTION KEY TO SWITCH TO FIELD PROPERTIES

With a field name selected in the top pane of the Design window, you can press the F6 function key to toggle to the field properties for the selected field. Continue to press F6 to cycle through the additional elements of the Access screen.

You notify the auditor that a date field is missing in your new table. Modify the table to add the new field. Refer to Figure 2.11 as you complete Step 4.

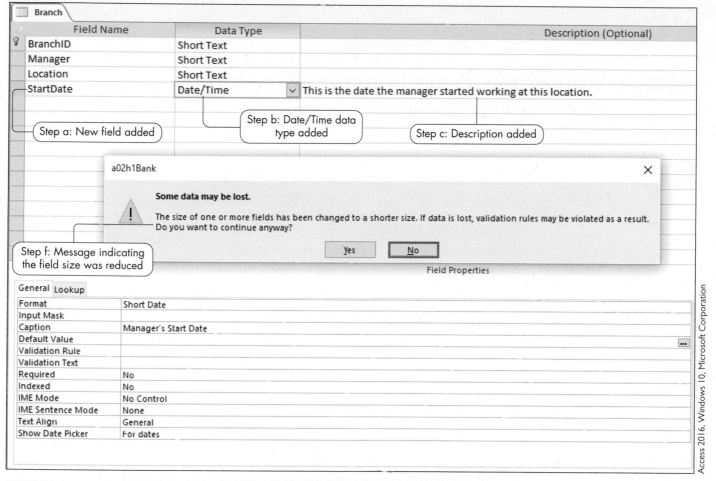

FIGURE 2.11 Adding a New Field to the Branch Table in Design View

a. Click in the first blank field row below the Location field name and type **StartDate**.

You added a new field to the table.

b. Press **Tab** to move to the Data Type column. Click the **Data Type arrow** and select **Date/Time**.

> **TIP: KEYBOARD SHORTCUT FOR DATA TYPES**
> You also can type the first letter of the data type, such as d for Date/Time, s for Short Text, or n for Number. To use the keyboard shortcut, click in the field name and press Tab to advance to the Data Type column. Next, type the first letter of the data type.

c. Press **Tab** to move to the Description column and type **This is the date the manager started working at this location.**

d. Click in the **Format box** in the Field properties pane, click the **arrow**, and then select **Short Date** from the list of date formats.

e. Click in the **Caption box** and type **Manager's Start Date.**

f. Click **Save** on the Quick Access Toolbar.

A warning dialog box opens to indicate that "Some data may be lost" because the size of the BranchID, Manager, and Location field properties were shortened (in the previous step). It asks if you want to continue anyway. Always read the Access warning! In this case, you can click Yes to continue because you know that the existing and anticipated data are no longer than the new field sizes.

g. Click **Yes** in the warning box.

STEP 5 ⟩⟩ MODIFY THE TABLE IN DATASHEET VIEW

As you work with the auditor, you will modify tables in the Bank database from time to time and add and modify records. Refer to Figure 2.12 as you complete Step 5.

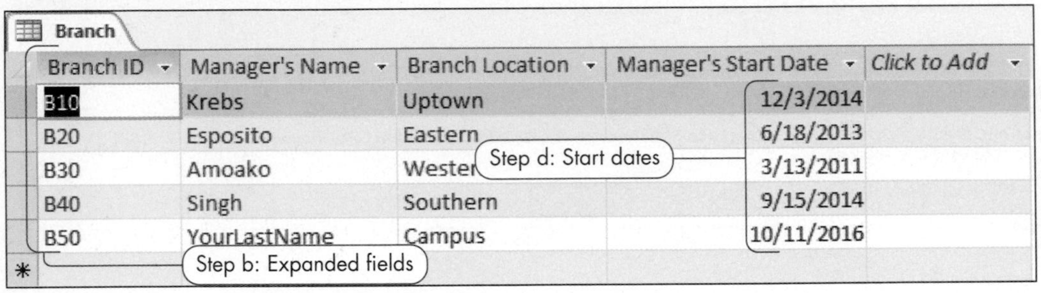

FIGURE 2.12 Start Dates Added to the Branch Table

a. Right-click the **Branch tab** and click **Datasheet View** from the shortcut menu.

The table displays in Datasheet view. The field captions display at the top of the columns, but they are cut off.

b. Position the pointer over the border between Branch ID and Manager's Name so that it becomes a double-headed arrow, and double-click the border. Repeat the process for the border between Manager's Name and Branch Location, the border between Branch Location and Manager's Start Date, and the border after Manager's Start Date.

The columns contract or expand to display the best fit for each field name.

c. Click inside the **Manager's Start Date** in the first record and click the **Date Picker** next to the date field. Use the navigation arrows to find and select **December 3, 2014** from the calendar.

You can also enter the dates by typing them directly into the StartDate field.

d. Type the start date directly in each field for the rest of the managers, as shown in Figure 2.12.

e. Click the **Close** ☒ at the top-right corner of the datasheet, below the Ribbon. Click **Yes** to save the changes.

> **TROUBLESHOOTING:** If you accidentally click Close on top of the Ribbon, you will exit Access completely. To start again, launch Access and click the first file in the Recent list.

f. Double-click the **Branch table** in the Navigation Pane to open the table. Check the start dates.

g. Click the **File tab**, click **Print**, and then click **Print Preview**.

Occasionally, users will print an Access table. However, database developers usually create reports to print table data.

h. Click **Close Print Preview** and close the Branch table.

i. Keep the database open if you plan to continue with the Hands-On Exercise. If not, close the database and exit Access.

Multiple-Table Databases

In Figure 2.2, the sample Bank database contains three tables—Customers, Accounts, and Branch. You created one table, the Branch table, in the previous section using Datasheet view and modified the table fields in Design view. You will create the two remaining tables using different methods—by importing data from external sources.

In this section, you will learn how to import data from Excel and Access, modify tables, create indexes, create relationships between tables, and enforce referential integrity.

Sharing Data

Most companies and organizations store some type of data in Excel spreadsheets. Often, the data stored in those spreadsheets can be more efficiently managed in an Access database. At other times, importing data from Excel and other applications can reduce the data entry effort for your database.

Import Excel Data

STEP 1 ❭❭ Access provides you with a wizard that guides you through the process of importing data from Excel.

> **To import an Excel spreadsheet to Access, complete the following steps:**
>
> 1. Click the External Data tab.
> 2. Click Excel in the Import & Link group. The Get External Data – Excel Spreadsheet dialog box opens, as shown in Figure 2.13.

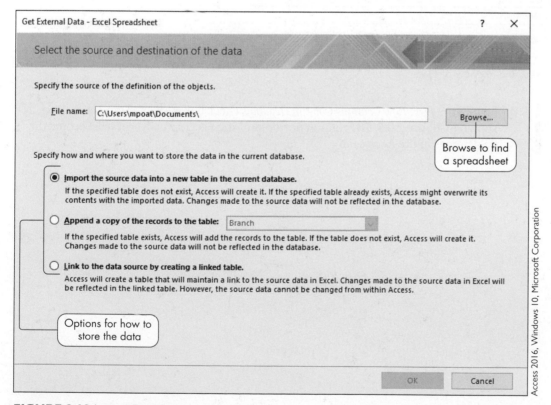

FIGURE 2.13 Import Excel Data

3. Click Browse to locate the Excel file you want to import, click the file to select it, and then click Open to specify this file as the source of the data.

4. Ensure the *Import the source data* option is selected, and click OK. The Import Spreadsheet Wizard launches.

5. Select the worksheet from the list of worksheets shown at the top of the dialog box, as shown in Figure 2.14 and then click Next.

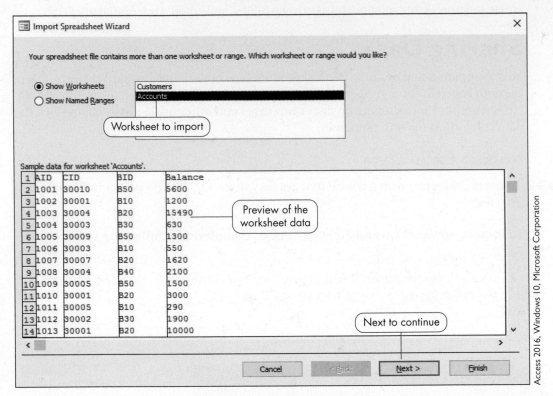

FIGURE 2.14 Available Worksheets and Preview of Data

6. Ensure the *First Row Contains Column Headings* check box is selected, and click Next, as shown in Figure 2.15. The column headings of the Excel spreadsheet will become the field names in the Access table.

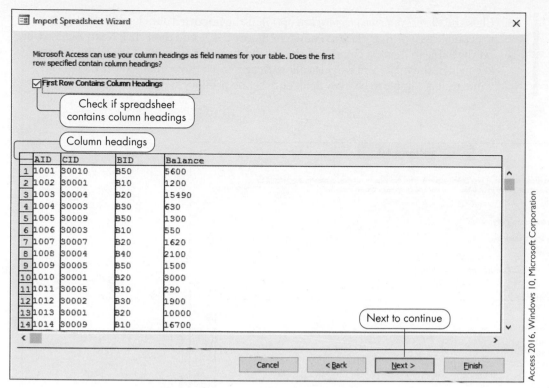

FIGURE 2.15 Excel Column Headings Become Access Field Names

> **7.** Change the field options for the imported data, as shown in Figure 2.16, and then click Next.

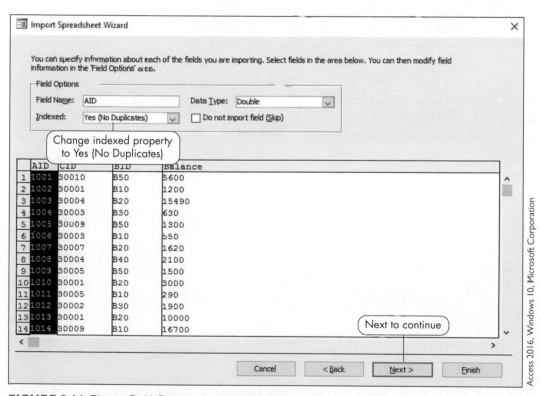

FIGURE 2.16 Change Field Options for Imported Data

8. Click the *Choose my own primary key* option if the imported data has a field that is acceptable as a primary key, as shown in Figure 2.17, and then click Next. Access will set the value in the first column of the spreadsheet (for example, AID) as the primary key field of the table. You can also allow Access to set the primary key if there is no value that is eligible to be a key field, or to set no primary key at all.

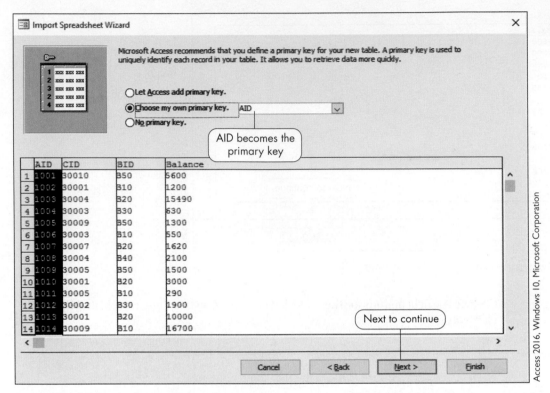

FIGURE 2.17 Set the Primary Key

9. Type the new table name in the Import to Table box, as shown in Figure 2.18, and then click Finish.
10. Click Close when prompted to Save Import Steps.

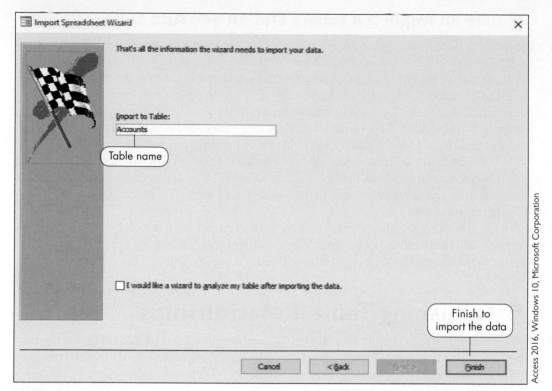

FIGURE 2.18 Enter a Table Name

> **TIP: LINKING TO EXTERNAL DATA**
> At times you might need to include a table in your database that already exists in another database. Instead of importing the data from this external source, you can create a link to it from within your database, and the table remains in the original database. You will be able to use the linked data as usual, without being able to modify the original table's design. You can also link to existing spreadsheets from your database without having to copy a large amount of data into your file.

Import Access Data

STEP 2 ▶▶ A wizard can also guide you as you import data from Access databases. You can import tables, queries, forms, reports, pages, macros, and modules from other databases. You can also modify the design of objects that are imported into your database.

> **To import an Access table into an existing database, complete the following steps:**
>
> 1. Click the External Data tab.
> 2. Click Access in the Import & Link group. The Get External Data – Access Database dialog box opens.
> 3. Ensure that the *Import tables, queries, forms, reports, macros, and modules into the current database* option is selected.
> 4. Click Browse to locate the Access database you want to import.
> 5. Click the file to select it, and then click Open to specify this file as the source of the data.
> 6. Select the table you want to import, and then click OK. (Click Select All if the database contains multiple tables and you want to import all of them, and then click OK.)

Modify an Imported Table's Design and Add Data

STEP 3 ⟩⟩ Importing data from other applications saves typing and prevents errors that may occur while entering data, but modifications to the imported tables will often be required. After you have imported a table, open the table and examine the design to see if changes need to be made. You may want to modify the table by renaming fields so that they are more meaningful. In the Bank database, for example, you could change the name of the imported AID field to AccountID to make it more readable and meaningful. Switch to Design view to modify the data types, field sizes, and other properties.

You may want to fit new fields into the imported tables or delete unnecessary fields from them. To create a new field between existing fields in Design view, click in the row below where you want the new field to be added, and then click Insert Rows in the Tools group on the Design tab.

STEP 4 ⟩⟩ After making the modifications, save your changes and switch back to Datasheet view to add or modify records. Any design changes you made such as to field sizes, captions, input masks, or other properties will now be implemented in the datasheet.

Establishing Table Relationships

STEP 5 ⟩⟩ The benefit of a relationship is to efficiently combine data from related tables for the purpose of creating queries, forms, and reports. In the example we are using, the customer data are stored in the Customers table. The Branch table stores data about the bank's branches, management, and locations. The Accounts table stores data about account ownership and balances.

The common fields that were determined in the design phase of the tables can now be used to establish relationships between them.

> **To create the relationship between the common fields of two tables, complete the following steps:**
>
> 1. Click the Database Tools tab.
> 2. Click Relationships in the Relationships group.
> 3. Drag the primary key field name from one table to the foreign key field name of the related table (for example, CustomerID in the Customers table to CustomerID in the Accounts table).
> 4. Set the desired options in the Edit Relationships dialog box, and click OK. Figure 2.19 shows the Bank database with relationships created by joining common fields.

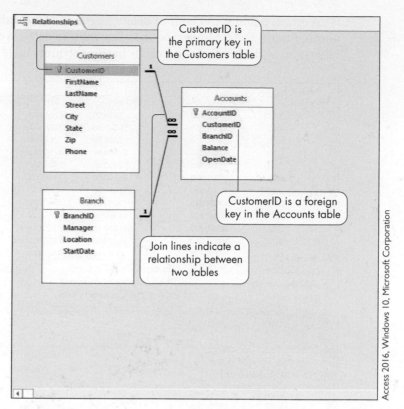

FIGURE 2.19 Relationships in the Bank Database

Access 2016, Windows 10, Microsoft Corporation

TIP: RETRIEVE DATA QUICKLY WITH INDEXING

When you set the primary key in Access, the Indexed property is automatically set to Yes (No Duplicates). The indexed property setting enables quick sorting in primary key order and quick retrieval based on the primary key. For non-primary key fields, it may be beneficial to set the Indexed property to Yes (Duplicates OK). Again, Access uses indexing to sort and retrieve data quickly based on the indexed field.

The primary key of a table plays a significant role when setting relationships. You cannot join two tables unless a primary key has been set in the primary table, which is one side of the relationship's join line. The other side of the relationship join line is most often the foreign key of the related table. A foreign key is a field in one table that is also the primary key and common field of another table. In the Bank database, CustomerID has been set as the primary key in the Customers table and also exists in the Accounts table. Therefore, a relationship can be set between the Customers table and the Accounts table, where CustomerID is the foreign key. Similarly, the Branch table can be joined to the Accounts table because BranchID has been set as the primary key in the Branch table, and BranchID is the foreign key in the Accounts table.

Enforce Referential Integrity

STEP 6 ▸▸ When you begin to create a relationship in Access, the Edit Relationships dialog box displays. The first check box, Enforce Referential Integrity, should be checked in most cases. **Referential integrity** enforces rules in a database that are used to preserve relationships between tables when records are changed.

When referential integrity is enforced, you cannot enter a foreign key value in a related table unless the primary key value exists in the primary table. In the case of the Bank database, the customer information is first entered into the Customers table before a customer's account information (which also includes CustomerID) can be entered into the Accounts table. If you attempt to enter an account prior to entering the customer information, an error will display, as shown in Figure 2.20. When referential integrity is enforced, usually you cannot delete a record in one table if it has related records in another table. For example, you may not want to delete a customer from the Customers table if he or she has active accounts in the Accounts table.

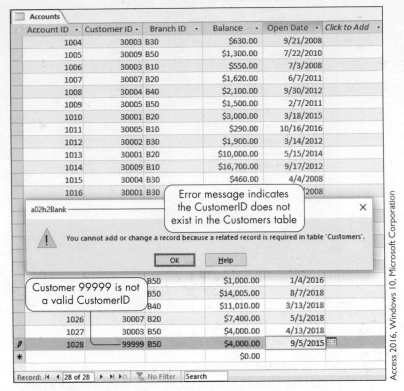

FIGURE 2.20 Error Message for Referential Integrity Violation

Set Cascade Options

When you create a relationship in Access and click the Enforce Referential Integrity check box, Access presents two additional options: Cascade Update Related Fields and Cascade Delete Related Records (see Figure 2.21). Check the ***Cascade Update Related Fields*** option so that when the primary key value is modified in a primary table, Access will automatically update all foreign key values in a related table. If a CustomerID is updated for some reason, all of the matching CustomerID values in the Accounts table will update automatically.

Check the ***Cascade Delete Related Records*** option so that when a record containing a primary key value is deleted in a primary table, Access will automatically delete all records in related tables that match the primary key. If one branch of a bank closes and its record is deleted from the Branch table, any account that is associated with this branch would then be deleted. Access will give a warning first to enable you to avoid the action of deleting records inadvertently.

Setting the Cascade Update and Cascade Delete options really depends on the business rules of an organization, and they should be set with caution. For example, if a branch of a bank closes, do you really want the accounts at that branch to be deleted? Another option might be to assign them to a different branch of the bank.

Establish a One-to-Many Relationship

Figure 2.21 also shows that the relationship that will be created will be a one-to-many relationship. Access provides three different relationships for joining tables: one-to-one, one-to-many, and many-to-many. The most common type by far is the one-to-many relationship. A ***one-to-many relationship*** is established when the primary key value in the primary table can match many of the foreign key values in the related table.

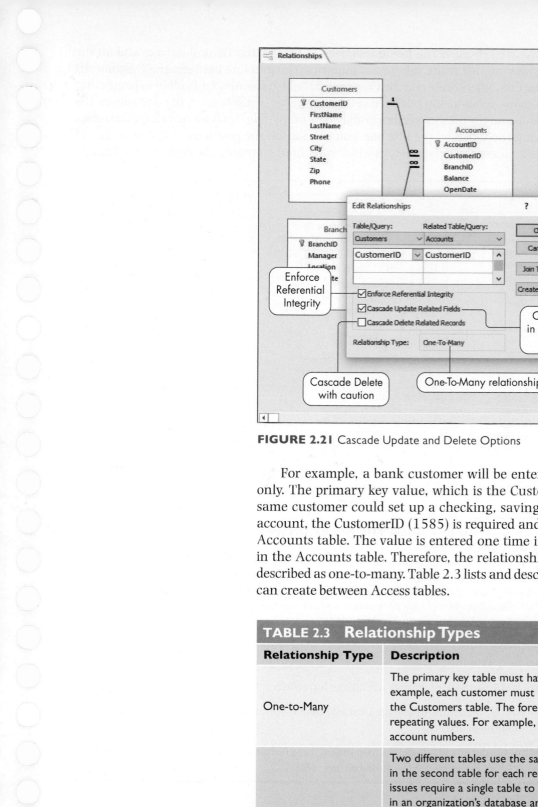

FIGURE 2.21 Cascade Update and Delete Options

For example, a bank customer will be entered into the Customers table one time only. The primary key value, which is the CustomerID number, might be 1585. That same customer could set up a checking, savings, and credit card account. With each account, the CustomerID (1585) is required and therefore will occur three times in the Accounts table. The value is entered one time in the Customers table and three times in the Accounts table. Therefore, the relationship between Customers and Accounts is described as one-to-many. Table 2.3 lists and describes all three types of relationships you can create between Access tables.

TABLE 2.3	Relationship Types
Relationship Type	**Description**
One-to-Many	The primary key table must have only one occurrence of each value. For example, each customer must have a unique identification number in the Customers table. The foreign key field in the related table may have repeating values. For example, one customer may have many different account numbers.
One-to-One	Two different tables use the same primary key. Exactly one record exists in the second table for each record in the first table. Sometimes security issues require a single table to be split into two related tables. For example, in an organization's database anyone in the company might be able to access the Employee table and find the employee's office number, department assignment, or telephone extension. However, only a few people need to have access to the employee's network login password, salary, Social Security number, performance review, or marital status, which would be stored in a second table. Tables containing this information would use the same unique identifier to identify each employee.
Many-to-Many	This is an artificially constructed relationship allowing many matching records in each direction between tables. It requires construction of a third table called a junction table. For example, a database might have a table for employees and one for projects. Several employees might be assigned to one project, but one employee might also be assigned to many different projects.

Figure 2.22 displays the Relationships window for the Bank database and all the relationships created using referential integrity. The join line between the CustomerID field in the Customers table and the CustomerID field in the Accounts table indicates that a one-to-many relationship has been set. The number 1 displays on the one side of the relationship and the infinity symbol displays the many side. You can rearrange the tables by dragging the tables by the title bar. You can switch the positions of the Branch and Accounts tables in the Relationships window without changing the relationship itself.

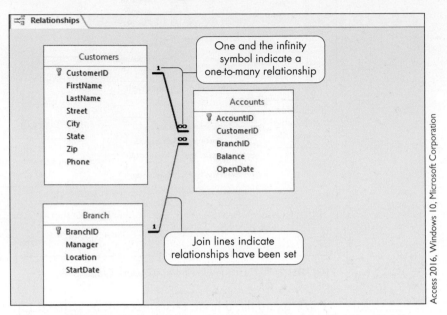

FIGURE 2.22 Relationships Window Displaying One-to-Many Relationships

---

TIP: NAVIGATING BETWEEN THE RELATIONSHIPS WINDOW AND A TABLE'S DESIGN

When you right-click a table's title bar in the Relationships window, the shortcut menu offers you the option to open the table in Design view. This is a convenient feature because if you want to link one table to another table, the joined fields must have the same data type. This shortcut enables you to check the fields and revise them if a table contains a field with the wrong data type.

Quick Concepts

4. Describe a scenario that may require you to import Excel data into Access. **p. 155**

5. What is the purpose of setting a relationship between two tables? **p. 160**

6. Why would you decide to use the Cascade Delete option (or not) when setting a relationship? **p. 162**

7. Specify two database tables that you might design that would contain a one-to-many relationship. Describe the relationship. **pp. 162–163**

Hands-On Exercises

Watch the Video
for this Hands-On
Exercise!

MyITLab®
HOE2 Training

2 Multiple-Table Databases

You created a new Bank database, and a new Branch table. Now you are ready to import additional tables—one from an Excel spreadsheet and one from an Access database. Assume that the data are formatted correctly and are structured properly so that you can begin the import process.

STEP 1 ›› IMPORT EXCEL DATA

You and the auditor have discovered several of Commonwealth's files that contain customer data. These files need to be analyzed, so you decide to import the data into Access. In this step, you import an Excel spreadsheet into the Bank database. Refer to Figure 2.23 as you complete Step 1.

CID	FirstName	LastName	Street	City	State	Zip	Phone	Click to Add
30001	Allison	Millward	2732 Baker Blvd.	Greensboro	NC	27492	5553345678	
30002	Bernett	Fox	12 Orchestra Terrace	High Point	NC	27494	5553585554	
30003	Clay	Hayes	P.O. Box 555	Greensboro	NC	27492	5559984457	
30004	Cordle	Collins	2743 Bering St.	Winston-Salem	NC	27492	5554472283	
30005	Eaton	Wagner	2743 Bering St.	Greensboro	NC	27492	555988334b	
30006	Kwasi	Williams	89 Jefferson Way	High Point	NC	27494	5554475565	
30007	Natasha	Simpson	187 Suffolk Ln.	Greensboro	NC	27493	5557753389	
30008	Joy	Jones	305 - 14th Ave. S.	Winston-Salem	NC	27493	5552587655	
30009	John	Nunn	89 Chiaroscuro Rd.	Greensboro	NC	27494	5559985557	
30010	Laura	Peterson	120 Hanover Sq.	Winston-Salem	NC	27492	5553346654	

All Access Obje... ⊚ «
Search...
Tables
  Branch
  Customers

Step e: Imported column headings

Access 2016, Windows 10, Microsoft Corporation

FIGURE 2.23 Imported Customers Table

a. Open *a02h1Bank_LastFirst* if you closed it at the end of Hands-On Exercise 1, and save it as **a02h2Bank_LastFirst**, changing h1 to h2.

b. Click **Enable Content** below the Ribbon to indicate that you trust the contents of the database.

c. Click the **External Data tab** and click **Excel** in the Import & Link group to launch the Get External Data – Excel Spreadsheet feature. Ensure that the *Import the source data into a new table in the current database* option is selected.

> **TROUBLESHOOTING:** Ensure that you click Excel in the Import & Link group to import the spreadsheet and not the Excel command in the Export group.

d. Click **Browse** and navigate to your student data files. Select the *a02h2Customers* workbook. Click **Open** and click **OK** to open the Import Spreadsheet Wizard.

e. Ensure that the *First Row Contains Column Headings* check box is checked to indicate to Access that column headings exist in the Excel file.

   The field names CID, FirstName, LastName, Street, City, State, ZIP, and Phone will import from Excel along with the data stored in the rows in the worksheet. You will modify the field names later in Access.

f. Click **Next**.

g. Ensure that CID is displayed in the Field Name box in Field Options. Click the **Indexed arrow** and select **Yes (No Duplicates)**. Click **Next**.

   The CID (CustomerID) will become the primary key in this table. It needs to be a unique identifier, so you must change the property to No Duplicates.

h. Click the **Choose my own primary key option**. Make sure that the CID field is selected. Click **Next**.

The final screen of the Import Spreadsheet Wizard asks you to name your table. The name of the Excel worksheet is Customers, and Access defaults to the worksheet name. It is an acceptable name.

i. Click **Finish** to accept Customers as the table name.

A dialog box opens prompting you to save the steps of this import to use again. If this is data that is to be collected in Excel and updated to the database on a regular basis, saving the import steps would save time. You do not need to save the import steps in this example.

j. Click **Close**.

The new table displays in the Navigation Pane of the Bank database.

k. Open the imported Customers table in Datasheet view and double-click the border between each of the field names to adjust the columns to Best Fit. Compare your table to Figure 2.23.

l. Save and close the table.

STEP 2 ›› **IMPORT DATA FROM AN ACCESS DATABASE**

The auditor asks you to import an Access database table that contains account information related to the accounts you are analyzing. You use the Import Wizard to import the database table. Refer to Figure 2.24 as you complete Step 2.

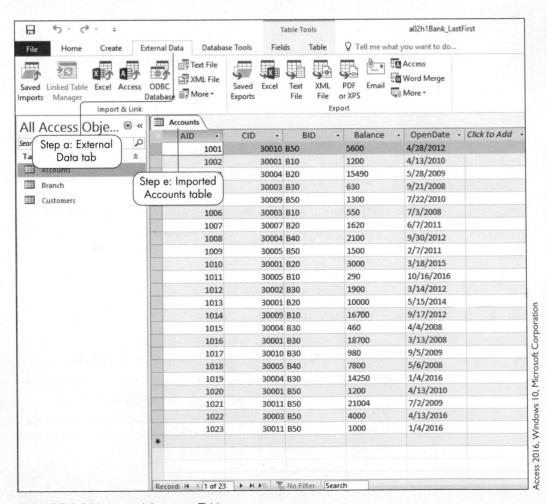

FIGURE 2.24 Imported Accounts Table

a. Click the **External Data tab** and click **Access** in the Import & Link group to launch the Get External Data – Access Database feature. Ensure that the *Import tables, queries, forms, reports, macros, and modules into the current database* option is selected.

b. Click **Browse** and navigate to your student data files. Select the *a02h2Accounts* database. Click **Open** and click **OK** to open the Import Objects dialog box.

c. Click the **Accounts table** for importing and click **OK**.

d. Click **Close** in the Save Import Steps dialog box.

The Navigation Pane now contains three tables: Accounts, Branch, and Customers.

e. Open the imported Accounts table in Datasheet view and compare it to Figure 2.24.

f. Close the table.

STEP 3 »» MODIFY AN IMPORTED TABLE'S DESIGN

When importing tables from either Excel or Access, the fields may have different data types and property settings than required to create table relationships. You will modify the tables so that each field has the correct data type and field size. Refer to Figure 2.25 as you complete Step 3.

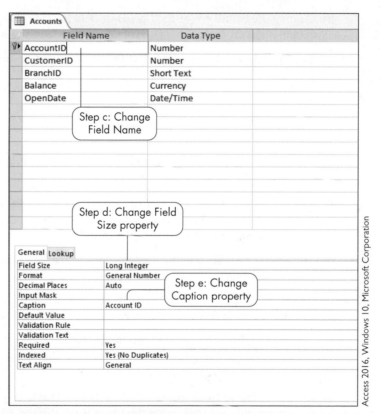

FIGURE 2.25 Modified Accounts Table Design

a. Right-click the **Accounts table** in the Navigation Pane.

b. Select Design view from the shortcut menu to open the table in Design view.

The Accounts table displays with the primary key AID selected.

c. Change the AID field name to **AccountID**.

d. Change the Field Size property to **Long Integer**.

Long Integer ensures that there will be enough numbers as the number of customers grows over time and may exceed 32,768 (the upper limit for Integer values).

e. Type **Account ID** in the Caption box for the AccountID field. The caption contains a space between Account and ID.

f. Click the **CID** field. Change the CID field name to **CustomerID**.

g. Change the Field Size property to **Long Integer**.

You can select the Field Size option using the arrow, or you can type the first letter of the option you want. For example, type l for Long Integer or s for Single. Make sure the current option is completely selected before you type the letter.

h. Type **Customer ID** in the Caption box for the CustomerID field. The caption contains a space between Customer and ID.

i. Click the **BID field**. Change the BID field name to **BranchID**.

j. Type **5** in the Field Size property box in the Field Properties.

k. Type **Branch ID** in the Caption property box for the Branch ID field.

l. Change the Data Type of the Balance field to **Currency**.

The Currency data type is used for fields that contain monetary values. In this case, changing the data type is not consequential; formatting the imported Balance field as Currency will not change the original data values.

m. Change the Data Type of the OpenDate field to **Date/Time** and set **Short Date** in the Format field property. Type **Open Date** in the Caption property box.

The OpenDate field stores the date that each account was opened.

n. Click **View** in the Views group to switch to Datasheet view. Read the messages and click **Yes** to each one.

In this case, it is OK to click Yes because the shortened fields will not cut off any data. Leave the table open.

o. Right-click the **Customers table** in the Navigation Pane and from the shortcut menu, select **Design View**.

p. Change the CID field name to **CustomerID**. Change the Field Size property of the CustomerID field to **Long Integer** and add a caption, **Customer ID**. Take note of the intentional space between Customer and ID.

The Accounts table and the Customers table will be joined using the CustomerID field. Both fields must have the same data type.

q. Change the Field Size property to **20** for the FirstName, LastName, Street, and City fields. Change the Field Size for State to **2**.

r. Change the data type for ZIP and Phone to **Short Text**. Change the Field Size property to **15** for both fields. Remove the @ symbol from the Format property where it exists for all fields in the Customers table.

s. Click the **Phone field name** and click **Input Mask** in Field Properties. Click the **ellipsis** on the right side to launch the Input Mask Wizard. Click **Yes** to save the table and click **Yes** to the *Some data may be lost* warning. Click **Finish** to apply the default phone number input mask.

The phone number input mask enables users to enter 6105551212 in the datasheet, and Access will display it as (610) 555-1212.

t. Click **Save** to save the design changes to the Customers table.

Now that you have created the Access tables, you discover that you need to add another customer and his account records to them. Refer to Figure 2.26 as you complete Step 4.

Customer ID	FirstName	LastName	Street	City	State	Zip	Phone	Click to Add
30001	Allison	Millward	2732 Baker Blvd.	Greensboro	NC	27492	(555) 334-5678	
30002	Bernett	Fox	12 Orchestra Terrace	High Point	NC	27494	(555) 358-5554	
30003	Clay	Hayes	P.O. Box 555	Greensboro	NC	27492	(555) 998-4457	
30004	Cordle	Collins	2743 Bering St.	Winston-Salem	NC	27492	(555) 447-2283	
30005	Eaton	Wagner	2743 Bering St.	Greensboro	NC	27492	(555) 988-3346	
30006 Kwasi		Williams	89 Jefferson Way	High Point	NC	27494	(555) 447-5565	
		Simpson	187 Suffolk Ln.	Greensboro	NC	27493	(555) 775-3389	
		Jones	305 - 14th Ave. S.	Winston-Salem	NC	27493	(555) 258-7655	
30009	John	Nunn	89 Chiaroscuro Rd.	Greensboro	NC	27494	(555) 998-5557	
30010	Laura	Peterson	120 Hanover Sq.	Winston-Salem	NC	27492	(555) 334-6654	
30011	YourName	YourName	800 University Ave.	High Point	NC	27494	(555) 447-1235	
* 0								

Step b: Enter yourself as a new customer

Access 2016, Windows 10, Microsoft Corporation

FIGURE 2.26 Customers Table Displaying the Added Customer ID 30011

a. Click **View** in the Views group to display the Customers table in Datasheet view.

The asterisk at the bottom of the table data in the row selector area is the indicator of a place to enter a new record.

b. Click next to the * in the **Customer ID field** in the new record row below 30010. Type **30011**. Fill in the rest of the data using your personal information as the customer. You may use a fictitious address and phone number.

Note the phone number format. The input mask you set formats the phone number.

c. Close the Customers table. The Accounts table tab is open.

TROUBLESHOOTING: If the Accounts table is not open, double-click Accounts in the Navigation Pane.

d. Click next to the * in the **Account ID field** in the new record row. Type **1024**. Type **30011** as the Customer ID and **B50** as the Branch ID. Type **14005** for the Balance field value. Type **8/7/2018** for the Open Date.

e. Add the following records to the Accounts table:

Account ID	Customer ID	Branch ID	Balance	Open Date
1025	30006	B40	$11,010	3/13/2018
1026	30007	B20	$7,400	5/1/2018

f. Close the Accounts table, but keep the database open.

The tables for the bank investigation have been designed and populated. Now you will establish connections between the tables. Look at the primary and foreign keys as a guide. Refer to Figure 2.27 as you complete Step 5.

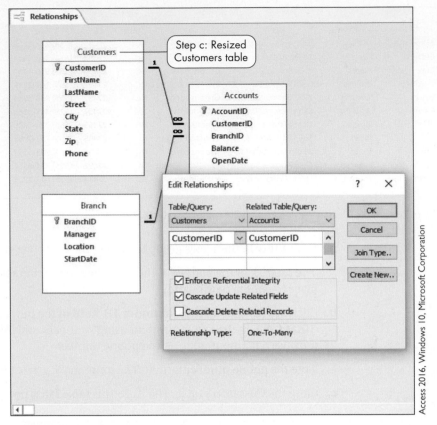

FIGURE 2.27 Relationships Between Tables

a. Click the **Database Tools tab** and click **Relationships** in the Relationships group.

   The Relationships window opens and the Show Table dialog box displays.

> **TROUBLESHOOTING:** If the Show Table dialog box does not open, click Show Table in the Relationships group on the Relationship Tools Design tab.

b. Double-click each of the three tables displayed in the Show Table dialog box to add them to the Relationships window. Click **Close** in the Show Table dialog box.

> **TROUBLESHOOTING:** If you have a duplicate table, click the title bar of the duplicated table and press Delete.

c. Click and drag the border of the Customers table field list to resize it so that all of the fields are visible. Arrange the tables as shown in Figure 2.27.

d. Drag the **BranchID field** (the primary key) in the Branch table onto the BranchID field (the foreign key) in the Accounts table. The Edit Relationships dialog box opens. Click the **Enforce Referential Integrity** and **Cascade Update Related Fields check boxes** to select them. Click **Create**.

   A black line displays, joining the two tables. It has a 1 at the end near the Branch table and an infinity symbol on the end next to the Accounts table. You have established a one-to-many relationship between the Branch and Accounts tables. Each single branch is connected with many accounts.

e. Drag the **CustomerID field** (the primary key) in the Customers table onto the CustomerID field (the foreign key) in the Accounts table. The Edit Relationships dialog box opens. Click the **Enforce Referential Integrity** and **Cascade Update Related Fields check boxes** to select them. Click **Create**.

You have established a one-to-many relationship between the Customers and Accounts tables. A customer will have only a single CustomerID number. The same customer may have many different accounts: Savings, Checking, Credit Card, and so forth.

> **TROUBLESHOOTING:** If you get an error message when you click Create, verify that the data types of the joined fields are the same. To check the data types from the Relationships window, right-click the title bar of a table and select Table Design from the shortcut menu. Modify the data type of the join fields, if necessary. Customer ID should be Number and Branch ID should be Short Text in both tables.

f. Click **Save** on the Quick Access Toolbar to save the changes to the relationships. Close the Relationships window.

STEP 6 ❯❯ ENFORCE REFERENTIAL INTEGRITY

The design of the Bank database must be 100% correct; otherwise, data entry may be compromised. Even though you are confident that the table relationships are set correctly, you decide to test them by entering some invalid data. If referential integrity is enforced, the invalid data will be rejected by Access. Refer to Figure 2.28 as you complete Step 6.

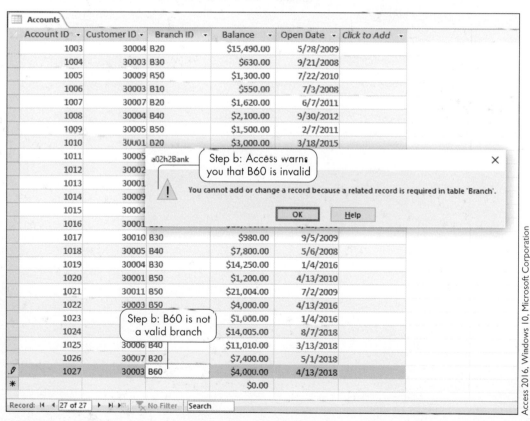

FIGURE 2.28 Referential Integrity Enforces Accurate Data Entry

a. Double-click the **Accounts table** to open it in Datasheet view.

b. Add a new record, pressing **Tab** after each field: Account ID: **1027**, Customer ID: **30003**, Branch: **B60**, Balance: **4000**, Open Date: **4/13/2018**. Press **Enter**.

You attempted to enter a nonexistent BranchID (B60) and were not allowed to make that error. A warning message is telling you that a related record in the Branch table is required, because the Accounts table and the Branch table are connected by a relationship with Enforce Referential Integrity checked.

c. Click **OK**. Double-click the **Branch table** in the Navigation Pane and examine the data in the BranchID field. Notice the Branch table has no B60 record. Close the Branch table.

d. Replace B60 with **B50** in the new Accounts record and press **Tab** three times. As soon as the focus moves to the next record, the pencil symbol disappears and your data are saved.

You successfully identified a BranchID that Access recognizes. Because referential integrity between the Accounts and Branch tables has been enforced, Access looks at each data entry item in a foreign key and matches it to a corresponding value in the table where it is the primary key. In Step b, you attempted to enter a nonexistent BranchID and were not allowed to make that error. In Step d, you entered a valid BranchID. Access examined the index for the BranchID in the Branch table and found a corresponding value for B50.

e. Close the Accounts table.

f. Close any open tables.

g. Keep the database open if you plan to continue with the Hands-On Exercise. If not, close the database and exit Access.

Single-Table Queries

A *query* enables you to ask questions about the data stored in a database and then provides the answers to the questions by creating subsets or summaries of data in a datasheet. If you wanted to see which customers currently have an account with a balance over $5,000, you could find the answer by creating an Access query.

In this section, you will use the Simple Query Wizard and Query Design view to create single-table queries that display only data that you select. Multitable queries will be covered in the next section.

Creating a Single-Table Query

Because data are stored in tables in a database, you always begin a query by determining which table (or tables) contain the data that you need. For the question about account balances over $5,000, you would use the Accounts table. You can create a single-table query in two ways—by using the Simple Query Wizard or the Query Design tool in the Queries group on the Create tab. While the Simple Query Wizard offers a step-by-step guide to creating a query, the Query Design tool allows for more flexibility and customization, and is often the preferred method for creating queries.

After you design a query, you run it to display the results in a datasheet. A query's datasheet looks like a table's datasheet, except that it is usually a subset of the fields and records found in the table on which it is based. The subset shows only the records that match the criteria that were added in the query design. The subset may contain different sorting of the records than the sorting in the underlying table. You can enter new records in a query, modify existing records, or delete records in Datasheet view. Any changes made in Datasheet view are reflected in the underlying table on which the query is based.

Create a Single-Table Select Query

Select queries are a type of query that displays only the fields and records that match criteria entered in the query design process.

> **To create a select query using the Query Design tool, complete the following steps:**
>
> 1. Click the Create tab.
> 2. Click Query Design in the Queries group on the Design tab.
> 3. Select the table you want for your query from the Show Table dialog box.
> 4. Click Add to add the table to the top pane of the query design and close the Show Table dialog box.
> 5. Drag the fields needed from the table's field list to the query design grid (or alternatively, double-click the field names); then add criteria and sorting options.
> 6. Click Run in the Results group on the Design tab to show the results in Datasheet view.

Use Query Design View

Query Design view is divided into two sections: The top pane displays the tables from which the data will be retrieved, and the bottom pane (known as the query design grid) displays the fields and the criteria that you set. In the query design grid, you select only the fields that contain the data you want in the query and arrange them in the order that you want them displayed in the query results. You add criteria to further limit (or filter) the records to display only those that you require in the results. The design grid also enables you to sort the records based on one or more fields. You can create calculated fields to display data based on expressions that use the fields in the underlying table. For example, you could calculate the monthly interest earned on each bank account by multiplying the Balance by an interest rate. If a query contains more than one table, the join lines between tables display as they were created in the Relationships window.

The query design grid (the bottom pane) contains columns and rows. Each field in the query has its own column and contains multiple rows. The rows allow you to control the query results.

- The Field row displays the field name.

- The Table row displays the data source (in some cases, a field occurs in more than one table, for example, when it is a join field; therefore, it is often beneficial to display the table name in the query design grid).

- The Sort row enables you to sort in ascending or descending order (or neither).

- The Show row controls whether the field will be displayed or hidden in the query results.

- The *Criteria row* is used to set the rules that determine which records will be selected, such as customers with account balances greater than $5,000.

Figure 2.29 displays the query design grid with the Show Table dialog box open. The Accounts table has been added from the Show Table dialog box. Figure 2.30 shows Design view of a sample query with four fields, with a criterion set for one field and sorting set on another. The results of the query display in Datasheet view, as shown in Figure 2.31.

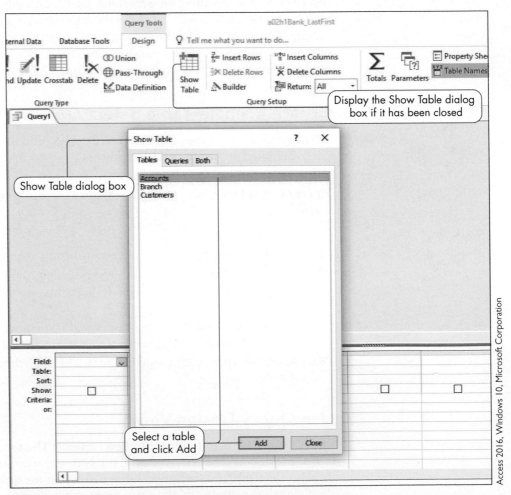

FIGURE 2.29 Query Design View with Show Table Dialog Box

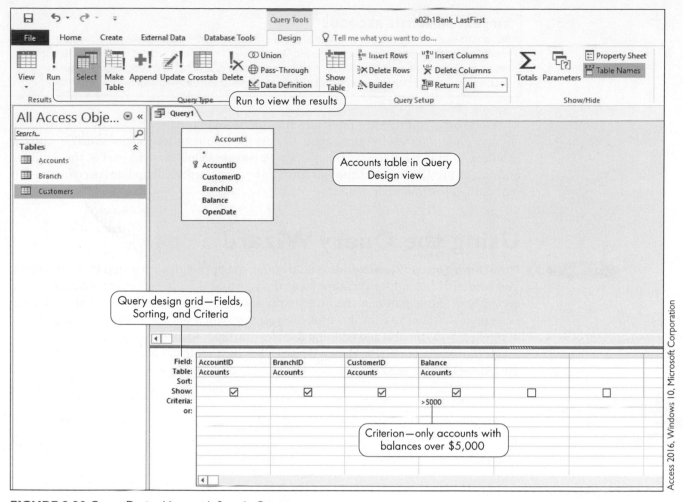

FIGURE 2.30 Query Design View with Sample Criterion

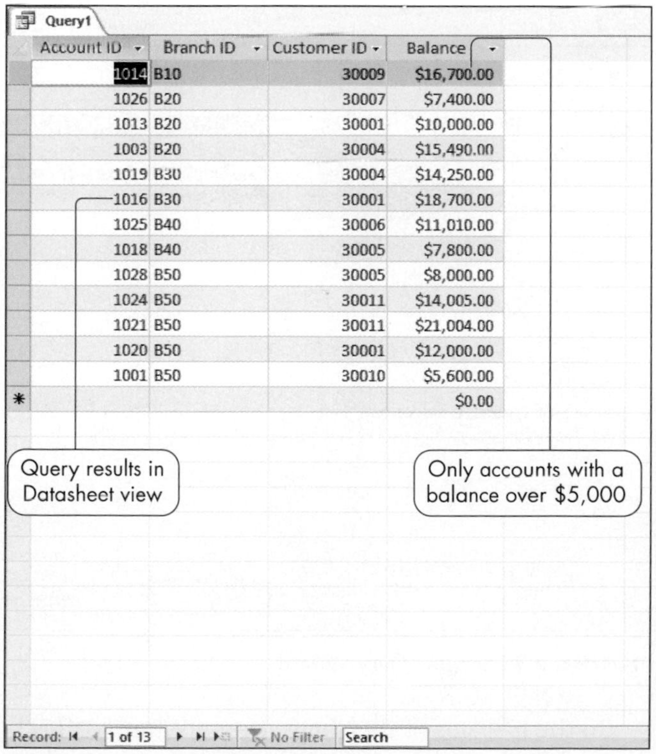

FIGURE 2.31 Query Results in Datasheet View

Each time you need to fine-tune the query, switch back to Design view, make a change, and then run the query again to view the results. After you are satisfied with the results, you may want to save the query so it becomes a permanent part of the database and can be used later. Each time you run a query, the results will update based on the current data in the underlying table(s).

Using the Query Wizard

STEP 1 The *Simple Query Wizard* guides you through query design with a step-by-step process. The wizard is helpful for creating basic queries that do not require criteria. However, even if you initially design the query with a wizard, you are able to modify it later in Design view. After the wizard completes, you can switch to Design view and add criteria as needed. You can also add additional tables and fields to an existing query when conditions change. To launch the Query Wizard, click the Create tab and click Query Wizard in the Queries group (see Figure 2.32).

FIGURE 2.32 Launching the Query Wizard

Access 2016, Windows 10, Microsoft Corporation

Select Simple Query Wizard in the New Query dialog box, as shown in Figure 2.33.

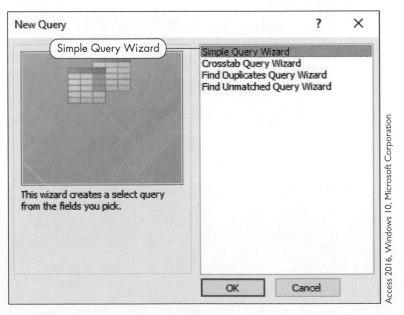

FIGURE 2.33 Simple Query Wizard

In the first step of the Simple Query Wizard dialog box, you specify the tables or queries and fields required in your query. When you select a table from the Tables/Queries arrow (queries can also be based on other queries), a list of the table's fields displays in the Available Fields list box (see Figures 2.34 and 2.35).

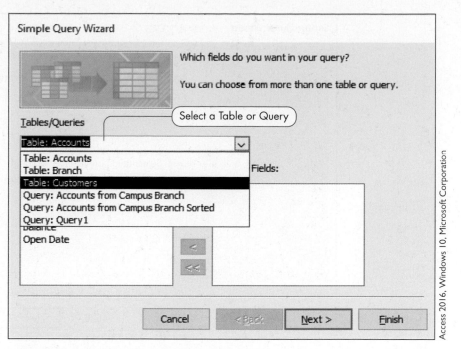

FIGURE 2.34 Specify Which Tables or Queries to Use

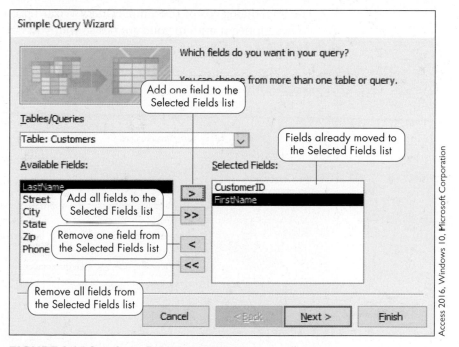

FIGURE 2.35 Specify the Fields for the Query

Select the necessary fields and add them to the Selected Fields list box using the directional arrows shown in Figure 2.35. In the next screen (shown in Figure 2.36), you choose between a detail and a summary query. The detail query shows every field of every record in the result. The summary query enables you to group data and view only summary records. For example, if you were interested in the total funds deposited at each of the bank branches, you would set the query to Summary, click Summary Options, and then click Sum on the Balance field. Access would then sum the balances of all accounts for each branch.

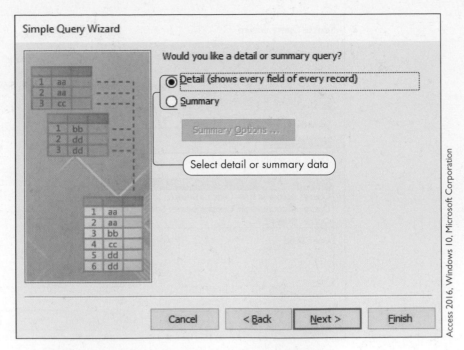

FIGURE 2.36 Choose Detail or Summary Data

The final dialog box of the Simple Query Wizard prompts for the name of the query. Assign descriptive names to your queries so that you can easily identify what each one does (see Figure 2.37).

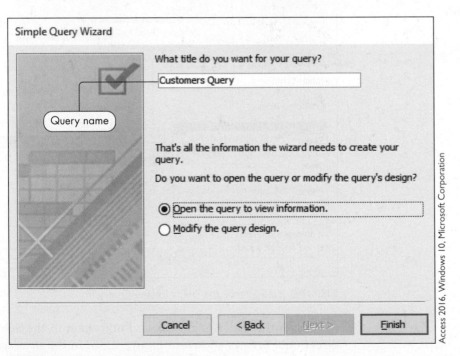

FIGURE 2.37 Name the Query

Specifying Query Criteria for Different Data Types

STEP 2 » You set criteria to limit the records to display only those that you require in the query results. When specifying a criterion for a query, you may need to include a delimiter—a special character that surrounds a criterion's value. The delimiter required is determined by the field data type. Text fields require quotation marks before and after the text; for example, "Campus" could be used to display customers from the Campus branch in the Bank database. Access automatically adds the quotation marks around text, but to ensure that the correct delimiter is used, you may want to include the delimiters yourself.

When the criterion is in a date field, you enclose the criterion in pound signs, such as #10/14/2018#. Access automatically adds the pound signs around dates, but to ensure that the correct delimiter is used, you may want to include the delimiters yourself. A date value can be entered using any allowed format, such as February 2, 2018, 2/2/2018, or 2-Feb-18. Use plain digits (no delimiter) for the criteria of a numeric field, currency, or AutoNumber. You can enter numeric criteria with or without a decimal point and with or without a minus sign. Commas and dollar signs are not allowed. You enter criteria for a Yes/No field as Yes or No. See Table 2.4 for query criteria and examples.

TABLE 2.4	Query Criteria	
Data Type	**Criteria**	**Example**
Text	"Harry"	For a FirstName field, displays only text that matches Harry exactly. The quotation marks can be typed, or Access will add them automatically.
Numeric	5000	For a Quantity field, displays only numbers that match 5000 exactly (do not specify commas, currency symbols, etc.).
Date	#2/2/2018#	For a ShippedDate field, shows orders shipped on February 2, 2018.
Yes/No	Yes	For a Discontinued field, returns records where the check box is selected, denoting Yes.

Pearson Education, Inc.

Use Wildcards

Wildcards are special characters that can represent one or more characters in a text value. Suppose you want to use a criterion to search for the last name of a customer, but you are not sure how to spell the name; however, you know that the name starts with the letters *Sm*. You can use a wildcard with a text value (such as Sm*) to search for the name.

You enter wildcard characters in text values in the Criteria row of a query. Therefore, if you want to search for names that start with the letters *Sm*, specify the criterion in the LastName field as *Sm**. All last names that begin with *Sm* would display in the results. Wildcard characters can be placed in the beginning, middle, or end of a text string. Table 2.5 shows more query criterion examples that use wildcards.

TABLE 2.5	Query Criteria Using Wildcards		
Character	**Description**	**Example**	**Result**
*	Matches any number of characters in the same position as the asterisk	Sm*	Small, Smiley, Smith, Smithson
?	Matches a single character in the same position as the question mark	H?ll	Hall, Hill, Hull
[ ]	Matches any single character within the brackets	F[ae]ll	Fall and Fell, but not Fill or Full
[!]	Matches any character not in the brackets	F[!ae]ll	Fill and Full, but not Fall or Fell

Pearson Education, Inc.

Use Comparison Operators in Queries

Comparison operators, such as equal (=), not equal (<>), greater than (>), less than (<), greater than or equal to (>=), and less than or equal to (<=), can be used in query criteria. Comparison operators enable you to limit the query results to only those records that meet the criteria. For example, if you only want to see accounts that have a balance greater than $5,000, you would type >5000 in the Criteria row of the Balance field. Table 2.6 shows more comparison operator examples.

TABLE 2.6	Comparison Operators in Queries
Expression	**Example**
=10	Equals 10
<>10	Not equal to 10
>10	Greater than 10
>=10	Greater than or equal to 10
<10	Less than 10
<=10	Less than or equal to 10

Pearson Education, Inc.

Work with Null

Sometimes finding null values is an important part of making a decision. For example, if you need to know which orders have been completed but not shipped, you would create a query to find the orders with a null (missing) ShipDate. The term that Access uses for a blank field is *null*. Table 2.7 provides two examples of when to use the null criterion in a query.

TABLE 2.7	Establishing Null Criteria Expressions	
Expression	**Description**	**Example**
Is Null	Use to find blank fields	For a SalesRepID field in the Customers table when the customer has not been assigned to a sales representative.
Is Not Null	Used to find fields with data	For a ShipDate field; a value has been entered to indicate that the order was shipped to the customer.

Pearson Education, Inc.

Establish AND, OR, and NOT Criteria

Remember the earlier question, "Which customers currently have an account with a balance over $5,000?" This question was answered by creating a query with a single criterion. At times, questions are more focused and require queries with multiple criteria. For example, you may need to know "Which customers from the Eastern branch currently have an account with a balance over $5,000?" To answer this question, you specify two criteria in different fields using the *AND condition*. This means that the query results will display only records that match *all* criteria. When the criteria are in the same row of the query design grid, Access interprets this as an AND condition. You can also use the AND logical operator to test two criteria in the same field, as shown in Table 2.8.

When you have multiple criteria and you need to satisfy only one, not all of the criteria, use the *OR condition*. The query results will display records that match any of the specified criteria. You can use the OR logical operator, and type the expression into the Criteria row, separating the criteria with the OR keyword. Table 2.8 shows an example of an OR condition created using this method. You can also type the first criterion into the Criteria row and then type the next criterion by using the Or row in the same field or a different field in the design grid (see Figure 2.38).

The NOT logical operator returns all records except the specified criteria. For example, "Not Eastern" would return all accounts except those opened at the Eastern branch.

TABLE 2.8 AND, OR, and NOT Queries

Logical Operator	Example	Result
AND	>5000 AND <10000	For a Balance field, returns all accounts with a balance greater than $5,000 and less than $10,000.
OR	"Eastern" OR "Campus"	For a Location field, returns all accounts that are at the Eastern or the Campus branch.
NOT	Not "Campus"	For a Location field, returns all records except those in the Campus branch.

Pearson Education, Inc.

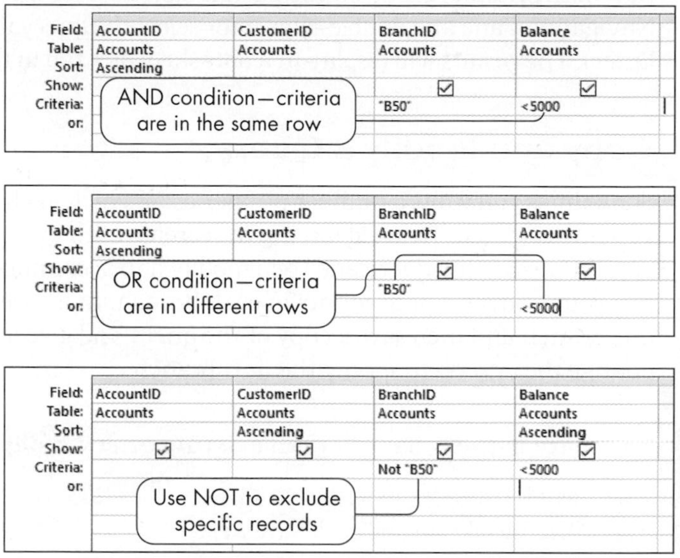

FIGURE 2.38 Query Design Views Showing the AND, OR, and NOT Operators

Access 2016, Windows 10, Microsoft Corporation

TIP: FINDING VALUES IN A DATE RANGE

To find the values contained within a date range, use the greater than (>) and less than (<) operators. For example, to find the values of dates on or after January 1, 2018, and on or before December 31, 2018, use the criterion >=1/1/2018 and <=12/31/2018. You can also use the BETWEEN operator to find the same inclusive dates, for example, BETWEEN 1/1/2018 and 12/31/2018.

Understanding Query Sort Order

The query sort order determines the order of records in a query's Datasheet view. You can change the order of records by specifying the sort order in Design view. When you want to sort using more than one field, the sort order is determined from left to right. The order of columns should be considered when first creating the query. For example, a query sorted by LastName and then by FirstName must have those two fields in the correct order in the design grid. When modifying sort order, it is sometimes necessary to rearrange fields, or add and delete columns in the query design grid.

To change order, add, or delete fields in the query design grid, complete one of the following steps:

- Change the order of a field: select the column you want to move by clicking the column selector. Click again and drag the selected field to its new location.

- Insert an additional column in the design grid: select a column and click Insert Columns in the Query Setup group on the Design tab. The additional column will insert to the left of the selected column.

- Delete a column: click the column selector to select the column and click Delete Columns in the Query Setup group, or press Delete on the keyboard.

Running, Copying, and Modifying a Query

Once your query is designed and saved, you run it to view the results. After you create a query, you may want to create a duplicate copy to use as the basis for creating a similar query. Duplicating a query saves time when you need the same tables and fields but with slightly different criteria.

Run a Query

There are several ways to run a query. One method is from within Design view; click Run in the Results group on the Design tab. Another method is to locate the query in the Navigation Pane and double-click it (or select the query in the Navigation Pane and press Enter). The results will display in a datasheet as a tab in the main window.

Copy and Modify a Query

Sometimes you want a number of queries in which each query is similar to another that you have created. To avoid having to recreate each query from scratch, you can create a copy of an existing query and then modify it to accommodate the new criteria. For example, you need a list of accounts in each branch. In a case like this, you create a query for one branch and then save a copy of the query and give it a new name. Finally, you would change the criteria to specify the next branch.

To create a query based on an existing query, complete the following steps:

1. Open the query you want to copy.
2. Click the File tab and click Save As.
3. Click Save Object As in the File Types section.
4. Ensure that Save Object As is selected in the Database File Types section and click Save As.
5. Type the name you want to use for the new query in the Save As dialog box and click OK (see Figure 2.39).
6. Switch to Design view of the copied query and modify the query criteria, as necessary.
7. Save and run the modified query.

TIP: COPYING THE QUERY IN THE NAVIGATION PANE
You can also right-click the original query in the Navigation Pane and from the shortcut menu, select Copy. Right-click in the empty space of the Navigation Pane again and then select Paste. Type a name for the new query in the Paste As dialog box and click OK.

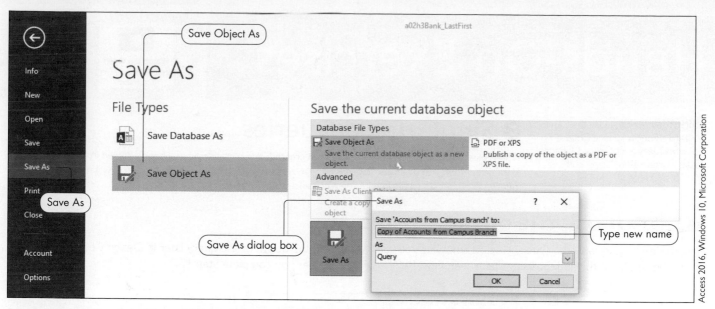

FIGURE 2.39 Using Save Object As to Save a Copy of a Query

Change Query Data

 STEP 3 >> Be aware that query results in the datasheet display the actual records that are stored in the underlying table(s). Being able to correct an error immediately while it is displayed in the query datasheet is an advantage. You can save time by not having to close the query, open the table, find the error, fix it, and then run the query again. However, use caution when editing records in query results since you will be changing the original table data.

Quick Concepts

8. Define a single-table query. Give an example. **p. 173**

9. Give an example of how to use the Criteria row to find certain records in a table. **p. 174**

10. Why would you use an OR condition in a query? **p. 180**

11. Why would you want to copy an existing query? **p. 182**

Hands-On Exercises

Watch the Video
for this Hands-On
Exercise!

MyITLab®
HOE3 Training

Skills covered: Use the Query
Wizard • Specify Query Criteria •
Specify Query Sort Order • Change
Query Data • Run, Copy, and
Modify a Query

3 Single-Table Queries

The tables and table relationships have been created, and some data have been entered in the Bank
database. Now, you begin the process of analyzing the bank data for the auditor. You will do so using
queries. You decide to begin with the Accounts table.

STEP 1 ›› USE THE QUERY WIZARD

You decide to start with the Query Wizard, knowing you can always alter the design of the query later in Design view. You will
show the results to the auditor using Datasheet view. Refer to Figure 2.40 as you complete Step 1.

Accounts from Campus Branch			
Account ID ▾	Customer ID ▾	Branch ID ▾	Balance ▾
1001	30010	B50	$5,600.00
1002	30001	B10	$1,200.00
Step e: Fields added to query			$15,490.00
1004	30003	B30	$630.00
1005	30009	B50	$1,300.00
1006	30003	B10	$550.00
1007	30007	B20	$1,620.00
1008	30004	B40	$2,100.00
1009	30005	B50	$1,500.00
1010	30001	B20	$3,000.00
1011	30005	B10	$290.00
1012	30002	B30	$1,900.00
1013	30001	B20	$10,000.00
1014	30009	B10	$16,700.00
1015	30004	B30	$460.00
1016	30001	B30	$18,700.00
1017	30010	B30	$980.00
1018	30005	B40	$7,800.00
1019	30004	B30	$14,250.00
1020	30001	B50	$1,200.00
1021	30011	B50	$21,004.00
1022	30003	B50	$4,000.00
1023	30011	B50	$1,000.00
1024	30011	B50	$14,005.00
Step h: 27 records displayed		B40	$11,010.00
1026	30007	B20	$7,400.00
1027	30003	B50	$1,000.00

Record: I◄ ◄ 1 of 27 ► ►I ►▣ ▼ No Filter | Search

Access 2016, Windows 10, Microsoft Corporation

FIGURE 2.40 Query Results Before Criteria Are Applied

a. Open *a02h2Bank_LastFirst* if you closed it at the end of Hands-On Exercise 2, and save it
as **a02h3Bank_LastFirst**, changing h2 to h3.

b. Click the **Create tab** and click **Query Wizard** in the Queries group.

The New Query dialog box opens. Simple Query Wizard is selected by default.

c. Click **OK**.

d. Verify that Table: Accounts is selected in the Tables/Queries box.

e. Click **AccountID** in the Available Fields list, then click **Add One Field** `>` to move it to
the Selected Fields list. Repeat the process with **CustomerID**, **BranchID**, and **Balance**.

The four fields should now display in the Selected Fields list box.

f. Click **Next**.

g. Confirm that Detail (shows every field of every record) is selected and click **Next**.

h. Name the query **Accounts from Campus Branch**. Click **Finish**.

This query name describes the data in the query results. Your query should have four fields: AccountID, CustomerID, BranchID, and Balance. The Navigation bar indicates that 27 records meet the query criteria.

STEP 2 ›› **SPECIFY QUERY CRITERIA AND SORT ORDER**

The auditor indicated that the problem seems to be confined to the Campus branch. You use this knowledge to revise the query to display only Campus accounts. Refer to Figure 2.41 as you complete Step 2.

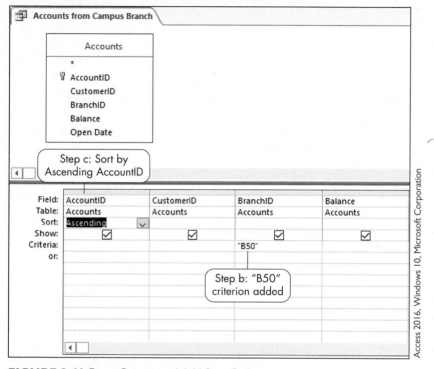

FIGURE 2.41 Enter Criteria and Add Sort Order

a. Click the **Home tab** and click **View** in the Views group.

The Accounts from Campus Branch query opens in Design view. You have created this query to view only those accounts at the Campus branch. However, other branches' accounts also display. You need to limit the query results to only the records of interest.

b. Click in the **Criteria row** (fifth row) in the BranchID column, type **B50**, and press **Enter**.

B50 is the BranchID for the Campus branch. Access queries are not case sensitive; therefore, b50 and B50 will produce the same results. Access adds quotation marks around text criteria after you press Enter, or you can type them yourself.

c. Click in the **Sort row** (third row) in the AccountID column and select **Ascending**.

d. Click **Run** in the Results group.

You should see nine records in the query results, all from Branch B50, sorted in ascending order by Account ID.

STEP 3 » CHANGE QUERY DATA AND RUN, COPY, AND MODIFY A QUERY

When the query results are on the screen, the auditor notices that some of the data are incorrect, and one of the accounts is missing. From your experience with Access, you explain to the auditor that the data can be changed directly in a query rather than switching back to the table. Refer to Figure 2.42 as you complete Step 3.

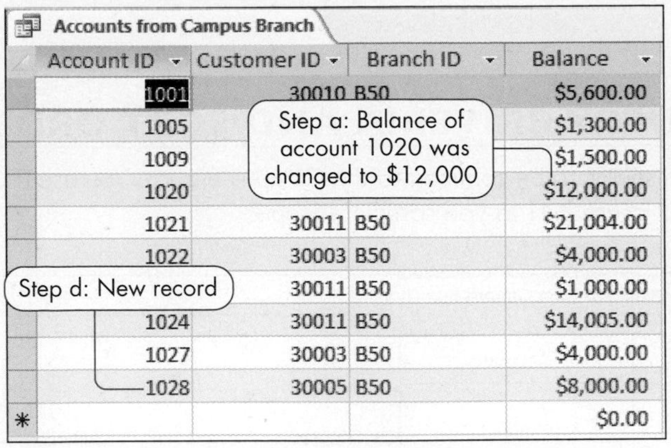

Access 2016, Windows 10, Microsoft Corporation

FIGURE 2.42 Changes Made in the Query Datasheet

a. Click in the **Balance field** in the record for account 1020. Change $1,200 to **$12,000**. Press **Enter**. Save and close the query.

You modified the record directly in the query results.

b. Double-click the **Accounts table** in the Navigation Pane

Only one account shows a $12,000 balance. The Account ID is 1020 and the Customer ID is 30001. The change you made in the Accounts table from the Campus Branch query datasheet automatically changed the data stored in the underlying table.

c. Open the Customers table. Notice the name of the customer whose CustomerID is 30001, Allison Millward. Close the Customers table.

d. Add a new record to the Accounts table with the following data: **1028** (Account ID), **30005** (Customer ID), **B50** (Branch ID), **8000** (Balance), and **8/4/2018** (Open Date). Press **Tab**.

> **TROUBLESHOOTING:** If the Accounts table is not open, double-click Accounts in the Navigation Pane.

The new record is added to the Accounts table.

e. Double-click the **Accounts from Campus Branch query** in the Navigation Pane.

Customer 30005 now shows two accounts: one with a balance of $1,500 and one with a balance of $8,000.

f. Click the **File tab**, click **Save As**, click **Save Object As**, and then click **Save As**. Type **Accounts from Campus Branch Sorted** as the query name. Click **OK**.

g. Click **View** in the Views group to return to Design view of the copied query.

h. Click in the **Sort row** of the AccountID field and select **(not sorted)**. Click in the **Sort row** of the CustomerID field and select **Ascending**. Click in the **Sort row** of the BalanceID field and select **Ascending**.

i. Click **Run** in the Results group.

Customer 30005 now shows two accounts with the two balances sorted in ascending order. Likewise, all other customers with more than one account are listed in ascending order by balance.

j. Save the query. Close the Accounts from Campus Branch Sorted query and close the Accounts table.

k. Keep the database open if you plan to continue with the Hands-On Exercise. If not, close the database and exit Access.

Multitable Queries

Multitable queries contain two or more tables, and enable you to take advantage of the relationships that have been set in your database. When you extract information from a database with a query, often you will need to pull data from multiple tables. One table may contain the core information that you want, while another table may contain the related data that make the query provide the complete results.

For example, the sample Bank database contains three tables: Customers, Accounts, and Branch. You connected the tables through relationships in order to store data efficiently and to enforce consistent data entry between them. The Customers table provides the information for the owners of the accounts. However, the Accounts table includes the balances of each account—the key financial information. Therefore, both the Customers and Accounts tables are needed to provide the information that you want: which Customers own which Accounts.

Creating a Multitable Query

There are several ways to create multitable queries. The simplistic method is to add tables to an existing query, or to copy an existing query and then add to it. You can also create a multitable query from scratch either using the Query Wizard or the Query Design tool.

Add Additional Tables to a Query

STEP 1 ⟩⟩ One way to create a multitable query is to add tables and fields to an existing query, for example to add branch or customer data to a query that includes account information.

> **To add tables to a saved query, complete the following steps:**
>
> 1. Open the existing query in Design view.
> 2. Add additional tables to a query by dragging tables from the Navigation Pane directly into the top pane of the query design window.
> 3. Add fields, criteria, and sorting options in the query design grid.
> 4. Run and save the query.

For example, the Branch and Customers tables were added to the query, as shown in Figure 2.43. The join lines between tables indicate that relationships were previously set in the Relationships window. With the additional tables and fields available, you can now add the customer's name (from Customers) and the branch location name (from Branch) rather than using CustomerID and BranchID in your results. The datasheet will contain more readily identifiable information than ID numbers for customers and locations.

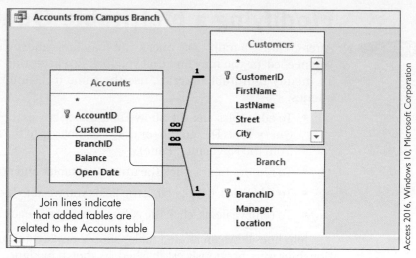

Access 2016, Windows 10, Microsoft Corporation

FIGURE 2.43 Two Additional Tables Added to a Query

Create a Multitable Query

STEP 2 ❯❯ Creating a multitable query from scratch is similar to creating a single-table query; however, choosing the right tables and managing the relationships in the query might require some additional skills. First, you should only use related tables in a multitable query. Related tables are tables that are joined in a relationship using a common field. Generally, related tables should already be joined in the Relationships window when you begin to create a multitable query. Using Figure 2.43 as a guide, creating a query with the Accounts and Branch tables would be acceptable, as would using Accounts and Customers tables, or Accounts, Branch, and Customers tables. All three scenarios include related tables. However, creating a query with only the Branch and Customers tables would not be acceptable because these tables are not directly related to one another (in other words, they do not have a common field).

To create a multitable query, complete the following steps:

1. Click the Create tab.
2. Click Query Design in the Queries group.
3. Add the tables you want in your query from the Show Table dialog box. Close the Show Table dialog box.
4. Drag the fields you want to display from the tables to the query design grid (or alternatively, double-click the field names); then add criteria and sorting options.
5. Click Run in the Results group on the Design tab to show the results in Datasheet view.

TIP: PRINT THE RELATIONSHIP REPORT TO HELP CREATE A MULTITABLE QUERY

When you create a multitable query, you only include related tables. As a guide, when the Relationships window is open, you can print the Relationship Report. Click the Database Tools tab, then click Relationship Report in the Tools group on the Relationship Tools Design tab. This report will provide a diagram that displays the tables, fields, and relationships in your database. The report is exportable to other formats such as Word if you want to share it with colleagues.

Modifying a Multitable Query

 After creating a multitable query, you may find that you did not include all of the fields you needed, or you may find that you included fields that are unnecessary to the results. To modify multitable queries, use the same techniques you learned for single-table queries.

- To add tables, use the Show Table dialog box in the Query Setup group on the Query Tools Design tab (or drag the tables into the top pane of the query design from the Navigation Pane).
- To remove tables, click the unwanted tables and press Delete.
- To add fields, double-click the fields you want to include.
- To remove fields, click the column selector of each field and press Delete.

Join lines between related tables should display automatically in a query if the relationships were previously established, as shown in Figure 2.43.

> **TIP: MULTITABLE QUERIES INHERIT RELATIONSHIPS**
>
> When you add two or more related tables to a query, join lines display automatically. You can delete a join line in a query with no impact on the relationship set in the database. Deleting a join line only affects the relationship in the individual query. The next time you create a query with the same tables, the relationships will be inherited from the database. And, if you open the Relationships window, you will find the join lines intact.

Add and Delete Fields in a Multitable Query

In Figure 2.44, three tables, as well as the join lines between the tables, display in the top pane of Design view. All the fields from each of the tables are now available for use in the query design grid. Figure 2.44 shows that Location (from the Branch table) replaced BranchID and LastName (from the Customers table) replaced CustomerID to make the results more useful. BranchID was deleted from the query; therefore, the "B50" criterion was removed as well. "Campus" was added to the Location field's Criteria row in order to extract the names of the branches rather than their BranchID numbers. Because criteria values are not case sensitive, typing "campus" is the same as typing "Campus" and both will return the same results. The results of the revised query are shown in Figure 2.45.

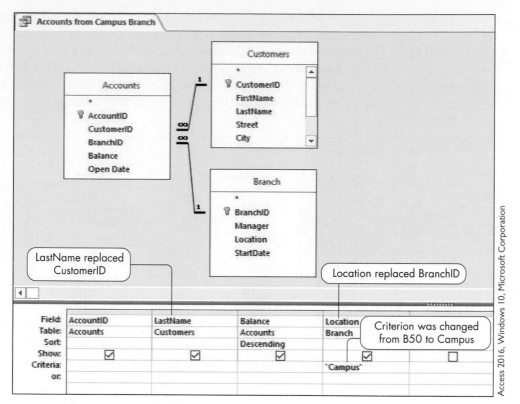

FIGURE 2.44 Modify the Query Design

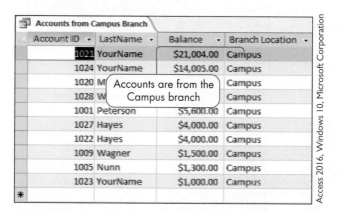

FIGURE 2.45 Datasheet View of a Multitable Query

Add Join Lines in a Multitable Query

In Figure 2.46, two tables are added to the query design, but no join line connects them. The results of the query will be unpredictable and will display more records than expected. The Customers table contains 11 records, and the Branch table contains 5 records. Because Access does not know how to interpret the unrelated tables, the results will show 55 records—every possible combination of customer and branch (11 × 5). See Figure 2.47.

To fix this problem, you can create join lines using existing tables if the tables contain a common field with the same data type. In this example, in which there is no common field, you can add an additional table that provides join lines between all three tables. You can add the Accounts table, which provides join lines between the two existing tables, Customers and Branch, and the added Accounts table. As soon as the third table is added to the query design, the join lines display automatically.

Over time, your databases may grow, and additional tables will be added. Occasionally, new tables are added to the database but not to the Relationships window. When queries are created with the new tables, join lines will not be established. When this happens, add join lines to create relationships with the new tables. Or you can create temporary join lines in the query design window. These join lines will provide a temporary relationship between tables (for that query only) and enable Access to interpret the query properly.

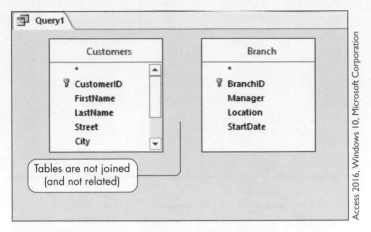

FIGURE 2.46 Query Design with Unrelated Tables

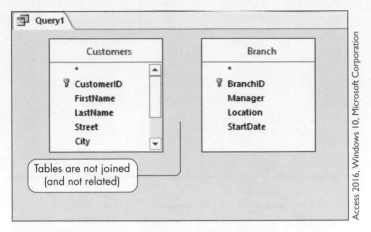

FIGURE 2.47 Query Results Using Unrelated Tables

Summarize Data Using a Multitable Query

 STEP 4 ⟩⟩ You can get valuable information from your database using a multitable query. For example, if you want to know how many accounts each customer has, you would create a new query and add both the Customers and Accounts tables to Design view. After you verify that the join lines are correct, you add the CustomerID field from the Customers table and the AccountID field from the Accounts table to the query design grid. When you initially run the query, the results show duplicates in the CustomerID column because some customers have multiple accounts.

> **To summarize this information (how many accounts each customer has), complete the following steps:**
>
> 1. Switch to Design view and click Totals in the Show/Hide group on the Query Tools Design tab. The Total row displays. Both fields show the Group By option in the Total row. The Total row enables you to summarize records by using functions such as Sum, Average, Count, etc.
> 2. Click in the Total row of the AccountID field, select Count from the list of functions, and run the query again. This time the results show one row for each customer and the number of accounts for each customer.

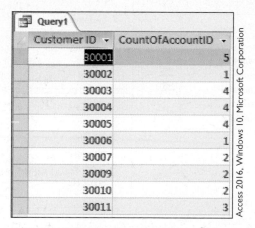

FIGURE 2.48 Datasheet Results with the Count of Accounts per Customer

Quick Concepts ✔

12. What is the advantage of creating a multitable query? *p. 188*

13. What is the benefit of summarizing data in a multitable query? *p. 193*

14. What is the result of creating a query with two unrelated tables? *p. 191*

Hands-On Exercises

Watch the Video
for this Hands-On
Exercise!

MyITLab®
HOE4 Training

4 Multitable Queries

Based on the auditor's request, you will evaluate the data further. This requires creating queries that are based on multiple tables rather than on a single table. You decide to open an existing query, add additional tables, and then save the query with a new name.

STEP 1 >> ADD ADDITIONAL TABLES TO A QUERY

The previous query was based on the Accounts table, but now you need to add information to the query from the Branch and Customers tables. You will add the Branch and Customers tables to the query. Refer to Figure 2.49 as you complete Step 1.

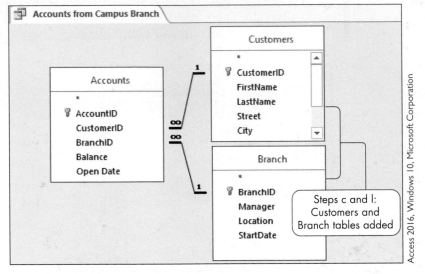

FIGURE 2.49 Add Tables to an Existing Query

a. Open *a02h3Bank_LastFirst* if you closed it at the end of Hands-On Exercise 3, and save it as **a02h4Bank_LastFirst**, changing h3 to h4.

b. Right-click the **Accounts from Campus Branch query** in the Navigation Pane and select **Design View** from the shortcut menu.

c. Drag the **Branch table** from the Navigation Pane to the top pane of the query design grid to the right of the Accounts table.

   A join line connects the Branch table to the Accounts table. The tables in the query inherit the relationship created earlier in the Relationships window.

d. Drag the **Location field** from the Branch table to the first empty column in the design grid.

   The Location field should be positioned to the right of the Balance field.

e. Click the **Show check box** below the BranchID field to clear the check box and hide this field from the results.

   The BranchID field is no longer needed in the results because the Location field provides the branch name instead. Because you deselected the BranchID Show check box, the BranchID field will not display the next time the query is run.

f. Delete the B50 criterion in the BranchID field.

g. Type **Campus** as a criterion in the Location field and press **Enter**.

Access adds quotation marks around Campus for you because Campus is a text criterion. You are substituting the Location criterion *(Campus)* in place of the BranchID criterion (B50).

h. Click in the AccountID field **Sort row**, click the arrow, and then click **(not sorted)**. Click in the **Sort row** of the Balance field. Click the arrow and select **Descending**.

i. Click **Run** in the Results group.

The BranchID field does not display in Datasheet view because you hid the field in Step e. Only Campus accounts display in the datasheet (10 records). Next, you will add the Customers LastName field to and delete the CustomerID field from the query.

j. Save the changes to the query design.

k. Click **View** in the Views group to return to Design view. Point over the column selector at the top of the BranchID field, and when a downward arrow displays, click to select it. Press **Delete**.

The BranchID field has been removed from the grid.

l. Drag the **Customers table** from the Navigation Pane to the top pane of the query design grid and reposition the tables so that the join lines are not blocked (see Figure 2.49).

The join lines automatically connect the Customers table to the Accounts table (similar to Step c above).

m. Drag the **LastName field** in the Customers table to the second column in the design grid.

The LastName field should be positioned to the right of the AccountID field.

n. Click the **column selector** in the CustomerID field to select it. Press **Delete**.

The CustomerID field is no longer needed in the results because we added the LastName field instead.

o. Click **Run** in the Results group.

The last names of the customers now display in the results.

p. Save and close the query.

STEP 2 **》 CREATE A MULTITABLE QUERY**

After discussing the query results with the auditor, you realize that another query is needed to show those customers with account balances of $1,000 or less. You create the query and view the results in Datasheet view. Refer to Figure 2.50 as you complete Step 2.

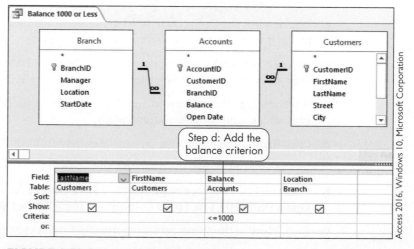

FIGURE 2.50 Create a Multitable Query

a. Click the **Create tab** and click **Query Design** in the Queries group.

b. Double-click the **Branch table name** in the Show Table dialog box. Double-click **Accounts** and **Customers** so that all three are added to Design view. Click **Close** in the Show Table dialog box.

Three tables are added to the query.

c. Double-click the following fields to add them to the query design grid: **LastName**, **FirstName**, **Balance**, and **Location**.

d. Type **<=1000** in the Criteria row of the Balance column.

e. Click **Run** in the Results group to see the query results.

Six records that have a balance of $1,000 or less display.

f. Click **Save** on the Quick Access Toolbar and type **Balance 1000 or Less** as the Query Name in the Save As dialog box. Click **OK**.

STEP 3 ›› **MODIFY A MULTITABLE QUERY**

The auditor requests additional changes to the Balance 1000 or Less query you just created. You will modify the criteria to display the accounts that were opened on or after January 1, 2011, with balances of $2,000 or less. Refer to Figure 2.51 as you complete Step 3.

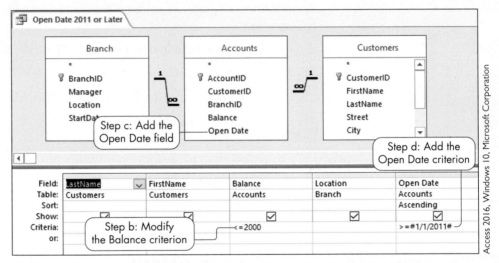

FIGURE 2.51 Query Using the And Condition

a. Click **View** in the Views group to switch the Balance 1000 or Less query to Design view.

b. Type **<=2000** in place of <=1000 in the Criteria row of the Balance field and press **Enter**.

c. Double-click the **Open Date field** in the Accounts table in the top pane of Design view to add it to the first blank column in the design grid.

d. Type **>=1/1/2011** in the Criteria row of the Open Date field and press **Enter** to extract only accounts that have been opened since January 1, 2011.

After you type the expression and then move to a different column, Access will add the # symbols around the date automatically.

e. Click **Run** in the Results group to display the results of the query.

Five records display in the query results.

f. Click the **File tab**, click **Save As**, click **Save Object As**, and then click **Save As**. Type **Open Date 2011 or Later** as the query name. Click **OK**.

g. Click **View** in the Views group to return to Design view of the copied query.

h. Click in the **Sort row** of the Open Date field and select **Ascending**.

i. Click **Run** in the Results group.

The records are sorted from the earliest open date on or after January 1, 2011, to the most recent open date.

j. Save and close the query.

STEP 4 » SUMMARIZE DATA USING A MULTITABLE QUERY

The auditor wants to know the number of accounts each customer has opened. You create a query using a Total row to obtain these data. Refer to Figure 2.52 as you complete Step 4.

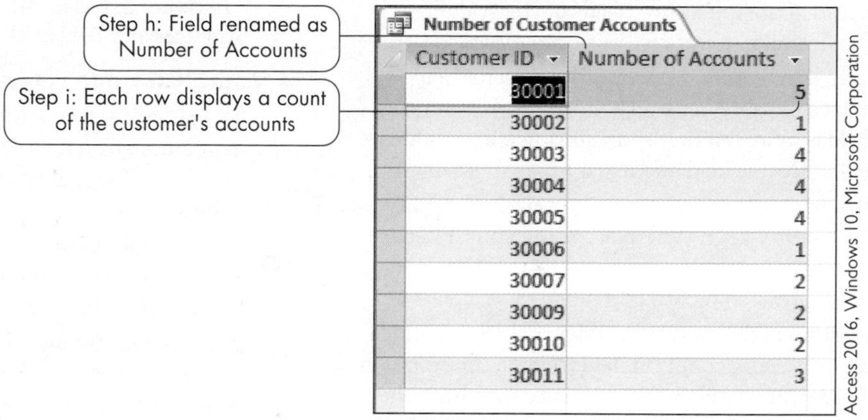

FIGURE 2.52 Number of Accounts per Customer

a. Click the **Create tab** and click **Query Design** in the Queries group.

b. Add the **Accounts table** and the **Customers table** to the top section of Design view. Click **Close** in the Show Table dialog box.

c. Double-click the **CustomerID** in the Customers table in the top section of Design view to add it to the first blank column in the design grid, and double-click the **AccountID** in the Accounts table to add it to the second column.

d. Click **Run** in the Results group.

The results show there are 28 records. Every account a customer has opened is displayed. The auditor wants only the total number of accounts a customer has, so you modify the query.

e. Click **View** in the Views group to return to Design view of the query.

f. Click **Totals** in the Show/Hide group.

Both columns show the Group By option in the Total row.

g. Click **Group By** in the Total row of the AccountID field and select **Count**.

h. Modify the AccountID field to read **Number of Accounts: AccountID**.

You typed a new field name followed by a colon that will display Number of Accounts in the datasheet when you run the query.

i. Click **Run** in the Results group. Resize the columns of the datasheet to fully display the results.

The results show one row for each customer and the number of accounts each customer has opened since the database was created.

j. Click **Save** on the Quick Access Toolbar and type **Number of Customer Accounts** as the query name. Close the query.

k. Close the database and exit Access. Based on your instructor's directions, submit a02h4Bank_LastFirst.

Chapter Objectives Review

After reading this chapter, you have accomplished the following objectives:

1. Design a table.

- Include necessary data: Consider the output requirements when creating table structure. Determine the data required to produce the expected information.
- Design for now and for the future: When designing a database, anticipate the future needs of the system and build in the flexibility to satisfy those demands.
- Store data in their smallest parts: Store data in their smallest parts for more flexibility. Storing a full name in a Name field is more limiting than storing a first name in a separate FirstName field and a last name in a separate LastName field.
- Determine primary keys: When designing your database tables, it is important to determine which field will uniquely identify each record in a table.
- Plan for common fields between tables: Tables are joined in relationships using common fields. Name the common fields with the same name and make sure they have the same data type.
- Design to accommodate calculations: Calculated fields are frequently created with numeric data. You can use date arithmetic to subtract one date from another to find the number of days, months, or years that have elapsed between them.

2. Create and modify tables and work with data.

- You can create tables in Datasheet view or Design view. Alternatively, you can import data from another database or an application such as Excel to create tables in an Access database.
- Determine data type: Data type properties determine the type of data that can be entered and the operations that can be performed on that data. Access recognizes 12 data types.
- Set a table's primary key: The primary key is the field that uniquely identifies each record in a table.
- Explore a foreign key: A foreign key is a field in one table that is also the primary key of another table.
- Work with field properties: Field properties determine how the field looks and behaves. Examples of field properties are the Field Size property and the Caption property.
- Create a new field in Design view: It may be necessary to add table fields that were not included in the original design process. While it is possible to add fields in Datasheet view, Design view offers more flexibility.
- Modify the table in Datasheet view: Datasheet view is used to add, edit, and delete records. Design view is used to create and modify the table structure by enabling you to add and edit fields and set field properties.

3. Share data.

- Import Excel data: You can import data from other applications such as an Excel spreadsheet.

- Import Access data: You can import data from another database by using the Import Wizard.
- Modify an imported table's design and add data: After importing a table, examine the design and make necessary modifications. Modifications may include changing a field name, adding new fields, or deleting unnecessary fields.

4. Establish table relationships.

- Use Show Table to add tables to the Relationships window. Drag a field name from one table to the corresponding field name in another table to join the tables.
- Enforce referential integrity: Referential integrity enforces rules in a database that are used to preserve relationships between tables when records are changed.
- Set cascade options: The Cascade Update Related Fields option ensures that when the primary key is modified in a primary table, Access will automatically update all foreign key values in a related table. The Cascade Delete Related Records option ensures that when the primary key is deleted in a primary table, Access will automatically delete all records in related tables that reference the primary key.
- Establish a one-to-many relationship: A one-to-many relationship is established when the primary key value in the primary table can match many of the foreign key values in the related table. One-to-one and many-to-many are also relationship possibilities, but one-to-many relationships are the most common.

5. Create a single-table query.

- Create a single-table select query: A single-table select query uses fields from one table to display only those records that match certain criteria.
- Use Query Design view: Use Query Design view to create and modify a query. The top portion of the view contains tables with their respective field names and displays the join lines between tables. The bottom portion, known as the query design grid, contains columns and rows that you use to control the query results.

6. Use the Query Wizard.

- The Query Wizard is an alternative method for creating queries. It enables you to select tables and fields from lists. The last step of the wizard prompts you to save the query.

7. Specify query criteria for different data types.

- Different data types require different syntax. Date fields are enclosed in pound signs (#) and text fields in quotations (" "). Numeric and currency fields require no delimiters.
- Use wildcards: Wildcards are special characters that can represent one or more characters in a text value. A question mark (?) is a wildcard that stands for a

single character in the same position as the question mark, while an asterisk (*) is a wildcard that stands for any number of characters in the same position as the asterisk.

- Use comparison operators in queries: Comparison operators such as equal (=), not equal (<>), greater than (>), less than (<), greater than or equal to (>=), and less than or equal to (<=) can be used in the criteria of a query to limit the query results to only those records that meet the criteria.

- Work with null: Access uses the term null for a blank field. Null criteria can be used to find missing information.

- Establish AND, OR, and NOT criteria: The AND, OR, and NOT conditions are used when queries require logical criteria. The AND condition returns only records that meet all criteria. The OR condition returns records meeting any of the specified criteria. The NOT logical operator returns all records except the specified criteria.

8. Understand query sort order.

- The query sort order determines the order of records in a query's Datasheet view. You can change the order of records by specifying the sort order in Design view.

- The sort order is determined from the order of the fields from left to right. Move the field columns to position them in left to right sort order.

9. Run, copy, and modify a query.

- Run a query: To obtain the results for a query, you must run the query. To run the query, click Run in the Results group in Design view. Another method is to locate the query in the Navigation Pane and double-click it. A similar method is to select the query and press Enter.

- Copy and modify a query: To save time, after specifying tables, fields, and conditions for one query, copy the query, rename it, and then modify the fields and criteria in the second query.

- Change query data: You can correct an error immediately while data is displayed in the query datasheet. Use caution when editing records in query results because you will be changing the original table data.

10. Create a multitable query.

- Add additional tables to a query: Open the Navigation Pane and drag the tables from the Navigation Pane directly into the top section of Query Design view.

- Create a multitable query: Multitable queries contain two or more tables enabling you to take advantage of the relationships that have been set in your database.

11. Modify a multitable query.

- Add and delete fields in a multitable query: Multitable queries may need to be modified. Add fields by double-clicking the field name in the table you want; remove fields by clicking the column selector and pressing Delete.

- Add join lines in a multitable query: If the tables have a common field, create join lines by dragging the field name of one common field onto the field name of the other table. Or you can add an additional table that will provide a join between all three tables.

- Summarize data using a multitable query: Use the total row options of a field such as Count to get answers.

Key Terms Matching

Match the key terms with their definitions. Write the key term letter by the appropriate numbered definition.

a. AND condition

b. AutoNumber

c. Caption property

d. Cascade Delete Related Records

e. Cascade Update Related Fields

f. Comparison Operator

g. Criteria row

h. Data redundancy

i. Data type

j. Field property

k. Foreign key

l. Multitable query

m. Null

n. One-to-many relationship

o. OR condition

p. Query

q. Referential Integrity

r. Simple Query Wizard

s. Wildcard

1. _____ Special character that can represent one or more characters in the criterion of a query. **p. 179**

2. _____ Characteristic of a field that determines how it looks and behaves. **p. 147**

3. _____ Returns only records that meet all criteria. **p. 180**

4. _____ A row in the Query Design view that determines which records will be selected. **p. 174**

5. _____ Determines the type of data that can be entered and the operations that can be performed on that data. **p. 145**

6. _____ Used to create a more understandable label than a field name label that displays in the top row in Datasheet view and in forms and reports. **p. 148**

7. _____ Enables you to ask questions about the data stored in a database and provides answers to the questions in a datasheet. **p. 173**

8. _____ The term Access uses to describe a blank field. **p. 180**

9. _____ A number that automatically increments each time a record is added. **p. 146**

10. _____ The unnecessary storing of duplicate data in two or more tables. **p. 143**

11. _____ When the primary key value in the primary table can match many of the foreign key values in the related table. **p. 162**

12. _____ A field in one table that is also the primary key of another table. **p. 147**

13. _____ An option that directs Access to automatically update all foreign key values in a related table when the primary key value is modified in a primary table. **p. 162**

14. _____ Rules in a database that are used to preserve relationships between tables when records are changed. **p. 161**

15. _____ Contains two or more tables, enabling you to take advantage of the relationships that have been set in your database. **p. 188**

16. _____ Returns records meeting any of the specified criteria. **p. 180**

17. _____ Provides a step-by-step guide to help you through the query design process. **p. 176**

18. _____ When the primary key value is deleted in a primary table, Access will automatically delete all foreign key values in a related table. **p. 162**

19. _____ Uses greater than (>), less than (<), greater than or equal to (>=), and less than or equal to (<=), etc. to limit query results that meet these criteria. **p. 180**

Multiple Choice

1. All of the following are suggested guidelines for table design *except*:
   - (a) Include all necessary data.
   - (b) Store data in its smallest parts.
   - (c) Avoid date arithmetic.
   - (d) Link tables using common fields.

2. Which of the following determines how the field names can be made more readable in table and query datasheets?
   - (a) Field size
   - (b) Data type
   - (c) Caption property
   - (d) Normalization

3. When entering, deleting, or editing input masks:
   - (a) The table must be in Design view.
   - (b) The table must be in Datasheet view.
   - (c) The table may be in either Datasheet or Design view.
   - (d) Data may only be entered in a form.

4. With respect to importing data into Access, which of the following statements is *true*?
   - (a) The Import Wizard works only for Excel files.
   - (b) The Import Wizard is found on the Create tab.
   - (c) You can assign a primary key while you are importing Excel data.
   - (d) Imported table designs cannot be modified in Access.

5. The main reason to set a field size in Access is to:
   - (a) Limit the length of values in a table.
   - (b) Make it possible to delete records.
   - (c) Keep your database safe from unauthorized users.
   - (d) Keep misspelled data from being entered into a table.

6. An illustration of a one-to-many relationship would be:
   - (a) An employee listed in the Employees table earns a raise so the Salaries table must be updated.
   - (b) A customer may have more than one account in an accounts table.
   - (c) Each employee in an Employees table has a matching entry in the Salaries table.
   - (d) An employee leaves the company so that when he is deleted from the Employees table, his salary data will be deleted from the Salaries table.

7. A query's specifications as to which tables to include must be entered on the:
   - (a) Table row of the query design grid.
   - (b) Show row of the query design grid.
   - (c) Sort row of the query design grid.
   - (d) Criteria row of the query design grid.

8. When adding date criteria to the Query Design view, the dates you enter must be delimited by:
   - (a) Parentheses ().
   - (b) Pound signs (#).
   - (c) Quotes (" ").
   - (d) At signs (@).

9. It is more efficient to make a copy of an existing query rather than to create a new query when which of the following is *true*?
   - (a) The existing query contains only one table.
   - (b) The existing query and the new query use the same tables and fields.
   - (c) The existing query and the new query have the exact same criteria.
   - (d) The original query is no longer being used.

10. Which of the following is *true* for the Query Wizard?
    - (a) No criteria can be added as you step through the Wizard.
    - (b) You can only select related tables as a source.
    - (c) Fields with different data types are not allowed.
    - (d) You are required to summarize the data.

Practice Exercises

1 Philadelphia Bookstore

FROM SCRATCH Tom and Erin Mullaney own and operate a bookstore in Philadelphia, Pennsylvania. Erin asked you to help her create an Access database to store the publishers and the books that they sell. The data for the publishers and books is currently stored in Excel worksheets that you decide to import into a new database. You determine that a third table—for authors—is also required. Your task is to create and populate the three tables, set the table relationships, and enforce referential integrity. You will then create queries to extract information from the tables. Refer to Figure 2.53 as you complete this exercise.

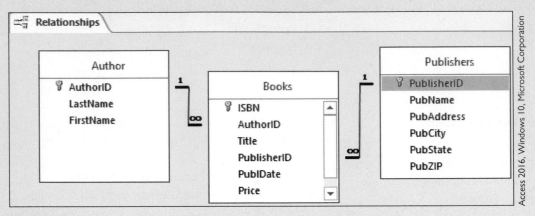

FIGURE 2.53 Books Relationships Window

a. Open Access and click **Blank desktop database**. Type **a02p1Books_LastFirst** in the **File Name box**. Click **Browse** to navigate to the location where you are saving your files in the File New Database dialog box, click **OK** to close the dialog box, and then click **Create** to create the new database.

b. Type **11** in the Click to Add column and click **Click to Add**. The field name becomes Field1, and *Click to Add* now displays as the third column. In the third column, type **Beschloss**, and then press **Tab**. Repeat the process for the fourth column; type **Michael R.** and press **Tab** two times. The insertion point returns to the first column where (New) is selected.

c. Press **Tab**. Type the rest of the data using the following table. These data will become the records of the Author table.

ID	Field1	Field2	Field3
1	11	Beschloss	Michael R.
(New)	12	**Turow**	**Scott**
	13	**Rice**	**Anne**
	14	**King**	**Stephen**
	15	**Connelly**	**Michael**
	16	**Rice**	**Luanne**
	17	*your last name*	*your first name*

d. Click **Save** on the Quick Access Toolbar. Type **Author** in the Save As dialog box and click **OK**.

e. Click **View** in the Views group to switch to Design view of the Author table.

f. Select **Field1**—in the second row—in the top portion of the table design and type **AuthorID** to rename the field. In the Field Properties section in the lower pane of the table design, type **Author ID** in the Caption box and verify that Long Integer displays for the Field Size property.

g. Select **Field2** and type **LastName** to rename the field. In the Field Properties section in the bottom portion of Design view, type **Author's Last Name** in the Caption box and type **20** as the field size.

h. Select **Field3** and type **FirstName** to rename the field. In the Field Properties section in the bottom portion of the table design, type **Author's First Name** as the caption and type **15** as the field size.

i. Click the **ID field row selector** (which displays the primary key) to select the row, and then click **Delete Rows** in the Tools group. Click **Yes** two times to confirm both messages.

j. Click the **AuthorID row selector**, and then click **Primary Key** in the Tools group to set the primary key.

k. Click **Save** on the Quick Access Toolbar to save the design changes. Click **Yes** to the *Some data may be lost* message. Close the table.

l. Click the **External Data tab** and click **Excel** in the Import & Link group to launch the Get External Data – Excel Spreadsheet feature. Verify that the *Import the source data into a new table in the current database* option is selected, click **Browse**, and then navigate to your student data folder. Select the *a02p1Books* workbook, click **Open**, and then click **OK**. This workbook contains two worksheets. Follow the steps below:

- Select the **Publishers worksheet** and click **Next**.
- Click the **First Row Contains Column Headings check box** to select it and click **Next**.
- Ensure that the PubID field is selected, click the **Indexed arrow**, select **Yes (No Duplicates)**, and then click **Next**.
- Click the **Choose my own primary key arrow**, ensure that PubID is selected, and then click **Next**.
- Accept the name Publishers for the table name, click **Finish**, and then click **Close** without saving the import steps.

m. Use the Import Wizard again to import the Books worksheet from the *a02p1Books* workbook into the Access database. Follow the steps below:

- Ensure that the Books worksheet is selected and click **Next**.
- Click the **First Row Contains Column Headings check box** to select it, and click **Next**.
- Click the **ISBN column**, click the down arrow, set the Indexed property box to **Yes (No Duplicates)**, and then click **Next**.
- Click the **Choose my own primary key arrow**, select **ISBN** as the primary key field, and then click **Next**.
- Accept the name Books as the table name. Click **Finish** and click **Close** without saving the import steps.

n. Right-click the **Books table** in the Navigation Pane and select **Design View**. Make the following changes:

- Click the **PubID field** and change the name to **PublisherID**.
- Set the caption property to **Publisher ID**.
- Change the PublisherID Field Size property to **2**.
- Click the **ISBN field** and change the Field Size property to **13**.
- Change the AuthorCode field name to **AuthorID**.
- Change the AuthorID Field Size property to **Long Integer**.
- Click the **ISBN field row selector** (which displays the primary key) to select the row. Click and drag to move the row up to the first position in the table design.
- Click **Save** on the Quick Access Toolbar to save the design changes to the Books table. Click **Yes** to the *Some data may be lost* warning.
- Close the table.

o. Right-click the **Publishers table** in the Navigation Pane and select **Design View**. Make the following changes:

- Click the **PubID field** and change the name to **PublisherID**.
- Change the PublisherID Field Size property to **2**.
- Change the Caption property to **Publisher's ID**.
- Change the Field Size property to **50** for the PubName and PubAddress fields.

- Change the Pub Address field name to **PubAddress** (remove the space).
- Change the PubCity Field Size property to **30**.
- Change the PubState Field Size property to **2**.
- Change the Pub ZIP field name to **PubZIP** (remove the space).
- Click **Save** on the Quick Access Toolbar to save the design changes to the Publishers table. Click **Yes** to the *Some data may be lost* warning. Close all open tables.

p. Click the **Database Tools tab** and click **Relationships** in the Relationships group. Click **Show Table**, if the Show Table dialog box does not open automatically. Follow the steps below:
- Double-click each table name in the Show Table dialog box to add it to the Relationships window and close the Show Table dialog box.
- Drag the **AuthorID field** from the Author table onto the AuthorID field in the Books table.
- Click the **Enforce Referential Integrity** and **Cascade Update Related Fields check boxes** in the Edit Relationships dialog box to select them. Click **Create** to create a one-to-many relationship between the Author and Books tables.
- Drag the **PublisherID field** from the Publishers table onto the PublisherID field in the Books table.
- Click the **Enforce Referential Integrity** and **Cascade Update Related Fields check boxes** in the Edit Relationships dialog box to select them. Click **Create** to create a one-to-many relationship between the Publishers and Books tables.
- Click **Save** on the Quick Access Toolbar to save the changes to the Relationships window, then in the Relationships group, click **Close**.

q. Click the **Create tab**, and then click **Query Wizard** in the Queries group. With Simple Query Wizard selected, click **OK**.
- Select the Publishers table, double-click to add **PubName**, **PubCity**, and **PubState** to the Selected Fields list. Click **Next**, and then click **Finish**. In Datasheet view, double-click the border to the right of each column to set the column widths to Best Fit. Click **Save** on the Quick Access Toolbar.

r. Click the **File tab**, click **Save As**, and then double-click **Save Object As**. Modify the copied query name to **New York Publishers Query**, and then click **OK**.
- Click **View** in the Views group on the Home tab to switch to Design view of the query. Click and drag the **Books table** from the Navigation Pane into the top pane of the query design window.
- Select the Books table, double-click **Title** and **PublDate** to add the fields to the query design grid.
- Click in the Criteria row of the PubState field, and type **NY**. Click the **Sort** cell of the PublDate field, click the arrow, and then click **Descending**.
- Click **Run** in the Results group (12 records display in the Datasheet sorted by PublDate in descending order). Double-click the border to the right of each column to set the column widths to Best Fit.
- Save and close the query.

s. Close the database and exit Access. Based on your instructor's directions, submit a02p1Books_LastFirst.

2 Employee Salary Analysis

The Morgan Insurance Company offers a full range of insurance services. They store all of the firm's employee data in an Access database. This file contains each employee's name and address, job performance, salary, and title, but needs to be imported into a different existing database. A database file containing two of the tables (Location and Titles) already exists; your job is to import the employee data from Access to create the third table. Once imported, you will modify field properties and set new relationships. The owner of the company, Victor Reed, is concerned that some of the Atlanta and Boston salaries may be below the guidelines published by the national office. He asks that you investigate the salaries of the two offices and create a separate query for each city. Refer to Figure 2.54 as you complete this exercise.

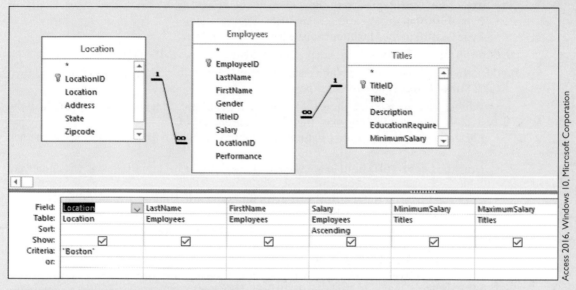

FIGURE 2.54 Boston Salaries Query Design

a. Open *a02p2Insurance* and save it as **a02p2Insurance_LastFirst**. Double-click the **Location table** and review the data to become familiar with the field names and the type of information stored in the table. Review the Titles table. Close both tables.

b. Click the **External Data tab**, click **Access** in the Import & Link group, and then complete the following steps:
  - Click **Browse** and navigate to the *a02p2Employees* database in the location of your student data files. Select the file, click **Open**.
  - Click **OK** in the Get External Data – Access Database dialog box.
  - Select the **Employees table**, and then click **OK**.
  - Click **Close** without saving the import steps.

c. Double-click the **Employees table** in the Navigation Pane, then click **View** in the Views group on the Home tab to switch to Design view of the Employees table. Make the following changes:
  - Ensure that the EmployeeID field is selected, and then click **Primary Key** in the Tools group.
  - Click the **LastName field** and change the Field Size property to **20**.
  - Change the Caption property to **Last Name**.
  - Click the **FirstName field** and change the Field Size property to **20**.
  - Change the Caption property to **First Name**.
  - Click the **LocationID field** and change the Field Size property to **3**.
  - Change the Caption property to **Location ID**.
  - Click the **TitleID field** and change the Field Size property to **3**.
  - Change the Caption property to **Title ID**.
  - Change the Salary field data type to **Currency** and change General Number in the Format property in field properties to **Currency**.
  - Save the design changes. Click **Yes** to the *Some data may be lost* warning.

d. Click **View** in the Views group to view the Employees table in Datasheet view and examine the data. Click any record in the Title ID and then click **Ascending** in the Sort & Filter group on the Home tab. Multiple employees are associated with the T01, T02, T03, and T04 titles.

e. Double-click the **Titles table** in the Navigation Pane to open it in Datasheet view. Notice that the T04 title is not in the list.

f. Add a new record in the first blank record at the bottom of the Titles table. Use the following data:
- Type **T04** in the TitleID field.
- Type **Senior Account Rep** in the Title field.
- Type **A marketing position requiring a technical background and at least three years of experience** in the Description field.
- Type **Four year degree** in the Education Requirements field.
- Type **45000** in the Minimum Salary field.
- Type **75000** in the Maximum Salary field.

g. Close all tables. Click **Yes** if you are prompted to save changes to the Employees table.

h. Click the **Database Tools tab** and click **Relationships** in the Relationships group, and then Click **Show Table**. Follow the steps below:
- Double-click each of the three table names in the Show Table dialog box to add it to the Relationships window and close the Show Table dialog box.
- Click and drag to adjust the height of the Employees table so that all fields display in each one.
- Drag the **LocationID field** in the Location table onto the LocationID field in the Employees table.
- Click the **Enforce Referential Integrity** and **Cascade Update Related Fields check boxes** in the Edit Relationships dialog box to select them. Click **Create** to create a one-to-many relationship between the Location and Employees tables.
- Drag the **TitleID field** in the Titles table onto the TitleID field in the Employees table (move the field lists by clicking and dragging their title bars as needed so that they do not overlap).
- Click the **Enforce Referential Integrity** and **Cascade Update Related Fields check boxes** in the Edit Relationships dialog box to select it. Click **Create** to create a one-to-many relationship between the Titles and Employees tables.
- Click **Save** on the Quick Access Toolbar to save the changes to the Relationships window and close the Relationships window.

i. Click the **Create tab** and click the **Query Wizard** in the Queries group. Follow the steps below:
- Select **Simple Query Wizard** and click **OK**.
- Select **Table: Employees** in the Tables/Queries box.
- Double-click **LastName** in the Available Fields list to move it to the Selected Fields list.
- Double-click **FirstName** in the Available Fields list to move it to the Selected Fields list.
- Double-click **LocationID** in the Available Fields list to move it to the Selected Fields list.
- Click **Next**.
- Type **Employees Location** as the query title and click **Finish**.
- Click **View** in the Views group on the Home tab to switch to Design view of the query. Click and drag the **Titles** table from the Navigation Pane into the top pane of the query design window.
- Double-click **Title** in the Titles table to add the field to the query design grid.
- Click the **Sort** cell of the LocationID field, click the arrow, and then click **Ascending**.
- Click **Run** in the Results group (311 records display in the Datasheet sorted by LocationID in ascending order). Double-click the border to the right of each column to set the column widths to Best Fit.
- Save and close the query.

j. Click the **Create tab** and click the **Query Wizard** in the Queries group. Follow the steps below:
- Select **Simple Query Wizard** and click **OK**.
- Select **Table: Location** in the Tables/Queries box.
- Double-click **Location** in the Available Fields list to move it to the Selected Fields list.
- Select **Table: Employees** in the Tables/Queries box.

- Double-click **LastName**, **FirstName**, and **Salary**.
- Select **Table: Titles** in the Tables/Queries box.
- Double-click **MinimumSalary** and **MaximumSalary**. Click **Next**.
- Ensure that the *Detail (shows every field of every record)* option is selected, and click **Next**.
- Type **Atlanta Salaries** as the query title and click **Finish**.

k. Click **View** in the Views group on the Home tab to switch to Design view of the Atlanta Salaries query.

- Click in the Criteria row of the Location field, and type **Atlanta**. Click the **Sort cell** of the Salary field, click the arrow, and then click **Ascending**.
- Click **Run** in the Results group. Review the data to determine if any of the Atlanta employees have a salary less than the minimum or greater than the maximum when compared to the published salary range. These salaries will be updated later.
- Save and close the query.

l. Right-click the **Atlanta Salaries query** in the Navigation Pane and from the shortcut menu, select **Copy**. Right-click a blank area in the Navigation Pane and select **Paste**. In the Paste As dialog box, type **Boston Salaries** for the query name. Click **OK**.

m. Right-click the **Boston Salaries query** in the Navigation Pane and select **Design View**. In the Criteria row of the Location field, replace Atlanta with **Boston**.

- Click **Run** in the Results group. Review the data to determine if any of the Boston employees have a salary less than the minimum or greater than the maximum when compared to the published salary range.
- Modify some data that have been incorrectly entered. In the query results, for the first employee, Frank Cusack, change the salary to **$48,700.00**; for Brian Beamer, **$45,900.00**; for Lorna Weber, **$45,700.00**; for Penny Pfleger, **$45,800.00**.
- Save and close the query.

n. Close the database and exit Access. Based on your instructor's directions, submit a02p2Insurance_LastFirst.

Mid-Level Exercises

1 My Game Collection

Over the years, you have collected quite a few video games, so you have cataloged them in an Access database, in the Games table. After opening the database, you will create two more tables—one to identify the game system (System) that runs your game and the other to identify the category or genre of the game (Category). Then, you will join each table in a relationship so that you can query the database.

a. Open *a02m1Games* and save the database as **a02m1Games_LastFirst**. Open the Games table and review the fields containing the game information. Close the table.

b. Click the **Create tab** and click **Table Design** in the Tables group.

c. Type **SystemID** for the first Field Name and select **AutoNumber** as the Data Type.

d. Type **SystemName** for the second Field Name and accept **Short Text** as the Data Type.

e. Set **SystemID** as the primary key. Add the caption **System ID**.

f. Change the SystemName Field Size property to **15**. Add the caption **System Name**, making sure there is a space between System and Name. Save the table as **System**. Switch to Datasheet view.

g. Add the system names to the System table as shown below, letting Access use AutoNumber to create the SystemID values. Close the table when finished.

System ID	System Name
1	XBOX 360
2	PS3
3	Wii
4	NES
5	PC Game
6	Nintendo 3DS

h. Click the **Create tab** and click **Table Design** in the Tables group. Type **CategoryID** for the first Field Name and select **AutoNumber** as the Data Type. Set the CategoryID as the primary key.

i. Type **CategoryDescription** for the second Field Name and accept **Short Text** as the Data Type. Change the Field Size property to **25**. Add the caption **Category Description**, making sure there is a space between Category and Description. Save the table as **Category**, saving the changes to the table design. Switch to Datasheet view.

j. Add the category descriptions to the Category table as shown below, letting Access use AutoNumber to create the CategoryID values. Close the table when finished.

CategoryID	Category Description
1	Action
2	Adventure
3	Arcade
4	Racing
5	Rhythm
6	Role-playing
7	Simulation
8	Sports

k. Click the **Database Tools tab** and click **Relationships** in the Relationships group. Display all three tables in the Relationships window and close the Show Table dialog box. Create a one-to-many relationship between CategoryID in the Category table and CategoryID in the Games table. Enforce referential integrity and cascade update related fields.

l. Create a one-to-many relationship between SystemID in the System table and SystemID in the Games table. Enforce referential integrity and cascade update related fields. Close the Relationships window, saving the changes.

m. Use the Query Wizard to create a simple query using the Games table. Add the following fields in the query (in this order): GameName, Rating. Save the query as **Ratings Query**.

n. Switch to Design view. Sort the Rating field in ascending order and run the query. Close the query, saving the changes.

o. Create a multitable query in Design view using all three tables. Add the following fields (in this order): GameName, CategoryDescription, Rating, SystemName, and DateAcquired.

p. Sort the query in ascending order by GameName and run the query. Save the query as **Game List Query** and close the query.

q. Copy the **Game List Query** and paste it into the Navigation Pane using the name **PS3 Games**. Modify the query in Design view by using **PS3** as the criterion for SystemName. Remove the sort by GameName and sort in ascending order by Rating. The query results should include 7 records.

r. Close the PS3 Games query, saving the changes. Assume you are going home for Thanksgiving and you want to take your **Wii** gaming system and games home with you—but you only want to take home games with a rating of **Everyone**.

s. Create a query named **Thanksgiving Games** that shows the name of the game, its rating, the category description of the game, and the system name for each. Run the query. The results of the query will tell you which games to pack. Close the query.

t. Close the database and exit Access. Based on your instructor's directions, submit a02m1Games_LastFirst.

2 The Prestige Hotel

The Prestige Hotel chain caters to upscale business travelers and provides state-of-the-art conference, meeting, and reception facilities. It prides itself on its international, four-star cuisine. Last year, it began a member reward club to help the marketing department track the purchasing patterns of its most loyal customers. All of the hotel transactions are stored in the database. Your task is to help the managers of the Prestige Hotels in Denver and Chicago identify their customers who stayed in a room last year and who had three persons in their party.

a. Open *a02m2Hotel* and save the file as **a02m2Hotel_LastFirst**. Review the data contained in the three tables. Specifically, study the tables and fields containing the data you need to analyze: dates of stays in Denver and Chicago suites, the members' names, and the numbers in the parties.

b. Import the location data from the Excel file *a02m2Location* into your database as a new table. The first row of the worksheet contains column headings. Set the LocationID Indexed property to **Yes (No Duplicates)** and set the Data Type to **Long Integer**. Select the **LocationID field** as the primary key. Name the table **Location**. Do not save the import steps.

c. Open the Relationships window and create a relationship between the Location table and the Orders table using the LocationID field. Enforce referential integrity and cascade update related fields. Create a relationship between the Orders and Members tables using the MemNumber field, ensuring that you enforce referential integrity and cascade update related fields. Create a relationship between the Orders and Service tables using the ServiceID field, ensuring that you enforce referential integrity and cascade update related fields. Save and close the Relationships window.

d. Open the Members table and use the Find command to locate Bryan Gray's name. Replace his name with your own first and last names. Locate Nicole Lee's name and replace it with your name. Close the table.

e. Create a query using the following fields: ServiceDate (Orders table), City (Location table), NoInParty (Orders table), ServiceName (Service table), FirstName (Members table), and LastName (Members table). Set the criteria to limit the output to **Denver**. Use the Between operator to show services only from **7/1/2017** to **6/30/2018**. Set the NoInParty criterion to **3**. Sort the results in ascending order by the ServiceDate.

f. Run the query and examine the number of records in the status bar at the bottom of the query. It should display 155. If your number of records is different, examine the criteria and make corrections.

g. Change the order of the query fields so that they display as FirstName, LastName, ServiceDate, City, NoInParty, and ServiceName. Save the query as **Denver Rooms 3 Guests**. Close the query.

DISCOVER

h. Copy the **Denver Rooms 3 Guests** query and paste it, renaming the new query **Chicago Rooms 3 Guests**.

i. Open the Chicago Rooms 3 Guests query in Design view and change the criterion for City to **Chicago**. Run the query and save the changes. It should display 179 results. Close the query.

DISCOVER

j. Review the criteria of the two previous queries and then create a third query named **Denver and Chicago Rooms 3 Guests**. Use the criteria from the two individual queries as a basis to create a combination AND–OR condition. The results will display guests in **Denver** or **Chicago** with **3** guests and service dates between **7/1/2013** and **6/30/2018**. The records returned in the results should equal the sum of the records in the two individual queries (334 records). Run, save, and close the query.

k. Close the database and exit Access. Based on your instructor's directions, submit a02m2Hotel_LastFirst.

3 New Castle County Technical Services

RUNNING CASE

New Castle County Technical Services (NCCTS) provides technical support for a number of companies in the greater New Castle County, Delaware area. Once you have completed the changes to the database tables and set the appropriate relationships, you will be ready to extract information by creating queries.

a. Open the database *a01m3NCCTS_LastFirst* and save it as a02m3NCCTS_LastFirst changing 01 to 02.

> **TROUBLESHOOTING:** If you did not complete the Chapter 1 case, return to Chapter 1, complete the case to create the database, and then return to this exercise.

b. Open the Call Types table in Design view. Before you create your queries, you want to modify some of the table properties:
  - Set the caption of the HourlyRate field to **Hourly Rate**.
  - View the table in Datasheet view, and save the changes when prompted.

c. Close the table.

d. Make the following additional changes to the tables:
  - Open the Calls table in Design view. Change the data type of the CallTypeID field to **Number**.
  - Set the caption of the HoursLogged field to **Hours Logged**.
  - Set the caption of the OpenedDate field to **Opened Date** and set the format to **Short Date**.
  - Set the caption of the ClosedDate field to **Closed Date** and set the format to **Short Date**.
  - Set the caption of the CustomerSatisfaction field to **Customer Satisfaction**.
  - View the table in Datasheet view, and save the changes when prompted. You will not lose any data by making this change, so click **Yes** in the message box when prompted. Close the table.
  - Open the Customers table in Design view. Set the field size of CompanyName to **50** and the caption to **Company Name**. View the table in Datasheet view, and save the changes when prompted. You will not lose any data by making this change, so click **Yes** in the message box when prompted. Close the table.
  - Open the Reps table in Design view. Set the caption of the RepFirst field to **Rep First Name**. Set the caption of the RepLast field to **Rep Last Name**. View the table in Datasheet view, and save the changes when prompted. Close the table.

e. Open the Relationships window. Create a join line between the Call Types and Calls tables, ensuring that you enforce referential integrity and cascade update related fields. Set a relationship between Reps and Calls and between Customers and Calls using the same options. Save and close the Relationships window.

f. Create a multitable query, following the steps below:
- Add the following fields (in this order): **CallID** (from Calls), **Description** (from Call Types), **CompanyName** (from Customers), and **RepFirst** and **RepLast** (from Reps).
- Run the query, and then modify it to add **HoursLogged** (from Calls).
- Sort the query by HoursLogged in ascending order. Set the criteria of the HoursLogged field to **Is Not Null** and run the query again.
- Modify the criteria of the HoursLogged field to **>=5** and **<=10**, the description to **Disaster Recovery**, and the rep to **Barbara**.
- Save the query as **Complex Disaster Recovery Calls_Barbara**. Run and then close the query.

g. Create a copy of the **Complex Disaster Recovery Calls_Barbara** query, and modify it following the steps below:
- Save the copy of the query as **Complex Network Installation Calls_Barbara**.
- Modify the query so that the description displays Barbara's network installation calls that logged between 5 and 10 hours.
- Save, run, and then close the query.

h. Close the database and exit Access. Based on your instructor's directions, submit a02m3NCCTS_LastFirst.

Beyond the Classroom

Database
Administrator
Position

GENERAL
CASE

FROM
SCRATCH

Create a database to keep track of candidates for open positions at Secure Systems, Inc., database management experts. Use the Internet to search for information about database management positions. One useful site is published by the federal government's Bureau of Labor Statistics. It compiles an Occupational Outlook Handbook describing various positions, the type of working environment, the education required, salary information, and the projected growth. The website is http://www.bls.gov/ooh. Research the necessary information in order to create the database using these requirements:

a. Create a new database named **a02b1Admin_LastFirst**.

b. Create three tables including the field names as follows, and in the specified orders:

- **Candidates (CandidateID, FirstName, LastName, Phone, Email)**.
- **JobOpenings (JobOpeningID, JobName, RequiredSkill, HourlyPayRate, DataPosted, Supervisor)**.
- **Interviews (InterviewSequenceID, CandidateID, JobOpeningID, InterviewedBy, DateOfInterview, Rank)**.

c. Set the data types, field properties, and a primary key for each table.

d. Set table relationships, and be sure to enforce referential integrity between them. Cascade update related fields

e. Add 10 candidates to the Candidates table.

f. Add a **Database Administrator** job and four other sample jobs to the JobOpenings table.

g. Add eight sample interviews—four for the Database Administrator position and four others. Rank each candidate on a scale of 1 to 5 (with 5 as the highest).

h. Create a query that lists the LastName, FirstName, JobOpeningID, InterviewedBy, DateOfInterview, and Rank fields. Display only Database Administrator interviews with a ranking of 3 or lower. Sort by LastName and then by FirstName. Run and save the query as **Database Admin Low Rank**. Close the query

i. Close the database and exit Access. Based on your instructor's directions, submit a02b1Admin_LastFirst.

A coworker explained that he was having difficulty with queries that were not returning correct results, and asked you to help diagnose the problem. Open *a02b2Traders* and save it as **a02b2Traders_LastFirst**. It contains two queries, *May 2018 Orders of Beverages and Confections* and *2018 Beverage Sales by Ship Country*. The May 2018 Orders of Beverages and Confections query is supposed to contain only information for orders shipped in May 2018. You find other shipped dates included in the results. Change the criteria to exclude the other dates. Run and save the query. Close the query.

The 2018 Beverage Sales by Ship Country query returns no results. Check the criteria in all fields and modify so that the correct results are returned. Run and save the query. Close the query.

Close the database and exit Access. Based on your instructor's directions, submit a02b2Traders_LastFirst.

Capstone Exercise

The Morris Arboretum in Chestnut Hill, Pennsylvania tracks donors in Excel. They also use Excel to store a list of plants in stock. As donors contribute funds to the Arboretum, they can elect to receive a plant gift from the Arboretum. These plants are both rare plants and hard-to-find old favorites, and they are part of the annual appeal and membership drive to benefit the Arboretum's programs. The organization has grown, and the files are too large and inefficient to handle in Excel. You will begin by importing the files from Excel into a new Access database. Then you will create a table to track donations, create a relationship between the two tables, and create some baseline queries.

Create a New Database

You will examine the data in the Excel worksheets to determine which fields will become the primary keys in each table and which fields will become the foreign keys.

a. Open the *a02c1Donors* Excel workbook, examine the data, and close the workbook.

b. Open the *a02c1Plants* Excel workbook, examine the data, and close the workbook.

c. Create a new, blank database named **a02c1Arbor_LastFirst**. Close the new blank table created automatically by Access without saving it.

Import Data from Excel

You will import two Excel workbooks into the database.

a. Click the **External Data tab** and click **Excel** in the Import & Link group.

b. Navigate to and select the *a02c1Donors* workbook to be imported.

c. Select the **First Row Contains Column Headings** option.

d. Set the DonorID field Indexed option to **Yes (No Duplicates)**.

e. Choose **DonorID** as the primary key when prompted and accept the table name Donors.

f. Import the *a02c1Plants* workbook, set the **ID field** as the primary key, and then change the indexing option to **Yes (No Duplicates)**.

g. Accept the table name Plants.

h. Change the ID field name in the Plants table to **PlantID**.

i. Open each table in Datasheet view to examine the data. Close the tables.

Create a New Table

You will create a new table to track the donations as they are received from the donors.

a. You will create a new table in Design view and save the table as **Donations**.

b. Add the following fields in Design view and set the properties as specified:
- Add the primary key field as **DonationID** with the **Number Data Type** and a field size of **Long Integer**.
- Add **DonorID** (a foreign key) with the **Number Data Type** and a field size of **Long Integer**.
- Add **PlantID** (a foreign key) as a **Number** and a field size of **Long Integer**.
- Add **DateOfDonation** as a **Date/Time** field.
- Add **AmountOfDonation** as a **Currency** field.

c. Switch to Datasheet view, and save the table when prompted. You will enter data into the table in a later step. Close the table.

Create Relationships

You will create the relationships between the tables using the Relationships window.

a. Open the Donors table in Design view and change the Field Size property for DonorID to **Long Integer** so it matches the Field Size property of DonorID in the Donations table. Save and close the table.

b. Open the Plants table in Design view and change the Field Size property for PlantID to **Long Integer** so it matches the Field Size property for PlantID in the Donations table. Save and close the table.

c. Identify the primary key fields in the Donors table and the Plants table and join them with their foreign key counterparts in the related Donations table. Enforce referential integrity and cascade and update related fields. Save and close the Relationships window.

Add Sample Data to the Donations Table

You will add 10 records to the Donations table.

a. Add the following records to the Donations table:

Donation ID	Donor ID	Plant ID	Date of Donation	Amount of Donation
10	8228	611	3/1/2018	$150
18	5448	190	3/1/2018	$ 55
6	4091	457	3/12/2018	$125
7	11976	205	3/14/2018	$100
1	1000	25	3/17/2018	$120
12	1444	38	3/19/2018	$ 50
2	1444	38	4/3/2018	$ 50
4	10520	49	4/12/2018	$ 60
5	3072	102	4/19/2018	$ 50
21	1204	25	4/22/2018	$120

b. Sort the Donations table by the AmountOfDonation field in descending order. Close the table.

Use the Query Wizard

You will create a query of all donations greater than $100 in the Donations table.

a. Add the DonorID and AmountOfDonation fields from Donations (in that order).

b. Save the query as **Donations Over 100**.

c. Add criteria to include only donations of more than $100.

d. Sort the query results in ascending order by AmountOfDonation.

e. Run the query.

f. Save and close the query.

Create a Query in Design View

You will create a query that identifies donors and donations.

a. Create a query that identifies the people who made a donation after April 1, 2018. This list will be given to the Arboretum staff so they can notify the donors that a plant is ready for pickup. The query should list the date of the donation, donor's full name (LastName, FirstName), phone number, the amount of the donation, and name of the plant they want (in that order). Add the tables and fields necessary to produce the query.

b. Sort the query by date of donation in descending order, then by donor last name in ascending order.

c. Run, close, and save the query as **Plant Pickup List**.

Copy and Modify a Query in Design View

You will copy a query and modify it to add and sort by a different field.

a. Copy the Plant Pickup List query and paste it using **ENewsletter** as the query name.

b. Open the ENewsletter query in Design view and delete the DateofDonation column.

c. Add the ENewsletter field to the first column of the design grid and set it to sort in ascending order, so that the query sorts first by ENewsletter and then by LastName.

d. Run, save, and close the query. Close the database and exit Access. Based on your instructor's directions, submit a02c1Arbor_LastFirst.

Using Queries to Make Decisions

LEARNING OUTCOME

You will create queries to perform calculations and summarize data.

OBJECTIVES & SKILLS: After you read this chapter, you will be able to:

CASE STUDY | Real Estate Investors

After completing their degrees in Business at Passaic County Community College (PCCC) and a weekend seminar in real estate investing, Donald Carter and Matthew Nevoso were ready to test their skills in the marketplace. Don and Matt had a simple strategy—buy distressed properties at a significant discount, then resell the properties for a profit. Based on their seminar, they knew to gather key information such as the asking price, the number of bedrooms, square feet, and days on the market. Because they are just starting out, they decided to consider less expensive houses.

Based on a tip from the real estate seminar, they decide to create a database using Access, using data from a variety of home listing services. They approached you to help them find houses that meet their criteria. This new database approach should hopefully help them acquire their first investment property.

Perform Calculations and Summarize Data Using Queries

First Name	Last Name	List Price	Square Feet	Listing	Sold	Price Per Sq Ft	Payment
Philip	DeFranco	$109,140.00	1133	10004	No	$96.33	$416.84
Chardae	Myles	$129,780.00	1132	10028	No	$114.65	$495.67
Makarem	Abdeljawad	$136,680.00	1375	10008	No	$99.40	$522.02
Meera	Shah	$138,990.00	1276	10016	No	$108.93	$530.85
StudentFirst	StudentLast	$140,693.00	1490	10069	No	$94.42	$537.35
Makarem	Abdeljawad	$140,904.00	1301	10061	No	$108.30	$538.16
Makarem	Abdeljawad	$142,380.00	1373	11028	No	$103.70	$543.80
Chardae	Myles	$163,737.00	1476	10910	No	$110.93	$625.36
Jaynish	Mody	$164,436.00	1850	10117	No	$88.88	$628.03
Jaynish	Mody	$166,320.00	1437	10082	No	$115.74	$635.23
Chardae	Myles	$166,552.00	1623	10851	No	$102.62	$636.12
Chardae	Myles	$166,800.00	1598	10014	No	$104.38	$637.06
Philip	DeFranco	$168,000.00	1680	10002	No	$100.00	$641.65
Chardae	Myles	$168,354.00	1651	10885	No	$101.97	$643.00
Philip	DeFranco	$174,230.00	1771	10104	No	$98.38	$665.44
StudentFirst	StudentLast	$174,720.00	1610	10921	No	$108.52	$667.31
Meera	Shah	$174,720.00	1694	11035	No	$103.14	$667.31
Chardae	Myles	$175,336.00	1855	10868	No	$94.52	$669.66
StudentFirst	StudentLast	$175,560.00	1562	11036	No	$112.39	$670.52
Meera	Shah	$176,176.00	1761	10025	No	$100.04	$672.87
Jaynish	Mody	$177,984.00	1707	10066	No	$104.27	$679.78
Chardae	Myles	$179,088.00	1837	10010	No	$97.49	$683.99
Chardae	Myles	$179,100.00	1946	11079	No	$92.03	$684.04
Chardae	Myles	$179,712.00	1854	10102	No	$96.93	$686.38
Chardae	Myles	$180,180.00	1896	10019	No	$95.03	$688.17
Makarem	Abdeljawad	$180,810.00	1667	10044	No	$108.46	$690.57
Total		**$167,100.47**		32		**$102.10**	

Record: 1 of 32   No Filter   Search

FIGURE 3.1 Real Estate Investors Property Database – Mortgage Payments Query

NameOfList	AvgOfSalePrice	Number Sold	DaysOnMarket
Algernon Listings	$324,697.22	18	23.50
FastHouse	$288,314.50	6	22.33
Houses 4 Sale	$218,039.00	2	23.50
Local Listings	$341,085.67	9	23.56
Major Houses	$235,757.88	8	24.75
Trullo	$236,885.21	19	26.05
Wholesaler	$276,654.92	26	26.12
Total		**88**	

FIGURE 3.2 Real Estate Investors Property Database – Results by Realtor Revised Query

CASE STUDY | Real Estate Investors

Starting File	Files to be Submitted
a03h1Property	**a03h1PropertyCheck_LastFirst** **a03h3Property_LastFirst**

Calculations and Expressions

There are going to be times, when manipulating data in an Access database, that you will want to perform calculations. A field storing the number of hours worked multiplied by a field storing the hourly pay rate will calculate the gross pay, for example. Unfortunately, calculations may not always be that easy. If you have received a paycheck, you realize your gross pay is not the same as the amount as your paycheck. Your net pay will be lower, due to common deductions such as Social Security, Medicare, federal and state income taxes, unemployment insurance, and union dues. Some deductions may be a flat rate, and others may be calculated based on the paycheck amount, so even what appears to be a simple calculation can be complex.

At first glance, you may not see an obvious location for you to enter a calculation in Access. However, Access includes many built-in calculations and functions. Calculations appear commonly in queries, but can also be added to tables, forms, and reports.

In this section, you will learn how to create a calculated field in a query. You will also format the calculations to enhance readability.

Creating a Query with a Calculated Field

Rather than performing a calculation outside of the database and then inputting the result into your database, you should instead store the components of the calculation in the database. Calculating values rather than inputting values will reduce errors and inconsistencies. If your database stored the hours worked and paycheck amount, both fields would have to be updated if there was a change in the hours the employee worked. However, if you store only the hours worked and calculate the paycheck amount, you do not have to worry about updating multiple fields. The next time the paycheck is calculated, the results will be updated and corrected.

As another example, a table might contain the times when employees clock in and out of work. You could create a calculation in a query to determine how many hours each employee worked by subtracting the ClockIn field from the ClockOut field. A combination of elements that produce a value is known as an ***expression***. A ***calculated field*** is a field that displays the result of an expression rather than data stored in a field.

You may find one or more of the following elements in a calculated field:

- Arithmetic operator (for example, *, /, +, or −)
- ***Constant***, a value that does not change (such as −20 or 3.14)
- Function (built-in calculations like Pmt)
- Identifier (the names of fields, controls, or properties)

Understand the Order of Operations

The ***order of operations*** determines the sequence by which operations are calculated in a mathematical expression. Evaluate expressions in parentheses first, then exponents, then multiplication and division, and, finally, addition and subtraction. You may remember PEMDAS (or the mnemonic device "Please Excuse My Dear Aunt Sally") from a math class. Table 3.1 shows some examples of the order of operations. Access uses the following symbols:

- Parentheses   ( )
- Exponentiation   ^
- Multiplication   *
- Division   /
- Addition   +
- Subtraction   −

Pearson Education, Inc.

TABLE 3.1 Examples of Order of Operations

Expression	Order to Perform Calculations	Output
=2+3*3	Multiply first and then add.	11
=(2+3)*3	Add the values inside the parentheses first and then multiply.	15
=2+2^3	Evaluate the exponent first, $2^3=2*2*2$ (or 8). Then add.	10
=10/2+3	Divide first and then add.	8
=10/(2+3)	Add first to simplify the parenthetical expression and then divide.	2
=10*2–3*2	Multiply first and then subtract.	14

Build Expressions

STEP 1 »» As mentioned earlier, expressions can contain a number of different elements. Expressions can be typed manually or inserted using Access tools.

The challenging part is typically creating the expression. Consider the following scenario. Your company plans on allowing customers to pay off their balance in 12 monthly payments. The balance is stored in your Access database in a field named Balance. To divide this into equal payments, you would type Balance/12 in the Field row of a blank column. For example, if the Balance field was $1,200, you divide by 12. You are left with a monthly payment of $100. See Figure 3.3 for an example of the Balance field added to a query.

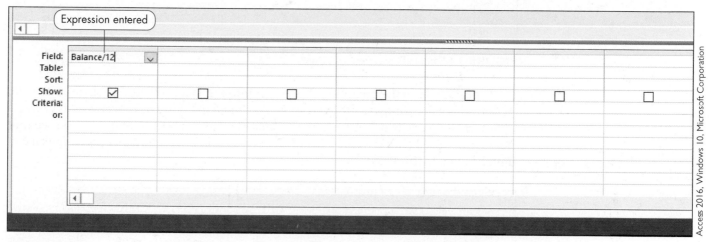

FIGURE 3.3 Balance Field in a Query

Access 2016, Windows 10, Microsoft Corporation

However, many companies will apply some sort of surcharge or add interest when customers pay balances off in installments. From your perspective as someone creating a query, this makes the calculation more complex. Your company may decide to add a surcharge of 20% (or, .20) of the balance. In this case, you will need to include a multiplication step in the above calculation. You will multiply the results by 1.20. Why multiply by 1.20 rather than .20? If you multiplied by .20 and divided by 12, you would only see the surcharge amount and not the total amount due for each payment. If the Balance field was $1,200, the monthly payment needs to be more than the $100 in the previous example.

If you multiply $1,200 by .20, you get a result of $20. The $20 does not represent the amount due, it represents the surcharge. Therefore, multiplying by 1.20 will give you the balance plus the surcharge. Dividing that by 12 gives you a monthly payment of $120. Note that there are multiple ways to implement this calculation, so this is not the only solution.

To create a calculated field within a query, complete the following steps:

1. Open the query in Design view.
2. Click the Field row (top row) of a blank column. Recall that the Field row is found in the bottom pane of the design.
3. Type the desired expression. See Figure 3.4 for an example of a query with an expression.
4. Click Run in the Results group to display the results in Datasheet view.

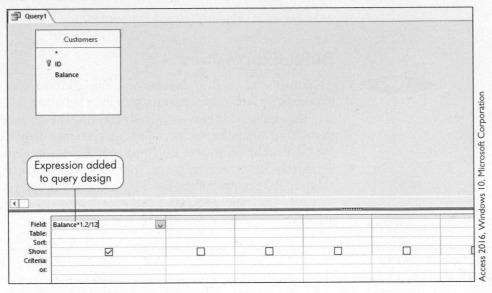

FIGURE 3.4 Sample Expression in a Query

When you type the preceding expression into the Field row and click another field, Access adds a few things to the expression. As shown in Figure 3.5, Access adds brackets [ ] around Balance, which Access uses to indicate a field name. In addition, you see that Access has added Expr1: to the start of the expression. This is how Access assigns a column heading to this field.

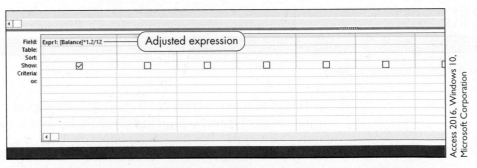

FIGURE 3.5 Modified Expression

If you were to run the query, the column heading would be *Expr1*. If you wanted to name this column MonthlySurcharge, you would start the expression with the name, followed by a colon, followed by the expression (or, if Expr1: already appears, replace Expr1 with the name and leave the colon in place). The column is renamed MonthlySurcharge in Figure 3.6.

Access 2016, Windows 10, Microsoft Corporation

FIGURE 3.6 Expression Renamed

The query results, as shown in Figure 3.7, display a decimal number in the MonthlySurcharge column. Notice that the results are not easy to read and should be formatted.

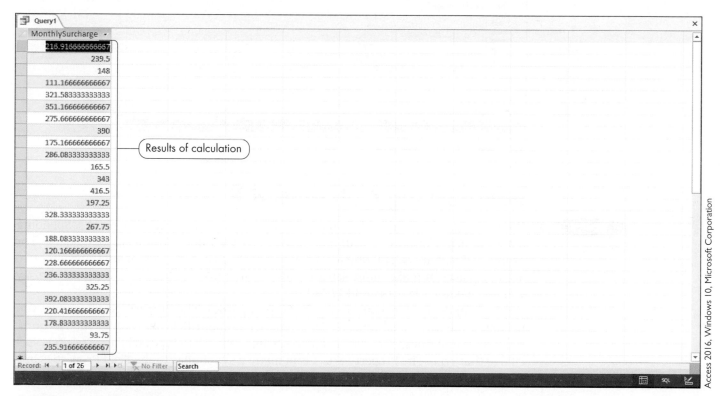

Access 2016, Windows 10, Microsoft Corporation

FIGURE 3.7 Unformatted Results

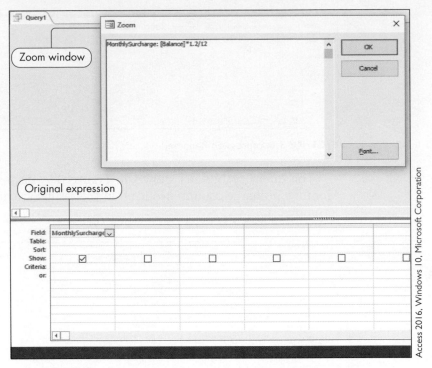

FIGURE 3.8 Zoom Window

Formatting Calculated Results

STEP 2 ›› When using calculated fields in queries, you may want to format the results. Spending a few moments formatting your output will make your query results more readable. For example, if you are calculating a net pay, you likely do not care about anything after two decimal places. It makes more sense to say you are making $980.15 a week than to say you are making $980.14983432743.

To format a field in a query, use the ***Property Sheet***. The Property Sheet enables you to change the way a field appears. For example, a numeric field has settings such as number format and number of decimal places, while other data types will have settings specific to that type. The Property Sheet is in many ways similar to the Field Properties in a table.

To format a field, complete the following steps:

1. Open the query in Design view.
2. Click the Field row of the field you want to format.
3. Click Property Sheet in the Show/Hide group on the Design tab.
4. Click the appropriate option and choose the setting desired. You can change the format by clicking the Format property arrow and selecting your desired format (such as Currency for numeric fields). For numeric fields, the Decimal Places property will allow you to choose the number of decimal places that display. To change the caption (which appears as the name of the column), click the text box next to the Caption property and type your desired column heading. Figure 3.9 shows the Property Sheet options related to a numeric field.
5. Close the Property Sheet, if desired, by clicking Close as shown in Figure 3.9. After using the Property Sheet, it will be displayed in the future when the query is opened in Design view, unless you close it. However, as most of your users will not be viewing the query in Design view, it should not matter either way if the Property Sheet is closed or not.

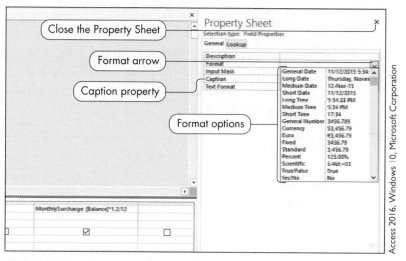

FIGURE 3.9 Property Sheet Options

Recovering from Common Errors

STEP 3 ▶▶ When creating calculated fields, there are a number of common errors that can occur. Learning how to recognize errors and recover from issues is important. Some common types of errors are shown below:

- Forgetting the colon between the column title and the formula

   A correct formula would look like this:

   MonthlySurcharge: [Balance]*1.2/12

   If you forget the colon, the formula looks like this instead:

   MonthlySurcharge [Balance]*1.2/12

   and you will get an invalid syntax error, indicating something is wrong with the way the formula is written, as shown in Figure 3.10.

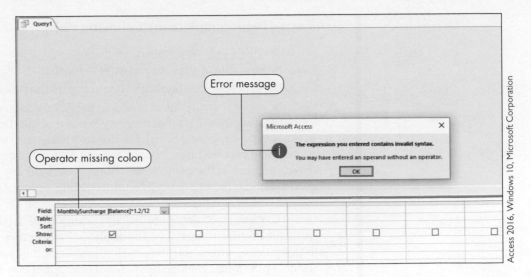

FIGURE 3.10 Syntax Error Warning

- Spelling a field name incorrectly

  If a field's name is Balance and you mistype it, you will get an error when you run the query. You may end up with a formula that looks like this:

  MonthlySurcharge: [Baalnce]*1.2/12

  When you run the query, you will be prompted by Access to give a value for Baalnce, as shown in Figure 3.11. This happens because Access does not know what Baalnce is.

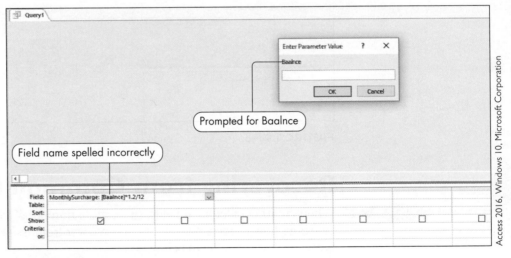

FIGURE 3.11 Result of Spelling Error in Field Name

- Forgetting the order of operations

  If you do not check your formulas, you may get bad values. For example, the following would not produce the expected output:

  NewMonthlyBalance: [Balance] + 100/12

  If you want addition to be done before division, you must remember the parentheses:

  NewMonthlyBalance: ([Balance] + 100)/12

Verifying Calculated Results

STEP 4 ⟩⟩ After your query runs, look at the field values in Datasheet view and look at the calculated values. You may find that the results do not make sense. In a real-world scenario, you will not be given step-by-step directions, and instead will apply critical thinking skills to your work. Access will calculate exactly what you tell it to calculate, even if you make logical errors in the calculation.

When you run a query, you need to analyze the results and ask yourself if the results make sense. Assume you are calculating a car payment for a $10,000 car, with monthly payments for 5 years. If your formula is incorrect, you may end up with a monthly payment result like $1,000. If you look at your results, you should say to yourself, "Does it make sense for me to pay $1,000 every month for five years to finance a $10,000 car?"

You can verify results with a calculator or by copying and pasting data into Excel. Recreate the calculations in Excel and compare the answers to the query results in Access. The Access calculated field, the calculator, and the Excel calculations should all return identical results.

Quick Concepts

1. What are the four types of elements that can appear as part of an expression in Access? *p. 218*

2. Briefly describe the order of operations. Give an example of how the order of operations makes a difference in a calculation. *p. 218*

3. How does Access respond when you spell a field name incorrectly in a query? *p. 224*

4. How can the Property Sheet make query results more readable? *p. 222*

Hands-On Exercises

Watch the Video
for this Hands-On
Exercise!

MyITLab®
HOE1 Training

Skills covered: Build
Expressions • Format Fields •
Recognize and Correct Common
Errors • Evaluate Results

1 Calculations and Expressions

Using the data from the homes for sale lists that Don and Matt acquired, you are able to help them target properties that meet their criteria. As you examine the data, you discover other ways to analyze the properties. You create several queries and present your results to the two investors for their comments.

STEP 1 »» BUILD EXPRESSIONS

You begin your analysis by creating a query using the Properties and Agents tables from the Property database. The Properties table contains all the properties the investors will evaluate; the Agents table contains a list of real estate agents who represent the properties' sellers. In this exercise, you will add requested fields and only show properties that have not been sold. You will then build an expression to calculate the price per square foot for each property. Refer to Figure 3.12 as you complete Step 1.

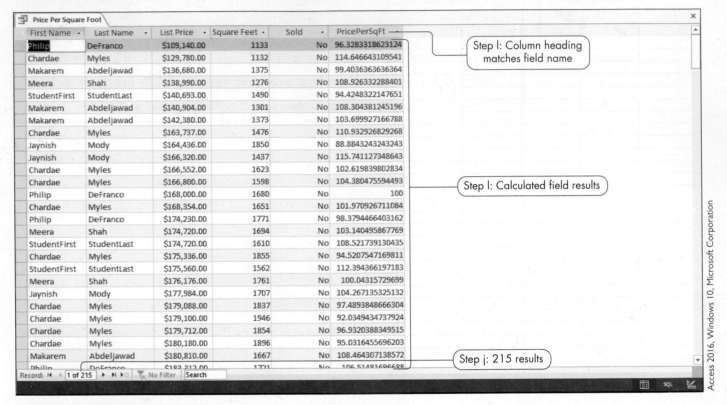

FIGURE 3.12 Modified Expression

a. Open *a03h1Property*. Save the database as **a03h1Property_LastFirst**.

> **TROUBLESHOOTING:** Throughout the remainder of this chapter and textbook, click Enable Content whenever you are working with student files.

> **TROUBLESHOOTING:** If you make any major mistakes in this exercise, you can close the file, open *a03h1Property* again, and then start this exercise over.

b. Open the Agents table and replace the name *Dilson Herrera* with your name. Close the table.

c. Click the **Create tab** and click **Query Design** in the Queries group to create a new query.

The Show Table dialog box opens so you can specify the table(s) and/or queries to include in the query design.

d. Select the **Agents table** and click **Add**. Select the **Properties table** and click **Add**. Click **Close** to close the Show Table dialog box.

e. Double-click the **FirstName** and **LastName fields** in the Agents table to add them to the query.

f. Double-click the **ListPrice**, **SqFeet**, and **Sold fields** in the Properties table to add them to the query.

g. Click **Run** in the Results group to display the results in Datasheet view.

A total of 303 properties appear in the results.

h. Switch to Design view. Type **No** in the Criteria row of the Sold field.

i. Click the **Sort row** in the ListPrice field. Click the **arrow** and select **Ascending**.

j. Click **Run** to see the results.

The 215 unsold properties appear in the datasheet, with the least expensive houses displayed first.

k. Click **Save** on the Quick Access Toolbar and type **Price Per Square Foot** as the Query Name in the Save As dialog box. Click **OK**.

l. Switch to Design view. Click the **Field row** of the first blank column of the query design grid. Right-click and select **Zoom** to show the Zoom window. Type **PricePerSqFt: ListPrice/SqFeet** and click **OK**.

Access inserts square brackets around the fields for you. The new field divides the values in the ListPrice field by the values in the SqFeet field.

m. Click **Run** in the Results group to view the results. Adjust column widths as necessary.

The new calculated field, PricePerSqFt, is displayed. Compare your results to those shown in Figure 3.12.

> **TROUBLESHOOTING:** If you see pound signs (#####) in an Access column, double-click the vertical line between column headings to increase the width.

> **TROUBLESHOOTING:** If, when you run the query, you are prompted for a value, cancel and return to Design view. Ensure that you have entered the formula from Step l in the first row of a blank column, not the criteria line.

n. Save the changes to the query and close the query.

Don and Matt would like the field formatted with two decimal places. You will change the format to Currency and add a caption to the calculated field. Refer to Figure 3.13 as you complete Step 2.

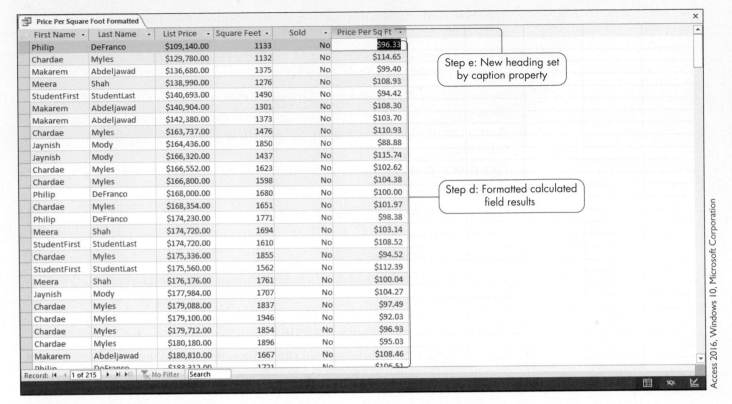

FIGURE 3.13 Modified Expression

a. Right-click the **Price Per Square Foot query** in the Navigation Pane and click **Copy**. Right-click in the Navigation Pane again and click **Paste**. Type **Price Per Square Foot Formatted** in the Paste As dialog box and click **OK**.

b. Open the Price Per Square Foot Formatted query in Design view.

c. Click the **PricePerSqFt calculated field cell**. Click **Property Sheet** in the Show/Hide group on the Design tab.

The Property Sheet displays.

d. Click the **Format property**. Click the **Format property arrow** and select **Currency**.

e. Click the **Caption property** and type **Price Per Sq Ft**. Press **Enter**. Close the Property Sheet.

f. Click **Run** to view your changes.

The calculated field values are formatted as Currency, and the column heading displays Price Per Sq Ft instead of PricePerSqFt.

g. Compare your result to Figure 3.13. Save the changes to the query.

A few errors arise as you test the new calculated fields. You check the spelling of the field names in the calculated fields because that is a common mistake. Refer to Figure 3.14 as you complete Step 3.

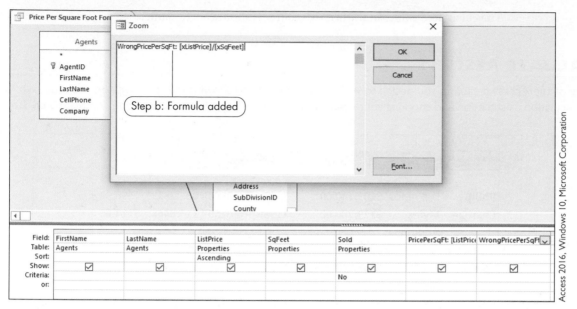

FIGURE 3.14 Incorrect Expression

a. Switch to Design view of the Price Per Square Foot Formatted query. Scroll to the first blank column of the query design grid and click the Field row.

b. Right-click and select **Zoom** to display the Zoom window. Type **WrongPricePerSqFt: xListPrice/xSqFeet**. Your formula should match Figure 3.14. Click OK in the Zoom window.

   Be sure that you added the extra *x*'s to the field names. You are intentionally misspelling the field names to see how Access will respond.

c. Click **Property Sheet** in the Show/Hide group of the Design tab. Click the **Format property**. From the menu, select **Currency**. Click the **Caption box** and type **Wrong Price Per Sq Ft**. Close the Property Sheet.

d. Click **Run** in the Results group.

   You should see the Enter Parameter Value dialog box. Access does not recognize xListPrice in the tables defined for this query in the first record. When Access does not recognize a field name, it will ask you to supply a value.

e. Type **100000** in the first parameter box. Press **Enter** or click **OK**.

   Another Enter Parameter Value dialog box displays, asking that you supply a value for xSqFeet. Again, this error occurs because the tables defined for this query do not contain an xSqFeet field.

f. Type **1000** in the second parameter box and press **Enter**.

   The query has the necessary information to run and returns the results in Datasheet view.

g. Examine the results of the calculation for Wrong Price Per Sq Ft.

   All of the records show 100 because you entered the values 100000 and 1000, respectively, into the parameter boxes. The two values are treated as constants and give the same results for all records.

h. Return to Design view. Display the Zoom window. Correct the errors in the WrongPricePerSqFt field by changing the formula to **WrongPricePerSqFt: [ListPrice]/[SqFeet]**. Click **OK**.

i. Run and save the query. Close the query.

The calculated values in the last two columns should be the same.

Because you are in charge of the Access database, you decide to verify your data prior to showing it to the investors. You use two methods to check your calculations: estimation and checking your results using Excel. Refer to Figure 3.15 as you complete Step 4.

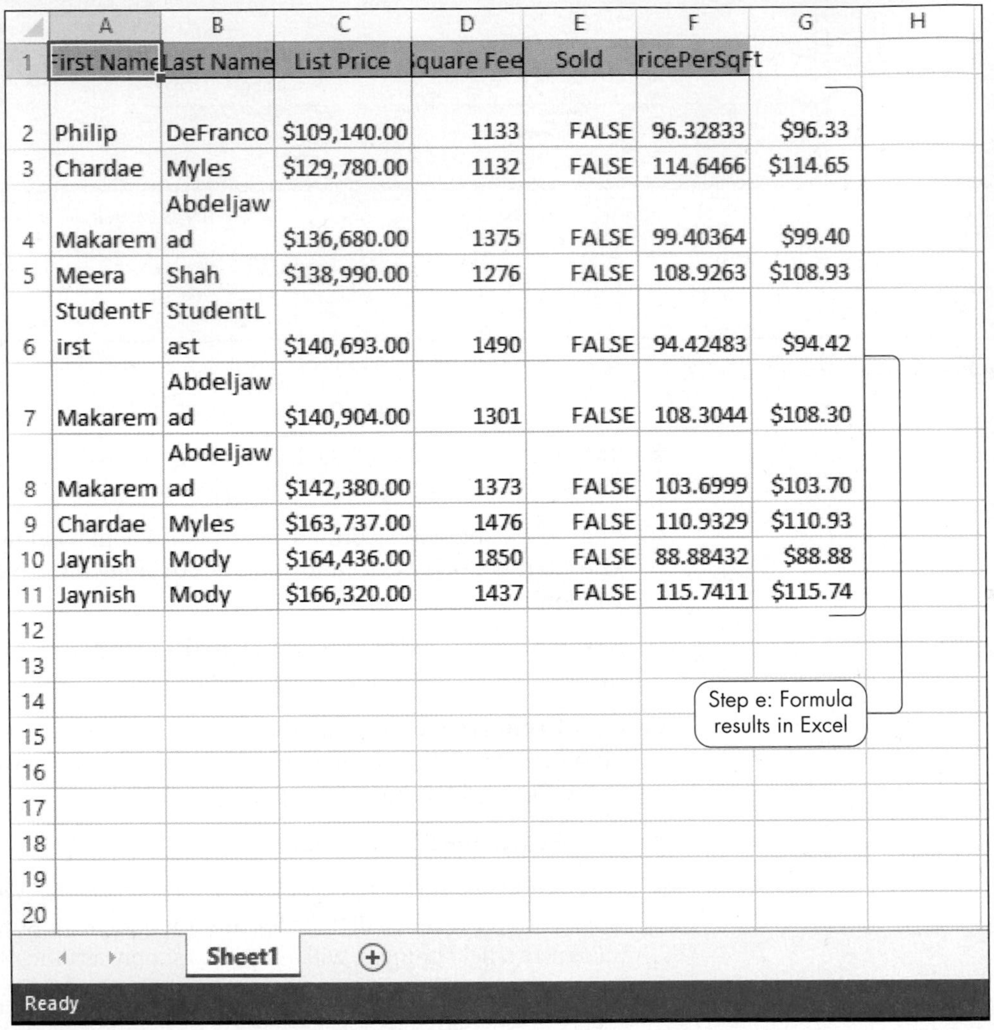

	A	B	C	D	E	F	G	H
1	First Name	Last Name	List Price	Square Fee	Sold	ricePerSqFt		
2	Philip	DeFranco	$109,140.00	1133	FALSE	96.32833	$96.33	
3	Chardae	Myles	$129,780.00	1132	FALSE	114.6466	$114.65	
4	Makarem	Abdeljaw ad	$136,680.00	1375	FALSE	99.40364	$99.40	
5	Meera	Shah	$138,990.00	1276	FALSE	108.9263	$108.93	
6	StudentF irst	StudentL ast	$140,693.00	1490	FALSE	94.42483	$94.42	
7	Makarem	Abdeljaw ad	$140,904.00	1301	FALSE	108.3044	$108.30	
8	Makarem	Abdeljaw ad	$142,380.00	1373	FALSE	103.6999	$103.70	
9	Chardae	Myles	$163,737.00	1476	FALSE	110.9329	$110.93	
10	Jaynish	Mody	$164,436.00	1850	FALSE	88.88432	$88.88	
11	Jaynish	Mody	$166,320.00	1437	FALSE	115.7411	$115.74	
12								
13								
14								
15								
16								
17								
18								
19								
20								

Step e: Formula results in Excel

Sheet1

Ready

Access 2016, Windows 10, Microsoft Corporation

FIGURE 3.15 Calculation Copied to Excel

a. Open the Price Per Square Foot query in Datasheet view. Examine the PricePerSqFt field.

One of the ways to verify the accuracy of the calculated data is to ask yourself if the numbers make sense.

b. Locate the 13th record with Philip DeFranco as the listing agent, an asking price of $168,000, and square footage of 1680. The result ($100.00) makes sense, since 168,000/1680 = 100.

TROUBLESHOOTING: If the 13th record is not the one listed above, ensure that you have sorted the query by the List Price in ascending order, as specified in Step 1i.

c. Open a new, blank workbook in Excel and then switch to Access. Select the first 10 records. Click **Copy** in the Clipboard group on the Home tab.

You will verify the calculation in the first 10 records by pasting the results in Excel.

d. Switch to Excel and click the **Paste** button in the Clipboard group on the Home tab.

The field names display in the first row, and the 10 records display in the next 10 rows. The fields are located in columns A–F. The calculated field results are pasted in column F as values rather than as a formula.

> **TROUBLESHOOTING:** If you see pound signs (#####) in an Excel column, double-click the vertical line between column headings to increase the width.

e. Click **cell G2**. Type **=C2/D2** and press **Enter**. Click **cell G2**, and click **Copy** in the Clipboard group. Select the **range G3:G11** and click **Paste** in the Clipboard group. Compare your results to Figure 3.15.

The formula divides the list price by the square feet. Compare the results in columns F and G. The numbers should be the same, except for the number of decimal places.

f. Save the Excel workbook as **a03h1PropertyCheck_LastFirst**. Close the file, and exit Excel. You will submit this file to your instructor at the end of the last Hands-On Exercise.

g. Keep the database open if you plan to continue with the next Hands-On Exercise. If not, close the database and exit Access.

The Expression Builder and Functions

In the last Hands-On Exercise, you calculated the price per square foot for real estate properties to help evaluate properties on the investment list. You were able to type the expression manually.

When you encounter more complex expressions, the ***Expression Builder*** tool can help you create more complicated expressions. The Expression Builder's size enables you to easily see complex formulas and functions in their entirety. In addition, it provides easy access to objects, operators, and functions.

In this section, you will learn how to create expressions with the Expression Builder. You also will learn how to use built-in functions.

Creating Expressions Using the Expression Builder

STEP 1 ❯❯ The Expression Builder helps you create expressions by supplying you with access to fields, operators, and functions. When you use the Expression Builder to help create expressions, you can eliminate spelling errors in field names. Another advantage is that when you insert a function, placeholders tell you which values belong where. Experienced users may have functions memorized, but new users have the Expression Builder to provide support.

Once you open the Expression Builder, the Expression Builder dialog box displays. The top portion is an empty rectangular box known as the expression box. The left column of the Expression Builder dialog box contains Expression Elements (see Figure 3.16), which include the built-in functions, objects from the current database (including tables), and common expressions.

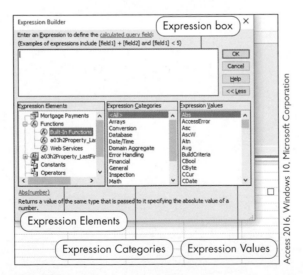

FIGURE 3.16 Expression Builder

The middle column displays the Expression Categories based on the item selected in the Expression Elements box (see Figure 3.16 above). For example, when the Built-In Functions item is selected in the Expression Elements box, the available built-in function categories, such as the Math category, are displayed in the Expression Categories box.

The right column displays the Expression Values, if any, for the categories that you selected in the Expression Categories box (see Figure 3.16 above). For example, if you click Built-In Functions in the Expression Elements box and click Date/Time in the Expression Categories box, the Expression Values box lists all of the built-in functions in the Date/Time category.

You can create an expression by manually typing text in the expression box or by double-clicking the elements from the bottom section in the Expression Builder dialog box.

To create an expression with the Expression Builder, complete the following steps:

1. Open a query in Design view (or create a new query).
2. Click the Field row of a blank column.
3. Click Builder in the Query Setup group of the Design tab to launch the Expression Builder.
4. Type the calculated field name and type a colon if you want to name the column. Although this is not required, as mentioned earlier in this chapter, this will change the title of the column in Datasheet view.
5. Type the name of a field (surrounded in [ ] brackets). Alternately, you can click the source table or query listed in the Expression Elements section and double-click the field you want. Using the second method will insert a field in a format resembling [Properties]![Beds] as shown in Figure 3.17. In this example, the table name Properties appears in brackets, followed by an exclamation point, followed by the field name Beds in brackets. As long as you do not have multiple fields with the same name, you can safely delete the table name and exclamation point (leaving you with [Beds] in this example). If you want to use operators (such as +) you can type those manually.
6. Repeat the previous step for each field you want to add to the calculation, remembering to take the order of operations into account. See Figure 3.17 as an example formula created in the Expression Builder.
7. Click OK to close the Expression Builder window.
8. Click Run in the Results group to view the results in Datasheet view.

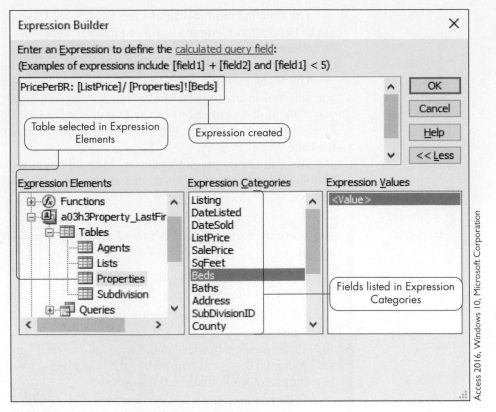

FIGURE 3.17 Expression Created in Expression Builder

Using Built-In Functions

A *function* is a predefined computation that performs a complex calculation. There are around 150 functions built into Access. If you are familiar with Excel, many of these will be familiar to you. Functions produce results based on inputs. Each input (such as a field name or a number) used to produce output for a function is known as an *argument*. Some functions have optional arguments, which are not required but may be necessary for your task.

Many of the tasks that are built-in would otherwise be difficult to perform. Figuring out the payment of a loan or determining the year portion of a date without functions would not be easy.

Once you identify what functionality is required, you can check the Built-In Functions in the Expression Builder to see if the function exists, or use search engines or Access Help. If the function exists, add the function to the expression box and replace «placeholder text» with the argument values. See Figure 3.18 for an example function inserted using the Expression Builder.

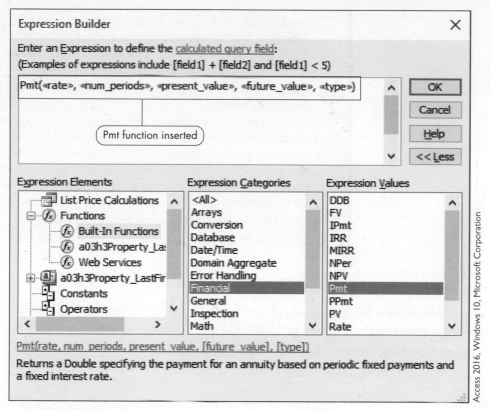

FIGURE 3.18 Function Inserted Using the Expression Builder

Functions work the same in Access, Excel, and programming languages (such as C#, Java, or Python). This chapter will demonstrate one function.

To create an expression containing a function with the Expression Builder, complete the following steps:

1. Open a query in Design view (or create a new query).
2. Click the Field row of a blank column.
3. Click Builder in the Query Setup group of the Design tab to launch the Expression Builder.
4. Type the calculated field name and type a colon if you want to name the column. Although this is not required, as mentioned earlier in this chapter, this will change the title of the column in Datasheet view.
5. Double-click Functions in the Expression Elements section of the window (see Figure 3.19). Click Built-In Functions. The list of available functions will appear in the Expression Categories box.
6. Locate and click the function category in the Expression Categories section, as shown in Figure 3.19. If you are unsure of the category, you can use Help or search through the category labeled <All>.

7. Double-click the function name in the Expression Values section to add it. Most functions include one or more placeholder text fields, text surrounded by «» symbols. These provide you guidance as to what data should be entered in each location. Notice an example of placeholder text in Figure 3.19.

8. Click a placeholder text element to select it, unless your function does not have placeholder text.

9. Type the number, field name, or calculation you want to replace the placeholder (for example, in Figure 3.19, the first placeholder text was replaced by .05/12). Note that you can also add a field by clicking the desired table or query listed in the Expression Elements section and double-clicking the field you want. In Figure 3.19, notice that [Properties]![ListPrice] has replaced the third placeholder. As discussed earlier, the table name and exclamation point can often be removed safely.

10. Click OK to close the Expression Builder window.

11. Click Run in the Results group to view the results in Datasheet view.

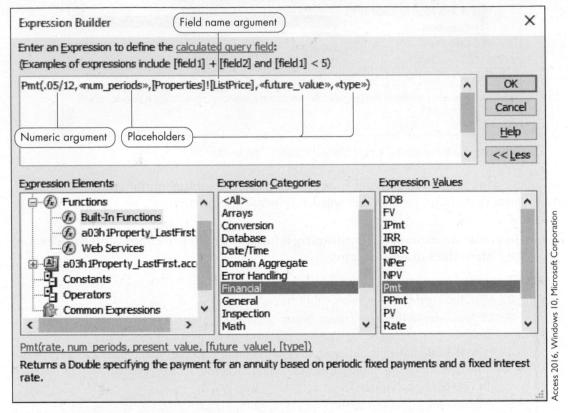

FIGURE 3.19 Expression with Some Arguments Filled In

Calculate a Loan Payment with the Pmt Function

 The ***Pmt function*** calculates the loan payment given the rate, number of periods (also known as term), and the present value of the loan (the principal). If necessary, two other arguments (future value and type) can be used, but they are not necessary for many calculations. The Pmt function uses the following syntax:

Pmt(rate, num_periods, present_value, future_value, type)

After inserting the function using the Expression Builder, you will supply at least the rate, num_periods, and present_value arguments. The arguments are as follows:

- **rate:** Interest rates are usually stated as yearly rates, so the rate must be converted to the rate per period. If a loan is paid monthly, divide the yearly rate by 12. Typically this is entered as a decimal followed by the division (for example, .05/12). It is also acceptable to enter this as a percentage (5%/12).

- **num_periods:** Multiply the number of years of the loan by the number of payments per year. The total number of payments for a monthly payment would be calculated as the number of years multiplied by 12.
- **present_value:** The amount of the loan.
- **future_value** and **type:** The last two arguments—future value and type—are both optional, so they are usually left blank or filled in with zero.

The following example shows how to use the Pmt function to calculate the payment for a loan with a 5% interest rate, paid 12 times a year. This loan will be paid for four years and has a present value of $12,500. Figure 3.20 shows how it appears in the Expression Builder.

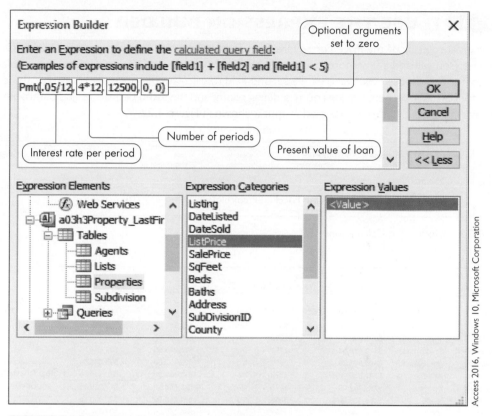

FIGURE 3.20 Pmt Function with Arguments Filled In

The Pmt function will return a negative value, as a loan payment is considered a debit. In this case, it returns −287.87. If you would like to display this as a positive number, place a negative sign in front of the loan amount.

Pmt(.05/12, 4*12, −12500, 0, 0)

By default, the column heading will display Expr1 for any calculated field, as shown in the first Hands-On Exercise. To change this, you can replace Expr1 with the desired column heading, followed by a colon (:), to the left of the calculation.

MonthlyPmt: Pmt(.05/12, 4*12, −12500, 0, 0)

Quick Concepts

5. List two benefits of using the Expression Builder to create expressions. **p. 232**

6. What is an example argument in the Pmt function? What does this argument do? **p. 236**

7. Given the following function: Pmt(.05/12, 5*12, 50000, 0, 0), how many years is the loan for and how much is the initial amount of the loan? **p. 237**

Hands-On Exercises

Watch the Video
for this Hands-On
Exercise!

MyITLab®
HOE2 Training

Skills covered: Use the
Expression Builder • Calculate a
Loan Payment with the Pmt Function

2 The Expression Builder and Functions

When Don and Matt ask you to calculate the price per bedroom and the price per room for each
property, you use the Expression Builder to make the task easier. You also create an additional calculated
field showing the estimated mortgage for each property.

STEP 1 ›› USE THE EXPRESSION BUILDER

You will create a copy of the Price Per Square Foot Formatted query from the previous Hands-On Exercise and paste it using a
new name. You will add a few more calculated fields to the new query. You will create one calculation to determine the price per
bedroom for each house. You will create a second field to calculate the price per room. For this calculation, you will assume that
each property has a kitchen, a living room, a dining room, and the listed bedrooms and bathrooms. The calculations you will create
are shown in Figure 3.21. Your expected output is shown in Figure 3.22.

Field:	FirstName	LastName	ListPrice	SqFeet	Sold	PricePerBR: [ListPrice]/[Beds]	PricePerRoom: [ListPrice]/([Beds]+[Baths]+3)
Table:	Agents	Agents	Properties	Properties	Properties		
Sort:			Ascending				
Show:	☑	☑	☑	☑	☑	☑	☑
Criteria:					No		
or:							

Step i: PricePerBR calculation

Step s: PricePerRoom
calculation

Access 2016, Windows 10, Microsoft Corporation

FIGURE 3.21 Expanded Calculations

	Mortgage Payments	List Price Calculations					
First Name ▾	Last Name ▾	List Price ▾	Square Feet ▾	Sold ▾	Price Per Bedroom ▾	Price Per Room ▾	
Philip	DeFranco	$109,140.00	1133	No	$54,570.00	$18,190.00	
Chardae	Myles	$129,780.00	1132	No	$64,890.00	$21,630.00	Step k: Caption set for first calculation
Makarem	Abdeljawad	$136,680.00	1375	No	$68,340.00	$22,780.00	
Meera	Shah	$138,990.00	1276	No	$69,495.00	$23,165.00	
StudentFirst	StudentLast	$140,693.00	1490	No	$70,346.50	$23,448.83	
Makarem	Abdeljawad	$140,904.00	1301	No	$70,452.00	$23,484.00	
Makarem	Abdeljawad	$142,380.00	1373	No	$71,190.00	$20,340.00	Step t: Caption set for second calculation
Chardae	Myles	$163,737.00	1476	No	$81,868.50	$27,289.50	
Jaynish	Mody	$164,436.00	1850	No	$82,218.00	$23,490.86	
Jaynish	Mody	$166,320.00	1437	No	$83,160.00	$27,720.00	
Chardae	Myles	$166,552.00	1623	No	$83,276.00	$23,793.14	
Chardae	Myles	$166,800.00	1598	No	$83,400.00	$27,800.00	
Philip	DeFranco	$168,000.00	1680	No	$84,000.00	$25,846.15	
Chardae	Myles	$168,354.00	1651	No	$84,177.00	$28,059.00	
Philip	DeFranco	$174,230.00	1771	No	$87,115.00	$29,038.33	
Meera	Shah	$174,720.00	1694	No	$87,360.00	$29,120.00	
StudentFirst	StudentLast	$174,720.00	1610	No	$87,360.00	$26,880.00	
Chardae	Myles	$175,336.00	1855	No	$87,668.00	$29,222.67	
StudentFirst	StudentLast	$175,560.00	1562	No	$87,780.00	$29,260.00	
Meera	Shah	$176,176.00	1761	No	$88,088.00	$25,168.00	
Jaynish	Mody	$177,984.00	1707	No	$88,992.00	$27,382.15	
Chardae	Myles	$179,088.00	1837	No	$89,544.00	$29,848.00	
Chardae	Myles	$179,100.00	1946	No	$89,550.00	$25,585.71	
Chardae	Myles	$179,712.00	1854	No	$89,856.00	$27,648.00	
Chardae	Myles	$180,180.00	1896	No	$90,090.00	$30,030.00	
Makarem	Abdeljawad	$180,810.00	1667	No	$90,405.00	$30,135.00	
Philip	DeFranco	$182,212.00	1721	No	$91,656.00	$30,552.00	

Record: ◄ ◄ 2 of 215 ► ►I ►☐ No Filter Search

Access 2016, Windows 10, Microsoft Corporation

FIGURE 3.22 Payment Calculation

a. Open *a03h1Property_LastFirst* if you closed it at the end of Hands-On Exercise 1, and save it as **a03h2Property_LastFirst**, changing h1 to h2.

b. Create a copy of the Price Per Square Foot Formatted query with the name **List Price Calculations**.

c. Open the List Price Calculations query in Design view. Click the **WrongPricePerSqFt field**. Click **Delete Columns** in the Query Setup group on the Design tab.

d. Click the **Field row** in the PricePerSqFt column and click **Builder** in the Query Setup group.

The Expression Builder dialog box opens, displaying the current formula.

e. Double-click the **PricePerSqFt field name** and type **PricePerBR**.

f. Double-click the **[SqFeet] field** in the expression and press **Delete**.

g. Click the **plus sign** ⊞ next to the a03h2Property_LastFirst database in the Expression Elements box to expand the list. Click the **plus sign** next to Tables and select the **Properties table**.

The fields from the Properties table are now listed in the middle column (Expression Categories).

h. Double-click the **Beds field** to add it to the expression box.

The expression now reads PricePerBR: [ListPrice]/[Properties]![Beds].

i. Highlight the **[Properties]! prefix** in front of *Beds* and press **Delete**.

The expression now reads PricePerBR: [ListPrice]/[Beds]. As the Beds field name is unique within our query, the table name is not necessary. Removing this makes the query easier to read. If a field named Beds appeared in more than one table in our query, removing the table name would cause problems.

j. Click **OK** and click **Run** to view the query results.

Notice that the column heading still reads Price Per Sq Ft. Also notice that the column's contents are formatted as Currency. These settings were copied when the query was copied.

k. Switch to Design view and ensure that the PricePerBR field is selected. Click **Property Sheet** in the Show/Hide group and change the **Caption** to **Price Per Bedroom**. Close the Property Sheet. Run the query and examine the changes.

The PricePerBR column now has an appropriate caption.

l. Switch to Design view. Select the entire **PricePerBR expression**, right-click the selected expression, and then select **Copy**. Right-click the **Field row** of the next blank column and select **Paste**.

You will edit the copied expression so that it reflects the price per room, assuming that the kitchen, living room, dining room, and the bedrooms and bathrooms will make up the number of rooms.

m. Click **Builder** in the Query Setup group.

n. Change the PricePerBR field name to **PricePerRoom**.

o. Add **an opening parenthesis** before the [Beds] portion of the formula. Type a **plus sign** after [Beds].

As you want the addition to be done first, enclose the addition in parentheses. The expression box should read PricePerRoom: [ListPrice]/([Beds]+

p. Click the **plus sign** next to the a03h2Property_LastFirst database in the Expression Elements box to expand the list. Click the **plus sign** next to Tables and select the **Properties table**.

The fields from the Properties table are now listed in the Expression Categories box.

q. Double-click the **Baths field** to add it to the expression box.

r. Type another plus sign after [Baths] and type **3** followed by a right parenthesis. In other words, you will type **+3)** in the expression box.

s. Delete the [Properties]! portion of the expression and click **OK** to close the Expression Builder.

The expression now reads PricePerRoom: [ListPrice]/([Beds]+[Baths]+3). Your final formula is the list price divided by the total number of rooms. The total number of rooms is the number of bedrooms (in the Beds field), plus the number of bathrooms (found in the Baths field), plus 3 (a constant representing the kitchen, living room, and dining room).

t. Click **Property Sheet** in the Show/Hide group. Type **Price Per Room** in the Caption box. Click the Format box, click the drop-down menu, and select **Currency**. Close the Property Sheet.

Compare your formulas to Figure 3.21. This figure has expanded the column widths for readability.

u. Run the query. Adjust column widths as necessary. Compare your results to Figure 3.22.

v. Save and close the query.

STEP 2 ⟫ CALCULATE A LOAN PAYMENT WITH THE PMT FUNCTION

Don and Matt feel like they are close to making an offer on a house. They would like to restrict the query to houses that cost $190,000 or less. They would also like to calculate the estimated mortgage payment for each house. You create this calculation using the Pmt function. You make the following assumptions: 80% of the sale price to be financed, a 30-year term, monthly payments, and a fixed 4.0% annual interest rate. Refer to Figures 3.23 and 3.24 as you complete Step 2.

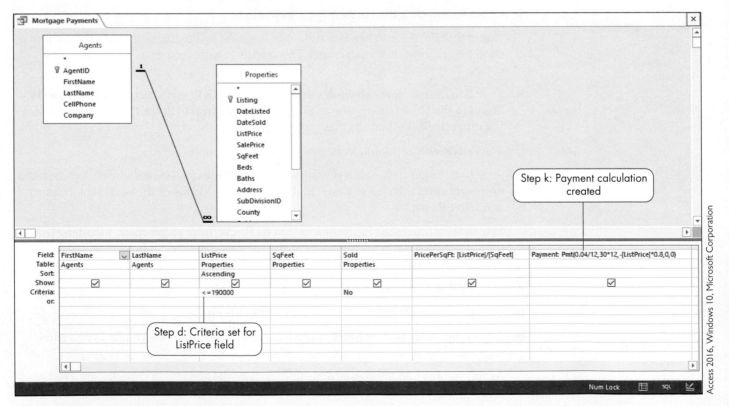

FIGURE 3.23 Mortgage Payments Design View

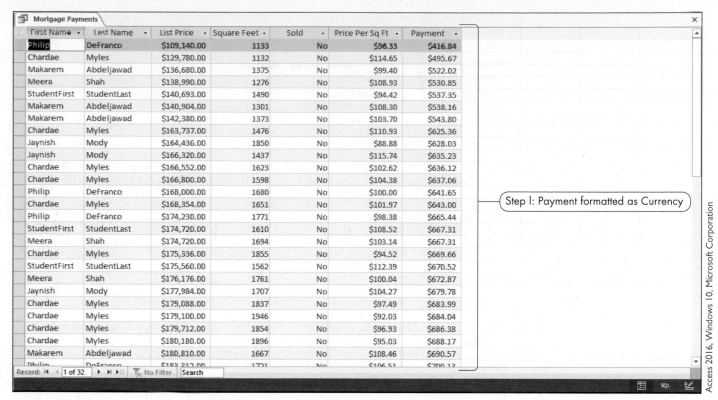

First Name	Last Name	List Price	Square Feet	Sold	Price Per Sq Ft	Payment
Philip	DeFranco	$109,140.00	1133	No	$96.33	$416.84
Chardae	Myles	$129,780.00	1132	No	$114.65	$495.67
Makarem	Abdeljawad	$136,680.00	1375	No	$99.40	$522.02
Meera	Shah	$138,990.00	1276	No	$108.93	$530.85
StudentFirst	StudentLast	$140,693.00	1490	No	$94.42	$537.35
Makarem	Abdeljawad	$140,904.00	1301	No	$108.30	$538.16
Makarem	Abdeljawad	$142,380.00	1373	No	$103.70	$543.80
Chardae	Myles	$163,737.00	1476	No	$110.93	$625.36
Jaynish	Mody	$164,436.00	1850	No	$88.88	$628.03
Jaynish	Mody	$166,320.00	1437	No	$115.74	$635.23
Chardae	Myles	$166,552.00	1623	No	$102.62	$636.12
Chardae	Myles	$166,800.00	1598	No	$104.38	$637.06
Philip	DeFranco	$168,000.00	1680	No	$100.00	$641.65
Chardae	Myles	$168,354.00	1651	No	$101.97	$643.00
Philip	DeFranco	$174,230.00	1771	No	$98.38	$665.44
StudentFirst	StudentLast	$174,720.00	1610	No	$108.52	$667.31
Meera	Shah	$174,720.00	1694	No	$103.14	$667.31
Chardae	Myles	$175,336.00	1855	No	$94.52	$669.66
StudentFirst	StudentLast	$175,560.00	1562	No	$112.39	$670.52
Meera	Shah	$176,176.00	1761	No	$100.04	$672.87
Jaynish	Mody	$177,984.00	1707	No	$104.27	$679.78
Chardae	Myles	$179,088.00	1837	No	$97.49	$683.99
Chardae	Myles	$179,100.00	1946	No	$92.03	$684.04
Chardae	Myles	$179,712.00	1854	No	$96.93	$686.38
Chardae	Myles	$180,180.00	1896	No	$95.03	$688.17
Makarem	Abdeljawad	$180,810.00	1667	No	$108.46	$690.57
Philip	DeFranco	$183,213.00	1721	No	$106.51	$700.13

Record: 1 of 32   No Filter   Search

Step I: Payment formatted as Currency

FIGURE 3.24 Mortgage Payments Results

a. Create a copy of the Price Per Square Foot Formatted query named **Mortgage Payments**.

b. Right-click **Mortgage Payments** and select **Design View**.

c. Delete the WrongPricePerSqFt field.

> **TROUBLESHOOTING:** If you do not see the WrongPricePerSqFt field, ensure that you copied the correct query.

d. Type **<=190000** in the Criteria row of the ListPrice column. Press **Enter**.

   The query, when it is run, will show only the houses that cost $190,000 or less.

e. Click the **Field row** of the first blank column. Click **Builder** in the Query Setup group to open the Expression Builder dialog box.

f. Double-click **Functions** in the Expression Elements box and select **Built-In Functions**.

g. Select **Financial** in the Expression Categories box.

h. Double-click **Pmt** in the Expression Values box.

   The expression box displays:

   Pmt(«rate», «num_periods», «present_value», «future_value», «type»)

i. Position the insertion point before the Pmt function. Type **Payment:** to the left of the Pmt function, with a space after the colon. The expression box now displays:

   Payment: Pmt(«rate», «num_periods», «present_value», «future_value», «type»)

Access 2016, Windows 10, Microsoft Corporation

j. Click each argument to select it and substitute the appropriate information. Make sure there is a comma between each argument.

Argument	Replacement Value
«rate»	.04/12
«num_periods»	30*12
«present_value»	[ListPrice]*.8
«future_value»	0
«type»	0

Note that the loan is a 30-year loan with 12 payments per year, hence the calculation for the number of payments. Also note, Don and Matt plan on financing 80% of the cost, putting 20% down. Therefore, you will multiply the list price by .8 (80%).

k. Click **OK**. Examine Figure 3.23 to make sure that you have entered the correct arguments.

l. Open the Property Sheet for the Payment field and change the format to **Currency**. Close the Property Sheet. Run the query.

Notice that the payment amounts are negative numbers (displayed in parentheses). You will edit the formula to change the negative payment values to positive.

m. Right-click the **Mortgage Payments tab** and select **Design View**. Click **Builder**. Add a **minus sign (−)** to the left of [ListPrice] and click **OK**.

By adding the negative sign in front of the ListPrice field, you ensure that the value is displayed as a positive number. The expression now reads:

Payment: Pmt(.04/12,30*12, −[ListPrice]*.8,0,0)

n. Run the query and examine the results. Adjust column widths as necessary.

The query displays a column containing the calculated monthly mortgage payment, formatted as currency, as shown in Figure 3.24.

o. Save and close the query. Keep the database open if you plan to continue with the next Hands-On Exercise. If not, close the database and exit Access.

Aggregate Functions

An *aggregate function* performs a calculation on an entire column of data and returns a single value. One example of an aggregate function is Sum.

Access refers to aggregate functions as Totals. Totals can be added to Datasheet view of a query, or they can be added to a query's Design view. Based on the data type, different aggregate functions will be available. Numeric fields are eligible for all of the functions, whereas Short Text fields are not. A list of common aggregate functions is shown in Table 3.2.

In the Property database, the average home price per county could be presented in a query or a report. This would give prospective buyers a good idea of home prices in their target counties. Almost every company or organization that uses a database will require some type of aggregate data.

TABLE 3.2	Common Aggregate Functions
Function	**Description**
Avg (Average)	Calculates the average value for a column.
Count	Counts the number of values in a column.
Max (Maximum)	Returns the item with the highest value.
Min (Minimum)	Returns the item with the lowest value.
Sum	Totals the items in a column.

Pearson Education, Inc.

In this section, you will learn how to create and work with aggregate functions. Specifically, you will learn how to use the Total row and create a totals query.

Adding Aggregate Functions to Datasheets

STEP 1 ►► Aggregate data helps users evaluate the values in a single record to the aggregate of all the records. If you are considering buying a property in Story County, Iowa, for $150,000, and the average price of a property in that county is $450,000, you know you are getting a good deal (or buying a bad property).

Access provides two methods of adding aggregate functions—a *Total row*, which displays the results of the aggregate function as the last row in Datasheet view of a table or query, and a totals query created in Query Design view. The totals query will be defined shortly.

The Total row method is quick and easy and has the advantage of showing the totals while still showing the individual records. Adding a Total row to a query or table can be accomplished by most users, even those who are not familiar with designing a query. Figure 3.25 shows the Total row added to Datasheet view of a query. In this image, the average of the List Price is displayed. The available aggregate functions are shown in the Price Per Sq Ft column. You can choose any of the aggregate functions that apply to numeric fields.

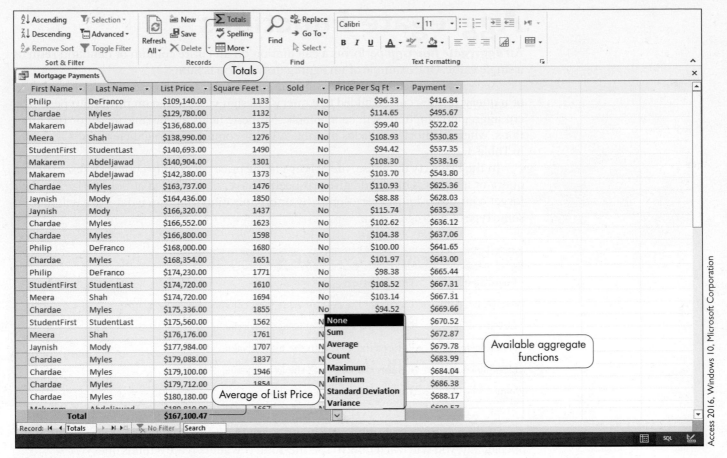

FIGURE 3.25 Total Row in Datasheet View

> **To add a Total row to the Datasheet view of a query or table, complete the following steps:**
>
> 1. View the query or table in Datasheet view.
> 2. Click Totals in the Records group on the Home tab. The Total row is added at the bottom of the datasheet, below the new record row.
> 3. Select one of the aggregate functions (such as Average, Count, or Sum) in the new Total row by clicking in the cell and clicking the arrow.

Creating Queries with Aggregate Functions

The total row, though useful, is limited. Many times, you may require in-depth statistics. Instead of wanting to see the average sale price for houses, you may want to see the average sale price by city. Instead of seeing the average price for every item your store sells, you may want to see the average price for each category. Using the total row in the previous example, this is not feasible. Another limitation of using the total row is that you might want to see the average sale price, minimum sale price, and maximum sale price. Using the previous method, this is difficult to do.

Another way to display aggregate functions requires changes to the query design. A *totals query* contains an additional row in the query design grid and is used to display aggregate data when the query is run. This provides two distinct advantages over the total row. The first allows you to show only the results of the aggregate functions (and not the detail), and the second enables you to see statistics by category.

Create a Totals Query

STEP 2 》》 Instead of showing detail, the overall statistics for the entire table or query may be displayed using a totals query. For example, if you want to see the number of listings, average value, and the average size in square feet for all properties in your table, you can use a totals query to get that data and not see details. Instead of having hundreds of rows of data with a summary row at the bottom (which could be missed), a totals query can display only the aggregate function results. Figure 3.26 shows a totals query in Design view, and Figure 3.27 shows the results.

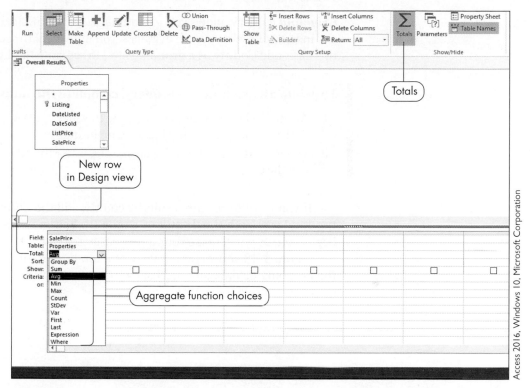

FIGURE 3.26 Totals Query Design View

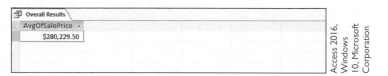

FIGURE 3.27 Totals Query Results

To create a totals query, complete the following steps:

1. Create a query in Design view and add the fields for which you want to get statistics.
2. Click Totals in the Show/Hide group on the Design tab. A new Total row displays in the query design grid between the Table and Sort rows. Notice that it defaults to Group By.
3. Click Group By and select the aggregate function you want applied for each field.
4. Display the Property Sheet (as done earlier in this chapter) and adjust settings to meet your requirements.
5. Click Run in the Results group to see the results.

Add Grouping to a Totals Query

Grouping a query allows you to summarize your data by the values of a field. For example, instead of seeing overall averages, you may want to see the results for each county. In this case, add County as a grouping level to see statistics by County.

To group an existing totals query, complete the following steps:

1. Add the field you want to group by to the query in Design view. For readability, the field should appear as the first field in the query.

2. Verify that the Total row displays Group By for the added field (see Figure 3.28), and run the query.

If you want to see the results by county, add the County field to the query and leave the Total row with the default of Group By. You may want to move this column to the beginning, as it will make your query easier to read.

Figure 3.28 shows Design view of a totals query with five columns, one of which is the grouping field. Figure 3.29 shows the results of this query. Notice that the resulting query shows one row for each county.

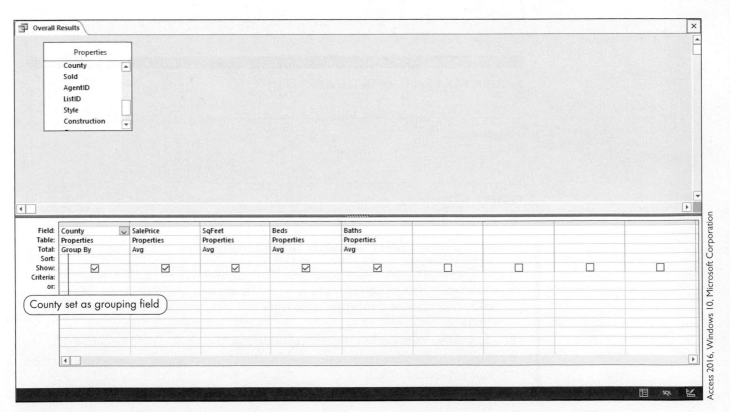

FIGURE 3.28 Grouped Totals Query Design View

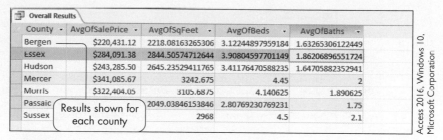

FIGURE 3.29 Grouped Totals Query Results

Add Conditions to a Totals Query

Totals queries can provide even better information if you add criteria. For example, if you wanted to see the number of houses, average price, and average square feet for only the sold properties, grouped by county, you can add the Sold field to the query. Set the criteria to Yes to indicate that the Sold field is yes.

To add conditions to an existing totals query, complete the following steps:

1. Double-click the field you want to limit by to add it to the design grid. The location of this field is not important, as it will not be displayed.
2. Select Where from the menu in the Total row.
3. Enter the condition.
4. Run the query.

Figure 3.30 shows a query with a condition added, and Figure 3.31 shows the results. Compare this to Figure 3.29 to see the change in results.

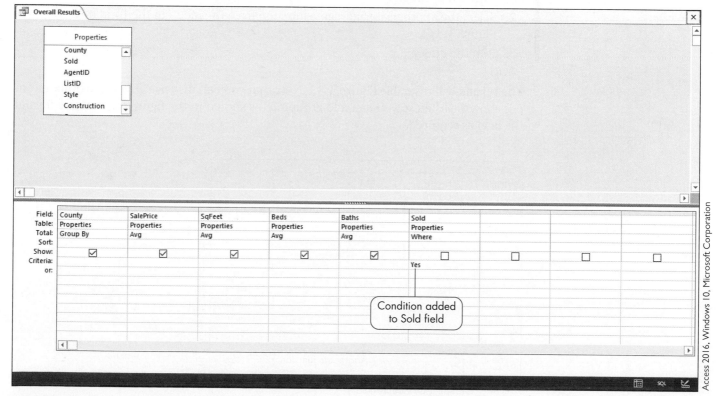

FIGURE 3.30 Totals Query with Condition Design View

Overall Results				
County	AvgOfSalePrice	AvgOfSqFeet	AvgOfBeds	AvgOfBaths
Bergen	$220,431.12	2223.11764705882	3.29411764705882	1.73529411764706
Essex	$284,091.38	2829.53846153846	3.96153846153846	1.94230769230769
Hudson	$243,285.50	2432.25	3	1.75
Mercer	$341,085.67	3440.55555555556	4.55555555555556	2
Morris	$322,404.05	3233.42857142857	4.33333333333333	1.9047619047619
Passaic	$219,325.20	2171.4	2.8	1.8
Sussex	$269,411.17	2610	3.83333333333333	2

Access 2016, Windows 10, Microsoft Corporation

FIGURE 3.31 Totals Query with Condition Results

TIP: MULTIPLE GROUPING LEVELS

At times, you may want to add multiple grouping fields. For example, instead of grouping by state, you might want to group by city. However, if you group by city, customers with the same city name in different states would be grouped together. For example, all 50 states have a location named Greenville. If you grouped by city, all customers with a city of Greenville, regardless of state, would appear as a group. This is probably not your intention. Instead, you probably would want to see results by city and state, and thus would want to add both fields to a query and select Group By.

Add a Calculated Field to a Totals Query

STEP 3 ▶▶ Calculated fields can also have aggregate functions applied to them. For example, you may want to calculate mortgage payments, and see the average of your calculation.

To apply an aggregate function to a totals query, complete the following steps:

1. Create the calculation you want to summarize, using any of the methods discussed earlier this chapter.
2. Select the appropriate aggregate function from the menu in the Total row (see Figure 3.32).
3. Run the query.

The results will resemble Figure 3.33. Note that you can also use any of the other methods shown earlier, so you can add grouping (as shown in the figures below) and format the field as required.

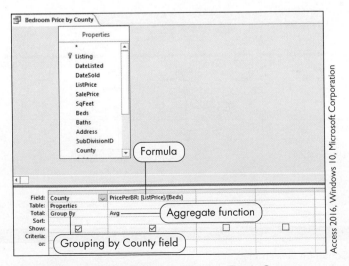

Access 2016, Windows 10, Microsoft Corporation

FIGURE 3.32 Adding Calculated Field to Totals Query

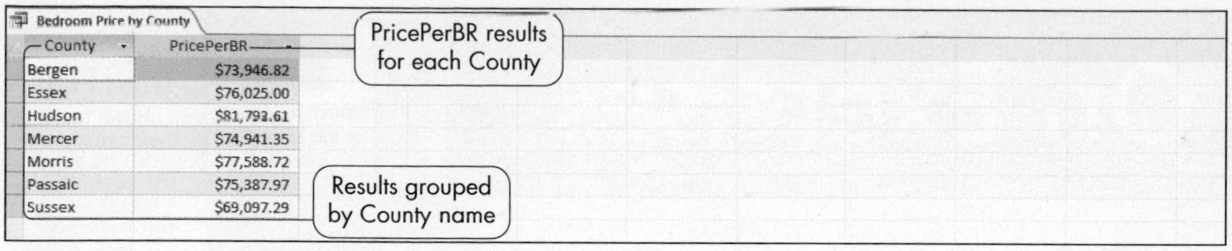

Bedroom Price by County
County
PricePerBR
Bergen $73,946.82
Essex $76,025.00
Hudson $81,793.61
Mercer $74,941.35
Morris $77,588.72
Passaic $75,387.97
Sussex $69,097.29
PricePerBR results for each County
Results grouped by County name

Access 2016, Windows 10, Microsoft Corporation

FIGURE 3.33 Calculated Field Results

Quick Concepts

8. What are the benefits of aggregate functions? List three examples of aggregate functions. ***p. 243***
9. How does a Total row change the display of the query's Datasheet view? ***p. 243***
10. What is a totals query? ***p. 244***
11. What would it mean if a query is "grouped by" state? ***p. 246***

Skills covered: Display a Total Row for a Query • Create a Totals Query • Add Grouping to a Totals Query • Add Conditions to a Totals Query • Add a Calculated Field to a Totals Query

3 Aggregate Functions

The investors decide it would be helpful to analyze the property lists they purchased. Some of the lists do not have homes that match their target criteria. The investors will either purchase new lists or alter their criteria. You create several totals queries to evaluate the property lists.

STEP 1 >> DISPLAY A TOTAL ROW FOR A QUERY

You begin your property list analysis by creating a total row in Datasheet view of the Mortgage Payments query. This will give you a variety of aggregate information for important columns. Refer to Figure 3.34 as you complete Step 1.

First Name	Last Name	List Price	Square Feet	Listing	Sold	Price Per Sq Ft	Payment
Philip	DeFranco	$109,140.00	1133	10004	No	$96.33	$416.84
Chardae	Myles	$129,780.00	1132	10028	No	$114.65	$495.67
Makarem	Abdeljawad	$136,680.00	1375	10008	No	$99.40	$522.02
Meera	Shah	$138,990.00	1276	10016	No	$108.93	$530.85
StudentFirst	StudentLast	$140,693.00	1490	10069	No	$94.42	$537.35
Makarem	Abdeljawad	$140,904.00	1301	10061	No	$108.30	$538.16
Makarem	Abdeljawad	$142,380.00	1373	11028	No	$103.70	$543.80
Chardae	Myles	$163,737.00	1476	10910	No	$110.93	$625.36
Jaynish	Mody	$164,436.00	1850	10117	No	$88.88	$628.03
Jaynish	Mody	$166,320.00	1437	10082	No	$115.74	$635.23
Chardae	Myles	$166,552.00	1623	10851	No	$102.62	$636.12
Chardae	Myles	$166,800.00	1598	10014	No	$104.38	$637.06
Philip	DeFranco	$168,000.00	1680	10002	No	$100.00	$641.65
Chardae	Myles	$168,354.00	1651	10885	No	$101.97	$643.00
Philip	DeFranco	$174,230.00	1771	10104	No	$98.38	$665.44
StudentFirst	StudentLast	$174,720.00	1610	10921	No	$108.52	$667.31
Meera	Shah	$174,720.00	1694	11035	No	$103.14	$667.31
Chardae	Myles	$175,336.00	1855	10868	No	$94.52	$669.66
StudentFirst	StudentLast	$175,560.00	1562	11036	No	$112.39	$670.52
Meera	Shah	$176,176.00	1761	10025	No	$100.04	$672.87
Jaynish	Mody	$177,984.00	1707	10066	No	$104.27	$679.78
Chardae	Myles	$179,088.00	1837	10010	No	$97.49	$683.99
Chardae	Myles	$179,100.00	1946	11079	No	$92.03	$684.04
Chardae	Myles	$179,712.00	1854	10102	No	$96.93	$686.38
Chardae	Myles	$180,180.00	1896	10019	No	$95.03	$688.17
Makarem	Abdeljawad	$180,810.00	1667	10044	No	$108.46	$690.57
Total		**$167,100.47**		**32**		**$102.10**	

Record: ◄ ◄ 1 of 32 ► ►I ►* ▼ No Filter Search

Step f: Average Price Per Sq Ft

Step f: Count of Listing

Step e: Average List Price

Access 2016, Windows 10, Microsoft Corporation

FIGURE 3.34 Totals Added to Datasheet View

a. Open *a03h2Property_LastFirst* if you closed it at the end of Hands-On Exercise 2 and save it as **a03h3Property_LastFirst**, changing h2 to h3.

b. Open the **Mortgage Payments query** in Design view. Drag the **Listing field** from the Properties table to the fifth column.

The Listing field is now in the fifth column, between the SqFeet and Sold fields. The other columns shift to the right.

> **TROUBLESHOOTING:** If you drag the Listing field to the wrong position, you can drag it again to the correct location.

c. Switch to Datasheet view. Click **Totals** in the Records group on the Home tab.

d. Click the **cell** that intersects the Total row and the List Price column.

e. Click the **arrow** and select **Average** to display the average value of all the properties that have not sold. Adjust column widths as necessary to ensure that all values are displayed.

The average list price of all properties is $167,100.47.

f. Click the **arrow** in the Total row in the Listing column and select **Count** from the list.

The count of properties in this datasheet is 32.

g. Click the **arrow** in the Total row in the Price Per Sq Ft column and select **Average** from the list.

The average price per square foot is $102.10.

h. Compare your results to Figure 3.34. Save and close the query.

STEP 2 ›› CREATE A TOTALS QUERY AND ADD GROUPING AND CONDITIONS

You create a totals query to help Don and Matt evaluate the properties in groups. Refer to Figure 3.35 and Figure 3.36 as you complete Step 2.

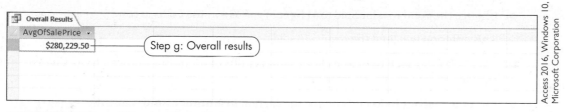

FIGURE 3.35 Overall Results Query Output

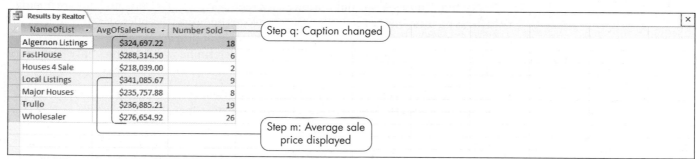

FIGURE 3.36 Results by Realtor Query Output

a. Click **Query Design** in the Queries group of the Create tab.

You create a new query in Query Design; the Show Table dialog box opens.

b. Click the **Properties table** in the Show Table dialog box and click **Add**. Close the Show Table dialog box.

c. Double-click the **SalePrice** and **Sold** fields to add them to the query.

d. Click **Totals** in the Show/Hide group of the Design tab to show the Total row.

A new row labeled Totals displays in the query design grid, between the Table and Sort rows. Each field has Group By listed in the new row by default.

e. Click the **Group By arrow** in the SalePrice column Total row and select **Avg**.

f. Click the **Group By arrow** in the Sold column Total row and select **Where**. Type **Yes** in the Criteria row.

This criterion will limit the results to sold houses only.

g. Click the **SalePrice field** and click **Property Sheet** in the Show/Hide group. Change the SalePrice format to **Currency**. Close the Property Sheet. Run the query and adjust the column width if necessary. Compare your results to Figure 3.35.

The results show an overall average of $280,229.50 for the sold properties in the database.

h. Click **Save** on the Quick Access Toolbar and type **Overall Results** in the Save As dialog box. Click **OK**. Close the query.

i. Click **Query Design** in the Query group of the Create tab to create a new query.

j. Add the Properties table and the Lists table from the Show Table dialog box. Close the Show Table dialog box.

k. Add the NameOfList field from the Lists table and the SalePrice, Listing, and Sold fields from the Properties table to the query.

l. Click **Totals** in the Show/Hide group to show the Total row.

A new row labeled Total appears between the Table and Sort rows.

m. Change the Total row for SalePrice to **Avg**.

n. Change the Total row for Listing to **Count**.

o. Change the Total row for Sold to **Where**. Type **Yes** in the Criteria row.

This criterion will limit the results to sold houses only.

p. Click the **SalePrice field** and click **Property Sheet** in the Show/Hide group. Change the SalePrice format to **Currency**.

q. Click the **Listing field** and change the caption to **Number Sold**. Close the Property Sheet. Run the query and widen the columns as shown in Figure 3.36.

Notice that Houses 4 Sale has the lowest average sale price. As Don and Matt are hoping to focus on inexpensive properties, they can focus on properties offered by this source. Notice also that the query results show the number of properties sold in each source, in addition to the average sale price. This will help determine which sources have been more effective.

r. Click **Save** on the Quick Access Toolbar and type **Results By Realtor** in the Save As dialog box. Click **OK**. Keep the query open for the next step.

The previous query shows the average value of the properties by realtor. However, Don and Matt learned at the seminar they attended that the longer a property has been on the market, the better your chances of negotiating a better price. You will revise the query to show, on average, how long each realtor takes to sell a house. Refer to Figure 3.37 as you complete Step 3.

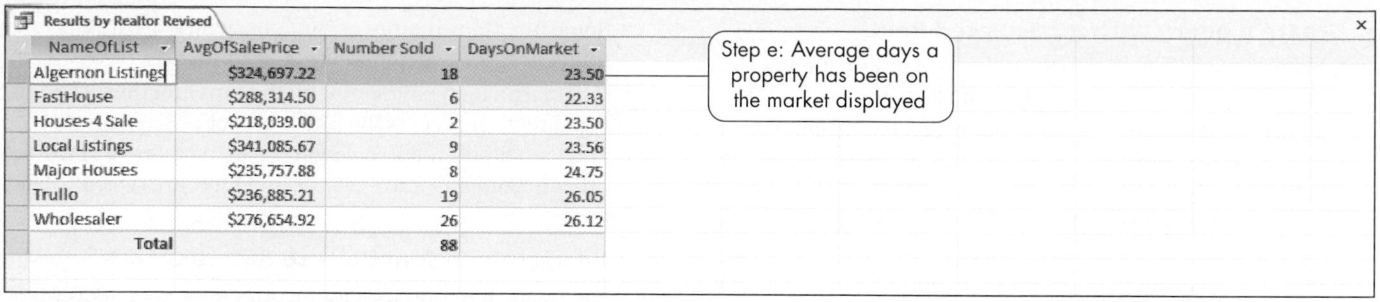

NameOfList	AvgOfSalePrice	Number Sold	DaysOnMarket
Algernon Listings	$324,697.22	18	23.50
FastHouse	$288,314.50	6	22.33
Houses 4 Sale	$218,039.00	2	23.50
Local Listings	$341,085.67	9	23.56
Major Houses	$235,757.88	8	24.75
Trullo	$236,885.21	19	26.05
Wholesaler	$276,654.92	26	26.12
Total		88	

Step e: Average days a property has been on the market displayed

FIGURE 3.37 Results by Realtor Revised Query Output

Access 2016, Windows 10, Microsoft Corporation

a. Click the **File tab**, select **Save As**, and click **Save Object As**. Click **Save As** and type **Results By Realtor Revised**. Click **OK**.

b. Click **Totals** in the Records group of the Home tab. Click in the Total row for the **NumberSold** column, click the arrow and select **Sum**.

The total number of houses sold (88) now displays at the bottom of the Number Sold column.

c. Switch to Design view. In the field row of the first blank column, type **DaysOnMarket: [DateSold]-[DateListed]** to create a new calculated field. Change the Total row from Group By to **Avg**.

The DaysOnMarket field will show the average number of days on the market for each sold listing.

d. Display the Property Sheet for the DaysOnMarket field and change the Format property to **Fixed**. Close the Property Sheet.

e. Run the query and examine the DaysOnMarket field. Adjust column widths as necessary. Compare your results to Figure 3.37.

Houses 4 Sale listings have an average of 23.50 days on the market. Since this is in-line with their competitors, it lets you know they are neither fast nor slow with sales.

f. Save and close the query.

g. Close the database and exit Access. Based on your instructor's directions, submit the following files:

a03h1PropertyCheck_LastFirst
a03h3Property_LastFirst

Chapter Objectives Review

After reading this chapter, you have accomplished the following objectives:

1. Create a query with a calculated field.

- Expressions can contain a combination of arithmetic operators, constants, functions, and identifiers.
- Understand the order of operations: Calculated fields follow the same order of operations as mathematical equations—parentheses, then exponentiation, then multiplication and division, and finally addition and subtraction.
- Build expressions: Expressions must be written in a certain way. Rules govern the way you give instructions to Access.

2. Format calculated results.

- Calculated results may not have the format you want; change the properties of a calculated field using the Property Sheet.

3. Recover from common errors.

- Common errors include forgetting the colon in the appropriate location, spelling errors, and misuse of the order of operations.

4. Verify calculated results.

- Always check the results of your equation; Access will check for errors in the way something is written, but not logic errors.

5. Create expressions using the Expression Builder.

- The Expression Builder will help you create complex expressions by enabling you to choose fields and built-in functions easily.
- Click the Builder icon to open the tool.

6. Use built-in functions.

- Access includes 150 built-in functions, or predefined computations that perform complex calculations.

- Some functions require arguments, which are inputs (often fields or constants) given to a function.
- Calculate a loan payment with the Pmt function: The Pmt function accepts the rate, number of payments, and loan amount and calculates a loan payment. Two other arguments, future value and type, are typically left as zero.

7. Add aggregate functions to datasheets.

- Aggregate functions, including functions such as Sum, Avg, and Count, perform calculations on an entire column of data and return a single value.
- The total row displays at the bottom of a query or table; it can perform any aggregate function on each column.

8. Create queries with aggregate functions.

- Create a totals query: Create a query as usual and click the Totals button in Design view.
- Add grouping to a totals query: Grouping enables you to summarize your data by the values of a field. For example, instead of showing overall averages, add County as a grouping field and see averages for each county.
- Add conditions to a totals query: Similar to other queries, conditions can be added to totals queries, such as only showing listings with the Sold field equal to No.
- Add a calculated field to a totals query: You can apply an aggregate function to the results of a calculation; for example, subtract one date from another, and calculate the overall average of the difference between those dates.

Key Terms Matching

Match the key terms with their definitions. Write the key term letter by the appropriate numbered definition.

a. Aggregate function
b. Argument
c. Calculated field
d. Constant
e. Expression
f. Expression Builder
g. Function

h. Grouping
i. Order of operations
j. Pmt function
k. Property Sheet
l. Total row
m. Totals query

1. _____ A combination of elements that produce a value. **p. 218**

2. _____ A field that displays the result of an expression rather than data stored in a field. **p. 218**

3. _____ A predefined computation that performs a complex calculation. **p. 234**

4. _____ A value that does not change. **p. 218**

5. _____ A method of summarizing data by the values of a field. **p. 246**

6. _____ An Access tool that helps you create more complicated expressions. **p. 232**

7. _____ Calculates the loan payment given the rate, number of periods (also known as term), and the present value of the loan (the principal). **p. 236**

8. _____ A way to display aggregate data when a query is run. **p. 243**

9. _____ The sequence by which operations are performed in a mathematical expression. **p. 218**

10. _____ A method to display aggregate function results as the last row in Datasheet view of a table or query. **p. 244**

11. _____ The location where you change settings such as number format and number of decimal places. **p. 222**

12. _____ The input used to produce output for a function. **p. 234**

13. _____ A calculation performed on an entire column of data that returns a single value. Includes functions such as Sum, Avg, and Count. **p. 243**

Multiple Choice

1. Which of the following *cannot* be used in a calculated field?

 (a) The number 12
 (b) An asterisk (*)
 (c) [HoursWorked] (a field in the current database)
 (d) All of these can be used in a calculated field

2. When creating a calculation, which of the following would be identified as an error by Access?

 (a) A field name spelled wrong in a calculation.
 (b) An incorrect formula (for example, adding two numbers instead of subtracting).
 (c) An order of operations error (for example, [HourlyPay] + 2 * [HoursWorked]).
 (d) A missing colon in the expression (for example: TotalHours [OTHours]+[RegHours]).

3. What is the result of the following expression?
2 * 5 + 8 - 6 / 2

 (a) 6
 (b) 15
 (c) 20
 (d) 23

4. Which of the following *cannot* be adjusted in the Property Sheet?

 (a) Caption
 (b) Mathematical expression
 (c) Number format (for example, displaying numbers as Currency)
 (d) Number of decimal places

5. Which of the following could *not* be done using an aggregate function?

 (a) Averaging a series of numbers
 (b) Calculating the payment amount of a loan
 (c) Counting the number of values that exist
 (d) Finding the smallest value

6. Which of the following can be added to a totals query?

 (a) Conditions
 (b) Grouping fields
 (c) Aggregate functions
 (d) All of the above can be added to a totals query.

7. Which statement about a totals query is true?

 (a) A totals query is created in Datasheet view.
 (b) A totals query may contain several grouping fields but only one aggregate field.
 (c) A totals query is limited to only two fields, one grouping field and one aggregate field.
 (d) A totals query may contain several grouping fields and several aggregate fields.

8. Which of the following statements is true?

 (a) A total order cost is an example of a common field to group by.
 (b) A last name is an example of a common field to group by.
 (c) For best results, add as many "group by" fields as possible.
 (d) None of the above statements is true.

9. If you want to calculate aggregate statistics about graduation rates for students in a college database, which of the following would provide the *least* useful information if you were to group by it?

 (a) Gender
 (b) High School
 (c) Race
 (d) Social Security Number

10. Which of the following about the Total row in Query design is *false*?

 (a) The Total row enables you to apply aggregate functions to the fields.
 (b) The Total row is hidden by default in all new queries.
 (c) The Total row is located between the Table and Sort rows.
 (d) The Total row applies only to non-numeric fields.

Practice Exercises

1 Conforto Insurance

The Conforto Insurance Agency is a mid-sized company with offices located across the country. Each employee receives an annual performance review. The review determines employee eligibility for salary increases and the annual performance bonus. The employee data is stored in an Access database, which is used to monitor and maintain employee records. Your task is to calculate the salary increase for each employee; you will also calculate the average salary for each position. Refer to Figure 3.38 as you complete this exercise.

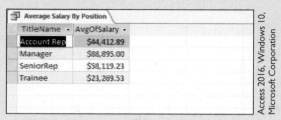

FIGURE 3.38 Average Salary by Position Results

a. Open *a03p1Insurance*. Save the database as **a03p1Insurance_LastFirst**.

b. Click the **Create tab** and click **Query Design** in the Queries group to create a new query. Select the **Employees table** and click **Add**. Select the **Titles table** and click **Add**. Click **Close** to close the Show Table dialog box.

c. Double-click the **LastName**, **FirstName**, **Performance**, and **Salary** fields from the Employees table to add them to the query. Double-click the **Increase** field from the Titles table to add it to the query.

d. Click the Field row of the first blank column in the query design grid and type
   NewSalary: [Salary]+[Salary]*[Increase] to create a calculated field that adds the existing salary to the increase.

e. Click **Run** in the Results group to run the query.

f. Switch to Design view. Ensure the NewSalary calculated field is selected. Click **Property Sheet** in the Show/Hide group to display the Property Sheet. Click the **Format property** in the Property Sheet. Click the **Format property arrow** and select **Currency**. Type **New Salary** in the Caption box.

g. Click **Run** in the Results group to view the results. Adjust column widths as necessary. Save the query as **Updated Salaries**. Close the query.

h. Click the **Create tab** and click **Query Design** in the Queries group to create a new query. Select the **Employees table** and click **Add**. Select the **Titles table** and click **Add**. Click **Close** to close the Show Table dialog box.

i. Double-click the **TitleName field** from the Titles table. Double-click the **Salary field** from the Employees table.

j. Click **Totals** in the Show/Hide group to display the Total row. Change the Total row for Salary to **Avg**. Leave the TitleName field set to Group By.

k. Click the **Salary field**. Click the **Format property** in the Property Sheet. Click the **Format property arrow** and select **Currency**.

l. Click **Run** in the Results group to view the results. Adjust column widths as necessary. Save the query as **Average Salary By Position** and compare your results to Figure 3.38. Close the query.

m. Close the database and exit Access. Based on your instructor's directions, submit a03p1Insurance_LastFirst.

2 South Bend Yachts

South Bend Luxury Motor Yachts, a local boat seller, hired a new Chief Financial Officer (CFO). The new CFO, Rosta Marinova, asked the financing department to provide her with some summaries. She would like to determine how much financing the company is currently offering, offer financing with interest to customers, and see aggregate purchase statistics for local cities. Refer to Figure 3.39 as you complete this exercise.

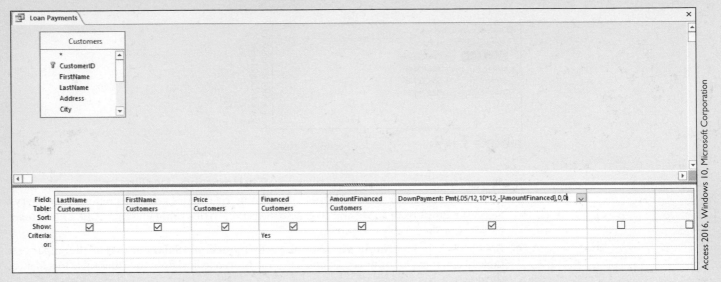

FIGURE 3.39 Loan Payments Design

a. Open *a03p2Boats* and save the database as **a03p2Boats_LastFirst**.

b. Click the **Create tab** and click **Query Design** in the Queries group to create a new query. Select the **Customers table** and click **Add**. Click **Close** to close the Show Table dialog box.

c. Double-click the **LastName**, **FirstName**, **Price**, **Financed**, and **AmountFinanced** fields.

d. Click the **Field row** of the first blank column and type **DownPayment: [Price]-[AmountFinanced]**.

e. Click **Run** in the Results group to run the query. Examine the results. Adjust column widths as necessary.

f. Click **Save** on the Quick Access Toolbar and type **Down Payment Amounts** as the Query Name in the Save As dialog box. Click **OK**.

g. Switch to Design view. Click the **Criteria row** for the Financed field and type **Yes**.

This will limit the results to financed boats. Boats that were not financed were paid for in full when purchased.

h. Click the **checkbox** on the Show row of the Financed field so it does not display when the query is run.

i. Sort the query by DownPayment in descending order by clicking the **Sort row** for the DownPayment field and selecting **Descending**.

j. Click **Property Sheet** in the Show/Hide group. In the Caption box, type **Down Payment**.

k. Click **Run** in the Results group to view the results. Adjust column widths as necessary. Notice that the column heading for the DownPayment field appears with a space in the name.

l. Save and close the query.

m. Click the **Create tab** and click **Query Design** in the Queries group to create a new query. Select the **Customers table** and click **Add**. Click **Close** to close the Show Table dialog box.

n. Double-click the fields **LastName**, **FirstName**, **Price**, **Financed**, and **AmountFinanced** to add them to the query.

o. Click the Field row of the first blank column. Click **Builder** in the Query Setup group to open the Expression Builder. Double-click **Functions**, and select **Built-In Functions**. Select **Financial**, and double-click **Pmt** in the Expression Values box.

p. Position the insertion point before the Pmt function. Type **DownPayment:** to the left of the function (including the colon).

q. Click each argument to select it, and substitute the appropriate information below. Once you have entered the information, click **OK**.

- **.05/12** for rate (5% interest, paid monthly).
- **10*12** for num_periods (10 year loan, 12 payments per year).
- Use **[AmountFinanced]** for the present_value.
- Use **0** in place of future_value and type.

r. Click **Property Sheet** in the Show/Hide group. In the Caption box, type **Monthly Payment**. Select **Currency** as the format.

s. Click the **Criteria row** for the Financed field and type **Yes**.

t. Click **Run** in the Results group to examine the results.

u. Click **Totals** in the Show/Hide group on the Design tab. Click Group By in the Monthly Payment column, click the drop-down menu, and select **Avg**.

v. Switch to Design view. Add a **minus sign** in front of [AmountFinanced] in the DownPayment calculation to display the results as positive numbers. Compare your design to Figure 3.39.

w. Click **Run** in the Results group to examine the results. Adjust column widths as necessary. Save the query as **Loan Payments** and close the query.

x. Close the database and exit Access. Based on your instructor's directions, submit a03p2Boats_LastFirst.

1 Small Business Loans

ANALYSIS CASE

FROM SCRATCH

You are the manager of a regional business loan department for the U.S. Small Business Administration office. You have decided to evaluate whether Access could be used in place of the Excel worksheet you are currently using. You will create a blank desktop database, add a table, add some sample customers, and import some recent data from an Excel spreadsheet. You will calculate the payments for the loans that are currently on the books by creating a query using the Pmt function. You will also summarize loans by the type of loan (M = Mortgage, C = Car, and O = Other).

a. Open Access and create a new blank desktop database named **a03m1Loans_LastFirst**.

b. Switch to Design view. Type **Customers** in the **Save As dialog box** and click **OK**.

c. Change the first Field Name to **CustomerID** and accept AutoNumber as the Data Type. Type **Company** in the second row and press **Tab**. Accept Short Text as the Data Type. Type **FirstName** in the third row and press **Tab**. Accept Short Text as the Data Type.

d. Type the remainder of the fields, selecting Short Text for the data type:

LastName	Short Text
City	Short Text
State	Short Text
Zip	Short Text

e. Verify that the first field is set as the primary key.

f. Switch to Datasheet view. Click **Yes** to save the table. Add the records as shown in the following table. Note that Access will assign an ID. Once you have typed the records, close the Customers table.

Company	FirstName	LastName	City	State	Zip
Jones and Co	Robert	Paterson	Greensboro	NC	27401
Elements, Inc.	Merve	Kana	Paterson	NJ	07505
Godshall Meats, LLC	Francisco	De La Cruz	Beverly Hills	CA	90210

DISCOVER

g. Click the **External Data tab** and click **Excel** in the Import & Link group. Click **Browse** to locate the *a03m1Loans* spreadsheet. Select the workbook and click **Open** at the bottom of the dialog box.

h. Ensure that *Import the source data into a new table in the current database.* is selected and click **OK**. Click **Next** three times, accepting the defaults, until you are asked to add a primary key. Click the *Choose my own Primary Key* option, and ensure **LoanID** is selected. Click **Next** once more and click **Finish**, accepting Loans as the table name. Click **Close** in the Get External Data dialog box.

i. Open the Loans table in Design view. Select the **InterestRate field** and change the format to **Percent**. Change the field size for the CustomerID field to **Long Integer**. Save and close the table, selecting **Yes** when prompted that some data may be lost.

j. Click the **Database Tools tab** and click **Relationships** in the Relationships group. Add both tables to the Relationships window and close the Show Table dialog box.

k. Drag the **CustomerID field** from the Customers table and drop it onto the **CustomerID field** in the Loans table. Check the **Enforce Referential Integrity** checkbox in the Edit Relationships dialog box and click **Create**. Save and close the Relationships window.

l. Create a query in Design view using the two tables. Add the **Company** field from the Customers table and the **LoanID, Amount, InterestRate, Term,** and **LoanClass fields** from the Loans table. Sort the query by LoanID in ascending order. Save the query as **Loan Payments**.

 m. Add a calculated field named **Payment** in the first blank column to calculate the loan payment for each loan, using the Expression Builder. Use the Pmt function. Insert the appropriate field names in place of the placeholder arguments. Assume that the loans have monthly payments (12 payments per year). Ensure that the payment displays as a positive number. Run the query. The first loan should have a value of 243.154499654298 (the extra decimal places will be removed shortly).

n. Switch to Design view and change the format for the Payment field to **Currency**. Run the query again to verify your change.

o. Click **Totals** in the Records group on the Home tab. Change the value for the Total row for the Amount column to **Sum** and the values for the InterestRate and Term to **Average**. Adjust column widths as necessary. Save and close the query.

p. Create a copy of Loan Payments. Save the new query as **Loan Payments Summary**.

q. Open the Loan Payments Summary query in Design view and rearrange the columns as follows: LoanClass, LoanID, Amount, and InterestRate. Delete columns Company, Term, and Payment. Click **Totals** in the Show/Hide group. Change the Total row for LoanID field to **Count**, for the Amount field to **Sum**, and for the InterestRate field to Avg. Run the query.

r. Switch to Design view and display the Property Sheet. For the LoanID field, change the caption to **Loans**. For the Amount field, change the caption to **Total Amount** and change the format to **Currency**. For the InterestRate field, change the caption to **Avg Interest Rate** and change the format to **Percent**. Run the query. Adjust column widths as necessary. Save and close the query.

s. Close the database and exit Access. Based on your instructor's directions, submit a03m1Loans_LastFirst.

2 Investment Properties

You are in charge of Dysan Investment's database, which contains all of the information on the properties your firm has listed and sold. Your task is to determine the length of time each property was on the market before it sold. You also have been tasked with calculating the sales commission from each property sold. Two agents will receive commission on each transaction: the listing agent and the selling agent. You also will summarize the sales data by employee and calculate the average number of days each employee's sales were on the market prior to selling and the total commission earned by the employees.

a. Open *a03m2Homes*. Save the database as **a03m2Homes_LastFirst**.

b. Create a new query, add the Agents, Properties, and SubDivision tables, and then add the following fields: from the Agents table, add the LastName field; from the Properties table, the DateListed, DateSold, SalePrice, SellingAgent, and ListingAgent fields; and from the SubDivision table, the Subdivision field.

DISCOVER

c. Add criteria to the table to ensure that the DateSold field is not empty (in other words, properties that have not been sold). You will need to use a condition involving Null to accomplish this. Format the SalePrice field as **Currency**. Save the query as **Sales Report**.

d. Create a calculated field using the Expression Builder named **DaysOnMarket** by subtracting DateListed from DateSold. This will calculate the number of days each sold property was on the market when it sold. Add a caption of **Days on Market**.

e. Calculate the commissions for the selling and listing agents using two calculated fields. The listing commission rate is 3.5% of the sale price, and the selling commission rate is 2.5% of the sale price. You can type these in directly or use the Expression Builder. Name the newly created fields **ListComm** and **SellComm**. Add captions of **Listing Commission** and **Selling Commission** and format the fields as **Currency**.

f. Run the query. Adjust column widths as necessary. Display the Total row. Calculate the average number of days on the market and the sum for the SalePrice and the two commission fields. Adjust column widths so all values are visible, and save and close the query.

g. Create a copy of the Sales Report query named **Sales Summary by Last Name**. Remove the DateListed, SellingAgent, ListingAgent, and Subdivision fields.

h. Display the Total row. Group by LastName and change the DateSold field Total row to **Where**, so the condition carries over. Show the sum of SalePrice, the average of DaysOnMarket, and the sum for both ListComm and SellComm. Change the caption for the SalePrice field to **Total Sales** and format the DaysOnMarket field as **Fixed**. Run the query. Adjust column widths as necessary.

i. Adjust the Total row in Datasheet view so it shows the sum of TotalSales. Adjust column widths as necessary. Save and close the query.

DISCOVER 🔍 **j.** Create a copy of the Sales Summary by Last Name query named **Sales Summary by Subdivision** and open the query in Design view. Remove the LastName field. Add the Subdivision field to the query and ensure the Total row is set to Group By. Sort the query results on the DaysOnMarket field in Ascending order. Limit the results to only return the top five values (hint: look in the Query Setup group of the Design tab).

k. Run the query and ensure only the top 5 values display. Save and close the query.

l. Close the database and exit Access. Based on your instructor's directions, submit a03m2Homes_LastFirst.

3 New Castle County Technical Services

RUNNING CASE

New Castle County Technical Services (NCCTS) provides technical support for a number of local companies. Part of their customer service evaluation involves logging how calls are closed and a quick, one-question survey given to customers at the end of a call, asking them to rate their experience from 1 (poor) to 5 (excellent). To evaluate the effectiveness of their operation, they asked you to create some queries to help evaluate the performance of the company.

a. Open the database you finished last chapter *a02m3NCCTS_LastFirst* and save the database as **a03m3NCCTS_LastFirst**.

> **TROUBLESHOOTING:** If you did not complete the Chapter 2 case, return to Chapter 2, complete the case to create the database, and then return to this exercise.

b. Create a new query in Design view. Select the rep first and last names from the Reps table, and the CallID and CustomerSatisfaction fields from the Calls table.

c. Group by the RepFirst and RepLast fields. Display the count of the CallID field and average for the CustomerSatisfaction field.

d. Change the caption for the CallID field to **Num Calls**.

e. Format the CustomerSatisfaction average in Standard format and change the caption to **Avg Rating**.

f. Add a new calculated field named **AvgResponse**. Subtract the OpenedDate from the ClosedDate. Format the field as **Fixed**. Display the average for this field.

g. Run the query. Adjust column widths to ensure all data is displayed. Save the query as **Tech Ratings** and close the query.

h. Create a new query in Design view. Select the Description field from the Call Types table, and the CallID and CustomerSatisfaction field from the Calls table.

i. Group by the Description field. Display the count of the CallID field and average for the CustomerSatisfaction field.

j. Change the caption for the CallID field to **Num Calls**.

k. Format the CustomerSatisfaction average in Standard format and change the caption to **Avg Rating**.

l. Run the query. Adjust column widths as necessary. Save the query as **Call Type Effectiveness** and close the query.

m. Create a new query in Design view. Select the CompanyName field from the Customers table, and the CallID and CustomerSatisfaction field from the Calls table.

n. Group by the CompanyName field. Display the count of the CallID field and average for the CustomerSatisfaction field.

o. Format the CustomerSatisfaction average in Standard format and change the caption to **Avg Rating**.

p. Change the caption for the CallID field to **Num Calls**.

q. Run the query. Display the Total row. Show the sum of the Num Calls column. Adjust column widths as necessary.

r. Save the query as **Customer Happiness** and close the query.

s. Close the database and exit Access. Based on your instructor's directions, submit a03m3NCCTS_LastFirst.

Beyond the Classroom

Denton Credit Union

GENERAL CASE

Open *a03b1Denton*, which contains data from a local credit union. Save the database as **a03b1Denton_LastFirst**. Replace Your Name in the Branch table with your first and last name.

Create a query to calculate how long each manager has worked for the credit union: Display the manager and start date, and create a calculated field named **YearsWithCompany** to determine the number of years each manager has been in his or her position. Hint: Find a built-in Date/Time function to use the current date, subtract the start date, and divide the result by 365.25 (Note: the .25 at the end accounts for leap years). Display the calculated field in Fixed format, and add a caption to the field to display Years With Company as the column heading. Adjust column widths in Datasheet view as necessary. Save the query as Longevity.

Create a totals query to summarize each customer's account balances. List the customer's last name and first name from the Customer table, and the sum of all account balances (found in the Account table), grouping by both the last and first name. Format the total of the balances as Currency and add a caption of **Total Balance**. Display the sum of the total balances in Datasheet view ($141,074), adjust column widths as necessary, and save the query as **Customer Balances**.

Create a totals query to show each city (found in the Customer table) and total account balances for each city. For example, the total amount for customers in Denton is $61,510. Format the sum of the Balance field as currency with a caption of **Total Balance**. Adjust column widths as necessary in Datasheet view. Save the query as **Balances by City**.

Close the database and exit Access. Based on your instructor's directions, submit a03b1Denton_LastFirst.

Too Many Digits

DISASTER RECOVERY

This chapter introduced you to calculated fields. Open the database *a03b2Interest* and save the database as **a03b2Interest_LastFirst**. Open the Monthly Interest Payments query in Datasheet view. Notice the multiple digits to the right of the decimal in the MonthlyInterest column; there should only be two digits. Search the Internet or Access Help to find a function that will resolve this rounding problem. You only want to display two digits to the right of the decimal. Display the Total row in Datasheet view and display the total of the MonthlyInterest field. Adjust column widths as necessary. Save and close the query. Close the database and exit Access. Based on your instructor's directions, submit a03b2Interest_LastFirst.

Capstone Exercise

Northwind Traders, an international gourmet food distributor, hired a new CEO. She asked for your assistance in providing summaries of data that took place before she started with the company. To help her with her strategic planning, you will create queries to perform data analysis. Based on your meeting, you plan on creating four queries. One query will find orders with major delays. Another query will summarize the cost impact of customer discounts. A third query will be used to help evaluate financing. The final query will calculate the total sales by country.

Database File Setup

You will open the Northwind Traders food database, use Save As to make a copy of the database, and then use the new database to complete this capstone exercise. You will add yourself to the employee database.

a. Locate and open *a03c1Food* and save the database as **a03c1Food_LastFirst**.

b. Open the Employees table. Add yourself as an employee. Fill in all information, with the hire date as the current date. Set your Title to **Technical Aide**, extension to **1144**, and the Reports To field to **Buchanan, Steven**. Leave the Photo and Notes fields blank.

c. Close the Employees table.

Shipping Efficiency Query

You will create a query to calculate the number of days between the date an order was placed and the date the order was shipped for each order. The result of your work will be a list of orders that took more than 30 days to ship. The salespeople will be required to review the records and report the source of the delay for each order. The CEO feels there may be issues with one of the shipping companies, and would like data to back that up.

a. Create a query using Query Design. From the Customers table, include the fields CompanyName, ContactName, ContactTitle, and Phone. From the Orders table, include the fields OrderID, OrderDate, and ShippedDate.

b. Run the query and examine the records. Save the query as **Shipping Efficiency**.

c. Add a calculated field named **DaysToShip** to calculate the number of days taken to fill each order. (Hint: The expression will include the OrderDate and the ShippedDate; the results will not contain negative numbers.)

d. Run the query and examine the results. Does the data in the DaysToShip field look accurate? Save the query.

e. Add criteria to limit the query results to include only orders that took more than 30 days to ship.

f. Add the Quantity field from the Order Details table and the ProductName field from the Products table to the query. Sort the query by ascending OrderID. When the sales reps contact these customers, these two fields will provide useful information about the orders.

g. Add the caption **Days to Ship** to the DaysToShip field. Switch to Datasheet view to view the results. Adjust column widths as necessary.

h. Save and close the query.

Order Summary Query

The CEO is considering the financial impact of discounts. She asked for a query showing the employee name, number of orders they have taken, and the total discount amount they have given customers. She hopes to see if there is a correlation between the discount offered and the number of sales.

a. Create a query using Query Design and add the Orders, Order Details, Products, and Customers tables. Add the fields OrderID and OrderDate from the Orders table. Set both fields' Total row to **Group By**.

b. Add a calculated field in the third column. Name the field **ExtendedAmount**. This field should multiply the quantity ordered (from the Order Details table) by the unit price for that item (from the Products table). This will calculate the total amount for each order. Format the calculated field as **Currency** and change the caption to **Total Dollars**. Change the Total row to **Sum**.

c. Add a calculated field in the fourth column. Name the field **DiscountAmount**. The field should multiply the quantity ordered, the unit price for that item, and the discount field (from the Customers table). This will calculate the total discount for each order. Format the calculated field as **Currency** and add a caption of **Discount Amt**. Change the Total row to **Sum**.

d. Run the query. Examine the results. Most customers should have a discount of 10% of the total dollars, but some customers will have no discount. Save the query as **Order Summary**. Return to Design view.

e. Add criteria to the OrderDate field so only orders made between 1/1/2016 and 12/31/2016 are displayed. Change the Total row to **Where**. This expression will display only orders that were placed in 2016.

f. Run the query and view the results. Adjust column widths as necessary. Save and close the query.

Order Financing Query

The CEO would like the salespeople to discuss financing with customers. In order to do so, she would like you to create a query showing the impact on price for prior orders. This way, the reps can give customers a comparison with an order they have already placed. For the moment, she is considering a 5% interest rate, paid over 12 months. She would like you to leave the results as negative numbers.

a. Create a copy of the Order Summary query named **Order Financing**.

b. Open the Order Financing query in Design view and remove the DiscountAmount field.

c. Add a new field using the Expression Builder named **SamplePayment**. Insert the Pmt function with the following parameters:
   - Use **.05/12** for the rate argument (5% interest, paid monthly).
   - Use the number **12** for the num_periods argument (12 months).
   - Use the calculated field **[ExtendedAmount]** for the present_value.
   - Use the value **0** for both future_value and type.

d. Change the Total row to **Expression** for the SamplePayment field.

e. Change the Format for the SamplePayment field to **Currency**.

f. Run the query and examine the results. Adjust column widths as necessary. The results appear as negative numbers, as requested. Save and close the query.

Order Summary by Country Query

The company is planning on opening up some shipping centers internationally. The previous CEO had been considering Brazil, Denmark, and Germany as potential shipping center locations, but he was working from older data. You will provide a list of total shipment value by country for the year before the current CEO started to best inform her decision making.

a. Create a copy of the Order Summary query named **Order Summary by Country**.

b. Open the query in Design view. Replace the OrderID field with the Country field from the Customers table.

c. Run the query and examine the summary records; there should be 21 countries listed.

d. Switch to Design view and change the sort order so that the country with the highest ExtendedAmount is first and the country with the lowest ExtendedAmount is last.

e. Run the query and verify the results. Note the ExtendedAmount field has a caption of Total Dollars, so this is the field the query will be sorted by.

f. Save and close the query.

g. Close the database and exit Access. Based on your instructor's directions, submit a03c1Food_LastFirst.

Creating and Using Professional Forms and Reports

LEARNING OUTCOMES
- You will develop and modify forms to input and manage data.
- You will create and modify reports to display and present information.

OBJECTIVES & SKILLS: After you read this chapter, you will be able to:

CASE STUDY | Coffee Shop Starts New Business

Coffee shop owner Ryung Park decided to use her knowledge of the coffee and retail industry to sell her specialty products to businesses around the country. She created an Access database to help track her customer, product, and order information.

Ryung created a database with tables to store data for customers, products, sales reps, and orders. She is currently using these tables to enter data and retrieve information. Ryung realizes that forms have an advantage over tables because they can be designed to display one record at a time—this can reduce potential data-entry errors. Ryung would like to create several reports so she can stay on top of her business by reviewing them each week. You have been hired to help Ryung create the new forms and reports that she needs.

Moving Beyond Tables and Queries

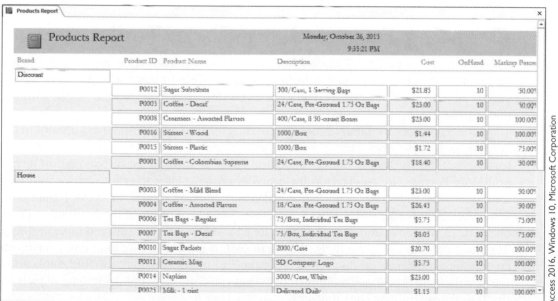

FIGURE 4.1 Coffee Shop Starts New Business Database

CASE STUDY | Coffee Shop Starts New Business

Starting File	Files to be Submitted
a04h1Coffee	a04h2Coffee_LastFirst
	a04h2Products_LastFirst

Form Basics

Most Access database applications use forms rather than tables for data entry and for finding information. A *form* is a database object used to add data to or edit data in a table. Three main reasons exist for using forms rather than tables for adding, updating, and deleting data:

- You are less likely to edit the wrong record by mistake.
- You can create a form that shows data from more than one table simultaneously.
- You can create Access forms to resemble the paper (or other types of) forms that users employ in their data entry processes.

When you are adding or editing data using a table with many records, you may navigate to the wrong record accidentally. A form is less likely to allow this type of error because most forms restrict entry to one record at a time.

Many forms require two tables as their record sources. For example, you may want to view a customer's details (name, address, email, phone, etc.) as well as all of the orders he or she has placed at the same time. This would require using data from both the Customers and the Orders tables in one form. Such a form enables a user to view two record sources at the same time and make changes—additions, edits, or deletions—to one or both sources of data. When a change is made in the form, the data in the underlying table (or tables) are affected. A form is really a mirror image of the data in the tables and simply presents a user-friendly interface for users of the database.

Access forms can be designed to emulate the paper documents already used by an organization. When paper forms are currently used to collect data, it is a good idea to design the electronic forms to resemble the paper forms. This will make the data entry process more efficient and ease the transition from paper form to electronic form

In this section, you will learn the basics of form design. You will discover multiple methods to create and modify Access forms.

Creating Forms Using Form Tools

Access provides a variety of options for creating forms. You will eventually develop a preference for one or two types of form layouts, but keep in mind that you have a good variety of options, if needed. You will want your forms to balance ease of use with the power to be effective.

Access provides 14 different tools for creating forms. You can find these options in the Forms group on the Create tab. The Forms group contains four of the most common form tools (Form, Form Design, Blank Form, and Form Wizard), a list of Navigation forms, and More Forms. The Navigation list provides six templates to create a user interface for a database; the More Forms list provides four additional form tools (Multiple Items, Datasheet, Split Form, and Modal Dialog). Select a table or query in the Navigation Pane, click one of the tools, and Access will create a form based on the selected table or query. The most common of these tools, the *Form tool*, is used to create data entry forms for customers, employees, products, and other types of tables. You can also find Application Parts, which are predefined building blocks that you can use to build database objects, in the Templates group on the Create tab.

A list of the Form tools available in Access is found in Table 4.1. Several of the tools will be covered in this chapter. Some tools will not be covered in detail, because they are not commonly used or because they are beyond the scope of this chapter (e.g., Form Design, Blank Form, Navigation forms, and Modal Dialog Form). Use Microsoft Access Help to find more information about Form tools not covered in this chapter.

TABLE 4.1 Form Tools in Access

Form Tool	Use
Form	Creates a form with a stacked layout that displays all of the fields in the record source.
Form Design	Creates a new blank form in Design view.
Blank Form	Creates a new blank form in Layout view.
Form Wizard	Creates a custom form based on your answers to a series of step-by-step questions.
Navigation	Creates user-interface forms that can also be used on the Internet. Six different Navigation form layouts are available from the list.
Split Form	Creates a two-part form with a stacked layout in one section and a tabular layout in the other.
Multiple Items	Creates a tabular layout form that includes all of the fields from the record source.
Datasheet	Creates a form that resembles the datasheet of a table or query.
Modal Dialog	Creates a custom dialog box that requires user input that is needed for a database object.

Pearson Education, Inc.

TIP: USABILITY TESTING

After a database object (such as a form) is finalized, it should be tested by both the database designer and the end users. The designer should be certain that the form meets any requirements the users have given him or her. The designer should also browse through the records to make sure the values in all records (and not just the first record) display correctly. After testing is completed by both designer and end users, the form should be modified and tested again before it is deployed with the database.

Ideally, a form should simplify data entry. Creating a form is a collaborative process between the database designer and the end users. This process continues throughout the life of the form, because the data needs of an organization may change over time. Forms designed long ago to collect data for a new customer account may not include an email or a website field; both the customer table and its associated form would have to be modified to include these fields. The designer needs to strike a balance between collecting the data required for use by the database and cluttering the form with extraneous fields. The database users generally offer good opinions about which fields should be on a form and how the form should behave. If you listen to their suggestions, your forms will function more effectively, the users' work will be easier, and the data will contain fewer data-entry errors.

After discussing the form with the users, it will help you to create the form in Access if you sketch the form first. After sketching the form, you will have a better idea of which form tool to use to create the form. After the form is created, use the sketch to determine which fields are required and what the order of the fields should be.

Identify a Record Source

Before you create a form, you must identify the record source. A **record source** (or data source) is the table or query that supplies the records for a form or report. Use a table if you want to include all the records from a single table. Create a query as the record source first if you need to filter the records in the source table, combine records from two or more related tables, or if you do not want to display all fields from the table(s) on your form. For example, if a sales rep wants to create a form that displays customers from a single state only—where his customers reside—he or she should base the form on a query.

Use the Form Tool

 As noted earlier, the Form tool is the most common tool for creating forms. A usable form can be created with a single click.

> **To use the Form tool, complete the following steps:**
> 1. Select a table or query in the Navigation Pane.
> 2. Click Form in the Forms group on the Create tab.

Based on the table or query selected, Access automatically creates a new form. You may need to modify the form slightly, but you can create a stacked layout form with just one click. A *stacked layout* displays fields in a vertical column for one record at a time, as shown in Figure 4.2. The other type of layout you can use is a *tabular layout*, which displays data horizontally across the page.

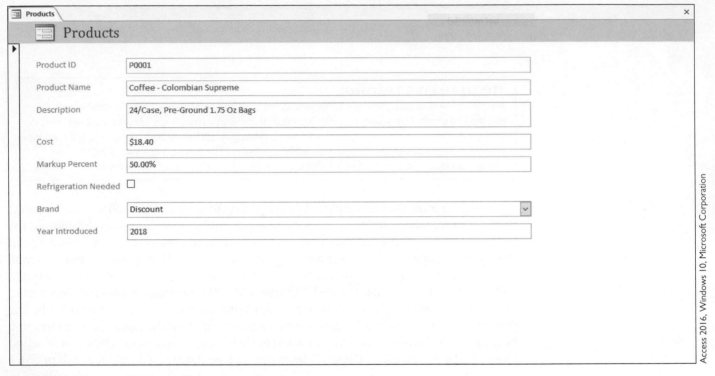

FIGURE 4.2 Form with a Stacked Layout

Understand Controls

Controls are the text boxes, buttons, labels, and other tools you use to add, edit, and display the data in a form or report. Notice in Figure 4.3 that each field has a label on the left and a text box on the right, both of which are referred to as controls. The form controls that display values are generally text box controls, and the boxes describing those values are label controls. In Figure 4.3, Product ID, Product Name, Description, etc. are label controls. The boxes containing the values for each field (P0001, Coffee–Colombian Supreme, etc.) are text box controls.

A *layout control* provides guides to help keep controls aligned horizontally and vertically and give your form a neat appearance, as shown in Figure 4.3.

There may be times when you will select controls in order to format, delete, or move them during your design process. To select an individual control, click the text box or the label as needed.

To select multiple controls to work with them simultaneously, complete one of the following steps:

- Click the first control, press and hold Ctrl, and then click the additional controls you want to include in the selection.
- Press Ctrl+A to select all of the controls on a form at one time.

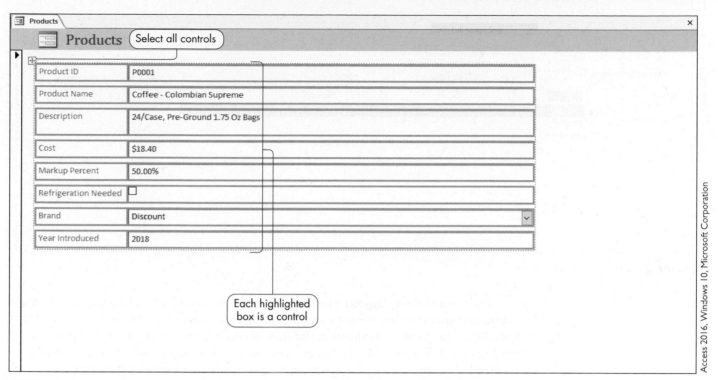

FIGURE 4.3 Form with Label and Text Box Controls

Work with Form Views

There are three different views of a form available. The first, **_Form view_**, is the user interface primarily used for data entry and modification. You cannot make changes to the form layout or design in Form view. Figure 4.4 shows a form in Form view. Notice that forms can be designed to include time-saving features such as drop-down lists and check boxes.

Access 2016, Windows 10, Microsoft Corporation

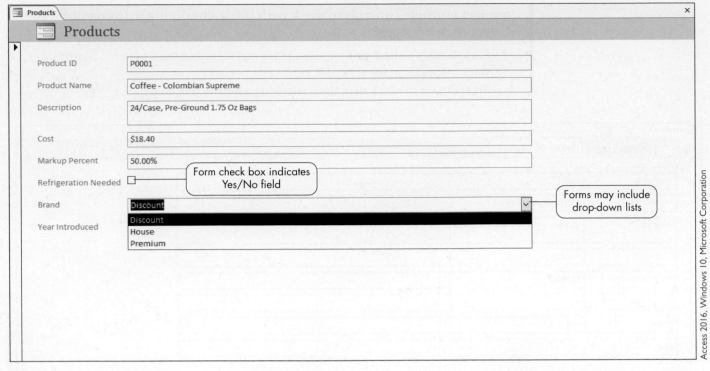

FIGURE 4.4 Form in Form View

The second view, ***Layout view***, enables you to make changes to the layout while simultaneously viewing the data in the form. Layout view is useful for testing the functionality of the form and adjusting the sizes of controls (text boxes and labels) as needed while viewing the data. When you create a form using the Form tool, Access opens the form in Layout view, ready for this type of customization, as shown in Figure 4.5.

Access 2016, Windows 10, Microsoft Corporation

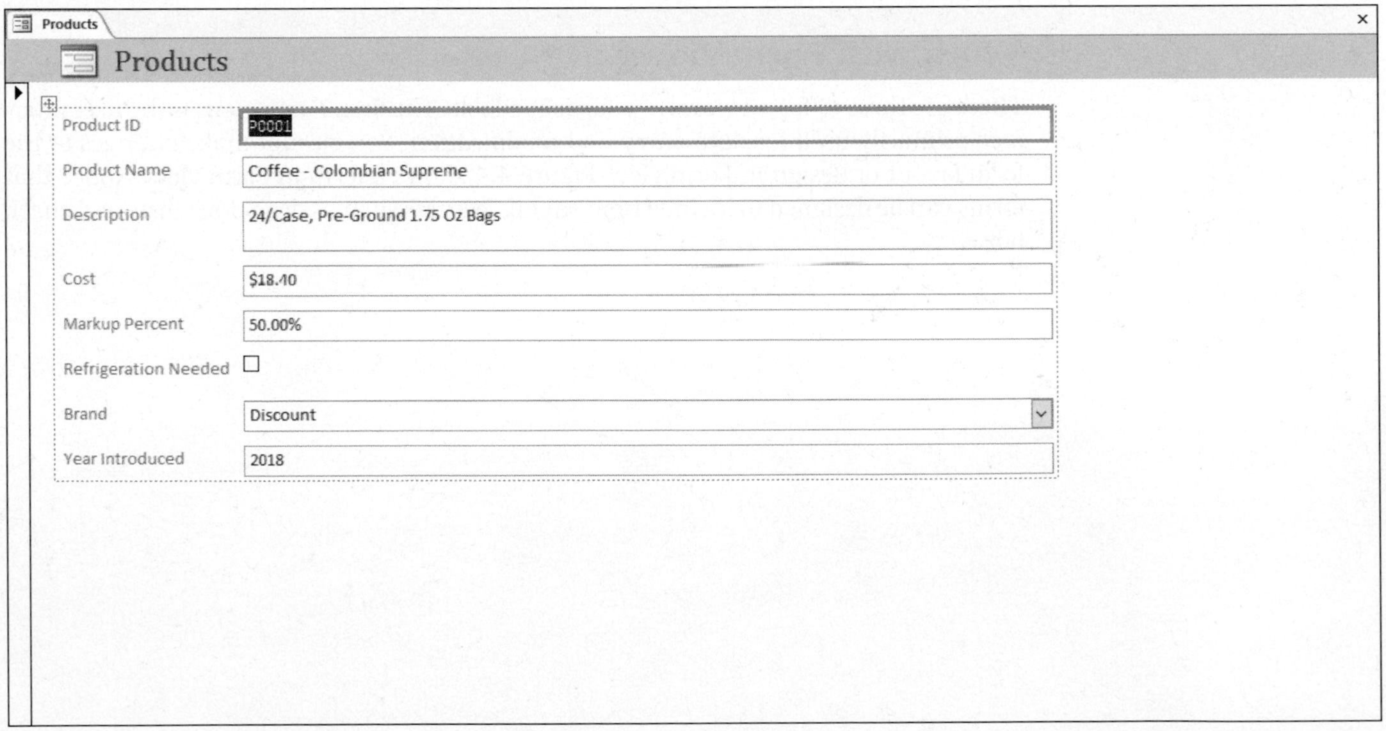

FIGURE 4.5 Form in Layout View

The third view, **Design view**, enables you to change advanced design settings that are not available in Layout view, such as removing a layout control, and gives you even more control over form design. Many forms can be made by toggling back and forth between Layout view for modifications and Form view for usability testing; however, Design view offers possibilities for more advanced adjustments. Figure 4.6 shows a form in Design view. Form views will be described in more detail later in this chapter.

To switch between the Form views, with the form open, click the View arrow in the Views group on the Home tab, and then select Form View, Layout View, or Design View. Alternatively, click the View buttons on the status bar at the bottom of the Access window, or right-click the form's window tab and select an option from the shortcut menu.

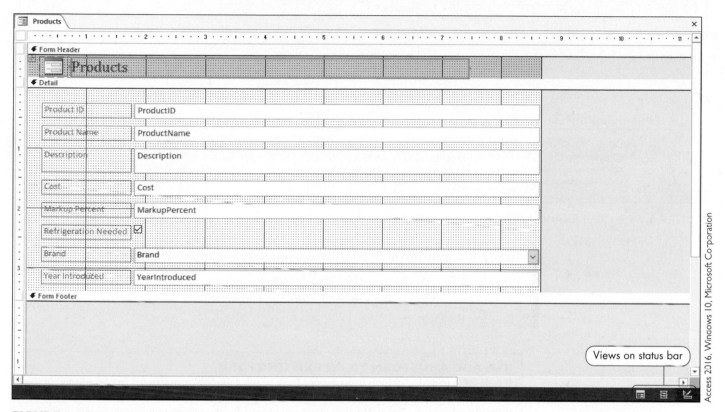

FIGURE 4.6 Form in Design View

Work with a Subform

When you use the Form tool to create a form, Access analyzes the table relationships in the database. If the table that the main form is based upon is related to another table, Access automatically adds a subform to the main form. The subform displays records in the related table, generally laid out in a datasheet format. For example, assume you have sales representatives stored in a Sales Reps table and related customer information stored in a Customers table. In this example, if you create a new form based on the Sales Reps table using the Form tool, Access will add a Customers subform to the bottom of the main form, displaying all customers assigned to each sales representative (see Figure 4.7). At times, you may want the subform as part of your form; at other times, you may want to remove it if it is not relevant to the requirements of the form design.

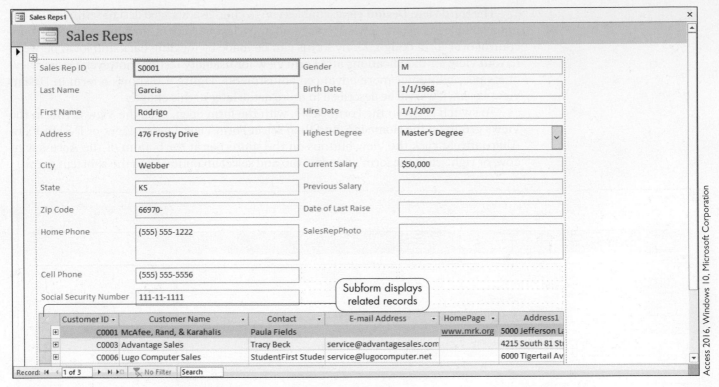

FIGURE 4.7 Sales Reps Form with Related Customers Subform

To remove a subform from a form, complete the following steps:

1. Click the View arrow in the Views group on the Home tab, and select Design View.
2. Click anywhere in the subform control and press Delete.
3. Save the form.

TIP: ADD A SUBFORM TO AN EXISTING FORM

It is possible to add a subform to an existing form by using the SubForm Wizard. In Design view of the form, in the Controls group, click the Subform/Subreport tool, and then click in the form where you want the subform to display. The wizard will prompt you for the record source and through the steps for creating the subform.

Create a Split Form

A *split form* combines two views of the same record source—by default; the top section is displayed in a stacked layout (Form view) and the bottom section is displayed in a tabular layout (Datasheet view). If you select a record in the top section of the form, the same record will be selected in the bottom section of the form and vice versa. For example, if you create a split form based on an Orders table, you can select an Order in the bottom (datasheet) section and then enter or edit the order's information in the top (Form view) section (see Figure 4.8). This gives you the option to navigate between orders more quickly in the bottom section, and then when you locate the one you need, you can move to the top section to work with the record in Form view; however, you can add, edit, or delete records in either section. The splitter bar divides the form into two halves. You can adjust the splitter bar up or down (unless this option is disabled).

To create a split form, complete the following steps:

1. Select a table or query in the Navigation Pane.
2. Click More Forms, and click Split Form in the Forms group on the Create tab.

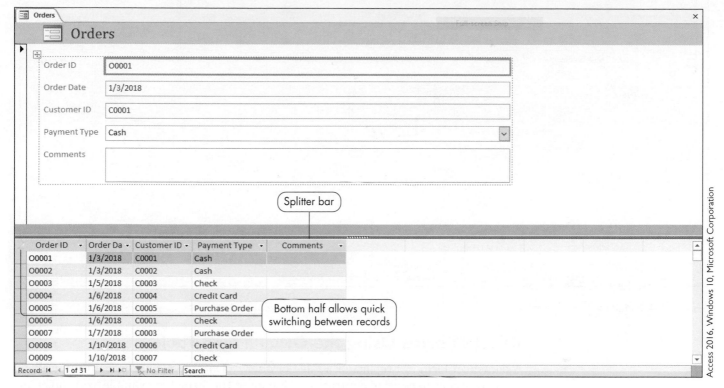

FIGURE 4.8 Split Form

Create a Multiple Items Form

A ***multiple items form*** displays multiple records in a tabular layout similar to a table's Datasheet view. However, a multiple items form provides you with more customization options than a datasheet, such as the ability to add graphical elements, buttons, and other controls. Figure 4.9 shows a multiple items form created from the Sales Rep table.

To create a multiple items form, complete the following steps:

1. Select a table or query in the Navigation Pane.
2. Click More Forms, and click Multiple Items in the Forms group on the Create tab.

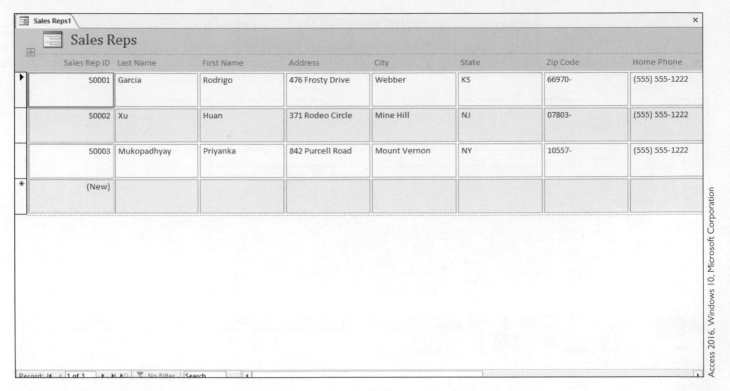

FIGURE 4.9 Multiple Items Form

Create Forms Using the Other Form Tools

A datasheet form is a replica of a table or query's Datasheet view except that it allows form properties to be set to control the behavior of the form. For example, you can create a datasheet form to display data in a table-like format but change the form's property so as not to allow a record to be deleted. This protects the data from accidental deletions while still providing users with the familiar Datasheet view.

> **TIP: FORM PROPERTIES**
> A form's Property Sheet enables you to control the behavior and formatting of controls in your forms. To access the Property Sheet, from Layout view or Design view, click Property Sheet in the Tools group on the Design tab. At the top of the Property Sheet, use the list arrow to select a control; you will see multiple tabs containing many individual attributes of the selected control that you can change. For example, the Format tab contains options for changing the styling of a control.

The Form Design tool and the Blank Form tools can be used to create forms manually from scratch in Design view or Layout view, respectively. Use these form types if you want to have complete control over your form's design. In either case, after opening a completely blank form, click Add Existing Fields in the Tools group on the Design tab, and then add the necessary fields by dragging and dropping them onto the blank form from the Field List pane.

The Navigation commands in the Forms group enable you to create user interfaces that have the look and feel of Web-based forms and enable users to open and close the objects of a database. For example, you can create a form that enables users to click buttons for the various forms, reports, and other objects that you want them to view in the database. This is an excellent way to simplify the database navigation for data-entry personnel who may not be that familiar with navigating in Access. These forms are also useful for setting up an Access database on the Internet.

The Modal Dialog Form tool can be used to create a dialog box. This feature is useful when you need to gather information from the user or provide information to the user, such as a message. Dialog boxes are common in all Microsoft Office applications.

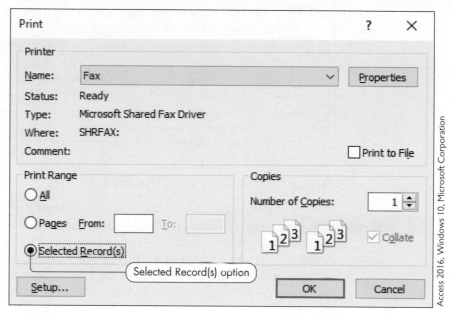

FIGURE 4.10 Print Selected Records Using a Form

Modifying Forms

As previously mentioned, Access provides different views for a form; most forms display
Layout, Form, and Design views. As you work with the form tools to create and modify
forms, you will need to switch between the three form views in Access. Much of your
design work can be done in Layout view; sometimes, you will need to switch to Design
view to use a more advanced feature, such as changing the order of the fields as you press
Tab to move from one to the next, or to use an option that is otherwise unavailable. Users
of the form will typically only work in Form view; there is little reason for a user to switch
to Layout or Design view, and these views can be disabled by the database designer to
protect the integrity of the form. Modifications to the form should ideally be done only by
a designated designer.

Use Form View to Edit Data

STEP 2 >> Use Form view to add, edit, and delete data in a form; the layout and design of the form
cannot be changed in this view. The Navigation bar at the bottom of the form provides
buttons to move between records, and you can click the New (blank) record button to
add a new record. You can move from one field to another field by pressing the Tab key or
clicking the desired field with your mouse.

Use Layout View to Modify Form Design

Use Layout view to alter the form design while viewing the data. The data is not editable
in this view. You use Layout view to add or delete fields in a form, change the order of
fields, modify field or form properties (such as which views are available), change the
control widths, and enhance a form by adding a theme or styling. Reviewing the data in

Layout view makes it easier to size controls, and to ensure that all data is visible in Form view. It is good practice to toggle back and forth between Layout view and Form view when making changes to the form's design.

TIP: USE THE FORM LAYOUT TOOLS TABS

Forms have a number of options that you can use in your design process. In Layout view, you have access to three contextual tabs on the Ribbon that provide a number of tools for modifying forms as follows:

- Design tab: Use this tab to make changes to the design of the form, such as applying themes, inserting headers and footers, and additional controls.
- Arrange tab: Use this tab to change the layout of a form, to move fields up or down, or to control margins.
- Format tab: Use this tab to work with fonts, font size, and colors, to add or remove bolding, italics, or underlining, adjust text alignment, or add a background image.

   Similarly, in Design view, the Form Design Tools tabs are available (Design, Arrange, and Format) with many of the same options you will find in Layout view.

Adjust Column Widths in a Form

When column widths are adjusted in a form with a stacked layout, all field sizes will increase and decrease in size together. Therefore, it is best to make sure that the columns are wide enough to accommodate the widest value in each field. For example, if a form contains information such as a customer's first name, last name, address, city, state, ZIP, phone, and email address, you will need to make sure the longest address and the longest email address are completely visible (because those fields are likely to contain the longest data values).

To increase or decrease column widths in a form with a stacked layout, complete the following steps:

1. Display the form in (Stacked) Layout view, and click the text box control of the first field to select it.
2. Point to the right border of the control until the pointer turns into a double-headed arrow. Drag the right edge of the control to the left or right until you arrive at the desired width.

   You will notice that all field sizes change as you change the width of the first field. All fields that are included in the layout will have a standard width. If you want to resize one specific field, you will remove that field from the layout control. Select the field and the label to be removed, right-click, and then from the shortcut menu, click Layout, and select Remove Layout. If you remove a field from the layout control, it stays on the form but can be moved and resized more freely.

Add and Delete Form Fields

STEP 3 ❯❯ There will be instances when you will want to add or delete form fields. At times, new fields may be added to tables and then need to be incorporated into forms. At other times, you may decide that while a field is present in a table, it is not necessary to display it to users in a form.

To add a field to a form, complete the following steps:

1. Display the form in (Stacked) Layout view, and click Add Existing Fields in the Tools group on the Design tab.

    A Field List pane displays at the right of the form. For a single-table form, you will see a list of fields from the table (record source). For a multiple-table form, click the plus sign (+) to the left of the appropriate table to expand it, and locate the desired field(s).

2. Click and drag the desired field to the precise location on the form, using the shaded line as a guide for positioning the new field. Alternatively, you can double-click a field to add it to the form; the field will be added below the selected field. The other fields will automatically adjust to make room for the new field, as shown in Figure 4.11.

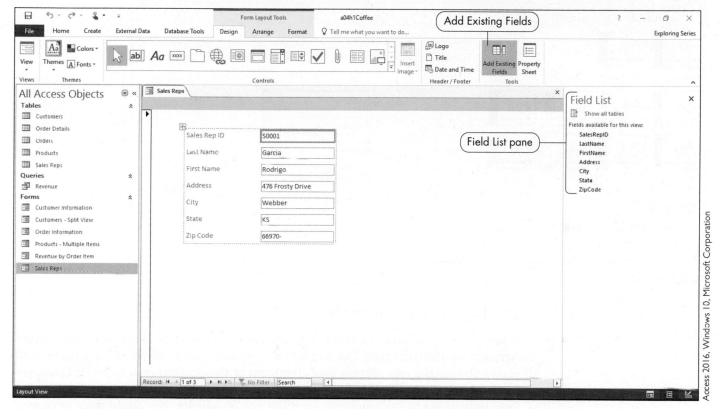

FIGURE 4.11 Add Fields to a Form

To delete a field from a form, complete the following steps:

1. Display the form in (Stacked) Layout view, and click the text box control of the field to be deleted (note the shaded border around the control).
2. Click Select Row in the Rows & Columns group on the Arrange tab in order to select the text box and its associated label. Alternatively, click the text box control, press and hold Ctrl, and then click the associated label control to select them both.
3. Press Delete.

The other fields will automatically adjust to close the gap around the deleted field.

Add a Theme to a Form

You can apply a theme to a form in order to give the form a more professional appearance. A ***theme*** is a defined set of colors, fonts, and graphics that can be applied to forms (or reports). In Layout or Design view, click Themes in the Themes group on the Design tab, point to a theme to see its name in the ScreenTip and a Live Preview of the theme in the form, and then click to select it. By default, the theme will be applied to all objects in your database.

Right-click a theme in the gallery to apply it to the current form only or to all the forms in your database that share a common theme. You can create customized themes and save them on your system so that they can be used again. Apply your custom settings, and then click the Save Current Theme command, as shown in Figure 4.12.

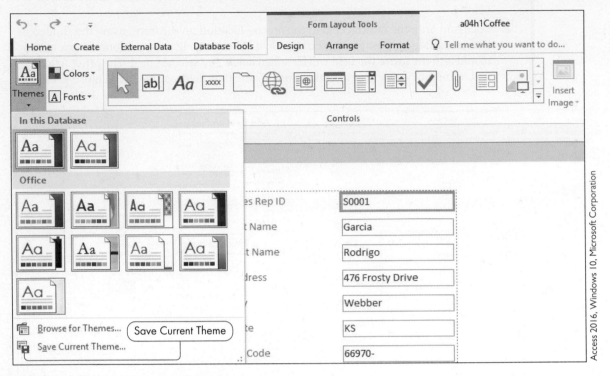

FIGURE 4.12 Add a Theme to a Form

Modify Form Controls

When you view a form in Layout view, the Form Layout Tools tab displays the Design, Arrange, and Format tabs. The Format tab contains a series of commands that enable you to change the font, display, and alignment of the controls on a form. At times, you may want to change the formatting of one or more controls. For example, if you have a form that shows the information about the sale of vehicles, you might want to emphasize the net profit of each transaction by changing the font or background color of the control.

From the Form Layout Tools Format tab, you can change a number of control attributes. Table 4.2 illustrates some of commands you would likely use.

TABLE 4.2 Common Formats for Form Controls	
Font size	Click the Font Size arrow in the Font group.
Font emphasis	Click Bold, Italic, or Underline in the Font group.
Alignment	Click Align Left, Center, or Align Right in the Font group.
Background color	Click the Background Color arrow in the Font group.
Font color	Click the Font Color arrow in the Font group.
Number format	Use the tools in the Number group to select number formats such as Currency, Percent, Comma formatting, or to increase or decrease decimal places.

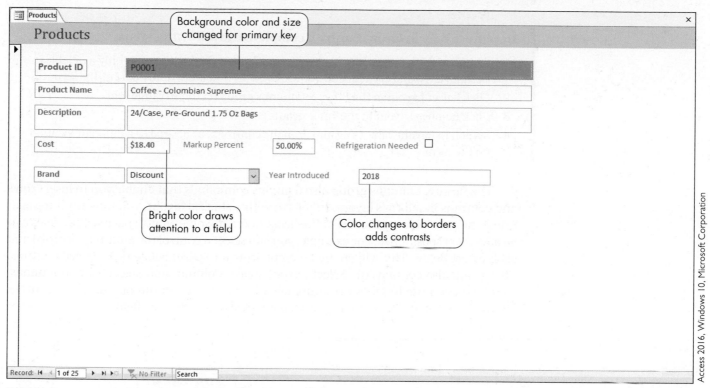

FIGURE 4.13 A Well-Designed Form with Styling

Working with a Form Layout

When you use one of the form tools to create a new form, Access adds a layout control to help align the fields. The layout control helps keep controls aligned in order to give your form a neat appearance. The layout control provides structure for the fields, but is somewhat restrictive. If you want to have more control over the location of your fields, you can remove the layout control and position the controls manually on the form.

To remove a control from a layout and reposition it, complete the following steps:

1. Select the field and the label to be removed, right-click, and from the shortcut menu, point to Layout and then select Remove Layout.
2. Drag and drop the control(s) as desired to a different location on the form.

Modify a Form Layout

STEP 4 >> You can use the tools on the Arrange tab to change the layout of a form, to move fields up and down, and to control margins. The Arrange tab displays in both Layout view and Design view.

The Table group of the Arrange tab contains commands that enable you to add gridlines to a form's layout, change the layout from stacked to tabular (and vice versa), or remove the layout (the Remove Layout command is available only in Design view).

To apply or change the layout of a form, complete the following steps:

1. Open the form in Layout or Design view.
2. Select multiple controls by clicking the first control, pressing and holding Ctrl, and then clicking the additional controls you want to include in the layout. To select all of the controls on a form, press Ctrl+A. If the controls already have a layout applied, click any control that is part of the layout, and click Select Layout in the Rows & Columns group on the Arrange tab.
3. Click Tabular or Stacked in the Table group on the Arrange tab.

To remove a form layout control, complete the following steps:

1. Switch to Design view (the Remove Layout option on the Ribbon is only available in Design view), and click any one of the controls that is currently part of the layout.
2. Click Select Layout in the Rows & Columns group on the Arrange tab.
3. Click Remove Layout in the Table group.
4. Switch to Layout view. Drag and drop the control(s) as desired to a different location on the form.

The Rows & Columns group also contains commands that enable you to insert rows and columns in a form's layout. In a form with a stacked layout, you may want to separate some controls from the rest of the fields, or create some empty space so that fields can be added or repositioned. For example, you can select a control (or multiple controls) and click Insert Below. This will create an empty row (or space) below the selected controls. This group also contains the Select Layout, Select Column, and Select Row commands, which you can use to select the entire layout, or a single column or row in a layout. In Figure 4.14, three empty rows have been inserted above the Cost field.

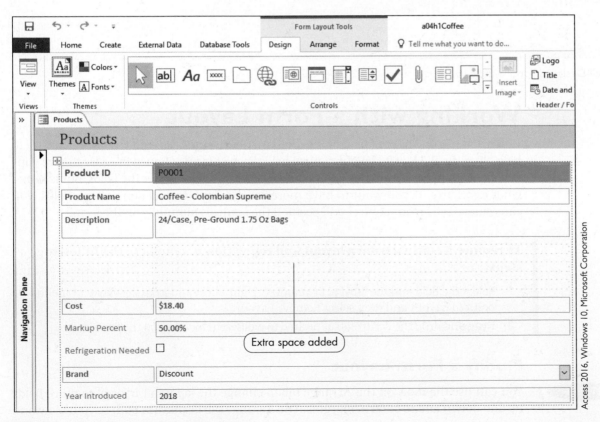

FIGURE 4.14 Rows Inserted in a Form Layout

> **TIP: APPLY A BACKGROUND IMAGE TO A FORM**
>
> To apply a background image to a form, open the form in Layout or Design view, and then click Background Image in the Background group on the Format tab. Next, click Browse to locate the image you want to apply to the form. Once the image has been applied to the form, you can change the properties of the image so that the image displays correctly. You can use the same technique to add a background image to a report.

Sorting Records in a Form

When a form is created using a Form tool, the sort order of the records in the form is initially dependent on the sort order of the record source—the underlying table or query. Tables are usually sorted by the primary key, whereas queries are generally sorted in a variety of ways. No matter how the records are initially sorted, you can modify the sort order in a form. Adding and removing sorts are shown in Figure 4.15.

FIGURE 4.15 Adding and Removing Sort Order

Access 2016, Windows 10, Microsoft Corporation

Sort by a Single Field

You can easily sort on a single field, in ascending or descending order. The sort order in a form can be different from the sort order of an underlying table or query.

> **To sort by a single field, complete the following steps:**
>
> 1. Open the form in Form view, and select the field by which you want to sort.
> 2. Click Ascending or Descending in the Sort & Filter group on the Home tab.

If you want to sort on multiple fields, you can create a query with a more advanced sort order, and then base the form on the query. Open the query in Design view, add the sort settings you want, save the query, and then use the query as the record source of the form. To remove the sort order in a form, open the form in Form view, then click Remove Sort in the Sort & Filter group on the Home tab.

Quick Concepts

1. How does a form simplify data entry (when compared to entering data into a table)? *p. 270*

2. What is the record source of a form? *p. 271*

3. What is the advantage of creating a form with a subform? *p. 275*

4. Why is using a layout control to keep your form fields in a neat arrangement sometimes a disadvantage? *p. 272*

Hands-On Exercises

Watch the Video for this Hands-On Exercise!

MyITLab®
HOE1 Training

1 Form Basics

After talking with Ryung about her data-entry needs, you decide to create several sample forms using different formats. You will show each form to Ryung to get feedback and see if she has any preferences.

STEP 1 ›› CREATE FORMS USING FORM TOOLS

You will create a number of forms using different layouts. Refer to Figure 4.16 as you complete Step 1.

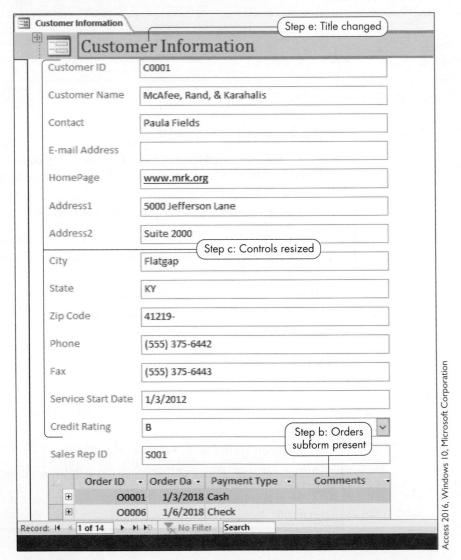

FIGURE 4.16 Customer Information Form

a. Open *a04h1Coffee* and save it as **a04h1Coffee_LastFirst**.

> **TROUBLESHOOTING:** Throughout the remainder of this chapter and textbook, click Enable Content whenever you are working with the student data files.

> **TROUBLESHOOTING:** If you make any major mistakes in this exercise, you can close the file, open *a04h1Coffee* again, and then start this exercise over.

b. Click the **Customers table** in the Navigation Pane to select the table but not to open it. Click the **Create tab**, and then click **Form** in the Forms group.

Access creates a new form with two record sources—Customers (with stacked layout, on top) and Orders (with datasheet layout, below). Access detected a one-to-many relationship between the Customers and Orders tables, and so it created a main form with its associated subform below it. The form opens in Layout view.

c. Ensure that the top text box containing *C0001* is selected. The text box is outlined with a shaded border. Move the pointer to the right edge of the shaded border until the pointer changes to a double-headed arrow. Drag the right edge to the left until the text box is approximately half of its original size.

All of the text boxes and the subform at the bottom adjust in size when you adjust the top text box. This is a characteristic of Layout view—enabling you to modify all controls at once.

> **TROUBLESHOOTING:** You may need to maximize the Access window or close the Navigation Pane if the right edge of the text box is not visible.

d. Ensure that the labels to the left of the text boxes display without being cut off. If they are cut off, adjust the size of the labels as you did in Step c.

e. Click **Save** on the Quick Access Toolbar, and then type **Customer Information** as the form name in the **Save As dialog box**. Click **OK**.

f. Click the **Customers title** at the top of the form to select it, click the title again, and then change the title to **Customer Information**. Press **Enter** to accept the change. Your form should now look like Figure 4.16. Save and close the form.

> **TROUBLESHOOTING:** If you make a mistake that you cannot easily recover from, consider deleting the form and creating it again. With the form closed, right-click the form name in the Navigation Pane, and from the shortcut menu, select Delete.

g. Verify that the Customers table is selected in the Navigation Pane. Click the **Create tab**, click **More Forms** in the Forms group, and then select **Split Form**.

Access creates a new form with a split view, one view in stacked layout and one view laid out like a datasheet.

h. Scroll down and click anywhere in the *Coulter Office Supplies* customer record in the bottom pane (datasheet) of the form (record 14).

The top pane shows all the information for this customer in a stacked layout view.

i. Click the **Customers title** at the top of the form to select it, click **Customers** again, and then change the title to **Customers - Split View**. Press **Enter** to accept the change.

j. Click **Save** on the Quick Access Toolbar and type **Customers - Split View** in the Form Name box Click **OK**. Close the form.

k. Click the **Products table** in the Navigation Pane. Click the **Create tab**, click **More Forms** in the Forms group, and then select **Multiple Items**.

Access creates a new multiple-item form based on the Products table. The form resembles a table's Datasheet view.

l. Click the **Products title** at the top of the form to select it, click **Products** again, and then change the title to **Products - Multiple Items**. Press **Enter** to accept the change.

m. Save the form as **Products - Multiple Items** and close the form.

n. Click the **Orders table** in the Navigation Pane. Click **Form** in the Forms group on the Create tab.

A form with a subform showing each line of the order is created.

o. Click the **Home tab**. Click the **View arrow** in the Views group, and select **Design View**. Click anywhere inside the subform and press **Delete**.

The subform is removed.

p. Switch to Form view to observe the change. Save the form as **Order Information**. Close all open objects.

STEP 2 ❯❯ **USE FORM VIEW TO EDIT DATA**

Now that you have created several forms, you will show Ryung how to test the forms for usability Refer to Figure 4.17 as you complete Step 2.

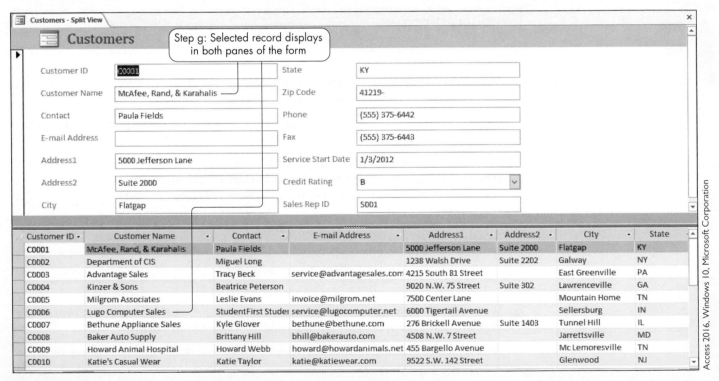

FIGURE 4.17

a. Right-click the **Customer Information form** in the Navigation Pane, and from the shortcut menu, select **Open**. Advance to the sixth customer, *Lugo Computer Sales*, using **Next record** on the Navigation bar at the bottom of the form.

> **TROUBLESHOOTING:** Two Navigation bars exist, the inside one for the subform and the bottom-most one for the main form. Make sure you use the bottom-most one that displays the record count of 14.

b. Double-click the **Customers table** in the Navigation Pane.

Two tabs now display in the main window. You will compare the table data and the form data while you make changes to both.

c. Verify that the sixth record of the Customers table is *Lugo Computer Sales*, which corresponds to the sixth record in the Customer Information form. Click the tabs to switch between the table and the form.

d. Click the **Customer Information tab** and replace *Adam Sanchez*, the contact for Lugo Computer Sales, with your name. Advance to the next record to save the changes. Click the **Customers tab** to see that the contact name changed in the table as well.

Changes to the Contact field and the other fields in the Customer Information form automatically change the data in the underlying table. Likewise, if you change data in the table, it will update automatically in the form.

> **TROUBLESHOOTING:** If the change from *Adam Sanchez* to your name does not display in the Customers table, check the Customer Information form to see if the pencil 🖉 displays in the left margin of the record. If it does, save the record by advancing to the next customer in the form and recheck to see if the name has changed in the underlying table.

e. Close the Customer Information form and the Customers table.

f. Open the Customers – Split View form. In the bottom pane of the split form, click **Lugo Computer Sales**, the sixth record. Notice that the top pane now displays the information for Lugo Computer Sales in a stacked layout. Notice also that there is an error in the email address—*service* is misspelled. In the top pane of the form, change the email address to **service@lugocomputer.net**.

g. Click another record in the bottom pane and then click back on **Lugo Computer Sales**, as shown in Figure 4.17.

The pencil disappears from the record selector box and the changes are saved to the table.

You will make some changes to the layouts based on feedback Ryung gave you after seeing the forms in action. You will also add a missing field to the main table and then add it to the form. Refer to Figure 4.18 as you complete Step 3.

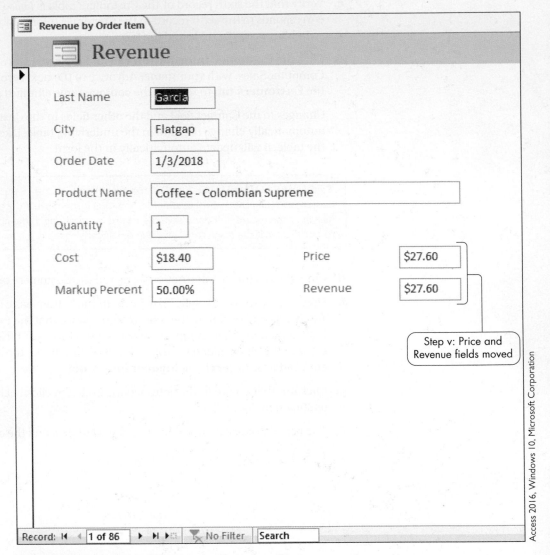

FIGURE 4.18 Completed Revenue by Order Item Form

a. Switch to Layout view with the Customers – Split View form open. Point to the **splitter bar**, the border between the top and bottom pane of the window. When the pointer shape changes to a double-headed arrow, drag the **splitter bar** until it almost touches the Sales Rep ID field. Save and close the form.

b. Open the Products – Multiple Items form in Layout view. Point to the bottom edge of **Product ID P0001** until the pointer shape changes to a double-headed arrow. Drag the bottom edge up to reduce the height of the rows so they are as tall as they need to be to accommodate the information.

Changing the height of one row affects the height of all the rows in the form.

c. Click anywhere in the **Cost column** and click **Select Column** in the Rows & Columns group on the Arrange tab. Press **Delete** to remove the column (alternatively, right-click in the column, and from the shortcut menu, select **Delete Column**). Delete the **MarkupPercent** column.

d. Click the **Refrigeration Needed label** to select it. Change the label to the abbreviation **Refrig?** Resize the column so it is wide enough to display the label text. Save and close the form.

e. Open the Customer Information form in Layout view.

f. Click the **Design tab**. Click **Themes** in the Themes group. Right-click the **Slice theme** and select **Apply Theme to This Object Only**.

The fonts and color scheme that are built into the theme are applied.

> **TROUBLESHOOTING:** You can determine which theme is named Slice by pointing to a theme in the gallery and waiting for a ScreenTip to display. The Office theme is displayed first and the others are displayed in alphabetical order after it.

g. Click the **Format tab**. Click **Shape Fill** in the Control Formatting group. Select **Light Turquoise, Background 2** under Theme Colors.

The background color of the CustomerID field changes to light turquoise. The theme colors in the palette are those built into the Slice theme.

> **TROUBLESHOOTING:** If you do not see Light Turquoise, Background 2 in the theme colors, ensure that you have selected the Slice theme.

> **TROUBLESHOOTING:** If the entire form background changes to turquoise, click Undo and ensure that only the Customer ID text box containing *C0001* is selected.

h. Select the **Customer Name field** (which should be *McAfee, Rand, & Karahalis*). Change the font size to **16**.

The customer name appears in a larger font, setting it apart from the other fields.

i. Save and close the form.

j. Right-click the **Customers table** in the Navigation Pane, and select **Design View**.

You will add the HomePage hyperlink field to the Customers table.

k. Click the **Address1 field** and click **Insert Rows** in the Tools group on the Design tab.

A new row is inserted above the Address1 field.

l. Type **HomePage** in the blank **Field Name box** and select **Hyperlink** as the Data Type.

m. Save and close the Customers table.

n. Right-click the **Customer Information form** in the Navigation Pane, and select **Layout View**.

You will add the HomePage field to the Customer Information form.

o. Click **Add Existing Fields** in the Tools group on the Design tab to display the Field List pane.

p. Click the **HomePage field**. Drag the field from the Field List pane to the form, below the E-mail Address field, until a shaded line displays between *E-mail Address* and *Address1* and then drop it. Close the Field List pane.

Access displays a shaded line to help you place the field in the correct location.

> **TROUBLESHOOTING:** If the placement of the field is incorrect, you can click Undo and try again. Alternatively, select the label and text box controls and use the Move Up or Move Down commands in the Arrange group.

q. Switch to Form view. Press **Tab** until you reach the HomePage field, type **www.mrk.org**, and then press **Tab**.

Because HomePage is a hyperlink field, Access formats it automatically in the form.

Save and close the form.

r. Click the **Revenue query** in the Navigation Pane. Click **Form** in the Forms group on the Create tab to create a new form based on this query.

The Revenue query is the record source for the form.

s. Switch to Design view. Click the first label, **Last Name**, press and hold **Ctrl**, and then click each of the other controls (alternatively, press Ctrl+A).

You have selected all label and text box field controls (from *Last Name* down to *Revenue*).

t. Click **Remove Layout** in the Table group on the Arrange tab. Switch back to Layout view.

> **TROUBLESHOOTING:** Recall that the Remove Layout option only displays on the Ribbon in Design view, so if you do not see the button, ensure that you are in Design view.

u. Resize the controls individually so they are approximately the same sizes as shown in Figure 4.18.

v. Click the **Price control**. Press and hold **Ctrl** and click the **Revenue control**, the **Price label**, and the **Revenue label**. Drag the fields to the locations shown in Figure 4.18. Switch to Form view.

w. Save the form as **Revenue by Order Item**. Close the form.

Ryung has an old Sales Reps form that she hopes you can make easier to read but keep in the vertical format. She tested the Customer Information form and likes the way it is working; however, she asks you to change the sort order to make it easier to find customers alphabetically by their names Refer to Figure 4.19 as you complete Step 4.

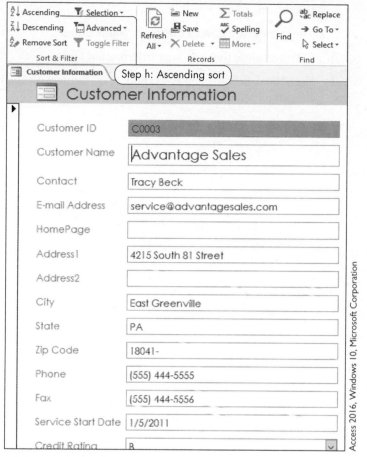

FIGURE 4.19

a. Open the Sales Reps form in Layout view. Notice that the form is not attractively laid out.

b. Click **Select All** in the Selection group on the Format tab.

All 14 controls are selected in the form.

c. Click **Tabular** in the Table group on the Arrange tab.

The controls are lined up horizontally across the top of the form.

d. Click **Stacked** in the Table group on the Arrange tab. Switch to Form view.

The controls are lined up vertically and the form is much easier to read.

e. Save and close the form.

f. Open the Customer Information form in Form view. Click **Next record** in the Navigation bar at the bottom several times to advance through the records.

Note that the customers are in Customer ID order.

g. Click **First record** in the Navigation bar to return to customer *McAfee, Rand, & Karahalis*.

h. Click in the **Customer Name text box**, and click **Ascending** in the Sort & Filter group on the Home tab.

Advantage Sales displays (Customer ID C0003), as it is the first customer name in alphabetical order, as shown in Figure 4.19.

i. Click **Next record** in the Navigation bar at the bottom of the form to advance through the records.

The records are now in Customer Name order.

j. Save and close the Customer Information form.

k. Keep the database open if you plan to continue with the Hands-On Exercise. If not, close the database, and exit Access.

Report Basics

By now, you know how to plan a database, create tables, establish relationships between tables, enter data into tables, and extract data using queries. In the previous section of this chapter, you learned how to create and modify several types of data-entry forms. In this section, you will learn how to create professional reports using the report-generating tools in Access.

A *report* is a document that displays information from a database in a format that outputs meaningful information to its readers. Access reports can be printed, viewed onscreen, or even saved as files, such as Word documents. You cannot use reports to change data in your database; a report is designed for output of information only based on data from tables or queries in your database (record sources).

The following are all examples of reports that might be created in Access:

- A telephone directory sorted by last name
- A customer report grouped by orders pending for each customer
- An employee list grouped by department
- A monthly statement from a bank
- A bill or invoice
- A set of mailing labels

Reports are used to help the reader understand and analyze information. For example, in a report you can group the customers together for each sales rep and highlight the customers who have not placed an order in six months. This is an example of using a list of customers from the Customers table together with other data in the database as an effective business analysis tool. To increase business, the sales reps could contact their customers who have not ordered in the past six months and review the findings with the sales manager. A sales report could then be run each month to see if the strategy has helped to produce any new business.

In this section, you will create reports in Access by first identifying a record source, then designing the report, and finally choosing a Report tool. You will learn how to modify a report by adding and deleting fields, resizing columns, and adding a theme. You will also learn about the report sections, the report views, and controls on reports.

Creating Reports Using Report Tools

Access provides five different report tools for creating reports. The report tools are located on the Create tab in the Reports group, as shown in Figure 4.20. The most common of the tools, the Report tool, is used to instantly create a tabular report based on a selected table or query. The Report Design tool is used to create a new blank report in Design view. This tool is used by advanced users who want to create a report from scratch with no help from Access. The Blank Report tool is used to create a new report in Layout view by inserting fields and controls manually to design the report. The Report Wizard tool will prompt you through a series of step-by-step screens and help you create a report based on your selections. The Labels tool is used to create printable labels using one of the pre-formatted templates provided by Access. Table 4.3 provides a summary of the five report tools and their usages. Once you create a report using one of the report tools, you can perform modifications in either Layout view or Design view.

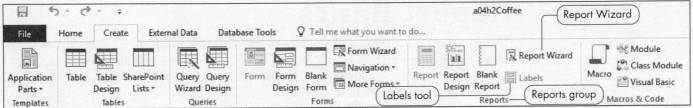

FIGURE 4.20 Reports Group on the Create Tab

Access 2016, Windows 10, Microsoft Corporation

TABLE 4.3 Report Tools and Their Usages	
Report Tool	**Usage**
Report	Create a tabular report showing all of the fields in the record source.
Report Design	Create a new blank report in Design view. Add fields and controls manually.
Blank Report	Create a new blank report in Layout view. Drag and drop to add fields and controls manually.
Report Wizard	Answer a series of step-by-step questions and Access will design a custom report for you.
Labels	Select a preformatted label template and create printable labels.

Pearson Education, Inc.

Before you create a report in Access, you should consider the following questions:

- What is the purpose of the report?
- Who will use the report?
- Which tables, queries, and fields are needed for the report?
- How will the report be distributed? Will users view the report directly from the Access database, or will they receive it through email, fax, or the Internet?
- Will the results be converted to Word, Excel, HTML, or another format?

In the Forms section of this chapter, you learned that it is helpful to talk to users and design a form before you launch Access. The same applies to creating an Access report. Users can give you solid input, and creating a design will help you determine which report tool to use to create the report.

The first step in planning your report is to identify the record source. You may use one or more tables, queries, or a combination of tables and queries as the report's record source. Sometimes, a single table contains all of the records you need for the report. Other times, you will incorporate several tables. When data from multiple related tables are needed to create a report, you can first create a single query (with criteria, if necessary) and then base the report on that query. Multiple tables used in a query must be related, as indicated with join lines.

Reports can contain text and numeric data as well as formatting, calculated fields, graphics, and so forth. For example, you can add a company logo to the report header. Be sure that you have appropriate permission to use any company logo, graphic, or photo in your reports in order to avoid inappropriate or illegal use of an asset.

Use the Report Tool

 The easiest way to create a report is with the Report tool. The **Report tool** is used to create a tabular report based on the selected table or query.

To create a report using the Report tool, complete the following steps:

1. Select a table or query in the Navigation Pane.
2. Click Report in the Reports group on the Create tab.

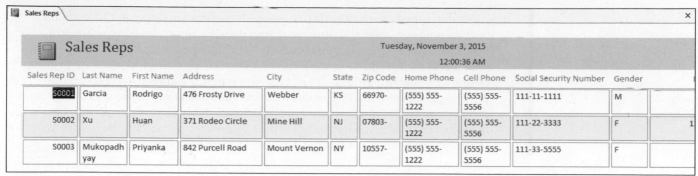

Sales Rep ID	Last Name	First Name	Address	City	State	Zip Code	Home Phone	Cell Phone	Social Security Number	Gender	
S0001	Garcia	Rodrigo	476 Frosty Drive	Webber	KS	66970-	(555) 555-1222	(555) 555-5556	111-11-1111	M	
S0002	Xu	Huan	371 Rodeo Circle	Mine Hill	NJ	07803-	(555) 555-1222	(555) 555-5556	111-22-3333	F	1
S0003	Mukopadh yay	Priyanka	842 Purcell Road	Mount Vernon	NY	10557-	(555) 555-1222	(555) 555-5556	111-33-5555	F	

Sales Reps — Tuesday, November 3, 2015 — 12:00:36 AM

FIGURE 4.21 Tabular Report Created with the Report Tool

Access 2016, Windows 10, Microsoft Corporation

Access creates a tabular layout report instantly. Notice that this type of report displays data horizontally in columns across the page, as shown in Figure 4.21.

If you prefer, you can display a report using a stacked layout, which displays fields in a vertical column. This type of report is less common, as it would result in longer printouts. The number of pages depends on the number of records in the record source.

Use the Report Wizard

The **Report Wizard** prompts you for input in a series of steps to generate a customized report. The wizard enables you to make certain customizations quickly and easily without having to be an expert in report design.

> **To create a report using the Report Wizard, complete the following steps:**
>
> 1. Select the report's record source (table or query) in the Navigation Pane, and click Report Wizard in the Reports group on the Create tab. The wizard opens with the selected table or query (the record source) displayed in the first dialog box. Although you chose the record source before you started, the first dialog box enables you to select fields from the selected source or additional tables or queries.
>
> 2. Click the Tables/Queries list arrow to display a list of available tables or queries, if you want to choose a different record source. Select the fields you want to include in the report. You can select an available field and then click `>` to add a single field to the Selected Fields list, `>>` to select all fields, `<` to remove a field, `<<` and to remove all fields from the report. See Figure 4.22. Set the desired fields and click Next.

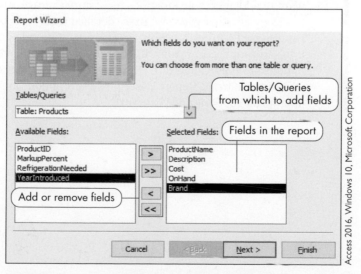

FIGURE 4.22 Selecting Fields in the Report Wizard

Access 2016, Windows 10, Microsoft Corporation

3. Apply the desired grouping in the next dialog box, shown in Figure 4.23. Grouping enables you to organize and summarize your data in a report, based on values in a field. For example, you can group products by their brand name and average the cost of products in each group. To group records in a report, select the field you want to group by and click Add One Field ▶ to add the new group. If you need a second or third grouping level, add those field names in order. The order in which you select the groups dictates the order of display in the report. In Figure 4.23, the products are grouped by the Brand field. Once you have selected the appropriate options, click Next. For a basic report, you would not select any grouping fields, and instead just click Next.

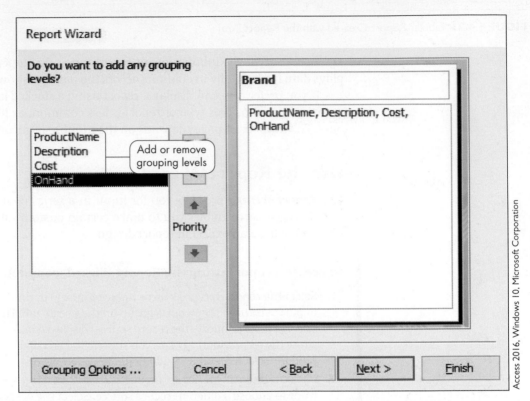

FIGURE 4.23 Grouping Options in the Report Wizard

4. Apply the desired sorting and summary options in the next dialog box. Figure 4.24 displays the sort options for a grouped report. You can click Summary Options if you want to add aggregate functions (e.g., sum, average, minimum, and maximum) and to specify whether you want to see detailed records on the report or only the aggregate results (see Figure 4.25). You can also choose to calculate values as percentages of totals in your report results. If no grouping is specified in your report, the summary options are not available. In Figure 4.25, no summary options are selected. Click OK to return to the Report Wizard. The sort options are the same as before. Set the appropriate options and click Next.

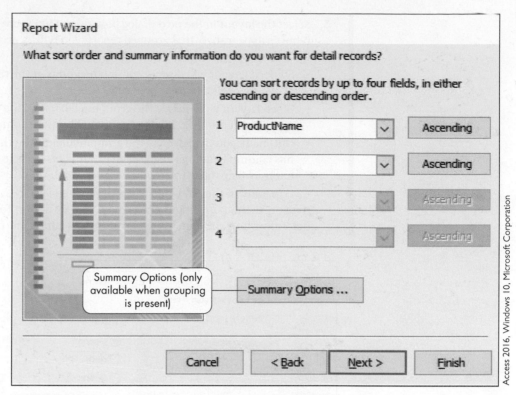

FIGURE 4.24 Sort and Summarize Grouped Data in the Report Wizard

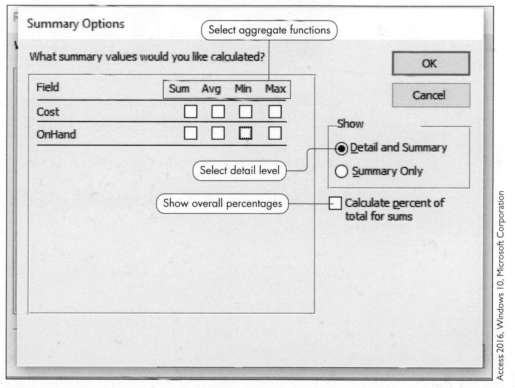

FIGURE 4.25 Summary Options Dialog Box

5. Select the layout in the next dialog box, shown in Figure 4.26, to determine the report's appearance. In a grouped report, you will be prompted to select the layout from three options:

- Stepped Layout will display column headings at the top of the page and keep the grouping field(s) in their own row.
- Block Layout will include the grouping field(s) in line with the data, saving some space when printing. It has one set of column headings at the top of each page.
- Outline Layout will display the grouping field(s) on their own separate rows and has column headings inside each group. This leads to a longer report when printing but may help make the report easier to read.

Clicking any of these layouts will give you a general preview in the preview area. In a report without grouping, the layouts are Columnar, Tabular, and Justified. You can determine how the data fits on a page by selecting Portrait or Landscape. Click Next.

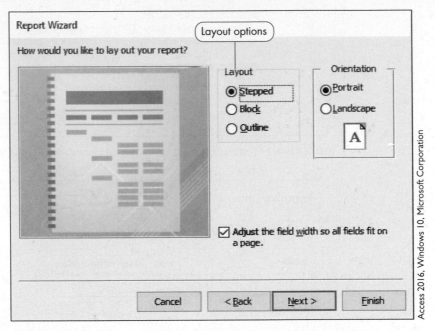

FIGURE 4.26 Layout Options for Grouped Data in the Report Wizard

6. Enter a report name and click Finish. Your grouped report will resemble Figure 4.27.

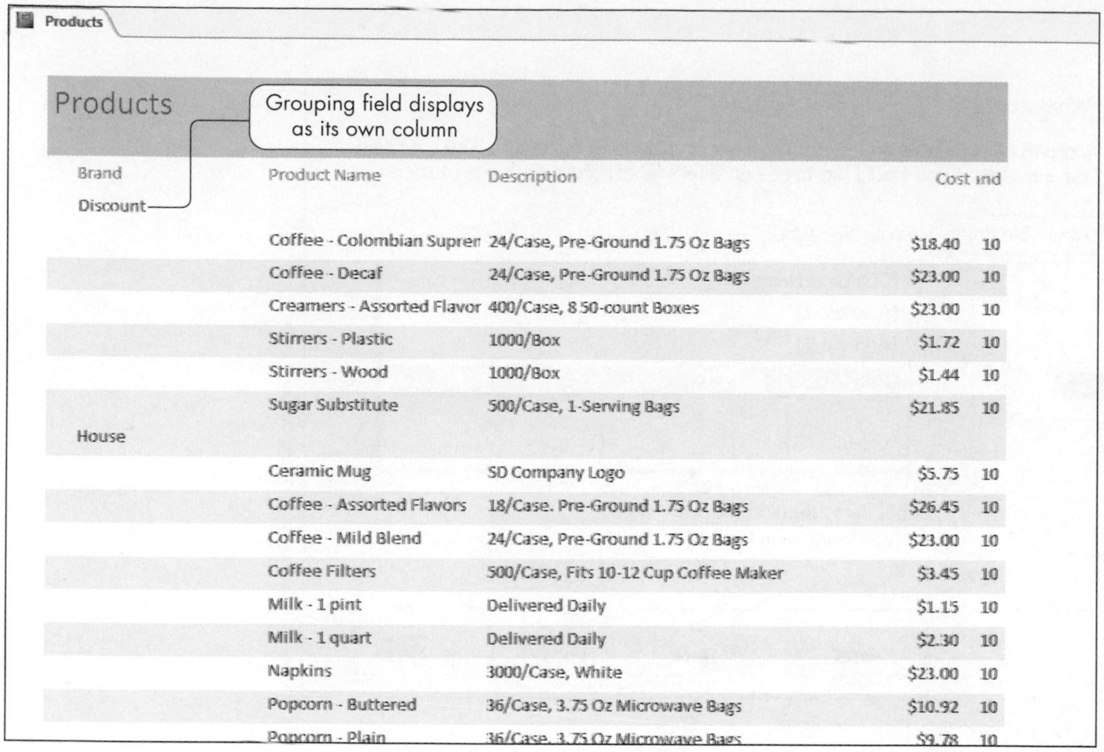

Access 2016, Windows 10, Microsoft Corporation

FIGURE 4.27 Grouped Report

Use the Label Wizard

The ***Label Wizard*** enables you to easily create mailing labels, name tags, and other specialized tags. A mailing label report is a specialized report that you can create and print with name-brand labels, such as Avery and many others. If you purchase a store brand label from an office supply store, it will generally state the comparable manufacturer and product number; the wizard provides a long list of both manufacturers and label sizes.

To use the Label Wizard, complete the following steps:

1. Select the table or query that you will use as the record source for the report.
2. Click Labels in the Reports group on the Create tab.
3. Select the manufacturer, product number, unit of measure, label type, and then click Next.
4. Select the font and color options, and then click Next.
5. Add the fields to the prototype label, as shown in Figure 4.28. You add the fields exactly as you would like them to display, including adding commas, spacing, and pressing Enter to move to the next line, where applicable.

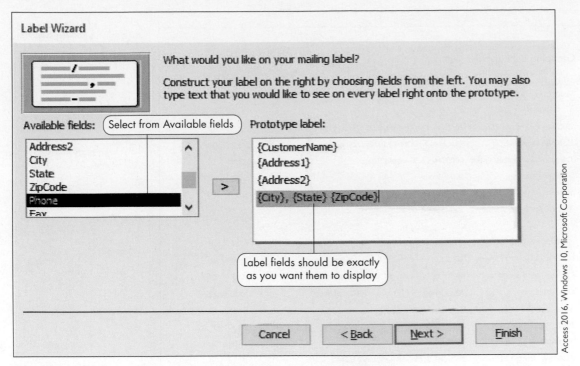

FIGURE 4.28 Create a Customers Prototype Label

6. Add sort fields; for example, you may want to sort by state or zip code, and then click Next.
7. Name the report and then click Finish to generate your label report. The results using the Customers table are shown in Figure 4.29.

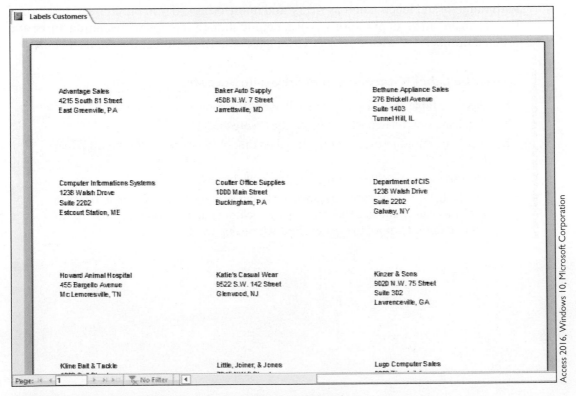

FIGURE 4.29 Customer Mailing Labels Created by Label Wizard

Using Report Views

As you work with the report tools to create and modify reports, you might need to switch between the four report views in Access—Report, Layout, Design, and Print Preview. Report view and Print Preview are generally used only for viewing or printing the report. To make modifications to a report, use Layout view and Design view. Most of the design work can be done in Layout view, but sometimes Design view is necessary to apply a more advanced feature, such as setting the tab order of the controls. To switch between the four views, click the View arrow in the Views group, and then select the desired view (alternatively, right-click the report tab, and from the shortcut menu, select the desired view).

View a Report in Report View

Report view enables you to view a report onscreen in a continuous page layout. However, because the data cannot be changed in Report view, it is simply a way of viewing the information without having to worry about accidentally moving a control. You can also use Report view to filter data, if necessary.

Print or Save a Report in Print Preview

STEP 2 ▶▶ *Print Preview* enables you to see exactly what the report will look like when it is printed. You cannot modify the design of the report or the data in Print Preview. By default, Print Preview will display all the pages in the report. Figure 4.29 displays the mailing labels report in Print Preview.

From Print Preview, you have the option to export and save the report to a different file type, such as Word. This is a useful option if you plan to share a report electronically but do not want to distribute the entire database. In the Data group, on the Print Preview tab, you will find a number of eligible file types, as shown in Figure 4.30. Select the option in the Data group, and then follow the onscreen prompts to export your report. Commonly used formats include Excel, Word, and Portable Document Format (PDF).

Portable Document Format (PDF) is a file type that was created for exchanging documents independently of software applications and operating system environments. In other words, you can email a report in PDF format to users running various operating systems, and they can open it even if they do not have Microsoft Access installed. PDF files open in Adobe Reader, a free downloadable program; recent versions of Windows have a built-in Reader program that displays PDF files as well.

Because databases contain a great deal of information, Access reports can become very long, requiring many pages to print. At times, reports can be formatted incorrectly, or blank pages might print in between each page of information. Be sure to troubleshoot your reports before sending them to the printer, or to recipients via email.

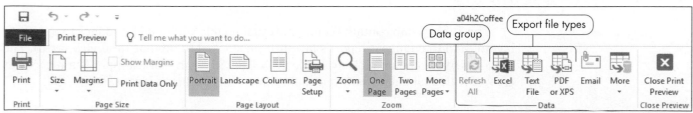

FIGURE 4.30 Data Group on Print Preview Tab

Access 2016, Windows 10, Microsoft Corporation

Alter a Report in Layout View

Use Layout view to alter the report design while still viewing the data. You should use Layout view to add or delete fields in the report, modify field properties, change the column widths, group, sort, and summarize data. The Page Setup tab presents options for setting the page size, orientation, and margins. Although you will be able to view your modifications along with the data in Layout view, you will still need to check the report in Print Preview to evaluate all the changes before printing it.

Modifying a Report

After you create a report by using one of the report tools, you may want to modify it. Some of the common changes you make in reports are adding and deleting controls, changing the arrangement, widths, and formatting of controls, and modifying the title. From either Layout or Design view, there are four tabs available for report modification:

- Design: Use this tab to make changes to the design of the report, such as adding fields, grouping and sorting records, changing themes, and inserting additional controls.
- Arrange: Use this tab to change the layout of a report, to move fields up and down, and to control margins and spacing.
- Format: Use this tab to work with fonts, font size, and colors, add or remove bolding, italics, or underlining, adjust text alignment, or add a background image or color.
- Page Setup: Use this tab to change paper size, margins, or page orientation, or to format reports into multiple columns.

Modify the Layout of a Report

STEP 3 ▶▶ The Arrange tab displays in both Layout view and Design view. Some key commands on the Arrange tab from Layout view are highlighted in Figure 4.31.

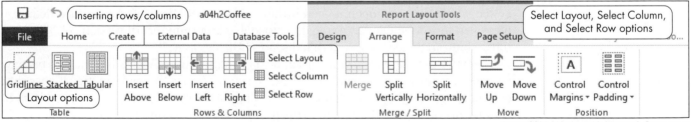

FIGURE 4.31 Report Layout Tools Arrange Tab

Access 2016, Windows 10, Microsoft Corporation

The Table group contains commands that enable you to add gridlines to a report's layout, and to change a report's layout from stacked to tabular (and vice versa). The Remove Layout command is available in Design view only. For example, if a report was created with a tabular layout, you could change it to a stacked layout.

> **To change a report's layout from tabular to stacked, complete the following steps:**
>
> 1. Open the report in Layout view and click the Arrange tab.
> 2. Click any text box in the Detail section of the report.
> 3. Click Select Layout in the Rows & Columns group.
> 4. Click Stacked in the Table group.

The Rows & Columns group contains commands that enable you to insert rows and columns inside a report's layout. In a report with a stacked layout, you may want to separate some controls from the rest of the fields, or create some empty space so that fields can be added or repositioned. For example, you can select a control (or multiple controls) and click Insert Below. This will create an empty row (or space) below the selected controls. This group also contains the Select Layout, Select Column, and Select Row commands, which you can use to select the entire layout, or a single column or row in a layout.

The Merge/Split group contains commands that enable you to merge and split the controls on a report. There are times when you might want to deviate from the basic row and column formats that the report tools create. For example, you can make a label such as *Product Name* display in two controls (Product and Name), with one positioned below the other, rather than in one single control.

The Move group contains commands to move a field up or down in a stacked layout. Moving controls up or down in a report may cause unexpected results; you can always click Undo if you need to reverse your changes.

The Position group contains commands to control the margins and the padding (the spacing between controls) in a report. The preset margin settings are convenient to use; ensure that if you change the margins, you preview the report to view the result.

Modify Report Controls

The Format tab contains a series of commands that enable you to change the font, display, and alignment of the controls on a report, as shown in Figure 4.32. The formatting tools in Access are similar to those in other Microsoft Office applications.

To format report controls, complete the following steps:

1. Open the report in Layout view (or Design view), then select the control(s) you want to format.
2. Click the Format tab, and click the formatting tools as desired.

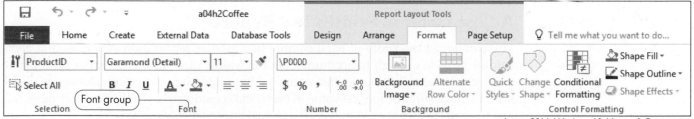

Access 2016, Windows 10, Microsoft Corporation

FIGURE 4.32 Report Layout Tools Format Tab

TIP: INSERT A LOGO IN A REPORT
To insert a logo in a report, open the report in Layout (or Design) view, and then click Logo in the Header / Footer group on the Design tab. In the Insert Picture dialog box, locate the image, click the file, and then click Open. The picture will display in the Report Header section; use the Property Sheet to modify the size and other attributes, if necessary.

Add a Field to a Report

At times, new fields may be added to tables and then need to be incorporated into reports. Alternatively, you might be creating a customized report and want to add fields individually. Adding a field to a report with a stacked or tabular layout is similar to adding a field to a form.

To add a field to a report, complete the following steps:

1. Open the report in Layout view, then click Add Existing Fields in the Tools group on the Design tab.

   The Field List pane displays at the right of the report. For a single-table report, you will be presented with a list of fields from the table (record source). For a multiple-table report, click the + (plus sign) to the left of the appropriate table to expand it, and locate the desired field(s).

2. Click and drag the desired field to the precise location on the report, using the shaded line as a guide for positioning the new field. Alternatively, you can double-click a field to add it to the report; the field will be added below the selected field. The other fields will automatically adjust to make room for the new field.

Delete a Field from a Report

You may decide that even though a field was available in a table or in a query that was used as the record source, it is not necessary to display it to users in a report. Not all fields in a database are necessarily relevant to reports that you create.

To delete a field from the Detail section of a report, complete the following steps:

1. Open the report in Layout view, and click the text box control of the field to be deleted (note the shaded border around the control).
2. Click Select Row in the Rows & Columns group on the Arrange tab in order to select the text box and its associated label. Alternatively, click the text box control, press and hold Ctrl, and then click the associated label control to select them both.
3. Press Delete.

The other fields will automatically adjust to close the gap around the deleted field.

Adjust Column Widths in a Report

You can adjust the width of each column in a tabular report individually so that each column is wide enough to accommodate the widest value in the field. For example, if a report contains first name, last name, address and city, and email address, you will need to make sure the longest value in each field is completely visible. Scroll through the records to ensure that all values can be viewed by report users.

To modify column widths in a tabular report, complete the following steps:

1. Open the report in Layout view, and click the text box control of the field you want to resize.
2. Point to the right border of the control until the pointer turns into a double-headed arrow. Drag the right edge of the control to the left or right until you arrive at the desired width.

Change Margins and Orientation

At times, you will want to print a report in Landscape orientation as opposed to Portrait; that decision will depend upon how many columns you want to display across the page, the widths of the fields, and other formatting considerations. The Page Setup tab presents options similar to those you may have used in Word. In the Page Size group, you can change the margins, and in the Page Layout group, you can work with Page Setup options, including setting the orientation of your report, as shown in Figure 4.33.

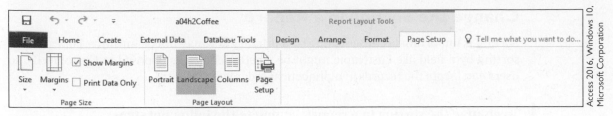

FIGURE 4.33 Report Layout Tools Page Setup Tab

Add a Theme to the Report

You can enhance the report's appearance by applying one of the built-in Access themes.

> **To apply a theme, complete the following steps:**
>
> 1. Open the report in Layout or Design view, and select Themes in the Themes group on the Design tab.
> 2. Point to a theme to see its name in the ScreenTip and a Live Preview of the theme in the report, and click to select it. By default, the theme will be applied to all objects in your database. Right-click a theme in the gallery to apply it to the current report only, or to all the reports in your database that share a common theme.

Work with a Report Layout Control

When you use one of the report tools to create a new report, Access will add a layout control to help align the fields. Layout controls in reports work similarly to layout controls in forms. The layout control provides guides to help keep controls aligned horizontally and vertically, and give your report a neat appearance. If you want to have more control over the location of your fields, you can remove the layout control and position the controls manually on the report.

> **To remove the layout control from a report, complete the following steps:**
>
> 1. Open the report in Design view (the option is not available on the Ribbon in Layout view), and click anywhere in the layout control you want to remove.
> 2. Click Select Layout in the Rows & Columns group on the Arrange tab.
> 3. Click Remove Layout in the Table group. All of the controls are still available in the report, but can now be managed individually.

You can add a layout control to a report by first selecting all the controls you want to include in the layout. To select multiple controls, click the first control, press and hold Ctrl, and then click the additional controls you want to include. To select all of the controls on a form, press Ctrl+A. Click Tabular or Stacked in the Table group.

Sorting Records in a Report

STEP 4 ›› When a report is created using the Report tool, the sort order of the records in the report is initially dependent on the sort order of the record source—similar to the way records are sorted in a form. The primary key of the record source usually controls the sort order. However, a report has an additional feature for sorting. While in Layout view or Design view, click Group & Sort in the Grouping & Totals group on the Design tab. The Group, Sort, and Total pane displays at the bottom of the report. This pane enables you to group records together and to override the sort order in the report's record source. Note that if you do not use the Report Wizard, this is generally how you would add grouping and totals to a report.

Change the Sorting in a Report

Sorting is important because sorting by a primary key may not be intuitive. For example, sorting by a field like LastName might be a better choice as opposed to CustomerID, so users can locate the records in alphabetical order by LastName.

> **To change the sorting in a report, complete the following steps:**
>
> 1. Open the report in Layout or Design view, and click Group & Sort in the Grouping & Totals group on the Design tab.
> 2. Click *Add a sort* and select the field by which you want to sort. The default sort order is ascending.
> 3. Add another sort by clicking *Add a sort* again. For example, you could sort first by Brand and then by ProductName, as shown in Figure 4.34.

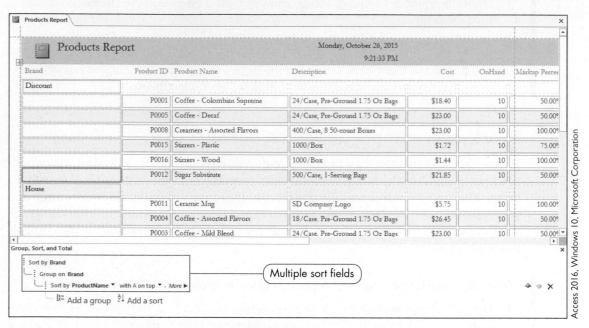

FIGURE 4.34 Report in Layout View with Two Sort Fields

Quick Concepts

5. What is the difference between Report view and Layout view? *p. 303*

6. What is the benefit of saving a report as another type of file? *p. 303*

7. Why is it important to view your reports in Print Preview? *p. 303*

8. Why would you decide to remove a report layout control when modifying a report? *p. 307*

9. Why is sorting the records in a report important? *p. 307*

Hands-On Exercises

Watch the Video
for this Hands-On
Exercise!

MyITLab®
HOE2 Training

2 Report Basics

You create a products report using the Access Report tool to help Ryung stay on top of the key information for her business. You will modify the column widths so that they all fit across one page. You will also use the Report Wizard to create additional reports that Ryung requires.

STEP 1 ›› CREATING REPORTS USING REPORT TOOLS

You use the Report tool to create an Access report to help Ryung manage her product information. This report is especially useful for determining which products she needs to order to fill upcoming orders. You also use the Report Wizard to determine sales by city. Refer to Figure 4.35 as you complete Step 1.

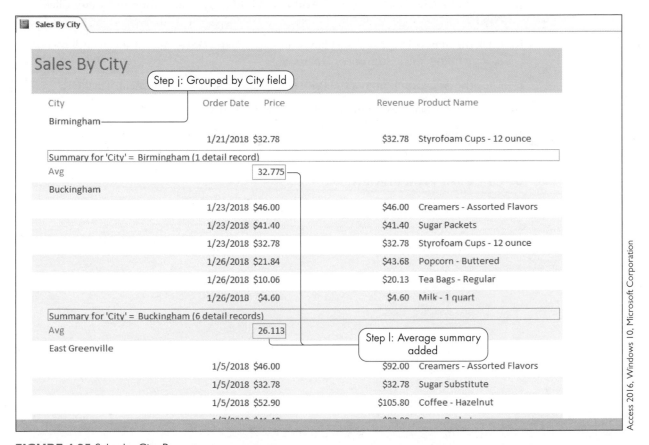

FIGURE 4.35 Sales by City Report

a. Open *a04h1Coffee_LastFirst* if you closed it at the end of Hands-On Exercise 1 and save it as **a04h2Coffee_LastFirst**, changing h1 to h2.

b. Select the **Products table** in the Navigation Pane. Click the **Create tab** and click **Report** in the Reports group.

Access creates a new tabular layout report based on the Products table. The report opens in Layout view ready for editing.

c. Click the **Products title** at the top of the report to select it, click again on **Products**, and then change the title to **Products Report**. Press **Enter** to accept the change.

d. Right-click the **Products report tab** and select **Print Preview**.

The report is too wide for the page; you will close Print Preview and change the orientation to Landscape.

e. Click **Close Print Preview** in the Close Preview group to return to Layout view.

f. Click the **Page Setup tab** and click **Landscape** in the Page Layout group.

The report changes to Landscape orientation. Most of the columns now fit across one page. You will make further revisions to the report later so that it fits on one page.

g. Save the report as **Products Report**. Close the report.

h. Select the **Revenue query** in the Navigation Pane. Click the **Create tab** and click **Report Wizard** in the Reports group.

The Report Wizard launches.

i. Click the **City field** and click **Add One Field** > to add the City field to the report. Repeat the same process for the **OrderDate**, **Price**, **Revenue**, and **ProductName fields**. Click **Next**.

j. Ensure that **City** is selected, click **Add One Field** > to add grouping by city. Click **Next**.

k. Click the **arrow** in the first sort box, and select **OrderDate**. Accept the default sort order as Ascending. Click **Summary Options**.

l. Click the **Avg check box** in the Price row to summarize the Price field. Click **OK**.

m. Click **Next**. Click **Next** again to accept the default layout.

n. Type **Sales by City** for the title of the report. Click **Finish**.

The report is displayed in Print Preview mode.

o. Click **Close Print Preview**.

p. Save and close the report.

The Products Report you created looks good, according to Ryung. However, she does not have Access installed on her home computer, and would like to have a copy of the report saved in PDF format so she can review it outside of the office. You will save a copy of the report for her Refer to Figure 4.36 as you complete Step 2.

Step a: Report in PDF format

Products Report

Sunday, November 4, 2015
9:24:45 PM

Product ID	Product Name	Description	Cost	Markup Percent	Refrigeration Needed	Brand
P0001	Coffee - Colombian Supreme	24/Case, Pre-Ground 1.75 Oz Bags	$18.40	50.00%	☐	Discount
P0002	Coffee - Hazelnut	24/Case, Pre-Ground 1.75 Oz Bags	$26.45	100.00%	☐	Premium
P0003	Coffee - Mild Blend	24/Case, Pre-Ground 1.75 Oz Bags	$23.00	50.00%	☐	House
P0004	Coffee - Assorted Flavors	18/Case. Pre-Ground 1.75 Oz Bags	$26.45	50.00%	☐	House
P0005	Coffee - Decaf	24/Case, Pre-Ground 1.75 Oz Bags	$23.00	50.00%	☐	Discount
P0006	Tea Bags - Regular	75/Box, Individual Tea Bags	$5.75	75.00%	☐	House
P0007	Tea Bags - Decaf	75/Box, Individual Tea Bags	$8.05	75.00%	☐	House
P0008	Creamers - Assorted Flavors	400/Case, 8 50-count Boxes	$23.00	100.00%	☐	Discount
P0009	Creamers - Liquid	200/Case, Individual Creamers	$17.25	100.00%	☑	Premium
P0010	Sugar Packets	2000/Case	$20.70	100.00%	☐	House
P0011	Ceramic Mug	SD Company Logo	$5.75	100.00%	☐	House
P0012	Sugar Substitute	500/Case, 1-Serving Bags	$21.85	50.00%	☐	Discount
P0013	Coffee Filters	500/Case, Fits 10-12 Cup Coffee Maker	$3.45	50.00%	☐	House
P0014	Napkins	3000/Case, White	$23.00	100.00%	☐	House
P0015	Stirrers - Plastic	1000/Box	$1.72	75.00%	☐	Discount
P0016	Stirrers - Wood	1000/Box	$1.44	100.00%	☐	Discount
P0017	Spoons	500/Box, White Plastic	$17.25	100.00%	☐	House
P0018	Popcorn - Plain	36/Case, 3.75 Oz Microwave Bags	$9.78	100.00%	☐	House
P0019	Popcorn - Buttered	36/Case, 3.75 Oz Microwave Bags	$10.92	100.00%	☐	House
P0020	Soup - Chicken	50 Envelopes	$11.50	100.00%	☐	Premium
P0021	Soup - Variety Pak	50 Envelopes	$13.80	100.00%	☐	Premium
P0022	Styrofoam Cups - 10 ounce	1000/Case	$19.55	50.00%	☐	House

Access 2016, Windows 10, Microsoft Corporation

FIGURE 4.36 Products Report Saved in PDF Format

a. Open the Products Report and on the **File** tab, click **Print**, and select **Print Preview**. Click **PDF or XPS** in the Data group on the Print Preview tab. Navigate to where you are saving your files, type the file name **a04h2Products_LastFirst**, ensure that *Open file after publishing* is selected, and then click **Publish**.

Windows will open the report in your system's default PDF viewer, which may be Adobe Reader or the Windows Reader app. Close the reader window. You will submit this file to your instructor at the end of the last hands-on exercise.

b. Ensure that you return to the Access window, and in the Export – PDF dialog box, click **Close** when prompted to save the export steps.

c. Click **Close Print Preview** and close the report.

Ryung realized the Products table is missing a field that she requires for her reports. She would like you to add the field to the table and update the report to include the new field. She would also like to make sure the report fits nicely across one landscape page. She also asked you to show her some sample color schemes Refer to Figure 4.37 as you complete Step 3.

Product ID	Product Name	Description	Cost	OnHand	Markup Percent	Refrig?	Brand
P0001	Coffee - Colombian Supreme	24/Case, Pre-Ground 1.75 Oz Bags	$18.40	10	50.00%	☐	Discount
P0002	Coffee - Hazelnut	24/Case, Pre-Ground 1.75 Oz Bags	$26.45	10	100.00%	☐	Premium
P0003	Coffee - Mild Blend	24/Case, Pre-Ground 1.75 Oz Bags	$23.00	10	50.00%	☐	House
P0004	Coffee - Assorted Flavors	18/Case. Pre-Ground 1.75 Oz Bags	$26.45	10	50.00%	☐	House
P0005	Coffee - Decaf	24/Case, Pre-Ground 1.75 Oz Bags	$23.00	10	50.00%	☐	Discount
P0006	Tea Bags - Regular	75/Box, Individual Tea Bags	$5.75	10	75.00%	☐	House
P0007	Tea Bags - Decaf	75/Box, Individual Tea Bags	$8.05	10	75.00%	☐	House
P0008	Creamers - Assorted Flavors	400/Case, 8 50-count Boxes	$23.00	10	100.00%	☐	Discount
P0009	Creamers - Liquid	200/Case, Individual Creamers	$17.25	10	100.00%	☑	Premium
P0010	Sugar Packets	2000/Case	$20.70	10	100.00%	☐	House
P0011	Ceramic Mug	SD Company Logo	$5.75	10	100.00%	☐	House
P0012	Sugar Substitute	500/Case, 1-Serving Bags	$21.85	10	50.00%	☐	Discount
P0013	Coffee Filters	500/Case, Fits 10-12 Cup Coffee Maker	$3.45	10	50.00%	☐	House
P0014	Napkins	3000/Case, White	$23.00	10	100.00%	☐	House
P0015	Stirrers - Plastic	1000/Box	$1.72	10	75.00%	☐	Discount

Products Retrospect — Step t: Retrospect theme applied

Products Report — Tuesday, November 3, 2015 — 9:32:32 AM

Access 2016, Windows 10, Microsoft Corporation

FIGURE 4.37 Products Retrospect Report

a. Right-click the **Products table** and select **Design View**.

You need to add the OnHand field to the Products table.

b. Click in the **MarkupPercent field**, and then click **Insert Rows** in the Tools group on the Design tab.

A new blank row displays above the MarkupPercent field.

c. Type **OnHand** in the Field Name box and select **Number** as the Data Type.

d. Save the table. Click **View** in the Views group to switch to Datasheet view.

The new OnHand column contains no data. Next, you will add some sample data to the new field for testing purposes only.

e. Type the number **10** for each item's OnHand value.

f. Close the Products table.

g. Right-click **Products Report** in the Navigation Pane, and select **Layout View**.

h. Click **Add Existing Fields** in the Tools group on the Design tab to open the Field List pane.

i. Drag the **OnHand field** from the Field List pane between the Cost and MarkupPercent fields. Close the Field List pane.

Because of the tabular layout control, Access adjusts all the columns to make room for the new OnHand field.

j. Display the report in Print Preview.

The report is still too wide for a single page.

k. Click **Close Print Preview**. Ensure that you are in Layout view.

l. Scroll to and then click anywhere in the **Year Introduced column**. Click the **Arrange tab** and click **Select Column** in the Rows & Columns group. Press **Delete** to remove the column.

The Year Introduced column is removed from the report.

m. Scroll to and then click the **ProductID column heading** and drag the right border to the left until the Product ID heading still fits, but any extra white space is removed.

n. Scroll to and then click the **Refrigeration Needed column heading** and rename the column **Refrig?**. Adjust the width of the *Refrig?* column heading so that any extra white space is removed.

o. Click **Themes** in the Themes group on the Design tab.

The available predefined themes display.

p. Right-click the **Organic theme** and select **Apply Theme to This Object Only**. Display the report in Print Preview.

Access reformats the report using the Organic theme. The report is still too wide for a single page. You will make further adjustments in the next steps.

q. Click **Close Print Preview** and save the report. Click the **File tab**, select **Save As**, select **Save Object As**, and then click **Save As**. Type **Products Organic** as the report name and click **OK**.

You saved the report with one theme. Now, you will apply a second theme to the report and save it with a different name.

r. Ensure that the report is in Layout view. You notice that the Brand column is extending over the dashed page break to its right and needs to be resized to fit on the page. Drag the right border of the Brand column to the left so that it fits inside the page break. Scroll down the report to ensure that all of the values in the column are visible. Narrow columns as required to ensure that all columns are fitting inside the dashed page break. Save the report.

s. Click **Themes** in the Themes group to apply a different theme. Right-click the **Retrospect theme** and select **Apply Theme to This Object Only**. Display the report in Print Preview.

If you do not apply the theme to this object only, all database objects will adopt the Retrospect theme.

t. Click **Close Print Preview**. Click the **File tab**, select **Save As**, select **Save Object As**, and then click **Save As**. Type **Products Retrospect** as the report name and click **OK**. Close the report.

You will be able to show Ryung two product reports with different themes applied.

Ryung would like the Products Report records to be sorted and grouped by Brand. You will change the sort order, group the records, and preview the report to see the results Refer to Figure 4.38 as you complete Step 4.

Products Report							✕
Step f: Report grouped by Brand							

Products Report

Monday, October 26, 2015
9:35:21 PM

Brand	Product ID	Product Name	Description	Cost	OnHand	Markup Percen
Discount						
	P0012	Sugar Substitute	500/Case, 1-Serving Bags	$21.85	10	50.00%
	P0005	Coffee - Decaf	24/Case, Pre-Ground 1.75 Oz Bags	$23.00	10	50.00%
	P0008	Creamers - Assorted Flavors	400/Case, 8 50-count Boxes	$23.00	10	100.00%
	P0016	Stirrers - Wood	1000/Box	$1.44	10	100.00%
	P0015	Stirrers - Plastic	1000/Box	$1.72	10	75.00%
	P0001	Coffee - Colombian Supreme	24/Case, Pre-Ground 1.75 Oz Bags	$18.40	10	50.00%
House						
	P0003	Coffee - Mild Blend	24/Case, Pre-Ground 1.75 Oz Bags	$23.00	10	50.00%
	P0004	Coffee - Assorted Flavors	18/Case. Pre-Ground 1.75 Oz Bags	$26.45	10	50.00%
	P0006	Tea Bags - Regular	75/Box, Individual Tea Bags	$5.75	10	75.00%
	P0007	Tea Bags - Decaf	75/Box, Individual Tea Bags	$8.05	10	75.00%
	P0010	Sugar Packets	2000/Case	$20.70	10	100.00%
	P0011	Ceramic Mug	SD Company Logo	$5.75	10	100.00%
	P0014	Napkins	3000/Case, White	$23.00	10	100.00%
	P0025	Milk - 1 pint	Delivered Daily	$1.15	10	100.00%

Access 2016, Windows 10, Microsoft Corporation

FIGURE 4.38 Products Report Grouped by Brand

a. Open **Products Report** in Layout view.

b. Click **Group & Sort** in the Grouping & Totals group on the Design tab.

The *Add a group* and *Add a sort* options display at the bottom of the report.

> **TROUBLESHOOTING:** If the options do not display, the Group, Sort, and Total pane may have been open. If the pane is closed after selecting the command, try clicking Group & Sort again.

c. Click **Add a sort**.

A new Sort bar displays at the bottom of the report.

d. Select **Brand** from the list.

The report is now sorted by Brand in ascending order (with Discount at the top).

e. Click **Add a group**.

f. Select **Brand** from the list.

The report is now grouped by Brand.

g. View the report in Report view. Save and close the report.

h. Close the database and exit Access. Based on your instructor's directions, submit the following:

a04h2Coffee_LastFirst

a04h2Products_LastFirst

Chapter Objectives Review

After reading this chapter, you have accomplished the following objectives:

1. Create forms using form tools.

- Identify a record source: A record source is the table or query that supplies the records for the form.
- Use the Form tool: The Form tool creates a basic form that opens in Layout view.
- Understand controls: Controls are the text boxes, buttons, labels, and other tools you use to add, edit, and display data in a form or report.
- Work with form views: Form view is a simplified interface used for data entry, but it allows no design changes. Layout view enables users to make changes to the layout while viewing the data in the form. Design view enables you to change advanced design settings that are not available in Layout view.
- Work with a subform: A subform displays data from a related table for each record in the main table.
- Create a split form: A split form combines two views of the same record source—one section is displayed in a stacked layout and the other section is displayed in a tabular layout.
- Create a multiple items form: This form displays multiple records in a tabular layout similar to a table's Datasheet view, with more customization options.
- Create forms using the other form tools: A datasheet form is a replica of a table or query's Datasheet view except that it still retains form properties. The Form Design tool and the Blank Form tools can be used to create a form manually. The Navigation option in the Forms group enables you to create user interface forms that have the look and feel of Web-based forms and enable users to open and close the objects of a database. The Modal Dialog Form tool can be used to create a dialog box.

2. Modify forms.

- Use Form view to edit data: Most users will work in Form view. This enables changes to data but not to design elements.
- Use Layout view to modify form design: Layout view enables you to change the design of a form while viewing data.
- Adjust column widths in a form: Column widths often need to be adjusted. Size the columns to accommodate the widest entry in a field.
- Add and delete form fields: Fields can be added to an existing form using the Field List. Fields can be removed by selecting the text box and the label controls and pressing Delete.
- Add a theme to a form: Themes can be applied to a single form or to all objects in the database.
- Modify form controls: The Format tab enables changes to the font, including bold, italic, underlining, font size, font color, font background, and alignment.

3. Work with a form layout.

- Modify a form layout: The Arrange tab displays in both Layout view and Design view, and enables you to change form layout, field order, and spacing options.

4. Sort records in form.

- Sort by a single field: Forms can be sorted by a single field in either ascending or descending order.

5. Create reports using report tools.

- Use the Report tool: Access has five report tools. The Report tool instantly creates a tabular report based on a table or query. The Report Design tool creates a new blank report in Design view. The Blank Report tool creates a new blank report so that you can insert controls and design the report manually in Layout view. The Report Wizard tool steps you through the process to create a report. The Labels tool creates a page of mailing labels using a template.
- Use the Report Wizard to create a report: The Report Wizard will guide you step by step through creating a report, prompting you for input and generating output. The wizard enables you to group records of a common type and summarize data in your reports.
- Use the Label Wizard: The Label Wizard can produce printable labels. Access includes predefined standard formats for common labels.

6. Use report views.

- View a report in Report view: Report view is ideal for viewing data onscreen. Neither data nor the design can be changed in this view.
- Print or save a report in Print Preview: Print Preview shows how the report will display when printed. It also enables you to save the report as a file in a number of formats, such as Word and PDF.
- Alter a report in Layout view: Layout view enables you to change the design of a report while viewing data.

7. Modify a report.

- Modify the layout of a report: The Arrange tab displays in both Layout view and Design view. The tools on the Arrange tab enable you to work with the layout of a report to give it a more uniform appearance.
- Modify report controls: The Format tab enables changes to the font, including bold, italic, underlining, font size, font color, font background, and alignment.
- Add a field to a report: Fields can be added to an existing report using the Field List.
- Delete a field from a report: Fields can be deleted either in Layout or Design view.
- Adjust column widths in a report: Column widths often need to be adjusted. Be sure to make the column wide enough to display the widest value in a field.

- Change margins and orientation: You can display the report in portrait or landscape mode and increase or decrease margin sizes.
- Add a theme to the report: Themes can be applied to a single report or to all objects in the database.
- Work with a Report Layout control: The Layout control keeps the fields neatly spaced, making it harder to move fields independently but keeping a standard format.

8. Sort records in a report.
- Change the sorting in a report: You can sort report records by a single or multiple fields.

Key Terms Matching

Match the key terms with their definitions. Write the key term letter by the appropriate numbered definition.

a. Control

b. Design view

c. Form

d. Form tool

e. Form view

f. Label Wizard

g. Layout control

h. Layout view

i. Multiple Items form

j. Portable Document Format (PDF)

k. Print Preview

l. Record source

m. Report

n. Report tool

o. Report view

p. Report Wizard

q. Split form

r. Stacked layout

s. Tabular layout

t. Theme

1. _____ A database object that is used to add data into or edit data in a table. **p. 270**

2. _____ Used to create data entry forms for customers, employees, products, and other tables. **p. 270**

3. _____ The table or query that supplies the records for a form or report. **p. 271**

4. _____ Displays fields in a vertical column. **p. 272**

5. _____ Displays fields horizontally. **p. 272**

6. _____ A text box, button, label, or other tool you use to add, edit, and display the data in a form or report. **p. 272**

7. _____ Provides guides to help keep controls aligned horizontally and vertically and give your form a uniform appearance. **p. 272**

8. _____ A simplified user interface primarily used for data entry; does not allow you to make changes to the layout. **p. 273**

9. _____ Enables users to make changes to a layout while viewing the data in the form or report. **p. 274**

10. _____ Enables you to change advanced design settings you cannot see in Layout view, such as removing a layout control. **p. 275**

11. _____ Combines two views of the same record source—one section is displayed in a stacked layout and the other section is displayed in a tabular layout. **p. 276**

12. _____ Displays multiple records in a tabular layout similar to a table's Datasheet view, with more customization options. **p. 277**

13. _____ A defined set of colors, fonts, and graphics that can be applied to a form or report. **p. 281**

14. _____ A database document that outputs meaningful information to its readers. **p. 295**

15. _____ Used to instantly create a tabular report based on the table or query currently selected. **p. 296**

16. _____ Prompts you for input and then uses your answers to generate a customized report. **p. 297**

17. _____ Enables you to easily create mailing labels, name tags, and other specialized tags. **p. 301**

18. _____ Enables you to determine what a printed report will look like in a continuous page layout. **p. 303**

19. _____ Enables you to see exactly what the report will look like when it is printed. **p. 303**

20. _____ A file type that was created for exchanging documents independent of software applications and operating system environment. **p. 303**

Multiple Choice

1. A report can be made from one or more tables or a query. The object(s) that a report is based on is known as the:

(a) Control.

(b) Record Source.

(c) Theme.

(d) Tabular Layout.

2. Which of the following statements is *false?*

(a) Both forms and reports can use tabular and stacked layouts.

(b) A stacked layout displays data in a vertical column.

(c) A tabular layout displays data horizontally.

(d) Stacked layouts are more common for reports because they use less paper when printed.

3. In order to summarize data in a report and override the sort order of the record source you would use:

(a) A text box.

(b) A button on a report.

(c) The Group, Sort, and Total Pane.

(d) A label on a report.

4. The simplest view you can use to modify control widths in a form is:

(a) Layout view.

(b) Form view.

(c) Design view.

(d) Print Preview.

5. Which of the following views provides you with the most flexibility in modifying forms and reports?

(a) Design view

(b) Layout view

(c) Form view/Report view

(d) Print Preview

6. Which of the following statements about reports is *false?*

(a) Reports can be saved to a file (such as a Word document) on your computer.

(b) Reports are primarily used to modify data.

(c) Reports can produce output in a number of ways, including mailing labels.

(d) Reports can be created simply by using the Report tool.

7. Use the _____ to see exactly what the printed report will look like before printing.

(a) Report tool

(b) Report Wizard

(c) Report view

(d) Print Preview

8. If you need to send a report to a user who does not have Microsoft Office available, which of the following file formats would be the best choice to ensure it can be opened?

(a) Word

(b) Excel

(c) Reader

(d) Portable Document Format (PDF)

9. Which of the following statements is *false?*

(a) Reports are generally used for printing, emailing, or viewing data on the screen.

(b) Layouts for forms and reports are the predefined sets of colors, fonts, and graphics.

(c) Forms are often used for inputting data.

(d) Forms and reports both include controls, such as text boxes, that can be resized.

10. Which of the following statements is *true?*

(a) You can group records to show a list of properties by state.

(b) You can sort records in reports but not in forms.

(c) A sort can only be set on one field at a time.

(d) You can either group or sort records (but not both).

Practice Exercises

1 Financial Management Prospects

You are working as a customer service representative for a financial management firm. Your task is to contact a list of prospective customers and introduce yourself and the services of your company. You will create a form to view, add, and update data for one customer at a time. After creating the form, you will customize it and add sorting. You will also create a report to display all of the information on one screen, for viewing purposes. Refer to Figure 4.39 as you complete this exercise.

FIGURE 4.39 Grouped and Sorted Leads Report

a. Open *a04p1Prospects*. Save the database as **a04p1Prospects_LastFirst**.

b. Click the **Leads table** in the Navigation Pane. Click the **Create tab,** and click **Form** in the Forms group.

   A new form based on the Leads table opens in Layout view.

c. Select the **ID text box** of record 1 and drag the right border to the left to resize the column to approximately half of its original width.

   The other text boxes will resize as well.

d. Change the title of the form to **New Leads**.

e. Click **Themes** in the Themes group of the Design tab. Apply the **Integral theme** to this form only.

f. Change the font size of the NetWorth text box control to **14** and change the Background Color to **Turquoise, Accent 3**.

g. Click **Select Row** in the Rows & Columns group on the Arrange tab. Click **Move Up** in the Move group until NetWorth displays above First.

> **TROUBLESHOOTING:** If the text box and the label do not move together, click Undo, ensure that both controls are selected, and then follow the instructions in Step g.

h. Save the form as **Leads Form**. Switch to Form view.

i. Navigate to Record 63. Enter your first and last names in the appropriate fields. Leave the Email field blank.

j. Click in the **Last field** and then click **Ascending** in the Sort & Filter group of the Home tab. Farrah Aaron should be the first record displayed unless your last name appears before hers alphabetically.

k. Save and close the form.

l. Click the **Leads table** in the Navigation Pane. Click the **Create tab**, click **More Forms** in the Forms group, and then select **Split Form**.

m. Modify the form title to read **Leads-Split Form**. Save the form as **Leads-Split Form** and close the form.

n. Click the **Leads table**. Click **Report** in the Reports group on the Create tab.

A new report is created based on the Leads table.

o. Make the fields as narrow as possible to remove extra white space. Change the report's orientation to **Landscape**.

p. Delete the **ID**, **Address**, and **City** columns from the report.

q. Ensure that **Group & Sort** is selected in the Grouping & Totals group on the Design tab. Group the records by **State** and sort them by **LastName** in ascending order. Close the Group, Sort, and Total pane.

r. Save the report as **Leads Report**. Close the report.

s. Close the database and exit Access. Based on your instructor's directions, submit a04p1Prospects_LastFirst.

2 Salary Analysis

The Human Resources department of the Comfort Insurance Agency has initiated its annual employee performance reviews. You will create a form for them to perform data entry using the Form tool and a multiple items form. You will create a report to display locations, and a report displaying employee salary increases by location. Additionally, you will save the salary increases report as a PDF file. Refer to Figure 4.40 as you complete this exercise.

Employee Compensation							×

Employee Compensation

Location	YearHired	LastName	FirstName	Salary	2018Increase	2018Raise
L01						
	2012	Abrams	Wendy	$47,500.00	3.00%	1425
	2008	Anderson	Vicki	$47,900.00	4.00%	1916
	2012	Bichette	Susan	$61,500.00	4.00%	2460
	2010	Block	Leonard	$26,200.00	3.00%	786
	2011	Brown	Patricia	$20,100.00	5.00%	1005
	2009	Brumbaugh	Paige	$49,300.00	3.00%	1479
	2011	Daniels	Phil	$42,600.00	3.00%	1278
	2010	Davis	Martha	$51,900.00	4.00%	2076
	2009	Drubin	Lolly	$37,000.00	3.00%	1110
	2011	Fantis	Laurie	$28,000.00	3.00%	840
	2009	Fleming	Karen	$41,100.00	3.00%	1233
	2008	Gander	John	$38,400.00	3.00%	1152
	2010	Grippando	Joan	$26,100.00	3.00%	783
	2012	Harrison	Jenifer	$44,800.00	3.00%	1344
	2011	Imber	Elise	$63,700.00	4.00%	2548
	2012	Johnshon	Billy	$21,800.00	5.00%	1090
	2012	Johnson	Debbie	$39,700.00	3.00%	1191

FIGURE 4.40 Employee Compensation Report

Access 2016, Windows 10, Microsoft Corporation

a. Open *a04p2Insurance*. Save the database as **a04p2Insurance_LastFirst**.

b. Click the **Locations table** in the Navigation Pane. Click the **Create tab,** and click **Form** in the Forms group.

c. Click the **View arrow** in the Views group on the Home tab, and select **Design View**. Click anywhere in the subform control, and press **Delete**. Switch to Layout view.

d. Ensure that the **LocationID text box** containing *L01* in Record 1 is selected. Drag the right border to the left to resize the column to approximately half of its original width. The other text boxes will resize as well.

e. Click **Themes** in the Themes group on the Design tab. Right-click the **Wisp theme,** and select **Apply Theme to This Object Only**.

f. Change the font size of the Location text box control (containing *Atlanta*) to **14**, and change the Background Color to **Green, Accent 6, Lighter 60%**.

g. Click **Select Row** in the Rows & Columns group on the Arrange tab. Click **Move Up** in the Move group until Location displays above LocationID.

h. Save the form as **Locations Data Entry**.

i. Click **Layout view**, and delete the **LocationID field**. Delete the **Office Phone label**. Move the **Office Phone field** to the row immediately below the Location field.

j. Add **LocationID** back to the form from the Field List, immediately below the Address field. Close the Field List pane.

k. Switch to Form view, and then save and close the form.

l. Click the **Locations table** in the Navigation Pane. Click the **Create tab,** and click **Report** in the Reports group.

m. Click the **LocationID label,** and drag the right border of the label to the left to reduce the size of the control to approximately half of its original size.

n. Repeat the sizing process with the **Zipcode label** and the **OfficePhone label**. Adjust the other column widths until there are no controls on the right side of the vertical dashed line (page break). Drag the control containing the page number to the left so that it is inside the page break.

o. Display the report in Report view. Verify that the report is only one page wide in Report view. Save the report as **Locations** and close the report.

p. Click the **Employees Query** in the Navigation Pane. Click the **Create tab,** and click **Report Wizard** in the Reports group. Respond to the prompts as follows:

- Add all the fields to the Selected Fields list. Click **HireDate,** and remove the field from the Selected Fields. Remove **YearHired** from the Selected Fields. Click **Next**.
- Accept grouping by Location. Click **Next**.
- Select **LastName** for the first sort order, and **FirstName** for the second (ascending order for both). Click **Summary Options**.
- Click **Sum** for Salary, **Avg** for 2018Increase, and **Avg** for YearsWorked. Click **OK**. Click **Next**.
- Accept the Stepped layout. Change Orientation to **Landscape**. Click **Next**.
- Type **Employee Compensation** for the title of the report. Click **Finish**.

q. Click **Close Print Preview**. Switch to Layout view.

r. Adjust the column widths so that all of the data values are visible and the columns all fit within the vertical dashed border (page break). Some of the text boxes and labels will need to be relocated; select the control to be moved and click and drag it to a new location.

s. Click **Themes** in the Themes group on the Design tab. Right-click the **Slice theme** and select **Apply Theme to This Object Only**. Adjust the label widths and report title so that they are fully visible. Scroll to the bottom of the report and move any text boxes, such as the page number control, so that they are inside the page break. Resize all text boxes and labels so that their values are fully visible.

t. Delete the **YearsWorked field** and **label**.

u. Click and drag **YearHired** from the Field List into the report layout. Drag and drop the column into the space immediately to the right of the Location column. Close the Field List. Display the report in Print Preview. Compare your report to Figure 4.40. Make adjustments as required.

v. Save the report as a PDF file named **a04p2Employee_Compensation_LastFirst**. Close the reader window.

w. Save and close the Employee Compensation report.

x. Create a Multiple Items form based on the Titles table. Resize the fields so that they are all visible onscreen without scrolling. Save the form as **Job Titles**. Close the form.

y. Close the database and exit Access. Based on your instructor's directions, submit the following:

a04p2Insurance_LastFirst

a04p2Employee Compensation_LastFirst

Mid-Level Exercises

1   Hotel Chain

ANALYSIS CASE

You are the general manager of a large hotel chain. You track revenue by categories, such as conference room rentals and weddings. You want to create a report that shows which locations are earning the most revenue in each category. You will also create a report to show you details of your three newest areas: St. Paul, St. Louis, and Seattle.

a. Open *a04m1Rewards*. Save the database as **a04m1Rewards_LastFirst**.

b. Select the **Members table,** and create a Multiple Items form. Save the form as **Maintain Members**.

c. Modify the form in Layout view as follows:
   - Change the MemNumber label to **MemID,** and reduce the MemNumber column width.
   - Adjust the column widths to eliminate extra white space.
   - Delete the form icon (the picture next to the title of the form) in the Form Header.

d. Change the sorting on the MemberSince control so that the members who joined most recently are displayed first.

DISCOVER

e. Click the **LastName field**. Change the Control Padding to **Wide**. (Hint: Search **Control Padding** in the *Tell me what you want to do...* box).

f. Save and close the form.

g. Select the **Revenue query,** and create a report using the Report Wizard. Answer the wizard prompts as follows:
   - Include all fields in the report.
   - Add grouping first by **City** and then by **ServiceName**.
   - Add a Sum to the Revenue field, and click the **Summary Only option**.
   - Select **Outline Layout**.
   - Name the report **Revenue by City and Service**.

h. Scroll through all the pages to check the layout of the report while in Print Preview mode.

i. Close Print Preview. Switch to Layout view, and delete the **NumInParty** and **PerPersonCharge** controls.

j. Change the font size, font color, and background color of the Sum control (found at the bottom of the report) so the control stands out from the other controls.

k. Change the font size, font color, and background color of the Grand Total control (found at the end of the report) so the control stands out as well.

l. Change the sort on the report, so that it sorts by city in descending order—that is, so that the last city alphabetically (St. Paul) is displayed first.

m. Examine the data in the report to determine and note which city (St. Paul, St. Louis, or Seattle) has the highest Sum of event revenue. You will use this information to modify a query. Save and close the report.

n. Modify the Totals by Service query so that the criteria for the City field is the city you determined had the highest sum of event revenue (St. Paul, St. Louis, or Seattle). Run, save, and close the query.

o. Create a report using the Report tool based on the Totals by Service query. Name the report **Targeted City**.

p. Close the report.

q. Close the database and exit Access. Based on your instructor's directions, submit a04m1Rewards_LastFirst.

FROM SCRATCH

You are helping to organize a benefit auction to raise money for families who lost their homes in a natural disaster. The information for the auction is currently stored in an Excel spreadsheet, but you have volunteered to import it into Access. You will create a database that will store the data from Excel in Access. You will create a form to manage the data-entry process. You also create two reports: one that lists the items collected in each category and one for labels so you can send the donors a thank-you letter after the auction.

a. Open Access, and create a new database named **a04m2Auction_LastFirst**. A new table displays with an ID column.

b. Switch to Design view. Type **Items** in the **Save As dialog box**, and click **OK**.

c. Change the ID Field Name to **ItemID**. Type **Description** in the second row, and press **Tab**. Set **Short Text** as the Data Type. Type **50** in the **Field Size property** in Field Properties.

d. Type the remainder of the fields and adjust the data types as shown:

Field Name	Data Type
DateOfDonation	**Date/Time**
Category	**Short Text**
Price	**Currency**
DonorName	**Short Text**
DonorAddress1	**Short Text**
DonorAddress2	**Short Text**

e. Open Excel. Open the *a04m2Items* file. Examine the length of the Category, Donor Name, Donor Address 1, and Donor Address 2 columns. Determine how many characters are needed for each field based on the longest value in each column, and round that value up to the nearest 5. For example, if a field needs 23 characters, you would round up to 25. You will use this to change field sizes in the table.

f. Change the field sizes for Category, DonorName, DonorAddress1, and DonorAddress2 to the sizes you chose in Step e. Save the table.

g. Copy and paste the 26 rows from the Excel spreadsheet into the Items table. To paste the rows, locate the * to the left of the first blank row, click the Record Selector, right-click the Record Selector, and then from the shortcut menu, select Paste. Resize the columns so all data is visible. Close the table.

> **TROUBLESHOOTING:** Once you have pasted the data, ensure that your chosen field sizes did not cause you to lose data. If so, update the field sizes, delete the records you pasted to the table, and then repeat Step g.

h. Verify that the Items table is selected in the Navigation Pane. Create a new form using the **Form** tool.

i. Change the layout of the form to **Tabular Layout**. Resize field widths to reduce extra space. It is acceptable for field values in the text boxes to display on two lines.

j. Change the title of the form to **Items for Auction**.

DISCOVER

k. Add conditional formatting so that each Price that is greater than 90 has a text color of **Green** (seventh column, first row below Standard Colors).

l. Save the form as **Auction Items Form**.

m. Switch to Form view. Create a new record with the following data. Note that the form will automatically assign an ItemID for you.

Description	DateOfDonation	Category	Price	DonorName	DonorAddress1	DonorAddress2
iPad	12/31/2018	House	$400	Staples	500 Market St.	Brick, NJ 08723

n. Add a sort to the form, so that the lowest priced items display first. Save and close the form.

o. Select the **Items table** in the Navigation Pane, and create a report using the Report Wizard. Include all fields except the two donor address fields, group by Category, include the Sum of Price as a Summary Option, accept the default layout, and then save the report as **Auction Items by Category**.

p. Switch to Layout view, and adjust the controls so that all data is visible. Adjust the widths of the controls until there are no controls extending over the right side of the vertical dashed line (page break). Preview the report to verify that the column widths are correct.

q. Sort the report so the least expensive item is displayed first in each group. Save and close the report.

DISCOVER

r. Create mailing labels based on the Avery 5660 template. Place the donor name on the first line, address (**DonorAddress1**) on the second, and city, state, and ZIP (**DonorAddress2**) on the third line. Sort the labels by **DonorName**. Name the report **Donor Labels**. After you create the labels, display them in Print Preview mode to verify that all values will fit onto the label template. Close the label report.

s. Close the database and exit Access. Based on your instructor's directions, submit a04m2Auction_LastFirst.

3 New Castle County Technical Services

RUNNING CASE

New Castle County Technical Services (NCCTS) provides technical support for a number of companies in the greater New Castle County, Delaware, area. Now that you have completed the database tables, set the appropriate relationships, and created queries, you are ready to create a form and a report.

a. Open the database *a03m3NCCTS_LastFirst* and save it as **a04m3NCCTS_LastFirst**.

> **TROUBLESHOOTING:** If you did not complete the Chapter 3 case, return to Chapter 3, complete the case, and then return to this exercise.

b. Create a split form based on the Calls table.

c. Apply the **Integral theme** to this form only.

d. Add the **Description field** by dragging and dropping it immediately below the CallTypeID (Hint: Click **Show all tables** in the Field List pane, and locate the field by expanding the **Call Types table**). Close the Field List pane. Switch to Form view and ensure that the records are sorted by CallID in ascending order.

e. Save the form as **Calls Data Entry**, and close the form.

f. Use the Report tool to create a basic report based on the Customer Happiness query.

g. Sort the records by the **Avg Rating field** in ascending order.

h. Apply the **Integral theme** to this report only.

i. Change the title of the report to **Customer Satisfaction Ratings**, and format the background color of the control to **Medium Gray** (under Standard Colors).

j. Set the font color of the title control to **Blue, Accent 2**, the font size to **20**, and the alignment to **Center**. Click the default logo in the report header and press **Delete**.

k. Switch to Report view. Save the report as **Customer Satisfaction Survey**, and close the report.

l. Close the database and exit Access. Based on your instructor's directions, submit a04m3NCCTS_LastFirst.

Beyond the Classroom

Create a Split Form
GENERAL CASE
FROM SCRATCH

This chapter introduced you to Access forms, including the split form. It is possible to convert an existing form into a split form if you know how to modify form properties. First, create a new database and name the file **a04b1Split_LastFirst**. Next, import only the Books table and Books form from the *a04b1BooksImport* database. To import the objects, click the **External Data tab** and click **Access** in the Import & Link group. Perform an Internet search to find the steps to convert a form to a split form. Use the information from the Internet to convert the Books form into a split form. Make sure the datasheet is in the bottom pane of the form. Delete the AuthorCode text box and label from the top pane of the form. Change the form so that it sorts by Title in ascending order. Increase the font size of the Title control to **14**, and change its background color to **Medium Gray** (under Standard Colors). Apply the **Integral** theme to this form only. Save the form as **Split Form Books**. Switch to Form view, and then close the form. Close the database and exit Access. Based on your instructor's directions, submit a04b1Split_LastFirst.

Properties by City
DISASTER RECOVERY

A co-worker is having difficulty with an Access report and asked you for your assistance. He was trying to fix the report and seems to have made things worse. Open the *a04b2Sales* database and save the file as **a04b2Sales_LastFirst**. Open the Properties Report in Report view. The report columns do not fit across one page. In addition, there is a big gap between two fields, and he moved the Beds and Baths fields so they are basically on top of one another. Add all of the fields to a tabular layout. Group the records first by City, and then by Beds in descending order. Within each group, sort the report by ListPrice in descending order. Change the report to Landscape orientation and adjust the column widths so they all fit across one page (inside the dashed vertical page break). Apply the Organic theme to this report only, and switch to Report view. Save the new report as **Properties by City**, close the report, and then delete the original **Properties Report** from the database (right-click the report in the Navigation Pane, and from the shortcut menu, select **Delete**). Close the database and exit Access. Based on your instructor's directions, submit a04b2Sales_LastFirst.

Capstone Exercise

Your boss asked you to prepare a schedule for each speaker for the national conference being hosted next year on your campus. She wants to mail the schedules to the speakers so that they can provide feedback on the schedule prior to its publication. You assure her that you can accomplish this task with Access.

Database File Setup

You need to copy an original database file, rename the copied file, and then open the copied database to complete this Capstone exercise. After you open the copied database, you replace an existing employee's name with your name.

a. Open the *a04c1_NatConf* database, and save it as **a04c1NatConf_LastFirst**.

b. Open the Speakers table.

c. Find and replace *YourName* with your own first and last name. Close the table.

Create and Customize a Form

You want to create a form to add and update the Speakers table. Use the Form tool to create the form and modify the form as required. You will also add a layout to an existing form.

a. Select the **Speakers table** in the Navigation Pane as the record source for the form.

b. Use the **Form tool** to create a new form with a stacked layout.

c. Change the form's title to **Enter/Edit Speakers**.

d. Reduce the width of the text box controls to approximately half of their original size.

e. Delete the **Sessions subform** control from the form.

f. View the form and the data in Form view. Sort the records by **LastName** in ascending order.

g. Save the form as **Edit Speakers**. Close the form.

h. Open the Room Information form in Layout view. Select all controls in the form, and apply the **Stacked Layout**.

i. Switch to Form view, and then save and close the form.

Create a Report

You will create a report based on the Speaker and Room Schedule query. You decide to use the Report Wizard to accomplish this task. You will also email the schedule to the presenters, so you will save the report as a PDF file.

a. Select the **Speaker and Room Schedule query** in the Navigation Pane as the record source for the report.

b. Activate the **Report Wizard**, and use the following options as you proceed through the wizard steps:
- Select all of the available fields for the report.
- View the data by Speakers.
- Accept LastName and FirstName as the grouping levels.
- Use **Date** as the primary sort field in ascending order.
- Accept the Stepped and Portrait options.
- Save the report as **Speaker Schedule**.
- Switch to Layout view, and apply the **Organic theme** to this report only.

c. Switch to Report view to determine whether all of the columns fit across the page. Switch to Layout view, and ensure that the column widths are adjusted accordingly.

d. Switch to Print Preview, and save the report as a PDF named **a04c1Speaker_LastFirst**.

e. Close the reader program that displays the PDF report, and return to Access. Close Print Preview. Save and close the report.

Add an Additional Field to the Query and the Report

You realize that the session start times were not included in the query. You add the field to the query and then create a new report with the Report Wizard to include the missing field.

a. Open the Speaker and Room Schedule query in Design view.

b. Add the **StartingTime field** from the Sessions table to the design grid, after the Date field. Run the query.

c. Save and close the query.

d. Click the **Speaker and Room Schedule query**. Activate the Report Wizard again and use the following options:
- Select all of the available fields for the report.
- View the data by Speakers.
- Use the LastName and FirstName fields as the grouping levels.
- Use **Date** as the primary sort field in ascending order.
- Use **StartingTime** as the secondary sort field in ascending order.
- Select the **Stepped** and **Portrait options**.
- Name the report **Speaker Schedule Revised**.
- Switch to Layout view and apply the **Facet theme** to this report only.

e. Adjust the widths of the columns and other controls so that all the data is visible and fits across the page. Switch to Report view to ensure that the adjustments were appropriate. Return to Layout view, and make any required changes.

f. Add spaces to the column heading labels so that all values display as two words where appropriate, for example, the label *LastName* should read **Last Name**, *RoomID* as **Room ID**, etc.

g. Save and close the report.

h. Close the database and exit Access. Based on your instructor's directions, submit the following:

a04c1NatConf_LastFirst
a04c1Speaker_LastFirst

Data Validation and Data Analysis

LEARNING OUTCOMES

- You will use data validation features to improve data entry.
- You will perform data analysis using advanced queries.

OBJECTIVES & SKILLS: After you read this chapter, you will be able to:

CASE STUDY | Implementing a New Database at Tommy's Shelter

Tommy Mariano operates a small animal shelter. He has been keeping records by hand, but due to a large turnover in volunteers, recordkeeping can be a challenge. He has decided to move to a database solution, and his hope is that this will help reduce errors. Though volunteers may still make mistakes, he believes that a well-designed database will prevent some common errors. As a volunteer, you have offered to create a database to assist him in this process. You have created the tables and done some data entry, and you will now work to make sure data validation takes place.

In addition to the problem of data entry, Tommy has been examining a lot of the data from his shelter by hand. As someone with some database experience, you know that advanced queries are the answer here. You will use advanced queries to help streamline his data gathering and reporting so Tommy can focus on what is important—finding homes for the animals in his shelter.

Reducing Errors and Extracting Better Information

AnimalType ▾	Gender ▾	Age ▾	DateFound ▾	Spayed/Neutered ▾	Notes ▾	Weight ▾	AdoptionFee ▾	Adopted ▾	
Bird	Female	1 year	4/25/2018	☐		2.12	100	☑	Ba
Cat	Male	2 year	3/7/2018	☐	White	12.04	$15.00	☑	V
Cat	Female	6 weeks	7/20/2018	☐	Black	12.58	$10.00	☑	Te
Dog	Female	5 years	5/15/2018	☑	Bichon Frise	12.93	$50.00	☑	Ji
Bird	Female	1 year	3/24/2018	☐		2.13	$15.00	☐	
Cat	Female	3 year	5/21/2018	☐	Black	12.47	$15.00	☑	Fl
Cat	Male	6 weeks	1/4/2018	☐	Orange	12.01	$40.00	☐	
Cat	Female	1 year	5/18/2018	☑	Black with white boots	12.45	$25.00	☐	M
Cat						12.46	$15.00	☑	St
Cat						12.88	$0.00	☐	
Cat						7.44	$25.00	☑	
Cat						12.32	$15.00	☑	Be
Bird						2.11	$15.00	☑	To
Cat	Female	2 years	11/7/2017	☑	Calico	12.72	$15.00	☐	
Bird	Male	1 year	5/27/2018	☐		2.20	$15.00	☑	Jc
Cat	Female	5 years	11/11/2017	☐	White	12.60	$15.00	☑	Ju

Microsoft Access ×

⚠ The maximum adoption fee is $50. Please double-check the adoption fee.

[OK]   [Help]

Access 2016, Windows 10, Microsoft Corporation

FIGURE 5.1 Tommy's Shelter Database—Validation Rule and Text

AnimalName ▾	AnimalType ▾	Age ▾	DateFound ▾	Notes ▾	Weight ▾	Rounded ▾
Leslie	Bird	1 year	4/25/2018		2.12	2
Edward	Cat	2 year	3/7/2018	White	12.04	12
Yolanda	Cat	6 weeks	7/20/2018	Black	12.58	13
Sully	Dog	5 years	5/15/2018	Bichon Frise	12.93	13
Emily	Bird	1 year	3/24/2018		2.13	2
Susan	Cat	3 year	5/21/2018	Black	12.47	12
Mark	Cat	6 weeks	1/4/2018	Orange	12.01	12
Tipsy	Cat	1 year	5/18/2018	Black with white boots	12.45	12
Christopher	Cat	2 years	9/24/2018	Black	12.46	12
Laura	Cat	2 years	8/1/2018	White	12.88	13
Leo	Cat	5 months	6/3/2018	Calico	7.44	7
Stephanie	Cat	5 years	4/5/2018	White	12.32	12
Lee	Bird	1 year	3/4/2018		2.11	2
Sylvia	Cat	2 years	11/7/2017	Calico	12.72	13
Marcus	Bird	1 year	5/27/2018		2.20	2
Judy	Cat	5 years	11/11/2017	White	12.60	13

Access 2016, Windows 10, Microsoft Corporation

FIGURE 5.2 Tommy's Shelter Database— Round Function

CASE STUDY | Implementing a New Database at Tommy's Shelter

Starting File	File to be Submitted
a05h1Tommys	a05h2Tommys_LastFirst

Data Validation in Tables

When filling out forms online, you may notice certain pieces of information are required. If you are attempting to purchase something, you will not be able to complete the purchase if you leave the credit card number blank. You may also notice that information you enter is checked for validity. On many sites, you cannot enter an email address without the @ sign. Some fields appear as drop-down menus. Instead of typing a state name, you may be given a menu offering only valid responses, from which you can choose one. Having a list helps narrow the possible answers as well as eliminates spelling and interpretation errors. Access contains validation features similar to those found in Web forms. Many of these features are found in the table settings; some are available in forms as well.

In this section, you will explore setting validation of data in tables to create more reliable data in your database. By setting up data validation, you reduce user errors, which is a key reason to use a database.

Establishing Data Validation

Data validation is a set of constraints or rules that help control data entered into a field. Access provides some data validation automatically. For example, you cannot enter text into a field with a Number data type or add two records with identical primary key values. Access provides a number of data validation methods to help minimize data entry errors. These can be found in the Field Properties pane in a table's Design view. This section will discuss many of these methods.

TIP: GOOD DATA VERSUS INCLUSION

When gathering data from users, your priority is often protecting data. A database may have fields storing the user's religion, gender, and/or citizen status. It is safer to protect your data and help guide your users by presenting them with options. For example, for a citizenship status field, you may let users type in a text box. However, if you let the users type whatever they want, you may get answers you are not expecting such as Green Card (technically a legal status, which is a different question). You can also imagine if you have a field named Sex and do not restrict values, users will write in all sorts of answers such as Yes (ask anyone who has ever had to perform data entry).

As a database administrator, you need to balance good data and inclusion. You do not want controversy to arise because users do not see an option for their gender, religion, or anything else. Sometimes it is best to look to what large companies do. For example, when you sign up for a Google account, you are given three options for Gender: Female, Male, or Other. Microsoft offers Female, Male, or Not Specified. Giving users a third option for Gender avoids excluding users who do not identify as female or male, while still protecting the integrity of your data. If you are unsure of how to proceed, you can always discuss this with your company's Human Resources Department.

Require a Field

 When a field is required, it simply means a field cannot be left without a value. Though this does not prevent incorrect data from being entered, it does at least prevent the user from accidentally missing a field. The default Required setting is No for most fields, which enables you to create a record with no data in those fields. To ensure the integrity of the records in a table, you should set the Required property to Yes for critical fields. Note any primary key fields will be required by virtue of being a primary key.

To change a field's Required property, complete the following steps:

1. Open the table in Design view.
2. Click the field you want to be required.
3. Click Required in the Field Properties pane.
4. Click the Required property box arrow found at the right of the box, and select Yes, as shown in Figure 5.3.
5. Save the table. Click No if prompted about data integrity rules.

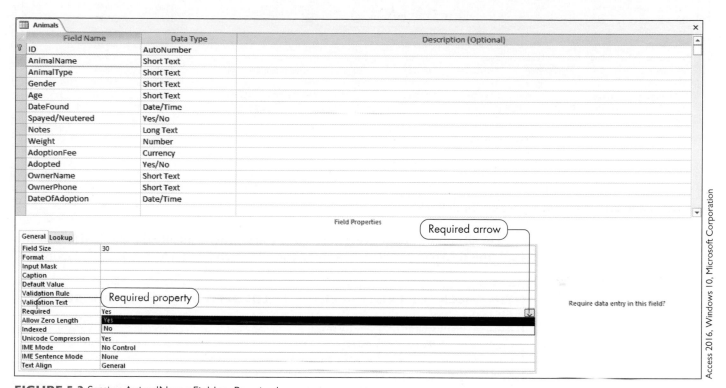

FIGURE 5.3 Setting AnimalName Field to Required

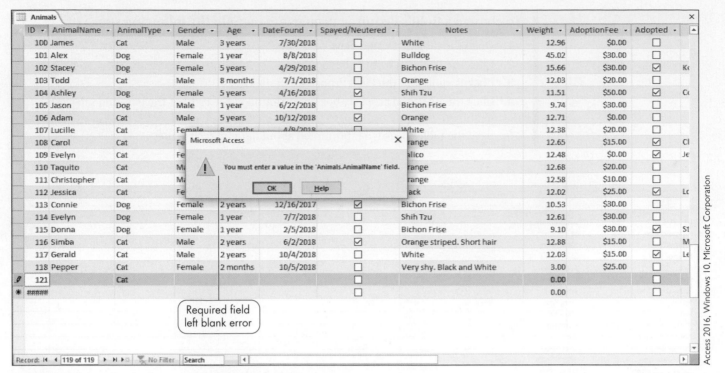

FIGURE 5.4 Results of a Required Field Being Left Blank

For all new records, Access will require you to enter data into the required field. If you leave this field blank during data entry, you will receive an error, as shown in Figure 5.4.

> **TIP: CHECK FOR EXISTING BLANK FIELDS BEFORE SETTING REQUIRED FIELDS**
>
> If you set the Required property to Yes after data has already been entered in a table, you will see the message, "Data integrity rules have been changed; existing data may not be valid for the new rules. This process may take a long time. Do you want the existing data to be tested with the new rules?" If an error arises, you will have to manually fix the data. You should use a filter to check for blank fields in the Datasheet view and resolve any inconsistencies before setting the Required property to Yes.

Add a Default Field Value

A *default value* specifies a value that is automatically entered into a field when a new record is added to a table. For example, if most of your customers live in North Dakota, you can set the default value of the State field to ND. When a majority of new records contain a common value, set a default value for that field to reduce data entry time.

To add or change a default value, complete the following steps:

1. Open the table in Design view.
2. Click the field for which you want to add a default value.
3. Click Default Value in the Field Properties pane, as shown in Figure 5.5.
4. Type the default value you want to add.

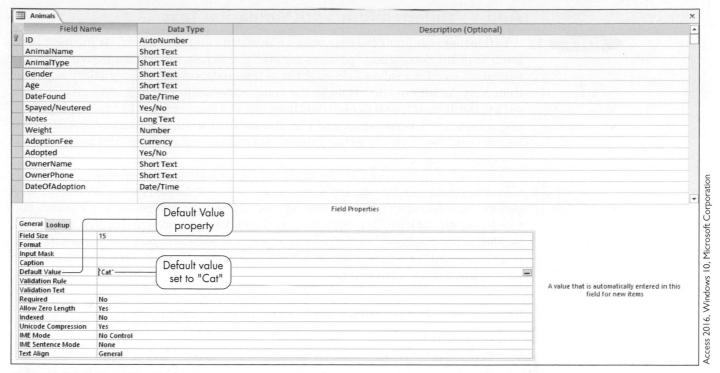

FIGURE 5.5 Default Value Property

For example, suppose the majority of the animals the shelter handles are cats. If you type Cat in the Default Value property, all new records entered in Datasheet view will display Cat, as shown in Figure 5.6. You can overwrite this default value if you have a different type of animal.

ID	AnimalName	AnimalType	Gender	Age	DateFound	Spayed/Neutered	Notes	Weight	AdoptionFee	Adopted
103	Todd	Cat	Male	8 months	7/1/2018	☐	Orange	12.03	$20.00	☐
104	Ashley	Dog	Female	5 years	4/16/2018	☑	Shih Tzu	11.51	$50.00	☑
105	Jason	Dog	Male	1 year	6/22/2018	☐	Bichon Frise	9.74	$30.00	☐
106	Adam	Cat	Male	5 years	10/12/2018	☑	Orange	12.71	$0.00	☐
107	Lucille	Cat	Female	8 months	4/9/2018	☐	White	12.38	$20.00	☐
108	Carol	Cat	Female	2 years	5/23/2018	☑	Orange	12.65	$15.00	☑
109	Evelyn	Cat	Female	2 years	10/29/2018	☑	Calico	12.48	$0.00	☑
110	Taquito	Cat	Male	3 year	7/29/2018	☐	Orange	12.68	$20.00	☐
111	Christopher	Cat	Male	7 weeks	4/12/2018	☐	Orange	12.58	$10.00	☐
112	Jessica	Cat	Female	8 months	11/25/2017	☐	Black	12.02	$25.00	☑
113	Connie	Dog	Female	2 years	12/16/2017	☑	Bichon Frise	10.53	$30.00	☐
114	Evelyn	Dog	Female	1 year	7/7/2018	☐	Shih Tzu	12.61	$30.00	☐
115	Donna	Dog	Female	1 year	2/5/2018	☐	Bichon Frise	9.10	$30.00	☑
116	Simba	Cat	Male	2 years	6/2/2018	☑	Orange striped. Short hair	12.88	$15.00	☐
117	Gerald	Cat	Male	2 years	10/4/2018	☐	White	12.03	$15.00	☑
118	Pepper	Cat	Female	2 months	10/5/2018	☐	Very shy. Black and White	3.00	$25.00	☐
* (New)		Cat				☐		0.00		☐

Default Cat appears in new record

Record: 1 of 118   No Filter   Search

FIGURE 5.6 Default Field Value of Cat

Add a Validation Rule with Validation Text

STEP 2 >> A ***validation rule*** limits the data values a user can enter into a field. At the most basic level, all of the comparison operators are available to help validate data. An appropriate validation rule for a salary field might be > 0 to make sure a person's salary is greater than zero. As with queries, you can use comparison operators, including greater than, (>) greater than or equal to (>=), less than (<), less than or equal to (<=), equal to (=), not equal to (<>), Between, In, and Like. If you violate a validation rule, Access does not let you continue until you either enter an appropriate value, or you discard the record you are entering.

You can help improve the user experience by providing ***validation text***, which provides a custom error message to the user when incorrect data is entered. Ideally, the validation text will explain which value is rejected, and why. If you have entered a validation rule to require salary to be greater than zero and the user enters an incorrect value, the validation text displays. A meaningful error message such as "You entered a negative salary. Salary must be greater than zero." would be helpful for users, as it provides specific feedback as to what went wrong.

> **To set up a validation rule, complete the following steps:**
>
> 1. Open the table in Design view.
> 2. Click the field for which you want to add a validation rule.
> 3. Click Validation Rule in the Field Properties pane.
> 4. Enter the validation rule, as shown in Figure 5.7. For example, *>0* or *Between 50 and 300*.
> 5. Enter a meaningful error message in the Validation Text property in the Field Properties pane, as shown in Figure 5.7 (optional, but recommended). This text will display when an incorrect value is entered, as shown in Figure 5.8.

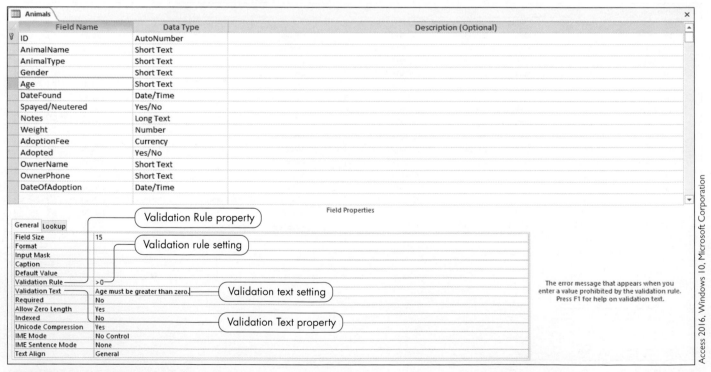

FIGURE 5.7 Setting Validation Rule and Text

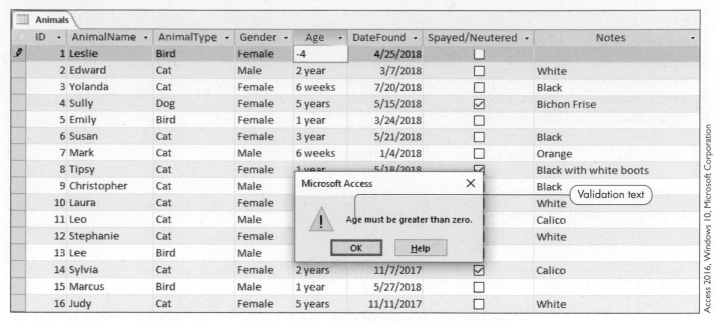

ID ▾	AnimalName ▾	AnimalType ▾	Gender ▾	Age ▾	DateFound ▾	Spayed/Neutered ▾	Notes ▾
1	Leslie	Bird	Female	-4	4/25/2018	☐	
2	Edward	Cat	Male	2 year	3/7/2018	☐	White
3	Yolanda	Cat	Female	6 weeks	7/20/2018	☐	Black
4	Sully	Dog	Female	5 years	5/15/2018	☑	Bichon Frise
5	Emily	Bird	Female	1 year	3/24/2018	☐	
6	Susan	Cat	Female	3 year	5/21/2018	☐	Black
7	Mark	Cat	Male	6 weeks	1/4/2018	☐	Orange
8	Tipsy	Cat	Female	1 year	5/18/2018	☑	Black with white boots
9	Christopher	Cat	Male				Black
10	Laura	Cat	Female				White
11	Leo	Cat	Male				Calico
12	Stephanie	Cat	Female				White
13	Lee	Bird	Male				
14	Sylvia	Cat	Female	2 years	11/7/2017	☑	Calico
15	Marcus	Bird	Male	1 year	5/27/2018	☐	
16	Judy	Cat	Female	5 years	11/11/2017	☐	White

Microsoft Access ✕

⚠ Age must be greater than zero.

OK   Help

Validation text

FIGURE 5.8 Validation Rule Violation

Validation rules only check values entered for a field. They do not prevent users from skipping the field. Unless you set the Required property to Yes, having a validation rule does not force data entry for the field. Therefore, if you add a validation rule to a field, you should also consider setting the Required property to Yes.

> **TIP: EXISTING DATA VIOLATE NEW VALIDATION RULE**
> If you add a validation rule to a table with existing records, some data in those records may violate the rule. For example, you might add validation to a hire date field, assuming it must be today or later. However, what about the users who are already hired and have hire dates in the past? When Access warns you that existing data may violate the new validation rule, you can click Yes to test the data. If your existing data will violate this rule, you should click No. If, however, adding a validation rule uncovers an underlying problem in the data, you can switch to Datasheet view and apply a filter to find the records in violation.

Controlling the Format of Data Entry

In addition to controlling what users enter into a data table, database designers can also control the format of the data entry. For example, a phone number might be stored in a Short Text field with a size of 14. The database designer might expect users to enter a number in a format such as (959) 555-6000. However, users could enter 959.555.6000, 9595556000, 959-555-6000, or even 99999999999 just as easily if there are no restrictions. Though this might not seem like a problem, inconsistent data will lead to problems with sorting, filtering, and queries.

An **input mask** restricts the data being input into a field by specifying the exact format of the data entry. Phone number and Social Security number are two common text fields that often use input masks. Figure 5.9 shows a field with a phone number input mask applied.

OwnerName	OwnerPhone	DateOfAdoption	Click to Add
Barbara Stevens	(__) ___-____	5/5/2018	
Veronica Chandler	(857) 670-2423	3/10/2018	
Terri Gonzalez	(711) 492-5550	8/8/2018	
Jigisha Bhalla	(236) 454-9264	6/11/2018	
Florence Blair	(300) 646-1104	6/14/2018	
Miguel Susanibar	(424) 750-6977	6/7/2018	
Stephanie Campbell	(351) 991-2011	10/22/2018	
Bernard Lane	(555) 422-4659	4/16/2018	

Input mask defines input format

Access 2016, Windows 10, Microsoft Corporation

FIGURE 5.9 Phone Number Input Mask

Create an Input Mask

STEP 3 >> The **Input Mask Wizard** is used to generate data restrictions (an input mask) for a field. Though you can type an input mask manually, they can be complicated. Access includes some common input masks automatically, including phone number, Social Security number, ZIP code, and more.

For example, the Social Security number input mask creates an input mask with three digits, a dash, two digits, another dash, and then four more digits. The Input Mask property for the field would appear as 000\-00\-0000;0;;_ in the Field Properties. As a result, when users enter data, they will see ###-##-####, which lets them know the expected format of the Social Security number.

> **To create an input mask using the wizard, complete the following steps:**
>
> 1. Open the table in Design view.
> 2. Click the field for which you want to add an input mask.
> 3. Click Input Mask in the Field Properties pane.
> 4. Click the ellipses at the end of the Input Mask row, as shown in Figure 5.10, to launch the Input Mask Wizard.
> 5. Choose one of the built-in input masks from the menu, as shown in Figure 5.11, and click Next. Note the input masks available will vary by data type; this figure shows the settings for a Short Text field.
> 6. Click Next to accept the default placeholder, or select one from the Placeholder character menu shown in Figure 5.12, and click Next. The placeholder will be the symbol shown in the field when data entry is performed.
> 7. Choose whether to store the symbols (such as the hyphen in a Social Security number) with the field data. It is a good idea to store the symbols with the data to avoid confusion later when you create queries and enter criteria for that field. Click Next.
> 8. Click Finish. The input mask now appears in the Input Mask property box. For example, a phone number field might appear as !\(999") "000\-0000;;_ as shown in Figure 5.13.

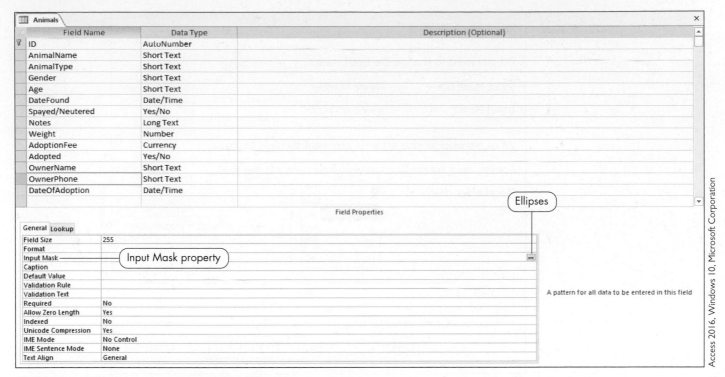

FIGURE 5.10 Ellipses to Launch Input Mask Wizard

FIGURE 5.11 Built-in Input Masks

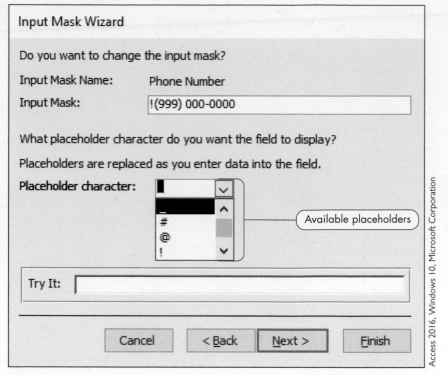

Input Mask Wizard

Do you want to change the input mask?

Input Mask Name: Phone Number

Input Mask: !(999) 000-0000

What placeholder character do you want the field to display?

Placeholders are replaced as you enter data into the field.

Placeholder character:

              _
              #   Available placeholders
              @
              !

Try It:

Cancel   < Back   Next >   Finish

FIGURE 5.12 Placeholder Characters

Field Name	Data Type	
ID	AutoNumber	
AnimalName	Short Text	
AnimalType	Short Text	
Gender	Short Text	
Age	Short Text	
DateFound	Date/Time	
Spayed/Neutered	Yes/No	
Notes	Long Text	
Weight	Number	
AdoptionFee	Currency	
Adopted	Yes/No	
OwnerName	Short Text	
OwnerPhone	Short Text	
DateOfAdoption	Date/Time	

General | Lookup

Field Size	255
Format	
Input Mask	!\(999") "000\-0000;;_
Caption	
Default Value	
Validation Rule	
Validation Text	

Phone number input mask

FIGURE 5.13 Input Mask for a Phone Number in Design View

Controlling Input with a Lookup Field

Input masks provide good validation for data, but at times you may want even more control. When looking at a datasheet, you may notice repetitive data. A field with a small number of repeated values may be better suited as a *lookup field*, which provides the user with a predefined list of values to choose from in a menu. For example, the shelter houses three types of animals: cats, dogs, and birds. Data entry would be faster and more accurate if the options for this field were limited to the three values in a drop-down list format. Changing the data type to a lookup field would present users with the three options and ensure uniformity and consistency of the data.

The options for a lookup field are often put in a separate table, which has been created ahead of time. This type of table is typically not bound by some of the best practices discussed in the book. This sort of table may just have a single field, which may or may not be set as the primary key. It may also be a table that does not have a relationship set up because it will not be used frequently in queries. For example, if an AnimalType field has the three options listed above, you should create a table to store the values. In this case, a separate table would contain three records, one for each option. The AnimalType field would be the primary key, and the field would not need any relationships created. Storing the options in a separate table makes it easier for users to update the list. To add another option, for example Snake, the user opens the separate table and adds a new record to the table. Figure 5.14 shows an example of a lookup field in Datasheet view.

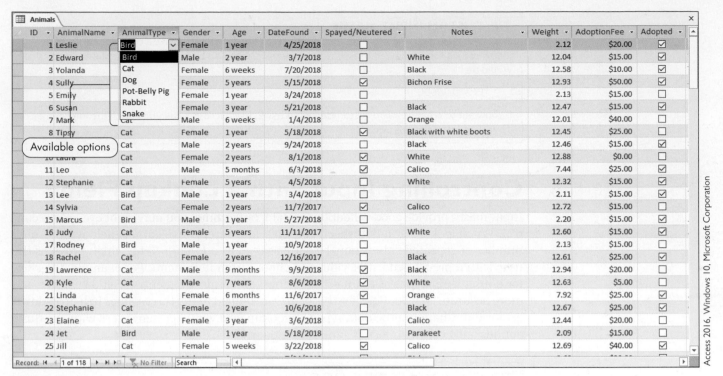

ID ▾	AnimalName ▾	AnimalType ▾	Gender ▾	Age ▾	DateFound ▾	Spayed/Neutered ▾	Notes ▾	Weight ▾	AdoptionFee ▾	Adopted ▾
1	Leslie	Bird ⌄	Female	1 year	4/25/2018	☐		2.12	$20.00	☑
2	Edward	Bird	Male	2 year	3/7/2018	☐	White	12.04	$15.00	☑
3	Yolanda	Cat	Female	6 weeks	7/20/2018	☐	Black	12.58	$10.00	☑
4	Sully	Dog	Female	5 years	5/15/2018	☑	Bichon Frise	12.93	$50.00	☑
5	Emily	Pot-Belly Pig	Female	1 year	3/24/2018	☐		2.13	$15.00	☐
6	Susan	Rabbit	Female	3 year	5/21/2018	☐	Black	12.47	$15.00	☑
7	Mark	Snake	Male	6 weeks	1/4/2018	☐	Orange	12.01	$40.00	☐
8	Tipsy	Cat	Female	1 year	5/18/2018	☑	Black with white boots	12.45	$25.00	☐
		Cat	Male	2 years	9/24/2018	☐	Black	12.46	$15.00	☑
10	Laura	Cat	Female	2 years	8/1/2018	☑	White	12.88	$0.00	☐
11	Leo	Cat	Male	5 months	6/3/2018	☑	Calico	7.44	$25.00	☑
12	Stephanie	Cat	Female	5 years	4/5/2018	☐	White	12.32	$15.00	☑
13	Lee	Bird	Male	1 year	3/4/2018	☐		2.11	$15.00	☑
14	Sylvia	Cat	Female	2 years	11/7/2017	☑	Calico	12.72	$15.00	☐
15	Marcus	Bird	Male	1 year	5/27/2018	☐		2.20	$15.00	☑
16	Judy	Cat	Female	5 years	11/11/2017	☐	White	12.60	$15.00	☑
17	Rodney	Bird	Male	1 year	10/9/2018	☐		2.13	$15.00	☐
18	Rachel	Cat	Female	2 years	12/16/2017	☐	Black	12.61	$25.00	☑
19	Lawrence	Cat	Male	9 months	9/9/2018	☑	Black	12.94	$20.00	☐
20	Kyle	Cat	Male	7 years	8/6/2018	☑	White	12.63	$5.00	☐
21	Linda	Cat	Female	6 months	11/6/2017	☑	Orange	7.92	$25.00	☑
22	Stephanie	Cat	Female	2 year	10/6/2018	☐	Black	12.67	$25.00	☑
23	Elaine	Cat	Female	3 year	3/6/2018	☐	Calico	12.44	$20.00	☐
24	Jet	Bird	Male	1 year	5/18/2018	☐	Parakeet	2.09	$15.00	☐
25	Jill	Cat	Female	5 weeks	3/22/2018	☑	Calico	12.69	$40.00	☑

Available options

Record: I◄ ◄ 1 of 118 ► ►I ►⊞ ⛉ No Filter   Search

FIGURE 5.14 Lookup Field

Access provides a Lookup Wizard to help you create a lookup field. The **Lookup Wizard** creates the menu of predefined values (lookup field) by asking you questions and using your answers to create the options list.

Create a Lookup Field

STEP 4 ▶▶ The first step in creating a lookup field is often to create a new table that will hold the options. As mentioned, it is usually best to look up the values in a table because the list can be easily updated.

> **To create a lookup field that references an existing table using the Lookup Wizard, complete the following steps:**
>
> 1. Open the table in Design view.
> 2. Click the field you want to change to a lookup and select Lookup Wizard from the list, as shown in Figure 5.15.
> 3. Click Next to accept the default *I want the lookup field to get the values from another table or query.*
> 4. Choose the table that contains the lookup values. Click Next.
> 5. Select the field (or fields) from the table for the lookup field, and click the ⟩ icon. Click Next.
> 6. Specify a sort order for the values. Click Next.
> 7. Adjust the column width for the lookup column. Columns should be wide enough to display the longest value. You may choose to *Hide key column*, although this is not necessary in cases where you only have a single field table. Click Next.
> 8. Name the lookup field. You can also choose to check the Enable Data Integrity check box, so users can only enter values found on the lookup list. Click Finish.
> 9. Click Yes if prompted that the table must be saved before the relationships can be created.

For the AnimalType field in the Animals table, shown previously in Figure 5.14, the table Types of Animals contains six records, as shown in Figure 5.16.

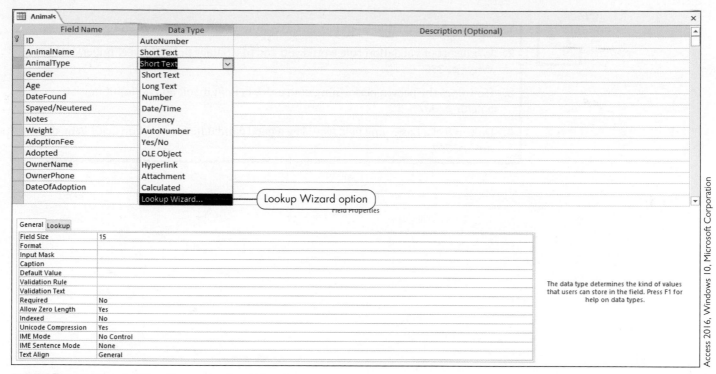

FIGURE 5.15 Changing Data Type to Lookup Wizard

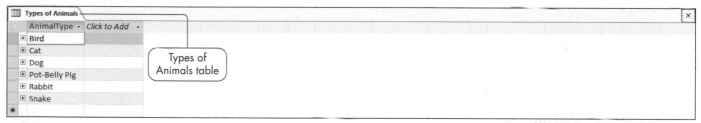

FIGURE 5.16 Table Containing Lookup Values

Modify a Lookup Field

STEP 5 ⟫ You can add, delete, or edit values in the lookup field to accommodate changing data needs. For example, if the shelter expands the types of animals it cares for to include rabbits, you open the Types of Animals table and add the new record to the bottom of the table. If the shelter needs to remove a type of animal, that is done in the same way. When you change the lookup field's source table, the options will be updated when the user tries to change data in the future.

1. Under what condition would you set a default value for a field? *p. 334*

2. What sort of validation rule would you add to a Salary field with a Number data type? Why? *p. 336*

3. How does the person performing data entry benefit if you add an input mask to a field? *p. 337*

4. Do you feel a LastName field would be a good candidate for a lookup field? Why or why not? *p. 341*

Hands-On Exercises

Watch the Video for this Hands-On Exercise!

MyITLab®
HOE1 Training

1 Data Validation in Tables

The purpose of the shelter database is to cut down on errors, so you will add some data validation rules to the tables. You will set default field values, set validation rules, create input masks, and establish a lookup field.

STEP 1 ›› REQUIRE A FIELD AND ADD A DEFAULT FIELD VALUE

You decide to review the Animals table and require the AnimalName field, as you do not want animals added to the database without names. You will also set the default value for the AnimalType field to Cat, as cats are the most common animal in the shelter. Refer to Figure 5.17 as you complete Step 1.

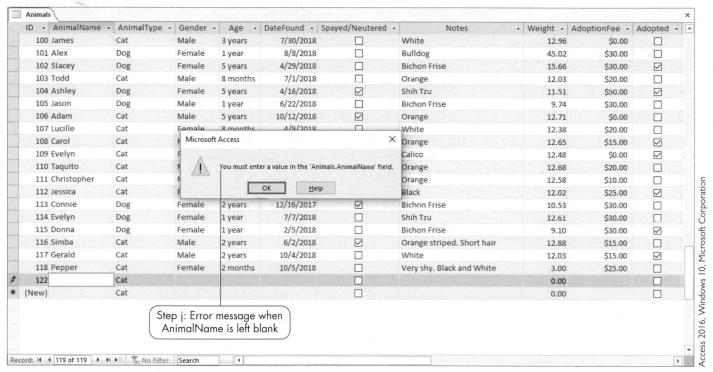

FIGURE 5.17 Changes to Animals Table

a. Open *a05h1Tommys*. Save the file as **a05h1Tommys_LastFirst**.

> **TROUBLESHOOTING:** If you make any major mistakes in this exercise, you can close the file, open *a05h1Tommys* again, and then start this exercise over.

> **TROUBLESHOOTING:** Throughout the remainder of this chapter and textbook, click Enable Content whenever you are working with student files.

b. Open the Animals table in Design view.

c. Click the **AnimalName field** in the design grid.

d. Click **Required** in the Field Properties pane. Click the Required property box arrow, and select **Yes** from the list.

An entry in the AnimalName field is now required for each animal.

e. Click the **AnimalType field**.

f. Click **Default Value** in the Field Properties pane, and type **Cat**.

Because most of the animals in the shelter are cats, you set the default value to Cat. You now will test the changes you made to the table design.

g. Click **Save** on the Quick Access Toolbar. Click **Yes** in response to the warning about testing the data integrity rules.

h. Switch to the Datasheet view of the Animals table. Click **New** in the Records group of the Home tab to add a new record. Ensure the AnimalType is displayed as Cat by default (see Figure 5.17).

i. Click the **Gender field** of the new record, and type **Female**. Type **2 months** in the Age field, and type **10/5/2018** in the DateFound field. Type **Very shy. Black and White** in the Notes field. Type **3** in the Weight field, and type **25** in the AdoptionFee field. The AnimalName, Spayed/Neutered, Adopted, OwnerName, OwnerPhone, and DateOfAdoption fields should be left blank.

To test data validation rules, you have left a required field blank.

j. Press **Tab** until you get an error message.

An error message appears, as shown in Figure 5.17, indicating that you must enter a value in the AnimalName field. This is because you made the AnimalName field a required field, so every record must contain a value in that field.

k. Click **OK**, click the **AnimalName field** for the new record you just typed, and then type **Pepper** in the AnimalName field. Click another record to save the new record. Notice you no longer see an error.

One issue Tommy reported was that volunteers have accidentally charged too much in adoption fees. The shelter keeps the fees low (under $50) to encourage adoption. You add a validation rule and validation text to enforce this rule. Refer to Figure 5.18 as you complete Step 2.

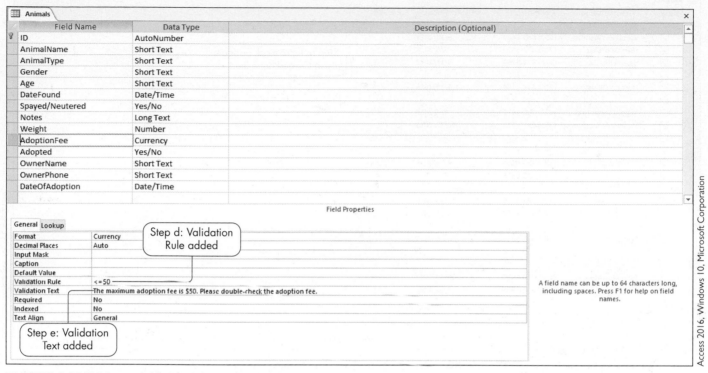

FIGURE 5.18 Validation Added to AdoptionFee field

a. Switch to Design view of the Animals table.

b. Click the **AdoptionFee field**.

c. Click **Validation Rule** in the Field Properties pane.

d. Type **<=50** in the Validation Rule property box.

The maximum adoption fee is $50. You have added a rule that notifies the user when a value that is not less than or equal to $50 (that is, greater than $50) is entered in the AdoptionFee field.

e. Click the **Validation Text property**, and type **The maximum adoption fee is $50. Please double-check the adoption fee.**

When a user enters an adoption fee that is too high, a message appears telling the user to modify the entry.

f. Compare your settings with Figure 5.18, and save the changes. Click **Yes** in response to the message about changed data integrity rules.

g. Switch to the Datasheet view of the Animals table.

h. Click the **AdoptionFee field** of the first record. Replace the current value with **51**, and press **Tab**.

The validation text you entered earlier appears.

i. Click **OK** in the error message box. Change the first record to **20** for the AdoptionFee field. Press **Tab**.

Because $20 is an acceptable value, you do not receive an error message.

You decide to add an input mask to the owner's phone number field so that all users follow a consistent data entry format. Refer to Figure 5.19 as you complete Step 3.

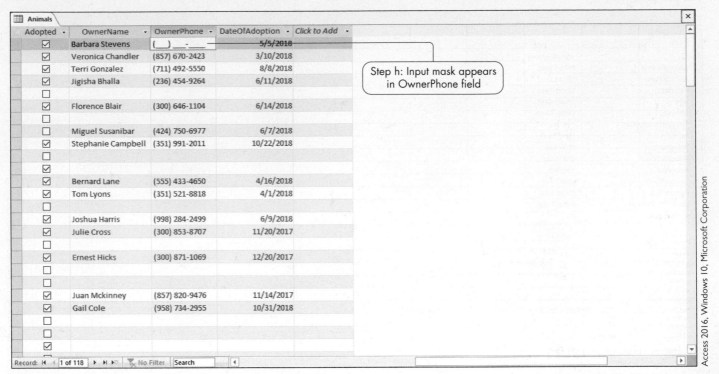

FIGURE 5.19 Input Mask for OwnerPhone Field

a. Switch to Design view of the Animals table.

b. Click the **OwnerPhone field** in the Field Name column.

c. Click **Input Mask** in the Field Properties pane. Click the **ellipses** on the right side of the Input Mask property box to open the Input Mask Wizard.

The Phone Number input mask is already selected.

d. Click **Try It** within the Input Mask Wizard dialog box. (___) ___-____ displays. Press **Home** to position the insertion point at the first character and type **5556667777** to verify that the mask displays the phone numbers as you want them displayed.

e. Click **Next** twice.

You accept the mask with the default placeholder character.

f. Click the **With the symbols in the mask, like this option**. Click **Next**, and click **Finish**.

The data will be stored in the Animals table with the symbols (the parentheses and the dash). This is important to note if you plan on querying the data later.

g. Save the table. Switch to the Datasheet view of the Animals table.

The phone numbers display in the preset format with parentheses and hyphens.

h. Type your phone number into the first record, replacing the existing phone number, to test the input mask. Press **Esc** to return the record to its original state.

Rather than typing in the name of an option (from a list of options) and risk the possibility of a misspelled or invalid animal type, you decide to create a lookup field that enables the volunteers to choose from a list. Refer to Figure 5.20 as you complete Step 4.

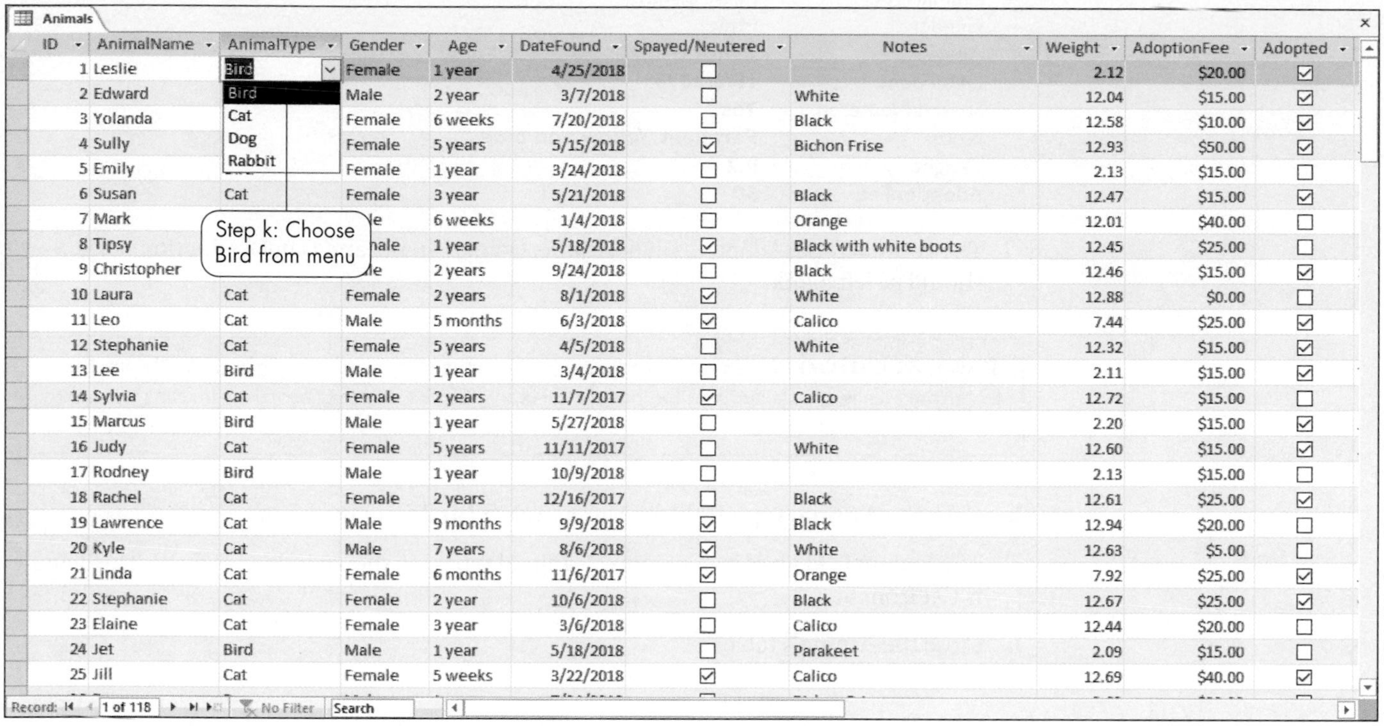

ID	AnimalName	AnimalType	Gender	Age	DateFound	Spayed/Neutered	Notes	Weight	AdoptionFee	Adopted
1 Leslie		Bird	Female	1 year	4/25/2018	☐		2.12	$20.00	☑
2 Edward		Bird	Male	2 year	3/7/2018	☐	White	12.04	$15.00	☑
3 Yolanda		Cat	Female	6 weeks	7/20/2018	☐	Black	12.58	$10.00	☑
4 Sully		Dog	Female	5 years	5/15/2018	☑	Bichon Frise	12.93	$50.00	☑
5 Emily		Rabbit	Female	1 year	3/24/2018	☐		2.13	$15.00	☐
6 Susan		Cat	Female	3 year	5/21/2018	☐	Black	12.47	$15.00	☑
7 Mark			le	6 weeks	1/4/2018	☐	Orange	12.01	$40.00	☐
8 Tipsy			nale	1 year	5/18/2018	☑	Black with white boots	12.45	$25.00	☐
9 Christopher			le	2 years	9/24/2018	☐	Black	12.46	$15.00	☑
10 Laura		Cat	Female	2 years	8/1/2018	☑	White	12.88	$0.00	☐
11 Leo		Cat	Male	5 months	6/3/2018	☑	Calico	7.44	$25.00	☑
12 Stephanie		Cat	Female	5 years	4/5/2018	☐	White	12.32	$15.00	☑
13 Lee		Bird	Male	1 year	3/4/2018	☐		2.11	$15.00	☑
14 Sylvia		Cat	Female	2 years	11/7/2017	☑	Calico	12.72	$15.00	☐
15 Marcus		Bird	Male	1 year	5/27/2018	☐		2.20	$15.00	☑
16 Judy		Cat	Female	5 years	11/11/2017	☐	White	12.60	$15.00	☑
17 Rodney		Bird	Male	1 year	10/9/2018	☐		2.13	$15.00	☐
18 Rachel		Cat	Female	2 years	12/16/2017	☐	Black	12.61	$25.00	☑
19 Lawrence		Cat	Male	9 months	9/9/2018	☑	Black	12.94	$20.00	☐
20 Kyle		Cat	Male	7 years	8/6/2018	☑	White	12.63	$5.00	☐
21 Linda		Cat	Female	6 months	11/6/2017	☑	Orange	7.92	$25.00	☑
22 Stephanie		Cat	Female	2 year	10/6/2018	☐	Black	12.67	$25.00	☑
23 Elaine		Cat	Female	3 year	3/6/2018	☐	Calico	12.44	$20.00	☐
24 Jet		Bird	Male	1 year	5/18/2018	☐	Parakeet	2.09	$15.00	☐
25 Jill		Cat	Female	5 weeks	3/22/2018	☑	Calico	12.69	$40.00	☑

Step k: Choose Bird from menu

Record: 1 of 118   No Filter   Search

Access 2016, Windows 10, Microsoft Corporation

FIGURE 5.20 Lookup for AnimalType Field

a. Switch to Design view of the Animals table.

b. Click the **AnimalType field**.

c. Click the **Data Type arrow** and choose **Lookup Wizard** from the list.

   The Lookup Wizard launches.

d. Verify that the *I want the lookup field to get the values from another table or query* option is selected. Click **Next**.

e. Click **Table: Types of Animals**, and click **Next**.

   This table was prefilled with animal types.

f. Click **AnimalType**, and click the ⟩ icon to move it to the Selected Fields box. Click **Next**.

g. Click the arrow in the first sort box, and select **AnimalType**. Click **Next**.

h. Click **Next** to accept the default column width.

   The column width should be fine here, but you could adjust to your preference.

i. Click **Finish**. Click **Yes** to save the table, and click **Yes** when prompted that some data may be lost.

   The Lookup Field has now been established.

j. Switch to the Datasheet view of the Animals table. Click **New** in the Records group of the Home tab to add a new animal using the following data, pressing **Tab** between each entry. Note that once you enter an AnimalName, you are given an ID automatically:

AnimalName	**Marco**
AnimalType	(leave blank)
Gender	**Male**
Age	**2 months**
DateFound	**10/6/2018**
Spayed/Neutered	**Yes**
Notes	**Parakeet. Yellow and blue**
Weight	**0.2**
AdoptionFee	**50**

The AnimalType, Adopted, OwnerName, OwnerPhone, and DateOfAdoption fields should be left blank.

> **TROUBLESHOOTING:** If you make a mistake in the middle of entering and start again, the ID automatically skips a number. Do not try to fix the ID; just add the record again using the next sequential number.

k. Click the **AnimalType field** for Marco. Select **Bird** from the menu.

The lookup field gives you a menu of animal types, as shown in Figure 5.20. The default is Cat from Step 1.

l. Close the Animals table.

<hr/>

STEP 5 ›› MODIFY A LOOKUP FIELD

After a few days of testing, you decide to modify the table containing the lookup values for the lookup field. Volunteers have pointed out the shelter does not have the facilities to care for snakes, but they can care for rabbits, which is not listed as an option. Refer to Figure 5.21 as you complete Step 5.

ID ▾	AnimalName ▾	AnimalType ▾	Gender ▾	Age ▾	DateFound ▾	Spayed/Neutered ▾	Notes ▾	Weight ▾	AdoptionFee ▾	Adopted ▾	
100	James	Cat	Male	3 years	7/30/2018	☐	White	12.96	$0.00	☐	
101	Alex	Dog	Female	1 year	8/8/2018	☐	Bulldog	45.02	$30.00	☐	
102	Stacey	Dog	Female	5 years	4/29/2018	☐	Bichon Frise	15.66	$30.00	☑	K
103	Todd	Cat	Male	8 months	7/1/2018	☐	Orange	12.03	$20.00	☐	
104	Ashley	Dog	Female	5 years	4/16/2018	☑	Shih Tzu	11.51	$50.00	☑	C
105	Jason	Dog	Male	1 year	6/22/2018	☐	Bichon Frise	9.74	$30.00	☐	
106	Adam	Cat	Male	5 years	10/12/2018	☑	Orange	12.71	$0.00	☐	
107	Lucille	Cat	Female	8 months	4/9/2018	☐	White	12.38	$20.00	☐	
108	Carol	Cat	Female	2 years	5/23/2018	☑	Orange	12.65	$15.00	☑	Cl
109	Evelyn	Cat	Female	2 years	10/29/2018	☑	Calico	12.48	$0.00	☑	Je
110	Taquito	Cat	Male	3 year	7/29/2018	☐	Orange	12.68	$20.00	☐	
111	Christopher	Cat	Male	7 weeks	4/12/2018	☐	Orange	12.58	$10.00	☐	
112	Jessica	Cat	Female	8 months	11/25/2017	☐	Black	12.02	$25.00	☑	Lo
113	Connie	Dog	Female	2 years	12/16/2017	☑	Bichon Frise	10.53	$30.00	☐	
114	Evelyn	Dog	Female	1 year	7/7/2018	☐	Shih Tzu	12.61	$30.00	☐	
115	Donna	Dog	Female	1 year	2/5/2018	☐	Bichon Frise	9.10	$30.00	☑	St
116	Simba	Cat	Male	2 years	6/2/2018	☑	Orange striped. Short hair	12.88	$15.00	☐	M
117	Gerald	Cat	Male	2 years	10/4/2018	☐	White	12.03	$15.00	☑	Le
118	Pepper	Cat	Female	2 months	10/5/2018	☐	Very shy. Black and White	3.00	$25.00	☐	
119	Marco	Bird	Male	2 months	10/6/2018	☑	Parakeet. Yellow and blue	0.20	$50.00	☐	
120	Thumper	Rabbit	Female	3 months	10/8/2018	☐	Extremely friendly. White	1.00	$25.00	☐	
*	#####					☐		0.00		☐	

Steps f–h: New record added

Record: ◄ ◄ 1 of 120 ▶ ▶ ▶* No Filter Search

Access 2016, Windows 10, Microsoft Corporation

FIGURE 5.21 New Record Added to Animals Table

a. Open the Types of Animals table in Datasheet view.

b. Click the **Snake** record. Click **Delete** in the Records group of the Home tab. Click **Yes** when prompted that you will not be able to undo this Delete operation.

c. Add a new row with **Rabbit** as the AnimalType.

d. Close the Types of Animals table.

e. Open the Animals table in Datasheet view.

f. Click **New** in the Records group of the Home tab to add a new record to the table. Accept the default ID and type **Thumper** as the value for the AnimalName field.

g. Select the menu for AnimalType. Notice that Snake is no longer an option, but Rabbit is. Select **Rabbit** for the AnimalType.

h. Type the rest of the data below, leaving any fields not mentioned blank:

Gender	**Female**
Age	**3 months**
DateFound	**10/8/2018**
Spayed/Neutered	**No**
Notes	**Extremely friendly. White**
Weight	**1**
AdoptionFee	**25**

i. Close the Animals table.

j. Keep the database open if you plan to continue with Hands-On Exercise 2. If not, close the database and exit Access.

Data Analysis Using Advanced Select Queries

Extracting and manipulating data is the center of the database experience. Creating multiple queries to extract similar information can result in wasted effort. For example, if you have one query to extract all information about dogs and one to extract all information about cats, you will be maintaining two similar queries and doubling your maintenance time. You can apply special conditions that enable you to make a query more versatile, so when a user runs a query, he or she is prompted for the criteria.

In addition to selecting information, Access includes a number of functions through the Expression Builder (as discussed in a previous chapter). There are many built-in functions you can use to perform a number of different tasks. You might be surprised at how many things can be done using a query.

In this section, you will create special queries to prompt the user for criteria when run. You will also use advanced functions in the Expression Builder to analyze data.

Customizing Output Based on User Input

Access provides a variety of query types to help business owners make decisions. To determine how many pets of a certain animal type were adopted at Tommy's this year, you could first construct a query with the relevant fields, and then enter Cat into the Criteria row of the AnimalType field. You could then save the query as Cat Adoptions. If you wanted to see the same information for dogs, you could copy the first query, rename the copy as Dog Adoptions, and then enter Dog into the Criteria row of the AnimalType field. However, you might ask yourself if there is a better way to handle this situation. The answer is yes—using a parameter query.

A **parameter query** is a query where the user provides the criterion at run time. It enables you to create a generic query and generate results based on the user's response. A parameter query reduces your development time because you can use the query repeatedly without modifying the design because only the criterion changes.

Create a Parameter Query

STEP 1 ›› A parameter query is not different from the queries you have used before—it is still a select query. The process to create it is very similar to the way you have created queries. However, it is unique in the way it asks the user to respond before completing its execution. You enter a phrase in brackets, for example [Enter animal type]. In this case, you have directed Access to prompt the user to enter the animal type, which will appear as a pop-up message when the query is run. Then, Access will display any values that match the user's data entry exactly. If you do not specify a comparison operator, Access will assume equal to.

If you want to be a little more flexible, you can combine a comparison operator with the parameter. For example, you may prefer to ask a user to enter a value that will serve as a minimum age. In this case, you would type >=[Enter Minimum Age]. Access will process this by displaying all values greater than or equal to the user's data entry. You can use any of the comparison operators you may have used in the past, including greater than (>), greater than or equal to (>=), less than (<), less than or equal to (<=), equal to (=), not equal to (<>), Between, In, and Like. Creating a parameter query is similar to creating most other queries; the major difference is in the criteria.

To create a parameter query, complete the following steps:

1. Click Query Design in the Queries group of the Create tab.
2. Choose the table or tables that contain the records that you want included in the query, and close the Show Table dialog box.
3. Drag the relevant fields from the table to the query design grid.
4. Click the Criteria row of the field that you want to filter. Enter the comparison operator followed by a phrase enclosed in brackets [ ] instructing the user what to enter, for example, [Enter Animal Type], as shown in Figure 5.22. When a user runs the query, the phrase you typed in brackets appears as a prompt in the Enter Parameter Value dialog box (see Figure 5.23). Note you can also add other criteria here as well.

To display the Query Parameters window, open the query in Design view, click Parameters on the Show/Hide group of the Design tab, and add the criteria. You can choose a data type for each parameter.

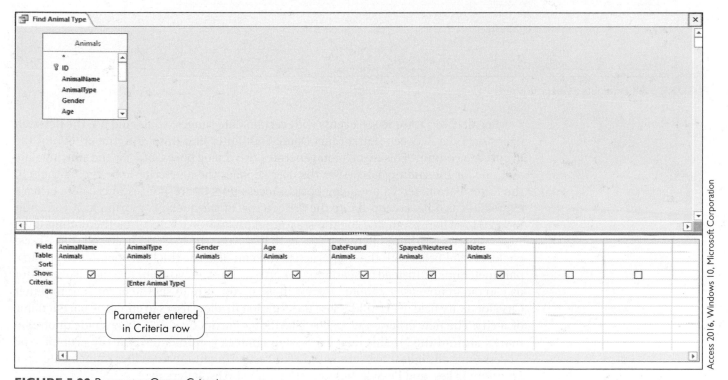

FIGURE 5.22 Parameter Query Criteria

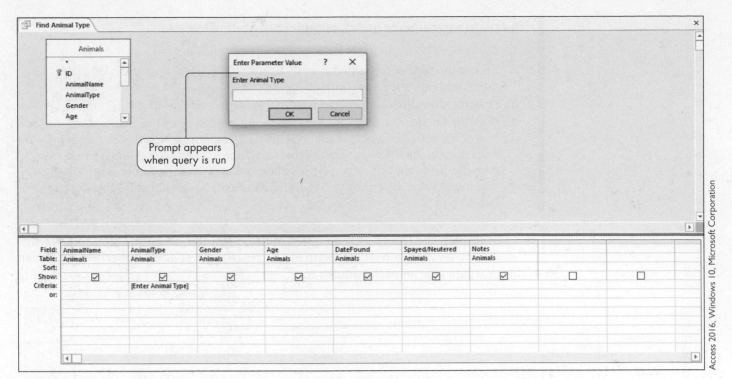

FIGURE 5.23 Parameter Query Prompt

Recall if you want to see events with certain date ranges, you could use the Between operator. Type Between [Enter Start Date] And [Enter End Date] into the criteria of the EventDate column. This expression generates two dialog boxes, one for the starting date and one for the ending date. After the user supplies the date criteria by typing them in the Enter Parameter Value dialog boxes, Access uses the responses to create a criteria expression as if it were typed into the Criteria row of the query. For example, if you enter 6/1/2017 when prompted for the starting date and 6/30/2017 as the ending date, Access interprets that as Between #6/1/2017# And #6/30/2017#. Recall that Access encloses date fields with the # character. You can also use the Like operator to create a parameter query. Instead of searching for an exact match, you can use the Like operator as you did in an earlier chapter. For example, if you were to set the parameter to [Enter City] for a City field, you could revise the criterion to allow users to enter the partial name of a city. The new criterion would be Like [Enter Partial City] & '*' (use single quotation marks around the *). This new expression enables you to enter P at the prompt, and Access finds all cities that begin with P. The results might include cities named Paterson, Pompton Lakes, and Passaic, but not cities named West Paterson.

You can also use multiple parameters within a single query. For example, you could prompt for a maximum adoption fee, and then prompt for gender. In this case, you would add one set of criteria to the AdoptionFee field and one to the Gender field.

This provides an additional level of control for parameter queries. If your users run queries and end up with no results, it may be because their input is not in the form the query expects.

Create a Parameter Report

The effectiveness of parameter queries can be extended to reports. By creating a report based on a parameter query, you automatically receive the benefits of a parameter query—adding flexibility that enables a user to control the content of the report. The creation of a parameter report is simple once the parameter query has been created.

To create a parameter report from an existing parameter query, complete the following steps:

1. Select a parameter query in the Navigation Pane.
2. Click Report in the Reports group of the Create tab. As the new report is being created, the Enter Parameter Value dialog box appears asking you to enter the criterion.
3. Enter a value, and click OK. If you only have one parameter, the report opens in Layout view. Otherwise, you will be prompted for the other parameters.
4. Save the report. Note each time the report is opened, you are prompted for new criteria.

Any other type of report can be created as well using the same process as you used in previous chapters. This can work well with labels reports, for example, if you want to generate labels for customers who live in a certain state or ZIP code.

Using Advanced Functions

Effective functions can make a huge difference in the power of a database. Database administrators may spend hours poring over Internet search results, trying to find a way to create a function to do something specific. Recall from an earlier chapter that there are a number of built-in functions in Access, each of which serve to perform some sort of calculation. Functions can include arguments, which are required to perform the calculation. Some arguments are required and some are optional. Some functions are relatively straightforward. For example, Sqr(Number) displays the square root of a field named Number.

Even without a background in Access, you may be able to guess what this function does. However, for more complex tasks, you may end up with some sort of long expression that would confuse most users. For example, the following function will find a space in the field FullName, and display the values that appear after the space:

Mid(FullName,InStr(1,FullName," ")+1,Len(FullName))

Many times, creating customized solutions for your users requires planning and research as well as combining multiple functions. These will not always be functions with which you are familiar. Once you identify what functionality is required, you can check the Built-In Functions in the Expression Builder to see if the function exists, or use search engines or Microsoft Help. If the function exists, add the function to the expression box and replace «placeholder text» with the argument values.

Use the Date Function

STEP 2 ▶▶ You performed simple date arithmetic in an earlier chapter. However, you started with a fixed date for the arithmetic. This is not always realistic. You may want to run the same query over and over and, based on the current date, perform some sort of calculation. To do so, you can use the ***Date function***, which calculates the current date. The Date function takes no parameters. For example, you could calculate days since a student's last payment using the Date function and subtracting the last PaymentDate from it. The Date function also is commonly used as a default value for date fields.

To insert the Date function in a query, you can either type it in the Field row of an existing query or complete the following steps:

1. Open a query in Design view (or create a new query).
2. Click the Field row of a blank column.
3. Click Builder in the Query Setup group of the Design tab to launch the Expression Builder.
4. Double-click Functions in the Expression Elements section of the Expression Builder window.
5. Click Built-In Functions.
6. Click Date/Time in the Expression Categories section of the window.
7. Double-click Date in the Expression Values section of the window (see Figure 5.24).
8. Click OK.
9. Replace Expr1 with a column name.

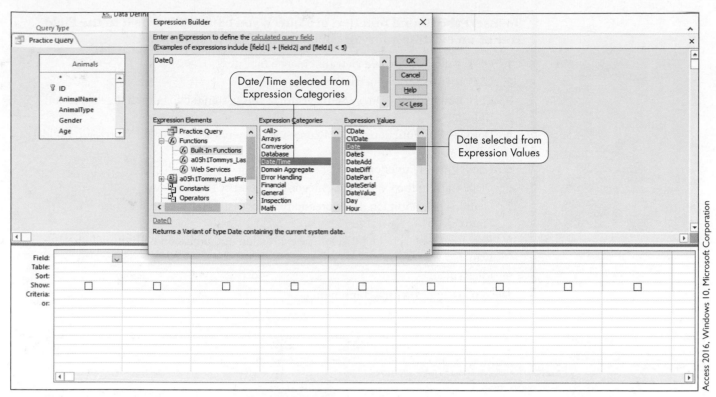

FIGURE 5.24 Date Function

> **TIP: DEFAULT A DATE FIELD TO TODAY**
> You can type Date() in the Default Value property in Table Design view to insert the current date
> when a new record is added. This type of default value is useful for many date fields where the
> person is inputting data for the current date, such as a hire date or an order date. In the future, the
> field will display the current date when data entry is performed.

Use the Round Function

The **_Round function_** displays a number rounded to a specific number of decimal places.
You may not want to round to the nearest whole number necessarily. You can round to a
different number of decimal places by changing the precision parameter. If you leave the
precision parameter blank, Access assumes the nearest whole number.

To insert the Round function in a query, you can either type it in the Field row of an existing query or complete the following steps:

1. Open a query in Design view (or create a new query).
2. Click the Field row of a blank column.
3. Click Builder in the Query Setup group of the Design tab to launch the Expression Builder.
4. Double-click Functions in the Expression Elements section of the Expression Builder window.
5. Click Built-In Functions.
6. Click Math in the Expression Categories section of the window.
7. Double-click Round in the Expression Values section of the window (see Figure 5.25).
8. Replace the placeholder text for the expression and precision with the values you want.
9. Click OK.
10. Replace Expr1 with a column name.

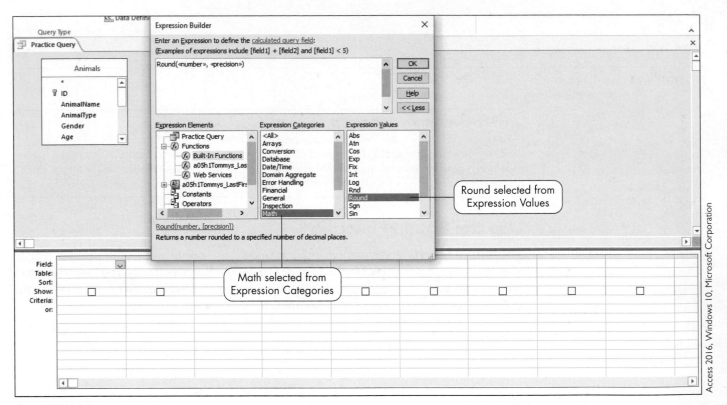

FIGURE 5.25 Round Function

For example, you might need to round animal weights to the nearest tenth of a pound. This can be accomplished using a query. See Figure 5.26. Notice the main function is written as Round([Weight],1). In this case, the Round function has two arguments. The first argument is the value to be rounded (the Weight field) and the second is to what decimal place (1, or the tenths). An animal weighing 25.05 pounds would be listed as 25.1 pounds, whereas an animal weighing 25.21 pounds would be listed as 25.2 pounds. See the results of the query in Figure 5.27.

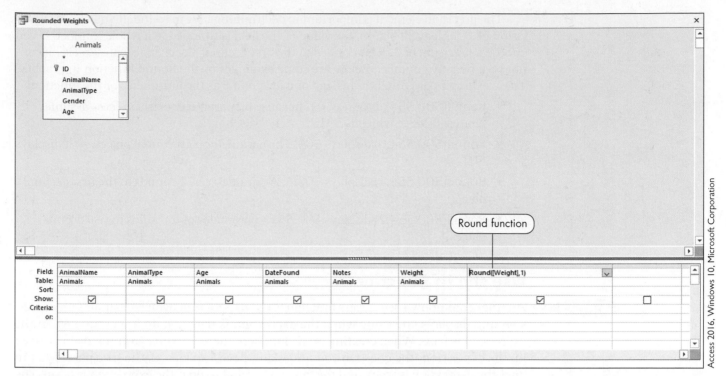

FIGURE 5.26 Round Function in Design View

AnimalName	AnimalType	Age	DateFound	Notes	Weight	Expr1
Leslie	Bird	1 year	4/25/2018		2.12	2.1
Edward	Cat	2 year	3/7/2018	White	12.04	12.0
Yolanda	Cat	6 weeks	7/20/2018	Black	12.58	12.6
Sully	Dog	5 years	5/15/2018	Bichon Frise	12.93	12.9
Emily	Bird	1 year	3/24/2018		2.13	2.1
Susan	Cat	3 year	5/21/2018	Black	12.47	12.5
Mark	Cat	6 weeks	1/4/2018	Orange	12.01	12.0
Tipsy	Cat	1 year	5/18/2018	Black with white boots	12.45	12.4
Christopher	Cat	2 years	9/24/2018	Black	12.46	12.5
Laura	Cat	2 years	8/1/2018	White	12.88	12.9
Leo	Cat	5 months	6/3/2018	Calico	7.44	7.4
Stephanie	Cat	5 years	4/5/2018	White	12.32	12.3
Lee	Bird	1 year	3/4/2018		2.11	2.1
Sylvia	Cat	2 years	11/7/2017	Calico	12.72	12.7
Marcus	Bird	1 year	5/27/2018		2.20	2.2
Judy	Cat	5 years	11/11/2017	White	12.60	12.6
Rodney	Bird	1 year	10/9/2018		2.13	2.1
Rachel	Cat	2 years	12/16/2017	Black	12.61	12.6
Lawrence	Cat	9 months	9/9/2018	Black	12.94	12.9
Kyle	Cat	7 years	8/6/2018	White	12.63	12.6
Linda	Cat	6 months	11/6/2017	Orange	7.92	7.9
Stephanie	Cat	2 year	10/6/2018	Black	12.67	12.7
Elaine	Cat	3 year	3/6/2018	Calico	12.44	12.4
Jet	Bird	1 year	5/18/2018	Parakeet	2.09	2.1
Jill	Cat	5 weeks	3/22/2018	Calico	12.69	12.7

Column contains weights rounded to 1 decimal place

Record: 1 of 120   No Filter   Search

FIGURE 5.27 Results of Round Function

The precision element is important in determining how to round. If you choose a precision of 0 (or leave it blank), the value of the field is rounded to a whole number. If you choose a precision of 1, it is rounded to the first decimal place, and so on. Precision cannot be a negative number. Below are some examples of the Round function in practice. These examples use numbers instead of a field name as the argument for the function:

- Round(500.554) displays 501. Because no parameter exists, Access assumes nearest integer, which is 501.

- Round(500.554,0) displays 501. The parameter is 0 decimal places, so it displays 501.

- Round(500.554,1) displays 500.6. A parameter of 1 rounds to the first decimal place.

- Round(500.554,2) displays 500.55. A parameter of 2 rounds to two decimal places.

Use the IIf Function

STEP 3 ❱❱ Another commonly used Access function is the **IIf function**, which evaluates an expression and displays one value when the expression is true and another value when the expression is false. When creating an IIf function, there are three arguments to be filled in: the expression (the question you are asking Access to check), the true part (what to do if the expression is true), and the false part (what to do if the expression is false). The expression is a statement that is evaluated to true or false. In your day-to-day life, you are constantly performing IIf statements. Based on the weather, you make a decision on whether to carry an umbrella. If the weather is rainy, you bring the umbrella. If the weather is not rainy, you leave the umbrella at home.

Create the Expression

The expression is often the most difficult part of creating an IIf statement. A condition is evaluated to determine the action. In the case of any condition, it is something that uses a comparison that is evaluated as yes or no. You can perform comparisons using the comparison operators mentioned earlier, including greater than (>), greater than or equal to (>=), less than (<), less than or equal to (<=), equal to (=), not equal to (<>), Between, In, and Like. The expression must be written so that it can evaluate as yes (or true) or no (or false) only. For example, Balance >= 10000 or City = "Sarasota" are valid expressions because they can be evaluated as true or false.

Create the Truepart and Falsepart Arguments

The truepart and falsepart are relatively straightforward. You type the values you want to appear. So, for example, if you want to display 25 as the result for a true condition, you would type 25 as the truepart argument. When using text and dates as the true or false results, you need to remember to include quotation marks (") around a text value, and pound signs (#) around a date value. You can find the IIf function through the Expression Builder in the Program Flow category of Built-In Functions.

To insert the IIf function in a query, you can either type it in the Field row of an existing query or complete the following steps:

1. Open a query in Design view (or create a new query).
2. Click the Field row of a blank column.
3. Click Builder in the Query Setup group of the Design tab to launch the Expression Builder.
4. Double-click Functions in the Expression Elements section of the Expression Builder window.
5. Click Built-In Functions.
6. Click Program Flow in the Expression Categories section of the window.
7. Double-click IIf in the Expression Values section of the window (see Figure 5.28).
8. Replace the placeholder text for the expression, truepart, and falsepart with the values you want.
9. Click OK.
10. Replace Expr1 with a column name.

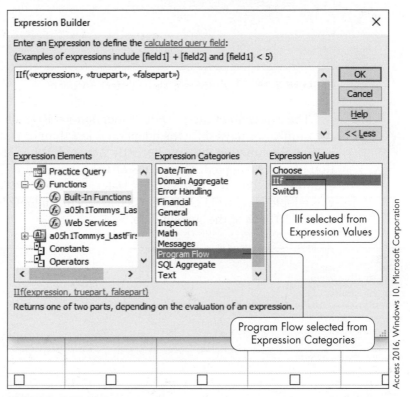

FIGURE 5.28 IIf Function

For example, if accounts with balances of $10,000 or more earn 3.5% interest, whereas accounts with balances below $10,000 earn 1.5% interest, the following IIf function could be created: IIf(Balance>=10000, .035, .015).

Another, slightly more complicated example would be if you categorize adopted pets based on when they were adopted. For recently adopted pets, you may want to display Recently Adopted. In this example, the truepart would be "Recently Adopted" (remember the quotes because it is text). The falsepart would be "Adopted" (again, in quotes). These are the values you want to display, depending on the evaluation of the expression. To create an expression that determines if the date of adoption is within (less than or equal to) 30 days of the current date, you will include the Date function and the DateOfAdoption field to create an expression: Date() – DateOfAdoption <=30. Putting it all together, the IIf function would be: IIf(Date()–DateOfAdoption <=30, "Recently Adopted", "Adopted"). The expression is shown in the Expression Builder in Figure 5.29.

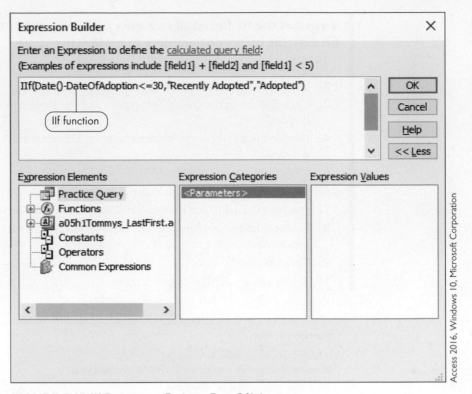

FIGURE 5.29 IIf Function to Evaluate DateOfAdoption

The expression Date() – DateOfAdoption <=30 evaluates each pet and determines if the number of days since the adoption is less than or equal to 30. When the expression is true, the function displays Recently Adopted. When the expression is false, the function displays Adopted. The results of the function are shown in Figure 5.30. For that example, the date it is run—that is, Date()—is 10/31/2018. You can see Stephanie, who was adopted on 10/31/2018, is listed as recently adopted because her adoption date was within 30 days of the current date.

AnimalName	DateOfAdoption	Status
Leslie	5/5/2018	Adopted
Edward	3/10/2018	Adopted
Yolanda	8/8/2018	Recently Adopted
Sully	6/11/2018	Adopted
Susan	6/14/2018	Adopted
Tipsy	6/7/2018	Adopted
Christopher	10/22/2018	Recently Adopted
Stephanie	4/16/2018	Adopted
Lee	4/1/2018	Adopted
Marcus	6/9/2018	Adopted
Judy	11/20/2017	Adopted
Rachel	12/20/2017	Adopted
Linda	11/14/2017	Adopted
Stephanie	10/31/2018	Recently Adopted
Stephen	2/5/2018	Adopted
Pearl	8/18/2018	Recently Adopted
Rosemary	6/13/2018	Adopted
Keith	3/25/2018	Adopted
Annie	5/19/2018	Adopted
Chris	5/7/2018	Adopted
Sue	6/12/2018	Adopted
Campeon	6/7/2018	Adopted
Carolyn	3/5/2018	Adopted
Eddie	4/15/2018	Adopted
Kimberly	4/18/2018	Adopted

Pet adopted in past 30 days listed as Recently Adopted

Record: 1 of 61   No Filter   Search

FIGURE 5.30 IIf Function Results

Your function to achieve this would be the following, assuming the Grade is stored in a field named Grade:

IIf(Grade >=90, "Honors", IIf(Grade >= 70, "Pass", "Fail"))

Access processes this as follows:

1. If Grade is greater than or equal to 90, display Honors.

2. If not (that is, Grade is less than 90), but Grade is greater than or equal to 70, display Pass.

3. If neither of those things are true, the Grade must be less than 70, so display Fail.

Use the IsNull Function

The *IsNull function* checks whether a field has no value. Null essentially means an absence of value. IsNull checks if a field has no value assigned. This can be useful in comparisons or as part of a query. In the Expression Builder, the IsNull function can be found in the Inspection category of Built-In Functions.

To insert the IsNull function in a query, you can either type it in the Field row of an existing query or complete the following steps:

1. Open a query in Design view (or create a new query).
2. Click the Field row of a blank column.
3. Click Builder in the Query Setup group of the Design tab to launch the Expression Builder.
4. Double-click Functions in the Expression Elements section of the Expression Builder window.
5. Click Built-In Functions.
6. Click Inspection in the Expression Categories section of the window.
7. Double-click IsNull in the Expression Values section of the window (see Figure 5.31).
8. Replace the placeholder text for the expression with the value you want to check.
9. Click OK.
10. Replace Expr1 with a column name.

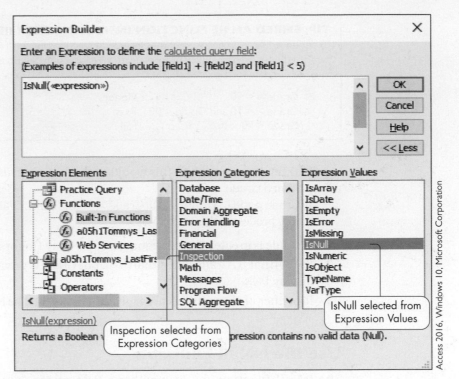

FIGURE 5.31 IsNull Function

For example, you may want to extract adoption date information about the pets in the database. For the sake of discussion, assume the database does not have a field named Adopted that stores as a Yes or No value whether the animal has been adopted. How would you extract only the pets that have not been adopted? You cannot use a criteria of AdoptedDate = 0. You would need to use the IsNull function to check if a value is missing.

When the IsNull function is added to a query, it displays one of two values. Access determines "is this value null?" If the value is null, it displays -1. If the value is not null—that is, it has a value—the function displays 0. For example, in Figure 5.32, the results of IsNull for Leslie's DateOfAdoption is 0 because she has an adoption date, whereas it is -1 for Emily, who does not have a value for the DateOfAdoption.

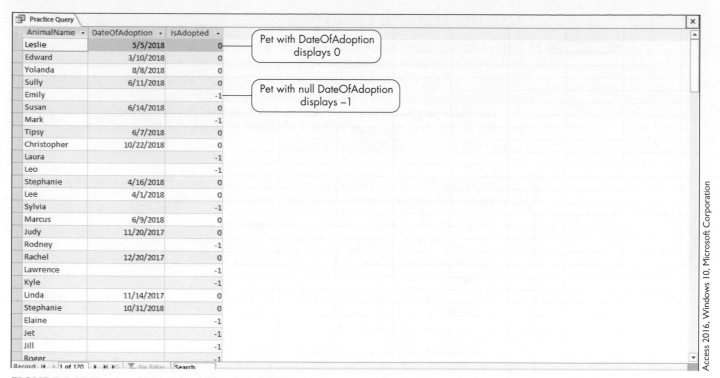

FIGURE 5.32 Results of IsNull Applied to DateOfAdoption Field

IsNull is frequently paired with criteria. After you have created a calculated column using the IsNull function, you could evaluate the results and display only certain values. You could display non-null values by setting the Criteria row to 0, or display null values by setting the Criteria row to -1. Figure 5.33 shows setting the criteria for the calculated IsAdopted field to 0, so it will only show pets with valid adoption dates.

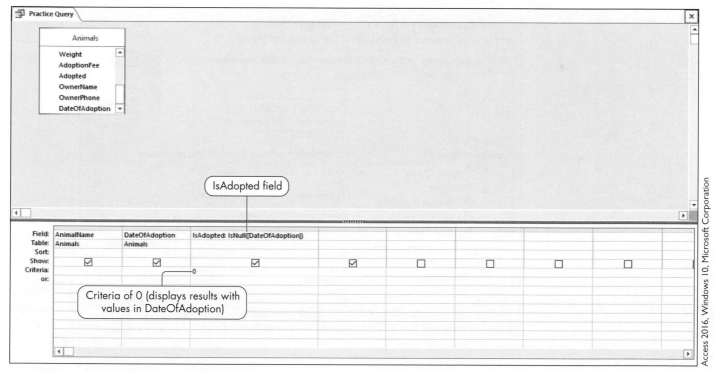

FIGURE 5.33 Setting Criteria for IsAdopted Field

Use the DatePart Function

 STEP 4 ›› Date manipulation is a task most database administrators will perform frequently. Users will typically seek out information with dates attached, whether it is finding orders placed in the last few days, or seeking out information about past transactions. Access has built-in functions to manipulate dates and perform date arithmetic.

The *DatePart function* is an Access function that examines a date and displays a portion of the date. You can find this function through the Expression Builder in the Date/Time category of Built-In Functions.

> **To insert the DatePart function in a query, you can either type it in the Field row of an existing query or complete the following steps:**
>
> 1. Open a query in Design view (or create a new query).
> 2. Click the Field row of a blank column.
> 3. Click Builder in the Query Setup group of the Design tab to launch the Expression Builder.
> 4. Double-click Functions in the Expression Elements section of the Expression Builder window.
> 5. Click Built-In Functions.
> 6. Click Date/Time in the Expression Categories section of the window.
> 7. Double-click DatePart in the Expression Values section of the window (see Figure 5.34).
> 8. Replace the placeholder text for the interval, date, firstdayofweek, and firstweekofyear with appropriate values.
> 9. Click OK.
> 10. Replace Expr1 with a column name.

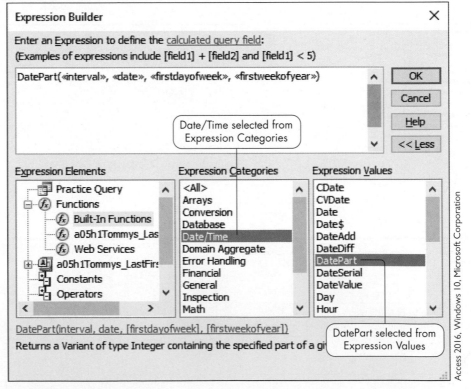

FIGURE 5.34 DatePart Function

DatePart is used to extract the year, month, or day, and a number of other intervals as well. You could use this function, for example, to find all pets adopted in the current month (for example, January), and send the owner a birthday card for the pet.

The function always displays a numeric value, so if you extract the month, you get a number from 1 (representing January) through 12 (representing December). If you extract the weekday, you get a number from 1 (representing Sunday) through 7 (representing Saturday). Table 5.1 shows the DatePart function parameters.

TABLE 5.1 Required DatePart Function Arguments

Function Portion	Explanation	
«interval»	The first argument, the interval, describes the portion of the date that you want to display. Here are some common values for the interval:	
	"yyyy"	Year
	"m"	Month (displays a number 1 through 12, 1 represents January)
	"d"	Day (displays a number, 1 through 366, representing the day of the year)
	"w"	Day of the Week (displays a number 1 through 7, 1 represents Sunday)
	"h"	Hour
	"n"	Minute
«date»	The second argument, the date, tells Access where to find the Date/Time information.	

Table 5.2 shows a few examples of the DatePart function being used on a Date/Time field named HireDate. For these examples, assume HireDate is 8/31/2018.

TABLE 5.2 Evaluating the DatePart Function

Function Portion	Resulting Value	Explanation
DatePart("yyyy",HireDate)	2018	August 31, 2018, has a year of 2018.
DatePart("m",HireDate)	8	August is the eighth month of the year.
DatePart("w",HireDate)	6	August 31, 2018, is a Friday (the sixth day of the week).

Pearson Education, Inc.

Calculated fields such as DatePart work like any other field when it comes to some of the tasks learned in earlier chapters. You can apply criteria (including using a parameter query). If you used the DatePart function to display the month number, you could add a criteria of a month number (for example, 1 for January), and only results from that month would appear. Likewise, if you use DatePart to display the month number, you could group by the calculated field. You would get one row for each month. Figure 5.35 shows the results of the animals grouped by the month each animal was found. The Month column was created using the DatePart function, as shown in Figure 5.36.

Found Month

Month	NumAnimals
1	9
2	7
3	14
4	12
5	20
6	10
7	14
8	6
9	7
10	13
11	5
12	3

Month 1 (January) has 9 animals

Access 2016, Windows 10, Microsoft Corporation

FIGURE 5.35 Query Showing Animals by Month

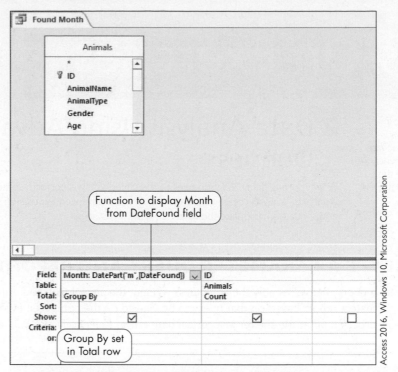

FIGURE 5.36 Grouping by DatePart Function Results

Access 2016, Windows 10, Microsoft Corporation

Quick
Concepts

5. Give an example of a query you might want to convert to a parameter query. **p. 352**

6. How does the precision argument change the way the Round function behaves? **p. 358**

7. You want to use the IIf function to display Yes for all applicants with a value of 700 or more in their CreditScore field, and No for all other applicants. What would be the value of the expression, truepart, and falsepart for this function? **p. 360**

8. What does the IsNull function do? **p. 363**

9. How would you direct the DatePart function to display only the year of a field named BirthDate? **p. 367**

Hands-On Exercises

Watch the Video
for this Hands-On
Exercise!

MyITLab®
HOE2 Training

Skills covered: Create a
Parameter Query • Create a
Parameter Report • Use the Date
Function • Use the Round Function
• Use the Ilf Function • Use the
IsNull Function • Use the DatePart
Function

2 Data Analysis Using Advanced Select Queries

After applying data validation rules to the tables, you will perform some advanced queries against the database. You will create a parameter query, use advanced Expression Builder functions, and use date arithmetic to manipulate the data.

STEP 1 ⟫ CREATE A PARAMETER QUERY AND REPORT

Tommy is hoping to create a query that will enable the volunteers to input the animal type and display all animals matching the type. He is hoping to also create a report based on that query to be viewed on the computer. In addition, he would like to create a query to display all animals dropped off at the shelter in a certain date range. Refer to Figure 5.37 as you complete Step 1.

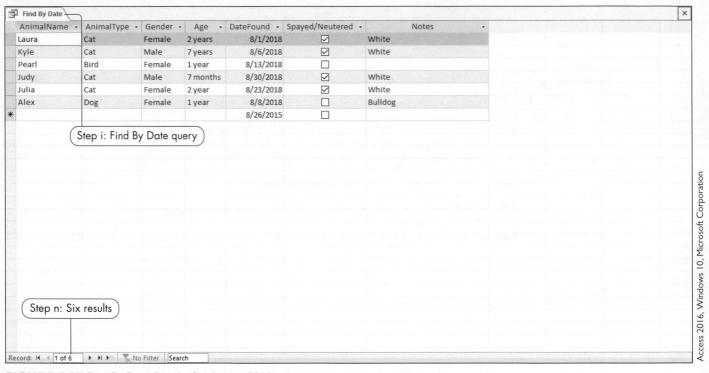

FIGURE 5.37 Find By Date Results for August 2018

a. Open *a05h1Tommys_LastFirst* if you closed it at the end of Hands-On Exercise 1, and save it as **a05h2Tommys_LastFirst**, changing h1 to h2.

b. Click the **Create tab**. Click **Query Design** in the Queries group to create a new query. Double-click the **Animals table** to add it to the query. Click **Close**.

c. Double-click each of the following fields to add them to the query: **AnimalName**, **AnimalType**, **Gender**, **Age**, **DateFound**, **Spayed/Neutered**, and **Notes**.

d. Type **[Enter Animal Type]** in the Criteria row for the AnimalType field.

e. Save the query as **Find Animal Type**. Run the query.

You are prompted to enter an animal type in a box labeled Enter Animal Type.

f. Type **Bird** at the prompt, and click **OK**.

All nine birds in the database are displayed, including Marco, who was entered in Hands-on Exercise 1.

g. Close the Find Animal Type query.

h. Double-click the **Find Animal Type query** to run the query again. Enter **Cat** when prompted, and click **OK**. Verify 86 records are displayed. Close the query.

i. Right-click the **Find Animal Type query**, and select **Copy**. Right-click a blank area of the Navigation Pane, and select **Paste**. Name the query **Find By Date**, and click **OK**.

j. Open the Find By Date query in Design view by right-clicking and selecting Design view.

k. Remove the criterion from the AnimalType field.

l. Type **Between [Enter Start Date] and [Enter End Date]** on the Criteria row for the DateFound field.

m. Save the query. Run the query.

You will be prompted for one date, and then for a second date.

n. Type **8/1/2018** when prompted to Enter Start Date, and click **OK**. Type **8/31/2018** when prompted to Enter End Date, and click **OK**. Verify six animals are displayed, as shown in Figure 5.37. Close the query.

o. Click the **Find Animal Type query**. Click the **Create tab**, and click **Report** in the Reports group.

You are prompted to Enter Animal Type.

p. Type **Bird** when prompted, and click **OK**.

The same nine records displayed earlier appear in report form. As this is designed to be viewed on screen and not printed, you will not worry about resizing fields.

q. Save the report as **Animal Report** and close the report.

Tommy has requested some modifications to the database that you can achieve using advanced functions. You will assist him by setting a default date and rounding animal weights. Refer to Figure 5.38 as you complete Step 2.

Rounded Weights							
AnimalName ▾	AnimalType ▾	Age ▾	DateFound ▾	Notes ▾	Weight ▾	Rounded ▾	
Leslie	Bird	1 year	4/25/2018		2.12	2	
Edward	Cat	2 year	3/7/2018	White	12.04	12	
Yolanda	Cat	6 weeks	7/20/2018	Black	12.58	13	
Sully	Dog	5 years	5/15/2018	Bichon Frise	12.93	13	
Emily	Bird	1 year	3/24/2018		2.13	2	
Susan	Cat	3 year	5/21/2018	Black	12.47	12	
Mark	Cat	6 weeks	1/4/2018	Orange	12.01	12	
Tipsy	Cat	1 year	5/18/2018	Black with white boots	12.45	12	
Christopher	Cat	2 years	9/24/2018	Black	12.46	12	
Laura	Cat	2 years	8/1/2018	White	12.88	13	
Leo	Cat	5 months	6/3/2018	Calico	7.44	7	
Stephanie	Cat	5 years	4/5/2018	White	12.32	12	
Lee	Bird	1 year	3/4/2018		2.11	2	
Sylvia	Cat	2 years	11/7/2017	Calico	12.72	13	
Marcus	Bird	1 year	5/27/2018		2.20	2	
Judy	Cat	5 years	11/11/2017	White	12.60	13	
Rodney	Bird	1 year	10/9/2018		2.13	2	
Rachel	Cat	2 years	12/16/2017	Black	12.61	13	
Lawrence	Cat	9 months	9/9/2018	Black	12.94	13	
Kyle	Cat	7 years	8/6/2018	White	12.63	13	
Linda	Cat	6 months	11/6/2017	Orange	7.92	8	
Stephanie	Cat	2 year	10/6/2018	Black	12.67	13	
Elaine	Cat	3 year	3/6/2018	Calico	12.44	12	
Jet	Bird	1 year	5/18/2018	Parakeet	2.09	2	
Jill	Cat	5 weeks	3/22/2018	Calico	12.69	13	

Record: 14 ◀ 1 of 120 ▶ ▶▶ ▶□ No Filter Search

Step k: Rounded field rounds Weight field to nearest whole number

Access 2016, Windows 10, Microsoft Corporation

FIGURE 5.38 Rounded Weights Query Results

a. Open the Animals table in Design view. Click the **DateFound field**.

b. Click **Default Value** in the Field Properties. Type **Date()** as the default value.

   The default value for all new records is the current date.

c. Switch to Datasheet view. Save the changes when prompted. Scroll to the new record at the bottom of the table.

   The first blank record has a default value of the current date. Note if you are working on this before 2018, your default date may be before some of the other dates.

d. Close the Animals table.

e. Click the **Create tab**. Click **Query Design** in the Queries group to create a new query. Double-click the **Animals table** in the Show Table dialog box. Click **Close**.

f. Double-click the **AnimalName**, **AnimalType**, **Age**, **DateFound**, **Notes**, and **Weight fields** to add them to the query.

g. Click the top row of the first column after the Weight field.

   You will create a new column to round the Weight field.

h. Click **Builder** in the Query Setup group. Double-click **Functions** in the Expression Elements section of the window. Click **Built-In Functions**. Click **Math** in the Expression Categories section of the Expression Builder.

i. Double-click **Round** in the Expression Values section.

   Round(«number», «precision») displays in the Expression Builder.

j. Remove «number», «precision» from the expression and replace it with **Weight**.

   Round(Weight) displays in the Expression Builder.

k. Click **OK**. Replace Expr1 in your new column with **Rounded**. Run the query. Check the Rounded column against the Weight column to make sure animal weights are rounded to the nearest whole number (see Figure 5.38).

l. Save the query as **Rounded Weights** and close the query.

STEP 3 ⟩⟩ USE IIF AND ISNULL FUNCTIONS

Tommy hopes to find data entry errors in his database. Due to the sheer number of volunteers, he has noticed mistakes in the database, and he would like an automated query to find any pets that are listed as adopted but do not have an owner name. You will help him to accomplish this by using an IsNull function inside an IIf function. Refer to Figure 5.39 as you complete Step 3.

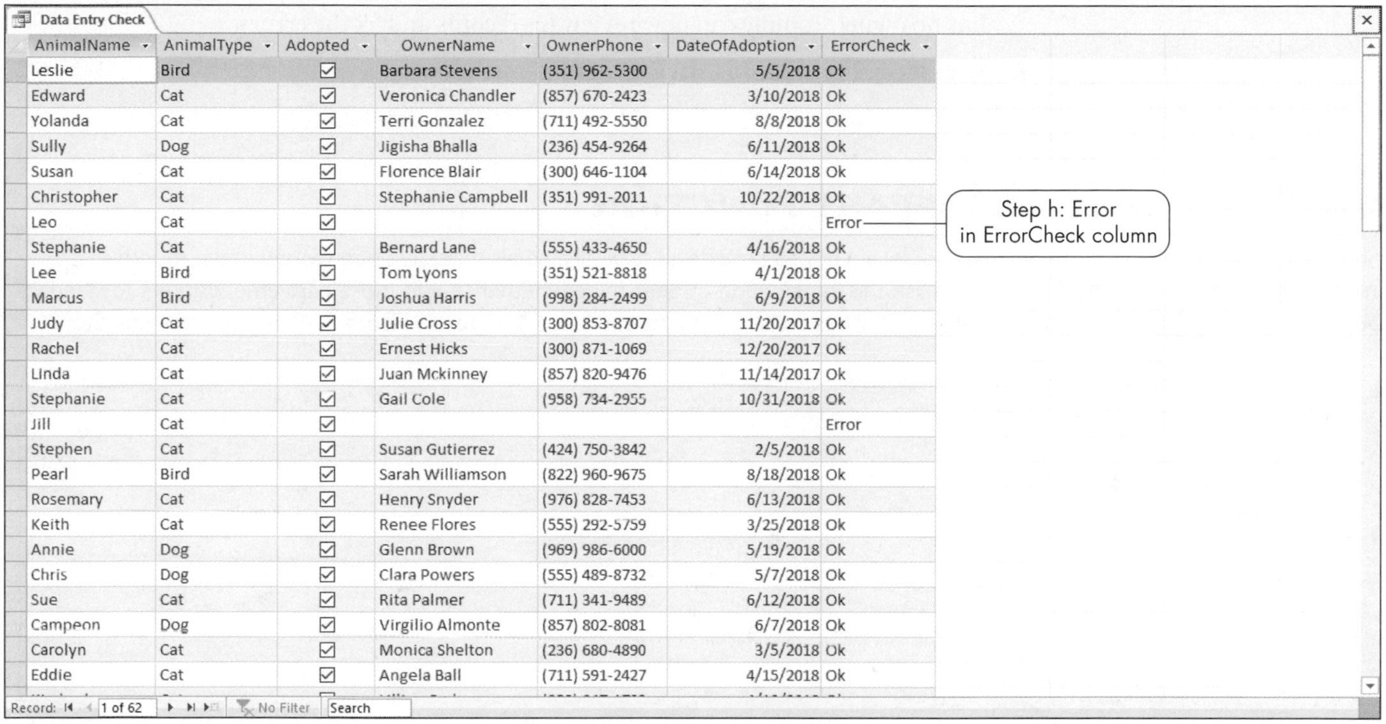

AnimalName	AnimalType	Adopted	OwnerName	OwnerPhone	DateOfAdoption	ErrorCheck
Leslie	Bird	☑	Barbara Stevens	(351) 962-5300	5/5/2018	Ok
Edward	Cat	☑	Veronica Chandler	(857) 670-2423	3/10/2018	Ok
Yolanda	Cat	☑	Terri Gonzalez	(711) 492-5550	8/8/2018	Ok
Sully	Dog	☑	Jigisha Bhalla	(236) 454-9264	6/11/2018	Ok
Susan	Cat	☑	Florence Blair	(300) 646-1104	6/14/2018	Ok
Christopher	Cat	☑	Stephanie Campbell	(351) 991-2011	10/22/2018	Ok
Leo	Cat	☑				Error
Stephanie	Cat	☑	Bernard Lane	(555) 433-4650	4/16/2018	Ok
Lee	Bird	☑	Tom Lyons	(351) 521-8818	4/1/2018	Ok
Marcus	Bird	☑	Joshua Harris	(998) 284-2499	6/9/2018	Ok
Judy	Cat	☑	Julie Cross	(300) 853-8707	11/20/2017	Ok
Rachel	Cat	☑	Ernest Hicks	(300) 871-1069	12/20/2017	Ok
Linda	Cat	☑	Juan Mckinney	(857) 820-9476	11/14/2017	Ok
Stephanie	Cat	☑	Gail Cole	(958) 734-2955	10/31/2018	Ok
Jill	Cat	☑				Error
Stephen	Cat	☑	Susan Gutierrez	(424) 750-3842	2/5/2018	Ok
Pearl	Bird	☑	Sarah Williamson	(822) 960-9675	8/18/2018	Ok
Rosemary	Cat	☑	Henry Snyder	(976) 828-7453	6/13/2018	Ok
Keith	Cat	☑	Renee Flores	(555) 292-5759	3/25/2018	Ok
Annie	Dog	☑	Glenn Brown	(969) 986-6000	5/19/2018	Ok
Chris	Dog	☑	Clara Powers	(555) 489-8732	5/7/2018	Ok
Sue	Cat	☑	Rita Palmer	(711) 341-9489	6/12/2018	Ok
Campeon	Dog	☑	Virgilio Almonte	(857) 802-8081	6/7/2018	Ok
Carolyn	Cat	☑	Monica Shelton	(236) 680-4890	3/5/2018	Ok
Eddie	Cat	☑	Angela Ball	(711) 591-2427	4/15/2018	Ok

Step h: Error in ErrorCheck column

Record: 1 of 62 — No Filter — Search

Access 2016, Windows 10, Microsoft Corporation

FIGURE 5.39 Data Entry Check Query Results

a. Click the **Create tab**. Click **Query Design** in the Queries group to create a new query. Double-click the **Animals table**. Click **Close**. Double-click the **AnimalName**, **AnimalType**, **Adopted**, **OwnerName**, **OwnerPhone**, and **DateOfAdoption fields** to add them to the query.

You will use a combination of an IIf and IsNull function to find animals that are listed as adopted but do not have owners listed.

b. Type **Yes** in the Criteria row of the Adopted field.

You will limit your query results to animals that are listed as adopted.

c. Click the top row of the first blank column following the DateOfAdoption column. Click **Builder** in the Query Setup group.

d. Double-click **Functions** in the Expression Elements section of the window. Click **Built-In Functions**. Click **Program Flow** in the Expression Categories section of the Expression Builder. Double-click **IIf** in the Expression Values section of the window.

IIf(«expression», «truepart», «falsepart») displays in the Expression Builder.

e. Click **«expression»**. Press **Delete**. Click **Inspection** in the Expression Categories section of the Expression Builder. Double-click **IsNull**.

IIf(IsNull(«expression»), «truepart», «falsepart») displays in the Expression Builder.

f. Click **«expression»**. Type **OwnerName**.

IIf(IsNull(OwnerName), «truepart», «falsepart») displays in the Expression Builder.

g. Click **«truepart»**. Type "**Error**". Click **«falsepart»**. Type "**Ok**".

IIf(IsNull(OwnerName), "Error", "Ok") displays in the Expression Builder.

h. Click **OK**. Replace Expr1 with **ErrorCheck**. Run the query and compare the results with Figure 5.39.

The first Error message appears for Animal #7 (Leo). Notice Leo is listed as adopted but has no owner. Tommy can now review his records and fix the errors.

i. Save the query as **Data Entry Check**. Close the query.

STEP 4 ⟫ **USE THE DATEPART FUNCTION**

Tommy has been asked by a local animal control agency to provide a list of all animals that have been found in the month of January in any year. The agency is hoping to use this information to determine whether to add more part-time workers for January. You will help him get a list of all animals the shelter has collected during any January. Refer to Figure 5.40 as you complete Step 4.

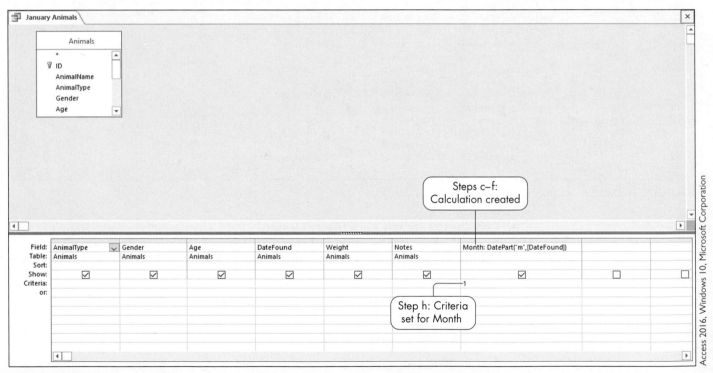

FIGURE 5.40 January Animals Design

a. Click the **Create tab**. Click **Query Design** in the Queries group to create a new query. Double-click the **Animals table**. Click **Close**. Double-click the **AnimalType**, **Gender**, **Age**, **DateFound**, **Weight**, and **Notes fields** to add them to the query.

b. Click the top row of the first blank column after the Notes field. Click **Builder** in the Query Setup group.

c. Double-click **Functions** in the Expression Elements section of the window. Click **Built-In Functions**, and click **Date/Time** in the Expression Categories section of the Expression Builder. Double-click **DatePart** in the Expression Values section of the window.

DatePart(«interval», «date», «firstdayofweek», «firstweekofyear») displays in the Expression Builder.

d. Click **«firstdayofweek»**, and press **Delete**. Repeat the process for **«firstweekofyear»** and the extra spaces and commas.

DatePart(«interval», «date») displays in the Expression Builder.

e. Click **«interval»**. Type **"m"**. Click **«date»**. Type **DateFound**.

DatePart("m",DateFound) now appears in the Expression Builder.

f. Click **OK**. Replace Expr1 with **Month**.

g. Run the query. Examine the new column.

The new column now contains a number corresponding to the number of the month of the year (for example, 1 for January and 12 for December).

h. Switch to Design view. Enter **1** in the Criteria row for the newly created column and compare your design with Figure 5.40. Run the query.

The nine animals found in the month of January appear.

i. Save the query as **January Animals**. Close the query.

j. Close the database and exit Access. Based on your instructor's directions, submit a05h2Tommys_LastFirst.

Chapter Objectives Review

After reading this chapter, you have accomplished the following objectives:

1. Establish data validation.

- Require a field: Required fields cannot be left without a value, and existing records do not have to be updated if you set this property.
- Add a default field value: A default field value automatically enters a value in a field, which is useful if a majority of new records have the same value.
- Add a validation rule with validation text: Validation rules limit the type or range of data that can be entered, and validation text provides more information when the user violates a validation rule.

2. Control the format of data entry.

- Create an input mask: Input masks specify the exact format of the data entry. You can use the wizard to create common input masks, such as Social Security number and phone number.

3. Control input with a lookup field.

- Create a lookup field: A field with a number of repeated values may be better suited as a lookup field, which provides the user with a finite list of values to choose from in a menu.
- Modify a lookup field: Lookup field options are usually in a separate table, so changes can be performed in that table.

4. Customize output based on user input.

- Create a parameter query: A parameter query is a select query where the user provides the criterion at run time.

It enables you to create a query for one situation and then expand it into a query for unlimited situations.

- Create a parameter report: Base a report on a query with parameters, and the same option to enter parameters at run time is available. This extends the effectiveness of the query to a report.

5. Use advanced functions.

- Use the Date function: The Date function calculates the current date. There are no parameters.
- Use the Round function: The Round function displays a number rounded to a specific number of decimal places. Different precision levels are available by changing the precision parameter.
- Use the IIf function: The IIf function evaluates an expression and displays one value when the expression is true and another value when the expression is false. The expression involves a comparison that can be evaluated as yes or no.
- Use the IsNull function: The IsNull function checks whether a field has no value.
- Use the DatePart function: DatePart enables you to isolate part of a date (day of the week, week number, month, year, etc.). A calculated field using DatePart can have criteria applied for it. Grouping also works well with the DatePart function.

Key Terms Matching

Match the key terms with their definitions. Write the key term letter by the appropriate numbered definition.

a. Data validation
b. Date function
c. DatePart function
d. Default value
e. IIf function
f. Input mask
g. Input Mask Wizard

h. IsNull function
i. Lookup field
j. Lookup Wizard
k. Parameter query
l. Round function
m. Validation rule
n. Validation text

1. _____ A function that calculates the current date. **p. 356**

2. _____ A function that checks whether a field has no value. **p. 363**

3. _____ A function that evaluates an expression and displays one value when the expression is true and another value when the expression is false. **p. 360**

4. _____ A function that examines a date and displays a portion of the date. **p. 366**

5. _____ A query where the user provides the criterion at run time. **p. 352**

6. _____ A set of constraints or rules that help control data entered into a field. **p. 332**

7. _____ A tool that helps you create a menu of predefined values by asking you questions and using your answers to create the options list. **p. 342**

8. _____ A setting that limits the data values a user can enter into a field. **p. 336**

9. _____ A setting that provides a custom error message to the user when incorrect data is entered. **p. 336**

10. _____ A way to provide the user with a predefined list of values to choose from in a menu. **p. 341**

11. _____ A setting that restricts the data being input into a field by specifying the exact format of the data entry. **p. 337**

12. _____ A function that returns a number rounded to a specific number of decimal places. **p. 357**

13. _____ A way to specify what value that is automatically entered into a field when a new record is added to a table. **p. 334**

14. _____ Used to generate data restrictions for a field. **p. 338**

Multiple Choice

1. Which of the following is *not* a data validation technique?
   (a) The Round function
   (b) Lookup fields
   (c) Default values
   (d) Input masks

2. Which of the following fields is *least likely* to be set to required?
   (a) A Social Security number in a taxpayer database
   (b) A student's first name in a college's database
   (c) The name of an emergency contact for a patient in a doctor's database
   (d) A license plate number in a Motor Vehicles office database

3. Which of the following enables users to choose from a list of options while entering data?
   (a) Lookup field
   (b) Validation text
   (c) Input mask
   (d) Parameter

4. The string of characters !\(999") "000\-0000;0;_ represents which of the following?
   (a) Lookup field
   (b) Validation text
   (c) Input mask
   (d) Parameter

5. A parameter query enables you to:
   (a) Specify criteria for a field when you run the query.
   (b) Find and display specific parts of a date, for example the month.
   (c) Restrict the data a user enters into a field, such as requiring the data to appear as a Social Security number.
   (d) Perform mathematical operations, such as rounding.

6. When would you use the Date function?
   (a) To display the current date
   (b) To display only the year from a date field
   (c) When doing math involving two date fields
   (d) To convert a value from a number into a date

7. Which of the following statements about the Round function is *false*?
   (a) The Round function has two parameters: the value you want to round and the precision.
   (b) A Round function with a precision of 1 rounds to the nearest integer.
   (c) A Round function without a precision parameter displays an integer.
   (d) Round(210.61,0) would display 211.

8. Which of the following statements is *false*?
   (a) The IsNull function works on date fields.
   (b) IsNull can be used to determine if a field has no value.
   (c) A null value means that the value is zero for any type of field.
   (d) All of the above are true.

9. Which of the following is *not* a valid condition for an IIf function?
   (a) Credits >= 60
   (b) State IN ("CA","WA","OR")
   (c) City <> "Nashua"
   (d) Between 10 and 22

10. Which of the following *cannot* be extracted by the DatePart function?
    (a) Weekday
    (b) Month
    (c) Year
    (d) All of the above can be extracted.

Practice Exercises

1 Willow Insurance Agency

The Willow Insurance Agency recently migrated to an Access database. Based on a recommendation from a colleague, the agency has hired you to consult on its database design. You will help to improve the quality of the data by implementing data validation and also create a query to help extract information. Refer to Figure 5.41 as you complete this exercise.

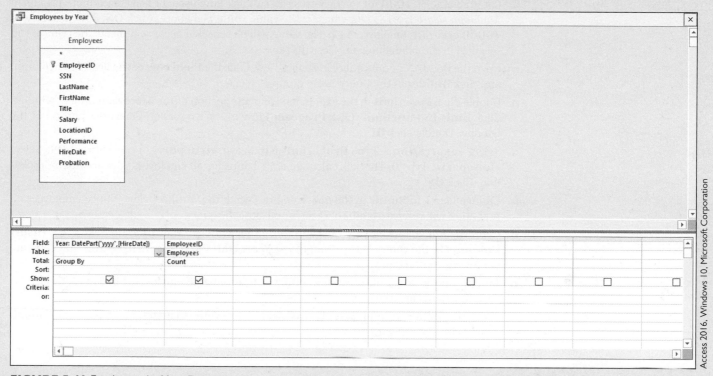

FIGURE 5.41 Employees by Year Design

a. Open *a05p1Willow*. Save the database as **a05p1Willow_LastFirst**.

b. Open the Employees table in Design view. Click the **Salary field**.

c. Click **Required** in the Field Properties pane. Click the arrow at the right of the row, and select **Yes**.

d. Click **Validation Rule** in the Field Properties pane. Type **>=18000**.

e. Click **Validation Text** in the Field Properties pane. Type **Minimum salary is $18,000**.

f. Click the **Title field**. Click **Default Value** in the Field Properties pane. Type **T03**. As most employees start as Trainees, this is a good choice for default value.

g. Click the **SSN field**. Click **Input Mask** in the Field Properties pane. Click the **ellipses** ⌊ ··· ⌋. Click **Yes** when prompted to save the table, and click **No** if asked if you want the existing data to be tested. Select **Social Security Number**, and click **Next** twice. When asked how you want to store the data, select the option for *With the symbols in the mask*. Click **Finish**.

h. Click the **LocationID field**. Click **Data Type**, and select **Lookup Wizard** from the list. Click **Next** to accept the default of getting values from another table or query. Click **Table: Location**, and click **Next**. Click **Location**, and click the ⌊ **>** ⌋ icon to add it to the Selected Fields. Click **Next**. Select **Location** for the sort order, and click **Next**. Click **Finish**. Click **Yes** in response to the prompt about saving the table.

i. Switch to Datasheet view. Click **New** in the Records group on the Home tab. Type an EmployeeID of **312**. Type a SSN of **999999999** (without the dashes), and notice Access fills dashes in automatically. Enter **Catt** for the last name and **Carrie** for the first name. Accept the default value of T03 for the Title field. Leave Salary blank.

j. Select **Miami** for LocationID. Notice this has an arrow at the right side of the field, which allows you to pick the name of the city from the values in the Location table because you set up a lookup. Type **Excellent** for **Performance** and **1/1/2018** for **HireDate**. Leave Probation unchecked.

k. Click EmployeeID **311**. You will receive an error message saying you must enter a value in the salary field because you set this field to required. Click **OK**.

l. Enter a value of **4000** for Carrie Catt's salary. Click Employee **311** again. You are prompted *Minimum salary is $18,000*, which is the value you typed above. Click **OK**. Type a salary of **40000** and click Employee **311**. The value will be accepted because it meets the criteria you specified in the validation rule. Close the table.

m. Open the Bonus Amounts query in Design view. Click the **Field row** of the first blank column, and click **Builder** in the Query Setup group.

n. Double-click **Functions** in the Expression Elements portion of the Expression Builder window. Click **Built-In Functions**. Click **Program Flow** in the Expression Categories portion of the window. Double-click **IIf**.

o. Select «**expression**». Type **Probation=No**. Select «**truepart**». Type **Salary*.05**. Select «**falsepart**». Type **0**. This will calculate a 5% bonus for all employees who are not on probation. Click **OK**.

p. Change Expr1 to **Bonus** in the new column. Switch to Datasheet view. Notice employees on probation will receive a bonus of 0. Save and close the query.

q. Open the Employees by Year query in Design view. Delete the HireDate field. Click **Insert Columns** in the Query Setup group. Type **Year: DatePart("yyyy",HireDate)** and compare your design with Figure 5.41.

r. Run the query. Notice the query now displays the number of employees hired in each calendar year. Save and close the query.

s. Close the database and exit Access. Based on your instructor's directions, submit a05p1Willow_LastFirst.

2 Physicians Center

The Paterson Physician Center asked you to improve its data entry process. Management wants to create a form to enroll new physicians. Because the data entry personnel sometimes misspell the members' specializations, you decide to create a lookup table. If all of the specialty areas are entered uniformly, a query of the data will produce accurate results. Before you create the form, you decide to apply some of the data validation techniques you learned. You will also create a parameter query to assist a doctor in finding potential new volunteers for studies. Refer to Figure 5.42 as you complete this exercise.

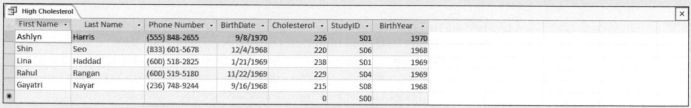

First Name	Last Name	Phone Number	BirthDate	Cholesterol	StudyID	BirthYear
Ashlyn	Harris	(555) 848-2655	9/8/1970	226	S01	1970
Shin	Seo	(833) 601-5678	12/4/1968	220	S06	1968
Lina	Haddad	(600) 518-2825	1/21/1969	238	S01	1969
Rahul	Rangan	(600) 519-5180	11/22/1969	229	S04	1969
Gayatri	Nayar	(236) 748-9244	9/16/1968	215	S08	1968
*				0	S00	

FIGURE 5.42 High Cholesterol Query Results

Access 2016, Windows 10, Microsoft Corporation

a. Open *a05p2Physicians*. Save the database as **a05p2Physicians_LastFirst**.

b. Open the Physicians table in Design view.

c. Click the **FirstName field** and change the Required property to **Yes** in the Field Properties pane. Do the same for the **LastName**, **State**, and **PhoneNumber fields**.

d. Click the **State field**. Click **Default Value**, and type **NJ**.

e. Click the **Specialization field**. Select **Lookup Wizard** in the Data Type box.

f. Respond to the wizard as follows:

- Select **I want the lookup field to get the values from another table or query**. Click **Next**.
- Select **Table: Specialization** as the lookup table. Click **Next**.
- Click the ⟩ icon to move Specialization to the Selected Fields box. Click **Next**.
- Click the arrow of the first sort box, and select **Specialization**. Click **Next**.
- Widen the column by dragging the right border to the right. Click **Next**.
- Click **Finish** to accept the default field name.
- Click **Yes** to save the table, and click **Yes** in response to the dialog boxes that display.

g. Close the table. Open the **Specialization table** in Datasheet view.

h. Click **New** in the Records group of the Home tab. Type **Pulmonary Disease** as the name of the specialization. Close the table.

i. Open the **Physicians table** in Datasheet view. Click the **Specialization field** and click the arrow to verify the new lookup field is working. For each physician, click the **Specialization arrow**, and select the correct specialization as listed below. Once you have completed that, close the table.

First Name	Last Name	Specialization
Takeo	Yamada	**Obstetrics**
Qiturah	Hamade	**Hematology**
Kazuo	Yamaguchi	**Pulmonary Disease**

j. Open the **High Cholesterol query** in Design view. Click **Criteria** for the BirthDate field. Type **Between [Start Date] and [End Date]** so the user is able to enter a start and end date.

k. Click the **Field row** of the first blank column. Type **BirthYear: DatePart("yyyy",BirthDate)**.

l. Run the query. You will be prompted for a Start Date and End Date. Type **1/1/1968** as the **Start Date** and **1/1/1971** as the **End Date**. You should see five results, as shown in Figure 5.42. Notice the year of birth is displayed as the final column. Save and close the query.

m. Click the **High Cholesterol** query in the Navigation Pane. Click **Report** in the Reports group of the Create tab. Type **1/1/1968** as the **Start Date** and **1/1/1971** as the **End Date**. The same results from the previous step display.

n. Click the **Page Setup** tab. In the Page Layout group, click **Landscape**. The results now fit on one page, left to right. Save the report as **High Cholesterol Report**, and close the report.

o. Close the database and exit Access. Based on your instructor's directions, submit a05p2Physicians_LastFirst.

Mid-Level Exercises

1 Hotel Chain

You are the general manager of a large hotel chain. Your establishment provides a variety of guest services ranging from rooms and conferences to weddings. The data entry accuracy of your staff could bear some improvement, so you have decided to move to Microsoft Access and implement several data validation techniques. You also will take advantage of Access's Expression Builder to help analyze data.

a. Open *a05m1Hotel*. Save the database as **a05m1Hotel_LastFirst**.

b. Open the Members table in Design view. Add a phone number input mask to the Phone field. Save and close the table.

c. Open the Location table in Design view. Change the Required property for the City and Address fields to **Yes**.

d. Convert the LastRenovation field to a Lookup Wizard. Look the values up in the Renovation table. Save and close the Location table.

e. Open the Orders table in Design view. Add a validation rule that requires the value of the NumInParty field to be less than or equal to 75. Set validation text to **Party sizes cannot exceed 75.** Save and close the Orders table.

f. Create a copy of the Average By Day query. Name the new query **Average By Month**.

g. Delete the ServiceDate field. Add a new column using the Expression Builder. Create a formula to extract the name of the month from the ServiceDate field using a combination of the DatePart and MonthName functions. Name the column **Month**, and move the Month field to the left of the NumInParty field.

h. Run the query. Save the query.

i. Create a copy of the Average By Month query. Name the new query **Average By Month and Year**.

j. Add a second grouping field between the Month and NumInParty fields. The field should display the four-digit year in the ServiceDate field. Run the query. Verify your results show both an April 2017 average as well as an April 2018 average. Name the new field **Year**. Sort by Year in ascending order. Save and close the query.

k. Close the database and exit Access. Based on your instructor's directions, submit a05m1Hotel_LastFirst.

2 Northwind Traders

You are the office manager of the Northwind Traders specialty food wholesaler. You will modify the company's Access database to help produce more reliable information. You create a lookup customers form in which data cannot be modified by users. You also create queries and reports to validate data.

a. Open *a05m2Traders*. Save the database as **a05m2Traders_LastFirst**.

b. Open the Employees table in Design view. Add a phone number input mask to the HomePhone field using the Input Mask Wizard.

c. Change the TitleOfCourtesy field to be a lookup field. Find values in the TitleOfCourtesy table. Sort by the TitleOfCourtesy field. Accept the default name. Save and close the table, ignoring the warning that data that may be lost.

d. Open the TitleOfCourtesy table in Datasheet view. Add the titles **Sr.**, **Sra.**, and **Srta.** on separate lines, as the company has hired a Spanish-speaking representative and may hire more. Save and close the table.

e. Open the Employees table in Datasheet view. Scroll to record 10 for Claudia Mendiola. Change her TitleOfCourtesy to **Srta.** by selecting it from the menu. Close the table.

f. Open the Customers table in Design view. Add an input mask to the CustomerID field so the user must enter five nonnumeric characters, and ensure the characters are converted to uppercase.

g. Switch to Datasheet view. Locate the record for the company with the name Around the Horn. Change the name of the company to **London Specialties**. Attempt to change the CustomerID to **99999**. If your input mask is working correctly, you will not be able to type it.

h. Change the CustomerID for London Specialties to **LONSP**. Close the table.

i. Create a copy of the Shipments By Vendor query. Name the query **Shipments By Vendor and Year**. Open the query in Design view.

j. Add a new field before Company Name. Extract the four-digit year from the ShippedDate field using a function and ensure the Total row is set to Group By. Name the column **Year**.

k. Add a parameter to the Year column so the user can type a year at run time and see one year's results at a time. The user should be prompted with the text **Enter Year**. Save and close the query.

l. Open the Revenue query in Design view. Create a new field named **Net** that calculates the difference between Revenue and TotalCost. Round the Net field to the nearest dollar.

m. Add a new field to the Revenue query that displays Profit when the value of the Net field is greater than zero and Loss when it is less than or equal to zero. Name the field **ProfitOrLoss**. Run the query and ensure orders with negative Net fields display Loss.

n. Save and close the query.

 o. Open Microsoft Word and open the *a05m2Traders* document from your data files. Save the document as **a05m2Traders_LastFirst**. Use the queries you created and modified to answer the questions in the Word document. Save and close the document.

p. Save and close the file. Based on your instructor's directions, submit a05m2Traders_LastFirst.

3 New Castle County Technical Services

RUNNING CASE

New Castle County Technical Services (NCCTS) provides technical support for a number of local companies. Your manager, Dora Marquez, has requested your assistance in creating a parameter query, a query that summarizes the calls by day of the week, and a query that rounds the hours a technician worked on a call.

This project is a running case. You will use the same database file across Chapters 5 through 10.

a. Open the database *a05m3NCCTS* and save the database as **a05m3NCCTS_LastFirst**.

b. Open the Calls table in Design view and click the **OpenedDate field**. Change the default value to display the current date (using the Date function). Change the field so it is required. Save the table. Click **No** when prompted to test the existing data with the new rules.

c. Switch to Datasheet view. Click the **Last record button** at the bottom of the datasheet to verify the new record (marked with a *) shows your current date as the default value. Close the table.

d. Open the **Calls By Type query** in Design view. Click the Criteria row of the CallTypeID field.

e. Add a parameter that displays **Enter Call Type Number** to the user. Run the query. Enter **1** when prompted. Verify 29 records are displayed. Save and close the query.

f. Create a new query in Query Design. Include the Calls table. Open Builder.

g. Insert the **DatePart function**. Display the day of the week for the OpenedDate field. Leave the other parameters as **0**.

h. Rename the field **Weekday**.

i. Add the **CallID field** to the query after the Weekday field.

j. Display the Totals row, and change the **Total row** for CallID to Count. Run the query. Verify Tuesday (weekday 3) has the lowest volume of calls. Save the query as **Calls By Day**, and close the query.

k. Open the **Customer Billing query** in Design view. Click the first empty column (following the HoursLogged column), and launch Builder. Round the **HoursLogged field** to a precision of **0**. Rename the column **Rounded**. Run the query, and verify the new column lists only whole numbers. Save and close the query.

l. Open the **Call Status query** in Design view. Click the first empty column and launch Builder. Insert the **IIf function**. The expression should check if the ClosedDate field is null, the result when true should display **Open**, and the result when closed should read **Closed**.

m. Rename the field **OpenOrClosed**. Run the query.

Notice the cases with a ClosedDate are listed as Closed in the OpenOrClosed column, while the cases with no ClosedDate are listed as Open. You can use a filter to verify. Save and close the query.

n. Close the database and exit Access. Based on your instructor's directions, submit a05m3NCCTS_LastFirst.

Beyond the Classroom

South Bend Luxury Motor Yachts

GENERAL CASE

You are working as a business intern with a luxury boat sales firm. Your supervisor, Tamika Catchings, asked for your advice on improving the company's Access database, based on your experience with Access. Open *a05b1Boats* and save it as **a05b1Boats_LastFirst**. Upon review, you found a few ways you can improve the database, and after approval from Tamika, you will make the changes. Given most customers are located in Indiana, you will set a default value of IN for the state field. You have also determined you should add a validation rule to the PurchaseDate field, requiring the purchase date to be greater than or equal to today's date. You have decided the purchase date in the Customers table should have a Short Date input mask. You will create a table with a single field storing the four boat types (Fishing, Other, Power, or Sail), using the boat type as the primary key. You will use this table as the source for a lookup list for the BoatType field in the Customers table. You will also create a query named Customers By Boat Type based on the Customers table, displaying the customer name, the boat type, and purchase date. You will add a parameter to the BoatType field so a user is prompted to enter a boat type and the query displays all customers with boats in that category. Close the database and exit Access. Based on your instructor's directions, submit a05b1Boats_LastFirst.

Moody Training

DISASTER RECOVERY

FROM SCRATCH

Amy Lee, owner of Moody Training, has an issue with her database. Her computer crashed and she did not have a backup. She would like you to help her recover her database, but all she has is a recent spreadsheet of job applicants. This will be a start in recovering from failure and helping rebuild the database. Start Access and create a new, blank desktop database named **a05b2Applicants_LastFirst**. Import the Excel spreadsheet *a05b2Applicants* contents into a new table, ensuring the first row contains column headings. Accept default data types. Select the SSN field as the primary key and save the table as **Applicants**. To help her recover, you will perform the following tasks:

- The SSN field should have an appropriate input mask applied to it.
- The LastName and FirstName fields should be required.
- New records should have a default value of the current date for the DateOfApplication field.
- Create a table named **DegreeTypes** containing the seven degree types found in the database (B.A., B.F.A., B.S., M.A., M.B.A., M.F.A., M.S.). This table should have one field (HighestDegreeType) and the table should be named **DegreeTypes**. Set the HighestDegreeType as the primary key.
- Change the HighestDegreeType field in the Applicants table to be a lookup field, getting values from the DegreeTypes table.
- Create a query named **Missing Degrees** to display the first name, last name, and email for all applicants with missing (null) highest degree names so they can be contacted via email for clarification. You will need to add a new, calculated field and set appropriate criteria so only the applicants with a null degree name appear. Name the calculated field MissingDegree and do not display it in the query results.

Close the database and exit Access. Based on your instructor's directions, submit a05b2Applicants_LastFirst.

Capstone Exercise

You work as the database manager at Replacements, Ltd. It has the world's largest selection of old and new dinnerware, including china, stoneware, crystal, glassware, silver, stainless steel, and collectibles. Your task is to add validation rules, create a form that data entry associates can use to add new items to the inventory, and create a new table to classify merchandise as china, crystal, or flatware. You will also use queries and reports to analyze existing data.

Database File Setup and Add New Table

You will save the database file with a new name and create a new table that will be the source for a lookup.

a. Open *a05c1Replace* and save it as **a05c1Replace_LastFirst**.

b. Use Design view to create a new table. Add **ProductLineID** as the first field name, with data type AutoNumber; add **ProductLineDescription** as the second field name, with data type Short Text and field size 10. Set the ProductLineID as the primary key. Save the table as **Product Lines**. Add three records: **China**, **Flatware**, and **Crystal**. Close the table.

Establish Data Validation

You will edit the Inventory table design to validate data. You will make two fields required and add a validation rule to a field. You will also make sure you test the validation to make sure the rules work as intended.

a. Open the Inventory table in Design view.

b. Set the OnHandQty and ProductLineID fields to **Required**.

c. Establish a validation rule for the OnHandQty field that requires the value to be greater than or equal to zero.

d. Create validation text for the OnHandQty: **The value of this field must be 0 or greater.**

e. Save the table. Switch to Datasheet view and test the data with the new rules.

f. Change the OnHandQty in the first record to **−3** and click another record. The validation text appears.

g. Press **Esc** to restore the original OnHandQty value. Close the Inventory table.

Control the Format of Data Entry

To help keep data input consistent, you will add input masks to the Phone fields in the Employees and Customer tables.

a. Open the Employees table in Design view.

b. Add a phone number input mask for the Phone field using the Input Mask Wizard.

c. Save and close the table.

d. Open the Customer table in Design view.

e. Add a phone number input mask for the Phone field using the Input Mask Wizard.

f. Save and close the table.

Control Input with a Lookup Field

You will convert the ProductLineID field in the Inventory table to a lookup field, using the new table you created previously as the source for the values in the lookup field.

a. Open the Inventory table in Design view.

b. Change the Data Type of the ProductLineID field to **Lookup Wizard**. Use the Product Lines table for the values in the lookup field, select both fields in the table, accept the default sort, hide the key field from the user, and then accept the default name ProductLineID.

c. Save the table, ignoring the warning about field size changes. Switch to Datasheet view.

d. Change the product line to **Crystal** in the first record, and click the second record. Change the first record back to **China**.

e. Close the table.

Customize Output Based on User Input

You will modify an existing query to add a parameter so employees doing data entry can quickly get a list of inventory below a certain level.

a. Open the Find Low Quantities query in Design view.

b. Add criteria for the OnHandQty field. The user should be prompted to Enter Threshold. The query should display all results between 1 and the parameter.

c. Run the query. Enter **2** when prompted to Enter Threshold. You should have two results.

d. Save and close the query.

Use Advanced Functions

You will modify the Rounded Prices query to round retail values for items in the inventory. You will also create a query to display employees who are in line for a performance review.

a. Open the Rounded Prices query in Design view.

b. Create a new column to round the Retail price of each item to the nearest dollar. Name the field **RoundedRetail**.

c. Create a new column to display **Luxury** for all items that have a RoundedRetail value of 100 or more and **Everyday** for items that are less than 100. Name the field **Class**.

d. Run the query. Ensure the correct values appear.

e. Save and close the query.

f. Open the Overdue Reviews query in Design view.

g. Add a new column to determine if an employee's performance review is overdue. If the employee's DateOfLastReview is null, it should display **Overdue**. If not, it should display nothing. Name the column **ReviewStatus**.

h. Add criteria of **Overdue** to the column you just created, so only the employees who are Overdue display.

i. Run the query. Ensure only employees with null DateOfLastReview display.

j. Save and close the query.

Perform Date Arithmetic

You will modify an existing query displaying daily totals to instead display monthly totals.

a. Open the Order Totals By Month query in Design view.

b. Change the first column so that instead of grouping by the order date, you group by the month. Use the DatePart function to extract the month from the date. Name the column **MonthNumber**.

c. Run the query. The first line should read 5 (as the month, representing May), with a total of $5,405.89.

d. Save and close the query.

e. Close the database and exit Access. Based on your instructor's directions, submit a05c1Replace_LastFirst.

Action and Specialized Queries

LEARNING OUTCOME You will use action queries to update, add, and delete data and create queries for specialized purposes.

OBJECTIVES & SKILLS: After you read this chapter, you will be able to:

CASE STUDY | Replacement China, Inc.

Replacement China, Inc., is an international firm that sells china, crystal, and flatware replacement pieces. You are the database administrator for Replacement China, Inc., and need to perform several important database operations. The most urgent is the need to increase retail prices for a key manufacturer, Spode China, by 5 percent. You will use an update query to make this price increase; you will create other action queries that make changes to the firm's database: adding records to and deleting records from existing tables, and making new tables from data in current tables.

Before you run the action queries, you decide to make a backup copy of the database. If a problem occurs with any of the queries, you will be able to recover data by reverting to the backup copy. In addition to backing up the database as a precaution, you will verify that the action queries identify the correct records before you run them, ensuring that the records will be processed as required.

You will create another special type of query known as the crosstab query; a crosstab query will summarize data in the Replacement China, Inc., database and help the managers evaluate the sales and other company statistics. Finally, you will create two queries that will reveal tables with missing data and tables with duplicate data.

Moving Beyond the Select Query

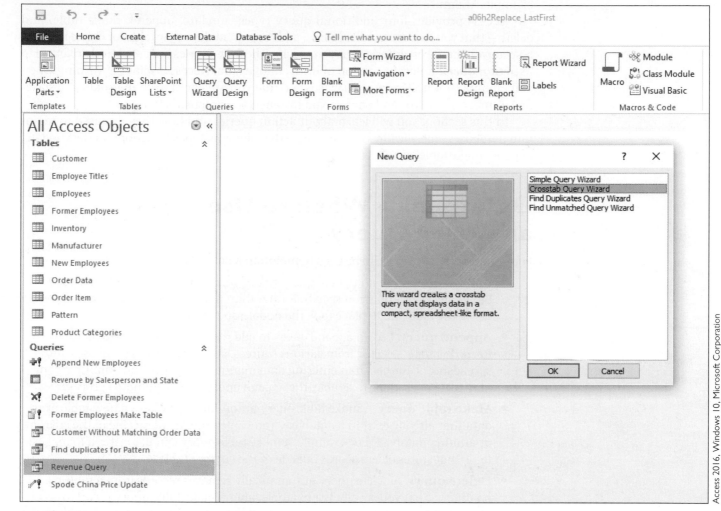

CHAPTER 6

FIGURE 6.1 Replacement China, Inc., Queries

CASE STUDY | Replacement China, Inc.

Starting File	File to be Submitted
a06h1Replace	a06h2Replace_LastFirst

Action Queries

When you create a new query, by default you are creating a select query. You begin your query design process by selecting the necessary tables and then selecting the required fields to add to the query design grid. A select query provides a subset of the data that answers questions that users ask about the data in their databases. A select query is also flexible; you can update the underlying table data if you notice an error in your data or discover a missing field value. Another advantage of a select query is that you can create a query for one condition—for example, banquet sales in Boston hotels—and then copy the query, rename the copy, and change the criteria to extract data for a second city, for example, Miami.

Access provides four additional query types—update, append, make table, and delete—that you can use to edit records, add records, make a new table, or delete records, respectively, based on criteria that you specify. The four queries are collectively referred to as *action queries*. Because action queries change data, Access displays a warning when you attempt to run them. Access warns you that you are about to change data in a specified number of records and enables you to cancel the proposed changes.

In this section, you will learn about action queries and how they are used to maintain databases. Specifically, you will create the following types of action queries: update, append, make table, and delete.

Determining When to Use an Action Query

Four main action queries can be used to maintain a database:

- **Update query.** Use an update query to update or change data automatically based on criteria that you specify. Rather than modifying data manually or by using the Find and Replace tool, the update query is fast and accurate.

- **Append query.** Use an append query to add records to an existing table. Records can be selected from various sources, such as external databases and spreadsheets. Rather than entering data manually or performing multiple copy-and-paste operations to a table, the append query is an automated process.

- **Make table query.** A make table query automatically creates a new table from data that already exist in a database. You can create the new table in the current or another database. For example, a make table query can use criteria to make a table that stores older records outside of the current table.

- **Delete query.** A delete query automatically removes records from a table based on criteria that you specify. For example, after a make table query is run to create records in another table, you may want to remove those same records from the current table.

Recognize the Benefits of Action Queries

One situation that requires an action query is when an end user is required to enter the same information into many records. For example, at Replacement China, Inc., if your objective is to locate orders with missing dates, you can replace every null date with a value manually by creating a select query to list them and then typing in today's date. Alternatively, you can convert the select query to an update query and enter today's date for all missing order dates automatically.

Another situation where an Access designer needs to create action queries is in a college's student database. When students enroll in a school or program, they are classified as current students and are entered into the Students table. After graduation, the school likely moves them to an Alumni table. An append query is the easiest way to copy records from one table to another. Use a delete query to remove the graduated students from the Students table to avoid storing the same data in two separate tables.

Back Up a Database When Testing an Action Query

STEP 1 ⟩⟩ Action queries locate and alter data that meet specific criteria. You cannot undo updates or deletions performed with an action query. Before running an action query, it is best to back up the entire database. This provides you with some insurance in case you need to recover from a mistake. Once you run an action query, you are committing yourself to an irreversible change.

Updating Data with an Update Query

An **update query** changes the data values in one or more fields for all records that meet specific criteria. For example, the phone company announces that all of your customers in a specific area code will now have a different area code. You can construct an update query to identify records of all customers who live in the specific area code and then change their existing area code to the new area code.

Create a Select Query Before Running an Update Query

After you back up your database and prior to updating data in a table, you will first want to locate the records that need to be modified. For example, you discover that one or more orders have a missing order date—key information required to process the order. To find orders with missing order dates, you can first create a select query and use criteria to locate the records with null date values.

To create a select query, complete the following steps:

1. Click Query Design in the Queries group on the Create tab.
2. Add the table that contains the order data to the query design, and add all fields to the query design grid.
3. Add any necessary criteria. As shown in Figure 6.2, Is Null is added as the criterion of the OrderDate field.
4. Run the query to see how many orders have a missing order date, as shown in Figure 6.3.

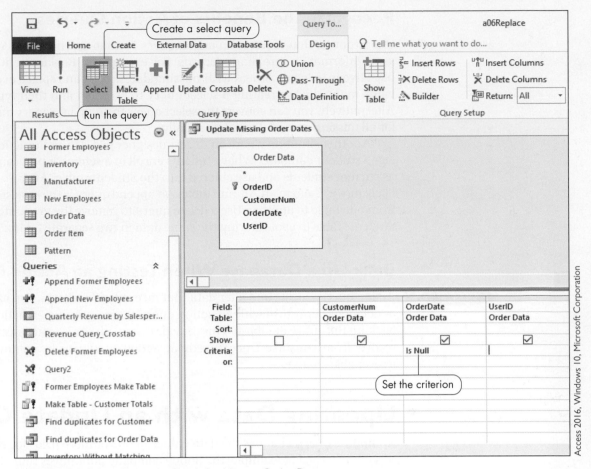

FIGURE 6.2 Select Query to Check for Missing Order Dates

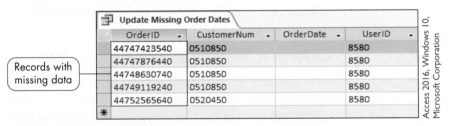

FIGURE 6.3 Query Results Display Records with Missing Dates

Convert a Select Query to an Update Query

STEP 2 ⟩⟩ Your goal is to update records with missing order dates. Once the records with missing order dates are located by a select query, you convert it to an update query and insert the current date into any record with a null order date so that the orders can be processed.

To create the update query, complete the following steps:

1. View the select query in Design view, as shown in Figure 6.2.
2. Click Update in the Query Type group.
3. Enter the new value into the Update To row. For example, type the Date() function into the Update To row of the OrderDate field, as shown in Figure 6.4.

The current date will be inserted into the OrderDate field for all records with a missing order date after you run the query.

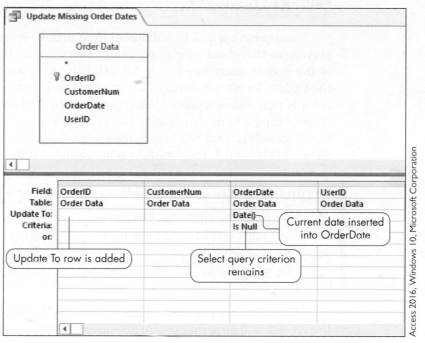

FIGURE 6.4 Update Query Created from a Select Query

Test an Update Query

STEP 3 ›› You can test an update query (before clicking Run) to verify that the correct number of records will be updated by switching to Datasheet view first. Once you run an update query, you cannot undo the modifications to your records, so it is important to view the eligible records beforehand. No updates will be made at this time.

To test an update query before running it, complete the following steps:

1. Click View in the Results group on the Design tab, and then click Datasheet view.
2. Examine the records in the datasheet carefully to ensure that the correct values will update when you run the query. Access only displays the columns that have a value in the Update To row.
3. Click View in the Views group of the Home tab, and click Design view.

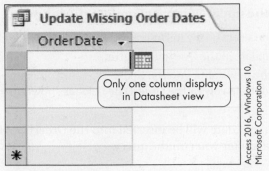

FIGURE 6.5 Datasheet View of an Update Query

Datasheet view will look different than usual—most of the columns that were displaying in Datasheet view of the select query are no longer shown in Datasheet view of the update query (see Figure 6.5). Only the field name and records that conform to the Update To criteria display. You can use this information to evaluate the number of records that will be updated when you run the update query. Look at the number of records shown in the Navigation bar at the bottom of the Datasheet view. If the number of records is what you expect, then it is safe to run the update query. In the example shown in Figure 6.5, the datasheet is indicating that there are five missing order dates.

To run the update query, complete the following steps:

1. Ensure that the query is in Design view.
2. Verify that Update is selected in the Query Type group.
3. Click Run in the Results group.
4. Click Yes to the warning message *Are you sure you want to update these records?*

The update query executes and replaces the current date in the order date field. The five records will have the current date inserted into the order date field after you click Yes to the Access message, as shown in Figure 6.6.

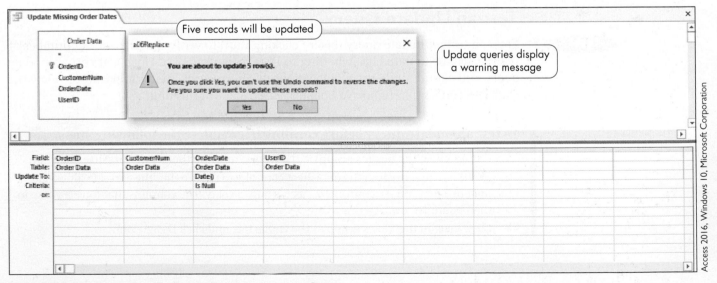

FIGURE 6.6 Warning Message Before Running an Update Query

Verify an Update Query

Running an action query from Design view does not display a view of the results; Access simply returns you to the query design window. No records (with the new data) are displayed. One method of verification is to try to locate the original records prior to their being updated and ensuring that those records no longer exist in their original state. In this example, you can select records where the order dates are null. In Design view of the Update Missing Order Dates query, click Select in the Query Type group. With Is Null as the criterion in the order date field, run the query. The query results show that there are no longer records with missing (null) order dates (see Figure 6.7).

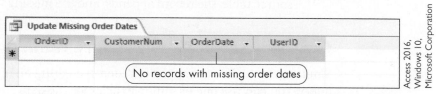

FIGURE 6.7 Verify the Data After Running the Missing Order Dates Update Query

---

TIP: DO NOT RERUN UPDATE QUERIES

After you run an action query, it might appear that nothing has happened except that the warning box disappears. You might be tempted to click Run again—but you should not; you may find that data is changed again unnecessarily. For example, if you created an update query to lower the sale price of all products by 15 percent, entering [Sale Price] * .85 into the Update To row for the sale price field would work correctly. However, running the query a second time would lower the price an additional 15 percent. In this case, the total reduction would be a 27.75 percent discount (lower than the intended 15 percent). If you run an update query inadvertently, you can restore your data from the backup copy of your database.

Adding Records to a Table with an Append Query

STEP 4 ⟩⟩ Another type of action query is the append query. An ***append query*** copies records from one or more tables—the source(s)—and adds them to an existing table—the destination. The appended records display in the destination table in primary key order, or they are added to the bottom of the table if no primary key exists. If any appended record violates the primary key rule or another rule created for the destination table, the record is rejected. For example, you might use an append query to copy employee records in the Replacement China, Inc., database. Suppose the company hires new employees each month. The company may place new hires into a Candidates table until the background checks are complete. Once the checks are completed, the candidates can be appended to the Employees table and then deleted from the Candidates table. Append queries are frequently used in conjunction with delete queries to move records from one table to another. If you use an append query to copy a record from one table to another, the original record still exists in the source table. The same data is now stored in two different places—a practice that should be avoided in a well-designed database. After the records meeting your criteria are copied into the destination table, you can use a delete query to remove them from the source table.

Often, organizations store current records (such as pending orders or periodic activities) in one table and then append them to a more permanent table after they are completed. The tables involved with an append query—the source and destination—usually contain the same field names. The rules for appending data from one table to another are as follows:

- Data types of the fields in both tables must match in most cases; however, some exceptions to this rule exist.

- All the normal rules for adding a new record to the destination table apply. For example, a record is not appended if a value is missing in the source table when the field in the destination table requires a value.
- The destination table should not contain an AutoNumber field. An AutoNumber in the source table should append to a Number field in the destination table.
- If a field from the source table does not exist in the destination table, Access leaves a blank in the Append To row, and you will need to manually specify the destination field name (or just delete the unneeded source field from the query design grid). If the destination table has nonrequired fields that are not in the source table, the record appends, and the missing field values are blank.

Create a Select Query Before Running an Append Query

Similar to an update query, the first step in creating an append query is to create a select query. You can use one or multiple tables for the data source. Next, select the fields you want to append from the table(s) to the query design grid. Enter the criteria to filter only the records you want to append. For example, if Replacement China, Inc., wants to move its former employees from the Employees table to the Former Employees table, you can create a select query, and then add criteria to find employees where the termination date is not null. The results of this select query are shown in Datasheet view in Figure 6.8.

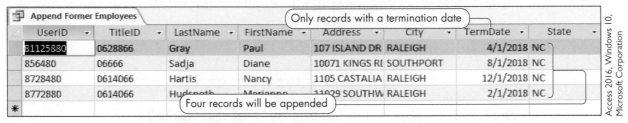

FIGURE 6.8 Verify the Data Before Running the Append Query

Set Append To Fields in an Append Query

After you verify that the correct records are selected, switch to Design view, and then change the select query to an append query.

> **To convert the select query to an append query, complete the following steps:**
> 1. Click Append in the Query Type group of the Design view.
> 2. Click the table name arrow, select the destination table, and then click OK. Figure 6.9 shows the Append dialog box, in which you specify the destination table.

When you convert a select query to an append query, Access removes the Show row in the query design grid and adds the Append To row in its place. If the fields in the source and destination tables are the same, Access automatically inserts the correct field names into the Append To row, as shown in Figure 6.10.

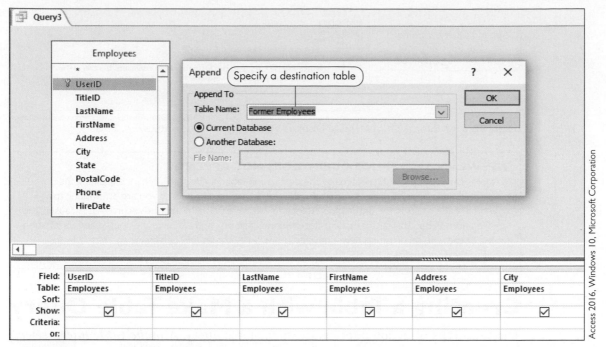

FIGURE 6.9 Create an Append Query

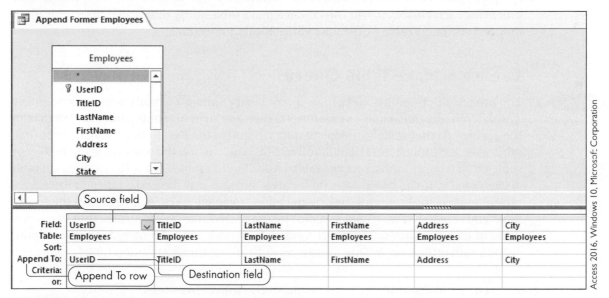

FIGURE 6.10 Source Fields Append to Destination Fields

Run an Append Query

If you want to preview the records to be appended before you run the query, click View in the Results group to double-check in Datasheet view. After verifying the records, switch back to Design view.

To run an append query, complete the following steps:

1. Click Run in the Results group in Design view. You will receive a message informing you that you are about to append the number of records selected, as shown in Figure 6.11.
2. Click Yes to continue. As with all the action queries, you cannot undo the action after it is run.
3. Save and close the append query if you intend to use it again.
4. Open the destination table and verify that the appended records are in the table.

Append Query warning message indicates only 4 rows will be appended.

a06Replace   ✕

⚠ **You are about to append 4 row(s).**

Once you click Yes, you can't use the Undo command to reverse the changes. Are you sure you want to append the selected rows?

[Yes]   [No]

Access 2016, Windows 10, Microsoft Corporation

FIGURE 6.11 Informational Message Displays When Append Query Runs

---

TIP: WHEN AN APPEND QUERY DOES NOT APPEND
If Access cannot append the records to the destination table, a message appears explaining the reasons why the append query failed. If the primary key value of a record you are attempting to append already exists in the destination table, you will not be able to add the record that is causing the key violation. When this failure occurs, close the message box and examine the source and destination tables. Locate the records that have duplicate primary key values and determine the best way to handle necessary changes.

Creating a Table with a Make Table Query

The third type of action query is the make table query. A *make table query* selects records from one or more tables and uses them to create a new table.

At Replacement China, Inc., the sales manager wants to know the total year-to-date orders for each customer. You can create a make table query that would insert this information into a new table—Customer Order Totals, for example.

Create a Make Table Query

The process of creating a make table query is very similar to creating an append query. The difference is that a make table query creates the structure of the table and then adds the records to that table. An append query requires the destination table to exist first; otherwise, it cannot append additional records. You can use the make table query to copy some or all records from a source table to a destination table even if the destination table does not exist. If the destination table exists and you run the make table query, Access prompts you before it deletes the original table. If you click Yes, Access deletes the source table and replaces it with data specified by the make table query. Ensure that you determine in advance that you want to create a new table with the records that meet your criteria rather than appending those records to an existing destination table.

To create a make table query, complete the following steps:

1. Create a select query; specify the tables and field names that you want to add to the new table to the query design window.
2. Specify the criteria that will result in selecting the correct records for your new table.
3. Click Make Table in the Query Type group of the Design view.
4. Specify the table name that you want to create in the Table Name box.
5. Click OK.

Figure 6.12 displays the design for a make table query that will copy summarized order data to a new table.

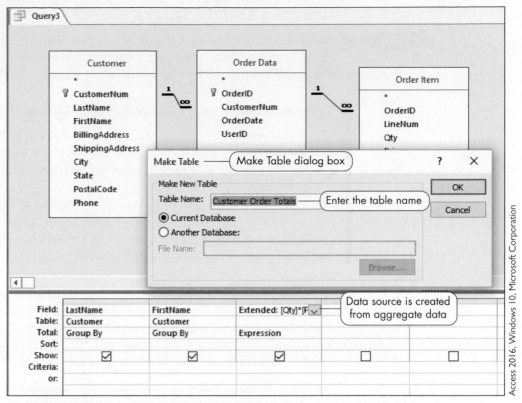

FIGURE 6.12 Make Table Query in Design View

Test and Run a Make Table Query

As with the other action queries, you should preview the datasheet prior to running the query to verify that the records are those that you intend to insert into a new table.

To test and run a make table query, complete the following steps:

1. Click View in the Results group to view the records in Datasheet view.
2. Verify that the previewed records are correct, and click View again to return to Design view.
3. Click Run in the Results group and Access displays a message warning you that you are about to append records to a new table.
4. Click Yes and the new table is created.
5. Open the new table, and verify the records are correct.
6. Save and close the query if you intend to use it again.

If you run the same make table query at a later date, the first table will be replaced with a new, up-to-date table.

Deleting Records with a Delete Query

The final type of action query is the delete query. A ***delete query*** selects records and removes them from a table. Sometimes it is necessary to identify and delete data in a database. For example, if you copy the Replacement China, Inc., database inactive customers from the Customers table to the Inactive Customers table using an append query, you will want to delete those records from the original Customers table. You should always take precautions prior to running a delete query. If you create a backup copy of the database prior to running a delete query, you can always recover from an error.

Create a Delete Query

STEP 6 The delete query begins the same way as all of the other action queries, with a select query. You can create a new select query or use one that already exists in your database, if it specifies the tables and field names that you need for the delete query.

To create a delete query, complete the following steps:

1. Create or select an existing select query; specify the tables and field names that you want to remove from the table in the query design window.
2. Specify the criteria in the fields that will result in deleting the correct records from your table.
3. Click Delete in the Query Type group of Design view.

   At this point, no records have been deleted, but you are simply specifying which records will be selected for deletion. You have changed the query type from a select to a delete query, but you will need to run the query before the actual deletions occur.

At Replacement China, Inc., there may be times when they want to remove orders that were incorrectly entered on a specific date. Figure 6.13 displays the criterion to delete the orders that were placed on 6/10/2018. If you fail to specify a criterion, Access will attempt to delete all of the records in the Orders table. Access displays a warning message and enables you to avoid running the delete query.

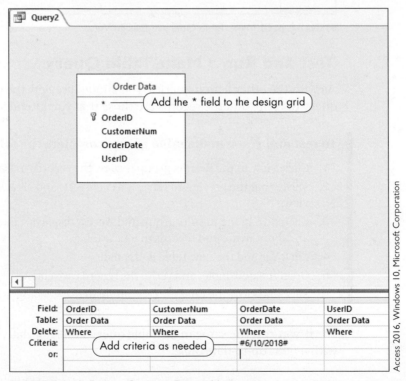

FIGURE 6.13 Delete Query in Design View

Test and Run a Delete Query

As with the other action queries, always preview the records to be deleted in Datasheet view prior to running the delete query. After you verify the number of records in the datasheet, run the query.

To test and run the delete query, complete the following steps:

1. Click View in the Results group to view the records in Datasheet view.
2. Verify that the previewed records are correct, and click View again to return to Design view.
3. Click Run in the Results group to run the query and delete the records.
4. Click Yes when the warning message appears. Verify the results of the delete query by opening the table to confirm that the records were deleted.
5. Save and close the query if you intend to use it again.

TIP: SAVING AND REUSING ACTION QUERIES

At times, you will use an action query one time for a specific task, such as a price change, and then you will close the query without saving it. However, there are times when you will want to reuse queries to append and delete records at certain intervals, or to make new tables as the needs of your database change. If you think you will use an action query on a regular basis, save it with an identifiable name in your database. Remember to preview records in Datasheet view before you run action queries.

TIP: ACTION QUERY ICONS

Access denotes the action queries differently from select queries by displaying a specific icon for each action query type in the Navigation Pane (see Figure 6.14). This may prevent users from accidentally running an action query and getting unexpected results. For example, if an update query is created to increase prices by 10 percent, running the query a second time would increase those prices again. Exercise caution when running action queries.

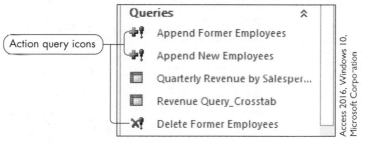

FIGURE 6.14 Action Query Icons

Quick Concepts

1. What is a benefit of creating a delete query? *p. 401*
2. What is a potential disadvantage of running an update query? How can you recover from an error that occurs when running this type of query? *p. 393*
3. When would you use a make table query as opposed to an append query? *p. 400*

Hands-On Exercises

Watch the Video
for this Hands-On
Exercise!

MyITLab®
HOE1 Training

Skills covered: Back Up a
Database • Create an Update
Query • Test an Update Query •
Create an Append Query • Create
a Make Table Query • Create a
Delete Query

1 Action Queries

Several maintenance tasks are required at Replacement China, Inc. Before work begins, you decide to back
up the database to make it easy to recover from a mistake. Each task requires an action query. After you
create and run each query, you verify the changes by checking the records in the modified table.

STEP 1 ▶▶ BACK UP A DATABASE

You will create a backup copy of the Replacement China, Inc., database before you create any action queries. If you make a mistake
along the way, revert to the original file and start again. Refer to Figure 6.15 as you complete Step 1.

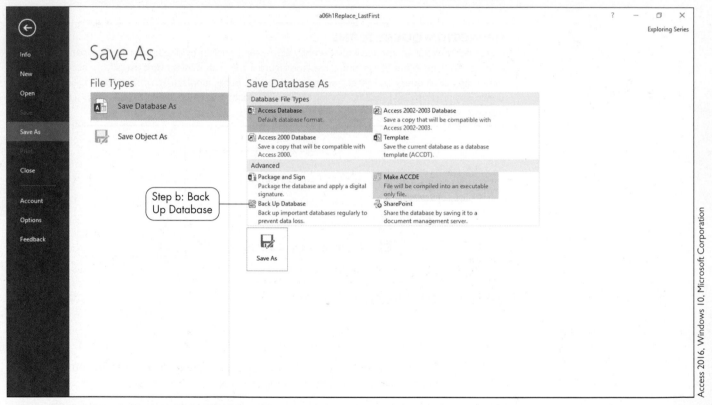

FIGURE 6.15 Create a Backup Copy of the Database

a. Open *a06h1Replace* and save it as **a06h1Replace_LastFirst**.

> **TROUBLESHOOTING:** Throughout the remainder of this chapter and textbook, click Enable
> Content whenever you are working with student files.

> **TROUBLESHOOTING:** If you make any major mistakes in this exercise, you can close the file,
> open *a06h1Replace* and then start this exercise over.

b. Click the **File tab**, click **Save As**, and then double-click **Back Up Database**.

Before you execute an action query, you should make a backup copy of the entire database.
If data is changed or deleted inadvertently, you can use the backup copy to recover it.

c. Click **Save** to accept the default file name for the backup copy of the a06h1Replace_LastFirst_*CurrentDate* database.

A backup copy of the database now exists in the folder where you store your exercise files.

d. Verify the backup file exists in your folder where you stored it.

STEP 2 >> **CREATE AN UPDATE QUERY**

One of your suppliers, Spode China, has increased its prices for the upcoming year. At Replacement China, Inc., you decide to increase your retail prices by the same amount for items supplied by Spode China. You create an update query to increase the retail price by 5 percent for those items only. Refer to Figure 6.16 as you complete Step 2.

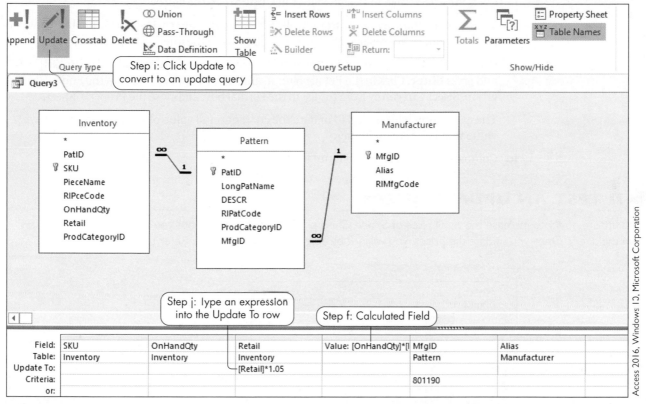

FIGURE 6.16 Create an Update Query

a. Click the **Create tab**, and then click **Query Design** in the Queries group.

The Show Table dialog box opens.

b. Double-click the **Inventory**, **Pattern**, and **Manufacturer tables** to add these tables to the query design space. Close the Show Table dialog box.

c. Add the SKU, OnHandQty, and Retail fields from the Inventory table; MfgID field from the Pattern table; and Alias field from the Manufacturer table to the design grid. Type **801190** in the Criteria row of the MfgID column.

You added the criteria to select only Spode China pieces for the price updates. The MfgID for Spode China is 801190.

d. Switch to Datasheet view and verify the correct records are selected.

The results include 1,129 Spode China records. No updates are made at this time; you are simply previewing the records to be updated in the next steps.

e. Switch to Design view. Click the **MfgID column**, and click **Insert Columns** in the Query Setup group.

A new blank column displays between Retail and MfgID.

f. Type **Value:[OnHandQty]*[Retail]** in the top (Field) row of the new blank column and press **Enter**. Click in the Value column, and then click **Property Sheet** in the Show/Hide group. Select **Currency** from the list in the Format box and close the Property Sheet.

You created a calculated field so that you can check the total value of the inventory before and after the update.

g. Switch to Datasheet view. Click **Totals** in the Records group. Advance to the last record in the datasheet.

h. Click in the **Total row** of the Value column, click the arrow, and then select **Sum**.

The total of the Value column is $911,415.88. The value after you update the prices by 5 percent will be $956,986.67 (911,415.88 × 1.05).

i. Click **View** to return to Design view. Click **Update** in the Query Type group.

You changed the query type from a select to an update query. The Sort and Show rows of the select query are replaced by the Update To row in the query design grid.

j. Click the **Update To row** under the Retail field in the query design grid. Type **[Retail]*1.05** and press **Enter**. Click in the Retail column, and click **Property Sheet** in the Show/Hide group. Select **Currency** from the list in the Format box, and close the Property Sheet.

The expression will be used to update the current retail value of these products with a value that is 5 percent higher.

k. Compare your screen with Figure 6.16.

STEP 3 ⟩⟩ TEST AN UPDATE QUERY

You created an update query to increase the retail price of Spode China products by 5 percent, but you want to verify the values before you run the query. Once you update the prices, you will not be able to undo the changes. Refer to Figure 6.17 as you complete Step 3.

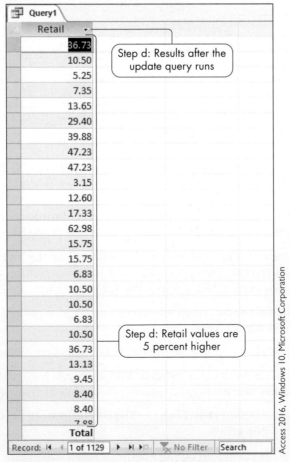

FIGURE 6.17 Query Results After Update

a. Switch to Datasheet view, and examine the records before running the query.

You should see a list of retail prices ($34.98, $10.00, $5.00, $7.00, etc.) but no other columns. Access only displays the columns that have a value in the Update To row. These are the current prices that will be updated.

b. Click **View** to return to Design view.

c. Click **Run** in the Results group to execute the query. Click **Yes** in response to the *You are about to update 1129 row(s)* warning.

Although it may seem as though nothing happened, your prices have changed.

d. View the results in Datasheet view.

The first four retail prices are now $36.73, $10.50, $5.25, and $7.35, as shown in Figure 6.17. These prices are 5 percent higher than the original retail prices you observed in Step a above.

e. Return to Design view. Click **Select** in the Query Type group.

f. Switch to Datasheet view.

The prices in the Retail column reflect the updated prices, and the bottom of the Retail column is now $956,986.67, which verifies that the update query worked correctly.

g. Return to Design view.

h. Click **Update** in the Query Type group to change it back to an update query. Save the query as **Spode China Price Update**. Close the query.

The query icon in the Navigation Pane indicates the query is an update query.

> **STEP 4** ›› **CREATE AN APPEND QUERY**

Replacement China, Inc., hired several new employees who were placed into the New Employees table for a 30-day probation period. The probation period is over, and now you want to add them to the Employees table. Refer to Figure 6.18 as you complete Step 4.

UserID	TitleID	LastName	FirstName	Address	City	State	PostalCode	Phone	HireDate
8965985	0626266	Thomasson	Aaron	5437 PRINCE CHARLES D	GIBSONVILLE	NC	27215	3368471364	9/3/18
8966000	0626266	Last	First	940 DEKALB PIKE	BLUEBELL	NC	27217	3368472393	9/11/18
8965990	063566	DePaul	Mason	376C GATE DR.	BURLINGTON	NC	27217	3363755307	11/9/18
8965995	0648266	Scott	Angie	101 BOSTON ST.	SALISBURY	NC	28146-8856	7048469158	9/10/18

Step i: Append query will add four records

FIGURE 6.18 Records to be Appended to the Employees Table

Access 2016, Windows 10, Microsoft Corporation

> **TROUBLESHOOTING:** You could make a backup copy of the database to revert back to the original data in the event of an error. You backed up the database at the beginning of this exercise, but you may want another backup in case the append query causes a problem. If you complete this step on the same day as you completed the last step, Access adds _(1) to the end of the backup file name to distinguish it from the earlier file name.

a. Open the New Employees table in Datasheet view. Type **8966000** in the **UserID field**; **0626266** in the **TitleID field**; your last name, first name, address, city, state, postal code, and phone number in the respective name fields; and **9/11/2018** in the **HireDate field**. Note that there are four new employees in the table.

b. Close the New Employees table.

c. Open the Employees table and note the total records in the Navigation bar at the bottom of the window.

The Navigation bar displays 115 current employees.

d. Close the Employees table.

e. Click the **Create tab**. Click **Query Design** in the Queries group. Double-click the **New Employees table**. Close the Show Table dialog box.

You have begun to create a select query.

f. Click **Append** in the Query Type group.

You changed the query design to an append query to add the four newly hired employees to the Employees table. The Append dialog box opens, prompting you to supply the destination table name.

g. Click the **Table Name arrow**, and select **Employees**. Verify the Current Database option is selected, and click **OK**.

The Append To row displays on the query design grid, ready for you to add fields. You need all of the fields in the New Employees table added to the Employees table.

h. Double-click the **title bar** of the New Employees table in the top pane of the Design view window. Double-clicking the title bar of the field list is a shortcut to ensure that all of the fields are selected. Drag the selected fields to the first field cell in the query design grid.

i. Click **View** in the Results group and preview the data you are about to append.

You should see 4 rows and 10 fields, as shown in Figure 6.18.

j. Click **View** in the Views group to return to Design view.

k. Click **Run** in the Results group to run the query. Click **Yes** in response to the *You are about to append 4 row(s)* warning.

Nothing obvious happens after the query runs; you will open the appended table to determine whether the four records were added to it.

l. Open the Employees table. Sort the table in descending order (Newest to Oldest) by the HireDate field and make sure the four newest records were added.

The Employees table should now contain a total of 119 employees. Your own name should be one of the top four records.

m. Click the **Query1 tab**, and click **Save** on the Quick Access Toolbar. Save the query as **Append New Employees**. Close the open objects. Save the design of the Employees table.

The query icon in the Navigation Pane indicates the query is an append query.

Replacement China, Inc., wants to create a Former Employees table for all employees who are no longer with the company. The records of these former employees are currently stored in the Employees table. You will move them to a Former Employees table. Refer to Figure 6.19 as you complete Step 5.

Former Employees					City	State	PostalCode	Phone	HireDate	TermDate	TermReason
UserID	TitleID										
81013580	0628866	W		PER	RALEIGH	NC	27615-5313	9198463129	6/1/2004	1/2/2009	Ret
81040480	0626266	Fangmeier	Angie	108 LOCHBERR	RALEIGH	NC	27615-2815	3362991750	1/31/2009	2/3/2010	Vol
81094880	0649066	Cox	Tim	1012 TRADERS	SAN FRANCISC	CA	94116-3039	9195671893	1/31/2009	3/4/2010	Term
81095180	0648266	Bowman	Jeanette	1018 WENTWO	SALISBURY	NC	28146-8856	9198512318	4/16/2001	4/5/2007	Vol
81100280	063566	Seeber	Carol	104 LITTLE RIVE	ROCKY MOUNT	NC	27801-3052	9198512318	7/21/2009	5/6/2012	Ret
81102780	0660466	Gregory	Joni	1010 MEADOW	SCOTIA	NY	12302	9198469158	1/20/1995	6/7/2009	Vol
81105580	0626266	Mesimer	John	1102 KINDLEY C	RALEIGH	NC	27609-2800	9197839369	12/25/2011	2/2/2012	Term
81105880	069266	Rhynes	Judy	100 CIRCLEVIEV	STEAMBOAT SF	CO	80488-1895	9103926711	12/12/1999	8/9/2005	Ret
81110980	0626266	Aaron	Bev	1102 BRITTLEY	RALEIGH	NC	27609-3625	9198472095	12/12/1999	9/10/2006	Vol

Step j: Nine records added to the Former Employees table

FIGURE 6.19 Former Employees Table Created by Make Table Query

Access 2016, Windows 10, Microsoft Corporation

a. Click the **Create tab**. Click **Query Design** in the Queries group.

b. Double-click the **Employees table** to add it to the query. Close the Show Table dialog box.

Some of the employees listed in the Employees table no longer work for Replacement China, Inc. You need to retain this information but do not want these records included in the Employees table; the records will be stored in an archive table named Former Employees.

c. Double-click the **title bar** of the Employees table in the top pane of the Design view window to select all the fields. Drag the selected fields to the first field box in the design grid.

d. Type **Is Not Null** in the Criteria row of the TermDate field, and press **Enter**.

This criterion will select only those employees with a value in the termination date field.

e. Display the results in Datasheet view.

You should find that nine employees are no longer with the company. These are the employees you want to move to a new table using a make table query.

f. Click **View** to switch back to Design view.

g. Click **Make Table** in the Query Type group.

The Make Table dialog box opens and prompts you for the name and storage location information for the new table. You will archive the out-of-date data, but the new table can reside in the same database.

h. Type **Former Employees** in the Table Name box. Make sure the Current Database option is selected. Click **OK**.

i. Click **Run** in the Results group to run the query. Click **Yes** in response to the *You are about to paste 9 row(s) into a new table* warning.

j. Open the Former Employees table to verify the nine former employees are present, as shown in Figure 6.19. Close the table.

> **TROUBLESHOOTING:** If your table did not come out properly, delete the query and the newly created table. You can try this query again by beginning from Step 5a. Be sure to check that the correct criterion is entered to locate employees with termination dates.

k. Save Query1 as **Former Employees Make Table**.

The query icon in the Navigation Pane indicates the query is a make table query.

l. Close the query.

STEP 6 » CREATE A DELETE QUERY

You moved the former employees from the Employees table to the Former Employees table in the Replacement China, Inc., database. Now you will delete the former employees from the Employees table. It is not good database design practice to have the same records stored in two different tables. Refer to Figure 6.20 as you complete Step 6.

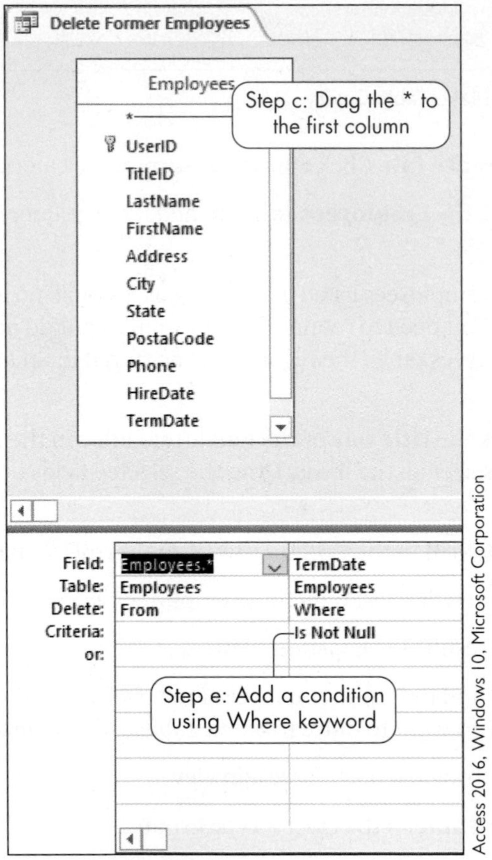

FIGURE 6.20 Delete Query to Remove Former Employees

a. Click the **Create tab**. Click **Query Design** in the Queries group.

b. Double-click the **Employees table** in the Show Table dialog box to add it to the query. Close the Show Table dialog box.

c. Drag the * from the Employees table field list to the first column of the query design grid.

The * field only takes up one column in the design grid. The * field represents all the fields in the Employees table. This is another shortcut for adding all of the fields to the query design grid in one step rather than one by one.

d. Drag the **TermDate field** from the Employees table to the second column of the query design grid.

When you use the * to add all of the fields to the query design grid simultaneously, you need to add the TermDate field separately in order to use it to set the criteria for the select query. The outcome of the query is no different than adding the fields to the query design grid in the conventional way.

e. Type **Is Not Null** in the Criteria row for the TermDate field. Click **View** to switch to Datasheet view.

You created a select query to make sure you have correctly identified the nine records for deletion prior to changing it to a delete query. Nine records are shown in Datasheet view.

f. Switch to Design view. Click **Delete** in the Query Type group.

The Delete row now contains *From* in the Employees.* column and *Where* in the TermDate column. This delete query will delete all records in the Employees table that have a termination date.

g. Click **Run** in the Results group. Click **Yes** in response to the *You are about to delete 9 row(s) from the specified table* warning.

You deleted the nine former employees from the Employees table.

h. Save the query as **Delete Former Employees**. Close the query.

i. Open the Employees table and verify that the number of total employees has been reduced from 119 to 110. Close the table.

j. Keep the database open if you plan to continue with the Hands-On Exercise. If not, close the database and exit Access.

Specialized Queries

Specialized queries exist in Access to help you to analyze and improve the integrity of the data in a database. Three specialized queries enable you to group and summarize data, find mismatched records, and locate duplicate records.

A crosstab query calculates data using a sum, average, or other function, and groups the results by two sets of values, one along the left side of the datasheet, and one across the top. For example, you can sum the revenues earned by each salesperson by month, quarter, or year.

A find unmatched query enables you to identify mismatched records. An unmatched record is a record in one table without a matching record in a related table. For example, you might want to locate customers who have no orders, or items for sale that have not been purchased with a find unmatched query.

A duplicate record is one where the same information is entered extraneously in a table, sometimes by data entry error, such as entering two customers with the same name or address. A find duplicates query will help you to locate those records so that you can make necessary corrections.

In this section, you will improve your effectiveness with a database by learning about three types of queries that are used for special conditions. You will create three specialized queries: a crosstab query to group and summarize data, a find unmatched query to find mismatched records, and a find duplicates query to locate duplicate records.

Summarizing Data with a Crosstab Query

STEP 1 ❯❯ You can present grouped and summarized data with a crosstab query. A ***crosstab query*** summarizes a data source (which can be a table or a query) into a grid of rows and columns (a datasheet). A crosstab query is usually created to show trends in values (e.g., sales) over time. For example, to evaluate the sales force at Replacement China, Inc., you can construct a crosstab query to examine the revenue generated by each salesperson over a specific period of time.

Group and Summarize Data

The grouping in a crosstab query comes from the definitions of row and column headings. A field selected as a ***row heading*** displays values from that field along the left side of a crosstab query datasheet. A ***column heading*** displays values from a selected field name along the top of a crosstab query. The summarizing or aggregating data in a crosstab query are displayed at the intersection of the rows and columns. The values that are displayed depend on which aggregate function you choose when you create the crosstab query—sum, average, and count are common examples. If you want to display the quarterly revenue for each salesperson for the current year, use the salespersons' names as the row headings, order dates as the column headings, and the total quarterly sales in dollars as the intersecting values. When you assign a date field to the column heading, Access gives you an option for summarizing by year, quarter, month, or date; in this case, you will summarize the Replacement China, Inc., data by quarter. You can also create additional levels of grouping by adding extra rows to the crosstab query.

Use the Crosstab Query Wizard

You will generally use the Crosstab Query Wizard to build a crosstab query, although you can build one from scratch using the query design grid. As with any query wizard, you first identify the source of the data that will be the basis of the crosstab query. Unlike other queries, you can only reference one object (table or query) as the data source in a crosstab query. Therefore, if you want to use fields stored in different tables, you must first combine the required data in a query. Once the data are combined in a single source, you can create the crosstab query.

To create a crosstab query, complete the following steps:

1. Click the Query Wizard in the Queries group on the Create tab.
2. Click Crosstab Query Wizard in the New Query dialog box.
3. Click OK, as shown in Figure 6.21.
4. Identify the data source, and click Next. You can display tables, queries, or both tables and queries by selecting the appropriate view option button (see Figure 6.22).
5. Identify up to three row heading fields in the next step of the wizard, as shown in Figure 6.23. To make a selection, double-click the field name, or click the field name, and click Add One Field $>$. Click Next. Access limits the number of row heading fields to three.
6. Select the field for the column headings, as shown in Figure 6.24. You can specify one field for column headings.
7. Click Next. If the field contains date data, this step will prompt you for the date interval (see Figure 6.25). Click Next. In this example, the sales data for each salesperson will be summarized by quarter.
8. Select the field to use in a calculation at the intersection of each row and column; then select which aggregate function to apply, such as Avg, Count, or Sum. You can have as many aggregate fields as you want, but more than two or three makes the crosstab query difficult to read. Click Next. Figure 6.26 shows the result of selecting the Revenue field and the Sum function.
9. Name the query and click an option to determine how you want to view the new query (see Figure 6.27).

Figure 6.28 shows the results of a crosstab query with the total quarterly sales for each salesperson. The Total of Revenue column displays totals for each salesperson for the entire year. To format the results as currency, you would need to modify the Format property of the Revenue field in Design view.

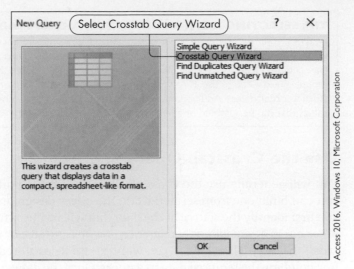

FIGURE 6.21 Open the Crosstab Query Wizard

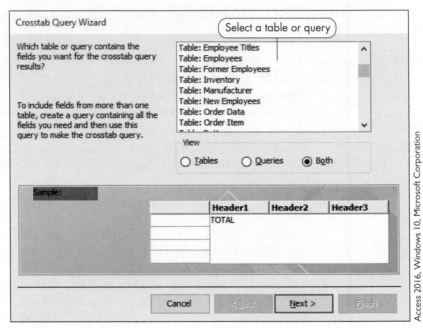

FIGURE 6.22 Select the Data Source

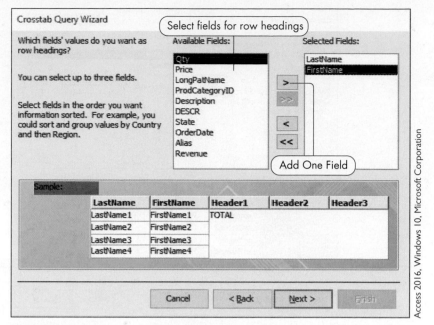

FIGURE 6.23 Select the Row Headings

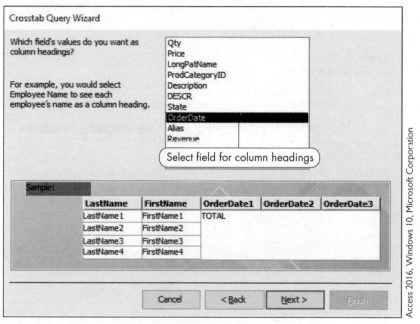

FIGURE 6.24 Select the Column Headings

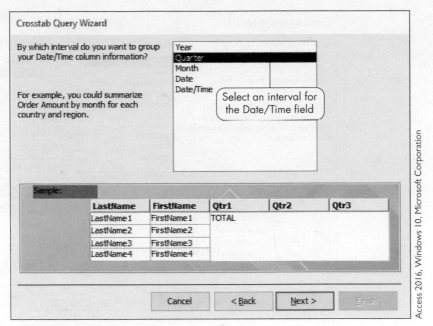

FIGURE 6.25 Specify the Date/Time Interval

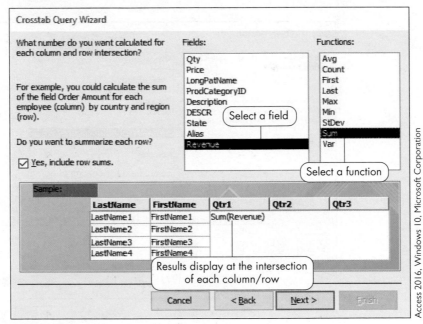

FIGURE 6.26 Select the Value to be Summarized

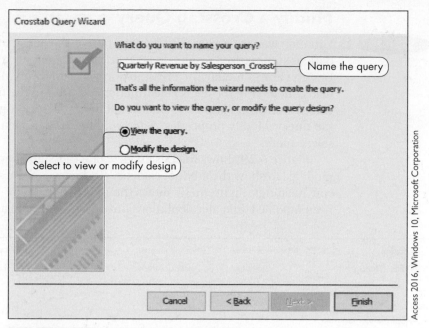

FIGURE 6.27 Name the Crosstab Query

LastName	FirstName	Total Of Rev	Qtr 2	Qtr 3
Abdel-Hameed W	ROBERT	19.995	19.995	
Ada...	...e	244.9	244.9	
Adams	Teresa	5...		...7
Albee	Sue	14...	...	...7
Allen	Sandra	398.855	351.865	46.99
Alphin	Rich	...	309.72	81.96
Alphin	Rick	...	311.92	27.495
Austin	JOY	1397.435	1397.435	
Austin	Judy	1299.215	844.35	454.865
Bailey	Jeanette	383.05	174.925	208.125
Bantel	Dick	26.995		26.995
Behnke	Zack	787.21	384.53	402.68
Behrend	Wynn	256.32	256.32	
Bolick	Violet	908.36	547.535	360.825
Bourbeau	Trevor	0	0	
Bremer	Tim	174.75	174.75	
Chesson	Susan	2956.375	2498.02	458.355
Chut Jr.	Susan	2104.9	451.185	1653.715
Cowan	Sherol	62.735		62.735
Dietz	Sally	37.975	37.975	
Dunn	Rudy	76.48	76.48	
Eichler	Ron	1337.635	225.17	1112.465
Eklund	Ron	589.535	392.67	196.865
Faggart	Robert	43.22	43.22	
Fairbanks	Rob	26.995	26.995	
Ferguson	Richard	207.34	150.275	57.065
Frantz	Rev. Charlie	117.43	108.44	8.99

Record: ◄ ◄ 1 of 93 ► ►I ► 🔾 No Filter Search

FIGURE 6.28 Crosstab Query Results in Datasheet View

Modify a Crosstab Query

 >> You may want to change the organization of the query to display different categories of data or summarized results. Instead of creating a new crosstab query, you can switch to Design view to modify the crosstab query design by changing row and column heading fields, modifying the aggregate function, or altering the field selection for the aggregate calculation. You also can include additional row heading (grouping) fields in the crosstab query. Modify properties, fields, and field order for a crosstab as you would in any select query.

Figure 6.29 shows the Design view of a crosstab query. The crosstab query has been modified to show the product category IDs instead of the salesperson's names as the first row headings. Figure 6.30 shows the Datasheet view of the crosstab query once it has been modified, and all calculations have been formatted as currency.

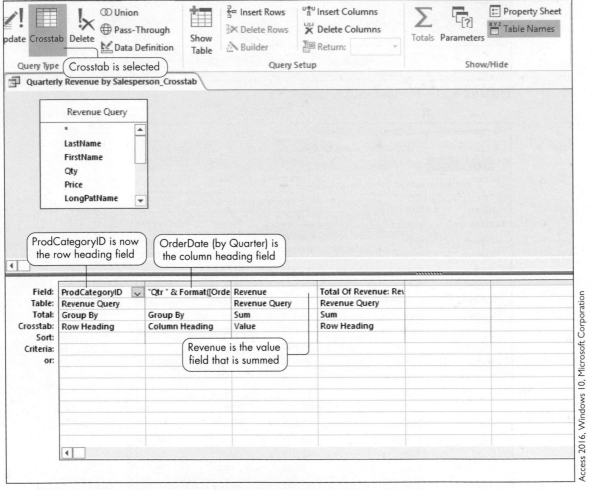

FIGURE 6.29 Crosstab Query in Design View

ProdCategor ▾	Total Of Revenue ▾	Qtr 2 ▾	Qtr 3 ▾
1	$31,114.33	$18,198.41	$12,915.93
2	$26,744.52	$14,471.53	$12,272.99
3	$15,026.88	$7,878.41	$7,148.46

FIGURE 6.30 Modified Crosstab Query Results in Datasheet View

Finding Duplicate Records with a Query

If two records with the same name and address exist in a table, it may indicate a duplicate entry. You might expect Access to restrict a user from entering more than one record into a table with the same name and address; however, because many tables use unique (primary key) values as the ID number for each record, as long as each ID (primary key value) is different, a user might be able to enter one, two, three, or more records with the same name and address (for example, two or more entries for the same customer). Access can create a query to display records that are potential duplicates, such as duplicated customer or order information.

Sometimes data is entered more than one time by mistake. However, not all duplicated data in a database are the result of errors. For example, if the CustomerID field is the unique identifier (primary key) in a Customer table, no two customers can have the same ID number. However, the same CustomerID field also exists as a foreign key field in the adjoining Orders table. Because of the one-to-many relationship between the Customer table and the Orders table, the CustomerID can repeat in the Orders table; thus one customer can place many orders. Repeating data values in a foreign key on the many side of a one-to-many relationship is standard database design—duplication is expected.

Additionally, some data values repeat naturally in a table. The city field will contain many records with duplicating values. The LastName field may contain records with the same name, such as Smith, Lee, or Rodriguez. Duplicated data values such as these are not errors, and duplicated data values are not always problematic; however, there may be occasions when you will need to find and manage unwanted duplicates.

Create a Find Duplicates Query Using the Wizard

STEP 3 ▶▶ You can use a *find duplicates query* to help identify duplicate values in a table. For example, if you inherit a poorly designed table (or import a spreadsheet into your database), with duplicate values in the field you propose to use as the primary key field, you might not be able to set a primary key. Once you identify the problem records, you can modify or delete them, and then set the primary key. Once the primary key is assigned, you can create appropriate relationships in the database, and enforce referential integrity between tables. Finding duplicate values and knowing what to do with them remains one of the challenges of good database design.

> **To create a find duplicates query, complete the following steps:**
>
> 1. Click the Query Wizard in the Queries group on the Create tab.
> 2. Select Find Duplicates Query Wizard in the New Query dialog box, and click OK.
> 3. Select the table or query that contains the data source for the query, such as Customer, and click Next (see Figure 6.31).
> 4. Identify the field or fields that might contain duplicate information, such as LastName and FirstName, as shown in Figure 6.32. Click Next.
> 5. Select additional fields you want to display in the query results, as shown in Figure 6.33. Click Next.
> 6. Name the query and select the option to determine how you want to view it initially (see Figure 6.34). Click Finish. The results are shown in Figure 6.35. The first two records for Susan Agner have the same address; therefore, one of them should probably be removed.

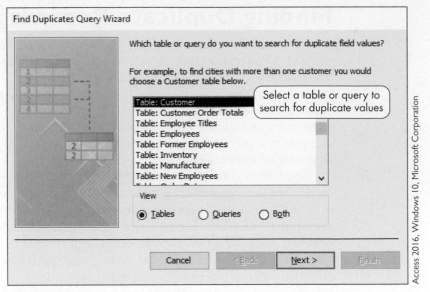

FIGURE 6.31 Find Duplicates Query: Select a Table or Query to Search for Duplicates

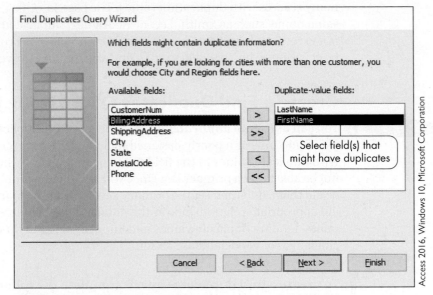

FIGURE 6.32 Find Duplicates Query: Select Fields to Display

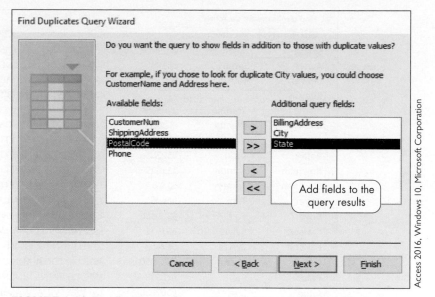

FIGURE 6.33 Find Duplicates Query: Select Additional Fields to Display

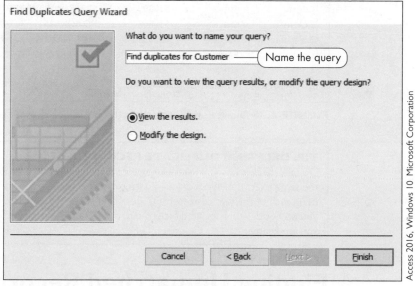

FIGURE 6.34 Name the Find Duplicates Query

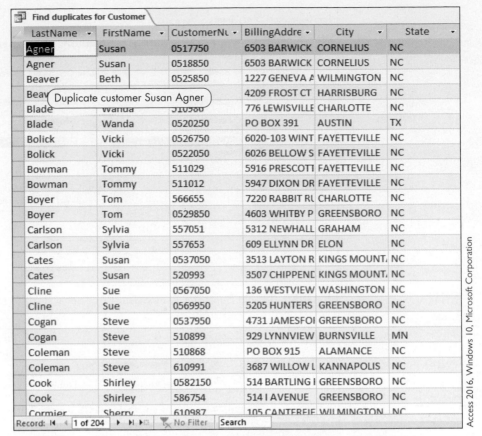

LastName ▾	FirstName ▾	CustomerNι ▾	BillingAddre ▾	City ▾	State ▾
Agner	Susan	0517750	6503 BARWICK	CORNELIUS	NC
Agner	Susan	0518850	6503 BARWICK	CORNELIUS	NC
Beaver	Beth	0525850	1227 GENEVA A	WILMINGTON	NC
Beav			4209 FROST CT	HARRISBURG	NC
Blade	Wanda	510980	776 LEWISVILLE	CHARLOTTE	NC
Blade	Wanda	0520250	PO BOX 391	AUSTIN	TX
Bolick	Vicki	0526750	6020-103 WINT	FAYETTEVILLE	NC
Bolick	Vicki	0522050	6026 BELLOW S	FAYETTEVILLE	NC
Bowman	Tommy	511029	5916 PRESCOTT	FAYETTEVILLE	NC
Bowman	Tommy	511012	5947 DIXON DR	FAYETTEVILLE	NC
Boyer	Tom	566655	7220 RABBIT RU	CHARLOTTE	NC
Boyer	Tom	0529850	4603 WHITBY P	GREENSBORO	NC
Carlson	Sylvia	557051	5312 NEWHALL	GRAHAM	NC
Carlson	Sylvia	557653	609 ELLYNN DR	ELON	NC
Cates	Susan	0537050	3513 LAYTON R	KINGS MOUNT.	NC
Cates	Susan	520993	3507 CHIPPEND	KINGS MOUNT.	NC
Cline	Sue	0567050	136 WESTVIEW	WASHINGTON	NC
Cline	Sue	0569950	5205 HUNTERS	GREENSBORO	NC
Cogan	Steve	0537950	4731 JAMESFOI	GREENSBORO	NC
Cogan	Steve	510899	929 LYNNVIEW	BURNSVILLE	MN
Coleman	Steve	510868	PO BOX 915	ALAMANCE	NC
Coleman	Steve	610991	3687 WILLOW L	KANNAPOLIS	NC
Cook	Shirley	0582150	514 BARTLING I	GREENSBORO	NC
Cook	Shirley	586754	514 I AVENUE	GREENSBORO	NC
Cormier	Sherry	610987	105 CANTERFIE	WILMINGTON	NC

Duplicate customer Susan Agner

Record: I◀ ◀ 1 of 204 ▶ ▶I ▶⊞ 🏷No Filter Search

Access 2016, Windows 10, Microsoft Corporation

FIGURE 6.35 Duplicated Customers in the Find Duplicates Query Results

---

TIP: DELETING DUPLICATE RECORDS

Double-check yourself when deleting duplicate records. For example, if two customers in a table have the same exact details but unique ID (primary key) values, records (such as orders) may be stored using each of the two customer IDs. Be sure that when you delete the duplicated customer record, you do not delete associated orders in a related table. Associate the orders with the customer ID that you are keeping.

Finding Unmatched Records with a Query

A *find unmatched query* compares records in two related tables and displays the records found in one table but not the other. In a student database, an instructor might want to find students with missing assignment grades. The find unmatched query would require two tables (Students and Grades) with a common field (StudentID) where one of the tables is missing information (Grades). The find unmatched query could become the source for a Missing Assignments Report.

Create a Find Unmatched Query Using the Wizard

STEP 4 ▶▶ It is possible for Replacement China, Inc., to run reports that show which customers did not place an order in the past week, or in the previous month, or in the past 12 months, or ever. No matter how you decide to handle this group of customers, it could be useful to know how many customers who receive your catalog have never placed an order.

In the Replacement China, Inc., database, management may want to know which items in their inventory are obsolete: items that the company stocks that have never been sold. You can create a find unmatched query to identify these obsolete items.

To create an unmatched query, complete the following steps:

1. Click the Query Wizard in the Queries group on the Create tab.
2. Select the Find Unmatched Query Wizard in the New Query dialog box, and click OK.
3. Select the table that will serve as the primary table source for this query (see Figure 6.36). Click Next. The first table is the one with the records you want to see in the results—for example, the one listing the inventory items that have never sold.
4. Select the second table that contains the related records—for example, the table that can show whether or not an inventory item was sold (see Figure 6.37). Click Next.
5. Click the appropriate field in each field list. Click Matching Fields to determine the matching field that will be used. Click Next. The find unmatched query only works if the two tables share a common field. Usually, the two tables are related to each other in a relationship. Access automatically recognizes the common field (see Figure 6.38).
6. Identify which fields to display in the query output. Use Add One Field $\boxed{>}$ to move the fields you want from the Available fields box to the Selected fields list, as shown in Figure 6.39. Click Next. In this case, three fields have been selected for the query.
7. Name the query (see Figure 6.40), and click Finish to view the results. Figure 6.41 displays the query results.

The results will show which items in the inventory have no sales. These items can be returned to the manufacturer, discounted in order to sell them, or used as a write-off.

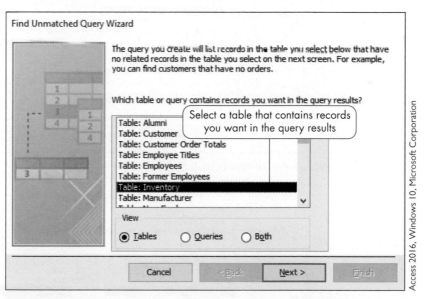

FIGURE 6.36 Find Unmatched Query Wizard: Select a Primary Table

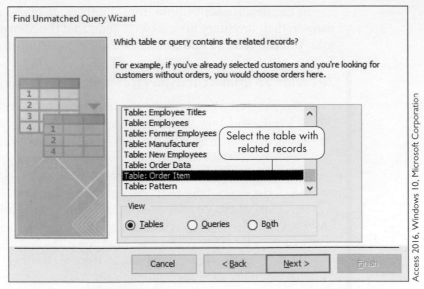

FIGURE 6.37 Find Unmatched Query Wizard: Select a Related Table

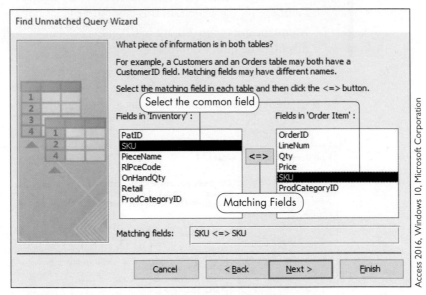

FIGURE 6.38 Find Unmatched Query Wizard: Identify the Common Field

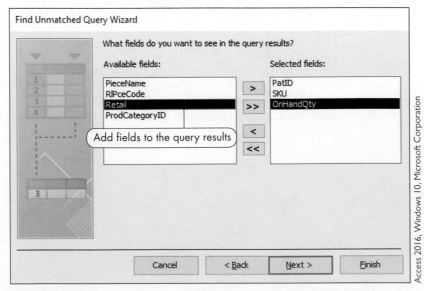

FIGURE 6.39 Find Unmatched Query Wizard: Select the Output Fields

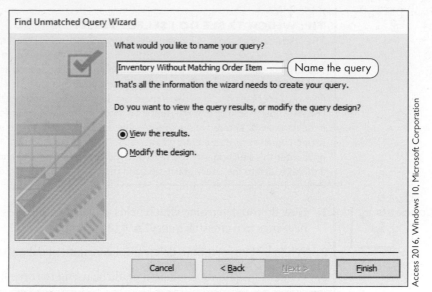

FIGURE 6.40 Find Unmatched Query Wizard: Name the Query

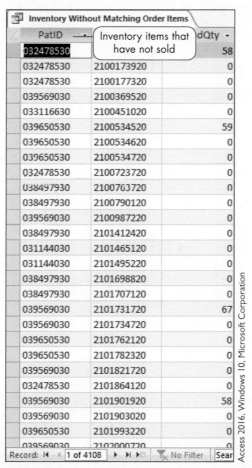

FIGURE 6.41 Find Unmatched Query Wizard: Results Displaying Obsolete Inventory

Quick Concepts

1. How do you determine which fields are good candidates for the row and column headings in a crosstab query? *p. 412*

2. When is it important to delete duplicate data in a database? *p. 419*

3. What is one situation where it could be useful to run a find unmatched query? *p. 422*

Hands-On Exercises

Watch the Video
for this Hands-On
Exercise!

MyITLab®
HOE2 Training

Skills covered: Use the
Crosstab Query Wizard • Modify
a Crosstab Query • Create a Find
Duplicate Records Query Using the
Wizard • Create a Find Unmatched
Query Using the Wizard

2 Specialized Queries

Replacement China, Inc., management has asked you to review their database and make a few
improvements. You create a crosstab query that summarizes their revenue by state to help them analyze
sales history. You also check tables for unmatched data and duplicate data using the built-in query tools.

STEP 1 ▶▶ **USE THE CROSSTAB QUERY WIZARD**

You want to analyze the revenue generated by each salesperson at Replacement China, Inc. You decide to group and analyze the
results by salesperson and by state. This type of summary can be accomplished using a crosstab query. Refer to Figure 6.42 as you
complete Step 1.

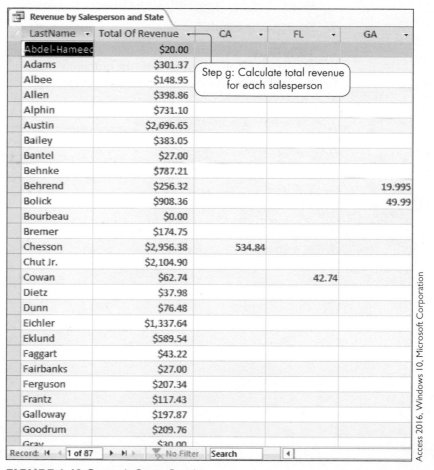

FIGURE 6.42 Crosstab Query Results

a. Open *a06h1Replace_LastFirst* if you closed it at the end of Hands-On Exercise 1, and save
   it as **a06h2Replace_LastFirst**, changing h1 to h2.

b. Click the **Create tab**. Click **Query Wizard** in the Queries group.

c. Click **Crosstab Query Wizard**. Click **OK**.

   The Crosstab Query Wizard opens.

d. Click **Queries** in the View section of the Crosstab Query Wizard dialog box. With *Query: Revenue Query* selected, click **Next**.

You selected the Revenue query as the data source that contains order data by salesperson and state. However, the data are not summarized the way you need it, so you will organize it using the crosstab query.

e. Double-click the **LastName field** in the Available Fields box to move it to the Selected Fields list. Click **Next**.

You selected the LastName field as the row headings. The query will summarize the data for each salesperson by last name.

f. Click the **State field** to select it as the column headings. Click **Next**.

The states will be listed across the top of the datasheet as column headings.

g. Click the **Revenue field** in the list to select it as the summarizing field. Click **Sum** in the Functions list to specify which aggregate function to perform. Click **Next**.

You directed the crosstab query to display the sum of revenue for each salesperson by state.

h. Change the query name to **Revenue by Salesperson and State**. Ensure that the *View the query* option is selected. Click **Finish**.

i. Examine the results.

The data show the sum of revenue for each salesperson in each state. However, the results are cumbersome to view; the numerous columns make the query difficult to read. You will modify the crosstab query in the next step.

The sales reps at Replacement China, Inc., asked you to change the column heading field from State to ProdCategoryID. This will help the sales reps identify the sales for each product category and also reduce the number of columns in the crosstab query. Refer to Figure 6.43 as you complete Step 2.

Step b: Sales by product category

LastName	Total Of Revenue	1	2	3
Abdel-Hameed	$20.00			19.995
Adams	$301.37	24.995	276.375	
Albee	$148.95	57.97	74.985	15.995
Allen	$398.86	16.995	97.48	284.38
Alphin	$731.10	230.915	316.385	183.795
Austin	$2,696.65	1257.525	742.005	697.12
Bailey	$383.05	0	174.925	208.125
Bantel	$27.00			26.995
Behnke	$787.21	200.18	491.515	95.515
Behrend	$256.32	126.35	46.99	82.98
Bolick	$908.36	515.845	184.555	207.96
Bourbeau	$0.00	0		
Bremer	$174.75	7.99	79.31	87.45
Chesson	$2,956.38	1399.245	963.945	593.185
Chut Jr.	$2,104.90	833.875	854.125	416.9
Cowan	$62.74	42.74	19.995	
Dietz	$37.98		37.975	
Dunn	$76.48	76.48		
Eichler	$1,337.64	719.055	505.82	112.76
Eklund	$589.54	121.915	74.95	392.67
Faggart	$43.22	9.995	33.225	
Fairbanks	$27.00	26.995		
Ferguson	$207.34	23.085	107.955	76.3
Frantz	$117.43	84.94		32.49
Galloway	$197.87	7.995	127.9	61.97
Goodrum	$209.76	71.975	88.29	49.49
Gray	$30.00			29.995

Record: I◄ ◄ 1 of 87 ► ►I ► No Filter   Search

FIGURE 6.43 Modified Crosstab Query Results

a. Switch to Design view.

b. Click the arrow in the Field row of the State column in the query design grid and select **ProdCategoryID**.

The columns now show the product category IDs rather than the state names, reducing the number of columns.

c. Click in the **Total of Revenue field**, open the Property Sheet, and then change the Format field property to **Currency**. Close the Property Sheet.

d. Click **Run** in the Results group to see the new results. Double-click the right border of the Total of Revenue column so the entire column displays.

e. Save the changes and close the query.

STEP 3 >> CREATE A FIND DUPLICATE RECORDS QUERY USING THE WIZARD

One of the data entry employees believes that duplicate entries may exist in the Pattern table. You create a query to find duplicates in the LongPatName field in the Pattern table. If duplicates do exist, the company will need to move all existing orders to one pattern and then delete the other pattern. Refer to Figure 6.44 as you complete Step 3.

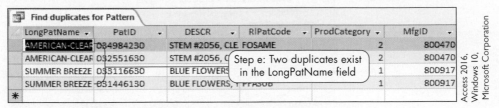

FIGURE 6.44 Results of the Find Duplicate Records Query

a. Click the **Create tab**. Click **Query Wizard** in the Queries group, and then select **Find Duplicates Query Wizard** to create a find duplicates query. Click **OK**.

b. Scroll down and click **Table: Pattern**. Click **Next**.

c. Double-click the **LongPatName** in the Available fields list to move it to the Duplicate-value fields box. Click **Next**.

d. Click Add All Fields >> to move the rest of the fields in the table from the Available fields box to the Additional query fields box. Click **Next**.

e. Click **Finish** to accept the default name, *Find duplicates for Pattern*, and the option to view the results.

   The query runs and opens in Datasheet view. It contains four records showing two duplicate LongPatName fields. Going forward, the company will need to make some changes to the database to correct this issue.

f. Save the query. Close the query.

The marketing manager at Replacement China, Inc., asked you to identify the customers who have records in the Customer table, but have not placed orders to date. You create a find unmatched query to find the customers who have no records in the Order Data table. The Marketing Department will contact these customers and offer them an incentive to place an order. Otherwise, it may no longer want to send catalogs to the inactive customers. Refer to Figure 6.45 as you complete Step 4.

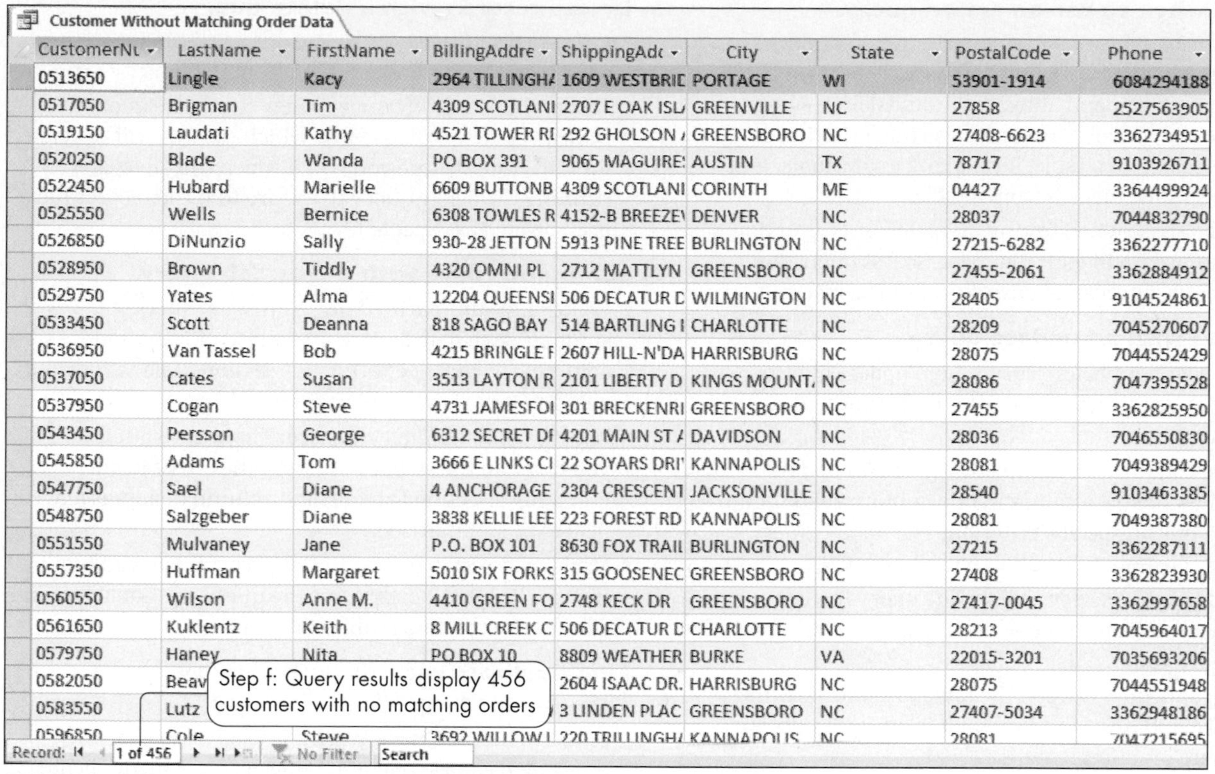

CustomerNu ▾	LastName ▾	FirstName ▾	BillingAddre ▾	ShippingAdc ▾	City ▾	State ▾	PostalCode ▾	Phone ▾
0513650	Lingle	Kacy	2964 TILLINGHA	1609 WESTBRIC	PORTAGE	WI	53901-1914	6084294188
0517050	Brigman	Tim	4309 SCOTLANI	2707 E OAK ISL	GREENVILLE	NC	27858	2527563905
0519150	Laudati	Kathy	4521 TOWER RI	292 GHOLSON /	GREENSBORO	NC	27408-6623	3362734951
0520250	Blade	Wanda	PO BOX 391	9065 MAGUIRE!	AUSTIN	TX	78717	9103926711
0522450	Hubard	Marielle	6609 BUTTONB	4309 SCOTLANI	CORINTH	ME	04427	3364499924
0525550	Wells	Bernice	6308 TOWLES R	4152-B BREEZE\	DENVER	NC	28037	7044832790
0526850	DiNunzio	Sally	930-28 JETTON	5913 PINE TREE	BURLINGTON	NC	27215-6282	3362277710
0528950	Brown	Tiddly	4320 OMNI PL	2712 MATTLYN	GREENSBORO	NC	27455-2061	3362884912
0529750	Yates	Alma	12204 QUEENSI	506 DECATUR C	WILMINGTON	NC	28405	9104524861
0533450	Scott	Deanna	818 SAGO BAY	514 BARTLING I	CHARLOTTE	NC	28209	7045270607
0536950	Van Tassel	Bob	4215 BRINGLE F	2607 HILL-N'DA	HARRISBURG	NC	28075	7044552429
0537050	Cates	Susan	3513 LAYTON R	2101 LIBERTY D	KINGS MOUNT.	NC	28086	7047395528
0537950	Cogan	Steve	4731 JAMESFOI	301 BRECKENRI	GREENSBORO	NC	27455	3362825950
0543450	Persson	George	6312 SECRET DI	4201 MAIN ST /	DAVIDSON	NC	28036	7046550830
0545850	Adams	Tom	3666 E LINKS CI	22 SOYARS DRI'	KANNAPOLIS	NC	28081	7049389429
0547750	Sael	Diane	4 ANCHORAGE	2304 CRESCENT	JACKSONVILLE	NC	28540	9103463385
0548750	Salzgeber	Diane	3838 KELLIE LEE	223 FOREST RD	KANNAPOLIS	NC	28081	7049387380
0551550	Mulvaney	Jane	P.O. BOX 101	8630 FOX TRAIL	BURLINGTON	NC	27215	3362287111
0557350	Huffman	Margaret	5010 SIX FORKS	315 GOOSENEC	GREENSBORO	NC	27408	3362823930
0560550	Wilson	Anne M.	4410 GREEN FO	2748 KECK DR	GREENSBORO	NC	27417-0045	3362997658
0561650	Kuklentz	Keith	8 MILL CREEK C	506 DECATUR C	CHARLOTTE	NC	28213	7045964017
0579750	Haney	Nita	PO BOX 10	8809 WEATHER	BURKE	VA	22015-3201	7035693206
0582050	Beav		2604 ISAAC DR.	HARRISBURG		NC	28075	7044551948
0583550	Lutz		3 LINDEN PLAC	GREENSBORO		NC	27407-5034	3362948186
0596850	Cole	Steve	3692 WILLOW L	220 TRILLINGH/	KANNAPOLIS	NC	28081	7047215695

Step f: Query results display 456 customers with no matching orders

Record: I◄ ◄ 1 of 456 ► ►I ►⊞ No Filter Search

FIGURE 6.45 Customers Who Have No Orders

a. Click the **Create tab**. Click **Query Wizard** in the Queries group. Click **Find Unmatched Query Wizard** in the New Query dialog box, and click **OK**.

Your goal in creating a find unmatched query is to find the customers who have not placed an order.

b. Ensure that Table: Customer is selected, and click **Next**.

You selected the Customer table as the first table, as you are trying to find customers who have not ordered.

c. Click **Table: Order Data**, and click **Next**.

You selected the Order Data table as the second table so you can find customers who have no orders listed in this table.

d. Click **Next** at the next screen.

Access identifies the common field (CustomerNum) that exists in both tables.

e. Click Add All Fields ⟩⟩ to add all of the fields to the query results. Click **Next**.

f. Click **Finish** to accept the default name and the option to view the results.

456 customers in the Customer table have not placed an order. This is a great opportunity to reach out to them to determine whether they would consider placing an order; alternatively, they may be eliminated from the company's catalog mailing list.

g. Save the query. Close the query.

h. Close the database and exit Access. Based on your instructor's directions, submit a06h2Replace_LastFirst.

Access 2016, Windows 10, Microsoft Corporation

Chapter Objectives Review

After reading this chapter, you have accomplished the following objectives:

I. Determine when to use an action query.

- Recognize the benefits of action queries: Action queries edit, add, or delete the data in a database. These four queries—update, append, make table, and delete—are used for updating records that meet certain criteria, for appending records to a table, for making a new table, and for deleting specific records from a table.
- Back up a database when testing an action query: Action queries change data in your database, so it is important to back up your database in case it needs to be restored.

2. Update data with an update query.

- Create a select query before running an update query: Use a select query to define the fields and criteria to be used in your update query.
- Convert a select query to an update query: An update query changes the data values in one or more fields for all records that meet a specific criterion. The update query defines precisely how field values will be updated.
- Test an update query: View the update query in Datasheet view to determine which records will be affected before you run it.
- Verify an update query: Open the table to determine the results of the updates. Verifying update query results is a good database practice.

3. Add records to a table with an append query.

- Create a select query before running an append query: Create a select query to define the fields and criteria to be used in an append query.
- Set Append To fields in an append query: An append query selects records from one or more tables and adds them to another table. The append query will define precisely how fields and records will be appended.
- Run an append query: If you need to verify the records to be appended, you can preview them in Datasheet view before you run the query. Open the appended table to ensure that the records have been added appropriately.

4. Create a table with a make table query.

- Create a make table query: A make table query selects records from one or more tables and uses them to create a new table.
- Test and run a make table query: View the make table query in Datasheet view to determine which records will be added to the new table before you run it. Open the new table to ensure that the records have been added appropriately.

5. Delete records with a delete query.

- Create a delete query: A delete query selects records from a table and then removes them from the table.
- Test and run a delete query: View the delete query in Datasheet view to determine which records will be deleted from the table before you run it. Open the table after running the delete query to ensure that the records have been deleted as expected.

6. Summarize data with a crosstab query.

- Group and summarize data: A crosstab query summarizes a data source into a grid of rows and columns (a datasheet); the intersection of each row and column displays valuable aggregate data.
- Use the Crosstab Query Wizard: The wizard guides you through the steps of creating the crosstab query, including selecting the row and column headings and the field to be summarized.
- Modify a crosstab query: In Design view, you can modify the row/column headings of the query, format fields, and summarize the data in different ways.

7. Find duplicate records with a query.

- Create a find duplicates query using the wizard: The Find Duplicates Query Wizard is used to help identify duplicated values in a table. However, not all duplicated data in a database are the result of an error. The wizard guides you through the steps of creating the query, including identifying which fields to search for duplicated data.

8. Find unmatched records with a query.

- Create a find unmatched query using the wizard: The Find Unmatched Query Wizard creates a query that compares records in two related tables and returns the records found in one table but not the other. The wizard guides you through the steps of creating the query, including identifying which fields to search for unmatched data.

Key Terms Matching

Match the key terms with their definitions. Write the key term letter by the appropriate numbered definition.

a. Action query

b. Append query

c. Column heading

d. Crosstab query

e. Delete query

f. Find duplicates query

g. Find unmatched query

h. Make table query

i. Row heading

j. Update query

1. _____ A query that compares records in two related tables, and then displays the records found in one table but not the other. **p. 422**

2. _____ A query that selects records from one or more tables (the source) and adds them to an existing table (the destination). **p. 397**

3. _____ A query that selects records from one or more tables and uses them to create a new table. **p. 400**

4. _____ A query that summarizes a data source into a few key rows and columns; the intersection of each row and column displays aggregate data. **p. 412**

5. _____ A query that selects records from a table and then removes them from the table. **p. 401**

6. _____ The field name used to display values along the left side of a crosstab query. **p. 412**

7. _____ The field name used to display values at the top of a crosstab query. **p. 412**

8. _____ A query that adds, updates, or deletes data in a database. **p. 392**

9. _____ A query that helps you identify repeated values in a table. **p. 419**

10. _____ A query that changes the data values in one or more fields for all records that meet specific criteria. **p. 393**

Multiple Choice

1. Which one of the following tasks *cannot* be completed with an action query?

   (a) Deleting records from a table

   (b) Updating records in a table

   (c) Finding duplicate values in a table

   (d) Creating a new table based on a group of selected records

2. Which statement is *true* about update queries?

   (a) Only database administrators can run update queries.

   (b) You can run an update query one time only.

   (c) You can only use an update query to change numeric values in a table.

   (d) Update queries should be executed with caution because you cannot undo their changes.

3. Which type of query would you run as a method of previewing the results of the other three?

   (a) Select query

   (b) Update query

   (c) Delete query

   (d) Append query

4. In a large products table that you have acquired from an external source, you find that there are repeating product IDs. You need to set ProductID as the primary key field in this table. What is the best way to resolve this problem?

   (a) Delete the duplicate product IDs manually.

   (b) Create a delete query to delete the repeating values.

   (c) Leave the table as is because there are already orders related to the duplicate product IDs.

   (d) Use a find duplicates query to locate duplicate product IDs. Delete the duplicates and associate all orders for that product to the remaining product ID.

5. Why is it important to monitor how many times an update query is executed?

   (a) Update queries are capable of changing values (such as prices) more than one time.

   (b) Update queries can be used to delete records from your tables.

   (c) It is not important; you can always undo the results of an update query.

   (d) An update query can erase your table and create a new one in its place.

6. When is it generally useful to run a delete query?

   (a) A delete query is usually run after an update query.

   (b) A delete query is usually run before an update query.

   (c) A delete query is usually run after an append or make table query.

   (d) A delete query should only be run when you need to delete data permanently from a database.

7. Why would you use an append query?

   (a) Because users need to be able to select records based on varied selection criteria

   (b) To determine which records may need to be deleted from the database

   (c) To summarize the data in a firm's database to help managers evaluate their financial position

   (d) To copy records from one table to another based on criteria that you specify

8. What is the easiest way to create a crosstab query?

   (a) Click Crosstab Query on the Create tab.

   (b) Use the Crosstab Query Wizard.

   (c) Create a grouping query in Design view and use that as a basis for the crosstab.

   (d) Create a select query and convert it to a crosstab query in Design view.

9. What is an unmatched record?

   (a) A record that contains the primary key in the one table

   (b) A record that requires deletion when running a delete query

   (c) A duplicated record that cannot be connected to a parent record

   (d) A record in one table without a related record in another table

10. What is the best way to find students who have not handed in a certain assignment?

    (a) Create a select query for assignments and compare the results with the student roster.

    (b) Create a select query of assignments and examine the results for missing dates.

    (c) Create a select query of assignments for the students in the class, and examine the results for missing student names for each assignment.

    (d) Create a find unmatched query using the student and assignment tables.

Practice Exercises

1 National Bank

You are the DBA for a national bank, working on a project to restructure the loans program. The bank has decided to increase mortgage loan rates by a half percent. You will use an update query to modify the mortgage rates. In addition, you will move all mortgage loans from the original loans table to a new mortgages table, and then delete the mortgages from the loans table. You will also create a query to determine which customers have multiple car or personal loans with the bank. Finally, you decide to summarize the payments made so that you can analyze the payments for car and personal loans by quarter. Refer to Figures 6.46 and 6.47 as you complete this exercise.

Access 2016, Windows 10, Microsoft Corporation

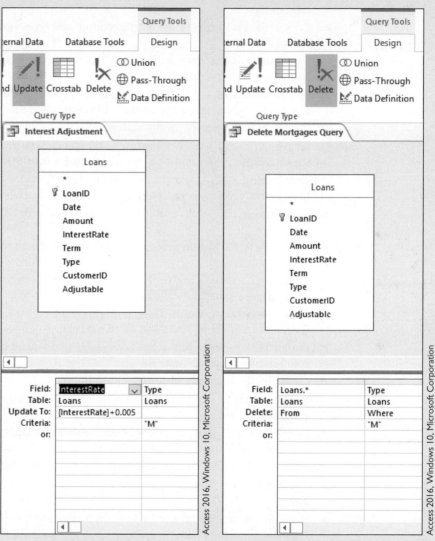

FIGURE 6.46 Update Query to Increase Mortgage Rates by 0.50 Percent

Access 2016, Windows 10, Microsoft Corporation

FIGURE 6.47 Query to Delete Mortgages from Loans Table

a. Open *a06p1Bank* and save it as **a06p1Bank_LastFirst**. Click **Save As** on the File tab, and double-click **Back Up Database**. Click **Save** to accept the default file name for the backup copy of the a06p1Bank_LastFirst_*CurrentDate* database.

b. Click **Query Design** in the Queries group on the Create tab. Double-click the **Loans table** in the Show Table dialog box to add it to the query. Close the Show Table dialog box.

c. Double-click the **LoanID**, **InterestRate**, and **Type fields**. Click **Run** in the Results group. Save the query as **Interest Adjustment**.

d. Switch to Design view. Type **"M"** in the **Criteria row** of the Type column.

   Entering *"M"* in the Criteria row of the Type column will filter out only those loans that are mortgages.

e. Click in the **Field row** of the fourth column, and type **NewRate: [InterestRate] + 0.0050**. Press **Enter**.

   You have created a new calculated field to determine the new proposed interest rate, which will increase by 0.50 percent.

f. Ensure the calculated field column is selected, and click **Property Sheet** in the Show/Hide group. Change the Format property to **Percent**. Close the Property Sheet.

g. Click **Run** in the Results group, and examine the results of the NewRate calculated field.

h. Switch to Design view. Click **Update** in the Query Type group. Click in the **Update To row** of the InterestRate field, and type **[InterestRate] + 0.0050**.

   The update query changes the existing interest rates to the higher interest rates that you calculated in the NewRate field. Compare your query design with Figure 6.46.

i. Click **View** in the Results group to verify that 12 records will be updated. Switch back to Design view.

j. Click **Run** in the Results group. Click **Yes** in response to the Warning box. Save and close the query.

k. Open the Loans table, and verify the Mortgage loan interest rates are 0.50 percent higher than in the original table. Close the table.

l. Click **Query Design** in the Queries group on the Create tab. Double-click the **Loans table** in the Show Table dialog box. Close the Show Table dialog box.

m. Double-click the **title bar** of the Loans table to select all the fields, and drag them to the first column in the query design grid.

n. Click **Run** in the Results group to run the query.

o. Switch back to Design view. Type **"M"** in the **Criteria row** of the Type column. Click **Run** in the Results group.

p. Switch back to Design view. Click **Make Table** in the Query Type group, and type **Mortgages** as the new table name. Accept the default setting of *Current Database*, and click **OK**.

q. Switch to Datasheet view to verify that only the 12 mortgage loans will be affected.

r. Switch to Design view. Click **Run** in the Results group. Click **Yes** in response to the Warning box.

s. Double-click the **Mortgages table** in the Navigation Pane. Verify that the 12 mortgages are in the table. Close the table.

t. Click **Delete** in the Query Type group on the Design tab of the make table query to change the make table query to a delete query.

u. Delete all the columns in the query design grid except the Type column.

v. Drag the *** field** from the Loans table to the first column in the query design grid. Compare your query design with Figure 6.47.

w. Click **Run** in the Results group. Click **Yes** in response to the Warning box.

x. Save the query as **Delete Mortgages Query**. Close the query.

y. Open the Loans table to verify that there are no mortgages (Type *M*) in the table. Close the table.

z. Click **Query Wizard** in the Queries group on the Create tab. Click **Find Duplicates Query Wizard**, and click **OK**.

aa. Click **Table: Loans**, and click **Next**. Add **CustomerID** and **Type** as the duplicate-value fields, and click **Next**. Add all additional fields as the additional query fields, and click **Next**.

ab. Accept the default name, and finish the query.

ac. Close the query.

ad. Click **Query Wizard** in the Queries group on the Create tab. Click **Crosstab Query Wizard**, and click **OK**.

ae. Click the **Queries option** in the View area, and click **Query: Loan Payments by Type**. Click **Next**.

af. Add the **LoanName** field for the row headings, and click **Next**. Click the **PaymentDate field** for the column headings, **Quarter** as the date interval, and the **AmountReceived field** for the column and row intersection. Sum the **AmountReceived field**. Click **Next**.

ag. Accept the default name, *Loan Payments by Type_Crosstab*, and finish the query.

The crosstab query displays the amounts received for car and personal loans by quarter.

ah. Close the query.

ai. Close the database and exit Access. Based on your instructor's directions, submit a06p1Bank_LastFirst.

You have been asked to modify a car dealership database that tracks employee data, sales records, and vehicle information. You will identify new hires in the database and move them to a separate table. You will also summarize data in the database and locate unmatched records. Refer to Figure 6.48 as you complete this exercise.

Vehicles Without Matching SalesAgreement								
VehicleID	VehicleYear	VehicleMake	VehicleModel	VehicleColor	VehicleCost	VehicleSalePrice	VehicleAquisitionDate	VehicleSoldDate
1000	2013	Honda	Accord	Gray	$25,000.00	$26,999.00	5/1/2018	
1002	2013	Honda	Accord	Red	$23,500.00	$27,500.00	5/5/2018	
1003	2012	Honda	Accord EX	Black	$24,900.00	$28,950.00	3/1/2018	
1004	2011	Honda	Civic	White	$11,300.00	$14,500.00	5/11/2018	
1007	2012	BMW	325i	White	$25,000.00	$32,000.00	4/26/2018	
1008	2013	BMW	528i	Black	$28,000.00	$35,900.00	5/20/2018	
1009	2010	BMW	M3	Red	$25,900.00	$31,500.00	5/29/2018	6/15/2018
*	(New)							

FIGURE 6.48 Vehicles Without Matching Sales Agreements

Access 2016, Windows 10, Microsoft Corporation

a. Open *a06p2Car* and save it as **a06p2Car_LastFirst**.

b. Click **Query Design** in the Queries group on the Create tab. Double-click the **Employees table** in the Show Table dialog box to add it to the query. Close the Show Table dialog box. Create a select query based on all of the fields from the Employees table. Add criteria to show only employees whose Active status is **"No"**. Run the query.

c. Convert the select query to a make table query. Name the new table **Hires Not Activated**. Run the query, and save it as **Make Table Query_Inactive**. Close the query. Open the Hires Not Activated table to verify the results.

d. Set the Active status of Employee ID 3 (*Jim Delsor*) in the Employees table to **No**. Close the table.

e. Make a copy of the Make Table Query_Inactive in the Navigation Pane, and name the copy **Append Query_Inactive**. Right-click the new append query, and from the shortcut menu, select **Design View**.

f. Change the query type to **Append**. Append records to the Hires Not Activated table. Modify the criteria to select Employee ID **3**, and delete the existing criterion. Run the query. Save and close the query.

g. Make a copy of the Append Query_Inactive in the Navigation Pane, and name the copy **Delete Query_Inactive**. Right-click the new delete query, and select **Design View** from the list.

h. Change the query type to **Delete**. Modify the criteria to show only employees whose Active status is **"No"**, and delete the existing criterion. Run the query. Save and close the query. Open the Employees table and note that the inactive employees are deleted. Close the table.

i. Create a crosstab query based on the Available Inventory query. Use the VehicleMake field for the row headings, the VehicleYear field for the column headings, and the VehicleSalePrice field for the column and row intersection. Average the VehicleSalePrice field. Save the query as **Available Inventory_Crosstab**.

j. Set the caption of the Total Of VehicleSalePrice: [VehicleSalePrice] field to **Average Sale Price**. Save and close the query.

k. Click **Query Wizard** in the Queries group on the Create tab. Click **Find Unmatched Query Wizard**, and click **OK**.

l. Create an unmatched query to display vehicles that have no sales agreement, and include all of the fields from the Vehicles table.

m. Select records where the VehicleID field in the Vehicles table does not have a match in the AgreementVehicleID field in the SalesAgreement table. Accept the default query name. Finish, and close the query.

n. Close the database and exit Access. Based on your instructor's directions, submit a06p2Car_LastFirst.

Mid-Level Exercises

1 Northwind Traders

Northwind Traders is a small international specialty foods distribution firm. Management has decided to close the North and South American operations and concentrate on European markets. They asked you to update certain customer records and to move all deactivated customers to another table. Once you move the records, you will delete them from the original table.

a. Open *a06m1Exporters* and save it as **a06m1Exporters_LastFirst**.

b. Create a select query based on all of the fields from the Customers table. Add criteria to show only customers in the **USA**. Run the query.

c. Change the query to an update query that replaces all instances of *USA* with **United States**. Run the query and save it as **Update US Customers**. Close the query.

d. Create a make table query that is based on all of the fields in the Customers table. Name the new table **Deactivated Customers**. Add criteria to select only **United States** customers. Run the query and save it as **Make Table Query**. Close the query.

e. Make a copy of the Make Table Query in the Navigation Pane, and name the copy **Append Query**. Right-click the new **Append Query**, and from the shortcut menu, select **Design View**.

f. Change the query type to **Append**. Append records to the Deactivated Customers table. Change the criteria of the Country field to **Venezuela**. Run the query. Save and close the query.

g. Make a copy of the Append Query in the Navigation Pane, and name the copy **Delete Query**. Right-click the new **Delete Query**, and from the shortcut menu, select **Design View**.

h. Change the query type to **Delete**. Change the Country criteria to **United States Or Venezuela**. Delete all the columns in the query design grid except the Country column. Run the query and click Yes in the message box. Save and close the query. Open the Deactivated Customers table to view the records added by the make table and append queries. Close the table.

i. Close the database and exit Access. Based on your instructor's directions, submit a06m1Exporters_LastFirst.

2 Hotel Chain

 You are assisting the general manager of a large hotel chain. You perform several tasks for the general manager, including calculating the total revenue for each service for each city where the chain has a hotel. You will also find duplicate names in the members table.

a. Open *a06m2Rewards* and save it as **a06m2Rewards_LastFirst**.

b. Create a crosstab query based on the Revenue query. Use the ServiceName field for the row headings, the City field for the column headings, and the Revenue field for the row and column intersection. Sum the Revenue field. Save the query as **Revenue_Crosstab**.

c. Format the Revenue and Total of Revenue crosstab values as **Currency**. Run the query. Save and close the Revenue_Crosstab query.

 **d.** Create a copy of the Revenue_Crosstab query and save it as **Revenue_Crosstab2**.

e. Modify the query so that the City field is used for the row headings and the ServiceName field is used for the column headings. Run the query, save the query, and then close it.

f. Create a find unmatched query that displays repeat members from Raleigh who have no matching orders. Records from the Repeat Members Club table should display in the results. Include all fields from the table. Run the query and save it as **Raleigh Members Without Matching Orders**.

g. Create a copy of the Raleigh Members Without Matching Orders query and save it as **Charlotte Members Without Matching Orders**.

h. Modify the query so that **Charlotte** members who have no matching orders are displayed in the results. Run, save, and then close the query.

i. Create a find duplicates query that displays any locations that have the same city and address. Display the LocationID field as an additional field in the third column of the query. Run the query and save it as **Find Duplicate Locations**.

j. Change the Address for LocationID 15 to **Downtown** in the query results. Close the query.

k. Close the database and exit Access. Based on your instructor's directions, submit a06m2Rewards_LastFirst.

3 New Castle County Technical Services

RUNNING CASE

New Castle County Technical Services (NCCTS) provides technical support for a number of companies in the greater New Castle County, Delaware area. Now that you have created a parameter query and used functions, you are ready to create action and specialized queries.

a. Open the database *a05m3NCCTS_LastOFirst* and save it as **a06m3NCCTS_LastFirst**.

> **TROUBLESHOOTING:** If you did not complete the Chapter 5 case, return to Chapter 5, complete the case, and then return to this exercise.

b. Create a select query based on all of the fields from the Calls table. Add criteria to display only closed dates between 1/1/2018 and 1/31/2018. Run the query.

c. Convert the select query to a make table query. Name the new table **Archived Calls**. Run the query and save it as **Make Table_Archive**. Close the query. Open the Archived Calls table to verify the results. Close the table.

d. Make a copy of the Make Table_Archive in the Navigation Pane, and name the copy **Append Table_Archive**. Right-click the new append query, and from the shortcut menu, select **Design View**.

e. Change the query type to **Append**. Append records to the Archived Calls table. Modify the existing criterion to append records with closed dates between 2/1/2018 and 2/28/2018. Run the query.

f. Save and close the query. Open the Archived Calls table to verify the results. Close the table.

g. Make a copy of the Append Table_Archive in the Navigation Pane, and name the copy **Delete Calls Query**. Right-click the new delete query, and from the shortcut menu, select **Design View**.

h. Change the query type to **Delete**. Modify the criteria to delete records with closed dates between 1/1/2018 and 2/28/2018. Run the query. Save and close the query. Open the Calls table and note that the calls closed in January and February are deleted. Close the table.

i. Create a crosstab query based on the Calls table. Use the CallTypeID field for the row headings, the CustomerSatisfaction field for the column headings, and the HoursLogged field for the row and column intersection. Average the HoursLogged field. Accept the default name and finish the query.

j. Format the [HoursLogged] and Total Of HoursLogged: [HoursLogged] fields as Fixed with two decimal places. Set the criteria of the CustomerSatisfaction field to **Is Not Null**. Run the query again. Widen the Total Of HoursLogged field to give it the best fit. Save and close the query.

k. Close the database and exit Access. Based on your instructor's directions, submit a06m3NCCTS_LastFirst.

Beyond the Classroom

Cover Letters and Résumé Tips

GENERAL CASE

You want to determine how many of the new employees in your database have no résumés on file with the Human Resources Department. You decide to create a make table query with their personal information so that they can be contacted by HR. Open *a06b1Resumes* and save it as **a06b1Resumes_LastFirst**. Create the query based on the New Employees table and include the following fields: FirstName, LastName, Email, DateOfHire, and ResumeOnFile (in that order). Set the criterion of the ResumeOnFile field to determine which employees have no résumés. Hide the ResumeOnFile field in the query results. Modify the query to create a table named **Missing Resume**. Save the query as **Missing Resume_Make Table**. Run the query to create the table and close the query. Close the database and exit Access. Based on your instructor's directions, submit a06b1Resumes_LastFirst.

Prohibit Duplicate Append

DISASTER RECOVERY ➕

Northwind Traders is an international specialty foods distributor that relies on an Access 2016 database to track customers and process its orders. A make table query moved all the owners from the Customers table to a new Customer Owners table. A colleague converted a copy of the make table query to an append query and ran it again (expecting it would not add another set of records). Unfortunately, it did add the same set of owners to the table, and now every owner is duplicated. Consider the best way to fix this problem. You need the append query so that you can run it when new owners are added to the database. However, running the append query should not add duplicate records to the Customer Owners table. Open *a06b2Food* and save it as **a06b2Food_LastFirst**. Correct the problem in the table that is allowing this type of error. Run the append query to ensure that duplicate records are no longer getting added to Customer Owners. Close the database and exit Access. Based on your instructor's directions, submit a06b2Food_LastFirst.

Capstone Exercise

Northwind Traders is a small international gourmet foods wholesaler. You will update the company's database by increasing the price of all of the beverage and dairy products. You will make a table of discontinued products. You will also summarize profits by salesperson and category and identify products that have no orders.

Database File Setup

You will prepare the database for changes by opening the original database file and saving a copy to use to complete this capstone exercise.

a. Open *a06c1Prices* and save it as **a06c1Prices_LastFirst**.

Identify and Update Selected Category Prices

Using a select query, you will identify all of the products with a category of beverage or dairy, and then use an update query to increase the prices of the products.

a. Create a select query that includes the CategoryID and CategoryName from the Categories table and the UnitPrice and ProductName fields from the Products table. Run the query and note the CategoryIDs for Beverages and Dairy.

b. Add the appropriate CategoryID criterion to limit the query output to only Beverages.

c. Convert the query to an update query. Update the UnitPrice for beverages only by increasing it by 5 percent. View the query in Datasheet view prior to running it to make sure you are updating the correct records. Return to Design view and run the query.

d. Update the UnitPrice for dairy products only by increasing it by 4 percent. View the query in Datasheet view prior to running it to make sure you are updating the correct records. Return to Design view and run the query.

e. Save the query as **Update Prices**. Close the query.

Create a New Table

You will identify the discontinued products and create a new table to store them.

a. Create a select query that identifies all of the discontinued products. Include all fields from the Products table.

b. Convert the select query to a make table query.

c. Name the new table **Discontinued Products**. Run the query.

d. Save the query as **Make Discontinued Products Table**. Close the query.

e. Make a copy of the Make Discontinued Products Table query and save it as **Append Discontinued Products Table**. Open the Append Discontinued Products Table query in Design view. Convert the make table query to an append query. The query will append to the Discontinued Products table.

f. Modify the criteria to append Boston Crab Meat as a product, using the SupplierID from the Products table. Run the query, save it, and then close it.

g. Make a copy of the Append Discontinued Products Table query and save it as **Delete Discontinued Products**. Open the Delete Discontinued Products query in Design view. Convert the append query to a delete query.

h. Modify the criteria to delete the discontinued products, as well as the record for Boston Crab Meat using its SupplierID. (*Hint:* There will be two criteria). Run, save, and then close the query.

Calculate Summary Statistics

You will create a crosstab query that shows profits by salesperson and category.

a. Open the Profit query in Design view and add the **LastName field** from the Employees table to the last column of the design grid. Run, save, and then close the query.

b. Use the query wizard to create a crosstab query based on the Profit query that shows total profit by LastName (row heading) and CategoryName (column heading). Accept the query name as **Profit_Crosstab**.

c. Modify the query to display **CategoryName** as a row heading field and **LastName** as a column heading field. Run, save, and then close the query.

Create a Find Unmatched Query

You will create a query to determine which products have no matching orders.

a. Create a query to find out if any of the products have no current order details. Add all of the fields from the Products table to the results.

b. Save the query as **Products With No Orders**. Run the query and close it.

c. Close the database and exit Access. Based on your instructor's directions, submit a06c1Prices_LastFirst.

Advanced Forms and Reports

LEARNING OUTCOME

You will use advanced form and report features to create customized solutions.

OBJECTIVES & SKILLS: After you read this chapter, you will be able to:

CASE STUDY | Yellowstone County Technical Services

Yellowstone County Technical Services is a small company that provides technical support for a number of businesses in Yellowstone County, Montana. You have been tasked with updating the customer tracking database to expand the input and output capabilities of the system. In your experience with the company, you have seen some of the common errors users make when performing data entry and have also seen what is effective and what is not effective in forms. In addition, you have seen which reports users utilize and have heard suggestions about changes they would like made.

You realize everyone benefits when you are proactive and help users prevent errors. In addition, finding ways to extract more information from the same amount of data is important as well. Being able to interpret and present the information in a database so management can use it can be what makes or breaks your career as a database administrator.

In your role as supervisor, you also want to lead your technicians by example, and implementing improvements in your database is a good start. After implementing the changes, you can use the database as a case study to train your technicians in effective database design.

Moving Beyond the Basics

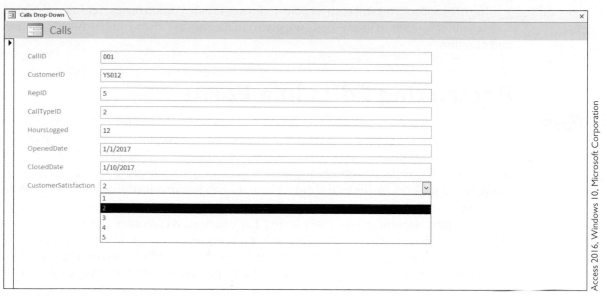

FIGURE 7.1 Yellowstone County Technical Services Form

Access 2016, Windows 10, Microsoft Corporation

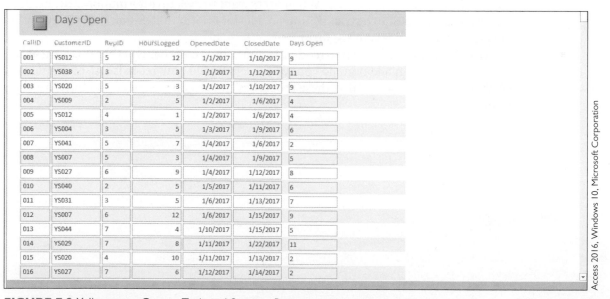

FIGURE 7.2 Yellowstone County Technical Services Report

Access 2016, Windows 10, Microsoft Corporation

CASE STUDY | Yellowstone County Technical Services

Starting Files	File to be Submitted
a07h1Yellowstone a07h2Logo	a07h2Yellowstone_LastFirst

Advanced Forms

For basic database solutions, a simple form created with the Form tool suffices. However, at times, you might want to go beyond the basics. There are a number of changes you can make to customize a form. For example, you can create a form that enables users to look up information but not change it, so a user cannot accidentally change data. You can convert a field from a text box to a menu. You can choose to adjust the sequence in which the fields are ordered as you press Tab. Access enables you to create and manipulate subforms, which show related records from other tables. Part of your goal when administering a database is to make the database easy to use, and well-designed forms provide that functionality.

In this section, you will restrict edits in forms, create combo boxes, set tab order, and create subforms. You will use Design view to make most of the changes in this section and chapter.

Restricting Edits in a Form

STEP 1 >> One method of protecting data in a database is to restrict casual users from editing the data. Representatives may look up information, such as a person's address or phone number, or review the details of an order. However, the people who want to look up information may be people you do not want adding, editing, and deleting records. When too many users make changes to the data, the data can become unreliable and difficult to maintain.

Most databases have data entry forms. For example, a customer form might be created in a database to enable customer information to be entered. If a mistake is made, data entry personnel can find the record with the mistake and fix the error. The form does not require permission or a password to make an edit. Perhaps other employees also want to look up information—for example, a phone number to contact a customer. The person making these calls should be able to look up the phone number of a customer without making any changes to the data. When users want to look up information without making changes, it is best to restrict editing on a form. A form that enables users to view but not change data is a ***read-only form***.

Before you change a form to read-only, you should consider whether this form will be used to edit data. In addition, do you want users to add new records? Also, should they be able to delete records? All of these properties can be adjusted once you have created a form.

To convert an existing form to a read-only form, complete the following steps:

1. Open the form in Layout view.
2. Click the Property Sheet in the Tools group on the Design tab.
3. Select Form in the Selection type box at the top of the Property Sheet.
4. Click the Allow Edits property on the Data tab.
5. Change the Allow Edits property to No, as shown in Figure 7.3.
6. Change the Allow Additions and Allow Deletions properties to No, as shown in Figure 7.3, if you want to restrict these types of changes.
7. Switch to Form view, and test the form by attempting to change data.
8. Save the form.

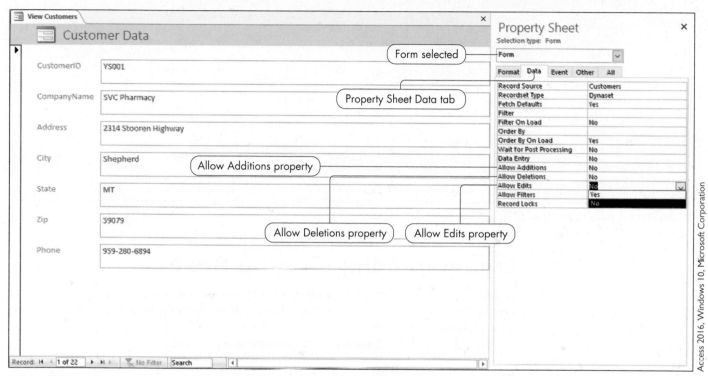

FIGURE 7.3 Changing a Form to Read-Only

If you changed the Allow Deletions property to No, you can see the results of this change when you attempt to click Delete in the Records group on the Home tab—Delete is no longer available. Likewise, if you have set the Allow Additions property to No, you cannot click New in the Records group on the Home tab. Figure 7.4 shows a read-only form in Datasheet view. Notice there are no obvious cues that this form cannot be used to edit data. It is suggested that you change the form title and name to indicate it is read-only. Otherwise, you can frustrate users who might open the form and wonder why they cannot change data.

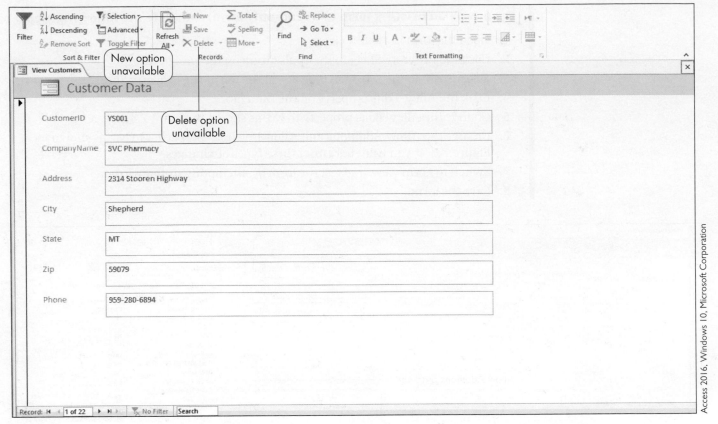

FIGURE 7.4 A Read-Only Form

Understanding Combo Boxes

If you create a form based on a table with a lookup field, the lookup field becomes a Combo Box control on the new form. A **Combo Box control** provides a menu displaying a list of options from which the user can choose a single value. If the combo box is not created automatically, you may want to create one yourself.

Convert a Text Box to a Combo Box

 At times, a text box on a form should be converted to a combo box. This can happen when the data you are collecting may not appear to contain repeating data at first. As you enter transactions over time, you may realize that a field does have repeating data and that a combo box may be appropriate. However, the desire to make input easier for the user should be weighed against creating a menu that is too long. For example, the State field will sometimes be a combo box. Fifty states and the District of Columbia make up the United States, and you may prefer not to have a menu containing 51 items. However, if you only need to reference a few states, you could do that as well.

> **To convert a text box to a combo box, complete the following steps:**
>
> 1. Open the form in Design view (or Layout view), and right-click the text box you want to convert.
> 2. Point to the Change To option, and select Combo Box from the shortcut menu, as shown in Figure 7.5.

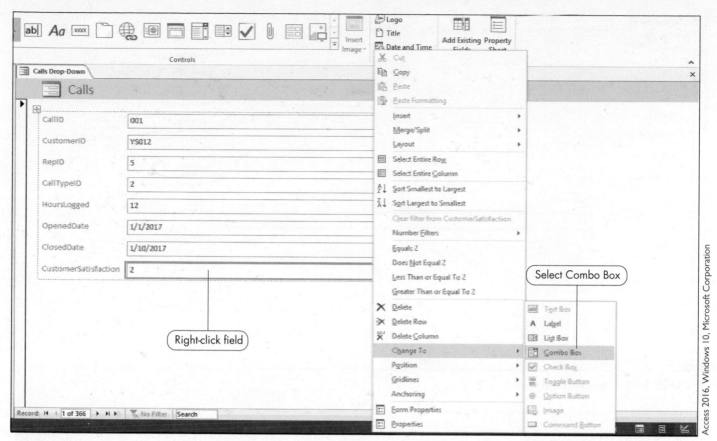

FIGURE 7.5 Changing a Field to a Combo Box

The field now displays with an arrow on the right side of the text box. It does not yet do anything, however. To enable the menu, you need to customize the combo box.

Customize a Combo Box

Once you have converted a text box to a combo box, you still have changes to make to enable the options. You should first create a new table and enter the values for the option list, much like you do for lookup fields. This way, the values can be found in an easy-to-edit location. Then, the source for the combo box can be set so the values displayed on the menu match those in your new table. Figure 7.6 shows properties you can set to customize a combo box, and Figure 7.7 shows how a combo box appears in Form view.

> **To set a source for a combo box, complete the following steps:**
> 1. Switch to Design view of the form.
> 2. Click the field you want to customize.
> 3. Click the Property Sheet in the Tools group on the Design tab.
> 4. Select a Row Source on the Data tab.
> 5. Switch to Form view to test the combo box.

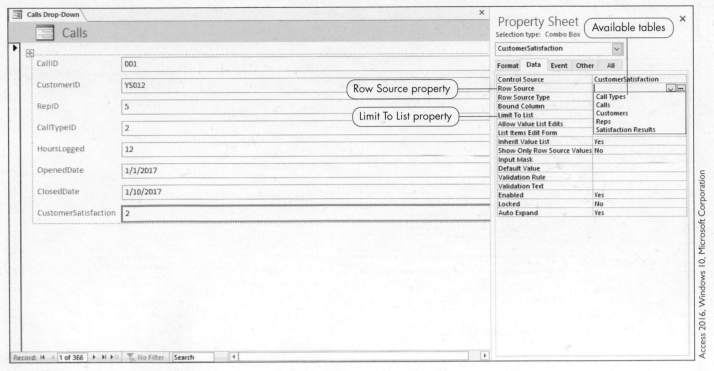

FIGURE 7.6 Combo Box Properties

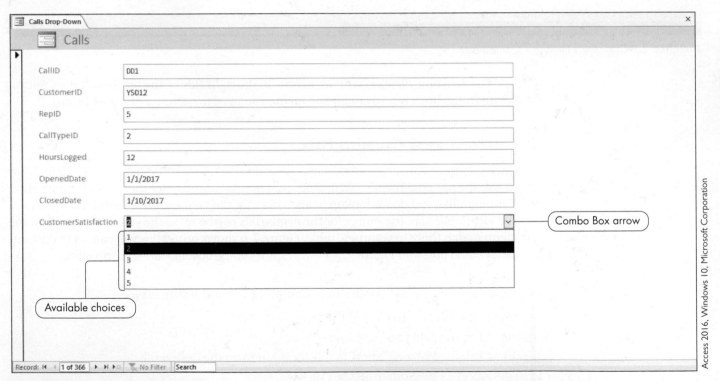

FIGURE 7.7 Combo Box in Form View

You may also want to ensure your users only enter values that exist in the menu. This way, they do not choose to enter a value you have not set as legal.

> **To limit the values to the contents of the source table, complete the following steps:**
>
> 1. Switch to Design view of the form.
> 2. Click the Property Sheet in the Tools group on the Design tab.
> 3. Change the Limit To List property to Yes on the Data tab.
> 4. Switch to Form view to test the combo box.

If you have set the Limit To List option and the user types a value not on the list, Access generates an error, as shown in Figure 7.8. Similar to lookup fields, storing values in a separate table makes it very easy to change the values accepted in a combo box if the values ever change. For example, you may have initially dealt with customers in Idaho, Montana, and Wyoming. If you ever want to add Oregon and Washington to the combo box, you can add new rows to the table storing the state names.

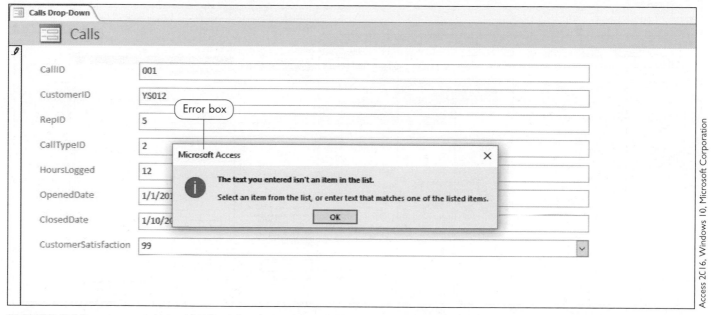

FIGURE 7.8 Response to a Value Not Found on List

Setting the Tab Order

 When entering data into a table, users often press Tab to advance from one field to the next. The *tab order* is the sequential advancing in a form from one field or control to the next when you press Tab. When working with forms, the designer must remember to check the tab order before delivering the form to the end users; when a form is created, the initial tab order is not necessarily the order that is most useful to the user.

Customize Tabbing

As you insert controls into a report, Access will set the tab order. At times, it will be set incorrectly. Access provides a tool that enables you to adjust the ordering. The tab order tool can attempt to automatically order the tabbing, which may fix the problem. However, if Access cannot fix the tabbing automatically, you can also set it manually. As a designer, you want to enable users to be as efficient as possible when entering data. Setting the tab order helps prevent errors and simplifies data entry.

To automatically set the tab order in a form, complete the following steps:

1. Switch to Design view.
2. Click Tab Order in the Tools group on the Design tab. This displays the Tab Order dialog box showing all the controls in each section of the form, as shown in Figure 7.9.
3. Ensure Detail is selected to display the tab order for the fields.
4. Click Auto Order if the form has a Stacked layout and you want to enter data from top to bottom.
5. Click OK to accept the changes.

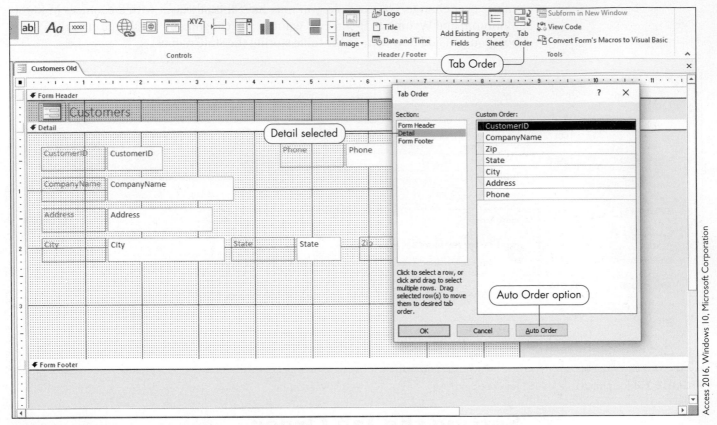

FIGURE 7.9 Tab Order for Form

Access does its best to set the tab order properly, but at times it does not work as you might require. For example, Auto Order does not work well if you have a form with multiple columns. In this case, you will need to customize the tab order.

To customize the tab order, complete the following steps:

1. Switch to Design view.
2. Click Tab Order in the Tools group on the Design tab.
3. Ensure Detail is selected to display the tab order for the fields.
4. Click the record selector to the left of a field name, and drag the field to the desired position in the tab order. For example, if two fields are next to each other but in the wrong order, click the second field and drag the second field on top of the first one.
5. Click OK to accept the changes.
6. Switch to Form view, and test the order by pressing Tab to advance through the fields on the form.

Remove a Tab Stop

At times, you want the tab order to skip a field completely. For example, if you add a calculated field to the form, you would not want to stop at this field. Calculated fields do not require data entry. Another example occurs when you have an AutoNumber field as the primary key. Your user does not add data to that field, so it should not have a tab stop.

To remove the Tab Stop property for a field, complete the following steps:

1. Switch to Layout view (or Design view).
2. Click the field you want to remove.
3. Click Property Sheet in the Tools group on the Design tab.
4. Click the Other tab in the Property Sheet.
5. Locate the Tab Stop property, and change the property setting to No, as shown in Figure 7.10.
6. Switch to Form view, and test the change by pressing Tab to advance through the fields on the form. The field you modified should be skipped when you press Tab.

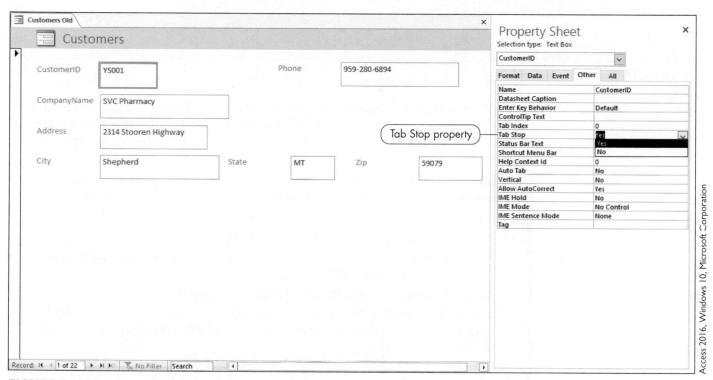

FIGURE 7.10 Removing a Tab Stop

Understanding Subforms

STEP 4 ⟩⟩ Relationships between tables usually exist in Access databases, which can lead to more complicated forms. In order to properly display information from multiple tables, a form will often have a *subform*, which is one form contained within another form. Subforms are generally laid out in a tabular fashion, as shown in Figure 7.11.

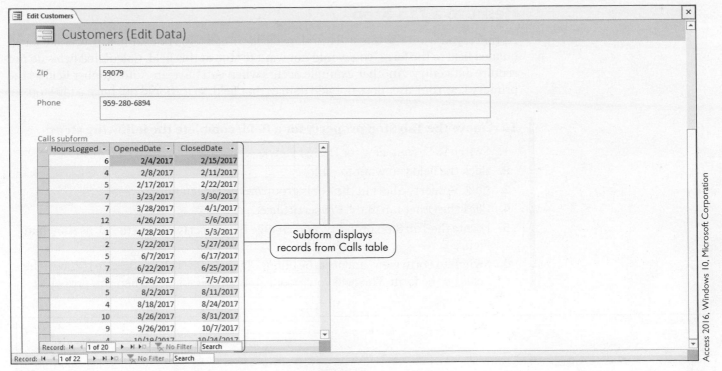

FIGURE 7.11 Form with a Subform

When you create a form using the Form Wizard, if a relationship exists, Access will create a form with a subform automatically. However, there may be times you need to add one manually. You can add a subform to an existing form using the Subform/Subreport tool.

To manually add a subform using the Subform/Subreport tool, assuming a relationship exists between the tables, complete the following steps:

1. Open the form in Design view.
2. Click the Subform/Subreport control in the Controls group on the Design tab, as shown in Figure 7.12. If it is not visible, click More at the lower right of the Controls box, as shown in Figure 7.13.
3. Draw the subform. It can be resized later as necessary.
4. Choose the source for the subform. You can use an existing form or view data in a table or query. Assuming you want to use a table, click Next, as shown in Figure 7.14.
5. Choose the appropriate fields from the table (or query) source, as shown in Figure 7.15. Click Next.
6. Choose the relationship you want to use, as shown in Figure 7.16. This step may not appear in certain cases. Click Next.
7. Accept the default name or create your own name for the subform. Click Finish.
8. Switch to Form view to see the results.

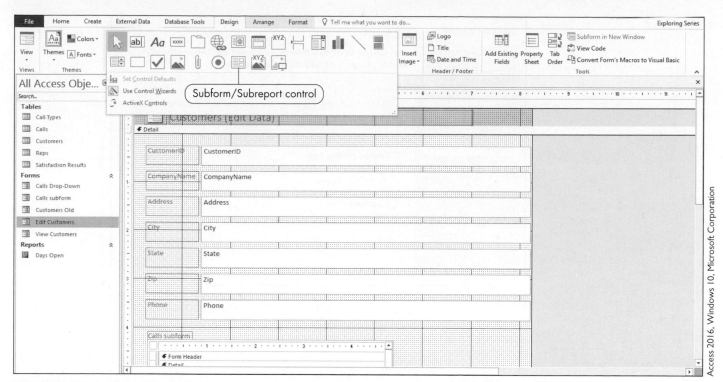

FIGURE 7.12 Subform/Subreport Control

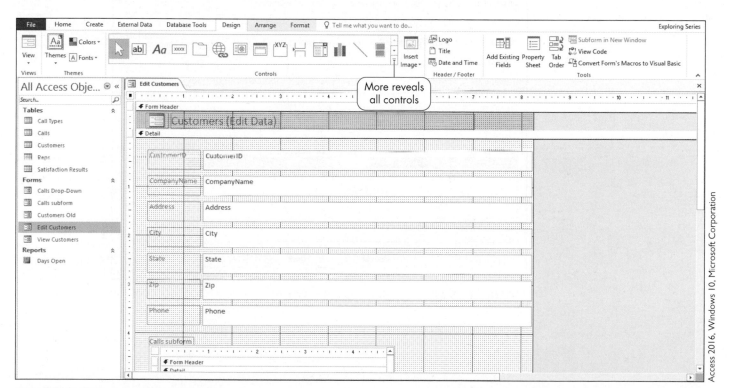

FIGURE 7.13 Showing More Controls

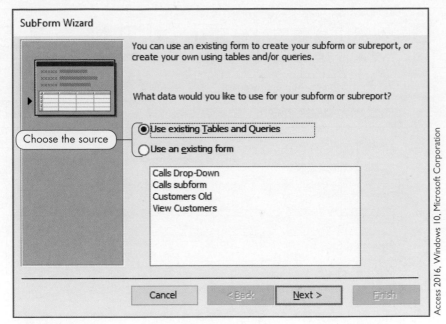

FIGURE 7.14 Selecting Source in SubForm Wizard

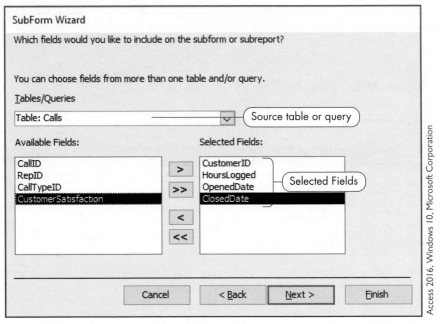

FIGURE 7.15 Selecting Fields in SubForm Wizard

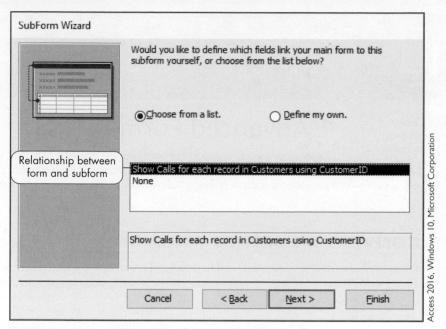

FIGURE 7.16 Selecting a Relationship in SubForm Wizard

You can change the size of the subform or the size of the fields in the subform as necessary. The subform will display in tabular fashion. The changes are easier to make in Layout view, as you can see the data as it appears in the subform, as shown in Figure 7.17.

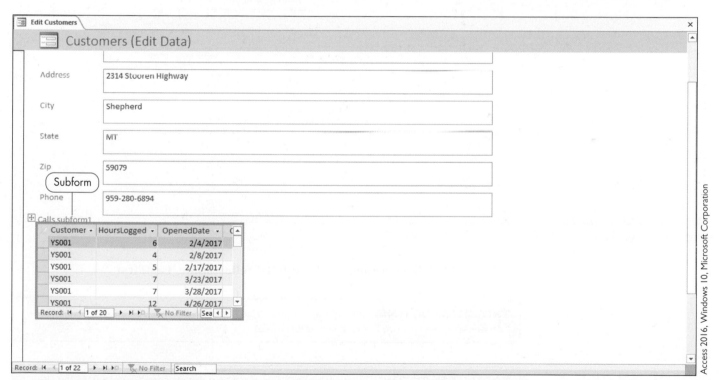

FIGURE 7.17 Subform in Form View

Quick Concepts

1. Why would you convert a form to be read-only? *p. 446*

2. How can you create a menu on an existing form? *p. 448*

3. Why is it important to ensure a form's tab order is logical? *p. 451*

4. What does a subform do? *p. 453*

Hands-On Exercises

Skills covered: Convert a Form to Read-Only • Convert a Text Box to a Combo Box • Customize a Combo Box • Customize Tabbing • Remove a Tab Stop • Create a Subform

1 Advanced Forms

You have decided to create a read-only form for customer data. You will also create a form with a drop-down menu to enable users to help record customer call satisfaction. You will repair an existing form that has problems with tab ordering. You will also create a form with a subform.

STEP 1 ›› CONVERT A FORM TO READ-ONLY

You have decided to use the Form tool to create a Customers form. This form will enable users to look up customer information. You will make this read-only so users do not accidentally make errors when looking up information. Refer to Figure 7.18 as you complete Step 1.

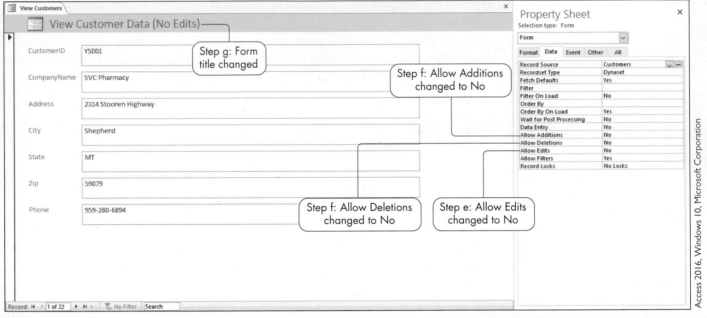

FIGURE 7.18 View Customers Form

a. Open *a07h1Yellowstone* and save it as **a07h1Yellowstone_LastFirst**.

> **TROUBLESHOOTING:** Throughout the remainder of this chapter and textbook, click Enable Content whenever you are working with student files.

> **TROUBLESHOOTING:** If you make any major mistakes in this exercise, you can close the file, open *a07h1Yellowstone* again, and then start this exercise over.

b. Select the **Customers table** in the Navigation Pane. Click the **Create tab**, and click **Form** in the Forms group.

   Access creates a new form based on the Customers table. The form opens in Layout view, ready to edit.

c. Click anywhere in the subform at the bottom of the window, click the border of the subform, and then press **Delete** to delete the subform.

> **TROUBLESHOOTING:** If you are prompted to confirm deleting of records, click No and ensure you have clicked the border before pressing Delete.

d. Click **Property Sheet** on the Design tab in the Tools group if it is not already displayed.

The Property Sheet displays on the right side of your screen.

e. Click the **Data tab** in the Property Sheet pane. Click the **Allow Edits box**, which currently displays *Yes*, and click the arrow at the right. Change the value to **No**.

f. Repeat Step e to change the **Allow Additions** and **Allow Deletions property values** to **No**. Close the Property Sheet.

g. Change the title of the form to **View Customer Data (No Edits)**. Compare your results with Figure 7.18.

h. Switch to Form view.

i. Attempt to type in the **CompanyName box**.

You should not be able to change the field value.

> **TROUBLESHOOTING:** If you are able to type in the CompanyName box, switch to Layout view, and check that you completed Step e.

j. Attempt to click the **New** and **Delete** buttons in the Records group on the Home tab.

You should not be able to add or delete a record.

> **TROUBLESHOOTING:** If you are able to click New or Delete, switch to Layout view, and check that you completed Step f.

k. Click **Save** in the Quick Access Toolbar, and save the form as **View Customers**. Close the form.

You will use the Form tool to create an Access form to help manage customer call data. This form will enable you to record customer data. You will implement this using a menu. Refer to Figure 7.19 as you complete Step 2.

FIGURE 7.19 Calls Drop-Down Form

a. Select the **Calls table** in the Navigation Pane. Click the **Create tab**, and click **Form** in the Forms group.

b. Right-click the **CustomerSatisfaction text box**, point to the **Change To option**, and then select **Combo Box** from the shortcut menu.

   The CustomerSatisfaction text box changes to a combo box with an arrow on the right side of the box.

c. Click **Property Sheet** in the Tools group on the Design tab if it is not already displayed.

d. Click the **Row Source property** on the Data tab of the Property Sheet, click the arrow at the right of the Row Source box, and then select **Satisfaction Results**.

e. Click the **Limit To List property**, and change the value to **Yes**.

f. Switch to Form view.

g. Click the **CustomerSatisfaction field**. Notice an arrow now appears on the right of the box. Click the arrow and notice values of 1, 2, 3, 4, and 5 appear, as shown in Figure 7.19.

h. Type the value **6** for the **CustomerSatisfaction field**, and press **Tab**.

   Access will display an error message that the text you entered is not an item in the list.

> **TROUBLESHOOTING:** If Access does permit the value to be entered, ensure you set the Limit To List property to Yes.

i. Click **OK**. Change the value for the first record's CustomerSatisfaction field to **2**, and press **Tab**.

   You will not receive an error message because the value is in range.

j. Save the form as **Calls Drop-Down**, and close the form.

The users of the current Edit Customers report have reported problems with the tab order. You will fix the tab order. You will also fix an old form so that the tabs appear in the correct order and remove a tab stop. Refer to Figure 7.20 as you complete Step 3.

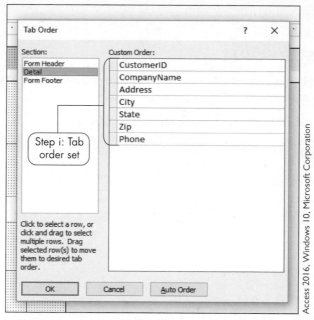

FIGURE 7.20 Tab Order for Customers Old Form

a. Open the **Edit Customers form** in Form view.

b. Press **Tab**.

   When you press Tab, the State field becomes active, rather than the CompanyName.

c. Press **Tab** five more times, noticing the order in which the fields appear.

   The fields are not displayed in a logical order.

d. Switch to Design view, and click **Tab Order** in the Tools group on the Design tab.

e. Ensure **Detail** is selected, and click **Auto Order**. Click **OK**.

   Notice State is no longer the second field on the list. The order now reflects the order of the fields, top to bottom. Because this is a Stacked Layout form, Access changes the tab order so it moves down one field at a time.

f. Switch to Form view. Press **Tab** six times, and verify that the tab order progresses in a logical order. Save and close the form.

g. Open the **Customers Old form** in Form view. Press **Tab**.

   The Phone field becomes active. You will switch the tab order so Phone is the last field to become active.

h. Switch to Design view. Click **Tab Order** in the Tools group on the Design tab. Ensure **Detail** is selected, and click **Auto Order**.

   Notice *Phone* is displayed at the top of the list, which would make it the first field displayed. This is not the logical order.

i. Click the record selector to the left of the Phone field. Drag the **Phone field** beneath the Zip field. Your tab order should match Figure 7.20. Click **OK**.

j. Click the **CustomerID field**. Display the Property Sheet, if it is not already displayed.

k. Click the **Other tab** in the Property Sheet. Locate the Tab Stop property, and change the property setting to **No**.

   You will no longer be able to access the CustomerID field by pressing Tab.

l. Switch to Form view. Tab through the fields.

The default field is now the CompanyName, and pressing Tab will bring you through Address, City, State, Zip, and Phone, in that order. Note pressing Tab does not bring you to the CustomerID field.

m. Save and close the form.

STEP 4 ›› CREATE A SUBFORM

The Edit Customers form does not display the related call information for each customer. You will modify it so the subform containing the information appears. Refer to Figure 7.21 as you complete Step 4.

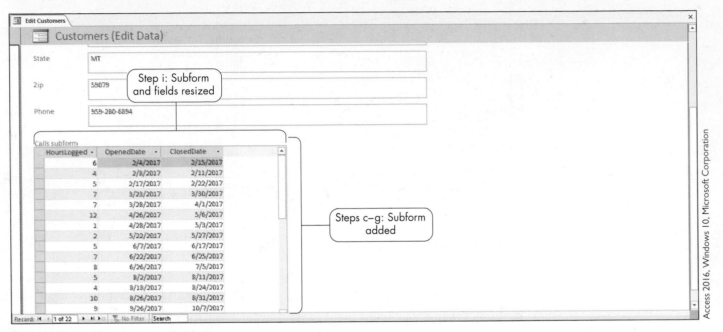

FIGURE 7.21 Edit Customers Subform

a. Open the **Edit Customers form** in Design view.

b. Click the **Subform/Subreport control** in the Controls group on the Design tab.

> **TROUBLESHOOTING:** If the Subform/Subreport control is not visible, click **More** at the lower right of the Controls box.

c. Draw a box in the location shown in Figure 7.21. The size does not matter, as it will be resized later.

The SubForm Wizard dialog box displays.

d. Click **Next** to accept the default *Use existing Tables and Queries* option.

e. Click the **Tables/Queries arrow**, and select **Table: Calls**. Double-click the **HoursLogged**, **OpenedDate**, and **ClosedDate fields**. Click **Next**.

f. Click **Next** to accept the default relationship.

g. Accept the default Calls subform name, and click **Finish**.

h. Switch to Layout view. Notice the Calls subform appears at the bottom of the screen.

i. Resize the subform and the fields to be approximately the size shown in Figure 7.21.

j. Save and close the form.

k. Keep the database open if you plan to continue with Hands-On Exercise 2. If not, close the database and exit Access.

Controls and Sections

As you work with tools to create and modify forms and reports, you will often switch between the three views in Access—Form or Report view, Layout view, and Design view. You use Layout view to perform most changes, but Design view gives you, as a designer, a higher level of control. Forms and reports have similar functionality in Design view, so the skills you use in forms can generally be applied to reports and vice versa.

Within each form or report, you find at least one *control*, which is an object on a form or report. Controls can display data, perform calculations, and add visual effects (such as boxes or lines).

In this section, you will work with advanced controls and sections in forms and reports.

Understanding Advanced Controls

When you use the form and report wizards to create basic objects, the resulting forms and reports contain a number of controls that were added automatically, such as a title, field values, and field names. Until this point, you probably did not concern yourself with the different types of controls. There are a number of different ways Access uses the word *control*, but remember at the most basic level, they are just objects on a form or report.

Controls fall into one of two categories. A ***bound control*** is any control that is connected to a field in a table or query. Bound controls are dynamic, in that the values update every time data is changed. This is how forms and reports display the most current information; they use controls that are bound to fields.

An ***unbound control*** is any control not tied to a specific field, and thus is generally unchanging. An unbound control is a decorative element, such as the title of the report or the label displaying the name of a field. Some other examples of unbound controls are lines, pictures, and other non-data-related elements.

For example, in Figure 7.22, notice there is one label and one value for each field in this record. The label CustomerID, for example, does not change and is, thus, an unbound control. The field value, in this case YS001, will change for each record and is, thus, a bound control.

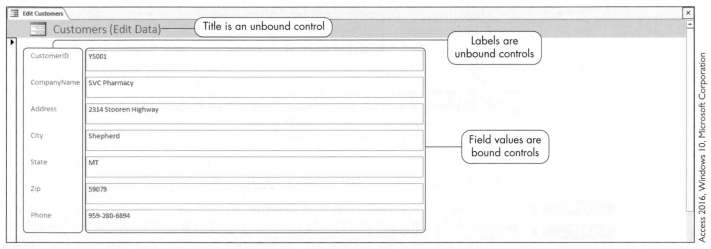

FIGURE 7.22 Bound and Unbound Controls in a Form

You can insert any control by clicking the Design tab and locating the control in the Controls group. There are a number of icons representing the controls, but each icon has a ScreenTip to identify the purpose. Remember, bound and unbound controls are the categories of controls, describing in effect if they are dynamic or not. They will not be identified as bound or unbound on the toolbar. Figure 7.23 shows some of the common controls found on the toolbar. Depending on your screen resolution, your view may vary slightly.

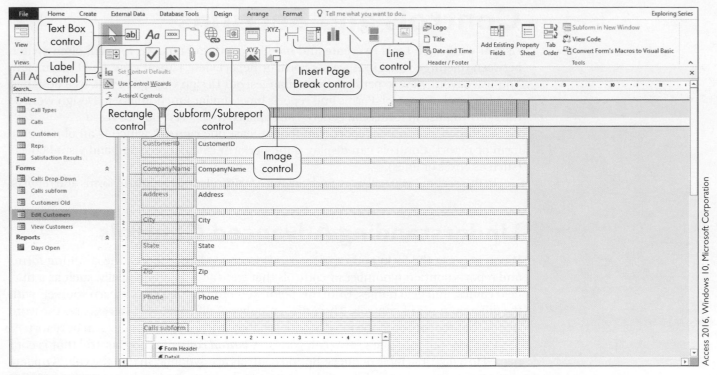

FIGURE 7.23 Common Controls

One common control is a Text Box control, which displays the data found in a record source (often, a table). Although the term *text box* may imply it only displays Short Text values, it can display numeric data, currency, and dates, depending on the field's data type. Because this is tied to a field and is dynamic, this is considered a bound control. Text boxes can also display the results of a calculation. A ***calculated control*** displays the result of an expression in a form or report. Calculated controls include simple math; aggregate functions such as Average, Count, and Sum; and functions created using the Expression Builder, and are typically inserted into a Text Box control.

The Label control is a word or phrase to describe the data associated with a text box. For a field in a form or report, the Label control defaults to the caption you set for a field. If you have not set a caption for a field, the label will default to the field name. Because this type of control does not change as you switch between records, it is an unbound control.

TIP: REMOVE THE TAB STOP FROM UNBOUND CONTROLS
In most cases, you will want to remove the tab stop from an unbound control. Unbound controls do not require data entry, so there is no reason for the insertion point to stop on them.

Add Emphasis to a Form or Report

When using the Form or Report tools to create an automatic form or report, you have a number of default controls. The title, the form/report icon, and each field are examples.

If you want to add emphasis to your form or report, the Line control and Rectangle control are two options. As the names imply, the Line control enables you to insert a line into your form or report, and the Rectangle control enables you to add a rectangle. After inserting these into an object, you can modify the shape to have a different line color, line thickness, and line type (such as dashed or dotted), and in the case of rectangles, the fill color. You will only find these options in Design view; they are not available in Layout view.

To add a Line or Rectangle control to a form or report, complete the following steps:

1. Switch to Design view.
2. Click the Design tab.
3. Select either the Line or Rectangle control in the Controls group. If it is not visible, click More at the lower right of the Controls box.
4. Drag from the desired start point to the desired end point to display your chosen control.

To format a Line or Rectangle control, use the appropriate options in the Control Formatting group on the Format tab, as shown in Figure 7.24. Choose the Shape Outline menu to change the color, thickness, and line type for a rectangle or line. Choose Shape Fill to add a fill color to a rectangle.

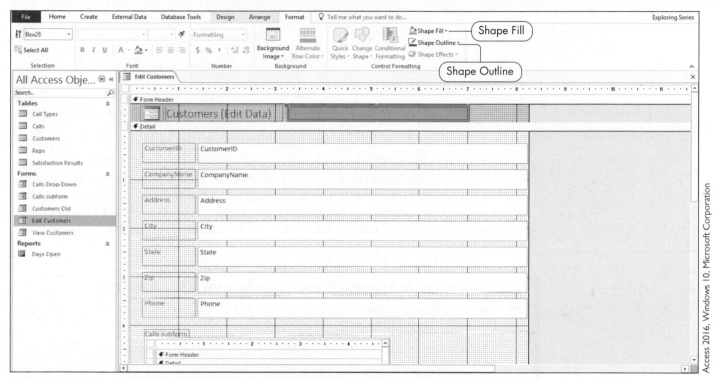

FIGURE 7.24 Formatting Options for a Rectangle Control

Add Text and Images to a Form or Report

Both forms and reports have the option to include text and images. In addition to the existing Label controls, you may want to add explanatory text to a form or report. Instead of (or in addition to) a validation rule, you can add text providing guidance for your users. As this text is not tied to a specific field and does not change, it is considered unbound. You can insert text inside of a form or report using a Label control.

To add text to a form or report, complete the following steps:

1. Switch to Design view.
2. Click the Design tab.
3. Click the Label control in the Controls group, as shown in Figure 7.25.
4. Drag from the desired start point to the desired end point.
5. Type the text you want to appear in the label.

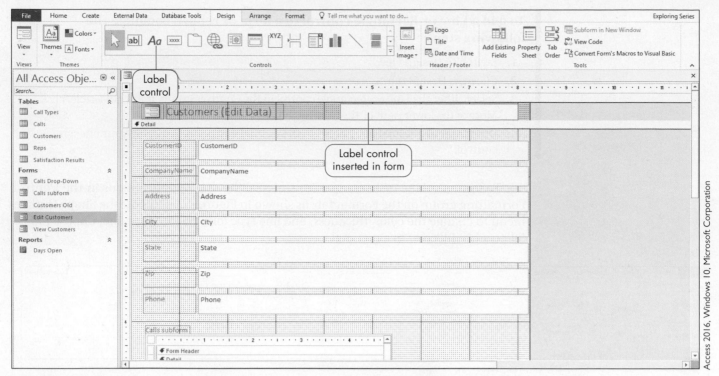

FIGURE 7.25 Label Control

Images can be useful especially when dealing with corporate forms and reports. Companies commonly use the same logo and colors on official publications. When creating a form or report, you can insert an image file containing the company logo or any other image. Often, the image is inserted in the header, so it displays once when printed or viewed on the screen. The header sections for forms and reports will be discussed later in this chapter.

To add an image to a form or report, complete the following steps:

1. Switch to Design view.
2. Click the Design tab.
3. Click the Image control in the Controls group, as shown in Figure 7.26. If it is not visible, click More at the lower right of the Controls box.
4. Drag from the desired start point to the desired end point. The Insert Picture dialog box appears.
5. Browse to the location containing the image.
6. Click the image you want to insert, and click Open.
7. Resize the image control as necessary.

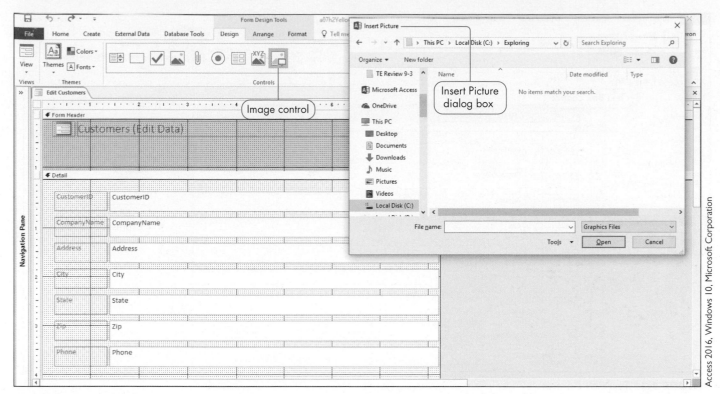

FIGURE 7.26 Image Control

Add a Calculated Control

Forms and reports based on a query can display calculated fields like any other field. However, some forms and reports are based on a table rather than a query. In this case, you can add a calculated field using a text box. The Expression Builder can be used similarly to how it is used in queries.

> **To add a calculated control to a form or report using the Expression Builder, complete the following steps:**
>
> 1. Switch to Design view and ensure the Design tab is selected.
> 2. Click the Text Box control in the Controls group, as shown in Figure 7.27.
> 3. Drag from the desired start point to the desired end point. The word *Unbound* appears in the text box. Access also displays a label by default, often to the left of the text box. You can choose to delete or modify the label as necessary.
> 4. Display the Property Sheet, if it is not displayed at the right side of your screen.
> 5. Click the Data tab on the Property Sheet, and click the ellipses [...] found next to the Control Source property to open the Expression Builder.
> 6. Create the desired expression.
> 7. Click OK.

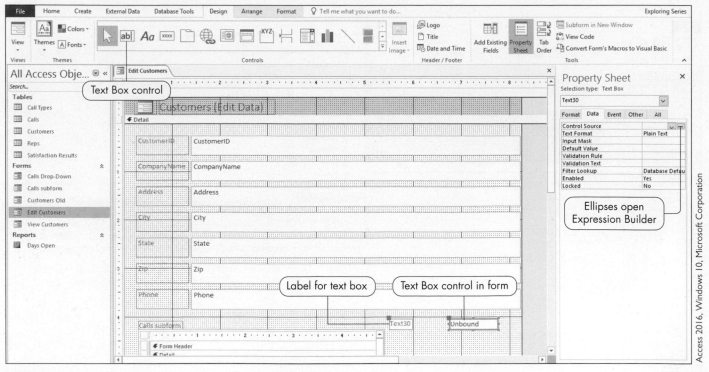

FIGURE 7.27 Text Box Control

When you add a new Text Box control to a report, you may find it puts the label in the same row as the data. In other words, the label, instead of appearing in a header, may appear in the data section, as shown in Figure 7.28. If this happens, you can click Tabular in the Table group on the Arrange tab while both the Label and Text Box controls are selected. The label will then move to a more appropriate location.

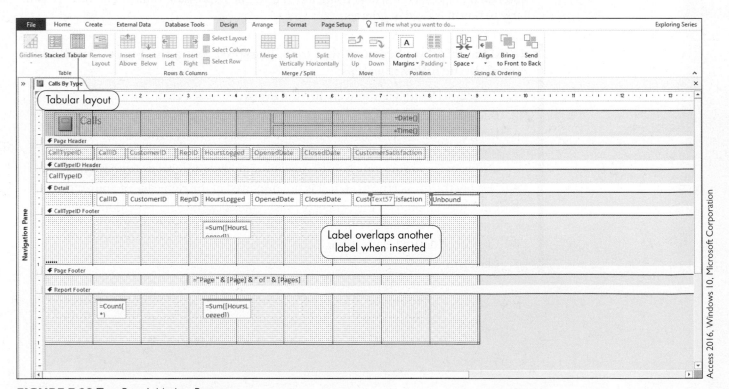

FIGURE 7.28 Text Box Added to Report

Note that if you are comfortable with functions, you do not have to use the Expression Builder. You could simply type the formula into the text box, preceded by an equal sign. For example, you could type =Date() to show the current date.

To format the results of a calculated control, complete the following steps:

1. Switch to Design view.
2. Click the text box you want to format.
3. Click Property Sheet in the Tools group on the Design tab.
4. Click the Format property on the Format tab of the Property Sheet to change the format. You will also find other options regarding formatting as well, such as a property for number of decimal places for a numeric field.

Add a Page Break Control

Pagination can be important for forms and especially reports. Instead of being unsure where a page will break when printed, you can add a page break at a certain location.

To add a page break to a form or report, complete the following steps:

1. Open the report in Design view.
2. Click the Insert Page Break control on the Design tab in the Controls group, as shown in Figure 7.29.
3. Click the section of the form or report where you want the page break. When you click the Insert Page Break control, the pointer changes to a crosshair with a small report icon (even in forms).
4. View the object in Print Preview to test the page break.

After you insert a page break on the form or report, a series of six dots [······] appears on the left margin (see Figure 7.29). To remove the page break, click the six dots and press Delete.

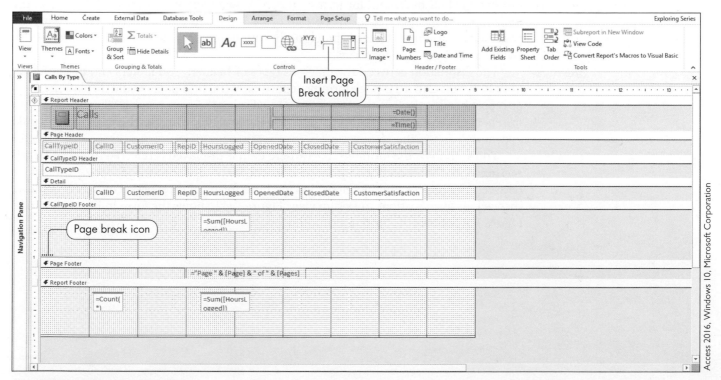

FIGURE 7.29 Page Break in Report

Understanding Sections

A *section* is a part of a form or report that can be manipulated separately from other parts of a form or report. Sections are visible in Design view. Each section can be collapsed or expanded as necessary. Forms and reports both have some common sections, as well as sections that differ only by the name of the object.

The *form header* is a section that displays one time at the top of the form. Likewise, the *report header* is a section that displays one time at the top of a report. If viewed on screen, both headers appear one time above the data in the object. If the form or report is printed, each of these headers will appear one time, on the first page of the printout. Column headings (labels) display in this section for reports as well as some types of forms.

Similarly, there are sections at the bottom of the object. The *form footer* is a section that displays one time at the bottom of a form. Likewise, the *report footer* is a section that displays one time at the bottom of the form or report. If viewed on screen, these footers appear one time underneath the data. If printed, they appear only on the final page of the printout, beneath any data. This section is left blank by default for forms and may contain an aggregate function (such as Count) for a report.

You may ask why page numbers were not mentioned. This is because the previous headers and footers only display once and thus would not be the appropriate choice to display page numbers. In addition to the previous sections, both forms and reports have a *page header*, a section that displays at the top of each page in a form or report. This is more commonly used for reports, as they are designed for printing. Page headers are switched off by default for forms but can be switched on as necessary. Likewise, the *page footer* appears once at the bottom of each page in a form or report. As with the page header, the page footer is much more common on reports. The page footer is also switched off by default for forms.

The distinction between the different types of headers and footers can be confusing at first. If you had a 10-page form or report, only the first page would display the form or report header. Each of the 10 pages would display the page header. Likewise, the form or report footer would appear once after the final record, whereas the page footer would appear on each of the 10 pages.

The section of the form or report where data is displayed is referred to as the *Detail section*. The Detail section can be seen as the body of the form or report. It displays between the header and footer sections in both forms and reports. Figure 7.30 shows the various form sections in Design view, Figure 7.31 shows the form in Form view, and Figure 7.32 shows the form in Print Preview.

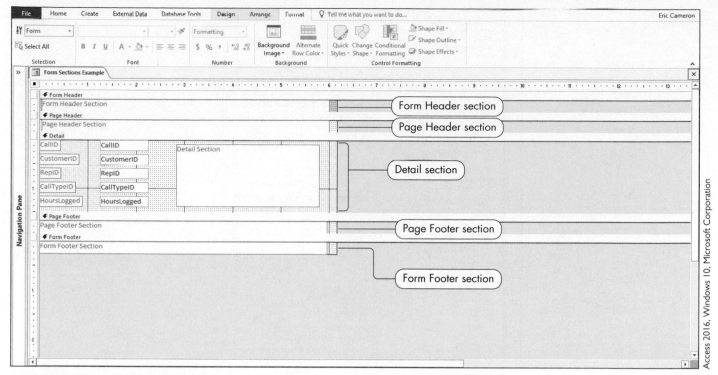

FIGURE 7.30 Form Sections in Design View

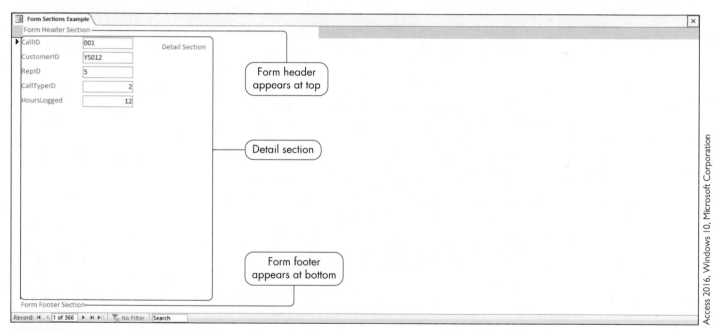

FIGURE 7.31 Form Sections in Form View

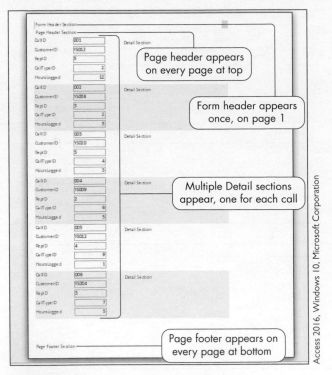

FIGURE 7.32 Form Sections in Print Preview

Reports are very similar to forms. Figure 7.33 shows the report sections in Design view, Figure 7.34 shows the sections in Report view, and Figure 7.35 shows the report in Print Preview.

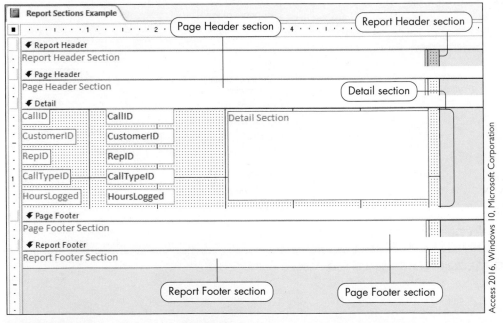

FIGURE 7.33 Report Sections in Design View

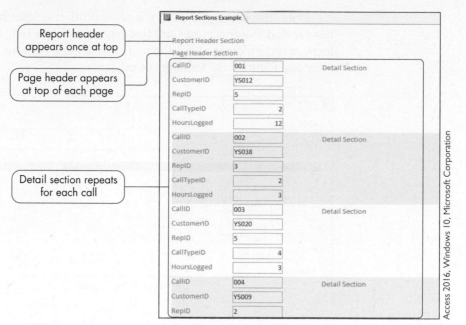

FIGURE 7.34 Report Sections in Report View

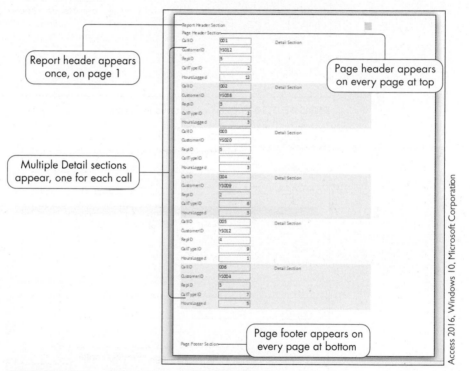

FIGURE 7.35 Report Sections in Print Preview

Show, Hide, and Resize Sections

Forms and reports display the Detail and Form/Report Header and Footer sections by default. Reports also include the page header/footer by default. All sections can be switched on and off using the same process.

To show or hide a section, complete the following steps:

1. Open the form or report in Design view.
2. Right-click a blank area of the form or report.
3. Select the section you want to show or hide—for example, Page Header/Footer.

Note that when you switch a section off, it deletes all controls in the section. The header and footer sections are tied together; if you hide the form or report header, the form or report footer also disappears. See Figure 7.36 for an illustration in Form Design view and Figure 7.37 for Report Design view.

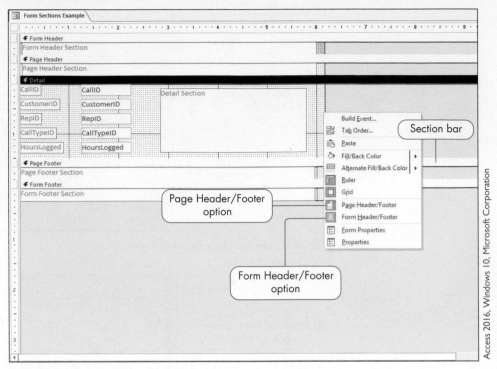

FIGURE 7.36 Displaying Sections in Forms

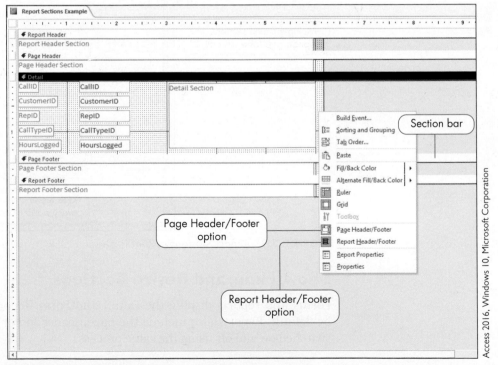

FIGURE 7.37 Displaying Sections in Reports

Within a form or report, you may want to change the height or width of portions of a section. The width is a global property. You cannot change the width of one section without changing it for the entire object. However, you can change the height of each section independently. In Figures 7.36 and 7.37, a *section bar* marks the top boundary of a section. You can expand or collapse the space between sections by moving the pointer over the section bar and dragging to the desired location. The top bar denotes the top boundary of the header. The bottom bar displays the top boundary of the footer. The gridlike area under the bars shows the space allotted to that section. If you decide that the allotted space for a particular section is not necessary, you can collapse that section fully so that the section bars are touching. The section remains in the report's design, but will not take up any room on the Print Preview or the printed page.

Add a Group Header/Footer to Reports

In addition to the sections previously listed, there is another header/footer set that exists. This header/footer set appear when grouping exists in a report. The *group header* is a section that appears one time for each unique value in the grouping, above the group. For example, if you group by a State field, there would be 50 separate groups and, therefore, the group header would appear 50 times. Unlike the previous headers, the group header will not be identified by the name. Instead, it will be identified by the field name followed by the word Header, so in the previous example, you would find a State Header section. Likewise, the *group footer* is a section that appears one time for each unique value in the grouping, below the group, and, therefore, would appear 50 times in the preceding example. This footer similarly would be named State Footer in this example. Note group headers and footers cannot be added to a form because forms do not support grouping.

If you use the Report Wizard to create a report, you may have specified grouping and thus would find a group header and/or footer in the report when you open in Design view. However, you can add a group header without the Report Wizard tool.

To add a group header to an existing report, complete the following steps:

1. Switch to Layout view.
2. Click Group & Sort in the Grouping & Totals group on the Design tab (if the Group, Sort, and Total pane is not displayed at the bottom of the screen, as shown in Figure 7.38).
3. Click Add a group in the Group, Sort, and Total pane at the bottom of the screen.
4. Select the field to group by.

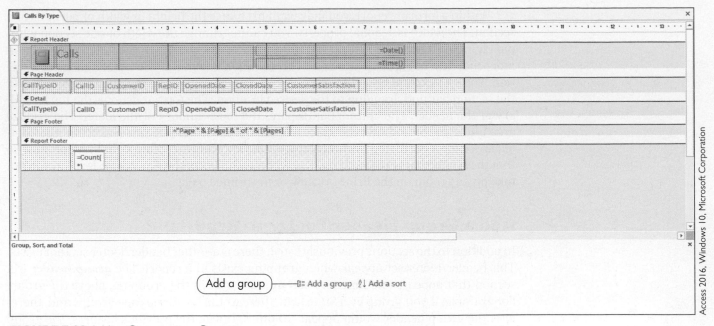

FIGURE 7.38 Adding Grouping to a Report

Note that even though you have done most of the work in this chapter in Design view, doing the grouping in Layout view saves you a few steps.

The Group Footer section does not show by default. It appears below the Detail section in Design view, but only when you select this option in the Group, Sort, and Total pane. The group footer is useful for totaling the data at the end of each group. If you want to display the total number of calls for each technician, this could be displayed in the group footer.

To display the group footer in an existing grouped report, complete the following steps:

1. Switch to Layout or Design view.
2. Click More on the Group, Sort, and Total pane.
3. Click the option to the right of *without a footer section* and select *with a footer section*, as shown in Figure 7.39.

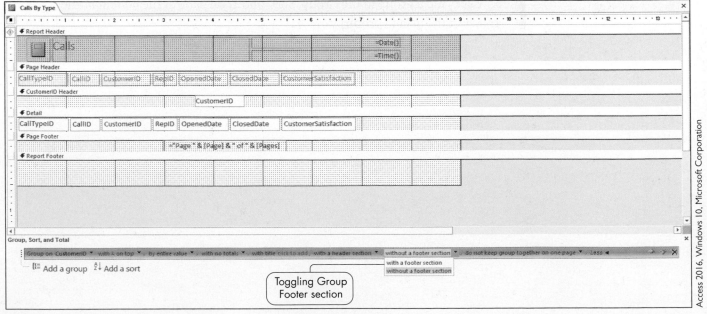

FIGURE 7.39 Displaying the Group Footer

Add Totals to a Footer

Often, reports require totals at the group level and/or at the grand total level. For example, a report might contain a count of the number of calls each technician has handled, and also display an overall total of the number of calls at the end of the report.

To add totals to a report that is grouped, complete the following steps:

1. Open the report in Design view.
2. Click More on the Group, Sort, and Total pane.
3. Click the option to the right of *without a footer section* and select *with a footer section*, as shown earlier in Figure 7.39.
4. Select the *with no totals* option, and select the field, the function, and the options, as shown in Figure 7.40.

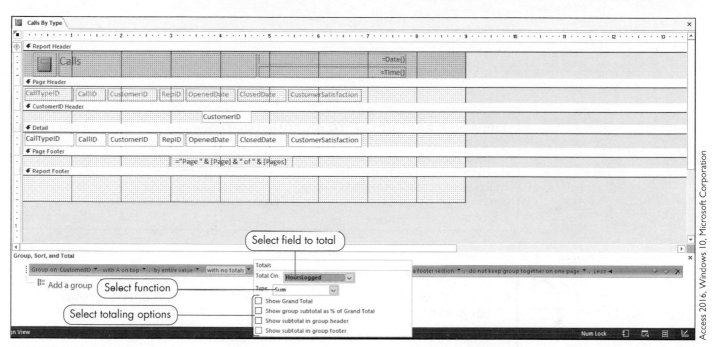

FIGURE 7.40 Adding Sum for HoursLogged Field

Figure 7.41 shows the sum for the HoursLogged field in Report view. Notice the total appears after Customer YS007, and then the next set of records for customer YS009 begin.

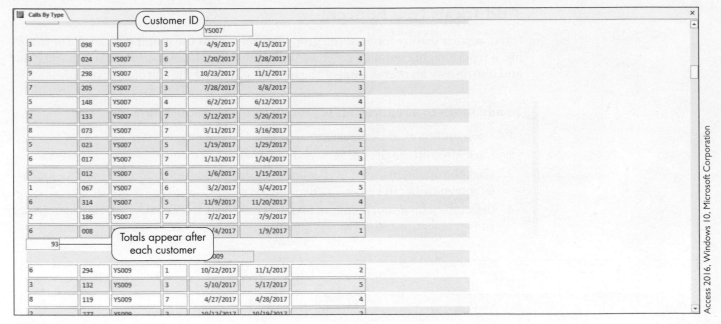

		Customer ID					
		YS007					
3	098	YS007	3	4/9/2017	4/15/2017		3
3	024	YS007	6	1/20/2017	1/28/2017		4
9	298	YS007	2	10/23/2017	11/1/2017		1
7	205	YS007	3	7/28/2017	8/8/2017		3
5	148	YS007	4	6/2/2017	6/12/2017		4
2	133	YS007	7	5/12/2017	5/20/2017		1
8	073	YS007	7	3/11/2017	3/16/2017		4
5	023	YS007	5	1/19/2017	1/29/2017		1
6	017	YS007	7	1/13/2017	1/24/2017		3
5	012	YS007	6	1/6/2017	1/15/2017		4
1	067	YS007	6	3/2/2017	3/4/2017		5
6	314	YS007	5	11/9/2017	11/20/2017		4
2	186	YS007	7	7/2/2017	7/9/2017		1
6	008			/4/2017	1/9/2017		1
93							
				009			
6	294	YS009	1	10/22/2017	11/1/2017		2
3	132	YS009	3	5/10/2017	5/17/2017		5
8	119	YS009	7	4/27/2017	4/28/2017		4
2	277	YS009	2	10/12/2017	10/19/2017		2

Totals appear after each customer

FIGURE 7.41 Report with Totals

> **TIP: ADD A PAGE BREAK TO A GROUP FOOTER**
>
> A page break is commonly used in a group footer. Doing so causes each group to print on a separate page. For example, if you had a report grouped by customer, the report would print each customer's data on a separate page (rather than continuing with the next customer on the same page). This type of report is useful when the information is distributed to each customer. In the case that a customer's information takes up more than one page, the page break is inserted after each customer's information.

Quick Concepts ✓

5. Explain the difference between a bound control and an unbound control. *p. 463*

6. List and briefly describe two controls found in the Controls group on the Design tab. *p. 464*

7. What is the purpose of a calculated control? *p. 464*

8. List and briefly describe the five default sections of a report. *p. 470*

9. What do the group header and footer do? *p. 475*

Access 2016, Windows 10, Microsoft Corporation

Hands-On Exercises

2 Controls and Sections

You have decided to modify reports to add calculations, and to modify the different header and footer sections of forms and reports to improve the print and on-screen readability.

STEP 1 >> **USE ADVANCED CONTROLS IN FORMS**

You will be making changes to an existing form and a calculated control to determine if a call is Open or Closed. Refer to Figure 7.42 as you complete Step 1.

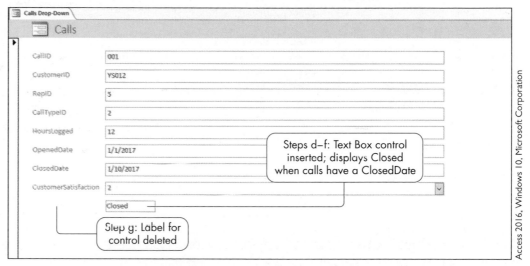

FIGURE 7.42 Calls Drop-Down Form

a. Open *a07h1Yellowstone_LastFirst* if you closed it at the end of Hands-On Exercise 1. Save the database as **a07h2Yellowstone_LastFirst**, changing h1 to h2.

b. Open the Calls Drop-Down form in Design view.

c. Drag the end of the Detail section (appearing right above the form footer) to about 4" on the vertical toolbar.

d. Click **Text Box** in the Controls group on the Design tab. Click beneath the last control in the form (CustomerSatisfaction) to insert the control. It should be placed approximately where it appears in Figure 7.42.

e. Display the Property Sheet, if it is not displayed. Click the **Data tab** on the Property Sheet, click the **Control Source box**, and then click the **ellipses** next to the Control Source property to display the Expression Builder.

f. Type **IIf(IsNull([ClosedDate]),"Open","Closed")** and click **OK**.

This expression will display Open when the ClosedDate is null (in other words, when no value exists in the ClosedDate field) and Closed otherwise.

g. Click the label for the new control (the word Text followed by a number), and press **Delete**.

h. Switch to Form view. Ensure the first few records display Closed. Click the **Last record Navigation button**, and ensure the last record in the table has a value of Open.

As the open calls are going to be the most recent, most older calls will be closed, whereas most new calls will be open. Compare your results with Figure 7.42.

i. Save and close the form.

STEP 2)) USE ADVANCED CONTROLS IN REPORTS

You will make changes to an existing report to display the number of days each call has been open. Refer to Figure 7.43 as you complete Step 2.

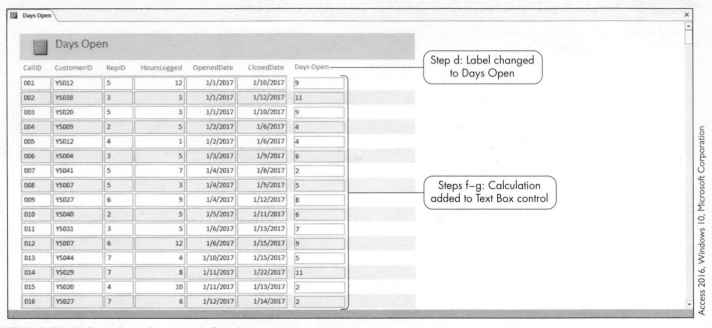

FIGURE 7.43 Days Open Report with Calculation

a. Open the Days Open report in Design view.

b. Click the **Text Box control** in the Controls group on the Design tab. Click to the right of the ClosedDate text box in the Detail section of the report to add a new field.

c. Click **Tabular** in the Table group on the Arrange tab.

The new field lines up after the final column in the report.

d. Click the **Label control** for the new column. Double-click to select the existing text. Press **Delete** to remove the existing text, and type **Days Open**.

e. Click the **Text Box control** for the new column (which currently displays the word *Unbound*). Display the Property Sheet, if it is not displayed.

f. Click the **Data tab** on the Property Sheet, and click **Control Source**. Click the **ellipses** to launch the Expression Builder.

g. Type **=[ClosedDate]-[OpenedDate]** in the Expression box. Click **OK**.

h. Switch to Report view. Verify the calculation correctly displays the number of days each call was open, as shown in Figure 7.43.

i. Save and close the report.

You will adjust an existing form by adding a logo to the form header and adding a page header. Refer to Figure 7.44 as you complete Step 3.

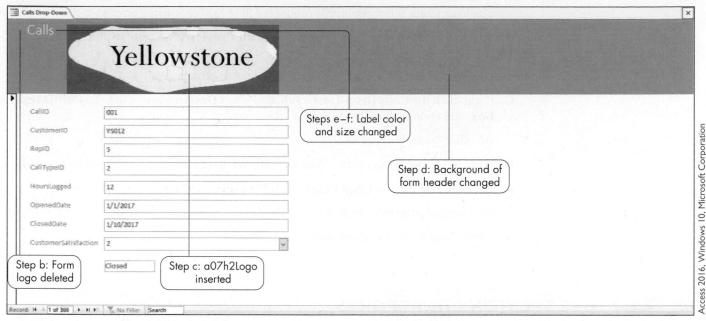

FIGURE 7.44 Updated Calls Drop-Down Form

a. Open the Calls Drop-Down form in Design view.

b. Click the **form logo** (to the left of the word Calls) in the Form Header section, and press **Delete**.

The form logo disappears.

c. Click the **Image control** in the Controls group on the Design tab. Click to the right of the word *Calls* in the form header. Browse to the location of your data files, and select *a07h2Logo*. Click **OK**.

> **TROUBLESHOOTING:** If you are unable to see the Image control in the Controls group on the Design tab, click More in the Controls group, and select the Image control.

A logo for Yellowstone appears in the report header.

d. Click the **gray background** of the Form Header section. Click the **Shape Fill arrow** in the Control Formatting group on the Format tab. Select **Blue, Accent 1** (first row, fifth column). Recall you can see the names for each color by pointing to a color and waiting for the ScreenTip to appear.

e. Click the **Calls label**. Click the **Font Color arrow** in the Font group on the Format tab. Select **White, Background 1** (first row, first column).

f. Click the **Font Size arrow** in the Font group on the Format tab. Change the size to **22**.

g. Switch to Form view, and compare your form with Figure 7.44.

h. Switch to Design view. Right-click a blank area, and select **Page Header/Footer** from the shortcut menu.

A Page Header section displays above the Detail section, and a Page Footer section displays below the Detail section.

i. Click the **Label control** in the Controls group on the Design tab. Click the left side of the Page Footer section. Type **Created by First Last**, replacing First with your first name and Last with your last name.

j. Switch to Form view.

The page footer is not displayed because it will only appear when printed.

k. Click the **File tab**, and click **Print**. Click **Print Preview**. Navigate to the second page.

The footer should appear on each page. You will notice the form is too wide to fit on one page left to right. When printed, this might lead to extra pages.

l. Right-click the **Calls Drop-Down tab**, and select **Design View**. Click the **CallID text box**, and change the width to **5.5"** on the top ruler.

All other controls adjust as well.

m. Point to the right edge of the Detail section, and drag it to about **7.5"** on the top ruler.

n. Click the **File tab**, and click **Print**. Click **Print Preview**.

As a printed page in Portrait is 8.5" wide, this report will now fit on one page left-to-right.

o. Click **Close Print Preview**, and save and close the form.

(**STEP 4**)) **USE SECTIONS IN REPORTS**

You will create a new report based on the Calls table and use the group headers and footers to summarize the data. Refer to Figure 7.45 as you complete Step 4.

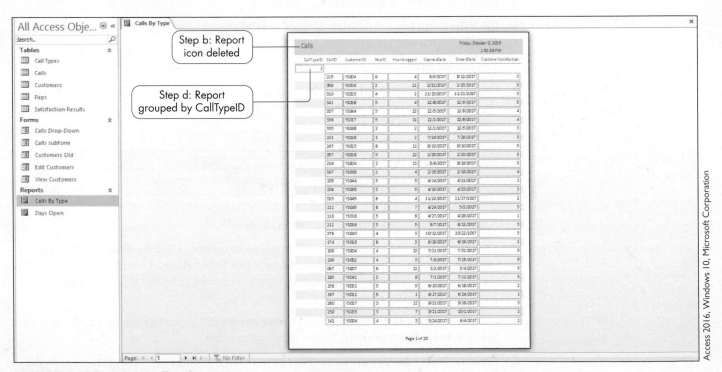

FIGURE 7.45 Final Calls by Type Report

a. Click the **Calls table**. Click the **Report tool** in the Reports group on the Create tab.

b. Delete the report icon (which appears to the left of the word *Calls*) from the report header.

c. Click **Group & Sort** in the Grouping & Totals group on the Design tab to display the Group, Sort, and Total pane at the bottom of the screen, if it is not already displayed.

The Group, Sort, and Total pane displays at the bottom of the report.

d. Click **Add a group** in the Group, Sort, and Total pane, and select **CallTypeID**.

The report will be grouped by the type of call.

e. Resize the RepID field so it takes up only as much room as necessary.

The report should fit on one page, left to right.

f. Switch to Design view.

Notice a CallTypeID Header appears between the Page Header and Detail sections.

g. Click **More** in the Group, Sort, and Total pane. Click the **without a footer section arrow** and select **with a footer section**.

A CallTypeID footer appears between the Detail and Page Footer sections.

h. Click the **HoursLogged text box**. Click **Totals** in the Grouping & Totals group on the Design tab, and select **Sum**.

A Sum function appears in both the CallTypeID Footer and the report footer.

i. Resize the CallTypeID footer and report footer to be about 1" tall. You can drag the border down until you see a 1 on the vertical ruler.

j. Resize the text boxes for the new sum fields to be about double the current height.

k. Click the **Insert Page Break control** ⸬ in the Controls group on the Design tab. Click the bottom of the CallTypeID footer.

Six small dots appear on the left of the CallTypeID footer.

l. Display the report in Print Preview.

> **TROUBLESHOOTING:** If you get an error message stating *The section width is greater than the page width, and there are no items in the additional space, so some pages may be blank.*, try making the rows slightly less tall.

All calls with a CallTypeID appear on page 1, with a total of 188 hours appearing on page 2. Due to the number of calls, your totals for CallTypeID 1 will appear on a page by itself. Scroll forward and notice a total of 208 hours for all calls with a CallTypeID of 2. Your results should resemble Figure 7.45.

m. Save the report as **Calls By Type**, and close the report.

n. Close the database and exit Access. Based on your instructor's directions, submit a07h2Yellowstone_LastFirst.

Chapter Objectives Review

After reading this chapter, you have accomplished the following objectives:

1. Restrict edits in a form.

- Read-only forms enable users to view but not change data to help prevent erroneous data entry. Forms can be set to restrict changes, additions, and/or deletions.

2. Understand combo boxes.

- Convert a text box to a combo box: A Combo Box control provides a menu that displays a list of options from which the user can choose a single value.
- Customize a combo box: Information can be looked up in a table or, less commonly, added manually to a combo box. You can restrict data entry to only the provided values.

3. Set the tab order.

- Customize tabbing: The tab order is the sequential advancing in a form from one field or control to the next when you press Tab. The tab order can be set automatically or manually.
- Remove a tab stop: Tab stops can be removed from any field. Often, they are removed from fields that do not require data entry.

4. Understand subforms.

- A form can display records from a related table using a subform.
- Subforms are generally laid out as a table and are used when a relationship exists between two tables.
- Subforms can be manually added to any form using the Subform/Subreport tool. Assuming a relationship exists between two tables, it is a straightforward process.

5. Understand advanced controls.

- A bound control is a category of control that is connected to a field in a table or query.
- An unbound control is a category of control not tied to a specific field, often decorative elements, such as titles, lines, pictures, and logos.
- Add emphasis to a form or report: The Line and Rectangle controls are among the options to add emphasis. Formatting can be adjusted as necessary.

- Add text and images to a form or report: Text can be added using a Label control, and images can be added using the Image control.
- Add a calculated control: A calculated control is placed inside a text box. It contains an expression that generates a calculated result. The Expression Builder can help create complex calculated controls.
- Add a Page Break control: You can specify exactly where to add a page break using the Page Break control.

6. Understand sections.

- A section is a part of a form or report that can be manipulated separately from other parts of the form or report. They are viewable in Design view.
- The Form Header section and the Report Header section are headers that display one time at the top of each form or report. The Form Footer and Report Footer sections are footers that display one time at the bottom of the form or report.
- The page header is a header that appears once at the top of each page in a form or report. The page footer is a footer that appears once at the bottom of each page in a form or report.
- The Detail section displays the records in the data source.
- Show, hide, and resize sections: You can show or hide any missing section in Design view by right-clicking and selecting the section. Section boundaries are marked by a section bar that can be dragged up or down to resize a section.
- Add a group header/footer to reports: The group header and footer sections appear once each time the grouping field value changes. Group headers and footers are only available in reports.
- Add totals to a footer: Group footers (hidden by default) are commonly used for totals.

Key Terms Matching

Match the key terms with their definitions. Write the key term letter by the appropriate numbered definition.

a.	Bound control	**k.**	Page header
b.	Calculated control	**l.**	Read-only form
c.	Combo Box control	**m.**	Report footer
d.	Control	**n.**	Report header
e.	Detail section	**o.**	Section
f.	Form footer	**p.**	Section bar
g.	Form header	**q.**	Subform
h.	Group footer	**r.**	Tab order
i.	Group header	**s.**	Unbound control
j.	Page footer		

1. _____ A form that enables users to view but not change data. **p. 446**

2. _____ A part of a form or report that can be manipulated separately from other parts of a form or report. **p. 470**

3. _____ A section that appears one time for each unique value in the grouping, below the group. **p. 475**

4. _____ A section that appears one time for each unique value in the grouping, above the group. **p. 475**

5. _____ A section that displays one time at the bottom of a form. **p. 470**

6. _____ A section that displays one time at the bottom of a report. **p. 470**

7. _____ A section that displays one time at the top of the form. **p. 470**

8. _____ A section that displays one time at the top of the report. **p. 470**

9. _____ A section that displays at the bottom of each page in a form or report. **p. 470**

10. _____ A section that displays at the top of each page in a form or report. **p. 470**

11. _____ An object on a form or report. **p. 463**

12. _____ Any control not tied to a specific field. **p. 463**

13. _____ Any control that is connected to a field in a table or query. **p. 463**

14. _____ A control that displays the result of an expression in a form or report. **p. 464**

15. _____ Marks the top boundary of a section. **p. 475**

16. _____ One form contained within another form. **p. 453**

17. _____ A control that provides a menu displaying a list of options from which the user can choose a single value. **p. 448**

18. _____ The section of the form or report where data is displayed. **p. 470**

19. _____ The sequential advancing in a form from one field or control to the next when you press Tab. **p. 451**

Multiple Choice

1. A form that is fully read-only permits you to:

   (a) Delete records.

   (b) Change data.

   (c) View records.

   (d) All of the above.

2. A menu can be created with a:

   (a) Calculated control.

   (b) Combo box.

   (c) Line control.

   (d) Section bar.

3. Which of the following statements about tab order is *false*?

   (a) Tab order can be automatically assigned by Access.

   (b) Fields can have their tab stop removed.

   (c) You can change the order in which fields appear when you press the Tab key.

   (d) None of the above are false.

4. Which of the following would most likely *not* be a subform?

   (a) A list of patients for a doctor

   (b) A list of orders for each customer

   (c) A list of employees for a location

   (d) A list of birth mothers for a child

5. A control displaying the value of a field from a table or query is a(n):

   (a) Bound control.

   (b) Calculated control.

   (c) Rectangle control.

   (d) Unbound control.

6. A control containing =Date() is most likely to be a:

   (a) Bound control.

   (b) Calculated control.

   (c) Rectangle control.

   (d) Page Break control.

7. Which of the following statements is *false*?

   (a) The Detail section displays the values of records.

   (b) A Label control is used for text, such as titles.

   (c) A calculated field is created with a Text Box control.

   (d) Forms cannot display calculated controls.

8. Which of the following prints once per report?

   (a) Form header

   (b) Group header

   (c) Page header

   (d) Report header

9. Which of the following prints on every page of a form?

   (a) Form header

   (b) Group header

   (c) Page header

   (d) Report header

10. Which of the following is available in a report but not in a form?

   (a) Detail section

   (b) Group Header section

   (c) Form Header/Report Header section

   (d) Page Footer section

Practice Exercises

1 La Vida Mocha

FROM SCRATCH 🍵 You are helping La Vida Mocha, a small coffee supply store, migrate to Access. You will help the company add data validation and create two forms, one for data entry and one for viewing data. Refer to Figure 7.46 as you complete this exercise.

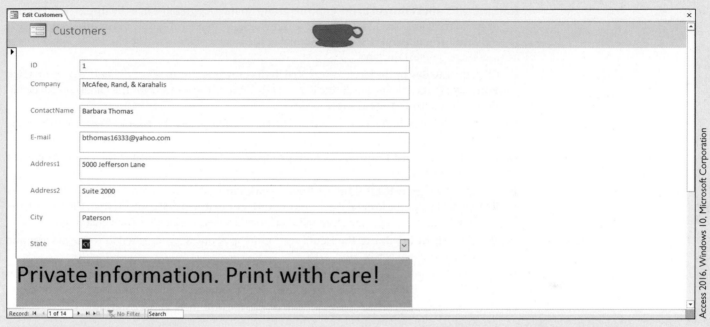

FIGURE 7.46 Edit Customers Form

a. Open Access and create a new blank desktop database named **a07p1Coffee_LastFirst**.

b. Import the text file *a07p1States* into a new table in the current database. Step through the wizard, naming the field **StateName** and choosing the StateName field as the primary key. Accept all other default properties. In the last step of the wizard, save the table as **State**.

c. Import the text file *a07p1Customers* into a new table in the current database. Step through the wizard, ensuring you check the **First Row Contains Field Names option** to select it, accept default field names, and choose **ID** when asked to select a primary key. In the last step of the wizard, name the table **Customers**.

d. Click the **Customers table** in the Navigation Pane. Click **Form** in the Forms group on the Create tab. Save the form as **Edit Customers**.

e. Right-click the **State text box**, point to **Change To**, and then select **Combo Box** from the shortcut menu. If the Property Sheet is not displayed at the right of the screen, click **Property Sheet** in the Tools group on the Design tab to display it.

f. Change the Row Source property to **State**. Change the Limit To List property to **Yes**. Switch to Form view.

g. Change the State for the first customer to **NJ**, press **Tab**, type **Paterson** in the City, press **Tab**, and type **07505** for Zip. You will notice the tab order is not logical (State, then City, then Zip).

h. Switch to Design view. Click **Tab Order** in the Tools group on the Design tab. Click **Detail** in the Section area of the Tab Order window. Click the **record selector** to the left of the State field, and drag it below the City field. Click **OK**.

i. Click the **Form Header section**. Click the **Image control** in the Controls group. If it is not visible, click More at the lower right of the Controls box to display all controls first. Click at about **6"** on the horizontal ruler in the Form Header section. Browse to the location of your data files and select *a07p1Mocha*.

j. Drag the **section bar** below the Form Footer section down to approximately **1"** on the vertical ruler.

k. Click the **Label control** in the Controls group on the Design tab. Click the **upper-left corner** of the Form Footer section (which is currently gray with dots in the background). Type the text **Private information. Print with care!** in the label. Click anywhere else in the Form Footer section to deselect the label.

l. Click the **border** of the label you created in the previous step to select the entire control. Click **Font Size** in the Font group on the Format tab. Change the font size for the Label control to **36**. Resize the control so it is about 8" wide.

m. Click **Font Color** in the Font group on the Format tab. Select the **Black, Text 1 color** in the first row.

n. Click **Background Color** in the Font group on the Format tab. Select the **Gold, Accent 4 color** in the first row.

o. Click the **Design tab**. Click **Insert Page Break control** in the Controls group. If it is not visible, click More at the lower right of the Controls box to display all controls first. Click along the left margin underneath the SalesRepID field to add a page break after each customer.

p. Drag the **right border** of the Detail section to be about **8"** wide. Switch to Form view and compare your form with Figure 7.46.

q. Click the **File tab**, and click **Print**. Click **Print Preview**. Notice only one customer appears on the first page. Click **Next Page** three times to notice how each page contains a single customer.

r. Save and close the form. Create a copy of the form named **View Customers**. Open View Customers in Design view.

s. Change the title at the top of the form to **Customers (View Only)**.

t. Display the Property Sheet. Ensure the menu at the top of the Property Sheet displays *Form*. Ensure the Data tab is displayed and change the options **Allow Additions**, **Allow Deletions**, and **Allow Edits** to **No** to create a read-only form. Switch to Form view and ensure you cannot add, change, or delete records.

u. Save and close the form.

v. Close **Table1**, choosing **No** when prompted to save.

w. Close the database and exit Access. Based on your instructor's directions, submit a07p1Coffee_LastFirst.

2 International Importers

You are a technical supervisor at International Importers. The technician who handles most Access tasks just went on paternity leave, and he was unable to address user changes before going on leave. You will create a form and report based on user requests. Refer to Figure 7.47 as you complete this exercise.

FIGURE 7.47 Products Report

a. Open *a07p2Importers*. Save the database as **a07p2Importers_LastFirst**.

b. Open the Products by Category form in Design view.

c. Click **Subform/Subreport** in the Controls group on the Design tab. If it is not visible, click More at the lower right of the Controls box to display all controls first. Click below the Description label along the left margin.

d. Answer the SubForm Wizard as follows:
   - Accept the default Use existing Tables and Queries, and click **Next**.
   - Select **Table: Products** from the Tables/Queries list. Double-click the **ProductName**, **QuantityPerUnit**, **UnitPrice**, **UnitsInStock**, and **UnitsOnOrder fields**. Click **Next**.
   - Accept the default relationship (Show Products for each record in Categories using CategoryID). Click **Next**.
   - Accept the default name of Products subform. Click **Finish**.

e. Switch to Layout view. Shrink the columns in the subform so all fields are displayed.

f. Right-click the **Category ID text box**. Point to **Change To**, and select **Combo Box** from the shortcut menu.

g. Click **Property Sheet** in the Tools group, if it is not displayed on the right side of your screen. Locate the Row Source Property. Click in the box, and click the arrow to the right of the box. Select **Categories** from the menu.

h. Locate the Limit To List property, and change the value to **Yes** so users can only input values found in the list.

i. Switch to Form view. Notice the arrow at the right side of the Category ID field, indicating you can now choose the Category ID from a menu. Close the form, saving all changes.

j. Open the Products report in Layout view. Click **Add a group** in the Group, Sort, and Total pane at the bottom of the screen. Select **CompanyName**. Notice the CompanyName field is not wide enough to display all values.

k. Switch to Design view. Change the width of the CompanyName field (displayed in the CompanyName Header) to **4"** on the horizontal ruler.

l. Click the **Text Box control** in the Controls group on the Design tab. Click to the right of the ProductCost box in the Detail section.

m. Click **Tabular** in the Table group on the Arrange tab to move the label to the Page Header section.

n. Double-click the **label** for the control (which currently displays the word *Text* followed by a number). Change the text in the label from the existing text to **Net**.

o. Double-click the **text box** for the new field (which currently displays *Unbound*) and type **=UnitPrice-ProductCost** in the box.

p. Click the **Format tab** on the Property Sheet. Change the format to **Currency**, and change the Decimal Places property to **2**. Close the Property Sheet.

q. Click the **Rectangle control** in the Controls group on the Design tab. If it is not visible, click More at the lower right of the Controls box to display all controls first. Draw a rectangle around the text box you just created (which currently displays =[UnitPrice]-[ProductCost]).

r. Click the **Format tab**. Click **Shape Fill** in the Control Formatting group. Select **Transparent**.

s. Switch to Report view. Compare your report with Figure 7.47.

t. Save and close the report.

u. Close the database and exit Access. Based on your instructor's directions, submit a07p2Importers_LastFirst.

Mid-Level Exercises

1 Red Cliffs City Hotels

ANALYSIS CASE

You are the general manager of a large hotel chain. You track revenue by categories: hotel rooms, conference rooms, and weddings. You will create a form that includes a menu for the state and the company logo in the header, uses the company colors, and has a correct tab order. You also plan on modifying a report so it displays the number of years that each customer has been a member.

a. Open *a07m1Rewards*. Save the database as **a07m1Rewards_LastFirst**.

b. Select the **Members table**, and create a form using the Form tool. Save the form as **Maintain Members**.

c. Switch to Design view. Change the State text box to a combo box.

d. Change the Row Source to **States**.

e. Delete the form logo and the Label control (containing the word *Members*) from the Form Header section.

f. Insert an Image control in the upper-left corner of the Form Header section. Insert the *a07m1Logo* file.

g. Change the background color of the Detail section to the orange color found in the first row (**Orange, Accent 6**).

DISCOVER

h. Select all the labels in the Detail section by drawing a box around them. Change the font color of the labels to **Black, Text 1**. Change the border width of the labels to **4 pt** and the border color to **Blue, Accent 1**.

i. Switch to Form view. Verify the tab order does not work as expected by pressing **Tab** to visit each field (State comes before City). Correct the tab order. Save and close the form.

j. Open the Members By State report in Design view.

k. Add a formula in the **Time as Member box** (which currently displays *Unbound*) to determine the number of years they have been a member. Use **#12/31/2017#** as the current date (recall dates must be surrounded by # signs), subtract the **MemberSince** field, and divide the result by **365**.

l. Change the format of the formula from the previous step using the Property Sheet, to display as **Standard format** with **1** decimal place.

m. Add grouping by the **State** field. Remove the State label from the Page Header section.

n. Switch to Report view. Ensure the values displayed make sense. For example, assuming a current date of 12/31/2017, member Melissa Remaklus has been a member since 11/8/2006, so she has been a member for slightly more than 11 years. Also notice after the members from Alaska (AK) there is a break before the members from Alabama (AL) due to the grouping you added.

o. Save and close the report.

★ p. Open the *a07m1Analysis* document in Word and save as **a07m1Analysis_LastFirst**. Use the database objects you created to answer the questions. Save and close the document.

q. Close the database. Exit Access. Based on your instructor's directions, submit the following files:

a07m1Rewards_LastFirst

a07m1Analysis_LastFirst

2 Replacement Parts

You are working as a stockperson in the warehouse for Replacement Parts. You have received an internship in the Information Technology Department. You have been tasked with making modifications to the company database. As you are hoping to move from being a stockperson to being a member of the technology staff, you want to impress and go above and beyond what has been asked of you.

a. Open *a07m2Replace*. Save the database as **a07m2Replace_LastFirst**.

b. Create a new form based on the Employees table using the Form tool. Save the form as **Employees Lookup**.

c. Delete the subform. Change the form to be read-only, ensuring users cannot add, delete, or edit records.

d. Change the title in the form header to **Employees (Lookup Only)**. Save and close the form.

e. Open the Customer Orders report in Design view.

f. Insert the *a07m2Logo* image using an Image control in the report header to the right of the Customer Orders text.

g. Change the option in the Group, Sort, and Total pane so the grouping on OrderID displays with a footer section. Change the option from *with no totals* to total on the **Qty field** and to show the subtotal in the group footer. Add a Label control at about 5" (to the left of the sum of the Qty field) in the OrderID footer that displays **Total Qty Ordered**.

h. Add a new Text Box control after the Price field in the Detail section. Click **Tabular** in the Table group on the Arrange tab.

i. Change the label for the new control to **Line Total**. Add a formula in the text box to multiply the **Qty** field by the **Price** field.

j. Change the format of the Line Total text box to **Currency**.

k. Use the **Line control** to add a horizontal line at the bottom of the OrderID footer that covers the entire width of the report. Hold **Shift** as you draw the line to help keep it straight.

l. Switch to Report view and ensure the Total Qty Ordered values appear correctly. Switch to Design view.

m. Change the shape outline's line type for the Total Qty Ordered text box—which currently displays =Sum([Qty])—in the OrderID footer to **Sparse Dots border**. Add a Special Effect of **Shadowed** using the Property Sheet. Save and close the report.

n. Close the database and exit Access. Based on your instructor's directions, submit a07m2Replace_LastFirst.

3 New Castle County Technical Services

RUNNING CASE

New Castle County Technical Services (NCCTS) provides technical support for a number of local companies. You will be creating a new form to enable call information to be added and deleted (but not modified). To ease data entry, you will convert the call type to a combo box. You will also modify an existing form to fix problems with the tabbing, add a subform, and make the form more attractive. You will then modify an existing report to add grouping by customer, display average satisfaction for each customer, and set the form so at the most one customer appears on a page.

This project is a running case. You will use the same database file across Chapters 5 through 10.

a. Open the database you finished last chapter *a06m3NCCTS_LastFirst* and save the database as **a07m3NCCTS_LastFirst**.

> **TROUBLESHOOTING:** If you did not complete the Chapter 6 case, return to Chapter 6, complete the case, and then return to this exercise.

b. Create a new form based on the Calls table using the Form tool. Change the form property for Allow Edits to **No**.

c. Change the **CallTypeID field** to a Combo Box, and set the row source to the **Call Types** table.

d. Save the form as **Call Logs**, and close the form.

e. Open the Customer Information form in Form view. Press **Tab** six times, and notice the inconsistent ordering of the fields. Switch to Design view.

f. Change the tab order so the fields display in the following order: **CustomerID**, **CompanyName**, **Address**, **City**, **State**, **Zip**, **Phone**.

g. Change the Tab Stop property for the CustomerID field to **No**.

h. Switch to Form view. Ensure the first field selected is now CompanyName, and when you press Tab, the fields appear in the order specified in Step f.

i. Switch to Design view. Create a new subform using the **Subform/Subreport control** beneath the Phone field label. You should include all fields from the Calls table, use the default relationship, and accept the default name for the subform.

j. Switch to Layout view, and resize the form to be as wide as necessary to display all the data.

k. Switch to Design view. Add a vertical **Line Control**, starting to the right of the CustomerID field in the Detail section and continuing down to the bottom of the page.

l. Add a **Label control** to the Form Header section at the **5"** mark. Type **New Castle County Technical Services** in the control, and change the font color to **Black, Text 1**.

m. Save and close the form.

n. Open the **Calls by Customer report** in Layout view. Add grouping by **CompanyName**.

o. Change the option so the CompanyName grouping appears **with a footer section**.

p. Display the average of the **CustomerSatisfaction** field, choosing the **Show subtotal in group footer** option.

q. Format the average of the CustomerSatisfaction field as **Standard** with **2** decimal places.

r. Switch to Design view and add a **Page Break control** to the bottom of the CompanyName footer.

s. Click in the Report Header section. Add a **Hyperlink control**. You plan on creating a link to the NCCTS website, but the website is not yet published, so you will create a link and modify it later. For the moment, the hyperlink should link to the address http://www.google.com and the text to display should be **Google**. Move the hyperlink to the **4"** mark.

t. Switch to Report view and click the **Google** link to test it. The link should open in your default browser. Close the browser and return to Access.

u. Switch to Print Preview. Ensure each page displays the average of the CustomerSatisfaction field for that customer, and each customer starts on a new page. Save and close the report.

v. Close the database and exit Access. Based on your instructor's directions, submit a07m3NCCTS_LastFirst.

Beyond the Classroom

Bank Reporting

You are working with the Fighting Irish Credit Union as a consultant. They have asked you to update a report you created. Open *a07b1Bank* and save it as **a07b1Bank_LastFirst**. Open the Loan Payments report in Design view. Add grouping by the Type field. Add a new calculated control with a label of MonthlyPmt, which calculates the monthly mortgage payment for each customer, assuming monthly payments for the loans (the number of years, annual rate, and loan amount are all fields already in the report). The results should be displayed as a positive number in Currency format with two decimal places. Display the Group Footer section. Add a label at the far left stating Averages, and show the average amount, the average interest rate, and the average term in the group footer using the Totals feature in the Group, Sort, and Total pane. Format the average term in Standard format with 2 decimal places. Add a Page Break control to the Type Footer (Group Footer) section beneath the Averages label. Save and close the report. Close the database and exit Access. Based on your instructor's directions, submit a07b1Bank_LastFirst.

Ramos Medical Care

As a recent graduate of a Medical Informatics program, you are working in the healthcare field at Ramos Medical Care. A database recently crashed, and you were able to restore the database from a backup. The data is correct, but your supervisor identified some form and report issues. Open *a07b2Ramos* and save it as **a07b2Ramos_LastFirst**. Address the following problems:

- The Patient Lookup form used to be read-only, and users could not change, add, or delete information from the form. In addition, there used to be a single box with a black border surrounding all the fields in the Detail section.
- The Intake form's tab order no longer works correctly. In addition, the State field used to be a menu, displaying the values found in the State Abbreviations table.
- The Medications by Room report used to be grouped by the patient's SSN, and was sorted by MedicationName.
- The Illness Statistics report prompts for "Date" every time it is opened, and no longer displays the current date in the page footer.

Close the database and exit Access. Based on your instructor's directions, submit a07b2Ramos_LastFirst.

Capstone Exercise

The Human Resources Department asked you to assist them in updating the database they are using. The department requires a form that can be used to find information but not change information. In addition, you will enhance an existing form and generate a report showing which employees report to each supervisor.

Database File Setup

You will save a copy of the original database and open the database to complete this capstone exercise.

a. Open *a07c1Prices*.

b. Save the database as **a07c1Prices_LastFirst**.

Create a Read-Only Form

You will create a form to view employees. Use the Form tool to create the form, and then switch the form to be read-only.

a. Select the **Employees** table and use the Form tool to create a new form.

b. Change the title to **View Employees**.

c. Delete the **Orders subform**.

d. Change the **Allow Edits**, **Allow Additions**, and **Allow Deletions** settings to **No**.

e. View the form in Form view and ensure you cannot edit, add, or delete records.

f. Save the form as **View Employees** and close the form.

Convert a Text Box to a Combo Box and Customize Tabbing

You will modify an existing form to implement a menu and fix the tab order.

a. Create a new table named **Countries**. Rename the default ID field to **Country**, and change the data type to **Short Text**. Enter two records, **UK** and **USA**. Close the table.

b. Open the Update Employees form in Design view.

c. Change the **Country** field to a combo box.

d. Set the Row Source to **Countries** and the Limit To List property to **Yes**.

e. Fix the tab order so the **Postal Code** field comes before the **Country** field. Save and close the form.

Add Controls to Forms and Reports and Use Sections

You were asked to add some privacy information to the bottom of the View Employees form and make some design changes. You were also asked to create a report for managers that shows the name of all employees who work for them and calculates the number of years the employees have been employed at the company.

a. Open the **View Employees form** in Design view. Increase the size of the Form Footer section and add a new Label control on the left side of the form footer that displays the text **Personnel information is considered private and printouts should be shredded after use**.

b. Change the font color to **Black, Text 1**, and bold the text.

c. Save and close the form.

d. Create a new report using the Report Wizard. From the Employees table, select the **FirstName**, **LastName**, **HireDate**, and **HomePhone fields** in that order. Accept all other default options.

e. Switch to Layout view. Add grouping by the **ReportsTo** field.

f. Switch to Design view. Switch the option to **with a footer section** in the Group, Sort, and Total pane. Use the pane to also display the count of the **First Name field** in the Group Footer section.

g. Add an **Insert Page Break control** at the bottom of the ReportsTo footer section.

h. Resize the Home Phone field so the right side lines up with the 6" on the horizontal ruler.

i. Add a new **Text Box control** to the right of the Home Phone box. Use **Tabular** in the Table group on the Arrange tab to place it correctly.

j. Change the label for the field to **Years Employed**.

k. Add a formula in the text box to calculate the number of years since the employee's hire date, assuming the current date is **#12/31/2017#**. Format the field as **Standard** with **1** decimal place.

l. Close and save the report. Close the database and exit Access. Based on your instructor's directions, submit a07c1Prices_LastFirst.

Get Connected

LEARNING OUTCOME

You will exchange data between Access and other Office applications or websites.

OBJECTIVES & SKILLS: After you read this chapter, you will be able to:

CASE STUDY | Property Management Data Exchange

The Blackwood Maintenance Service (BMS) is a property management company located in Pineville, North Carolina. The owners would like to attract new customers by expanding the services they offer. Many of the properties that are maintained by BMS belong to residents' associations.

Your task is to contact the board members of each association and ask them if you can send information about the new services. You will also ask permission to send the homeowners a flyer by regular mail.

After contacting each association, you send the association manager a list of the new services that BMS can offer the homeowners. In addition, you create a list of homeowners who BMS will contact by mail. Each association has its own preferred format, so you prepare the information in a variety of ways. Information is also received by BMS in a variety of formats that you incorporate as new data into the database.

Exchanging Data Between Access and Other Applications

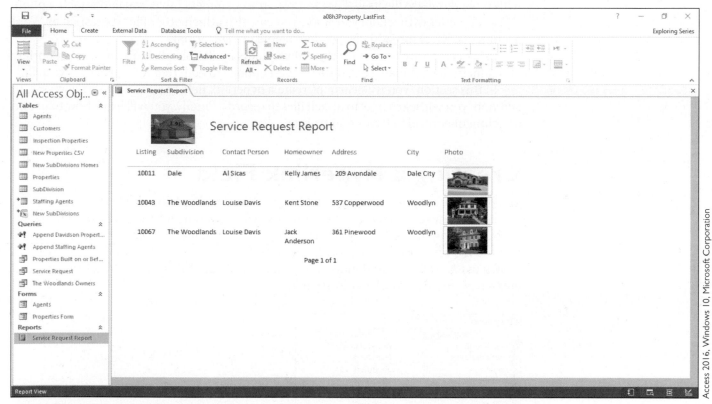

FIGURE 8.1 Property Management Data Exchange Database

CASE STUDY | Property Management Data Exchange

Starting Files	Files to be Submitted
a08h1Property	a08h3Property_LastFirst
a08h1Agents (folder)	a08h2Woodlands_LastFirst
a08h1Photos (folder)	a08h2Service_LastFirst.xlsx
a08h2Propexport	a08h2Sub_LastFirst
a08h3Propstaff	a08h2Service_LastFirst.pdf
a08h3Propinspect	a08h2Propexport_LastFirst
a08h3Propnew	

Connect Access to External Files

At times, it is advantageous to connect to data that exists separately from an Access database. Access supports the ***hyperlink*** data type that enables you to link to a file on your computer, to a webpage on the Internet, or to an email address. When you click a hyperlink field value in Datasheet view, Access launches the program required and displays the file you specified or opens the webpage defined by the URL you entered. A ***uniform resource locator (URL)*** is the location of a website or webpage on the Internet. If the hyperlink is an email address, Access launches a new email window and automatically enters the email address in the To field.

Access also offers you the option of attaching files to records in a database through an attachment field. An attachment field enables you to attach multiple files of different types. Rather than links that direct you outside of your database, attachments are stored within the database file itself. For example, in a customers table, you can attach a photo of a key contact with whom you work. You can also attach other file types, such as Word documents, Excel spreadsheets, or documents in PDF format.

Users can easily work with these documents by double-clicking on the appropriate attachment field. A dialog box displays with options to add, remove, open, or save a file.

In this section, you will learn to create a hyperlink field to store website addresses. In addition, you will learn how to attach files to records. Finally, you will learn how to use an attachment control in forms and reports.

Creating a Hyperlink Field

If you are working in a customers table, you can add a hyperlink field in Design view (or Datasheet view) of the table to store the customers' website locations (URLs). Figure 8.2 shows the hyperlink data type selection for the field name CustomerWebsite. After you add the hyperlink field, save the changes and then add the URLs in the datasheet, as shown in Figure 8.3. Additionally, you could add a hyperlink field that, when clicked, creates a new email message to a customer.

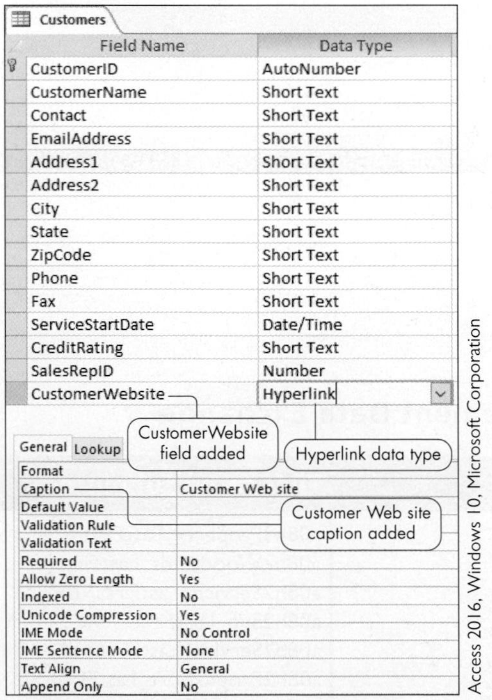

FIGURE 8.2 Creating a Hyperlink Field

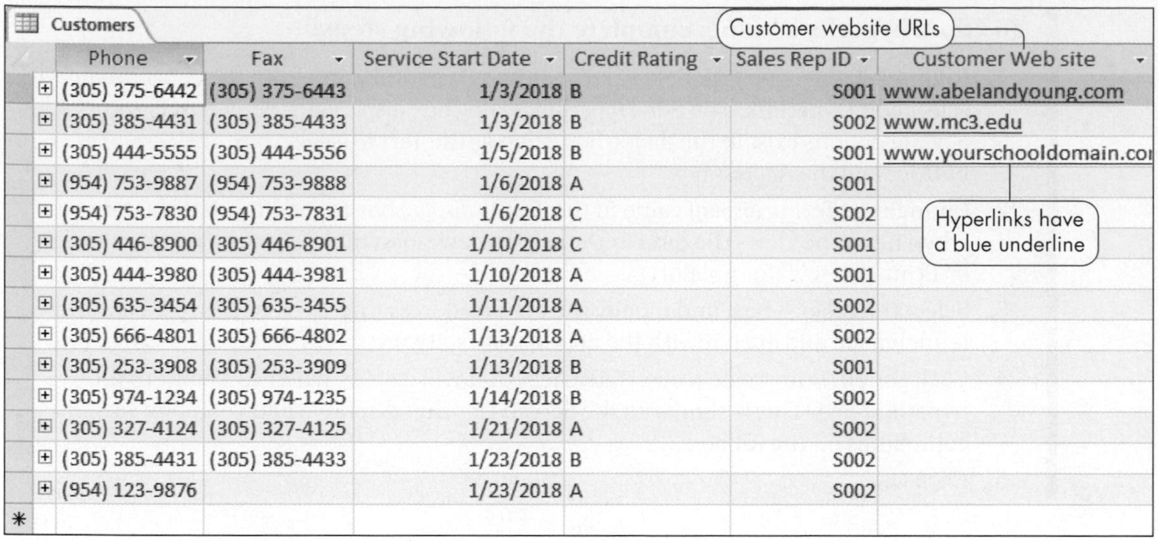

Phone	Fax	Service Start Date	Credit Rating	Sales Rep ID	Customer Web site
⊞ (305) 375-6442	(305) 375-6443	1/3/2018	B	S001	www.abelandyoung.com
⊞ (305) 385-4431	(305) 385-4433	1/3/2018	B	S002	www.mc3.edu
⊞ (305) 444-5555	(305) 444-5556	1/5/2018	B	S001	www.yourschooldomain.com
⊞ (954) 753-9887	(954) 753-9888	1/6/2018	A	S001	
⊞ (954) 753-7830	(954) 753-7831	1/6/2018	C	S002	
⊞ (305) 446-8900	(305) 446-8901	1/10/2018	C	S001	
⊞ (305) 444-3980	(305) 444-3981	1/10/2018	A	S001	
⊞ (305) 635-3454	(305) 635-3455	1/11/2018	A	S002	
⊞ (305) 666-4801	(305) 666-4802	1/13/2018	A	S002	
⊞ (305) 253-3908	(305) 253-3909	1/13/2018	B	S001	
⊞ (305) 974-1234	(305) 974-1235	1/14/2018	B	S002	
⊞ (305) 327-4124	(305) 327-4125	1/21/2018	A	S002	
⊞ (305) 385-4431	(305) 385-4433	1/23/2018	B	S002	
⊞ (954) 123-9876		1/23/2018	A	S002	

FIGURE 8.3 Hyperlink Fields

Add a Hyperlink Field in Design View

STEP 1 ≫ You can access information about customers or organizations you are working with from within an Access table—the addresses, phone numbers, or contact information—by adding hyperlinks to their websites. For example, if you have a database that contains a customers table, you can add a hyperlink field to store the website address of each customer.

> **To add a hyperlink field in Design view, complete the following steps:**
> 1. Open the table in Design view, and add the new field name to the table.
> 2. Select Hyperlink from the Data Type list.
> 3. Save the changes, and switch to Datasheet view.
> 4. Add the data values (URLs, email addresses, etc.) to the new hyperlink field.

Click a hyperlink value and Access launches the appropriate program, such as a Web browser, Word, or Excel, and enables you to interact with the file. If you make any changes to the file, save the changes within the host application. For example, if you launch an Excel workbook from within Access, you can make changes to the file, and then save your changes in Excel.

Edit a Hyperlink in Datasheet View

STEP 2 ≫ At times, you will need to modify a hyperlink field if the URL changes, or if you want to modify the ScreenTip or the text that displays. When you attempt to edit a hyperlink by clicking it, you will launch the software application; therefore, you need to use a different process to edit the hyperlink.

To edit a hyperlink value, complete the following steps:

1. Right-click the hyperlink field value, point to Hyperlink, and from the shortcut menu, select Edit Hyperlink. The Edit Hyperlink dialog box displays, as shown in Figure 8.4. Several options exist in the dialog box, such as the *Text to display* box, the *ScreenTip* button, and the *Address* box.

2. Change the *Text to display* value in the *Text to display* box to modify what the user sees when he or she views the data in Datasheet view (for a table), Form view (for a form), or Print Preview (for a report).

3. Select the *Address* box, and modify the actual address that Access uses to locate and launch a file and open it with the appropriate software.

4. Click *ScreenTip* to create a descriptive text that will display when you point to the hyperlink text. This is similar to the ScreenTips that display when you point to commands on the Ribbon.

5. Click OK.

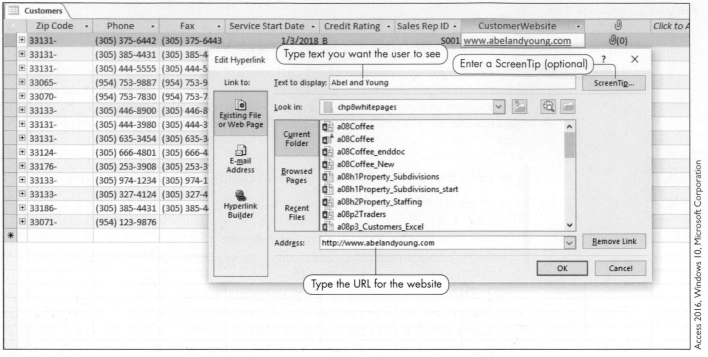

FIGURE 8.4 Edit Hyperlink Dialog Box

TIP: PRESS F2 TO EDIT HYPERLINK VALUES IN THE DATASHEET

To edit the text of a hyperlink value in a datasheet, press Tab or the Arrow keys to navigate to the value in the field you want to edit. With the value selected, press the F2 function key and when the blinking insertion point displays, edit the value and then press Enter or Tab.

TIP: ALTERNATIVE TO A HYPERLINK FIELD

At times, end users may prefer not to work with data as active hyperlinks. It is possible to accidentally click to launch a website or a program when you only want to edit the hyperlink. For this reason, some database designers define hyperlink fields as text fields. Users can still store the URLs, email addresses, and file name paths as field values, but the references will not automatically launch any software when clicked. Users must copy and paste the text value into an appropriate application, such as a Web browser.

Other options for manipulating a hyperlink field (such as Copy Hyperlink) exist in the shortcut menu that displays when you right-click a hyperlink; however, editing and removing a hyperlink field are the most commonly used.

Adding an Attachment Field

An Access database is primarily used to store and analyze data and to retrieve information. This data is usually typed directly into the tables or entered using an Access form. Sometimes you may want to store a reference to an external file—an image, a scanned document, an Excel spreadsheet, a PDF document—and then be able to open that file from within Access. These situations can be handled by adding an attachment field to a table. An *attachment field* is similar to an attachment in an email; you can use an Access attachment field to attach multiple files of different types, and then launch those files from within Access. The files are actually copied into the database itself. Keep in mind that Access is not able to analyze the data within these external files; Access can only open the files. To work with a file, you need to use the program associated with it.

The size of your database grows when you attach files. If the database grows too large, you can remove some attachments, resize the files, and reattach the files in a smaller format. Remember to compact your database after you add and remove attachments.

To monitor the file size of a database, complete the following steps:

1. Compact the database.
2. Check the size of the database file:
   - Click the File tab, and from the Info page, click View and edit database properties.
   - Note the file size on the General tab of the Properties dialog box.
3. Add or remove the file attachment(s).
4. Check the size of the database file again.

Create an Attachment Field in Design View

STEP 3 ⟫ At times, you may want to store external files—pictures, documents, spreadsheets, PDF files—and then be able to open them from within Access. To handle these situations, you can create attachment fields in Access tables. For example, if you are working with a customers table and want to store a photo of the business owner, the office building, and the master contract in Access, you can add a new field such as CustomerFiles. In Design view, select the data type Attachment, as shown in Figure 8.5, and save the changes.

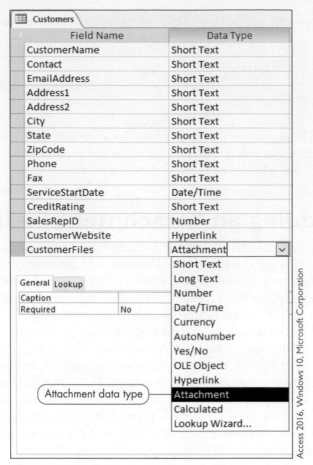

FIGURE 8.5 Create an Attachment Field in Design View

Add or Edit Attachments in Datasheet View

STEP 4 ⟩⟩ Once you have created the attachment field, you can add files to the new field in Datasheet view. Suppose you have a database that stores all the customer information for your business. You want to store a photo of the owner, a photo of the exterior of the main building, a map with directions to the business, and a Word document containing the price structure for each company. You can attach all of the files relating to each customer's record. Once you add the attachments, a paperclip icon with the number of files attached displays in the New Attachment column. In Figure 8.6, all records, except record 6, show (0) attachments because no files are attached yet. You can edit existing attachments later on as the requirements of the database change.

To attach a file (or files) to a record, complete the following steps:

1. Double-click the attachment field's paperclip icon to open the Attachments dialog box, as shown in Figure 8.7.
2. Click Add to add the attachment.
3. Use the Choose File dialog box to locate and select the file to attach.
4. Click Open to attach the file to the record.
5. Click Add again to add the next file and each additional file.
6. Click OK to close the Attachments dialog box. The paperclip icon indicates how many files are attached to the current record.
7. Click the record below the current record to save the attached files.

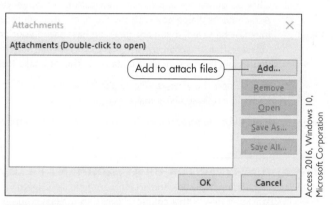

Customers				
CustomerID ▾	Customer Name ▾	Customer Web site ▾	📎	Click to Add ▾
⊞ C0001	Abel & Young	Abel and Young	📎(0)	
⊞ C0002	Department of CIS	www.mc3.edu	📎(0)	
⊞ C0003	Advantage Sales	www.yourschooldomain.cor	📎(0)	
⊞ C0004	Kinzer & Sons		📎(0)	
⊞ C0005	Milgrom Associates		📎(0)	
⊞ C0006	Lugo Computer Sales		📎(2)	
⊞ C0007	Bethune Appliance Sales		📎(0)	
⊞ C0008	Baker Auto Supply		📎(0)	
⊞ C0009	Howard Animal Hospital		📎(0)	
⊞ C0010	Katie's Casual Wear		📎(0)	
⊞ C0011	Little, Joiner, & Jones		📎(0)	
⊞ C0012	Kline Bait & Tackle		📎(0)	
⊞ C0013	Computer Informations Sys		📎(0)	
⊞ C0014	Coulter Office Supplies		📎(0)	
＊	(New)		📎(0)	

Paperclip icon indicates an Attachment field

Number of files is indicated in parentheses

Access 2016, Windows 10, Microsoft Corporation

FIGURE 8.6 Datasheet View Showing Attachments

Attachments ✕

Attachments (Double-click to open)

Add to attach files

Add...
Remove
Open
Save As...
Save All...

OK   Cancel

Access 2016, Windows 10, Microsoft Corporation

FIGURE 8.7 Attachments Dialog Box

To view or edit attached files, complete the following steps:

1. Double-click the attachment field's paperclip icon to open the Attachments dialog box.
2. Select the file to modify.
3. Click Open. For example, if you click the photo of the owner, and then click Open, you can modify the photo using your computer's default picture manager software.
4. Save and close the file once the change has been made.
5. Click OK in the Attachments dialog box.
6. Click Yes in the Save Attachment dialog box to save your changes (see Figure 8.8).
7. Click the record below the current record to save the changes.

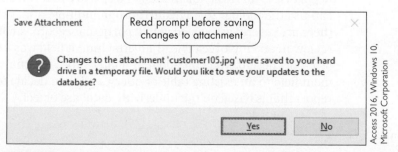

Save Attachment ✕

Read prompt before saving changes to attachment

❓ Changes to the attachment 'customer105.jpg' were saved to your hard drive in a temporary file. Would you like to save your updates to the database?

Yes   No

Access 2016, Windows 10, Microsoft Corporation

FIGURE 8.8 Save Attachment Message

Remove Attachments in Datasheet View

 STEP 5 ❯❯ Attachments can increase the file size of your database substantially. It is important to remove unnecessary or incorrect attachments from database objects to avoid excessive bloat.

To remove an attached file, complete the following steps:

1. Double-click the attachment field's paperclip icon to open the Attachments dialog box.
2. Select the file to remove, and click Remove.
3. Click OK.
4. Click the record below the current record to save the changes.

Table 8.1 details the available options in the Attachments dialog box.

TABLE 8.1	Using the Attachments Dialog Box
Add	Click to add one or more files to a record.
Remove	Click to remove previously attached files.
Open	Click to launch the appropriate application and open the file. If you try to close the Attachments dialog box with the file open, you will receive a warning that your changes may not be saved. If you are sure you have saved your changes, click OK. You will receive a message that the changes were saved to your hard drive in a temporary file. Access asks if you would like to save your updates to the database (refer to Figure 8.8).
Save As	Use to save the attached file to a local storage location. You must remember to add it back into the database if you make changes.
Save All	Save all of the attachments in a record to a local, temporary folder.

> **TIP: ADD A HYPERLINK OR ATTACHMENT FIELD IN DATASHEET VIEW**
> In addition to adding hyperlink and attachment fields in Design view of a table, you can also add them in Datasheet view with a couple of clicks. In the last column of the datasheet, click *Click to Add* in the column header. Click Hyperlink or Attachment to set the data type for the new field, and then rename the field as desired. Save the table.

Adding Attachment Controls to Forms and Reports

In a form or report, you can interact with attachments using an attachment control. An ***attachment control*** is a control that enables you to manage attached files in forms and reports. If the attachment is a photo, the control displays the photo as you navigate through the records. If the attachment is a document, you will only see an icon representing the application (such as Word) that was used to create the file. In Form view and Report view, an Attachment toolbar displays when you click the attachment control. You can use the toolbar to navigate through multiple attachments in a form or report when there are several associated with a particular record, such as a photo and a performance review in an employee table. If an attachment field was not included in the original form or report design, you can add it at a later time. Alternatively, you might add an attachment field to an existing table or query, and then decide to include that field in a form or report that is based on the underlying database object.

Add an Attachment Control to a Form

 STEP 6 ⟩⟩ When you add an attachment control to a form, you can interact with attachments such as photos and files that are associated with the individual records.

To add an attachment control to a form, complete the following steps:

1. Open the form in Layout view.
2. Click Add Existing Fields in the Tools group on the Design tab.

   In the Field List pane, the attachment field displays as a parent field with three child fields. The expand symbol (+) enables you to expand and the collapse symbol (-) enables you to collapse the child fields.
3. Drag the parent field name from the Field List pane to the form, and then drop it in the desired location, as shown in Figure 8.9. Access adds the bound attachment control and the associated label to the form.
4. Resize the bound control to ensure that the images display correctly.

Save the changes, and then switch to Form view (see Figure 8.10). When the attachment control is in place, click the control to view the Attachment toolbar. The Attachment toolbar displays arrows that enable you to advance through multiple attachments. The Attachment toolbar also has a paperclip icon that you can click to open the Attachments dialog box. This dialog box is the same one that opens when you click an attachment field in a table. Return to Layout view for additional modifications if necessary.

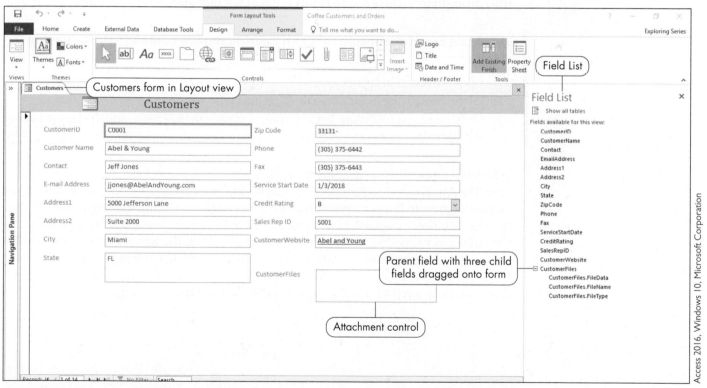

FIGURE 8.9 Add an Attachment Control to a Form

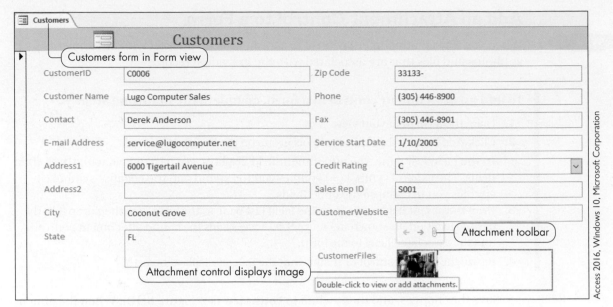

FIGURE 8.10 Attachment Control in Form View

Add an Attachment Control to a Report

 **STEP 7** >> When you add an attachment control to a report, you can interact with attachments such as photos and files that are associated with individual records. An attachment control can be added to an existing report if it was not included in the original report design.

> **To add an attachment control to an existing report, complete the following steps:**
>
> 1. Open the report in Layout view.
> 2. Click Add Existing Fields in the Tools group on the Design tab.
> 3. Drag the parent field name from the Field List pane to the report, and then drop it in the desired location.

When the report is viewed in Print Preview, the attachment field displays the first file only. The Attachment toolbar does not display in Print Preview. Usually, attachments are viewed by users in Report view of the report. To use the Attachment toolbar and advance through multiple attachments in a report, switch to Report view. Click the control to view the Attachment toolbar, as shown in Figure 8.11. Click the arrows on the Attachment toolbar, to navigate from one attachment to another, or click the paperclip icon to open the Attachments dialog box. You should reduce the size of the attachment control in a report because a report usually displays multiple records on one page.

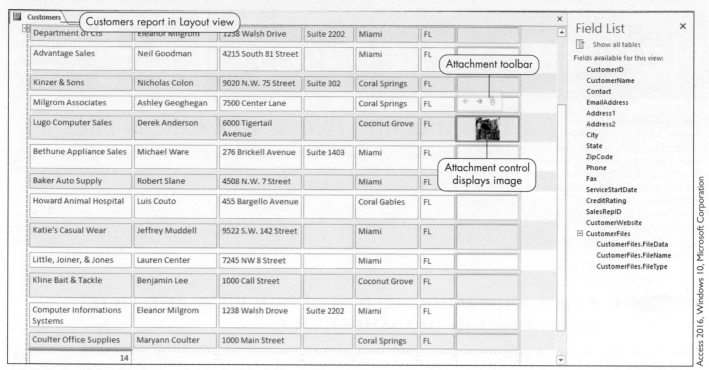

FIGURE 8.11 Attachment Control Added to a Report's Layout View

Quick Concepts

1. What is the major difference between a linked file and an attachment? *p. 498*

2. What is a potential disadvantage of storing attachments in your databases? *p. 507*

3. Why is the Attachment toolbar useful in a form or a report? *p. 504*

Hands-On Exercises

Watch the Video for this Hands-On Exercise!

MyITLab®
HOE1 Training

Skills covered: Add a Hyperlink Field in Design View • Enter Hyperlinks in Datasheet View • Edit a Hyperlink in Datasheet View • Create an Attachment Field in Design View • Add Attachments in Datasheet View • Remove an Attachment in Datasheet View • Add an Attachment Control in Layout View • Use an Attachment Control in a Form

1 Connecting Access to External Files

Blackwood Maintenance Service wants to add a link to the website for each subdivision's school district. You will also add a photo of each property that BMS now serves. Finally, you will add a photo and related documents to the record of each BMS agent.

> **STEP 1** ›› **ADD A HYPERLINK FIELD IN DESIGN VIEW AND ENTER HYPERLINKS IN DATASHEET VIEW**

Create a new field that will link to the school district's website for each subdivision served by Blackwood. Refer to Figure 8.12 as you complete Step 1.

SubDivision

Steps f–h: Type School District URLs in Datasheet view

SubD	SubDivision	Contact Person	Pool			School District
1	Fair Brook	Irma Stark	Yes	No	No	http://abss.k12.nc.us
2	King's Forest	Red Donner	No	Yes	Yes	http://www.gcnc.com/pages/ncgc
3	Dale	Al Sicas	Yes	Yes	Yes	http://www.gcnc.com/pages/ncgc
4	Eagle Valley	Tony Salvatores	No	No	No	http://www.orange/k12.nc.us
5	Running Brook	Jerry Kudash	Yes	Yes	No	http://www.orange/k12.nc.us
6	North Point	Reggie Elder	No	Yes	Yes	http://abss.k12.nc.us
7	Red Canyon	Kevin Kellie	Yes	No	No	http://abss.k12.nc.us
8	Seeley Lake	Glen Hughes	Yes	Yes	Yes	http://www.gcnc.com/pages/ncgc
9	The Links	Hugh Hyatt	Yes	No	Yes	http://abss.k12.nc.us
10	The Estates	Deb Dahl	No	No	No	http://www.orange/k12.nc.us
11	The Orchards	John Erthal	Yes	Yes	Yes	http://www.gcnc.com/pages/ncgc
12	The Pines	Ralph Borden	Yes	Yes	No	http://abss.k12.nc.us
13	Water Valley	Jansen Kunkelman	No	Yes	Yes	http://www.orange/k12.nc.us
14	The Woodland	Louise Davis	No	No	No	http://www.orange/k12.nc.us

Access 2016, Windows 10, Microsoft Corporation

FIGURE 8.12 Enter Hyperlinks in Datasheet View

a. Open *a08h1Property* and save it as **a08h1Property_LastFirst**.

> **TROUBLESHOOTING:** Throughout the remainder of this chapter and textbook, click Enable Content whenever you are working with student files.

> **TROUBLESHOOTING:** If you make any major mistakes in this exercise, you can close the file, open *a08h1Property* again, and then start this exercise over.

b. Open the Agents table and replace *Your_Name* with your name in both the FirstName and LastName fields. Close the Agents table.

c. Open the SubDivision table in Design view. In the blank field row below the BikeTrail field name, type **SchoolDistrict**. Click the **Data Type arrow**, and select **Hyperlink**.

d. Type **School District** in the Caption property box in the Field Properties pane of the Table Design view.

e. Save the changes to the table. Switch to Datasheet view.

You are ready to add the school districts' website addresses to the new hyperlink field.

f. Type **http://abss.k12.nc.us** into the School District field for records 1, 6, 7, 9, and 12.

Fair Brook, North Point, Red Canyon, The Links, and The Pines are all located in the Alamance-Burlington School System.

g. Type **http://www.gcnc.com/pages/ncgc** into the School District field for records 2, 3, 8, and 11.

King's Forest, Dale, Seeley Lake, and The Orchards are in the Guilford District.

h. Type **http://www.orange.k12.nc.us** into the School District field for the remaining records (records 4, 5, 10, 13, and 14).

The remaining subdivisions are in the Orange County School District.

> **TROUBLESHOOTING:** If you make a mistake, do not click in the School District field to correct it. Instead, click in the BikeTrail column and press Tab to select the field that contains an error. Retype the information.

i. Click the **School District hyperlink** in record 1. The browser opens and the school district's website opens. Close the browser window.

j. Widen the School District field so that all data is displayed, and then compare your screen with Figure 8.12.

STEP 2 ›› EDIT A HYPERLINK IN DATASHEET VIEW

You realized that you entered an incorrect URL for the Guilford schools. The current URL contains a typographical error. You will fix the links in this step so that the URL links to schools in North Carolina. Refer to Figure 8.13 as you complete Step 2.

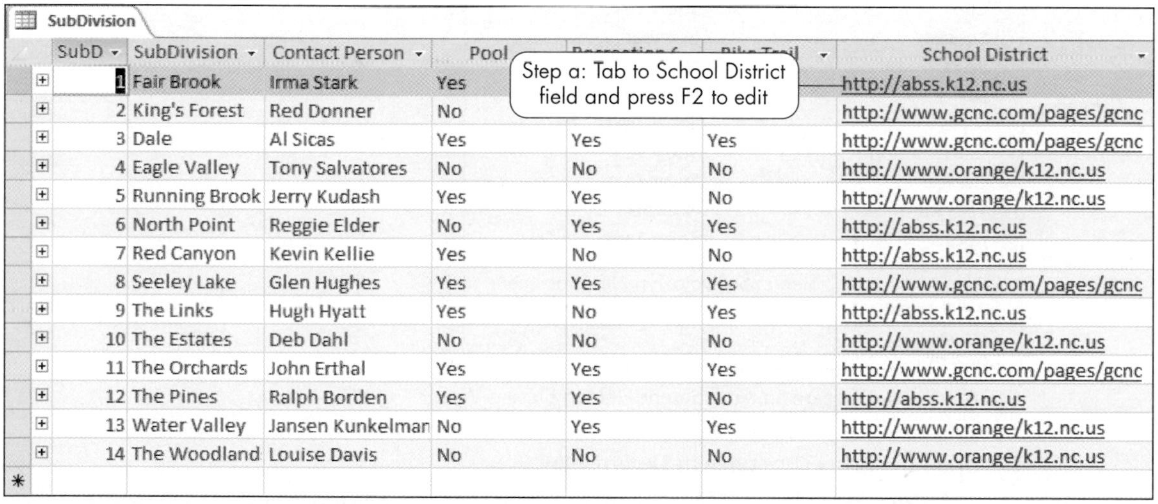

SubD ▾	SubDivision ▾	Contact Person ▾	Pool	Recreation (	Bike Trail ▾	School District ▾
1	Fair Brook	Irma Stark	Yes			http://abss.k12.nc.us
2	King's Forest	Red Donner	No			http://www.gcnc.com/pages/gcnc
3	Dale	Al Sicas	Yes	Yes	Yes	http://www.gcnc.com/pages/gcnc
4	Eagle Valley	Tony Salvatores	No	No	No	http://www.orange/k12.nc.us
5	Running Brook	Jerry Kudash	Yes	Yes	No	http://www.orange/k12.nc.us
6	North Point	Reggie Elder	No	Yes	Yes	http://abss.k12.nc.us
7	Red Canyon	Kevin Kellie	Yes	No	No	http://abss.k12.nc.us
8	Seeley Lake	Glen Hughes	Yes	Yes	Yes	http://www.gcnc.com/pages/gcnc
9	The Links	Hugh Hyatt	Yes	No	Yes	http://abss.k12.nc.us
10	The Estates	Deb Dahl	No	No	No	http://www.orange/k12.nc.us
11	The Orchards	John Erthal	Yes	Yes	Yes	http://www.gcnc.com/pages/gcnc
12	The Pines	Ralph Borden	Yes	Yes	No	http://abss.k12.nc.us
13	Water Valley	Jansen Kunkelman	No	Yes	Yes	http://www.orange/k12.nc.us
14	The Woodland	Louise Davis	No	No	No	http://www.orange/k12.nc.us

Step a: Tab to School District field and press F2 to edit

Access 2016, Windows 10, Microsoft Corporation

FIGURE 8.13 Edit a Hyperlink Field in Datasheet View

a. Click in the **BikeTrail column** of record 2, and press **Tab** until the School District field is selected. Press **F2**, and edit the link so it reads **http://www.gcnc.com/pages/gcnc**.

The *ncgc* segment of the hyperlink was changed to *gcnc*. The hyperlink is enclosed with pound signs (#), which Access uses to activate the link when clicked.

b. Click in the **BikeTrail column** of record 3 to save your changes.

You will use another method to edit the remaining Guilford URLs.

c. Right-click the **http://www.gcnc.com/pages/ncgc** hyperlink in record 3, point to **Hyperlink**, and then select **Edit Hyperlink** from the shortcut menu.

The Edit Hyperlink dialog box opens.

d. Change the *ncgc* segment of the hyperlink to **gcnc** in the Address field at the bottom of the dialog box. Click **OK** to accept your changes, and press ↓ to save your changes.

The Text to display changes.

e. Edit the remaining Guilford URLs (change *ncgc* to **gcnc**) using the Edit Hyperlink dialog box. Compare your results with Figure 8.13.

f. Close the SubDivision table.

STEP 3 » CREATE AN ATTACHMENT FIELD IN DESIGN VIEW

BMS has collected photos of its properties for the past several years. The photos are stored in a folder where employees can access them as needed. The owners have asked you to create an attachment field so you can attach each photo to its corresponding property. Refer to Figure 8.14 as you complete Step 3.

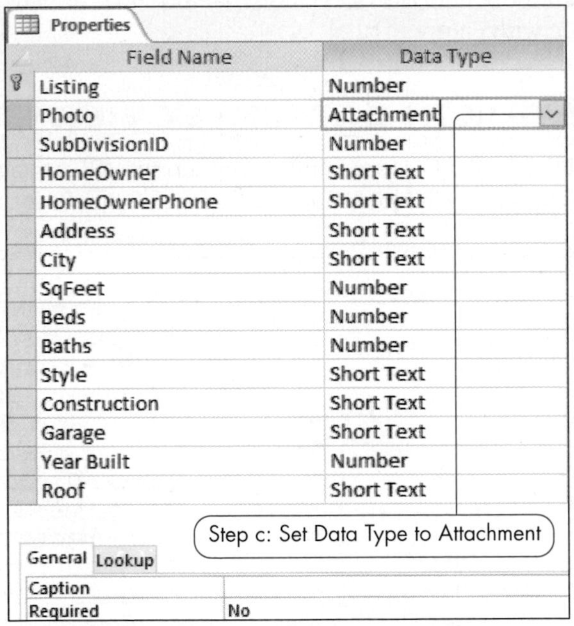

Access 2016, Windows 10, Microsoft Corporation

FIGURE 8.14 Create an Attachment Field in Design View

a. Open the Properties table in Design view.

You will add an attachment field that enables you to attach the photos of the properties.

b. Click the **SubDivisionID field row selector**, and click **Insert Rows** in the Tools group.

A new row is added between Listing and SubDivisionID.

c. Type **Photo** in the Field Name column, and select **Attachment** as the data type.

d. Save the changes to the table design. Switch to Datasheet view.

The new attachment field displays a paperclip symbol with a (0), indicating no attachments are in any of the property records.

You will attach four photos to their corresponding properties. Having these photos attached to the properties enables the agents to access them when working with the property owners. Refer to Figure 8.15 as you complete Step 4.

FIGURE 8.15 Add Attachments in Datasheet View

a. Double-click the **paperclip icon** in the Photo field in the record for listing 10011 to open the Attachments dialog box.

b. Click **Add**. Locate the *10011* photo in the a08h1Photos folder. Double-click the file to add it to the Attachments dialog box.

The file displays in the Attachments dialog box.

c. Click **OK** to close the Attachments dialog box. Click the record for listing 10012 to save the record.

d. Double-click the **paperclip** in record 11 to open the Attachments dialog box again. Double-click the *10011* photo to open your computer's default photo software.

Compare your screen with Figure 8.15.

e. Close the photo software, and click **OK** in the Attachments dialog box.

f. Double-click the **paperclip** in listing *10043*.

g. Click **Add** in the Attachments dialog box, and then locate and attach photo *10043* to the record. Click **OK**.

h. Double-click the **paperclip** in listing *10067*, and attach photo *10067* to the record.

i. Select the record for listing 10025. Double-click the **paperclip** to open the Attachments dialog box. Click **Add**, and add photo *10025* to the Attachments dialog box. Click **OK**. Click the record for listing 10026 to save the record.

STEP 5)) REMOVE AN ATTACHMENT IN DATASHEET VIEW

One of the properties was sold, and the new owners are not going to use BMS to manage their property. You decide to remove the photo from this property's record. Refer to Figure 8.16 as you complete Step 5.

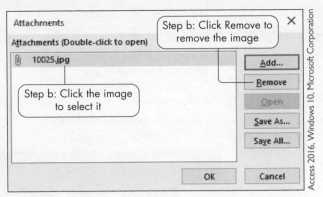

FIGURE 8.16 Remove an Attachment in Datasheet View

a. Double-click the **paperclip** in listing 10025 to open the Attachments dialog box.

b. Click *10025.jpg*, and click **Remove**.

The photo has been removed from the Attachments dialog box.

c. Click **OK** to close the Attachments dialog box, and click the record below to save the record.

d. Close the Properties table.

e. Click the **File tab**, and click **Compact & Repair Database**.

You decide to compact the database because adding and removing attachments can increase the size of the database.

STEP 6)) ADD AN ATTACHMENT CONTROL IN LAYOUT VIEW

BMS asks you to create a report showing the properties with an outstanding service request. You decide to include a photo of each property, but only a thumbnail will display in the report. Refer to Figure 8.17 as you complete Step 6.

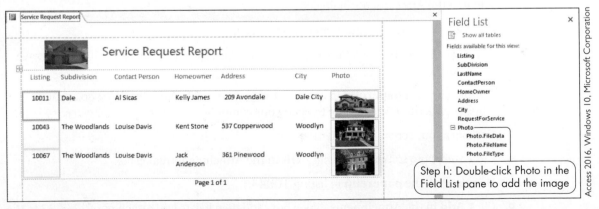

FIGURE 8.17 Attachment Field in a Report

a. Open the Service Request query in Design view. Change the criterion in the LastName field from *Your_Name* to your last name.

b. Switch to Datasheet view, and examine the query results.

Three properties display with your last name as the agent. The Photo field is missing; you will return to Design view to add it to the query design.

c. Switch to Design view.

d. Drag the **Photo field** from the Properties table, and drop it into the first blank field cell in the query design grid.

> **TROUBLESHOOTING:** If you drag one of the three child fields, delete the column, and try again. Make sure you add the parent photo field, the field with a (+) or (−) symbol to its left.

e. Switch to Datasheet view, and examine the query results again. Save and close the query.

f. Double-click **Service Request Report**, and switch to Layout view.

g. Click **Add Existing Fields** in the Tools group on the Design tab.

h. Click **Dale City** to select the City column. Double-click **Photo** in the Field List pane to add the field to the right side of the report.

> **TROUBLESHOOTING:** If you double-click one of the three child fields, click Undo and try again. Make sure you double-click the parent photo field, the field with a (+) or (−) symbol to its left.

The Photo field is added as the last column on the right of the report. Most of the photos are positioned on the right side of the right margin line. You will resize the other columns to reduce the layout width to one page.

i. Close the Field List pane. Reduce the width of the Listing column by dragging the right border of the Listing column heading to the left.

j. Reduce the width of the City column until no photos are positioned on the second page (ensure that they are inside the dashed page break).

k. View the report in Print Preview.

All the fields now fit onto one page.

l. Click **Close Print Preview** in the Close Preview group. Save and close the report.

STEP 7 ›› **USE AN ATTACHMENT CONTROL IN A FORM**

BMS wants to add a photo of each agent to the database. They also want to attach the latest performance evaluation to each employee's record. Refer to Figure 8.18 as you complete Step 7.

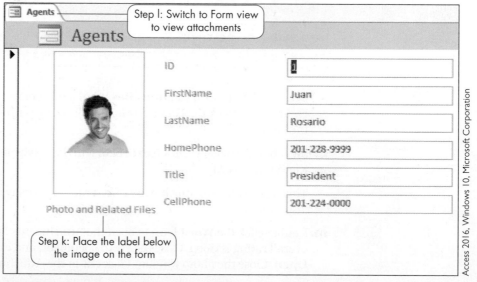

FIGURE 8.18 Attachment Control in a Form

a. Open the Agents table in Design view. Add a field named **RelatedFiles** in the first blank field row under CellPhone. Select **Attachment Data Type**. In the Field Properties section, type **Photo and Related Files** in the Caption property.

You added an attachment field to store the photo and performance review for each agent.

b. Save the table changes, and then switch to Datasheet view.

c. Double-click the **paperclip** in the first record, for Juan Rosario. The Attachments dialog box opens. Click **Add**. Locate and open the a08h1Agents folder. Double-click *juan* to attach it. Click **OK** to close the Attachments dialog box, and click another record to save the current record.

The paperclip now shows that (1) file is attached to Juan's record. Next, add a photo and a Word file to Kia Hart's record.

d. Double-click the **paperclip** in Kia Hart's record to open the Attachments dialog box. Click **Add**. Locate the *kia* photo, and attach it to the record by double-clicking the file. Click **Add** again, and attach the document *Kia Hart Performance Evaluation*. Click **OK** to close the Attachments dialog box, and click another record to save the current record.

Kia's record should indicate (2) attachments.

e. Attach the remaining agents' photos to their records. Use the photo named *your_name* for your photo. Attach the *Your_Name Performance Evaluation* document to your record as well. Close the table.

f. Open the Agents form in Design view. Click the **ID field** to activate the Layout Selector (the small square with a cross inside, located to the left of the first field).

You will move all the fields to the right.

g. Click **Layout Selector**, and drag the fields as a group to the right. Use Figure 8.18 (the completed form) as a guide as you reposition the fields.

h. Click **Add Existing Fields** in the Tools group on the Design tab to open the Field List pane.

i. Drag the **RelatedFiles field** to the left of the fields you just moved.

The field is added to the left side of the form. You will reposition the label and the control separately.

j. Drag the **RelatedFiles control** to the top of the form using the small solid square at the top left of the control. Resize the control using Figure 8.18 (the completed form) as a guide.

> **TROUBLESHOOTING:** If the label follows the attachment control, release the mouse button and try again. Verify you are dragging the attachment using the small solid square.

k. Drag the **Photo and Related Files label** to the bottom of the control, as shown in Figure 8.18. Click the **Format tab**, and click **Center** in the Font group to center-align the label text.

l. Switch to Form view. Click **Next record** in the Navigation bar to advance to record 2, Kia Hart's record.

This record has two attachments. The Word file displays as an icon, and the photo is not displayed.

m. Double-click the **Word icon** to open the Attachments dialog box. Click **Open**. Kia's overall rating is Good. Close the Word document, and exit Word. Click *Kia.jpg*, and click **Open**. Close the photo window. Click **OK** in the Attachments dialog box.

n. Click the **Attachment control** to activate the Attachment toolbar. Click **Forward** (the right arrow) to display the next attachment.

Kia's photo displays.

o. Click **Next record** in the Navigation bar to advance to your record. Double-click the Attachment control to open the Attachments dialog box. Click each attachment, and click **Open** to view each file. Close the Word and photo windows. Close the Attachments dialog box when you are finished.

p. Save and close the form.

q. Keep the database open if you plan to continue with the next Hands-On Exercise. If not, close the database and exit Access.

Export Data to Office and Other Applications

Using Access to collect and store data and to extract and analyze information is useful for any organization. But what happens when information must be shared with the other departments, or with other companies that might not have the software or whose employees might not be familiar with Access? One way to deliver information is via hard copies. However, this does not work if the recipients want to manipulate the data themselves, or to analyze it further from a different angle. A common way to distribute data stored in an Access database is to export it to another application.

In this section, you will learn how to export Access data to Excel and Word. Because these two applications are part of the Microsoft Office suite, exporting from Access is straightforward. In addition to exporting to Excel and Word, you will also learn how to create a PDF or XPS document and how to export objects from one Access database to another Access database.

Exporting Data to Excel

Several reasons exist for Access users to export data to Excel. One is to take advantage of Excel's charting capabilities. Another reason is to test different scenarios with the data and to analyze the results. This type of analysis enables managers to predict future trends. Manipulating data in Excel is preferable to changing data in Access. You want the raw data in Access to stay the same! A final reason for exporting to Excel is to be able to distribute the Access data to users who do not have Access or who do not know how to use Access. Exporting data from Access to Excel is generally uncomplicated because the data in Access is usually structured in a manner that Excel understands.

Select a Record Source to Export to Excel

If the record source you want to export to Excel is a table, such as the Customers table shown in Figure 8.19, then the export-to-Excel process is fast and easy. When you export a table to Excel, the field names become the column headings and the table records become the rows in the Excel spreadsheet. You can export an entire Access table to Excel or only the records that you select; records can be selected individually in a table, or the table can be filtered to display a subset of the records before the export is initiated.

	CustomerID	Customer Name	Contact	E-mail Address	Address1	Address2	City	State	Custome
⊞	C0001	Abel & Young	Jeff Jones	jjones@AbelAndYoung.com	5000 Jefferson Lane	Suite 2000	Miami	FL	Abel and Yo
⊞	C0002	Department of CIS	Eleanor Milgrom		1238 Walsh Drive	Suite 2202	Miami	FL	www.mc3.e
⊞	C0003	Advantage Sales	Neil Goodman	service@advantagesales.com	4215 South 81 Street		Miami	FL	www.yours
⊞	C0004	Kinzer & Sons	Nicholas Colon		9020 N.W. 75 Street	Suite 302	Coral Springs	FL	
⊞	C0005	Milgrom Associates	Ashley Geoghegan	ageoghegan@milgrom.net	7500 Center Lane		Coral Springs	FL	
⊞	C0006	Lugo Computer Sales	Derek Anderson	service@lugocomputer.net	6000 Tigertail Avenue		Coconut Grove	FL	
⊞	C0007	Bethune Appliance Sales	Michael Ware	bethune@bethune.com	276 Brickell Avenue	Suite 1403	Miami	FL	
⊞	C0008	Baker Auto Supply	Robert Slane	rslane@bakerauto.com	4508 N.W. 7 Street		Miami	FL	
⊞	C0009	Howard Animal Hospital	Luis Couto	lcouto@howardanimals.net	455 Bargello Avenue		Coral Gables	FL	
⊞	C0010	Katie's Casual Wear	Jeffrey Muddell	katie@katiewear.com	9522 S.W. 142 Street		Miami	FL	
⊞	C0011	Little, Joiner, & Jones	Lauren Center	lcenter@ljj.com	7245 NW 8 Street		Miami	FL	
⊞	C0012	Kline Bait & Tackle	Benjamin Lee	blee@klineb&t.com	1000 Call Street		Coconut Grove	FL	
⊞	C0013	Computer Informations Sys	Eleanor Milgrom	emilgrom@cis.edu	1238 Walsh Drove	Suite 2202	Miami	FL	
⊞	C0014	Coulter Office Supplies	Maryann Coulter	mcoulter@coulter.com	1000 Main Street		Coral Springs	FL	
✻	(New)								

FIGURE 8.19 Customers Table in Access Before Exporting to Excel

When you export a table from Access, all of the columns and the designated records in the table are exported, even if the table is open and not all of the data is visible (as shown in Figure 8.19). If no records are selected or filtered in advance, all of the records are exported. In this example, the end result is a new Excel worksheet containing all of the columns and all of the records in the Customers table, as shown in Figure 8.20.

FIGURE 8.20 Customers Table Exported to Excel

Export a Query to Excel

STEP 1 ›› If you want to export only a subset of a table such as Customers, you can filter a table or select specific records before exporting. Alternatively, you can create a query to then export to Excel. For example, if you only need the address fields for customers in a certain zip code, you can create a query, and then export the query records to Excel.

To export a query to Excel, complete the following steps:

1. Select the query in the Navigation Pane (or open the query first).
2. Click Excel in the Export group on the External Data tab. Access opens the Export – Excel Spreadsheet dialog box (shown in Figure 8.21) to guide you through the export process.
3. Specify the file name and destination and the format for the exported file.
4. Specify whether to export the data with formatting and layout.
5. Specify if you want to open the destination file after the export operation is complete.
6. Specify if you want to export only the selected records (if you have selected one or more records in the datasheet).
7. Click OK.

The Excel spreadsheet will display (see Figure 8.22). Once you are finished reviewing the exported Excel spreadsheet, and then return to the Access window, one final screen requires a response. In Figure 8.23, Access asks you, *Do you want to save these export steps?* Click to select the *Save export steps* check box if you want to repeat the same export process at a later time. Saving export steps is useful if you need to repeatedly export the same query. The saved steps are stored under Saved Exports in the Export group.

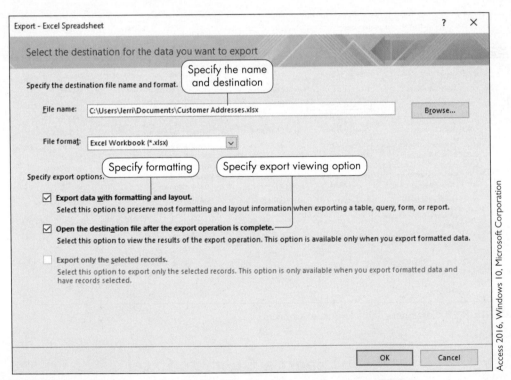

FIGURE 8.21 Export – Excel Spreadsheet Dialog Box

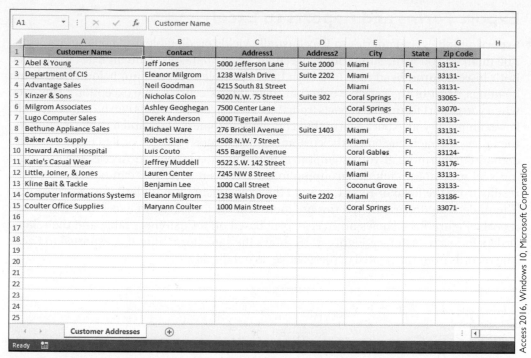

FIGURE 8.22 Customer Addresses Query Exported to Excel

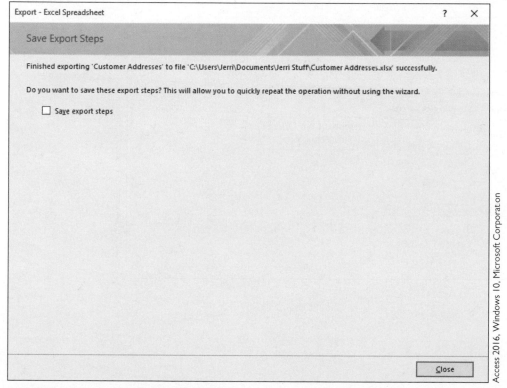

FIGURE 8.23 Save Export Steps Dialog Box

Export Forms and Reports to Excel

Exporting tables and queries to Excel usually yields predictable and consistent results. The main reason is the similarity between an Access datasheet and an Excel worksheet. Both have column headings, and both have multiple rows of data below the column headings. Most of the cells have data in them (blank cells are the exception). However, when you export forms and reports from Access to Excel, the results can be unpredictable. For example, if you export a form that contains customers' data and a subform showing the orders for each customer, the customers' data exports but the orders (subform data) do not. Furthermore, if you attempt to export a grouped report in Access, the grouping in Excel may not match the grouping in the Access report. You can either accept the results from the form or report, or redo the export using the underlying record source. The underlying tables and queries are more reliable for export to Excel than forms and reports. Figure 8.24 shows an Access form based on a Customers table and the related Orders for each customer. Figure 8.25 shows the same form after it is exported to Excel. The records from the related (Orders) table do not display.

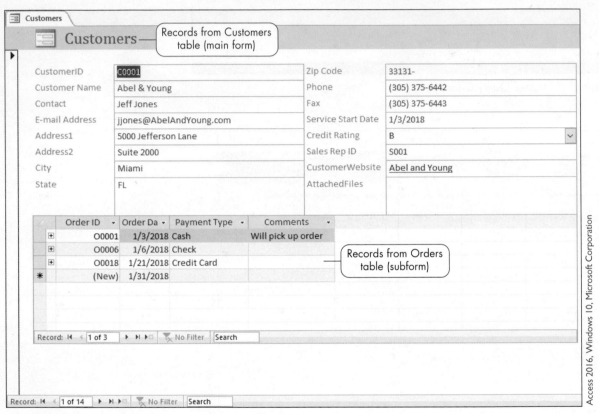

FIGURE 8.24 Customers with Orders Form in Access

FIGURE 8.25 Customers with Orders Form Exported to Excel

Exporting Data to Word

The process for exporting data from Access to Word is similar to that for exporting data to Excel. Generally, you are not able to analyze the data in Word as you can in Excel. When you export an object from Access to Word, Access creates a file in the Rich Text Format. ***Rich Text Format (RTF)*** is a format that enables documents created in one software application to be opened with a different software application. The RTF format was introduced in 1987 by Microsoft and is now supported by Windows, Macintosh, open source, Unix, and other environments. RTF is a useful format for basic formatted text documents, such as instruction manuals, résumés, letters, and other documents. These documents support special text formatting, such as bold, italic, and underline. RTF documents also support left-, center-, and right-justified text. Furthermore, font specifications and document margins are supported in RTF documents. Once the data is exported to Word, you will most likely use the data as is for reporting purposes rather than for analysis. Although you can modify the data in the table cells, those changes do not update the totals or other calculated fields (as they do in Excel).

When you export data from Access to Word, the RTF format is used and the file's extension is .rtf. Word is the default software application for the .rtf extension; once the RTF file is opened in Word, you can convert it to the Word file format.

> **To convert an RTF file to the Word file format, complete the following steps:**
>
> 1. Click the File tab on the Word Ribbon.
> 2. Click Save As.
> 3. Change the *Save as type* to Word Document.

From that point forward, the document retains the Word format.

Select a Record Source to Export to Word

The objects you select to export from Access to Word should have a tabular layout, such as tables, queries, and tabular reports.

Although other object types do export to Word, the results are unpredictable and poorly formatted. If you are uncertain about which type of objects to export to Word, select any object in Access and export it to Word to see if it is properly formatted. If the data is usable, you can keep the Word document. If the data is not what you wanted, just close the file without saving and try again with a different layout. For example, if you want to export a products table from an Access database into a Word document, as shown in Figure 8.26, the export-to-Word process is fast and easy. For the Products table, the field names become the column headings and the records become the table rows in the RTF file.

When you export tabular reports to Word, Access preserves the report's grouping aggregate functions, although some of the formatting may be lost. Columnar forms and reports do not export to Word properly. You should test the export of these objects to see if they produce usable data.

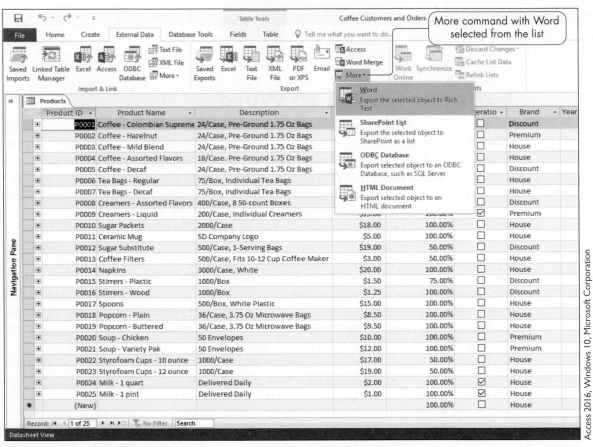

FIGURE 8.26 Product Data in Access

Export Tables and Queries to Word

 » Exporting tables and queries to Word is similar to exporting tables and queries to Excel.

> **To export a table or query to Word, complete the following steps:**
>
> 1. Select the table or query in the Navigation Pane (or open the table or query first), and click the External Data tab.
> 2. Click More in the Export group.
> 3. Select Word. Access opens the Export – RTF dialog box (shown in Figure 8.27) to guide you through the export process.
> 4. Specify the file name, destination, and format for the exported file.
> 5. Specify if you want to open the destination file after the export operation is complete.
> 6. Specify if you want to export only the selected records (if you have selected one or more records in the datasheet).
> 7. Click OK.

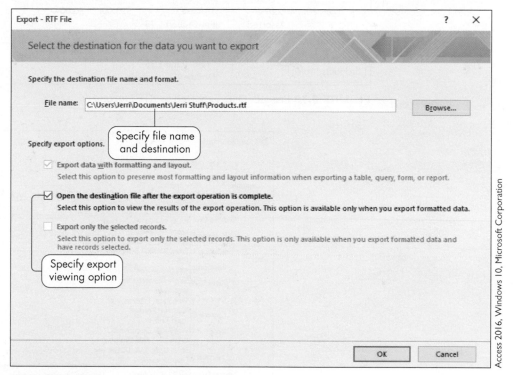

FIGURE 8.27 Export – RTF File Dialog Box

Modify an RTF File in Word

After you export an Access table to an RTF file, such as a products table, you can edit the file in Word and add additional text to the content. For example, if you want to send the exported products table to a few vendors to check current prices, you can add additional lines above the table to change the document to a memo format, as shown in Figure 8.28.

When you save an RTF file, you can change the file type to Word Document so that you can take full advantage of Word's features and formatting tools (see Figure 8.29).

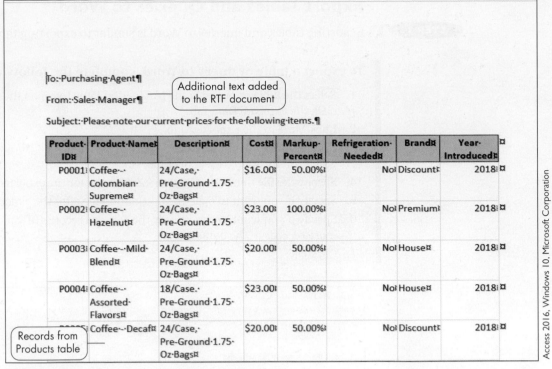

To: Purchasing Agent¶

From: Sales Manager¶

Additional text added to the RTF document

Subject: Please note our current prices for the following items.¶

Product ID¤	Product Name¤	Description¤	Cost¤	Markup Percent¤	Refrigeration Needed¤	Brand¤	Year Introduced¤	¤
P0001¤	Coffee - Colombian Supreme¤	24/Case, Pre-Ground 1.75 Oz Bags¤	$16.00¤	50.00%¤	No¤	Discount¤	2018¤	¤
P0002¤	Coffee - Hazelnut¤	24/Case, Pre-Ground 1.75 Oz Bags¤	$23.00¤	100.00%¤	No¤	Premium¤	2018¤	¤
P0003¤	Coffee - Mild Blend¤	24/Case, Pre-Ground 1.75 Oz Bags¤	$20.00¤	50.00%¤	No¤	House¤	2018¤	¤
P0004¤	Coffee - Assorted Flavors¤	18/Case, Pre-Ground 1.75 Oz Bags¤	$23.00¤	50.00%¤	No¤	House¤	2018¤	¤
P0005¤	Coffee - Decaf¤	24/Case, Pre-Ground 1.75 Oz Bags¤	$20.00¤	50.00%¤	No¤	Discount¤	2018¤	¤

Records from Products table

FIGURE 8.28 Product Data Exported to RTF Document

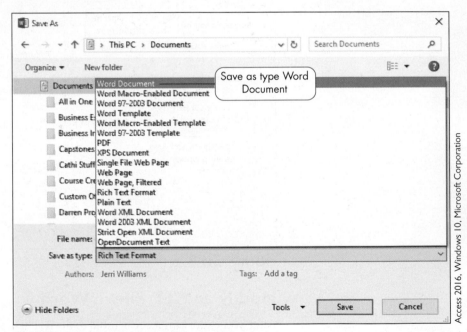

FIGURE 8.29 Save As Dialog Box in Word

Exporting Data to a PDF or XPS Document

Exporting data from Access to a PDF or XPS document is similar to exporting data to Word, except that you are not typically able to edit the exported documents. When you export from Access to Word or Excel, you can modify the exported files.

When you export Access data to a PDF or XPS document, you are not required to purchase a commercial software application to view the information. Both PDF and XPS documents can be opened by their respective document readers. Both readers are available as free downloads to users. ***Portable Document Format (PDF)*** is a file format created by Adobe Systems in 1993 for document exchange independent of software application and operating system environment. PDF documents can be viewed with Adobe Reader, which is available online at https://get.adobe.com/reader/. Reader, a Windows application, is an alternative to Adobe Reader, and is available in the Store. You can access the Store by clicking the Store icon on the Windows 10 taskbar. ***XML Paper Specification (XPS)*** is a file format designed by Microsoft to display a printed page on screen identically on any computer platform. The XPS format is considered an alternative to PDF. An XPS document can be viewed with an XPS Viewer, which may be preinstalled with your operating system; otherwise, various free XPS viewers are available online.

Export to a PDF or XPS Document

STEP 4)) Tables, queries, forms, and reports can be exported to a PDF or XPS document. However, the number of pages should be checked after the objects are exported. For example, if you attempt to export a single record from a form, you will be surprised to find the results contain all the records in the record source; you cannot selectively export form records. Reports tend to be better choices for creating PDF and XPS documents, particularly if they do not need modification or data analysis. Documents in PDF or XPS format are generally intended for reviewing and printing.

> **To export to a PDF or XPS document, complete the following steps:**
> 1. Select the object that you want to export, and click the External Data tab.
> 2. Click PDF or XPS in the Export group. The Publish as PDF or XPS dialog box opens, as shown in Figure 8.30.
> 3. Select the folder where the document should be saved, type the name of the exported document, and then select the document type, either PDF or XPS Document.
> 4. Ensure that the *Open file after publishing* check box is selected.
> 5. Click Publish to create the document.

A document opens using the reader associated with the document type (PDF or XPS). The document contains multiple pages if the source has multiple pages. If the document is too wide, then two pages may be required to display one page of data. See Figure 8.31 as an example of a PDF document and Figure 8.32 as an example of an XPS document.

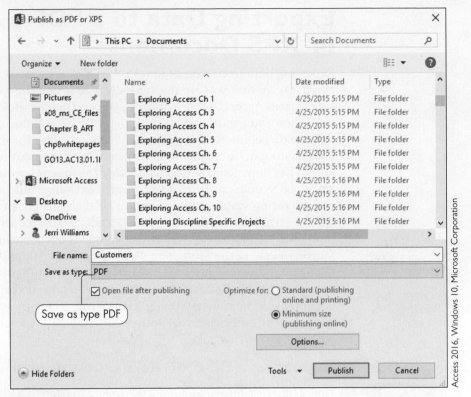

FIGURE 8.30 Publish as PDF or XPS Dialog Box

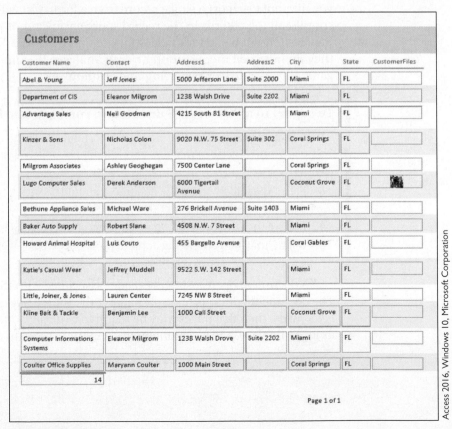

FIGURE 8.31 PDF Document Created from an Access Report

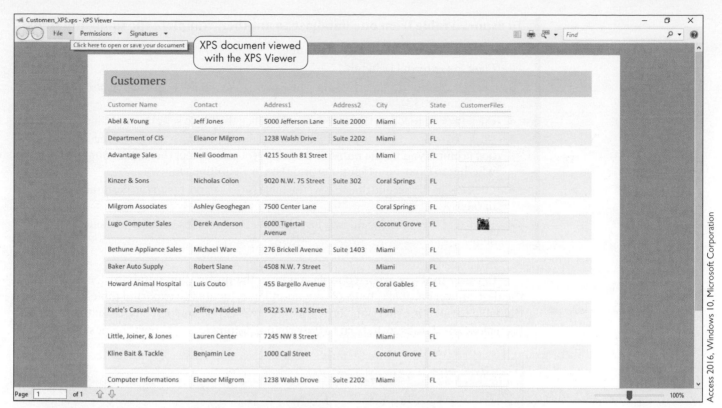

FIGURE 8.32 XPS Document Created from an Access Report

TIP: VIEWING XPS DOCUMENTS

XPS documents can be viewed with your browser (e.g., Microsoft Edge) or Reader if an XPS Viewer has not been installed. XPS documents are not as widely used and distributed as PDF documents. For that reason, PDF documents are the preferred format when exporting this type of document from Access.

Exporting Objects to Another Access Database

After you create a database for one purpose, you may be able to use the structure of certain objects in a different database. For example, if you are designing databases for businesses, you will notice that many business databases require an employees table, a customers table, and an orders table. Companies often need a data entry form for each of those three tables. There may be common reports that can also be exported from one database to another—for example, an employee list report or a customer list report. Exporting objects from one Access database to another saves time because you do not have to create the objects (tables, forms, reports) from scratch. However, you might have to modify the imported objects slightly to match the requirements of the new database.

When you export tables to another database, the Export dialog box asks if you want to export the data along with the definition (e.g., the field names, data types, etc.). Generally, you will not want the data exported to the new database. After the tables are successfully exported, you can delete unwanted fields and add new fields to create the table structure you need for the new purpose. Forms and reports may need to be modified as well.

Export Tables to Another Database

STEP 5 ▶▶ Before you can export a table to another database, you must first create the new database if one does not already exist.

To export a table from one database to another, complete the following steps:

1. Select the table in the Navigation Pane.
2. Click the External Data tab.
3. Click Access in the Export group. The Export – Access Database dialog box displays (see Figure 8.33).
4. Click Browse to locate the destination file, click the file to select it, and then click Save.
5. Click OK to proceed to the next dialog box, shown in Figure 8.34. The second dialog box prompts you for the name of the table (you can accept the default name) and whether to export the Definition and Data or Definition Only.
6. Click OK in the second dialog box; the table is then exported to the destination database.
7. Return to the Access window. Close the Save Export Steps window without saving the steps.

To verify that the exported table is now in the destination database, locate and open the destination database. In the Navigation Pane, locate the exported table. Double-click the table to open it. After you verify the table was exported correctly, close the table, and then close the database. Return to the original database and export the next object.

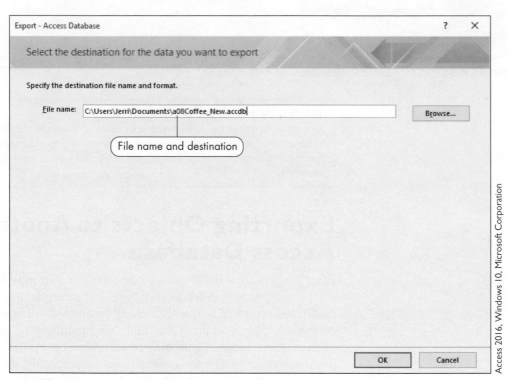

FIGURE 8.33 Export – Access Database Dialog Box

FIGURE 8.34 Export to Access Dialog Box

Export Other Objects to Another Database

STEP 6 >> In addition to tables, you may find that you can share queries, forms, and reports that you have designed with other databases.

> **To export other objects from one Access database to another database, complete the following steps:**
>
> 1. Select the object (query, form, or report) in the Navigation Pane.
> 2. Click the External Data tab.
> 3. Click Access in the Export group. The Export – Access Database dialog box displays (see Figure 8.33).
> 4. Click Browse to locate the destination file, click the file to select it, and then click Save.
> 5. Click OK to proceed to the next dialog box. The second dialog box prompts you for the name of the object (you can accept the default name or type a new name).
> 6. Click OK in the second dialog box; the object is then exported to the destination database.
> 7. Return to the Access window. Close the Save Export Steps window without saving the steps.

Verify that the exported object is in the destination database by opening the destination database. In the Navigation Pane, locate the exported object. After you verify the object was exported correctly, return to the original database, and then open the original database to export the next object.

Quick Concepts

4. What is one advantage of exporting Access data to Excel? *p. 516*

5. Why would you want to export an Access report to PDF format? *p. 529*

6. Why would you decide to export the definition of a table to a different database, but not the data? *p. 529*

Hands-On Exercises

Watch the Video
for this Hands-On
Exercise!

MyITLab®
HOE2 Training

Skills covered: Export a Query to Excel • Export a Report to Excel • Export a Query to Word •Modify an RTF File in Word • Export to a PDF or XPS Document • Export a Table to Another Database • Export a Form to Another Database

2 Exporting Data to Office and Other Applications

Blackwood Maintenance Service wants to contact the homeowners from the subdivisions they serve to tell them about their new services. You will export data to several different formats, depending on the preference of each subdivision's contact person. Some prefer an Excel spreadsheet, some prefer a Word document, one prefers PDF, and one prefers data in an Access table.

STEP 1 ›› EXPORT A QUERY TO EXCEL

You will create a new query that lists all the homeowners in The Woodlands subdivision and export it to an Excel spreadsheet. Refer to Figure 8.35 as you complete Step 1.

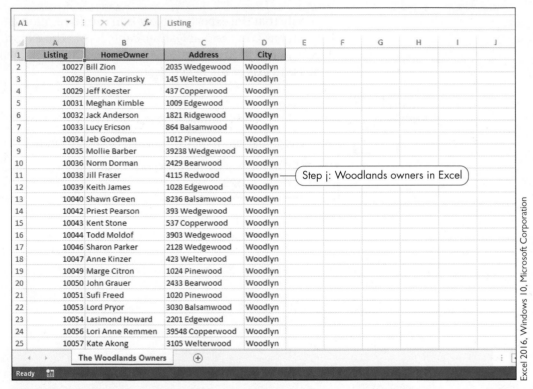

FIGURE 8.35 Woodlands Query Exported to Excel

a. Open *a08h1Property_LastFirst* if you closed it at the end of Hands-On Exercise 1, and save it as **a08h2Property_LastFirst**, changing the h1 to h2.

b. Click the **Create tab**, and click **Query Design** in the Queries group. Add the Properties table to the query design, and close the Show Table dialog box.

c. Double-click the **SubDivisonID**, **Listing**, **HomeOwner**, **Address**, and **City fields** to add them to the query design grid.

d. Type **14** into the Criteria row of the SubDivisionID field. Click the **Show check box** to deselect it. Save the query as **The Woodlands Owners**.

You entered 14 in the Criteria row, which represents The Woodlands subdivision.

e. Run the query, and widen the columns of the query so that all the data values are visible.

When you export to Excel, the Excel spreadsheet columns will be the same width as the Access columns, so it is important that all data display before exporting.

f. Click the **External Data tab**, and click **Excel** in the Export group. Click **Browse** to navigate to where you save your homework files. Type **a08h2Woodlands_LastFirst** in the File name box. Click **Save**.

> **TROUBLESHOOTING:** If you inadvertently click Excel in the Import & Link group, cancel the dialog box and click Excel in the Export group.

g. Click the **Export data with formatting and layout** and **Open the destination file after the export operation is complete check boxes** in the Export – Excel Spreadsheet dialog box to select them. Click **OK**.

A new Excel spreadsheet window opens showing The Woodlands owners' data.

> **TROUBLESHOOTING:** If you attempt to create an Excel file that already exists, Access displays the message, *Do you want to replace the existing one?* If you attempt to create an Excel file that is already open, Access displays a warning, *Microsoft Office Access can't save the output data.* Close the open Excel file and try again.

h. Return to the Access window. Click **Close** to close the Save Export Steps window without saving the export steps.

i. Save and close the query.

j. Review the workbook to ensure that all records have been exported as expected. Close the workbook and exit Excel. You will submit this file at the end of the last Hands-On Exercise.

You want to send the Service Request Report to one of the BMS subcontractors. You will export the report to Excel. Refer to Figure 8.36 as you complete Step 2.

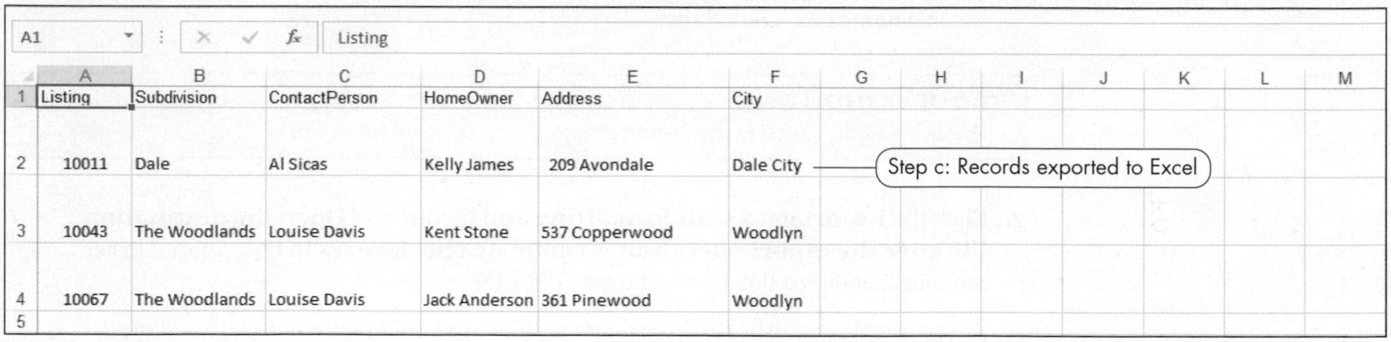

	A	B	C	D	E	F	G	H	I	J	K	L	M
1	Listing	Subdivision	ContactPerson	HomeOwner	Address	City							
2	10011	Dale	Al Sicas	Kelly James	209 Avondale	Dale City							
3	10043	The Woodlands	Louise Davis	Kent Stone	537 Copperwood	Woodlyn							
4	10067	The Woodlands	Louise Davis	Jack Anderson	361 Pinewood	Woodlyn							
5													

A1 ▾ : × ✓ fx | Listing

Step c: Records exported to Excel

FIGURE 8.36 Report Exported to Excel

Excel 2016, Windows 10, Microsoft Corporation

a. Double-click the **Service Request Report** in the Navigation Pane to open it.

   You will export this report to Excel.

b. Click **Excel** in the Export group on the External Data tab.

c. Click **Browse** and navigate to where you save your homework files. Change the file name to **a08h2Service_LastFirst**. Click **Save**. Click the **Open the destination file after the export operation is complete check box** in the Export – Excel Spreadsheet dialog box to select it. Click **OK**.

   A new Excel spreadsheet window opens, showing the Service Request Report data. The photos are missing, and the report title was deleted.

d. Return to the Access window. Click **Close** to close the Save Export Steps window without saving the export steps.

e. Close the Access report.

f. Close the workbook and exit Excel. You will submit this file at the end of the last Hands-On Exercise.

You will create a query showing all homes with a tile roof built in or before 1997; these roofs may need to be repaired or replaced. Export the query results to Word. You will modify the exported document to include the typical memo elements. Refer to Figure 8.37 as you complete Step 3.

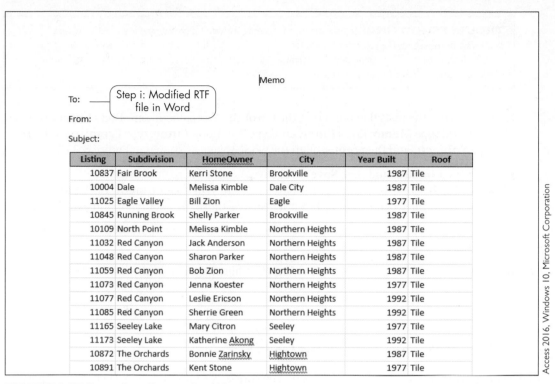

FIGURE 8.37 Query Data Exported to Word

a. Click the **Create tab**, and click **Query Design** in the Queries group. Add the Properties table and the SubDivision table to the query design, and close the Show Table dialog box.

b. Double-click the fields **Listing**, **HomeOwner**, **City**, **Year Built**, and **Roof** in the Properties table.

c. Click and drag **SubDivision** from the SubDivision table to the second column in the query design grid.

The other fields shift to the right to make room for the SubDivision field.

d. Type **<=1997** in the Criteria row of the YearBuilt column, and type **Tile** in the Criteria row of the Roof column.

You only want to see properties with a tile roof that were built on or before 1997.

e. Save the query as **Properties Built on or Before 1997**.

f. Run the query. Widen the columns of the query so that all the data values are visible.

When you export to Word, the columns show all the data if the column widths are wide enough in Access and the total width of the exported table does not exceed the Word document width.

g. Click the **External Data tab**, click **More** in the Export group, and then select **Word** from the displayed list.

You will use the list of properties to create a memo to send to the roofer so he can inspect the roofs for damage.

h. Click **Browse** and navigate to where you save your homework files. Type **a08h2Sub_LastFirst** in the File name box. Click **Save**. Click the **Open the destination file after the export operation is complete check box** in the Export – RTF File dialog box to select it. Click **OK**.

Although you are exporting to Word, the file is saved in an RTF format. A new Word window opens, showing the Properties Built on or Before 1997 data.

> **TROUBLESHOOTING:** If you attempt to create a Word file that already exists, Access displays the message, *Do you want to replace the existing one?* If you attempt to create a Word file that is already open, Access displays a warning; *Microsoft Office Access can't save the output data.* Close the open Word file and try again.

i. Ensure that the insertion point is at the top of the Word document. Press **Enter** one time, and type **Memo**. Press **Enter**, and type **To:**. Press **Enter**, type **From:**, press **Enter**, type **Subject:**, and then center-align the word *Memo*, as shown in Figure 8.37.

j. Click the **File tab**, and click **Save As** to save the new Word document as **a08h2Sub_LastFirst**. Change the *Save as type* to **Word Document**. Click **Save**. Click **OK** in the warning dialog box if it displays. Close the document and exit Word.

k. Return to the Access window. Click **Close** to close the Save Export Steps window without saving.

l. Save and close the query. You will submit this file at the end of the last Hands-On Exercise.

STEP 4 ›› EXPORT TO A PDF OR XPS DOCUMENT

You want to send the Service Request Report to one of the BMS contractors. The contractor asks that you send him the report in PDF format file because he does not have Microsoft Office on his machine. Refer to Figure 8.38 as you complete Step 4.

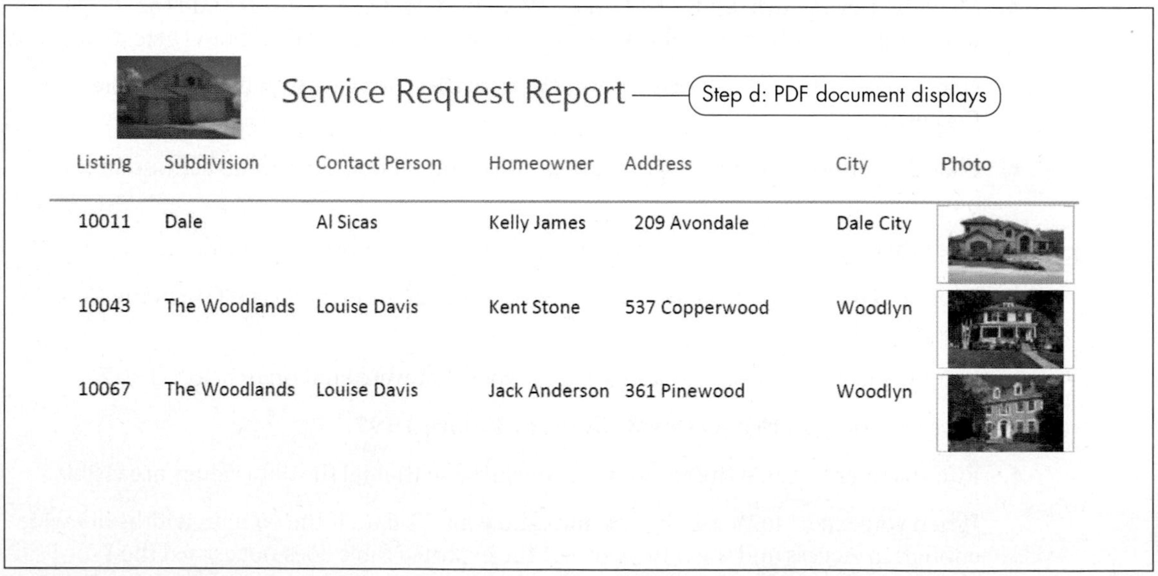
Service Request Report

Listing	Subdivision	Contact Person	Homeowner	Address	City	Photo
10011	Dale	Al Sicas	Kelly James	209 Avondale	Dale City	
10043	The Woodlands	Louise Davis	Kent Stone	537 Copperwood	Woodlyn	
10067	The Woodlands	Louise Davis	Jack Anderson	361 Pinewood	Woodlyn	

Access 2016, Windows 10, Microsoft Corporation

FIGURE 8.38 Service Request Report Exported to PDF

a. Select the **Service Request Report** in the Navigation Pane.

You will use this report to create a PDF document.

b. Click **PDF or XPS** in the Export group on the External Data tab.

c. Navigate to where you save your homework files.

d. Change the file name to **a08h2Service_LastFirst**, and ensure that **PDF** is selected for the *Save as type*. Click **Publish**.

A new PDF document is created in the folder where you are saving your files and opens in the reader window. The images display in the PDF document, whereas they did not display in the Excel file.

> **TROUBLESHOOTING:** You might notice another file by the same name already in the file list, as it was used to export Excel data in a previous step.

e. Close the reader window.

f. Click **Close** to close the Save Export Steps window without saving. You will submit this file at the end of the last Hands-On Exercise.

STEP 5 ›› EXPORT A TABLE TO ANOTHER DATABASE

Blackwood's landscaping contractor asked you for a list of all properties for which BMS provides landscaping services. Because his office manager knows Access, he asks you to send him the information in an Access database. Refer to Figure 8.39 as you complete Step 5.

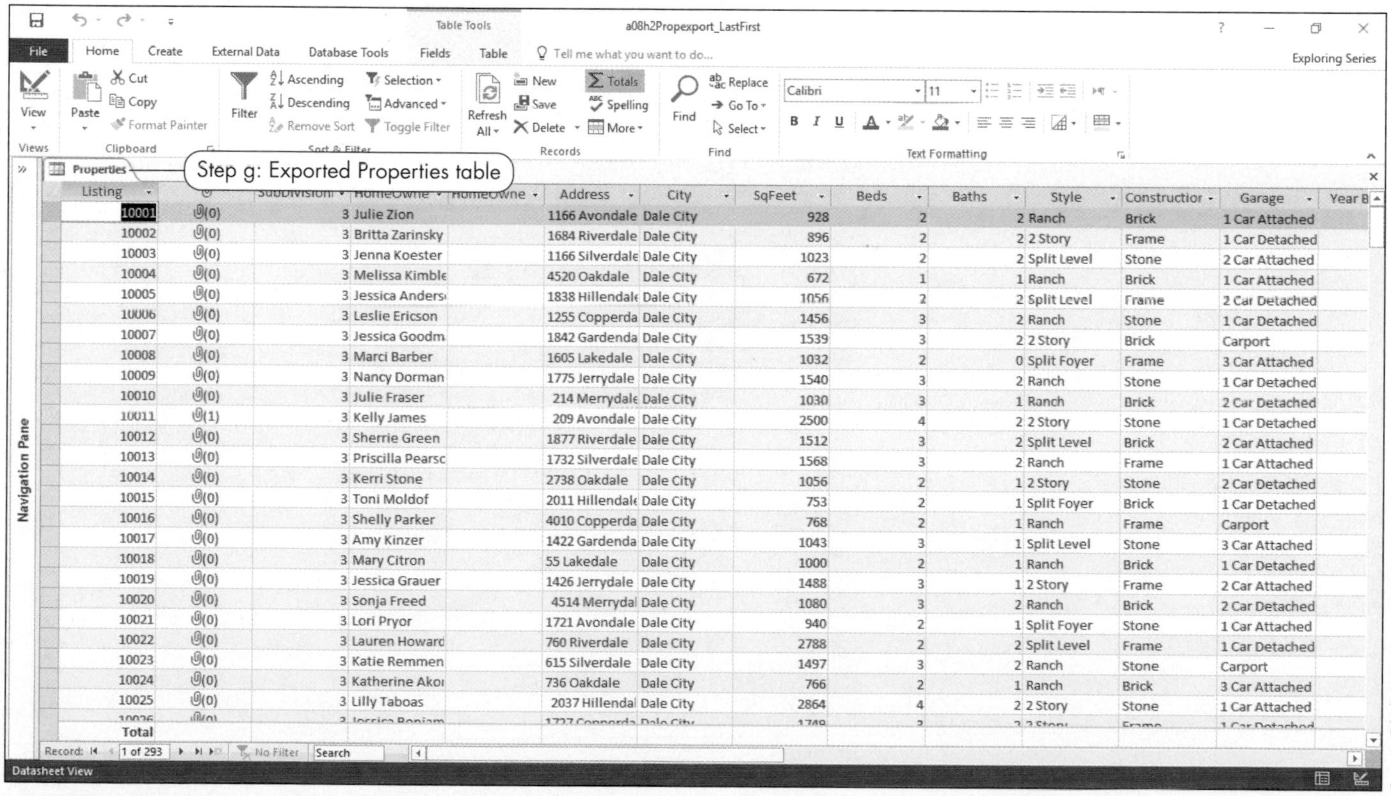

FIGURE 8.39 Destination Database with the Properties Table

a. Close the a08h2Property_LastFirst database. Open the *a08h2Propexport* database and save it as **a08h2Propexport_LastFirst**. Verify that this database does not contain any tables. Close a08h2Propexport_LastFirst. Open *a08h2Property_LastFirst*.

b. Select, but do not open, the **Properties table** in the Navigation Pane.

c. Click the **External Data tab**, and click **Access** in the Export group.

The Export – Access Database dialog box displays.

d. Click **Browse** and navigate to where you saved the a08h2Propexport_LastFirst database. Select the **a08h2Propexport_LastFirst** database, and click **Save**. When you return to the Export – Access Database dialog box, click **OK**.

The Export dialog box displays, prompting for additional information about the table you are exporting.

e. Confirm that *Properties* is in the *Export Properties to* box. Accept the **Definition and Data option**. Click **OK**.

You are sending the properties data to the landscaping contractor.

f. Click **Close** to close the Save Export Steps window without saving.

Next, you want to verify that the table is in the destination database.

g. Close a08h2Property_LastFirst. Locate *a08h2Propexport_LastFirst* and open the database. Open the Properties table.

Compare your findings with Figure 8.39.

h. Close the a08h2Propexport_LastFirst database.

i. Open the *a08h2Property_LastFirst* database.

The landscaping contractor would like you to send him a form to make it easier to work with the properties data. You will use the Form tool to quickly make a form with stacked layout. You will export the form to the same destination database as in Step 5. Refer to Figure 8.40 as you complete Step 6.

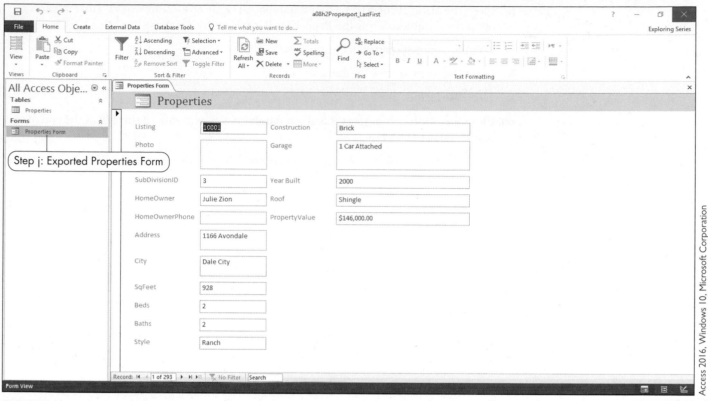

FIGURE 8.40 Destination Database with the Properties Form

a. Click to select the **Properties table** in the Navigation Pane in the a08h2Property_LastFirst database.

b. Click the **Create tab**, and click **Form** in the Forms group.

   Access creates a new stacked layout form based on the Properties table.

c. Reduce the width of the Listing control by clicking on the right border and dragging it to the left. Reduce the width by approximately half. All of the fields in the column will be resized.

d. Select the last four fields—text boxes and labels: **DateServiceStarted**, **RequestForService**, **SellingAgent**, and **ListingAgent**—one at a time and press **Delete** to delete the fields from the form.

e. Save the form as **Properties Form**. Close the form. Select the **Properties Form** in the Navigation Pane.

f. Click the **External Data tab**, and click **Access** in the Export group.

   The Export – Access Database dialog box displays.

g. Click **Browse** and navigate to where you saved the a08h2Propexport_LastFirst database. Select the **a08h2Propexport_LastFirst database**, and click **Save**. When you return to the Export – Access Database dialog box, click **OK**.

   The Export dialog box displays, prompting you to type the name of the form you are exporting.

h. Confirm that *Properties Form* is in the *Export Properties Form to* box. Click **OK**.

You accept the default name Properties Form.

i. Click **Close** to close the Save Export Steps window without saving.

Next you want to verify that the form is in the destination database.

j. Close the a08h2Property_LastFirst database. Locate *a08h2Propexport_LastFirst* and open the database. Verify the Properties Form is in the database.

Compare your screen with Figure 8.40.

k. Open the form to view the data.

l. Close the form.

m. Close the a08h2Propexport_LastFirst database. You will submit this file at the end of the last Hands-On Exercise.

n. Keep Access open if you plan to continue with the Hands-On Exercise. If not, exit Access.

Import and Link Data in Access Databases

In the previous section, you learned about the benefits of exporting information from Access to Excel, Word, PDF, or XPS, and from one Access database to another. Sometimes you need the opposite process—*importing* data into Access, which enables you to copy external data directly into your databases. A variety of data file formats can be imported into Access. Alternatively, you can create links to use data from Access databases and Excel worksheets, without importing it into your databases.

When you work with Access, much of the data entry is achieved by typing directly into the tables or forms. However, at times, you may want to import Access database objects from another database into your Access database. Importing tables from external databases is a convenient way to reuse data from other sources; you can modify an imported table or its records, or append the data to an existing table. You can also import and use other database objects, such as queries, forms, and reports in existing databases.

You may receive data in Excel spreadsheets that can be imported directly into your Access database. Once the Excel data is imported into Access, you can append it to an existing table and save a lot of data entry time. Alternatively, you can use the imported Excel data as a stand-alone table.

You may also want to import and use text files in your Access databases rather than typing the data that originates from this type of source file.

In this section, you will learn how to link a table from one Access database to another. You will also learn to use Excel data in a database by creating a link to and importing an Excel worksheet. Finally, you will learn how to import data into Access using a text file.

Linking to an Access Table

When a table in another database is relevant to your database, two options are available to provide access to that data in your database. One is to import the table from the external database into your database; the other is to create a link to a table in another Access database. Importing a table from an external database provides direct access to the data, but also increases the size of your database. If the table you are importing is very large, you might want to consider linking it to your database. **Linking** enables you to connect to a table without having to import the table data into your database. You can only link to the tables in another Access database; you cannot link to queries, forms, reports, macros, or modules.

When you link to a table in another Access database, Access creates a linked table that maintains a connection to the source table. You cannot change the structure of a linked table in the destination database (e.g., you cannot add or delete a field in a linked table, and you cannot modify the data type of a field). However, any changes you make to the data in the destination database are reflected in the linked table in the source database, and vice versa.

The ability to link to Access tables is important because databases are sometimes intentionally split so that nontable objects reside in one database, and tables reside in another. To join the two databases, links are created from the database *without* tables to the database *with* tables. Users can add, delete, and edit data (in the linked tables) as if the tables reside in the first database (when they actually reside in the second).

Examine the Tables in the Source Database

STEP 1 ❯❯ Before you link to tables in another Access database, it is best to examine the tables in the source database first. Open the table that contains the information you need, as shown in Figure 8.41. Make sure the contents, field names, and other elements are correct prior to linking to the table.

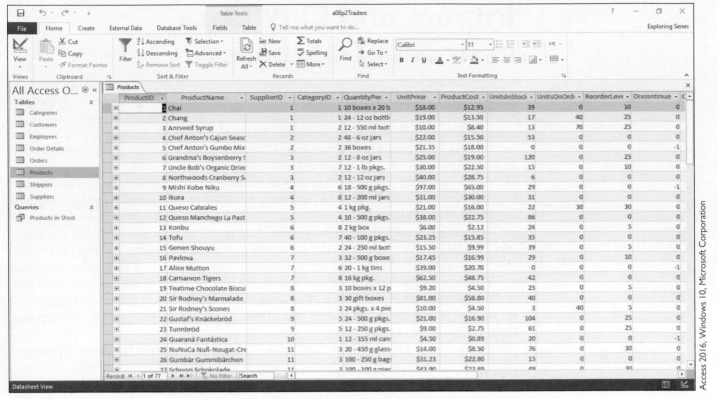

ProductID	ProductName	SupplierID	CategoryID	QuantityPer	UnitPrice	ProductCost	UnitsInStock	UnitsOnOrd	ReorderLeve	Discontinue	C
1	Chai	1	1	10 boxes x 20 b	$18.00	$12.95	39	0	10	0	
2	Chang	1	1	24 - 12 oz bottl	$19.00	$13.50	17	40	25	0	
3	Aniseed Syrup	1	2	12 - 550 ml bot	$10.00	$8.40	13	70	25	0	
4	Chef Anton's Cajun Seasc	2	2	48 - 6 oz jars	$22.00	$15.50	53	0	0	0	
5	Chef Anton's Gumbo Mix	2	2	36 boxes	$21.35	$18.00	0	0	0	-1	
6	Grandma's Boysenberry S	3	2	12 - 8 oz jars	$25.00	$19.00	120	0	25	0	
7	Uncle Bob's Organic Driec	3	7	12 - 1 lb pkgs.	$30.00	$22.50	15	0	10	0	
8	Northwoods Cranberry Sa	3	2	12 - 12 oz jars	$40.00	$28.75	6	0	0	0	
9	Mishi Kobe Niku	4	6	18 - 500 g pkgs.	$97.00	$65.00	29	0	0	-1	
10	Ikura	4	8	12 - 200 ml jars	$31.00	$30.00	31	0	0	0	
11	Queso Cabrales	5	4	1 kg pkg.	$21.00	$16.00	22	30	30	0	
12	Queso Manchego La Past	5	4	10 - 500 g pkgs.	$38.00	$22.75	86	0	0	0	
13	Konbu	6	8	2 kg box	$6.00	$2.12	24	0	5	0	
14	Tofu	6	7	40 - 100 g pkgs.	$23.25	$15.85	35	0	0	0	
15	Genen Shouyu	6	2	24 - 250 ml bot	$15.50	$9.99	39	0	5	0	
16	Pavlova	7	3	32 - 500 g boxe	$17.45	$16.99	29	0	10	0	
17	Alice Mutton	7	6	20 - 1 kg tins	$39.00	$20.70	0	0	0	-1	
18	Carnarvon Tigers	7	8	16 kg pkg.	$62.50	$48.75	42	0	0	0	
19	Teatime Chocolate Biscui	8	3	10 boxes x 12 p	$9.20	$4.50	25	0	5	0	
20	Sir Rodney's Marmalade	8	3	30 gift boxes	$81.00	$58.80	40	0	0	0	
21	Sir Rodney's Scones	8	3	24 pkgs. x 4 pie	$10.00	$4.50	3	40	5	0	
22	Gustaf's Knäckebröd	9	5	24 - 500 g pkgs.	$21.00	$16.90	104	0	25	0	
23	Tunnbröd	9	5	12 - 250 g pkgs.	$9.00	$2.75	61	0	25	0	
24	Guaraná Fantástica	10	1	12 - 355 ml can:	$4.50	$0.89	20	0	0	-1	
25	NuNuCa Nuß-Nougat-Cre	11	3	20 - 450 g glass	$14.00	$8.50	76	0	30	0	
26	Gumbär Gummibärchen	11	3	100 - 250 g bag:	$31.23	$22.80	15	0	0	0	
27	Schoggi Schokolade	11	3	100 - 100 g piec	$43.90	$22.89	49	0	30	0	

FIGURE 8.41 Products Table in External Database

Link to an Access Table

 STEP 2 >> After you examine the data in the source table—the data you want to link to Access—you are ready to create a link from within your Access database. To add the new data into your existing table, you can append all or only a subset of the new table records to your table. You accomplish this by creating an append query based on the linked Access table. An append query is an action query that adds records to an existing table.

> **To link to an Access table in another database, complete the following steps:**
>
> 1. Click the External Data tab.
> 2. Click Access in the Import & Link group. The Get External Data – Access Database dialog box opens, as shown in Figure 8.42.
> 3. Click *Link to the data source by creating a linked table*.
> 4. Click Browse to locate the Access database you want to link to.
> 5. Click the file to select it, and click Open to specify this file as the source of the data.
> 6. Ensure that the *Link to the data source by creating a linked table* option is selected, and click OK. The Link Tables dialog box displays, as shown in Figure 8.43.
> 7. Select the table you want to link to, and click OK. Click Select All if the database contains multiple tables and you want to link to all of them.

Once the link is created, you will see a special arrow icon next to the table name in the Navigation Pane that indicates the table is linked to an Access table (see Figure 8.44). Because the name of the linked table, Products, is the same as that of a table that already exists in your Access database, Access adds the number 1 to the end of the table name. Therefore, Access renames the linked table Products1. If you link to another table with the same name, Products, Access renames the third table Products2. To distinguish the linked Products table from the existing Products table, the second table could be renamed (as Traders Products, for example), as shown in Figure 8.45.

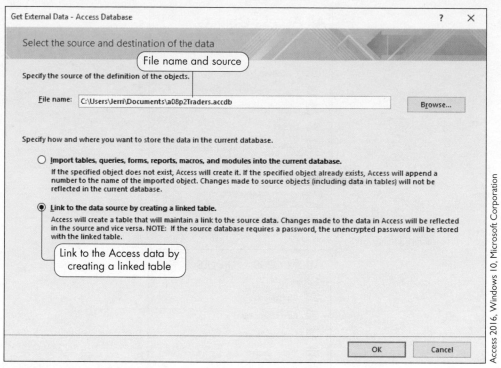

FIGURE 8.42 Get External Data – Access Database Dialog Box

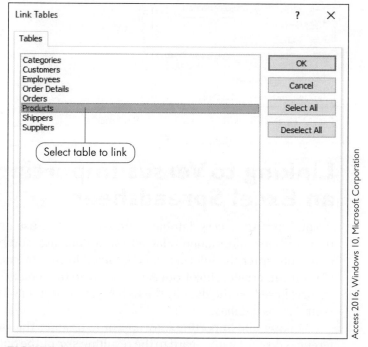

FIGURE 8.43 Link Tables Dialog Box

FIGURE 8.44 Link to Access Table

FIGURE 8.45 Link to Access Table – Renamed

Linking to Versus Importing an Excel Spreadsheet

If you have an Access database and you want to use data from an Excel spreadsheet that contains information related to your database, you have three options: (1) you can manually enter the information contained in the spreadsheet into the database tables, (2) you can create a link from Access to Excel that enables you to update tables or create reports based on the data in the Excel spreadsheet, or (3) you can import the data into your Access database.

Linking and importing may appear to produce the same results; however, some differences do exist with regard to the resulting size of the database and the ability to modify data. Linking enables you to view the Excel data without increasing the size of the Access database. Linking does not enable you to update data from within Access; if errors exist in the worksheet, you must correct the errors in Excel and redisplay the linked table in Access. Importing an Excel worksheet enables you to modify the data in the imported table, which is a separate and distinct copy of the Excel worksheet.

Examine the Format of an Excel Spreadsheet

STEP 3 » Before linking to the spreadsheet, you want to be sure the data is organized so that the import will be successful. First open the spreadsheet in Excel and examine the data, as shown in Figure 8.46. The data should be in continuous rows and columns with no blank rows, columns, or extraneous explanatory text. Ideally, the column headings and data formats should be an exact match to those in your database and in the same order, particularly if you are planning to merge the linked spreadsheet into an existing table. For example, the data in the Excel spreadsheet contains titles in cells A1 and A2 and a blank row in row 3. These first three rows will not import or link properly and should be deleted prior to importing or linking the data (see Figure 8.47). It is a good idea to create a backup copy of the original spreadsheet before altering the spreadsheet to prepare it for linking or importing. This enables you to look up the original data in case this information is needed at another time.

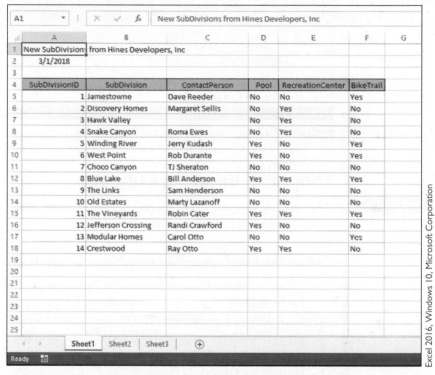

FIGURE 8.46 Property SubDivisions Spreadsheet to Import into Access

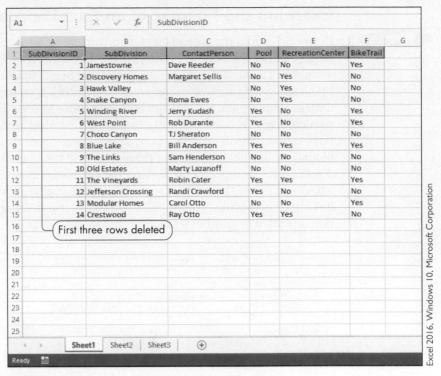

	A	B	C	D	E	F	G
1	SubDivisionID	SubDivision	ContactPerson	Pool	RecreationCenter	BikeTrail	
2	1	Jamestowne	Dave Reeder	No	No	Yes	
3	2	Discovery Homes	Margaret Sellis	No	Yes	No	
4	3	Hawk Valley		No	Yes	No	
5	4	Snake Canyon	Roma Ewes	No	Yes	No	
6	5	Winding River	Jerry Kudash	Yes	No	Yes	
7	6	West Point	Rob Durante	Yes	No	Yes	
8	7	Choco Canyon	TJ Sheraton	No	No	No	
9	8	Blue Lake	Bill Anderson	Yes	Yes	Yes	
10	9	The Links	Sam Henderson	No	No	No	
11	10	Old Estates	Marty Lazanoff	No	No	No	
12	11	The Vineyards	Robin Cater	Yes	Yes	Yes	
13	12	Jefferson Crossing	Randi Crawford	Yes	No	No	
14	13	Modular Homes	Carol Otto	No	No	Yes	
15	14	Crestwood	Ray Otto	Yes	Yes	No	

First three rows deleted

FIGURE 8.47 Excel Spreadsheet After Modification

Link to an Excel Spreadsheet

STEP 4 ≫ After you modify the Excel spreadsheet so the data will properly link to Access, you are ready to create a link from within Access.

To link the Excel spreadsheet to Access, complete the following steps:

1. Click the External Data tab, and click Excel in the Import & Link group. The Get External Data – Excel Spreadsheet dialog box launches, as shown in Figure 8.48.
2. Click Browse to locate the Excel file you want to link to, click the file to select it, and then click Open to specify this file as the source of the data.
3. Click the *Link to the data source* option, and click OK. The Link Spreadsheet Wizard launches, as shown in Figure 8.49.
4. Select the worksheet from the list of worksheets if there is more than one sheet shown at the top of the dialog box, and click Next.
5. Ensure that *First Row Contains Column Headings* is selected, and click Next. The column headings of the Excel spreadsheet become the field names in the Access table.
6. Enter the new table name in the Linked Table Name box, as shown in Figure 8.50, and click Finish.

Because Access can only link to one sheet at a time, you might have to create multiple links, one for each worksheet. Make sure you label the links with descriptive names.

Once the link is created, you will see a special arrow icon next to the table name in the Navigation Pane that indicates the table is linked to the Excel file (see Figure 8.51). Double-click the table name and the table opens. The data looks similar to data in the other tables, even though the data resides in an external Excel file. Although you have the linked table open in Access, you can still open the file in Excel (and vice versa).

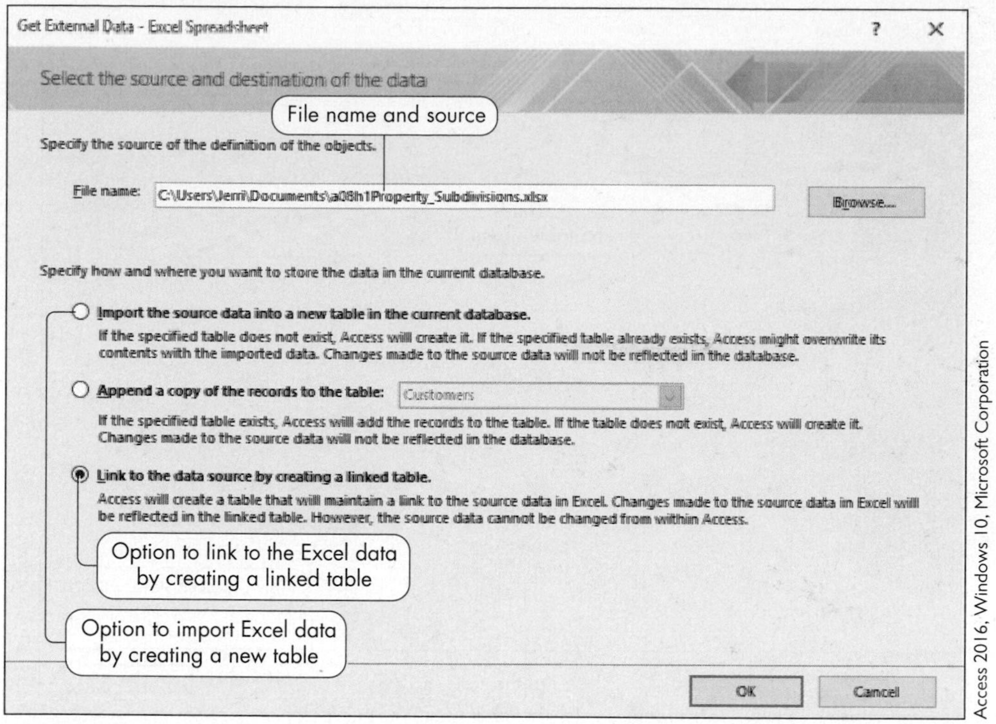

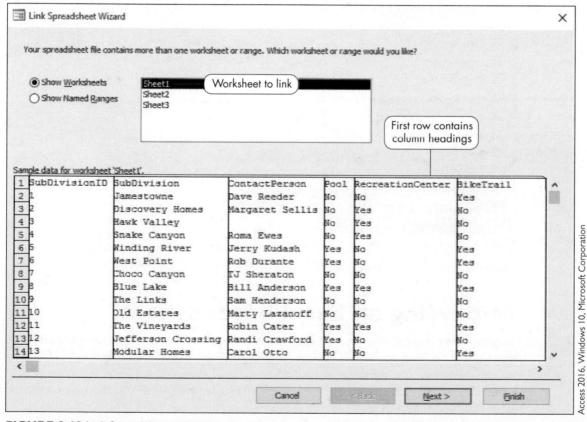

FIGURE 8.48 Get External Data – Excel Spreadsheet Dialog Box

FIGURE 8.49 Link Spreadsheet Wizard

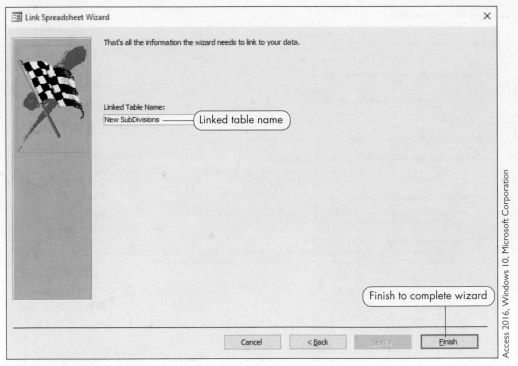

FIGURE 8.50 Specify Linked Table Name

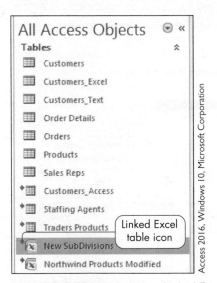

FIGURE 8.51 Icon Indicates Linked Excel Table

Importing an Excel Spreadsheet

Suppose you receive data in an Excel spreadsheet from another branch of your company and want to work with it in your Access database. In addition to linking to an Excel spreadsheet, you can import a spreadsheet into your Access database. Importing a large Excel worksheet may increase the database file size substantially; however, one reason why you would import an Excel spreadsheet is because you have more control over the imported data. The imported spreadsheet is actually a copy of the original spreadsheet, with no dependency on the external source. For that reason, you are able to manipulate the data as necessary once it is available in your database.

Import a Spreadsheet into Access

STEP 5 ⟩⟩ After you examine the Excel spreadsheet to determine that the data will properly import to Access (see Figure 8.52), you are ready to create the imported table.

To import the Excel spreadsheet to Access, complete the following steps:

1. Click the External Data tab.

2. Click Excel in the Import & Link group. The Get External Data – Excel Spreadsheet dialog box launches, as shown in Figure 8.48.

3. Click Browse to locate the Excel file you want to import, click the file to select it, and then click Open to specify this file as the source of the data.

4. Ensure that the *Import the source data* option is selected, and click OK. The Import Spreadsheet Wizard launches.

5. Select the worksheet from the list of worksheets if there is more than one sheet shown at the top of the dialog box, and click Next.

6. Click the First Row Contains Column Headings check box, and click Next two times (see Figure 8.53). The column headings of the Excel spreadsheet become the field names in the Access table.

7. Click the *Choose my own primary key* option if the imported data has a field that is acceptable as a primary key (as shown in Figure 8.54), and click Next. Access sets the value in the first column of the spreadsheet (for example, CustomerID) as the primary key field of the table. You can also allow Access to set the primary key if no value that is eligible to be a key field exists, or to set no primary key at all.

8. Enter the new table name in the Import to Table box, as shown in Figure 8.55, and click Finish.

9. Click Close when prompted to Save Import Steps.

FIGURE 8.52 Customers Spreadsheet Prepared for Import

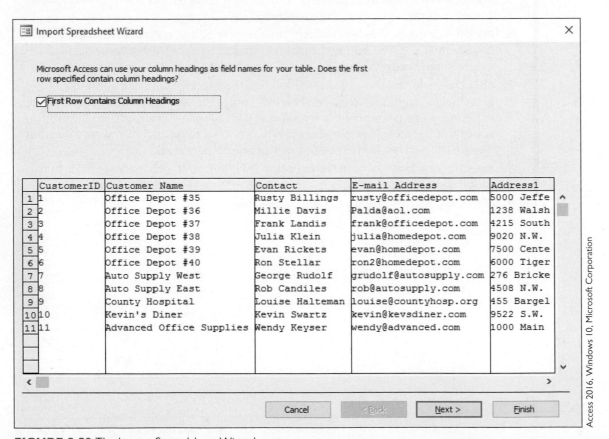

FIGURE 8.53 The Import Spreadsheet Wizard

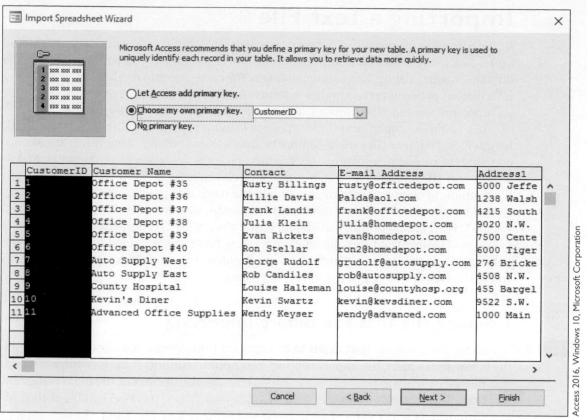

FIGURE 8.54 Choose My Own Primary Key Option

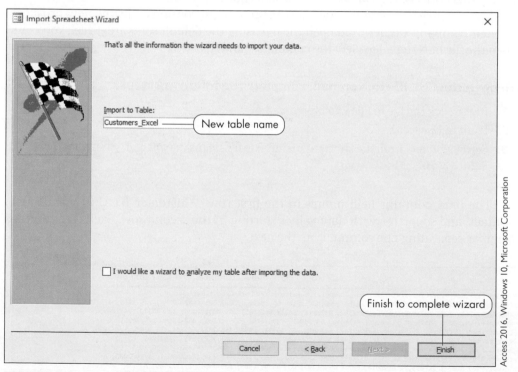

FIGURE 8.55 Import to Table Box

Importing a Text File

In the preceding examples, you learned how to link to a table in another Access database and to link to and import an Excel spreadsheet. In this example, you will import a text file directly into an existing Access database. ***Text files*** are common methods of exchanging information between two computer systems. Text files are usually created by computer software, not manually by humans, and usually contain consistent formatting.

The two most common text file types are comma-separated values (CSV) and fixed-length files. ***CSV text files*** use a comma to separate one column from the next column, enabling the receiving software to distinguish one set of field values from the next. ***Fixed-length text files*** allocate a certain number of characters for each field. A fixed-length file containing company data might contain the fields Company Name with 25 characters allocated, Address with 20 characters allocated, City with 20 characters allocated, Region with 2 characters allocated, and Postal Code with 10 characters allocated. Any values with fewer than the allocated characters have spaces added to the end of the value, and any value that is longer than its allocated characters is cut off at the position where the characters exceed the maximum allowed.

Examine the Text File Before Importing

STEP 6 If you receive a text file that needs to be imported into Access, you should examine the file before performing the import routine. You need to confirm that the contents of the text file are relevant to your database. Also, verify that the format of the file is consistent and that the fields and data values correspond to your Access tables. A text file of the CSV type usually has a .csv extension. If you double-click a CSV file, Excel, the default software application associated with CSV files, opens the file. You can examine the file using Excel. Alternatively, you can view the file in its native format.

For example, suppose the file NewCustomers.csv contains a list of new prospects for your company. Rather than open the file using the default software, Excel, you could open the file in Notepad to view the comma-separated text.

To open the CSV file in Notepad, complete the following steps:

1. Right-click the file in File Explorer.
2. Point to *Open with.*
3. Select Notepad from the shortcut menu. The file opens in Notepad, as shown in Figure 8.56.

The data contains field names in the first row—Customer ID, Customer Name, Contact, and so forth—with data values starting in the second row. Each row contains commas separating one column from the next.

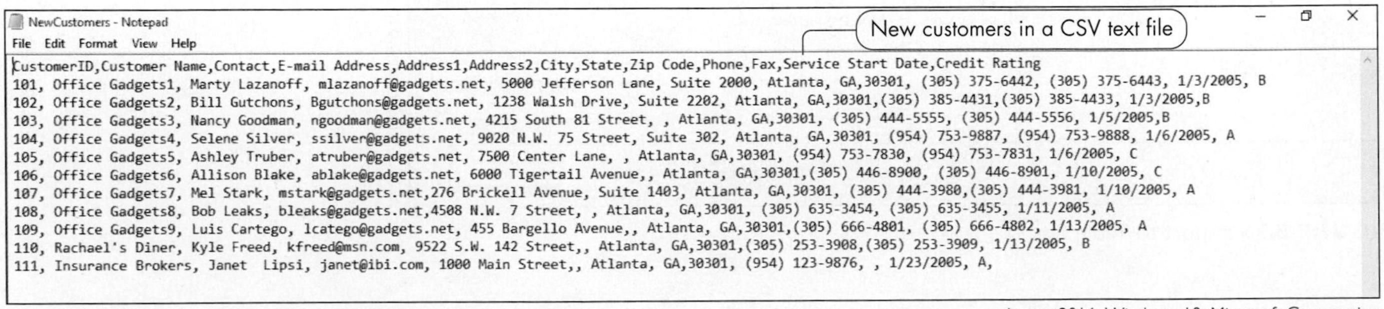


```
CustomerID,Customer Name,Contact,E-mail Address,Address1,Address2,City,State,Zip Code,Phone,Fax,Service Start Date,Credit Rating
101, Office Gadgets1, Marty Lazanoff, mlazanoff@gadgets.net, 5000 Jefferson Lane, Suite 2000, Atlanta, GA,30301, (305) 375-6442, (305) 375-6443, 1/3/2005, B
102, Office Gadgets2, Bill Gutchons, Bgutchons@gadgets.net, 1238 Walsh Drive, Suite 2202, Atlanta, GA,30301,(305) 385-4431,(305) 385-4433, 1/3/2005,B
103, Office Gadgets3, Nancy Goodman, ngoodman@gadgets.net, 4215 South 81 Street, , Atlanta, GA,30301, (305) 444-5555, (305) 444-5556, 1/5/2005,B
104, Office Gadgets4, Selene Silver, ssilver@gadgets.net, 9020 N.W. 75 Street, Suite 302, Atlanta, GA,30301, (954) 753-9887, (954) 753-9888, 1/6/2005, A
105, Office Gadgets5, Ashley Truber, atruber@gadgets.net, 7500 Center Lane, , Atlanta, GA,30301, (954) 753-7830, (954) 753-7831, 1/6/2005, C
106, Office Gadgets6, Allison Blake, ablake@gadgets.net, 6000 Tigertail Avenue,, Atlanta, GA,30301,(305) 446-8900, (305) 446-8901, 1/10/2005, C
107, Office Gadgets7, Mel Stark, mstark@gadgets.net,276 Brickell Avenue, Suite 1403, Atlanta, GA,30301, (305) 444-3980,(305) 444-3981, 1/10/2005, A
108, Office Gadgets8, Bob Leaks, bleaks@gadgets.net,4508 N.W. 7 Street, , Atlanta, GA,30301, (305) 635-3454, (305) 635-3455, 1/11/2005, A
109, Office Gadgets9, Luis Cartego, lcatego@gadgets.net, 455 Bargello Avenue,, Atlanta, GA,30301,(305) 666-4801, (305) 666-4802, 1/13/2005, A
110, Rachael's Diner, Kyle Freed, kfreed@msn.com, 9522 S.W. 142 Street,, Atlanta, GA,30301,(305) 253-3908,(305) 253-3909, 1/13/2005, B
111, Insurance Brokers, Janet  Lipsi, janet@ibi.com, 1000 Main Street,, Atlanta, GA,30301, (954) 123-9876, , 1/23/2005, A,
```

FIGURE 8.56 CSV File Opened with Notepad

Access 2016, Windows 10, Microsoft Corporation

Import a Text File into Access

STEP 7 » After you examine the data in the CSV file, you are ready to import the data into your Access database.

> **To import a text file into an Access database, complete the following steps:**
>
> 1. Click the External Data tab.
> 2. Click Text File in the Import & Link group. The Get External Data – Text File dialog box launches, as shown in Figure 8.57.
> 3. Click Browse to locate the CSV file you want to import (e.g., NewCustomers.csv), click the file to select it, and then click Open to specify this file as the source of the data.
> 4. Ensure that the *Import the source data into a new table* option is selected, and click OK. The Import Text Wizard dialog box displays, as shown in Figure 8.58.
> 5. Click Next to proceed through the questions in the wizard.
> 6. Click the *First Row Contains Field Names* check box, and click Next two times.
> 7. Click the *Choose my own primary key* option, and click Next. Access sets the value in the first field name of the text file as the primary key field of the table by default. Otherwise, you can specify a different value. You can also allow Access to set the primary key if no value that is eligible to be a key field exists, or to set no primary key at all.
> 8. Enter the new table name in the *Import to Table* box, and click Finish.
> 9. Click Close when shown the Save Import Steps prompt. The new table displays in the Navigation Pane, as shown in Figure 8.59.

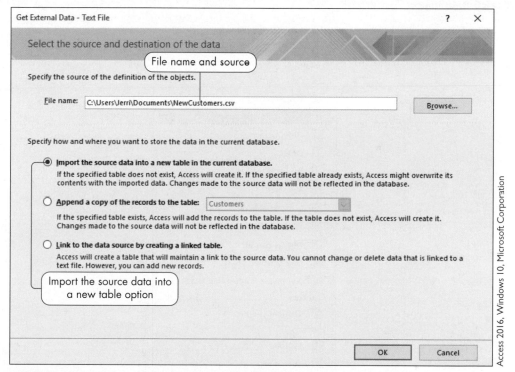

FIGURE 8.57 Get External Data – Text File Dialog Box

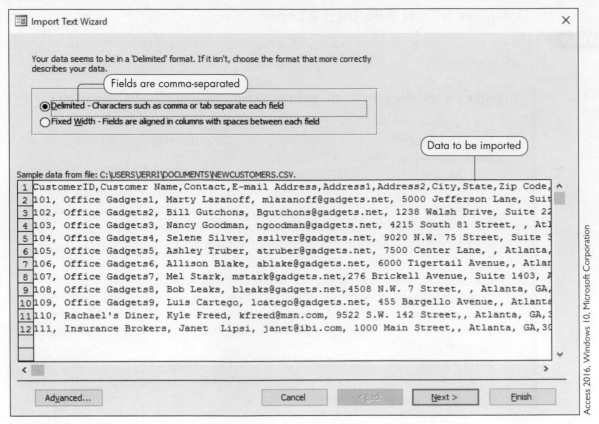

FIGURE 8.58 Import Text Wizard

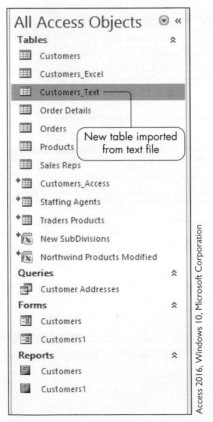

FIGURE 8.59 Table Imported from CSV File

7. What would be a benefit of linking a table to your database rather than importing it? **p. 546**

8. Why is it important to examine a spreadsheet before importing it into Access? **p. 543**

9. How is the data organized in a CSV file? **p. 553**

Hands-On Exercises

Watch the Video
for this Hands-On
Exercise!

MyITLab®
HOE3 Training

Skills covered: Examine the
Tables in the Source Database
• Link to an Access Table • Examine
the Format of an Excel Spreadsheet
• Link to an Excel Spreadsheet
• Examine and Import a Spreadsheet
into Access • Examine the Text File
Before Importing • Import a Text
File into Access

3 Importing and Linking Data in Access Databases

Blackwood Maintenance Service is adding additional subdivisions to its portfolio. It will need several new employees to manage the new subdivisions—you will review the list of agents provided in an Access database and link it to the BMS database. BMS has obtained some subdivision information in an Excel spreadsheet, which you will link and import to the database. Another spreadsheet containing potential properties to be inspected also needs to be imported. Finally, BMS purchased a list of properties that might need its services. You will import the CSV list into the current database.

STEP 1 ❯❯ EXAMINE THE TABLES IN THE SOURCE DATABASE

BMS needs to hire additional agents. It received an Access database from a staffing company with a list of possible agents. You will need to review the data first before you add the data to the Blackwood database. Refer to Figure 8.60 as you complete Step 1.

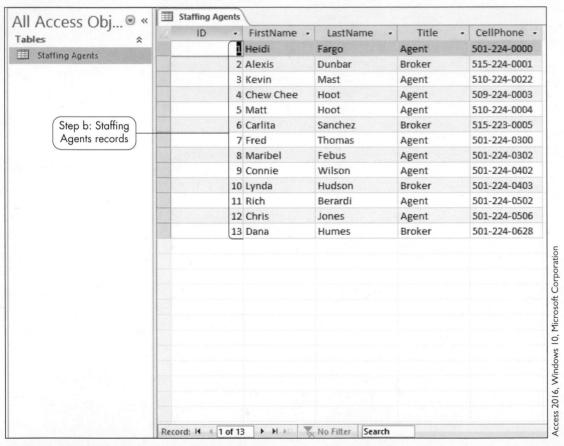

FIGURE 8.60 Open the Source Database and Table

a. Open the *a08h3Propstaff* database file.

Access opens a08h3Propstaff database, and the Staffing Agents table displays in the Navigation Pane.

b. Open the Staffing Agents table in Datasheet view.

Thirteen agents are in the table.

c. Close the Staffing Agents table. Save the database as **a08h3Propstaff_LastFirst**. Close the database.

After examining the data from the staffing company, Blackwood management wants to link the data to its database. You will create a link to the table in the staffing database; you will then append the data to the Agents table in the Blackwood database. Refer to Figure 8.61 as you complete Step 2.

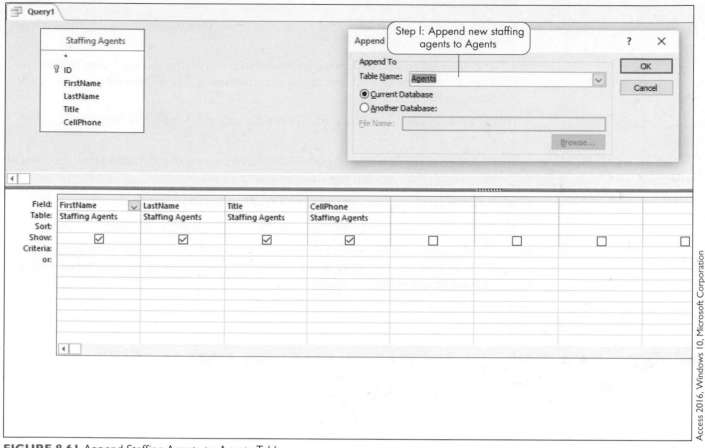

FIGURE 8.61 Append Staffing Agents to Agents Table

a. Open *a08h2Property_LastFirst* and save it as **a08h3Property_LastFirst**, changing h2 to h3.

b. Click the **External Data tab**, and click **Access** in the Import & Link group.

c. Click **Browse** to locate the *a08h3Propstaff_LastFirst* database. Click the file to select it, and click **Open**.

d. Select the **Link to the data source option**, and click **OK**.

e. Select the **Staffing Agents table** in the Link Tables dialog box, and click **OK**.

   You created a link to the Staffing Agents table in the staffing database. Note the arrow next to the table icon that indicates that the table is linked.

f. Double-click the **Staffing Agents table** in the Navigation Pane.

   The table contains the same 13 records that are in the staffing database. You are now prepared to add the new agents to the Agents table so that all of the agents can be merged into one table.

g. Close the Staffing Agents table.

h. Click the **Create tab**, and click **Query Design** in the Queries group. Add Staffing Agents to the query design, and close the Show Table dialog box.

   You created a select query, which you will convert to an append query.

i. Double-click the **title bar** of the Staffing Agents table to select all the fields. Drag the fields to the query design grid.

j. Switch to Datasheet view.

The new staffing agents are listed as expected.

k. Switch back to Design view.

l. Click **Append** in the Query Type group, and select **Agents** using the Table Name arrow. Click **OK**.

The *Append to* row displays in the query design grid with the corresponding field names listed. Some of the new IDs are the same as the existing IDs. You decide to remove the ID field from the append query.

m. Click the column selector at the top of the ID column. Press **Delete** to remove the column.

n. Click **Run** in the Results group to add the staffing agents to the Agents table. Click **Yes** in the message that says you are about to append 13 rows to the Agents table.

o. Save the query with the name **Append Staffing Agents**. Close the query.

p. Double-click the **Agents table** to verify the new agents are in the table.

The ID numbers of the appended agents are automatically assigned by the Agents table, as the ID field has the data type AutoNumber. Note that some of the missing data, such as home phone numbers, will need to be added later.

q. Close the table.

STEP 3 ›› **EXAMINE THE FORMAT OF AN EXCEL SPREADSHEET**

You will open the list of new subdivisions that BMS received in an Excel spreadsheet format and decide whether you want to add the information to your existing subdivision table. Refer to Figure 8.62 as you complete Step 3.

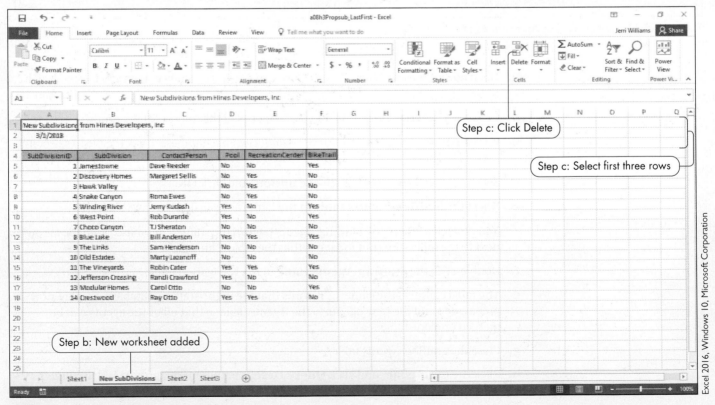

FIGURE 8.62 Copied Excel Worksheet to Be Modified

a. Open the Excel workbook *a08h3Propsub* and save it as **a08h3Propsub_LastFirst**.

You need to decide if the data will fit into the existing subdivision table and whether the data is formatted properly and does not contain extraneous rows.

b. Click **Enable Editing** in the Excel window if it displays. Right-click the **Sheet1 tab**. Select **Move or Copy**. Select **Sheet2** in the *Before sheet:* box, and click to select the **Create a copy check box**. Click **OK**. Double-click the copied sheet tab, rename the worksheet **New SubDivisions**, and then press **Enter**.

The new worksheet is the second worksheet.

c. Click and drag the **row headers** to select the first three rows of the worksheet. Click **Delete** in the Cells group on the Home tab, as shown in Figure 8.62.

The first row of a spreadsheet that is being linked or imported must contain column headings that can be recognized as field names by Access.

d. Click **cell A17**, which contains *The contact for Hawk Valley just resigned*. Press **Delete**.

There should not be any data after the last row of formatted data.

e. Save and close the workbook, and exit Excel.

The Excel spreadsheet can now be linked to the Access database.

STEP 4 ⟩⟩ **LINK TO AN EXCEL SPREADSHEET**

You will create a link to the new subdivisions worksheet, and then use the linked worksheet to create a new table in the database. Refer to Figure 8.63 as you complete Step 4.

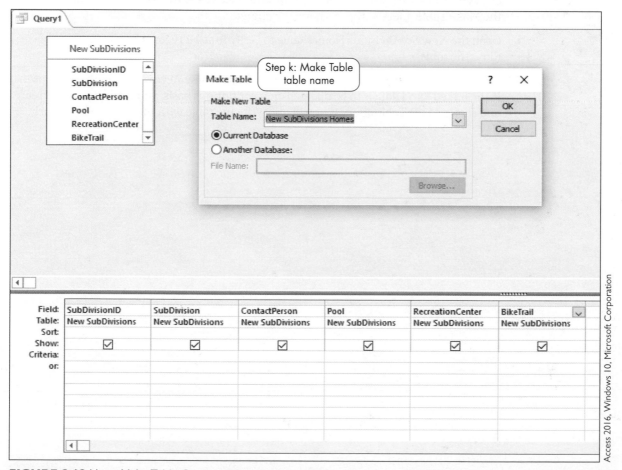

FIGURE 8.63 Use a Make Table Query to Create a New Table

a. Return to the Access window, and then click the **External Data tab**.

b. Click **Excel** in the Import & Link group.

c. Click **Browse** to locate the spreadsheet *a08h3Propsub_LastFirst*. Click **Open**.

d. Select the **Link to the data source option**, and click **OK**.

e. Select **New SubDivisions** in the Show Worksheets box of the Link Spreadsheet Wizard. Click **Next**.

You selected the revised worksheet for the link.

f. Click the **First Row Contains Column Headings check box** to select it. Click **Next**.

g. Accept the name *New SubDivisions* for the Access linked table name. Click **Finish**. Click **OK** in the message box that displays.

The Excel linked icon displays next to the New SubDivisions table.

h. Click the **Create tab**, and click **Query Design** in the Queries group. Add the New SubDivisions table to the query design, and close the Show Table dialog box.

You decide to create a new table from the linked spreadsheet using a Make Table query.

i. Add all the fields from the New SubDivisions table to the query design grid. Switch to Datasheet view to examine the records.

There are 14 records in the query results.

j. Switch back to Design view.

k. Click **Make Table** in the Query Type group. Type **New SubDivisions Homes** in the Table Name box, as shown in Figure 8.63. With the Current Database option selected, click **OK**. Click **Run** in the Results group, and click **Yes** to the warning message. Close the Make Table query without saving the changes.

l. Open the New SubDivisions Homes table to verify that 14 records display in the table. Close the table.

The Excel spreadsheet data has been used to create a new Access table in the database. If the linked Excel data is to be updated on a continuous basis, you could decide to create and save a Make Table query that will overwrite the table with the new data regularly.

STEP 5 ›› EXAMINE AND IMPORT A SPREADSHEET INTO ACCESS

Blackwood received an Excel spreadsheet containing a list of potential new properties to be inspected. You need to examine the data prior to adding it to BMS's database; for now, the imported data will be used as a stand-alone table. Refer to Figures 8.64 and 8.65 as you complete Step 5.

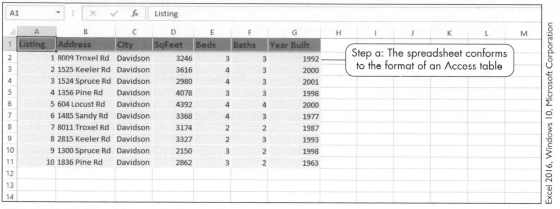

FIGURE 8.64 Spreadsheet to Be Imported into Access

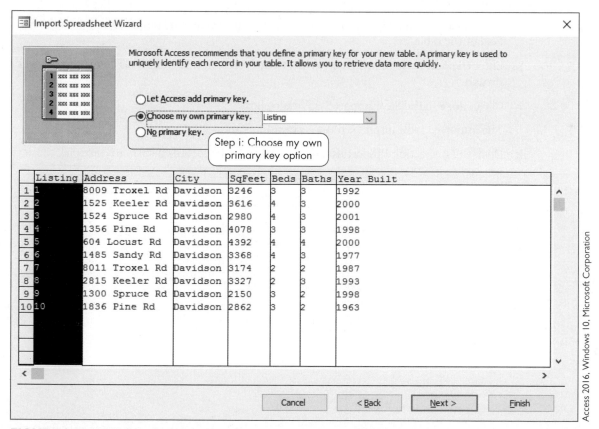

FIGURE 8.65 Importing a Spreadsheet to Access

a. Open the *a08h3Propinspect* workbook.

The spreadsheet conforms to the format of an Access table, so you do not need to make any changes to it at this time.

b. Close the workbook and exit Excel without making any changes to the file.

c. Return to the Access window, and then click the **External Data tab**.

d. Click **Excel** in the Import & Link group.

e. Click **Browse** to locate the spreadsheet *a08h3Propinspect*. Click **Open**.

f. Ensure that the *Import the source data into a new table in the current database* option is selected, and click **OK**.

g. Ensure that *First Row Contains Column Headings* is checked, and click **Next** in the Import Spreadsheet Wizard.

The first row of the spreadsheet contains column headings that will be used as the field names for the Access table.

h. Click **Next**.

i. Click the **Choose my own primary key option**, verify that Listing displays as the primary key, and then click **Next**.

Access sets the value in the first column of the spreadsheet, Listing, as the primary key field of the table.

j. Enter the new table name, **Inspection Properties**, in the Import to Table box, and click **Finish**.

k. Click **Close** in the Save Import Steps dialog box.

The imported table displays in the Navigation Pane.

l. Open the Inspection Properties table to verify that 10 records display in the table. Close the table.

Blackwood management wants to add additional properties from the city of Davidson to its database. You want to examine the data prior to adding it to the database. The new data is in a text file with the CSV format. Refer to Figure 8.66 as you complete Step 6.

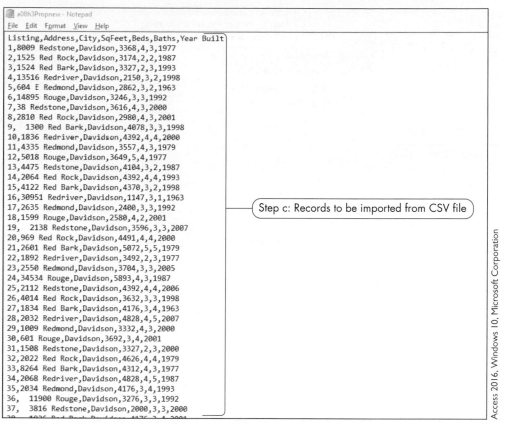

FIGURE 8.66 CSV File Opened in Notepad

a. Open *a08h3Propnew* using File Explorer.

b. Exit Excel without making any changes to the file.

Note that the file has consistent formatting for importing into Access.

c. Right-click the *a08h3Propnew* file in File Explorer, point to **Open with**, and then select **Notepad** from the shortcut menu.

You use Notepad to examine the file in its native format.

d. Close Notepad.

The BMS owners want to import and then append the Davidson properties to the Properties table in the Blackwood database. The Listing values will have to be modified when the data is appended so that they are higher than the existing values in the table. Refer to Figure 8.67 as you complete Step 7.

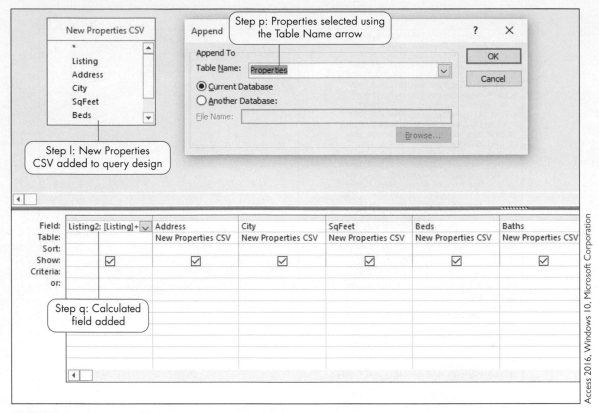

FIGURE 8.67 Append CSV Records to an Access Table

a. Return to Access. Click the **External Data tab**.

b. Click **Text File** in the Import & Link group.

c. Click **Browse** to locate the *a08h3Propnew* file. Click **Open**.

d. Ensure that *Import the source data into a new table in the current database* option is selected, and click **OK**.

   The Import Text Wizard starts. Delimited should be selected by default.

e. Click **Next** to accept the default options in this dialog box.

f. Click the **First Row Contains Field Names check box**. Click **Next**.

g. Click **Next** to accept the default field options in this dialog box.

h. Click the **No primary key option**. Click **Next**.

   When the records are appended to an existing table in the database, a unique value will be assigned to each of the imported records.

i. Type the new table name, **New Properties CSV**, in the Import to Table box, and click **Finish**.

j. Click **Close** in the Save Import Steps dialog box.

   The imported table displays in the Navigation Pane.

k. Open the Properties table. Scroll down through the table and note that the existing Listing numbers consist of five digits. Close the table.

When the imported records are appended to an existing table in the database, similar values will be assigned to each of the records.

l. Click the **Create tab**, and click **Query Design** in the Queries group. Add **New Properties CSV** to the query design, and close the Show Table dialog box.

You created a select query, which you will convert to an append query.

m. Double-click the **title bar** of the New Properties CSV table to select all the fields. Drag the fields to the query design grid.

n. Switch to Datasheet view.

58 new properties are listed as expected.

o. Switch to Design view.

p. Click **Append** in the Query Type group, and select **Properties** using the Table Name arrow. Click **OK**.

The *Append to* row displays in the query design grid with the corresponding field names listed. The new listing values need to be modified so they conform to the format of the existing listings. You decide to add 11300 to each new listing number using a calculated field.

q. Select the **Listing field name** in the first column. Type the calculated field:

Listing2:[Listing]+11300.

r. Switch to Datasheet view to see the results of the calculated field.

All of the listing values are now higher than the listing numbers of the existing properties.

s. Switch to Design view.

t. Click **Run** in the Results group to add the new (Davidson) properties to the Properties table.

u. Click **Yes** in response to the *You are about to append 58 row(s)* message.

v. Save the query with the name **Append Davidson Properties**. Close the query.

w. Close the database and exit Access. Based on your instructor's directions, submit:

a08h3Property_LastFirst
a08h2Woodlands_LastFirst
a08h2Service_LastFirst.xlsx
a08h2Sub_LastFirst
a08h2Service _LastFirst.pdf
a08h2Propexport_LastFirst

Chapter Objectives Review

After reading this chapter, you have accomplished the following objectives:

1. Create a hyperlink field.

- Add a hyperlink field in Design view: A hyperlink in a table or form launches the appropriate software and enables you to interact with the file.
- Edit a hyperlink in Datasheet view: Edit a hyperlink value if it navigates to an incorrect webpage, file, or location.

2. Add an attachment field.

- Create an attachment field in Design view: An attachment field stores a reference to an external file, and you can open that file from within Access.
- Add or edit attachments in Datasheet view: Manage your attachments from the datasheet using the Attachments dialog box.
- Remove attachments in Datasheet view: Attachments can be removed using the Attachments dialog box.

3. Add attachment controls to forms and reports.

- Add an attachment control to a form: An attachment control enables you to manage attached files in forms.
- Add an attachment control to a report: You can also manage attached files in reports. In a report, only the first file displays in Print Preview; to use the Attachment toolbar and advance through multiple attachments in a report, switch to Report view.

4. Export data to Excel.

- Select a record source to export to Excel: Tables, queries, forms, and reports can all be exported to Excel if their formats are compatible with spreadsheets.
- Export a query to Excel: Tables and queries tend to export well to Excel as their datasheet formats are compatible with spreadsheets.
- Export forms and reports to Excel: Subforms or grouped data may not export or display correctly.

5. Export data to Word.

- Select a record source to export to Word: Data that has been exported to Word cannot always be manipulated or analyzed.
- Export tables and queries to Word: Export objects that have a tabular layout (e.g., tables and queries).
- Modify an RTF file in Word: When an object is exported to Word, Access creates a file in Rich Text Format that opens in Word by default. You can save the file in the Word document format.

6. Export data to a PDF or XPS document.

- Export to a PDF or XPS document: PDF and XPS documents can be opened by their respective readers, and do not require Microsoft Office to be installed on your system.

7. Export objects to another Access database.

- Export tables to another database: After you create a table for one database, you may be able to use it again (definition or both definition and data) for another database.
- Export other objects to another database: There may be common queries, forms, or reports that could also be exported from one database to another.

8. Link to an Access table.

- Examine the tables in the source database: Ensure that the data and format are relevant to your database.
- Link to an Access table: Linking lets you connect to a table without having to import the table data into your database.

9. Link to versus import an Excel spreadsheet.

- Examine the format of an Excel spreadsheet: Ensure that the data will display properly in Access; delete extraneous or blank rows.
- Link to an Excel spreadsheet: Create a link from Access to Excel that enables you to view Excel data in Access.

10. Import an Excel spreadsheet.

- Examine the spreadsheet before importing to ensure that the data will display properly in Access.
- Import a spreadsheet into Access: Import the data into your Access database to evaluate it before appending it to the tables.

11. Import a text file.

- Examine the text file before importing: Ensure that the data is eligible to be separated into columns and is consistent from row to row.
- Import a text file into Access: You are able to manipulate the data after it is imported into Access without changing the original text file.

Key Terms Matching

Match the key terms with their definitions. Write the key term letter by the appropriate numbered definition.

a. Attachment control
b. Attachment field
c. CSV text file
d. Fixed-length text file
e. Hyperlink
f. Importing

g. Linking
h. Portable Document Format (PDF)
i. Rich Text Format (RTF)
j. Text file
k. Uniform resource locator (URL)
l. XML Paper Specification (XPS)

1. _____ A file format developed by Microsoft and designed to display a printed page on screen identically on any computer platform. **p. 525**

2. _____ Uses a comma to separate one column from the next column, enabling the receiving software to distinguish one set of field values from the next. **p. 550**

3. _____ Data type that enables you to quickly link to a file on your computer or to a webpage on the Internet. **p. 498**

4. _____ A common method of exchanging data between two computer systems. **p. 550**

5. _____ The location of a website or webpage on the Internet. **p. 498**

6. _____ Process that enables you to connect to a table or spreadsheet without having to import the data into your database. **p. 539**

7. _____ A format that enables documents created in one software application to be opened with a different software application. **p. 521**

8. _____ This process may result in increasing the size of the Access database substantially. **p. 539**

9. _____ A file format created by Adobe Systems for document exchange independent of software application and operating system environment. **p. 525**

10. _____ You can use this field to store multiple files of various formats and then launch those files from within Access. **p. 525**

11. _____ Allocates a certain number of characters for each field. **p. 550**

12. _____ A control that enables you to manage attached files in forms and reports. **p. 504**

Multiple Choice

1. Which statement is *true* about hyperlink fields?

(a) Hyperlinks cannot be used to launch webpages.

(b) Hyperlinks cannot launch Excel spreadsheets or Word documents.

(c) You can edit a hyperlink value in Datasheet view.

(d) You can edit a hyperlink value in Design view.

2. Which statement is *true* about attachments?

(a) You can attach only one file per record in a table.

(b) You can use attachment files in forms and reports, but you must first define the attachment field in the underlying table.

(c) Attached photos display as thumbnails in queries.

(d) Attachment files do not increase the size of an Access database.

3. You need to attach an employee's photo to his record in the Employees table. What is the correct action?

(a) Open the Employees table, add a hyperlink field, and then attach the photo to the employee's record in Datasheet view of the table.

(b) Open the Employees table, add an attachment field, and then attach the photo to the employee's record in Design view of the table.

(c) Open the Employees table, add an attachment field, and then attach the photo to the employee's record in Datasheet view of the table.

(d) Open the Employees table, add a lookup field, and then look up the photo on the Internet.

4. What is the primary difference between an imported table and a linked table?

(a) Data in an imported table can be modified from Access; data in a linked table cannot be modified.

(b) A linked table increases the size of the database, but an imported table does not.

(c) Users cannot create queries with a linked table.

(d) The data in imported tables resides inside the database; the data in linked tables resides outside the database.

5. You have exported an Access table to a PDF file because:

(a) You cannot create reports in Access.

(b) It can be viewed by a user who does not know Access or does not own the software.

(c) Data cannot be formatted in Access.

(d) The Access database has grown too large.

6. What is the default format when you export data to Word?

(a) PDF

(b) RTF

(c) DOC

(d) DOCX

7. What is the main difference between a PDF document and an XPS document?

(a) PDF does not require reader software to open the documents.

(b) PDF documents can be opened with an Internet browser.

(c) XPS documents show a replica of what the printed document looks like.

(d) One format was created by Adobe (PDF) and the other by Microsoft (XPS).

8. You have linked an Excel spreadsheet named *Inventory* to your database. It displays in the Navigation Pane as:

(a) The Inventory table with a special icon to its left.

(b) The Inventory form.

(c) The Inventory report.

(d) The Inventory query.

9. Which type of object(s) can be exported from one database to another?

(a) Tables only

(b) Tables and queries

(c) All objects

(d) Reports only

10. Importing a text file requires the data to be:

(a) Separated by delimiters, such as commas.

(b) Stored in a CSV file.

(c) 999 rows or less.

(d) In Word file format.

Practice Exercises

1 Houston Bank Customer Updates

As database administrator for Houston Bank, your manager wants you to attach photos of the customers to the records in the Customers table. You create an attachment field in the Customers table and then attach photos to each record. You create an email hyperlink field for the customers and add an email address to the table. You add the photo attachment control to a form, and export a report and a query to various file formats. Finally, you remove attachments and edit a hyperlink in a datasheet. Refer to Figures 8.68 and 8.69 as you complete this exercise.

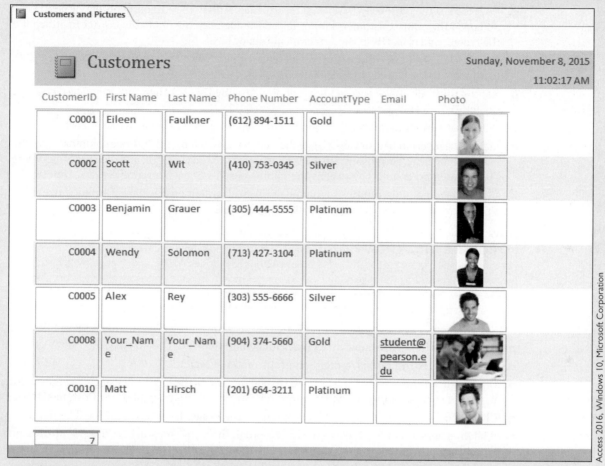

FIGURE 8.68 Hyperlink and Attachment Control in a Report

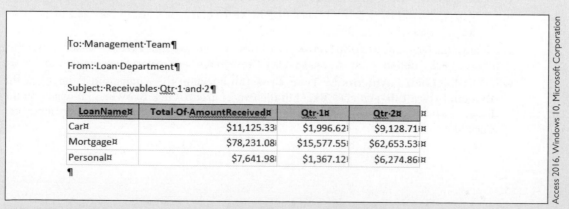

FIGURE 8.69 Loan Payments by Type_Crosstab Query Exported to Word

a. Open *a08p1Bank* and save it as **a08p1Bank_LastFirst**.

b. Open the Customers table in Datasheet view, and replace *Your_Name* with your name. Switch to Design view.

c. Type **Email** in the first blank row of the Field Name column. Select **Hyperlink** as the Data Type.

d. Add another field, **Photo**, under Email, and then select **Attachment** as the Data Type.

e. Save the table. Switch to Datasheet view.

f. Type your email address into the Email column of the eighth record.

g. Double-click the **paperclip** in the first record. Click **Add** in the Attachments dialog box. Locate and open the a08p1Customer_Photos folder. Double-click the photo file *C0001* to attach it to the record, and click **OK** in the Attachments dialog box.

h. Double-click the **paperclip** in the second record. Click **Add**. Double-click the photo file *C0002* to attach it to the record, and click **OK**.

i. Repeat until all of the records have photos attached. Use either the provided picture for CustomerID C0008, or attach a photo of yourself.

j. Click the **Create tab**, and click **Report** in the Reports group to create a new report.

k. Modify the report in Layout view. Delete the Address, City, State, and Zip Code columns by clicking each column heading, pressing **Shift**, clicking the first text box below it, and then pressing **Delete**. Delete the empty columns by clicking the column heading of each one and pressing **Delete**.

l. Resize the remaining columns so that all of the fields will fit on one page. Display the report in Print Preview to verify that all columns fit on one page.

> **TROUBLESHOOTING:** If empty columns remain in the report in Layout view, click the empty column heading of each one, and press Delete. If the report does not fit on one page, switch to Design view, and drag the page numbers text box to the left. Reduce the width of the report grid until the report fits on one page.

m. Save the report as **Customers and Pictures**. Close the report. Close the Customers table.

n. Double-click the **Customers and Loans form**, and switch to Layout view.

o. Click **Add Existing Fields** in the Tools group on the Design tab.

p. Double-click **Photo** in the Field List pane to add the field to the form. Click and drag the control to move it so that it is aligned with the top and immediately to the right of the CustomerID field.

q. Click **Add Existing Fields** in the Tools group on the Design tab to close the Field List pane.

r. Switch to Form view. Navigate to the last record in the form, Record 11. Click the **photo**, and when the Attachment toolbar displays, click the **paperclip** (Manage Attachments). In the Attachments dialog box, click **Remove**, and then click **OK** to remove the photo.

s. Save and close the form.

t. Select the **Customers and Pictures report** in the Navigation Pane.

u. Click the **External Data tab**, and click **PDF or XPS** in the Export group. Navigate to the folder where you are saving your files.

v. Change the file name to **a08p1Bank_LastFirst**, and ensure that **PDF** is selected as the *Save as type*. Click **Publish**. Close the reader. Click **Close** in the Save Export Steps window in Access.

w. Select the **Loan Payments by Type_Crosstab** query in the Navigation Pane. Click the **External Data tab**, and click **Excel** in the Export group. Click **Browse** to navigate to the location where you are saving your files. Type **a08p1Bank_LastFirst** in the File name box. Click **Save**.

x. Click the **Export data with formatting and layout** and **Open the destination file after the export operation is complete check boxes** in the Export – Excel Spreadsheet dialog box. Click **OK**. Exit Excel. Click **Close** in the Save Export Steps window in Access.

y. Select the **Loan Payments by Type** report in the Navigation Pane. Click the **External Data tab**, and click **Excel** in the Export group. Click **Browse** to navigate to the location where you are saving your files. Type **a08p1BankReport_LastFirst** in the File name box. Click **Save**.

z. Click the **Open the destination file after the export operation is complete check box** in the Export – Excel Spreadsheet dialog box. Click **OK**. Save the workbook and exit Excel. Click **Close** in the Save Export Steps window in Access.

aa. Select the **Loan Payments by Type_Crosstab** query in the Navigation Pane. Click the **External Data tab**, click **More** in the Export group, and then select **Word** from the list. Click **Browse** to navigate to the location where you are saving your files. Type **a08p1Bank_LastFirst** as the file name. Ensure that the *Save as type* is Rich Text Format. Click **Save** to return to the Export – RTF File dialog box. Click the **Open the destination file after the export operation is complete check box** to select it. Click **OK**.

ab. Verify that the data exported correctly to Word, press **Enter**, and then type the **To**, **From**, and **Subject** lines, as shown in Figure 8.69.

ac. Click the **File tab**, and click **Save As**. Navigate to the location where you are saving your files, and type **a08p1Bank_LastFirst** as the file name. Change the file type to **Word Document**. Click **Save**. Click **OK** in the compatibility message box if it displays. Close the Word document. Click **Close** in the Save Export Steps window in Access.

ad. Open the Customers table. Double-click the **paperclip** for Record 8, CustomerID C0008. In the Attachments dialog box, click **Remove**, and click **OK**.

ae. In the same record, right-click the email address, point to **Hyperlink**, and then select **Edit Hyperlink** from the shortcut menu. Change the email address to **student@pearson.edu**. Click **OK**. Press the down arrow to move to the next record. Close the table.

af. Close the database and exit Access. Based on your instructor's directions, submit:

a08p1Bank_LastFirst.accdb

a08p1Bank_LastFirst.pdf

a08p1Bank_LastFirst.xlsx

a08p1BankReport_LastFirst.xlsx

a08p1Bank_LastFirst.docx

2 Break Room Suppliers, Inc.

Break Room Suppliers, Inc., provides coffee, tea, beverages, and snacks to businesses in its area. In an effort to expand their business, the owners have obtained several customer-prospect lists. You will link and import the prospect lists into Access so the owners can determine how best to use them in their database. You will also import an Excel spreadsheet containing newly developed sales rep information. Finally, you will export a products table and form to an external database. Refer to Figure 8.70 as you complete this exercise.

CustomerID	Customer Name	Contact	E-mail Address	Address1	Address2	City	State	Zip Code	Phone	Fax
1	Drinks On Us	Jeff Jones	jeff@drinksonus.net	5000 Jefferson Lane	Suite 2000	Miami	FL	33131-	(305) 375-6442	(305) 375-
2	Water Department	Ed Milgrom		1238 Walsh Drive	Suite 2202	Miami	FL	33131-	(305) 385-4431	(305) 385-
3	Advantage Foods	Nancy Goodman	service@advantagesales.com	4215 South 81 Street		Miami	FL	33131-	(305) 444-5555	(305) 444-
4	Kinzer Snackfood	Selene Silver	selene@kinzer.com	9020 N.W. 75 Street	Suite 302	Coral Springs	FL	33065-	(954) 753-9887	(954) 753-
5	Juice & Associates	Ashley Truber	truber@juiceassoc.net	7500 Center Lane		Coral Springs	FL	33070-	(954) 753-7830	(954) 753-
6	Allisons Restaurant	Allison Blake	allison@allrest.com	6000 Tigertail Avenue		Coconut Grove	FL	33133-	(305) 446-8900	(305) 446-
7	Meats & Sauces	Mel Stark	mstark@meatsinc.com	276 Brickell Avenue	Suite 1403	Miami	FL	33131-	(305) 444-3980	(305) 444-
8	Three Bakers	Bob Leaks	bob@3bakers.com	4508 N.W. 7 Street		Miami	FL	33131-	(305) 635-3454	(305) 635-
9	County Hospital	Luis Cartego	luis@countyhosp.com	455 Bargello Avenue		Coral Gables	FL	33124-	(305) 666-4801	(305) 666-
10	Katie's Diner	Katie Mast	katie@msn.com	9522 S.W. 142 Street		Miami	FL	33176-	(305) 253-3908	(305) 253-
11	Advanced Office Supplies	Maryanne Ross	maryanne@advanced.com	1000 Main Street		Coral Springs	FL	33071-	(954) 123-9876	

FIGURE 8.70 Customers Imported from Another Access Database

a. Open *a08p2Coffee* and save it as **a08p2Coffee_LastFirst**.

b. Open the Excel workbook *a08p2Custexcel*, and verify that the content and formatting of the worksheet is compatible with an Access table. Exit Excel. You will link the worksheet to your database.

c. Click the **External Data tab**, and click **Excel** in the Import & Link group.

d. Click **Browse** in the Get External Data – Excel Spreadsheet dialog box, and locate the file *a08p2Custexcel*.

e. Select the file, and click **Open** to return to the Get External Data dialog box.

f. Click the **Link to the data source by creating a linked table option**. Click **OK**.

g. Click the **First Row Contains Column Headings check box** to select it. Click **Next**.

h. Confirm **Customers_Excel** is the Linked Table Name. Click **Finish**. Click **OK** in the message box.

i. Double-click the **Customers_Excel table** in the Navigation Pane to view the customer records. Close the table.

j. Open the Excel workbook *a08p2Repsexcel*, and verify that the content and formatting of the worksheet is compatible with an Access table. Exit Excel. You will import the worksheet to your database.

k. Click the **External Data tab**, and click **Excel** in the Import & Link group.

l. Click **Browse** in the Get External Data – Excel Spreadsheet dialog box, and locate the file *a08p2Repsexcel*.

m. Select the file, and click **Open** to return to the Get External Data dialog box.

n. Ensure that the **Import the source data into a new table in the current database option** is selected, and click **OK**.

o. Click the **First Row Contains Column Headings check box** to select it. Click **Next** two times.

p. Click the **Choose my own primary key option**, and verify that Sales Rep ID is selected. Click **Next**.

q. Confirm **Sales Reps** is the *Import to Table* name. Click **Finish**. Click **Close** in the Save Import Steps dialog box.

r. Double-click the **Sales Reps table** in the Navigation Pane to view the records. Close the table.

s. Open the database *a08p2Custaccess*. Open the Customers_Access table, and examine the contents. You will link your database to this table. Close the table, and close the database.

t. Return to the *a08p2Coffee_LastFirst* database. Click the **External Data tab**. Click **Access** in the Import & Link group.

u. Click **Browse** in the Get External Data – Access Database dialog box, and locate the file *a08p2Custaccess*.

v. Select the file, and click **Open** to return to the Get External Data dialog box.

w. Click the **Link to the data source by creating a linked table option** to select it. Click **OK**.

x. Click **Customers_Access** in the Link Tables dialog box. Click **OK**.

y. Double-click the **Customers_Access table** in the Navigation Pane to view the customer records. Close the table.

z. Open File Explorer, right-click *a08p2Custtext*, point to **Open with**, and then select **Notepad** from the shortcut menu. Examine the content of the .csv file. You will import this data into your database. Close Notepad, and return to the *a08p2Coffee_LastFirst* database.

aa. Click the **External Data tab**. Click **Text File** in the Import & Link group.

ab. Click **Browse** in the Get External Data – Text File dialog box, and locate the file *a08p2Custtext*.

ac. Select the file, and click **Open** to return to the Get External Data dialog box. Verify that the *Import the source data into a new table in the current database* option is selected. Click **OK**.

ad. Click **Next** when the Import Text Wizard displays.

ae. Click the **First Row Contains Field Names check box** to select it. Click **Next**.

af. Click **Next** to confirm the field options.

ag. Click the **No primary key option** in the next dialog box. Click **Next**.

ah. Change the *Import to Table* name to **Customers_Text**. Click **Finish**. Click **Close** in the Save Import Steps dialog box. Close the window.

ai. Double-click the **Customers_Text table** in the Navigation Pane to view the customer records. Close the table.

aj. Close the a08p2Coffee_LastFirst database. Open the *a08p2Custaccess* database, and save it as **a08p2Custaccess_LastFirst**. Close a08p2Custaccess_LastFirst. Open *a08p2Coffee_LastFirst*. Select, but do not open, the **Products table** in the Navigation Pane.

ak. Click the **External Data tab**, and click **Access** in the Export group.

al. Click **Browse** to locate the destination database file. Select the *a08p2Custaccess_LastFirst* database, and click **Save**. When you return to the Export – Access Database dialog box, click **OK**.

am. Confirm that **Products** is in the *Export Products to* box. Accept the **Definition and Data option**. Click **OK**.

an. Click **Close** to close the Save Export Steps window without saving.

ao. Select, but do not open, the **Products form** in the Navigation Pane.

ap. Click the **External Data tab**, and click **Access** in the Export group.

aq. Click **Browse** to locate the destination database file. Select the *a08p2Custaccess_LastFirst* database, and click **Save**. When you return to the Export – Access Database dialog box, click **OK**.

ar. Confirm that Products is in the *Export Products to* box. Click **OK**.

as. Click **Close** to close the Save Export Steps window without saving.

at. Close the database and exit Access. Based on your instructor's directions, submit:

a08p2Coffee_LastFirst

a08p2Custaccess_LastFirst

Mid-Level Exercises

1   Morrison Arboretum

The Morrison Arboretum at NC University wants to add a few new features to its database. They want to add photos of the plants to the Plant Descriptions table and a hyperlink field that points to a website that describes each plant. You also want to create a report showing the plant names, the corresponding hyperlinks, and the plant photos. You export this report to Word and notice that the photos do not display in the Word document; instead, you publish the report as a PDF document to distribute via email to members. Finally, you export a query to Excel to be used as a mailing list.

a. Open the file *a08m1Arbor*, and save it as **a08m1Arbor_LastFirst**.

b. Create a new hyperlink field named **PlantLink** in the Plant Descriptions table below the PlantName field.

c. Create a new attachment field named **Picture** in the Plant Descriptions table below the PlantLink field.

DISCOVER

d. Visit Wikipedia.org and search for **viburnum**. Copy the URL and paste it into the correct PlantLink field in Datasheet view.

e. Use the Attachments dialog box to add the appropriate photo for each plant. The photos are stored in the a08m1Plant_Photos folder.

f. Create a basic report based on the Plant Descriptions table. Set the title of the report as **Plants with Links and Pictures**.

g. Center the report title text in the control, and delete the logo to the left of the title control. Switch to Design view and drag the right edge of the report to the 8.25-inch mark and then change the page layout to **Landscape**. Save the report as **Plants with Photos**. Close the report. Export the *Plants with Photos* report to Word, in RTF format, and save the document in Word format as **a08m1Plants_LastFirst**. Note that no pictures were exported, and exit Word. Close the Save Export Steps window without saving the export steps.

h. Publish the report in PDF format, and save the document as **a08m1Plants_LastFirst**. View the PDF report in your reader program, note that the pictures were exported, and then close the reader. Close the Save Export Steps window without saving the export steps.

i. Export the query ENewsletter Members to Excel to use as mailing list. Select **Export data with formatting and layout** and **Open the destination file after the export operation is complete**. Save the workbook as **a08m1Email_LastFirst**. Review the exported data, and close Excel. Close the Save Export Steps window without saving the export steps. Import the Excel spreadsheet back into the database as a linked table named **ENewsletter List**, using the first row headings as field names.

j. Open the linked ENewsletter List table, and close the table.

k. Close the database and exit Access. Based on your instructor's directions, submit:

    a08m1Arbor_LastFirst.accdb

    a08m1Email_LastFirst.xlsx

    a08m1Plants_LastFirst.docx

    a08m1Plants_LastFirst.pdf

2 Hotel Services

ANALYSIS CASE

As the database manager of a hotel chain, you monitor the services ordered using a summary query. The hotel chain's manager asks you to send him a summary of the Raleigh location orders as an Excel spreadsheet. He also asks you to export the Repeat Members Club table to a different database. Several hotels in Los Angeles are for sale, and you decide to import their order data to determine their activity levels.

a. Open *a08m2Hotel* and save it as **a08m2Hotel_LastFirst**. Open *a08m2Hotelexport*. Save the database as **a08m2Hotelexport_LastFirst**. Close a08m2Hotelexport_LastFirst, and return to the a08m2Hotel_LastFirst database.

b. Export the Repeat Members Club table to another Access database, a08m2Hotelexport_LastFirst. Verify that the table was exported correctly, and return to the a08m2Hotel_LastFirst database. Do not save the export steps.

c. Modify the Summary by ServiceID query so that it displays only orders from location 3 (which is Raleigh). Save, run, and then close the query. Export the query to Excel, and save the workbook as **a08m2Raleighorders_LastFirst**.

d. Review the exported data, and close Excel. Do not save the export steps. Import the Excel spreadsheet back into the database as a linked table named **Raleigh Property Updates**, with the first row headings as field names. Open the Raleigh Property Updates table, and close the table. Do not save the import steps.

e. Open *a08m2Ordersexcel.xslx*, and review the data in the spreadsheet. Exit Excel, and return to a08m2Hotel_LastFirst. Import the Excel spreadsheet as a table named **Orders_Excel** with the first row as column headings and OrderID as the primary key field. Do not save the import steps.

f. Open *a08m2Ordersaccess*, and review the data in the Orders_Access table. Close a08m2Ordersaccess, and return to a08m2Hotel_LastFirst. Create a link to the **Orders_Access** table in the a08m2Ordersaccess database. Do not save the import steps.

g. Open *a08m2Orderstext.csv*, and review the data. Exit Excel, and return to a08m2Hotel_LastFirst. Import the data as **Orders_Text** from the a08m2Orderstext.csv text file using the first row headings as field names and **OrderID** as the primary key field into the database. Do not save the import steps.

h. Save a copy of the file *a08m2Orderstext* as **a08m2Orderstext_LastFirst** with the text file format (.txt). Edit the file using the Notepad program to delete the first record, *OrderID 4001*, and reimport the modified text file into your database as **Orders_Text**. Overwrite the original table when prompted.

i. Close the database and exit Access. Based on your instructor's directions, submit:
a08m2Hotel_LastFirst
a08h2Hotelexport_LastFirst

3 New Castle County Technical Services

RUNNING
CASE

New Castle County Technical Services (NCCTS) provides technical support for a number of companies in the greater New Castle County, Delaware area. Now that you have completed form and report design, you are ready to share data between Access and other applications.

a. Open the database *a07m3NCCTS_LastFirst* and save it as **a08m3NCCTS_LastFirst**.

> **TROUBLESHOOTING:** If you did not complete the Chapter 7 case, return to Chapter 7, complete the case, and then return to this exercise.

b. Create a Hyperlink field named **EmailAddress** in the last position of the Customers table.

c. Type the email address **ITDept@SVCPharm.com** in the first record of the Customers table datasheet, and close the table.

d. Create an Attachment field named **RepPhoto** in the last position of the Reps table.

e. Add the photo named *a08m3Barbara* to the first record of the Reps table datasheet, and close the table.

f. Export the Calls by Customer report to Excel using the file name **a08m3Service CallsGrouped_LastFirst**. Open the destination file after the export operation is complete. When the file opens in Excel, press Ctrl+A to select the entire worksheet, and set the font color to Automatic.

g. Save the Excel workbook and close it. Return to the Access window, and do not save the export steps.

h. Export the Calls_Crosstab query to Word in RTF format using the file name **a08m3CallsCrosstab_LastFirst**. Open the destination file after the export operation is complete. When the file opens in Word, save a copy as a Word document using the same file name.

i. Click the Layout tab, click the Orientation arrow in the Page Setup group, and then click Landscape. Ensure that the insertion point is at the top of the document, press Enter, and then type **Average Hours Logged by Call Type and Customer Satisfaction Rating**.

j. Save the Word document and close it. Return to the Access window, and do not save the export steps.

k. Import the Excel workbook named *a8m3CallGroups* into a new table in the database. Select CallTypeID as the primary key, and import the table using the name **Call Groups**.

l. Close the database and exit Access. Based on your instructor's directions, submit:

a08m3NCCTS_LastFirst

a08m3ServiceCallsGrouped_LastFirst.xlsx

a08m3CallsCrosstab_LastFirst.docx

Beyond the Classroom

Exporting from Access

The *a08b1China* database contains data from an international china, crystal, flatware, and collectibles firm. This chapter introduced you to the power of data sharing. You now know how to import and export data using many different types of file formats. The database contains a query, Orders More Than $150, which displays revenue information. Export the query and save it as a Word document in the Word format as **a08b1China_LastFirst**. At the top of the document, write a brief memo to your instructor that lists at least five formats that are available for exporting data from Access. Use the Internet to research which formats are most popular among computer users. Add that information to your memo. Exit Word, close the database, and then exit Access. Based on your instructor's directions, submit the Word document a08b1China_LastFirst.

Workplace Etiquette

You have discovered that some of the new employees in the *a08b2Etiquette* database require an in-service on workplace etiquette. Open *a08b2Etiquette* and save it as **a08b2Etiquette_LastFirst**. Modify the Require Etiquette Inservice query so that only employees who have *not* had etiquette training display in the results. Export the query results to Excel. Save the Excel workbook as **a08b2Etiquetteinservice_LastFirst**. Close Excel. Close the database and exit Access. Based on your instructor's directions, submit the Excel workbook a08b2Etiquetteinservice_LastFirst.

Capstone Exercise

You work as an associate database manager at Replacement China, Inc. This firm specializes in finding difficult-to-replace, no-longer-manufactured china, crystal, silver, and collectibles. You add a hyperlink field that will store a URL for each manufacturer's website. The HR Department manager wants to store a photo and the most recent performance review for each employee. You also export select inventory items in three different formats. Finally, you import information from Excel, Access, and text files.

Database File Setup

You will make a copy of the original database file, rename the copy, and then open the copy. After you open the copied database, you will replace an existing employee's name with your name.

a. Open *a08c1Replace* and save it as **a08c1Replace_LastFirst**.

b. Open the Employees table.

c. Navigate to record 21 and replace *Your_Name* with your name. Save the record and close the table.

Create Attachment and Hyperlink Fields

You will add a hyperlink field to the Manufacturer table to store each company's website address. You will also add an attachment field to the Employees table to store the employee's performance reviews and photos.

a. Create a new field in the Manufacturer table after RlMfgCode named **Website** with the Hyperlink data type. Save the table.

b. Switch to Datasheet view, add the website **http://www.lenox.com** to the Lenox China record (7), and then add **http://www.waterford.com** to the Waterford Crystal record (14). Click each link to make sure it launches a browser and locates the appropriate website. Close the table.

c. Create a new field in the Employees table after HireDate named **Files** with the Attachment data type. Save the table.

d. Switch to Datasheet view and use the Find command to locate the record for UserID **822680**. Add the Word document named *822680* and the picture file named *822680* to the Files field. The files are located in the a08c1Reviews folder. Additional attachments will be added in the future.

e. Create a basic form based on the Employees table that will open in Layout view. Delete the subform. Navigate to the record for UserID 822680 (record 21) and use the Attachment toolbar to display the Word document and the picture file.

f. Save the form as **Employees**. Close the form and the table.

Export a Filtered Table to Excel, Word, and PDF

You filter the Inventory table and then export the records to three formats: Excel, Word, and PDF. This information will be used to get prices on items that have no on-hand quantity.

a. Use Filter by Selection to display records in the Inventory table where the Category equals *Crystal*. Filter the records further to display Crystal where the OH (on-hand) value equals *0* (three records will display). Leave the filtered table open for the next three steps.

b. Export the filtered records to an Excel file. Save the file as **a08c1Crystal_LastFirst**. Do not save the export steps.

c. Export the same filtered records to a Word file. Open the destination file after the export operation is complete. Press **Enter** one time and add the title **Crystal with 0 on hand** to the Word file. Format the title as Bold. Save the file as a Word document with the name **a08c1Crystal_LastFirst**. Do not save the export steps.

d. Export the filtered records to a PDF document. Save the file as **a08c1Crystal_LastFirst**. Do not save the export steps.

e. Close the Inventory table without saving the changes.

Import and Link Data from Excel, Access, and a Text File

You import new customer records from Excel and Access. You also import customer records from a text file.

a. Create a linked table in the database by importing the workbook named *a08c1Customers*. Use the first row of the Customers1 worksheet as row headings and accept all other default options.

b. Create a linked table in the database by importing the Customers2 table from the database named *a08c1Customers*.

c. Create a table in the database by importing the text file named *a08c1Textcust*. Use the first row of the file as field names, **CustomerNum** as the primary key, and name the table **Customers Text**. Accept all other default options.

d. Close the database and exit Access. Based on your instructor's directions, submit:

a08c1Replace_LastFirst
a08c1Crystal_LastFirst.xlsx
a08c1Crystal_LastFirst.docx
a08c1Crystal_LastFirst.pdf

Access

Fine-Tuning the Database

LEARNING OUTCOMES
- You will protect and optimize your database using advanced Access database tools.
- You will demonstrate a basic understanding of database normalization.

OBJECTIVES & SKILLS: After you read this chapter, you will be able to:

CASE STUDY | The Metropolitan Zoo

You have been working at the Metropolitan Zoo for the past two months, performing data entry and creating forms and reports for the Access database. Now that you are familiar with the functions of the database, you have suggested to your supervisor Selene Platt that you can improve the design and performance of the database.

Given your expertise in Access, you will run some diagnostic utilities to check the performance. You know there are many ways a database can perform at a less-than-ideal level. You will also look to improve security on the database and reduce repetition of data.

CHAPTER 9

Analyzing and Improving Database Performance

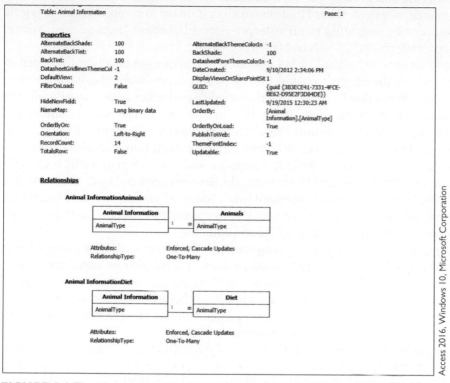

FIGURE 9.1 The Metropolitan Zoo Database—Documenter Report

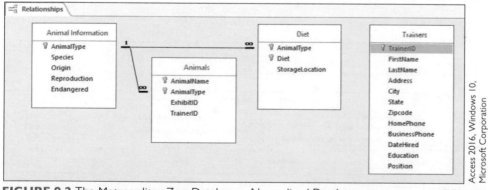

FIGURE 9.2 The Metropolitan Zoo Database—Normalized Database

CASE STUDY | The Metropolitan Zoo

Starting Files	Files to be Submitted
a09h1Zoo a09h1ZooAnalyzer a09h3Normalization	a09h1ZooAnalyzer_LastFirst a09h1ZooDocumenter_LastFirst a09h1ZooSplit_LastFirst_be a09h2ZooExecutable_LastFirst a09h3Normalization_LastFirst

Built-In Analysis and Design Tools

As new tables, queries, forms, and reports are added to a database, the performance of the database may decline. This slower performance may be due to the fact that Access databases are often created by users who lack formal training in database design. For example, a user who creates a database with 10 tables might not understand how to join the tables to produce efficient results and thus end up with repetition of data, poor performance, and data entry errors. Even if a database is well designed, deficiencies causing poor performance may exist. Some IT administrators may try to compensate for a poorly designed database by migrating to an enterprise-level Database Management System (DBMS), such as Microsoft SQL Server, MySQL, or Oracle.

Moving to an enterprise-level DBMS may have a positive net effect on the speed of processing; however, the design problems that existed in Access will still exist. It is best to resolve the design issues first in Access and then evaluate whether Access can handle the processing demands of the database. If it can, other reasons to use Access rather than move to an enterprise-level DBMS may exist. These reasons include wizards to help create tables, forms, and reports and a graphical user interface (GUI) that is intuitive to Access users. Also, Access can run on a desktop computer and does not require its own dedicated server as enterprise-level DBMS programs do. Another reason is cost. Microsoft SQL Server and Oracle are much more expensive than Access. If you recommend migrating to one of those solutions, it is best to be sure it is worth the investment. MySQL, though free, still requires more expertise than an Access database.

Sometimes, you can fix problems using the built-in Access tools. For example, you can split an Access database into two database files. If a number of users are accessing the same database, splitting the database may improve performance. One file would contain all the tables and reside on a server, while the other would reside with each user. Each user could create his or her own queries, forms, and reports on local machines but still access the same tables everyone else is using.

Access provides three useful tools that database administrators can use to analyze and improve database performance—the Database Documenter tool, the Performance Analyzer tool, and the Table Analyzer tool. Figure 9.3 shows the tools available on the Database Tools tab.

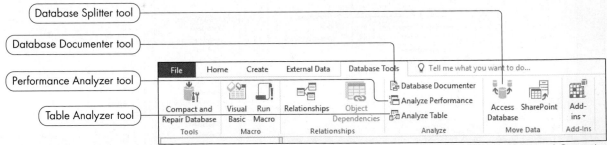

Access 2016, Windows 10, Microsoft Corporation

FIGURE 9.3 Database Analysis Tools

In this section, you will learn how to use these three tools. You will also learn how to split an Access database into two databases using the Database Splitter tool.

Using the Database Documenter Tool

The *Database Documenter* creates a report that contains detailed information for each selected object in a database. The tool creates a report showing the field names, data types, properties, indexes, and permissions for each of the selected objects. This can be helpful in a number of ways. New hires can become familiar with the structure of the database if you provide them a report. If someone will be working on a database, having this sort of documentation handy as he or she becomes familiar with a database is invaluable. You can also use this tool to get details that are not necessarily apparent by looking at an object. The tool can provide information about when an object was last modified, or even when a field in a table was last modified. This can help fix problems related to unintentional (or even intentional) problems introduced by a user. Obviously, the larger the database, the more useful the tool can be. You may not need this level of information for a database with two tables, but this is more important the larger your database grows.

Run the Database Documenter

STEP 1 ›› If you run the Database Documenter tool for the Zoo database discussed in this chapter, the report generated can be as long as 99 pages if every option is selected. In other words, important information can be missed due to the sheer amount of data. Before running the Documenter, you should narrow the options so only the pertinent information is displayed. A number of options are available, including choosing which objects to analyze and what level of detail to show. You will most commonly run the Documenter to gather information about tables.

> **To run the Database Documenter, complete the following steps:**
>
> 1. Click Database Documenter in the Analyze group on the Database Tools tab.
> 2. Select objects to include in the report (see Figure 9.4). Each tab in the Documenter dialog box represents a database object that can be documented.
> 3. Click Options (as shown in Figure 9.4) to display the Print Table Definition dialog box and select the appropriate options, as shown in Figure 9.5. A brief explanation of each of these options is listed in Table 9.1.
> 4. Click OK to generate the report after you have selected the objects to analyze.

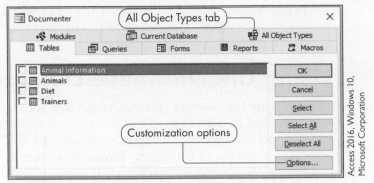

FIGURE 9.4 Database Documenter Dialog Box

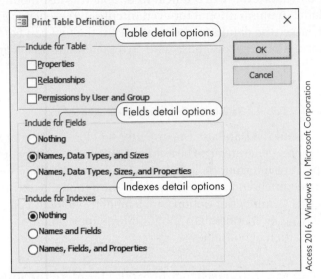

FIGURE 9.5 Print Table Definition Dialog Box

TABLE 9.1	Database Documenter Options Found in Print Table Definition Dialog Box
Option	**Function**
Include for Table: Properties	Documents table properties, including number of records, date of last update, and formatting.
Include for Table: Relationships	Documents table relationships, including which fields are common between tables and type of relationship, such as one to many.
Include for Table: Permissions by User and Group	Shows permissions for the tables based on users and/or groups. If your database does not have user-based permissions, deselect this option.
Include for Fields: Nothing	Includes no detail about the fields in the selected tables.
Include for Fields: Names, Data Types, and Sizes	Includes field names, data types, and field sizes for each field in the selected tables.
Include for Fields: Names, Data Types, Sizes, and Properties	Includes field names, data type, and field size for each field in the selected tables and options such as whether a zero-length value (or null value) is allowed, column width, and text alignment. This makes the report much longer.
Include for Indexes: Nothing	Includes no detail about the indexes in the selected tables.
Include for Indexes: Names and Fields	Includes the names of all indexes and the fields with which they are associated.
Include for Indexes: Names, Fields, and Properties	Includes the names of all indexes, the fields with which they are associated with, and the index properties, including the number of distinct index values and whether the index is required and must be unique. This makes the report much longer.

The Documenter creates a report that contains detailed information about the tables and other selected objects in your database; the report opens in Print Preview mode, as shown in Figure 9.6. Although the Documenter starts in Print Preview mode, you can save the report in a number of formats, including as a PDF or XPS file, as shown in Figure 9.6. This is especially useful when sharing the results with someone else electronically.

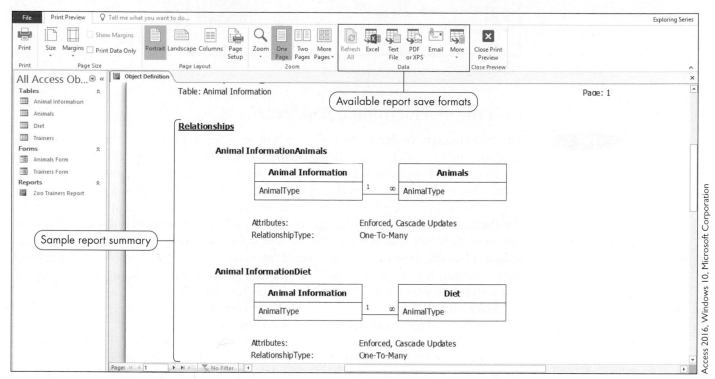

FIGURE 9.6 Database Documenter Report

Using the Performance Analyzer Tool

The Database Documenter is useful for listing the properties of each object in a database. However, the Documenter does not identify flaws in the design of the database. The ***Performance Analyzer*** evaluates each object in a database and makes recommendations for optimizing the database. Figure 9.7 shows the Performance Analyzer dialog box, where you can select what to analyze.

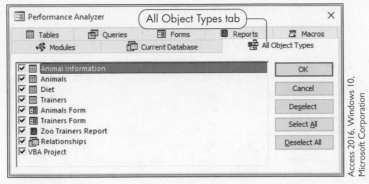

FIGURE 9.7 Performance Analyzer Options

Run the Performance Analyzer

STEP 2 >> The Performance Analyzer lists three kinds of analysis results—recommendations, suggestions, and ideas. When you click an item in the Analysis Results list, information about the proposed optimization is displayed in the Analysis Notes box, as shown in Figure 9.8. A recommendation will be marked with an exclamation point and is a change that will improve your database with little risk. Recommendations can be fixed automatically with the Performance Analyzer. A suggestion is marked by a question mark and will have potential trade-offs that you should consider before performing them. Ideas are labeled with a lightbulb; these must be performed manually by you. Before implementing any of these changes, you should read the information provided in the Analysis Notes box and if you are unsure, spend a little time doing research online first.

Some common ideas you may see include changing data types, relating a table to other tables in your database, and saving your database as a MDE file. A known bug in Access is that the Performance Analyzer suggests creating an MDE file when it should say ACCDE file. This suggestion refers to an Access Database Executable, which will be discussed later in this chapter. Aside from those common ideas, you likely will not have other major suggestions at this point.

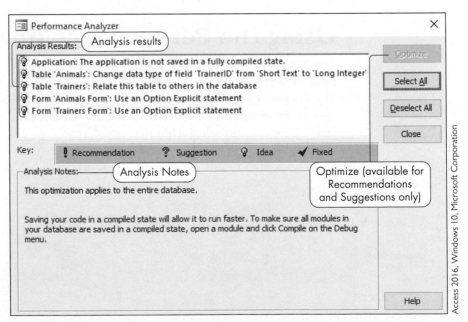

FIGURE 9.8 Performance Analyzer Results

> **To launch the Performance Analyzer, complete the following steps:**
>
> 1. Click Analyze Performance in the Analyze group on the Database Tools tab.
> 2. Select the appropriate objects to analyze. The Tables tab is selected by default, as they are the most likely cause of slowdowns.
> 3. Click OK.

The Performance Analyzer does not catch all possible database problems. Though a useful tool, the Performance Analyzer may miss some issues, so think of this tool as a supplement to your own analysis, not a replacement for it.

TIP: BACK UP DATABASE BEFORE OPTIMIZING

Before optimizing your database by making the changes suggested by the Performance Analyzer, it is best to back up your database. That way, you can revert back to the copy if the optimization yields unexpected results.

Add an Index

One common suggestion made by the Performance Analyzer is to add an index. This is a simple change to a field (or fields) in a table that could improve performance when implemented. An *index* is a setting for a field that reduces the time it takes to run queries and reports. It is similar to the index in the back of a textbook in that it provides a convenient way to find information quickly. If you wanted to find where a topic is introduced in this book, you could flip through page by page, but you would probably instead turn to the index and find out what pages reference your topic. An index works similarly for the database.

Generally, you should add an index to any field that will be searched or sorted often. For example, in a college database, a student's name would likely be indexed, but not a phone number. However, in a cell phone service provider's database, a phone number would probably be indexed because customer service representatives would use it to find a customer. Adding an index saves time searching, but will increase the time it takes to add information to the database. A database of the size of the Zoo database may not require an index, but in a larger project this is a common suggestion of the Performance Analyzer tool.

Using the Table Analyzer Tool

The *Table Analyzer* analyzes the tables in a database and makes suggestions to minimize duplication of data. This can involve splitting existing tables into smaller, related tables, with each table focused on a single topic of information. If the Table Analyzer is able to find improvements, updating information is faster and easier because fewer data changes are required. Second, only the minimum information is stored; therefore, the database is smaller. Finally, the database stores more reliable data because data is not repeated, and, therefore, will be more consistent.

Although the Table Analyzer will provide suggestions for changes, you can adjust settings such as table names, location of fields, and table relationships as you use the wizard. The third section of this chapter discusses the way database professionals minimize duplication without using the Table Analyzer tool.

Run the Table Analyzer

STEP 3 ➤➤ The Table Analyzer often produces additional tables in your database as it optimizes the way your data is stored. As you walk through the process, you can take some control of the process by deciding which fields should be included in new tables created by the Table Analyzer Wizard, or you can choose to let the wizard decide on your behalf. The wizard will offer suggestions, but it is best to think about whether they make sense in your database.

To use the Table Analyzer Wizard, complete the following steps:

1. Click the Database Tools tab, and select Analyze Table.
2. Click Next twice to advance past the introductory pages.
3. Select a table (see Figure 9.9), and click Next.
4. Click Next to let the wizard propose changes to the table. If no changes are recommended, Access will inform you and enable you to exit the wizard.
5. Rename tables by clicking the Rename Table, as shown in Figure 9.10, to clearly define the table content. You can also drag fields from one table to another if what Access suggests does not match what you have in mind. Click Next.
6. Confirm the primary keys in each proposed table, as shown in Figure 9.11. If you want to mark a field as a primary key, select it, and click Set Unique Identifier. To have Access create a primary key field for you, click in the table, and click Add Generated Key. Click Next.
7. Correct any inconsistent data, if prompted. If there are no problems with inconsistent data, this step does not appear. However, if there are errors (such as the same animal having two different origins declared in two different records), this will be indicated, as shown in Figure 9.12.
8. Choose whether or not to create a query that simulates the original table. If you choose to create the query, Access will manipulate your database so your existing queries, forms, and reports do not need to be rebuilt. In a database without any of these objects, you should select not to create the query.
9. Close the help window that appears.

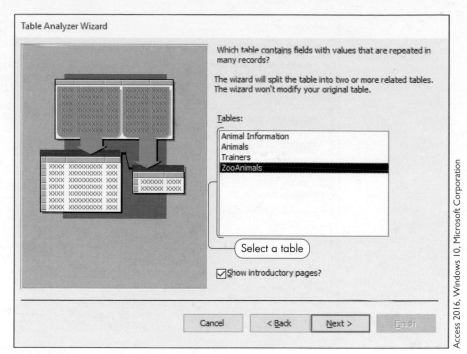

FIGURE 9.9 Choosing a Table to Analyze

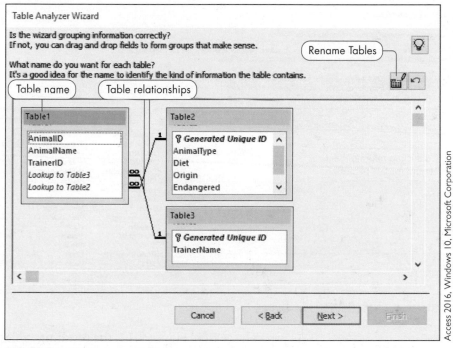

FIGURE 9.10 Renaming Tables

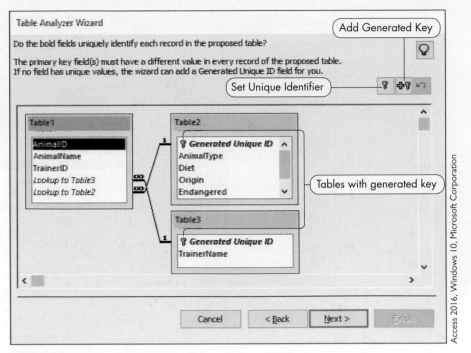

FIGURE 9.11 Identifying Primary Keys

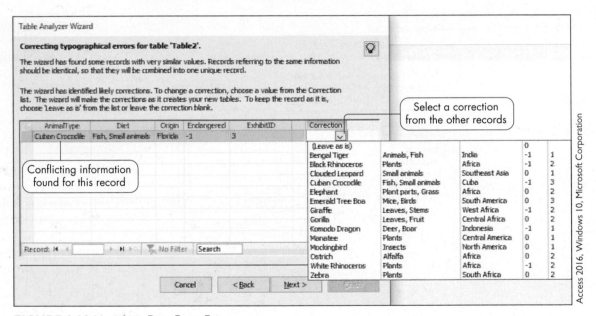

FIGURE 9.12 Identifying Data Entry Errors

As you can see from Figure 9.13, the resulting tables may not always make sense at first glance. The tool has suggested to break a table containing information about animal diets into four tables. There are reasons this makes sense, which is discussed later in the chapter, but it can be a challenge to understand why Access is making the suggestion.

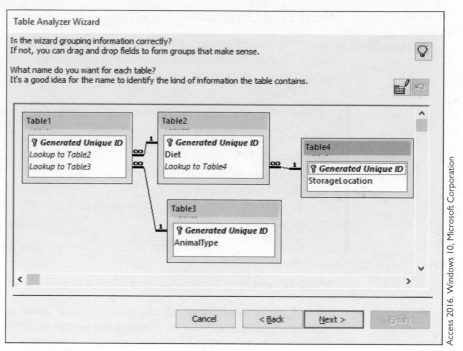

FIGURE 9.13 A Complicated Analyzer Result

After the Table Analyzer Wizard is finished, you should examine the new table structure. Click the Database Tools tab, and click Relationships in the Relationships group. From there, you can review and modify the table relationships. You could also use the Database Documenter tool to generate a new set of documentation for reference.

Using the Database Splitter Tool

A single-file Access database may work fine for a small office with a handful of users. However, when the number of users grows beyond that, you can use the **Database Splitter** tool, which enables you to split a database into two files: a back-end and a front-end database. A **back-end database** contains the tables of the database. A **front-end database** contains the queries, forms, and reports of the database. You could then have multiple front-end databases using one back-end database.

Splitting a database provides a few advantages. The main advantages of splitting an Access database are improved reliability, security, and flexibility. By storing the back-end database on a server, the tables of the database will be backed up with the server, thus improving reliability. In addition, if the front-end database is corrupted, it also should not affect the back-end database because they are two separate files. Security is improved because the security on the server is often better than that of a client machine. Finally, allowing each user to modify his or her own front-end database adds flexibility. Instead of trying to manage queries, forms, and reports in a single-file database, the database administrator can allow each user to manage his or her own front-end database, which does not affect other users.

Run the Database Splitter

STEP 4 ❯❯ Once you have made the decision to split a database, the important decision is to choose where to store the back-end database. As discussed, storing the back-end database on a server would allow multiple users to use the tables.

> **To start the Database Splitter, complete the following steps:**
>
> 1. Click Access Database in the Move Data group of the Database Tools tab.
> 2. Click Split Database.
> 3. Choose the folder and name for the new back-end database. Be aware Access will often default to your Documents folder, so make sure the correct folder is selected. The default name will be the original name plus "_be" for "back-end."
> 4. Click Split.
> 5. Click OK.

Work with a Front-End Database

After Access creates the back end, the front-end database remains open. The tables that existed in the original database have been replaced with linked tables with the same table names. Linked tables have an arrow icon to indicate they are linked to another Access database (see Figure 9.14). When you point to a table name, a ScreenTip shows the path to the physical table to which your front-end database is linked. As users add data to the linked tables using the front-end database, the data becomes available to other users of the back-end tables.

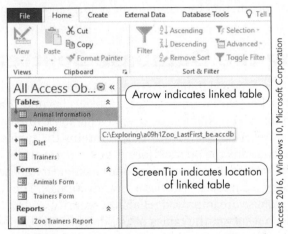

FIGURE 9.14 Linked Tables

> **TIP: ERRORS OPENING FRONT-END DATABASES**
> Note that if you use the front-end database on a different machine, or if you move the files into a different folder, you may get an error stating network access has been interrupted or the file path is not valid. If the database linking fails, you can right-click any linked table and select Linked Table Manager. Click Select All, and click OK to update the location of the back-end database.

TIP: COMPARE DATABASES

Business editions of Microsoft Office 2016 include a tool called Database Compare, which was introduced in Office 2013. This tool is not part of Access; instead, it is a tool you can launch from your Start screen or Start menu. As the name implies, you can compare two database files to see the difference. Refer to Online Help for more assistance with the tool.

Quick Concepts

1. Describe three reasons to use the Database Documenter tool. **p. 581**

2. Define the three possible result types the Performance Analyzer tool might propose. **p. 584**

3. How does the Table Analyzer tool make you more productive? **p. 586**

4. Why would a database administrator decide to split a database? **p. 589**

Hands-On Exercises

 Watch the Video for this Hands-On Exercise!

 MyITLab® HOE1 Training

Skills covered: Run the Database Documenter • Run the Performance Analyzer • Run the Table Analyzer • Run the Database Splitter • Work with a Front-End Database

1 Built-In Analysis and Design Tools

The Metropolitan Zoo database has been working well, but you decide to examine the database to see if improvements can be made. Before you begin, you will create a report of the database relationships for your reference. You will use some built-in tools to analyze the database; you also decide to split the database into two files to allow different users to create their own queries, forms, and reports.

STEP I ⟩⟩ **RUN THE DATABASE DOCUMENTER**

You will create a report with the Database Documenter to show information on relationships in the Zoo database. You will save this report as a PDF file for your reference. Refer to Figure 9.15 and Figure 9.16 as you complete Step 1.

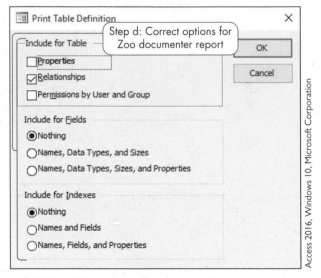

FIGURE 9.15 Database Documenter Options

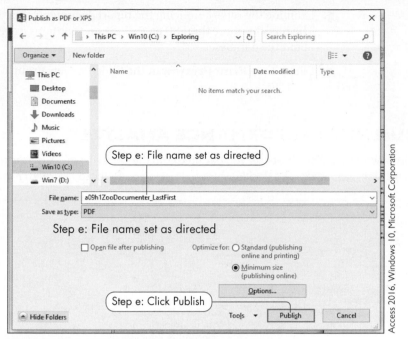

FIGURE 9.16 Publish Options for Documenter Report

a. Open *a09h1Zoo*. Save the database as **a09h1Zoo_LastFirst**.

> **TROUBLESHOOTING:** If you make any major mistakes in this exercise, you can close the file, open *a09h1Zoo* again, and then start this exercise over.

b. Click **Database Documenter** in the Analyze group on the Database Tools tab. Click the **All Objects Types tab**.

The complete set of objects in the database, including the forms, reports, properties, and relationships, are available to select

c. Click **Select All** on the All Object Types tab, and click **Options**.

d. Ensure the Relationships box in the *Include for Table* section is checked. Click the **Properties** and **Permission by User and Group check boxes** to deselect them. Click **Nothing** in the Include for Fields section, and click **Nothing** in the Include for Indexes section. Your dialog box should resemble Figure 9.15. Click **OK**. Click **OK** to run the report.

You have changed the options so only the required information is present in the report.

e. Select **PDF or XPS** in the Data group on the Print Preview tab. Type **a09h1ZooDocumenter_LastFirst** for the file name. Click the **Open file after publishing check box** to deselect it, and click **Publish** to save the file, as shown in Figure 9.16. You will submit this file to your instructor at the end of the last Hands-On Exercise.

> **TROUBLESHOOTING:** If the report opens in Adobe Acrobat Reader or another tool, close the program and return to Access.

f. Click **Close** on the next screen, which prompts you to save the steps.

g. Examine the report, noticing the report documents the relationships on the first page. The report is more than 80 pages long and contains extremely detailed information about the database.

h. Click **Close Print Preview** in the Close Preview group to close the report.

RUN THE PERFORMANCE ANALYZER

To evaluate the performance of the Zoo database, you decide to run the Performance Analyzer tool. You will review the recommendations, suggestions, and ideas, and decide which to implement. Refer to Figure 9.17 as you complete Step 2.

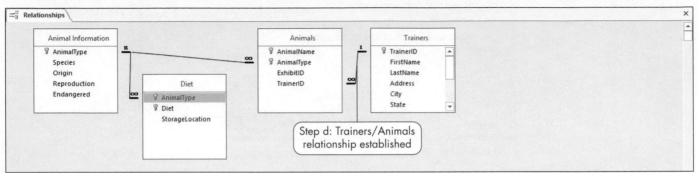

FIGURE 9.17 Zoo Database Relationships

Access 2016, Windows 10, Microsoft Corporation

a. Click the **Database Tools tab**, and click **Analyze Performance** in the Analyze group.

b. Click the **All Object Types tab**, click **Select All**, and then click **OK** to start the Performance Analyzer.

The results window displays ideas to improve the Zoo database.

c. Review the results of the Performance Analyzer, and click the idea regarding relating Trainers to another table. This relationship should be established. Click **Close** to close the Performance Analyzer dialog box.

You decide to establish relationships between the Trainers and Animals tables.

d. Click **Relationships** in the Relationships group on the Database Tools tab, and create a relationship between the Trainers and Animals tables, using the common field TrainerID. Click the **Enforce Referential Integrity** and **Cascade Update Related Fields check boxes** to select them, and click **Create**.

Your relationships should now match Figure 9.17. The tables may appear in a different order or of a different height in your database.

e. Save and close the Relationships window.

f. Repeat the procedure in Steps a and b above to run the Performance Analyzer again and see if the results are different this time.

The idea to relate tables is gone.

g. Close the Performance Analyzer dialog box, and close the database.

You decide to test the design of the tables in the Zoo database. To do this, you will open an older version of the database, run the Table Analyzer, and then compare the results with the current database. Refer to Figure 9.18 as you complete Step 3.

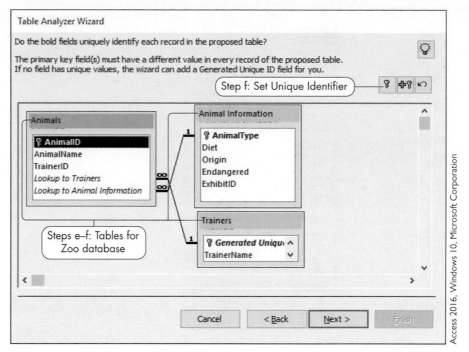

FIGURE 9.18 Unique Identifiers for Tables

a. Open *a09h1ZooAnalyzer*. Save the database as **a09h1ZooAnalyzer_LastFirst**.

b. Click the **Database Tools tab**, and click **Analyze Table** in the Analyze group.

The Table Analyzer Wizard starts.

c. Click **Next** twice to skip the information steps.

Access displays a screen asking you to select tables.

d. Click **Next** twice.

The ZooAnimals table was selected by default, and the wizard has suggested it be split into three tables.

e. Click the **Rename Table** icon, type **Animals** as the name of Table1, and then click **OK**. Select **Table2**, and use the same process to rename Table2 **Animal Information**. Select **Table3**, and rename it **Trainers**. Click **Next**.

f. Click the **AnimalID field** in the Animals table, and click **Set Unique Identifier** 🔑 to set the primary key. Click the **AnimalType field** in the Animal Information table, and use the same process to set the primary key. Compare your screen with Figure 9.18, and click **Next**.

Note that Access correctly identified the primary key for the Trainers table.

g. Select the **No, don't create the query option**, and click **Finish**. Click **OK** in response to the warning message.

There are still some repetition issues in the Diet field, but the Table Analyzer did reduce repetition of data.

h. Close the database. You will submit this file to your instructor at the end of the last Hands-On Exercise.

You decide to split the Zoo database to see if the performance of the database improves. You use the Database Splitter to divide the database into a front-end and a back-end file. Refer to Figure 9.19 as you complete Step 4.

FIGURE 9.19 Split Database

a. Open *a09h1Zoo_LastFirst*. Save the database as **a09h1ZooSplit_LastFirst**.

The new database is displayed.

b. Click the **Database Tools tab**, and click **Access Database** in the Move Data group.

The Database Splitter Wizard starts.

c. Click **Split Database**. Accept **a09h1ZooSplit_LastFirst_be** as the file name, and click **Split**.

The Database Splitter splits the database into two files. You will submit the back-end file to your instructor at the end of the last Hands-On Exercise.

d. Click **OK**.

The database is split successfully. Notice arrows now appear to the left of each table, indicating they are stored in the back-end database.

e. Open the tables and the other objects to verify the database is working properly. Ensure the tables have arrows to the left of them, as shown in Figure 9.19.

f. Close the a09h1ZooSplit_LastFirst database.

g. Keep the a09h1Zoo_LastFirst database open if you plan to continue with the next Hands-On Exercise. If not, save and close the database, and exit Access.

Database Security

Computer security can be defined as the protection of data from unauthorized access, modification, or destruction and can be divided into two general categories: physical security and logical security. Physical security involves protecting assets you can touch, such as computers, storage devices, backup devices, and the office safe. Logical security protects the information that resides on the physical devices, including databases and other computer software. Security measures should be taken to protect your assets against both physical and logical threats.

In this section, you will learn several techniques available in Access to keep your database application safe.

Controlling Navigation

To simplify data entry, a database designer can create a menu for their users, highlighting commonly used objects. This can be accomplished using a ***navigation form***, a tabbed menu system that ties the objects in the database together so that the database is easy to use. This can also help secure the database, as objects can be hidden from user view. The interface displays a menu enabling a nontechnical person to open various objects within the database and to move easily from one object to another.

Create a Navigation Form

STEP 1 ▶▶ When you create a navigation form, you drag and drop forms and reports onto tabs. An important point to note here is that a navigation form is designed for forms and reports only; dragging tables and queries will result in objects not being part of the navigation and will likely confuse users.

An added benefit of a navigation form is that it can be easily converted to a Web form if the Access database is deployed on a company intranet or on the Internet. Navigation forms have the look and feel of forms you might find on a website such as Amazon or a mobile application.

To create a navigation form, complete the following steps:

1. Click Navigation in the Forms group on the Create tab, as shown in Figure 9.20.
2. Select one of the form layouts.
3. Drag the forms and/or reports from the Navigation Pane onto [Add New], as shown in Figure 9.21.
4. Switch to Form view, click each tab to view and test each form or report, and save the navigation form.

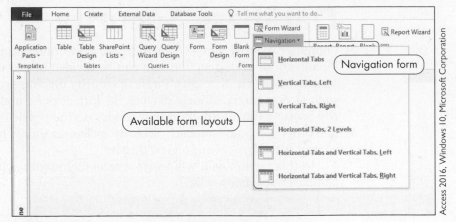

FIGURE 9.20 Creating a Navigation Form

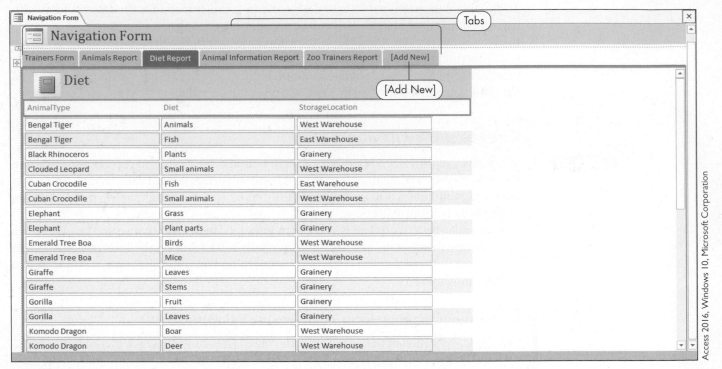

FIGURE 9.21 Navigation Form in Layout View

By default, Access will use the name of each form or report to identify the tab. In other words, if you drag a report named Animals to [Add New], the new tab is named Animals. To modify the tab name, double-click the name and replace the text.

Start a Navigation Form Automatically

As mentioned earlier, one advantage of navigation forms is the ability to give the users guidance and help make sure they are using the forms and reports they should be. However, if they have to figure out which form to open to get to the navigation form, there still may be confusion. To integrate a navigation form as seamlessly as possible, you can set an option so the navigation form opens automatically when the database is opened. Note this can be done with any form, not just a navigation form.

To start a form automatically when the database is opened, complete the following steps:

1. Click the File tab.
2. Click Options.
3. Click Current Database in the left pane.
4. Click the Display Form arrow, and select the name of the navigation form, as shown in Figure 9.22.
5. Click OK to close the Access Options window.

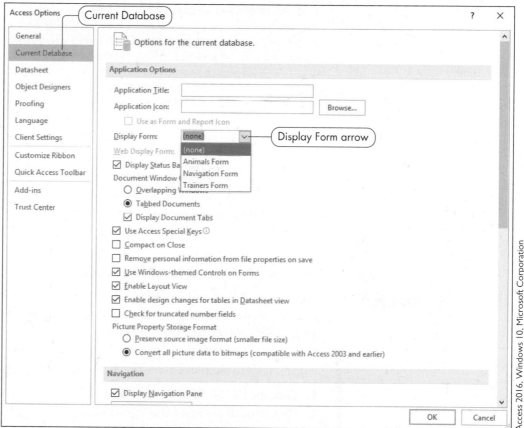

FIGURE 9.22 Starting a Form Automatically

Encrypting and Password Protecting a Database

Access incorporates encryption methods to help keep your databases secure. ***Encryption*** makes the data unreadable to anyone except those who possess the key (password). Because the point of encryption is to protect your data, choose a good password when setting up encryption. Encrypting a database is especially useful if you intend to distribute your database via email or store your database on removable media such as a USB flash drive.

Adding a password to an Access database prevents unauthorized access to the file. Passwords typically include a combination of letters and numbers. A good password should be impossible for unauthorized users to guess. An example of a weak password is the word *password*. A stronger password is *eXploring!2016*. Notice the password includes a capital letter, a number, and a special character, which make the password harder to guess. Including capital letters, numbers, and special characters help to make the password more secure. You can also improve security by using longer passwords and avoiding words found in a dictionary.

TIP: PASSWORD SECURITY

Writing down the password on a sticky note and leaving it on your monitor is not a good choice for protecting a truly secure password. If you write down your passwords, store them in a secure location such as a locked file cabinet or a safe.

You can download or purchase an application to manage your passwords or use a secure online password manager. Of course, those tools require a password, so make sure you do not forget the password that protects your passwords.

TIP: LOST YOUR PASSWORD?

A number of software applications exist that attempt to find a password for a database. However, the more secure the password, the longer it takes to recover. It may take days or weeks for a password to be recovered, but that is better than losing data permanently. Also, keep in mind that the same tool you can use to recover a legitimately lost password can be used by anyone, so a strong password helps prevent unauthorized access.

Add a Password to a Database

 STEP 2 ⟫ Adding a password and encryption to a database requires the database to be opened in exclusive mode. Opening the database in exclusive mode guarantees that you are the only one currently using the database.

To open a database in exclusive mode, complete the following steps:

1. Click the File tab, and click Open.
2. Click Browse to display the Open dialog box.
3. Locate and click the database, click the Open arrow at the bottom of the dialog box, and then select Open Exclusive from the list (see Figure 9.23).

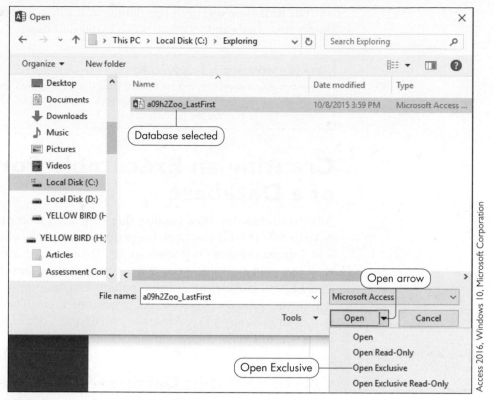

FIGURE 9.23 Open Exclusive Option

> **To assign a password to a database after it is opened in exclusive mode, complete the following steps:**
>
> 1. Click the File tab.
> 2. Click Encrypt with Password, as shown in Figure 9.24.
> 3. Type and verify the password for this database, and click OK.

FIGURE 9.24 Encrypting a Database

The next time you open this database, it will prompt for a password to access. Keep the password safe and secure to protect your database.

> **TIP: REMOVING A PASSWORD**
> To remove a password, you must open the database using the Open Exclusive option. Click the File tab, and click Decrypt Database. In the Unset Database Password dialog box, type the password, and click OK to remove the password.

Creating an Executable Form of a Database

After a database has been created, there are times where the database administrator will have to help correct mistakes. Users may accidentally change, delete, or rename objects and find the database no longer works. To protect your users from accidentally making these types of mistakes, you can create an ***Access Database Executable (ACCDE)*** file. This file will prohibit users from making design and name changes to forms or reports within the database, and prohibit users from creating new forms and reports. In addition, if there is any VBA code, users can execute, but cannot modify, the code. Note that users can still make changes to tables and queries in this case.

Create an Access Database Executable

STEP 3 ➤➤ Creating an Access Database Executable is a straightforward process. It saves your existing database with the new file extension, making a copy of the last saved version of your database.

To create an ACCDE file, complete the following steps:

1. Click the File tab.
2. Click Save As.
3. Double-click Make ACCDE (see Figure 9.25). The Save As dialog box opens.
4. Type a file name (or accept the default). Click Save.

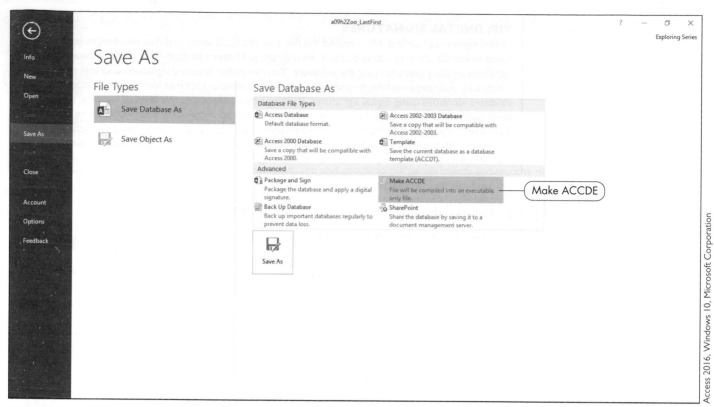

FIGURE 9.25 Creating an Access Database Executable

You cannot create an Access Database Executable file unless you have clicked Enable Content. As these files can cause potentially dangerous code to be executed, you first should ensure that the file is trustworthy. When the database has been converted to an Access Database Executable, it cannot be converted back to its source format (.accdb). Therefore, keep your original database in a safe place. Without your original database, you would not be able to make changes to forms or reports.

TIP: ACCDE COMPATIBILITY ISSUES

When an ACCDE file is created, it will either be created as a 32-bit executable or a 64-bit executable. If you are familiar with computer hardware, you will recognize this as the word size. Access will generate an ACCDE for the word size corresponding to your Office installation, If a co-worker cannot open your ACCDE file, mismatched word sizes is the likely cause. You can check the word size of your installation by clicking File, selecting Account, and selecting About Access. The first line will state either 32-bit or 64-bit. If this is a problem within your organization, you may want to work with your technical support personnel to make sure the Office installation is standard across your organization.

Implement First Normal Form

STEP 1 ❱❱ A table is defined as being in ***first normal form (1NF)*** if it contains no repeating groups or repeating columns. In the book example, the Title column might be replaced with Title1, Title2, and Title3. This might appear to correct the repeating groups problem because each cell contains one piece of information; however, this type of design still violates 1NF and must be corrected. In this example, it is still difficult to find data efficiently.

Violations of the 1NF rule come in many forms. For example, you cannot have multiple values in the same field. Each of the following would be violations of 1NF:

- An Authors field listing multiple authors separated by commas like *Poatsy, Cameron, Williams*

- An Address2 field listing the city, state, and ZIP together such as *Paterson, NJ 07501*

- An Instructor field that contains the following values for the same class on two lines:

  Poatsy

  Cameron

Likewise, you cannot have multiple columns in the same record that store the same sort of data. A table with an Author1 field set to *Poatsy*, Author2 field set to *Cameron*, and Author3 field set to *Williams* is a violation of 1NF.

Each of those examples has a common thread: They make it difficult to find specific pieces of information, and that is the essence of the repeating groups problem. Tables containing repeating groups make it more difficult to add new entries, update existing entries, and properly extract information when running queries. For example, to see the information for *Digital Fortress*, you could create a filter or query searching for those results. However, Access considers them to be part of the same record, and you would also see the book *The Lost Symbol*. As a matter of fact, when you attempt to filter your data (as shown in Figure 9.31), two book names are listed as one piece of data. Similar problems would exist with queries searching for a specific book. In other words, there is no easy way to only show the information for *Digital Fortress*. This occurs because all the books by one author are contained in the same record.

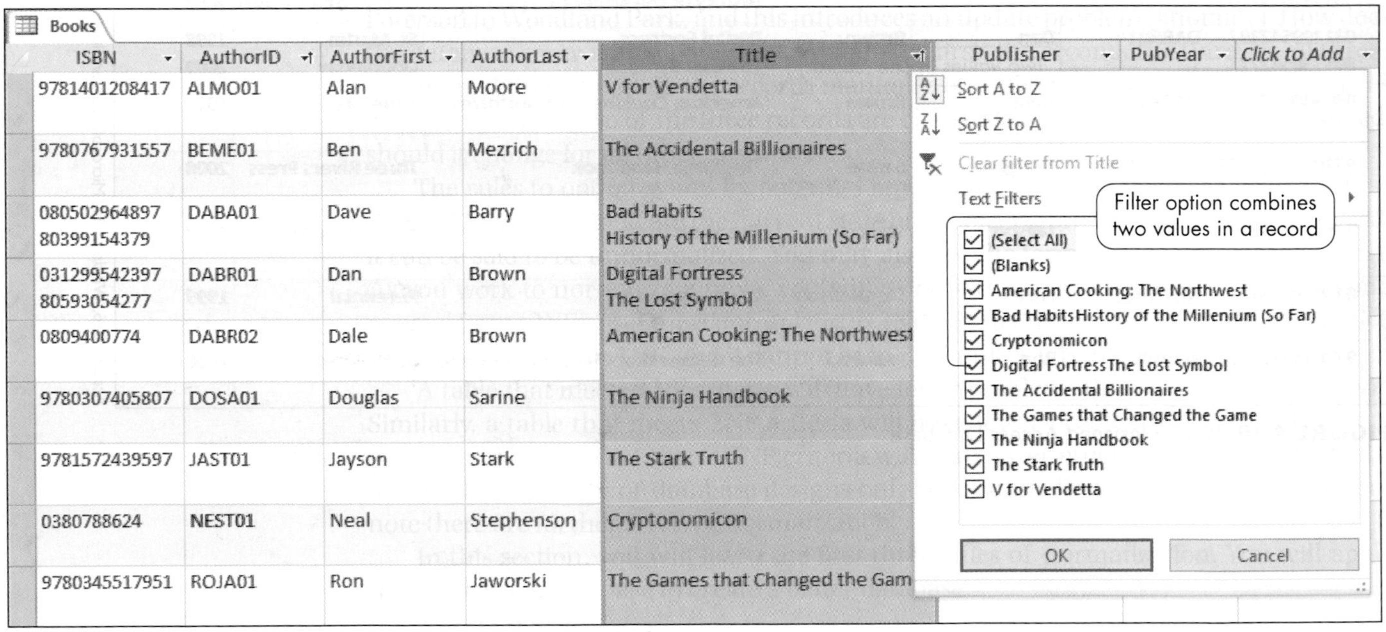

FIGURE 9.31 Filter Issues with Repeating Groups

To fix a table that has repeating groups, change the table so each unique piece of information is stored on a separate record in the same field. Any columns should have the missing information added, even if this leads to repetition. You can do this in Excel before importing to Access, or alternately add rows in Access and separate the repeating data into individual rows.

Figure 9.32 shows the Books table in Access after it has been put into first normal form; the single Brown row has been split into two rows, and the books by the same author have been separated. Now each book has its own record.

FIGURE 9.32 Books Table in First Normal Form (1NF)

At this point, although the table is in 1NF, it still has redundancy issues. In fact, redundancy has been introduced into the table. However, because normalization is a process, further normalization will remove the introduced redundancies.

There are many other ways data can violate 1NF. Note that even database professionals may struggle with normalization, so your goal should be to become familiar with the process.

Understanding Second Normal Form

Most bookstore databases contain information about location and quantity in stock. Therefore, the earlier example has been expanded to include three extra fields, as shown in Figure 9.33. For the purposes of this example, assume the bookstore has two locations, one in the town of Paterson and another one in the town of Wanaque. Because this more realistic version of the table has the location added, a problem now exists. Notice in Figure 9.33 that the ISBN cannot be the primary key for this table because the same book (with the same ISBN) can appear in both locations. In this case, a good option is to use a combination of two fields as the primary key. The composite key for this table would be ISBN plus the location, which uniquely identifies each row.

FIGURE 9.33 Expanded Books Table

Implement Second Normal Form

STEP 2 » A table is in *second normal form (2NF)* if it meets 1NF criteria and all non-key fields are functionally dependent on the entire primary key. A *non-key field* is defined as any field that is not part of the primary key. *Functional dependency* occurs when the value of one field is determined by the value of another. For example, in a government database, given a Social Security number, you can determine a person's first and last name, but the opposite is not true. Given a first and last name, you cannot determine the Social Security number because many people can share the same name. In this case, the first and last names are functionally dependent upon the Social Security number.

A table with a single-field primary key is usually in 2NF. Because many tables have a single-field primary key, 2NF often requires no changes to a table. However, some tables have a *composite key*, a primary key that is made of two or more fields. Tables with a composite key may require some changes.

Because the table referenced above has a composite key, to bring the table into 2NF, you must ensure all fields are functionally dependent on the entire primary key. Some fields are functionally dependent on both the ISBN and location. For example, to determine the number of books on hand for any specific title, both the ISBN and the location are required. Similarly, to determine the aisle in which a book is stored, both the ISBN and the location are required. However, some fields, such as Title, are only dependent on the ISBN component. Regardless of whether a book is in Paterson or Wanaque, a book with an ISBN of 0312995423 is always *Digital Fortress*. The same goes for the rest of the fields.

TIP: OTHER ISSUES FIXED BY SECOND NORMAL FORM

For simplicity's sake, this example focused on composite key issues. Other situations exist in which 2NF may require changes. In Figure 9.32, just adding an AutoNumber field labeled as the primary key would not solve the issue that the ISBN would still determine some of the information, and the combination of ISBN and location would determine other information. Examples will focus on the composite key issues that 2NF fixes.

Second normal form tells you that when fields are functionally dependent upon part of a primary key, remove those fields from the table. Most of the time, this results in new tables, though it is possible to move fields into another existing table. Notice earlier in Figure 9.32 that all the information related to the book *Digital Fortress* is repeated—the AuthorFirst, AuthorLast, Title, Publisher, and PubYear. It would be very easy for inconsistent data to occur in this case. To resolve the problem, two tables are created: Books and Stock. The Books table contains the fields ISBN, AuthorID, AuthorFirst, AuthorLast, Title, Publisher, and PubYear. The primary key of this table is ISBN. See Figure 9.34. The Stock table contains the fields ISBN, Location, OnHand, and Aisle, as shown in Figure 9.35. The primary key for this table is a composite key, the combination of ISBN and Location. In the Stock table, as explained above, all fields are dependent on both components of the primary key. In addition, notice that the data, once divided into two tables, has less repetition of book information.

ISBN	AuthorID	AuthorFirst	AuthorLast	Title	Publisher	PubYear
9781401208417	ALMO01	Alan	Moore	V for Vendetta	DC Comics	2005
9780767931557	BEME01	Ben	Mezrich	The Accidental Billionaires	Anchor Books	2009
0805029648	DABA01	Dave	Barry	Bad Habits	Henry Holt & Co.	1987
9780399154379	DABA01	Dave	Barry	History of the Millenium (So Far)	G. P. Putman's Sons	2007
080...		Dale	Brown	American Cooking: The Northwest	Time Life	1970
031...		Dan	Brown	Digital Fortress	St. Martin	1998
9780593054277	DABR01	Dan	Brown	The Lost Symbol	Doubleday	2009
9780307405807	DOSA01	Douglas	Sarine	The Ninja Handbook	Three Rivers Press	2008
9781572439597	JAST01	Jayson	Stark	The Stark Truth	Triumph Books	2007
0380788624	NEST01	Neal	Stephenson	Cryptonomicon	Perennial	1999
9780345517951	ROJA01	Ron	Jaworski	The Games that Changed the Game	ESPN Books	2010

(Callout: Each book appears in one record only)

FIGURE 9.34 Books Table in Second Normal Form (2NF)

Stock

ISBN	Location	OnHand	Aisle
0312995423	Paterson	2	5
0312995423	Wanaque	3	1
0380788624	Paterson	1	1
		1	4
		1	8
9780307405807	Paterson	1	3
9780345517951	Paterson	2	1
9780399154379	Wanaque	1	2
9780593054277	Paterson	11	3
9780593054277	Wanaque	5	4
9780767931557	Paterson	11	5
9780767931557	Wanaque	6	5
9781401208417	Paterson	2	5
9781572439597	Wanaque	1	6

Book information no longer repeated for each location

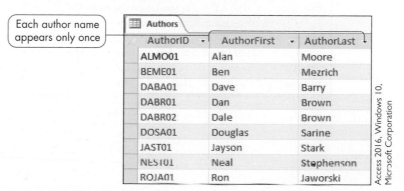

FIGURE 9.35 Stock Table Created from Books Information

Understanding Third Normal Form

A ***transitive dependency*** occurs when the value of one non-key field is functionally dependent on the value of another non-key field. AuthorFirst and AuthorLast in the example are dependent on AuthorID and, therefore, are an example of a transitive dependency. Whenever you know the AuthorID, the AuthorFirst and AuthorLast are automatically known. This can lead to repetition within a database, and therefore must be fixed.

Implement Third Normal Form

STEP 3 A table is in ***third normal form (3NF)*** if it meets 2NF criteria and no transitive dependencies exist. Therefore, to conform to 3NF, AuthorFirst and AuthorLast must be moved to another table, as shown in Figure 9.36. The new Authors table contains three fields: AuthorID, AuthorFirst, and AuthorLast. The Books table can now reference the author using the AuthorID field, as shown in Figure 9.37. The Books table is in 3NF because the transitive dependency was removed. In effect, moving to 3NF requires some work, as a new table is created and data is moved. For a large database, this may require creation of a Make Table query (see the Action Queries section of this textbook for more information). In the worst case, this could require large amounts of tedious data entry. However, the trade-off is less repeated data, which leads to fewer anomalies. For example, if you had a typographical error for an author's name (say, Steven King instead of Stephen King), you would only change the spelling in one place to correct it.

Each author name appears only once

Authors

AuthorID	AuthorFirst	AuthorLast
ALMO01	Alan	Moore
BEME01	Ben	Mezrich
DABA01	Dave	Barry
DABR01	Dan	Brown
DABR02	Dale	Brown
DOSA01	Douglas	Sarine
JAST01	Jayson	Stark
NEST01	Neal	Stephenson
ROJA01	Ron	Jaworski

FIGURE 9.36 Author Table Created from Books Information

ISBN	AuthorID		Publisher	PubYear
9781401208417	ALMO01	V for Vendetta	DC Comics	2005
9780767931557	BEME01	The Accidental Billionaires	Anchor Books	2009
0805029648	DABA01	Bad Habits	Henry Holt & Co.	1987
9780399154379	DABA01	History of the Millenium (So Far)	G. P. Putman's Sons	2007
0312995423	DABR01	Digital Fortress	St. Martin	1998
9780593054277	DABR01	The Lost Symbol	Doubleday	2009
9780307405807	DOSA01	The Ninja Handbook	Three Rivers Press	2008
9781572439597	JAST01	The Stark Truth	Triumph Books	2007
0809400774	NEST01	American Cooking: The Northwest	Time Life	1970
0380788624	NEST01	Cryptonomicon	Perennial	1999
9780345517951	ROJA01	The Games that Changed the Game	ESPN Books	2010

> Author name is no longer repeated for each book

FIGURE 9.37 Books Table in Third Normal Form (3NF)

Another way to handle a conversion to 3NF is to delete fields that may not be necessary. In this specific case, the AuthorID field is important. In other cases, ask yourself if there is an extra field that can be eliminated. Table 9.2 presents a summary of the three normal forms covered in this chapter.

TABLE 9.2   Normalization Summary

Form	What It Does	Notes
First Normal Form	Removes repeating groups	Introduces redundancy, which is fixed by later normal forms.
Second Normal Form	Removes dependencies on part of a composite primary key	Commonly an issue when a table has a composite key. If the primary key is a single field, a table is often in 2NF. Changes usually result in added tables.
Third Normal Form	Removes dependencies on any field that is not a primary key	Changes usually result in new tables.

TIP: CITY, STATE, ZIP, 3NF?

For most locations in the United States, if you have the ZIP code, you can look up the city and state. This might lead you to believe that this is a transitive dependency. However, on some rare occasions, this is not true. For example, the ZIP code 42223 covers parts of Christian County, Kentucky, and Montgomery County, Tennessee. In this case, the same ZIP code not only crosses county borders, it also crosses state lines! Note that in this case, this oddity has to do with an army base that crosses state borders. Due to issues such as these, it is safe to consider a database with the city, state, and ZIP in the same table to be in 3NF.

On the other hand, if you have two customers who live in North Brunswick, New Jersey, one person doing data entry might type it into the database as North Brunswick and the other may abbreviate it as N Brunswick. If you created a filter or query to locate all towns listed as North Brunswick, only one of those two customers would appear. The argument for putting ZIP in a separate table is to avoid issues such as that.

Finalizing the Design

Once you have created new tables, you will create relationships between the tables. This should be done after completion of the normalization process. The tables should be connected, and the Enforce Referential Integrity option should be checked. Remember, the purpose of normalization is to remove repetition, but you still have to be able to retrieve data. Relationships make that possible in a multiple-table database.

Create Relationships

STEP 4 ≫ Figure 9.38 shows the relationships in the Books database after normalization. The relationships are not set up automatically, so you should set this up as you did in an earlier chapter. Once the relationships have been set up, the flow of information becomes more obvious. Notice the Authors table now has a plus symbol to the left of each record, and clicking it displays the books associated with that author, as shown in Figure 9.39.

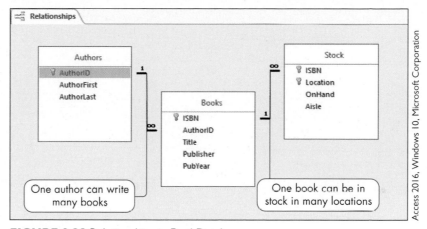

FIGURE 9.38 Relationships in Final Database

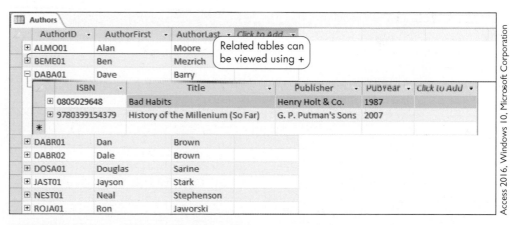

FIGURE 9.39 Related Tables in Datasheet View

Creating relationships can also be a way to test your normalization. Normalization should not result in data loss, so if you cannot create a relationship between the tables, there is likely an issue with the way you have normalized. It may be frustrating to see an error saying a relationship cannot be created, but this is Access's way of letting you know there is a problem. To fix the problem, you will need to determine which records in one table do not match the records in another table. For example, you might have a book assigned to an author that does not exist, and you can fix that by assigning the book to a valid author.

Quick Concepts

8. What is the purpose of normalizing a database? *p. 608*

9. What problems does first normal form fix? *p. 610*

10. What problems does second normal form fix? *p. 612*

11. What problems does third normal form fix? *p. 613*

Hands-On Exercises

Skills covered: Implement First Normal Form • Implement Second Normal Form • Implement Third Normal Form • Create Relationships

3 Database Normalization

Your job at the Metropolitan Zoo has been fun and challenging. You have been making daily updates to the Zoo's database with the help of your boss, Selene Platt. Based on your understanding of the rules of normalization, you decide to recommend some design changes to the database.

STEP 1 » IMPLEMENT FIRST NORMAL FORM

Selene has asked you to review the table structure to see if any changes should be made. You decide to apply the rules of normalization to the Animals table. Refer to Figure 9.40 as you complete Step 1.

AnimalName	AnimalType	Origin	Endangered	ExhibitID	TrainerID	TrainerName
Anny	Mockingbird	North America	☐	1	1	Asha
Archie	Zebra	South Africa	☐	2	3	Elizabeth
Bronstein	Komodo Dragon	Indonesia	☑	1	3	Elizabeth
Cara	Manate~~Step c: Diet field deleted~~ica	☐	1	1	Asha
Cassandra	Emerald Tree Boa	South America	☐	3	1	Asha
Cassandra	Ostrich	Africa	☐	2	2	Keisha
Dietre	Clouded Leopard	Southeast Asia	☐	1	2	Keisha
Farunn	White Rhinoceros	Africa	☑	2	2	Keisha
Khamen	Cuban Crocodile	Cuba	☑	3	3	Elizabeth
Palom	Black Rhinoceros	Africa	☑	2	2	Keisha
Perenolde	Komodo Dragon	Indonesia	☑	1	1	Asha
Pocho	Cuban Crocodile	Cuba	☑	3	4	Ruben
Rakshiri	Bengal Tiger	India	☑	1	4	Ruben
Sindall	Bengal Tiger	India	☑	1	4	Ruben
Sophie	Giraffe	West Africa	☑	2	2	Keisha
Stampy	Elephant	Africa	☐	2	3	Elizabeth
Uhkloc	Gorilla	Central Africa	☐	2	4	Ruben
Zhevra	Zebra	South Africa	☐	2	4	Ruben

Access 2016, Windows 10, Microsoft Corporation

FIGURE 9.40 Animals Table in First Normal Form (1NF)

a. Open *a09h3Normalization*. Save the database as **a09h3Normalization_LastFirst**.

b. Open the Animals table in Datasheet view. Look for repeating groups in the Animals table.

The Diet field has multiple values separated by commas. This qualifies as a repeating group. This information will be added to a new table and removed from this table.

For simplicity's sake, the information for animal diets has been preloaded to a table called Diet, so removing the Diet field from the Animals table is required to conform to 1NF.

c. Switch to Design view. Click the **row selector** for the Diet field, and click **Delete** on the Home tab in the Records group. Click **Yes** when asked for confirmation, and switch to Datasheet view. Click **Yes** when prompted to save.

Your Animals table should now match Figure 9.40, and the table now meets 1NF criteria. You deleted the Diet field because it contained repeating values. Repeating values violate 1NF.

d. Open the Diet table in Datasheet view.

For the purposes of this exercise, the data is already in the Diet table. This table has been provided to expedite the normalization process.

After you remove the Diet field, you will examine the Animals table and convert to second normal form. Refer to Figure 9.41 as you complete Step 2.

AnimalName ▾	AnimalType ▾	ExhibitID ▾	TrainerID ▾	TrainerName ▾
Anny	Mockingbird	1	1	Asha
Archie	Zebra	2	3	Elizabeth
Bronstein				Elizabeth
Cara	Manatee	1	1	Asha
Cassandra	Emerald Tree Boa	3	1	Asha
Cassandra	Ostrich	2	2	Keisha
Dietre	Clouded Leopard	1	2	Keisha
Farunn	White Rhinoceros	2	2	Keisha
Khamen	Cuban Crocodile	3	3	Elizabeth
Palom	Black Rhinoceros	2	2	Keisha
Perenolde	Komodo Dragon	1	1	Asha
Pocho	Cuban Crocodile	3	4	Ruben
Rakshiri	Bengal Tiger	1	4	Ruben
Sindall	Bengal Tiger	1	4	Ruben
Sophie	Giraffe	2	2	Keisha
Stampy	Elephant	2	3	Elizabeth
Uhkloc	Gorilla	2	4	Ruben
Zhevra	Zebra	2	4	Ruben

(Callout: Step e: Origin and Endangered fields deleted)

Access 2016, Windows 10, Microsoft Corporation

FIGURE 9.41 Animals Table in Second Normal Form (2NF)

a. Close the Diet table. Examine the Animals table and notice there are two animals named Cassandra.

This table has a composite key (the combination of AnimalName and AnimalType), so you must check to make sure it is in 2NF.

b. Switch to Design view for the Animals table.

Origin, Diet, and Endangered are all determined by AnimalType and are attributes of a type of animal, not a specific animal. ExhibitID, TrainerID, and TrainerName are attributes of a specific animal. Fields will need to be removed to satisfy 2NF.

c. Open the Animal Information table in Datasheet view. Note this table includes the Origin and Endangered fields as well as other fields regarding animals.

In a real-world scenario, you would need to create a separate table for this information, but the Animal Information table is provided so you do not have to perform data entry.

d. Close the Animal Information table.

e. Examine the Animals table. This table is not in 2NF because some fields are dependent on part of the primary key. Click the **row selectors** for the Origin and Endangered fields, and click **Delete** in the Records group of the Home tab, clicking **Yes** in response to the warning.

You deleted these two fields because they are not functionally dependent on the entire primary key.

f. Save the Animals table. Switch to Datasheet view.

Your table should match Figure 9.41.

All the remaining fields are functionally dependent on the entire primary key. Therefore, the table now meets 2NF criteria.

The final step to improve the zoo's Animals table is to convert to third normal form: The value of a non-key field cannot be functionally dependent on the value of another non-key field. Refer to Figure 9.42 as you complete Step 3.

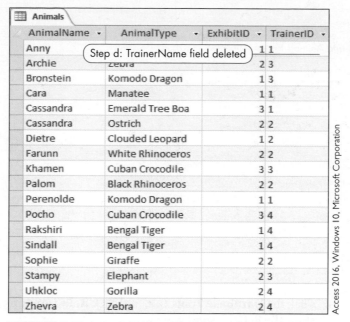

AnimalName	AnimalType	ExhibitID	TrainerID
Anny		1	1
Archie	Zebra	2	3
Bronstein	Komodo Dragon	1	3
Cara	Manatee	1	1
Cassandra	Emerald Tree Boa	3	1
Cassandra	Ostrich	2	2
Dietre	Clouded Leopard	1	2
Farunn	White Rhinoceros	2	2
Khamen	Cuban Crocodile	3	3
Palom	Black Rhinoceros	2	2
Perenolde	Komodo Dragon	1	1
Pocho	Cuban Crocodile	3	4
Rakshiri	Bengal Tiger	1	4
Sindall	Bengal Tiger	1	4
Sophie	Giraffe	2	2
Stampy	Elephant	2	3
Uhkloc	Gorilla	2	4
Zhevra	Zebra	2	4

Step d: TrainerName field deleted

Access 2016, Windows 10, Microsoft Corporation

FIGURE 9.42 Animals Table in Third Normal Form (3NF)

a. Look for any non-key field values in the Animals table that are functionally dependent on another non-key field value.

TrainerName (non-key) is functionally dependent on TrainerID (non-key). If you know the TrainerID, you can determine the TrainerName. For example, if you enter value 1 for the TrainerID, then the trainer's name will always be Asha. A table named Trainers already exists.

b. Switch to Design view in the Animals table.

c. Delete the TrainerName field, clicking **Yes** in response to the warning.

You delete the TrainerName field because it is functionally dependent on the TrainerID field and therefore is not allowed in the Animals table. Normally, this would then require you to set up a new table, but as you already have a Trainers table, you can simply delete the TrainerName field. Note that this may not always be the case.

d. Switch to Datasheet view, saving the table. Compare your results with Figure 9.42.

The table now meets 3NF criteria.

e. Close the Animals table.

You will now create relationships for the tables in the database. Due to the changes you made to the design, you will add relationships to ensure the database functions correctly. Refer to Figure 9.43 as you complete Step 4.

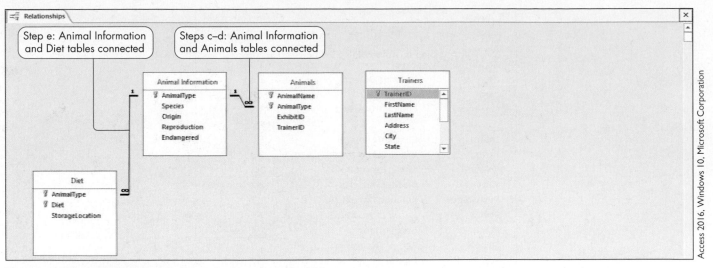

FIGURE 9.43 Zoo Relationships

a. Click the **Database Tools tab**, and click **Relationships** in the Relationships group to show the Relationships window.

> **TROUBLESHOOTING:** If all the tables are not closed, you will get a warning about tables being locked. If you receive this warning, exit the Relationships window, close all open tables, and repeat Step a.

b. Click **Show Table**. Click each **table**, and click **Add**. Once you have added all four tables, click **Close** to close the Show Table dialog box.

c. Drag the **AnimalType field** from the Animal Information table to the AnimalType field in the Animals table.

The Animals and Animal Information tables are related by the common AnimalType field.

d. Select the **Enforce Referential Integrity** and **Cascade Update Related Fields options**. Click **Create** to create this relationship.

e. Repeat Steps c and d to connect the AnimalType field in the Animal Information table to the AnimalType field in the Diet table. Compare your results with Figure 9.43.

You may also notice the Animals and Trainers tables are not yet linked. You are leaving these tables unlinked intentionally as you want to discuss the contents with your supervisor.

> **TROUBLESHOOTING:** There are three tables with an AnimalType field. If you cannot create the relationship, make sure you are connecting the AnimalType in the Animals and Trainers tables.

f. Save the relationships and close the Relationships window.

g. Close the database and exit Access. Based on your instructor's directions, submit the following:

a09h1ZooAnalyzer_LastFirst

a09h1ZooDocumenter_LastFirst

a09h1ZooSplit_LastFirst_be

a09h2ZooExecutable_LastFirst

a09h3Normalization_LastFirst

Chapter Objectives Review

After reading this chapter, you have accomplished the following objectives:

1. Use the Database Documenter tool.

- Run the Database Documenter: Database Documenter creates a report containing detailed information for each selected object. Database Documenter can be run on specific objects (for example, only tables, or only forms and reports). Users can select varying levels of detail.

2. Use the Performance Analyzer tool.

- Run the Performance Analyzer: Performance Analyzer evaluates a database and makes optimization recommendations.
- Add an index: Performance Analyzer may recommend adding an index, which will speed up searches such as queries or filters.

3. Use the Table Analyzer tool.

- Run the Table Analyzer: The Table Analyzer helps minimize duplication of information.
- The Table Analyzer includes a wizard that enables you to split tables, rename newly created tables, rearrange fields in the new tables, and create relationships.

4. Use the Database Splitter tool.

- Run the Database Splitter: The Database Splitter tool is useful when the number of database users grows beyond a few. The tool splits a database into two files—a front-end database containing queries, forms, and reports, and a back-end database containing tables. Splitting a database may improve the speed of data processing. The back-end database is generally on a server.
- Work with a front-end database: The front-end database is typically on each user's machine. The front-end database enables users to create their own queries, forms, and reports. The front end links to back-end tables, which can be shared between users.

5. Control Navigation.

- Create a navigation form: Navigation forms help users open important forms and reports quickly. Choose one of six prebuilt layouts. Drag and drop forms and reports directly on tabs. A navigation form can be easily converted to a Web form.

- Start a navigation form automatically: Navigation forms can start automatically when a database opens to help provide guidance to users.

6. Encrypt and password protect a database.

- Add a password to a database: Encryption alters digital information using an algorithm, making it unreadable without the key (secret code). Encrypted databases are very difficult to break into. Encryption is suggested especially if a database is sent via email or put on removable storage such as a USB drive.

7. Create an executable form of a database.

- Create an Access Database Executable: An Access Database Executable, or ACCDE, file is an executable form of the database—objects such as forms, reports, and VBA code cannot be changed. Saving as an ACCDE file adds an extra layer of protection.

8. Understand first normal form.

- Implement first normal form: The first step to normalizing a table removes repeating groups.

9. Understand second normal form.

- Implement second normal form: Requires 1NF. The criteria are that all non-key fields must be functionally dependent on the entire primary key. If no composite key exists, the table is often in 2NF.

10. Understand third normal form.

- Implement third normal form: Requires 2NF. Converting a database to third normal form removes transitive dependencies, or dependencies on non-key fields.

11. Finalize the design.

- Create relationships: After normalization, relationships exist between your tables. If a table cannot be connected to others, there is likely a problem with your normalization.

Key Terms Matching

Match the key terms with their definitions. Write the key term letter by the appropriate numbered definition.

a. Access Database Executable (ACCDE)
b. Anomaly
c. Back-end database
d. Composite key
e. Database Documenter
f. Database Splitter
g. Encryption
h. First normal form (1NF)
i. Front-end database

j. Functional dependency
k. Navigation form
l. Non-key field
m. Normalization
n. Performance Analyzer
o. Second normal form (2NF)
p. Table Analyzer
q. Third normal form (3NF)
r. Transitive dependency

1. _____ A type of database file that prohibits users from making design and name changes to forms or reports within the database, and prohibits users from creating new forms and reports. **p. 602**

2. _____ A tabbed menu that ties the objects in the database together so that the database is easy to use. **p. 597**

3. _____ A primary key that is made up of two or more fields. **p. 612**

4. _____ A tool that creates a report containing detailed information for each selected object. **p. 581**

5. _____ An error or inconsistency that occurs when you add, edit, and delete data. **p. 608**

6. _____ A tool that evaluates the tables in a database and normalizes them for you. **p. 586**

7. _____ Any field that is not part of the primary key. **p. 612**

8. _____ A database that contains the queries, forms, and reports of the database. **p. 589**

9. _____ A database that contains the tables of the database. **p. 589**

10. _____ A tool that enables you to convert a database into two files, a back-end database and a front-end database. **p. 589**

11. _____ A tool that evaluates a database and then makes recommendations for optimizing the database. **p. 583**

12. _____ A condition that occurs when the value of one non-key field is functionally dependent on the value of another non-key field. **p. 613**

13. _____ A criterion satisfied when a table contains no repeating groups or repeating columns. **p. 610**

14. _____ A criterion satisfied when a table meets 2NF criteria and no transitive dependencies exist. **p. 613**

15. _____ A criterion satisfied when a table that meets 1NF criteria and all non-key fields are functionally dependent on the entire primary key. **p. 612**

16. _____ The process of efficiently organizing data so that the same data is not stored in more than one table, and that related data is stored together. **p. 608**

17. _____ The process of altering digital information using an algorithm to make it unreadable to anyone except those who possess the key (or secret code). **p. 600**

18. _____ A condition that occurs when the value of one field is determined by the value of another. **p. 612**

Multiple Choice

1. The Database Documenter:

   (a) Lists the properties of selected objects in the database.
   (b) Suggests ways the database can be optimized.
   (c) Searches for rows of repeating data and suggests design changes to improve performance.
   (d) Is a wizard that provides step-by-step instructions on the creation of tables and forms.

2. Which tool makes recommendations for optimizing a database?

   (a) Database Documenter
   (b) Database Splitter
   (c) Performance Analyzer
   (d) Table Analyzer

3. What might be an outcome of running the Table Analyzer tool?

   (a) A report listing information about the tables (such as data types and field names)
   (b) Two files—a front-end and a back-end database
   (c) An optimized set of tables
   (d) A password-protected database

4. Which of the following is typically stored in a back-end database after it has been split?

   (a) Forms
   (b) Queries
   (c) Tables
   (d) All of the above are typically stored in a back-end database.

5. Which of the following is *true* about encrypted databases?

   (a) Database encryption alters the contents of the database so that it cannot be opened without a password.
   (b) Encrypted databases can be broken into with ease.
   (c) Passwords cannot be removed from a database.
   (d) Databases can be encrypted but not have a password assigned.

6. Which password is strongest?

   (a) 12345
   (b) Ginger125
   (c) mypassword
   (d) eXploring!2016

7. What is the benefit of creating an Access Database Executable?

   (a) The database will be protected against hackers.
   (b) Users cannot change forms and reports.
   (c) Table contents cannot be modified.
   (d) The navigation in the database will be greatly improved.

8. Which of the following statements about normalization is *false*?

   (a) A database in 3NF must also be in 2NF.
   (b) There are only three normal forms.
   (c) Normalization reduces repetition of data.
   (d) The Table Analyzer can help normalize tables.

9. Which normal form will remove dependencies on a non-key field?

   (a) 1NF
   (b) 2NF
   (c) 3NF
   (d) None of these

10. Normalization can be defined as:

    (a) Eliminating repetition of data.
    (b) Adding a layer of security to a database.
    (c) Combining tables together to form a single table.
    (d) A database with multiple tables.

Practice Exercises

1 Info Labs

Info Labs, a clinical studies company in Mississippi, employs 14 employees; most employees fall in the categories of manager, account rep, or trainee. The employee database holds information about each employee, including salary, gender, title, and location. You have been asked to review the database to see if the employee table was designed properly. Refer to Figure 9.44 as you complete this exercise.

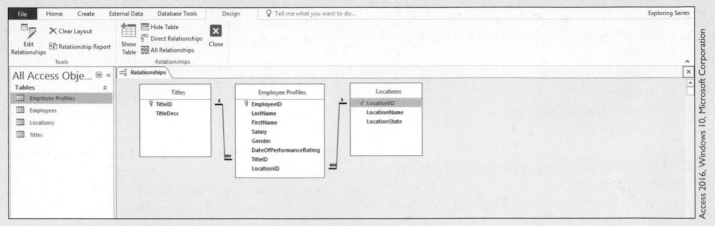

FIGURE 9.44 Clinic Database Relationships

a. Open *a09p1Clinic*. Save the database as **a09p1Clinic_LastFirst**.

b. Open the Employees table in Datasheet view and examine the data. Determine if the data meets the three normalization rules: 1NF, 2NF, and 3NF.

c. Close the Employees table. You decide to use the Table Analyzer for help with normalizing the Employees table.

d. Click **Analyze Table** in the Analyze group on the Database Tools tab. When the first wizard screen appears, click **Next** twice.

e. Accept the default **Employees table** when the *Which table contains fields with values that are repeated in many records?* screen appears. Click **Next** twice.

f. Verify the Employees table has been split into three tables on the next screen. Click **Table1**, click **Rename Table**, and then type **Employee Profiles** as the new name of this table. Click **OK**.

g. Click **Table2**, click **Rename Table**, and then type **Locations** as the new name of this table. Click **OK**.

h. Click **Table3**, click **Rename Table**, and then type **Titles** as the new name of this table. Click **OK**.

i. Click **Next**.

j. Click **LocationID** in the Locations table, and click **Set Unique Identifier** to set LocationID as the primary key.

k. Click **EmployeeID** in the EmployeeProfiles table, and click **Set Unique Identifier** to set EmployeeID as the primary key.

l. Click **Next**. Accept the default *No, don't create the query option*, and click **Finish**. Click **OK** when the information message appears.

m. Review the new tables and confirm that the Analyzer moved fields from the Employees table into the two new lookup tables. Close all the tables.

n. Click **Relationships** on the Database Tools tab in the Relationships group. Click **All Relationships** to reveal the relationships created by the Table Analyzer. Your relationships should match Figure 9.44. Close the Relationships window, and click **No**.

o. Click the **File tab**, and click **Encrypt with Password**. Access displays the message *You must have the database open for exclusive use*. Click **OK**. Close the database.

p. Use the Open command on the File tab to locate the *a09p1Clinic_LastFirst* database. Click the database, click the Open arrow at the bottom of the dialog box, and then select Open Exclusive from the list.

q. Click the **File tab**, and click **Encrypt with Password**. Type **eXploring!2016** as the password. Click **OK**. Click **OK** in response to the *Row level locking will be ignored* message.

r. Close the database and reopen it. Type **eXploring!2016** in the Enter database password box.

s. Close the database and exit Access. Based on your instructor's directions, submit a09p1Clinic_LastFirst.

2 Metropolitan Zoo

The Metropolitan Zoo invites its patrons to become members of the zoo. For a donation of $50 per year for an individual, or $100 for a family membership, members are entitled to special discounts and member-only promotions. Your task is to review the database to review the tables for normalization errors, check the performance, create a lookup field, and save the database as an Access Database Executable. Refer to Figure 9.45 as you complete this exercise.

FIGURE 9.45 Zoo Database Navigation Form

a. Open *a09p2Members*. Save the database as **a09p2Members_LastFirst**.

b. Open the Members table, and examine the data. Determine if the data meets the three normalization rules: 1NF, 2NF, and 3NF.

Problems exist in the Members table, especially with the Membership fields.

c. Close the Members table. You decide to normalize the table manually.

d. Click **Query Design** in the Queries group on the Create tab. Double-click the **Members table** to add it to the query design, and click **Close** in the Show Table dialog box.

e. Double-click the **MembershipTypeID**, **MembershipTypeName**, and **MembershipDonation** fields to add them to the query design grid. Click **Run** in the Results group to run the query. Take note of the repeating rows of data.

f. Switch to Design view. Click **Totals** in the Show/Hide group to eliminate the duplicate rows. Run the query.

Only the unique rows show in the results. There are only two unique rows.

g. Switch to Design view. Click **Make Table** in the Query Type group, and type **MemberTypes** in the Table Name box. Click **OK**. Click **Run** in the Results group to create the MemberTypes table. Click **Yes** to the warning message.

You created a second table (MemberTypes) to help normalize the Members table.

h. Save the query as **Create Member Types**, and close the query.

i. Open the **MemberTypes table** in Design view. Set the **MembershipTypeID field** as the primary key. Save and close the table.

j. Open the **Members table** in Design view, and complete the following steps:
- Change the MembershipTypeID data type to **Lookup Wizard**.
- Click **Next** in the first Lookup Wizard step, select **Table: MemberTypes** in the next step, and then click **Next**.
- Click >> to include all fields in the Lookup field. Click **Next** three times.
- Click **Finish**, and click **Yes** to save the table. The two tables are now joined using the MembershipTypeID field.

k. Switch to Datasheet view. Click the **MembershipTypeID field** in the first row, and verify the Lookup field is working.

You can choose either of the two membership types from the menu. Next, you will delete the redundant fields in the Members table.

l. Switch to Design view. Select the **MembershipTypeName** and **MembershipDonation fields**. Click **Delete Rows** in the Tools group. Click **Yes** to confirm the deletion. Save and close the table.

m. Select the **Animals table**. Click the **Create tab**, and select **Form** to create a form based on the Animals table. Save the form with the default name and close the form.

n. Create forms for the Members and MemberTypes tables using the same method as Step m. Delete the subform that appears as part of the MemberTypes form. Save the forms with the default name, and close the forms.

o. Click the **Create tab**, and select **Report** to create a basic report based on the Members table using the Report tool. Save with the default name, and close the report.

p. Click the **Navigation arrow** in the Forms group, and select **Horizontal Tabs**. Drag the **Animals form**, **Members form**, **MemberTypes form**, and **Members report**, in that order, to the navigation form.

q. Double-click the **fourth tab**, and type **Summary**. Switch to Form view, and click each tab to ensure the form works. Compare your results with Figure 9.45. Close the navigation form, saving with the default name when prompted.

r. Click the **Database Tools tab**, and click **Analyze Performance**. Click the **All Object Types tab**, click **Select All**, and then click **OK**. The first idea in the Results window suggests you save your application as an MDE file.

Recall when Access suggests you create MDE files, it should refer to ACCDE files. This is a known inconsistency in the program.

s. Click **Close** to close the dialog box.

t. Click the **File tab**, and click **Save As**. Double-click **Make ACCDE**. Change the name to **a09p2MembersExecutable_LastFirst**. Click **Save**.

u. Close the database and exit Access. Based on your instructor's directions, submit the following:

a09p2Members_LastFirst

a09p2MembersExecutable_LastFirst

Mid-Level Exercises

1 The Computer Store

ANALYSIS CASE

Bytes and Bits, a computer store based in Florida, sells computer products to individuals and small businesses. You have been hired to assist with the daily computer operations, including management of the order processing database. Your plan is to analyze the database, create a front end for the users, and transfer the tables to a back-end database. After splitting the database, you will create a navigation form to open the database objects.

a. Open *a09m1Computers*. Save the database as **a09m1Computers_LastFirst**.

b. Open the Database Documenter. Click **Options**, and uncheck all options in the Include for Table section. Select the **Names, Data Types, and Sizes option** in the Include for Fields section, and select **Nothing** in the Include for Indexes section. Click **OK**. Click the **check box** next to the **Customers table** to select it, and click **OK**. In the generated report, take note of the Size (the third column) of each field. Notice the values for the ZipCode and PhoneNumber field sizes in the Customers table are very large.

 c. Click **Close Print Preview** in the Close Preview group. Open the **Customers table** in Design view, and adjust the field size to an appropriate size. The field size for the ZipCode and PhoneNumber fields should be large enough to accommodate all data but small enough so users cannot type extra characters. Save and close the table.

d. Click **Access Database** in the Move Data group, and click **Split Database** to split the database into a front-end and a back-end database. Save the split database in the same folder as your other solution files, accepting the default file name. The Navigation Pane shows linked table icons to the left of each table.

e. Open the **Customers table**, and type your first and last names as the next customer, leaving the other fields blank. Close the table.

f. Open the *a09m1Computers_LastFirst_be* database, and open the Customers table. Verify your name is in the Customers table. Close the back-end database.

> **TROUBLESHOOTING:** If you open the front-end database at a later time on a different computer, you may get an error stating the file path is not valid. Use the techniques learned in a previous chapter to link the front-end database to the back-end database.

g. Create three objects in the a09m1Computers_LastFirst database: a form named **Customers** based on the Customers table using the Form tool, a form named **Products** based on the Products table using the Form tool, and a report named **Customer List** based on the Customers table using the Report tool. Close all objects.

h. Create a navigation form using the **Vertical Tabs, Left template**. Add the **Customers form**, followed by the **Products form**, followed by the **Customer List report**, followed by the **Products List report**.

i. Test the navigation form in Form view. Save the form with the default name, and close the form.

j. Add the navigation form to the Display Form option in the Current Database portion of the Access Options so the navigation form opens when the database opens.

DISCOVER

k. Locate and change the option in the Access Options so that the Navigation Pane does not display when the database is opened.

l. Close the database and exit Access. Based on your instructor's directions, submit the following:
   a09m1Computers_LastFirst
   a09m1Computers_LastFirst_be

The owners of Boats for All Seasons have asked you to assist in improving their database. They have plans for some additional forms and reports and also modifications to their main table. They are having a problem with the database when customers who bought boats from them years ago return to purchase again. The owners are unsure how to record a second transaction for the same customer. They have also asked for any other suggestions you may have for making the database more secure.

a. Open *a09m2Boats*. Save the database as **a09m2Boats_LastFirst**.

b. Open the Customers table and review the contents of the table.

Notice customer 2 (Frank Billingslea) is the same as customer 62, with identical addresses. James Windon (30 and 63) and Kathy Mcdowell (35 and 61) also have repeated information. In the following steps, you will split the customers table into two tables: a Customers table and a BoatPurchases table.

c. Open the Customer Purchases query and examine the results. The owners are trying to use this query to input purchases. They are confused because the boat purchase data is mixed with the Customers table. Also, some of the customers have not purchased a boat yet. You will fix the problem in the following steps.

d. Modify the Customer Purchases query so it only shows values that are not null in the BoatType field. Run the query. Your query should list only customers who purchased a boat (56 records).

e. Switch to Design view. Click **Make Table** in the Query Type group, and type **BoatPurchases** in the Table name box. Click **OK**. Run the query, and click **Yes** at the warning. Save and close the query.

f. Open the BoatPurchases table in Design view, and change the CustomerID Data Type to **Number**. Save the table, and switch to Datasheet view. Sort the records by CustomerID in ascending order, locate the three customers who purchased more than one boat (Billingslea, Windon, and Mcdowell), and then update their CustomerIDs so that both purchases show the smaller ID. For example, change the second Billingslea CustomerID from 62 to **2**.

DISCOVER

g. Switch to Design view, and change the CustomerID field to a Lookup Wizard displaying CustomerID, LastName, and FirstName from the Customers table, sorted by LastName and then by FirstName, both in ascending order. Hide the key column. Accept the default field name. Save the table, and click **Yes** at the prompt.

h. Switch to Datasheet view. The customer LastName and FirstName should display when you click the arrow at the right of any CustomerID field. Verify that the name in column 1 matches the names in columns 2 and 3. If it does, switch to Design view and delete the **LastName** and **FirstName fields**. These two fields were for reference only until you verified that the data matched. Save and close the BoatPurchases table.

i. Open the Customers table in Design view, and delete the **BoatType**, **BoatPurchaseDate**, and **BoatPurchaseAmount fields**.

This information is not required in the Customers table because it now exists in the BoatPurchases table.

j. Save the table, and switch to Datasheet view. Sort the table by LastName in ascending order. Locate the three customers who purchased more than one boat (Billingslea, Windon, and Mcdowell), and delete the three duplicate records with the larger CustomerID. For example, delete the second Billingslea record with a CustomerID of 62.

k. Close the database and reopen using the Open Exclusive option. Encrypt the database with a password of **exploring**.

l. Create a new form using the Form tool and a new report using the Report tool based on the BoatPurchases table. Save with the default name and close each object.

m. Save the database as an Access Database Executable. Type **a09m2BoatsExecutable_LastFirst** for the file name.

n. Display the options for the database. In the Current Database tab, change the Application Title to **Boats for All Seasons**, and click the option for **Compact on Close** to select it. Notice the title bar now displays Boats for All Seasons.

o. Close the database and exit Access. Based on your instructor's directions, submit the following:

a09m2Boats_LastFirst

a09m2BoatsExecutable_LastFirst

3 New Castle County Technical Services

RUNNING CASE

New Castle County Technical Services (NCCTS) provides technical support for a number of local companies. A new hire will be working with you on the database, so to help prepare her, you will create a report to document the relationships for her, and you will split the database into two files so both of you can use the database on the NCCTS network. You will also create a navigation form and set it to open automatically. You will additionally create an Access Database Executable and add a password to help protect the database from accidental changes. Finally, you will apply your knowledge of normalization to analyze whether the database can be optimized.

This project is a running case. You will use the same database file across Chapters 5 through 10.

a. Open *a08m3NCCTS_LastFirst* and save the database as **a09m3NCCTS_LastFirst**.

> **TROUBLESHOOTING:** If you did not complete the Chapter 8 case, return to Chapter 8, complete the case to create the database, and then return to this exercise.

b. Use the Database Documenter tool to create a report displaying the relationships. Save the report as a PDF file named **a09m3NCCTSRelationships_LastFirst** and close Print Preview.

c. Create a new navigation form using the **Vertical Tabs, Right** layout. Include the **Customer Information form** and Calls by Customer report, in that order from top to bottom. Save the report as **NCCTS Navigation** and close the form.

d. Use the Table Analyzer tool to evaluate the **Customers table** and move through the steps. Notice the tool suggests you split the City and State fields into one table, and the Zip in another. You will leave this window open for reference for the moment.

 e. Open Microsoft Word. Write a short memo to your supervisor explaining what the Table Analyzer has suggested, and whether you think it is a good suggestion. Make sure you discuss normalization as part of your explanation. Save the document as **a09m3NCCTSMemo_LastFirst** and close Word.

f. Cancel the Table Analyzer, as you will not make any changes without discussing with your supervisor.

g. Create an Access Database Executable from the database, using the name **a09m3NCCTSExecutable_LastFirst** as the file name.

h. Close the database. Reopen the **a09m3NCCTSExecutable_LastFirst** database in exclusive mode. Encrypt the database, entering the password **eXploring!2016** in both boxes.

i. Set the **NCCTS Navigation form** to open automatically each time the database is opened.

j. Use the Database Splitter tool to split the database into a front-end and back-end database. Save the back-end database with the default name of **a09m3NCCTSExecutable_LastFirst_be**.

k. Close the database and exit Access. Based on your instructor's directions, submit the following:

a09m3NCCTS_LastFirst

a09m3NCCTSRelationships_LastFirst

a09m3NCCTSMemo_LastFirst

a09m3NCCTSExecutable_LastFirst

a09m3NCCTSExecutable_LastFirst_be

Beyond the Classroom

Mint Condition

You and your partner Keith have a small business selling baseball cards online through eBay. As the more computer-savvy partner, you created an Access database with records of the cards you have in stock. You and Keith both prefer a different interface, so you have decided it is best to split the database and provide Keith with his own front-end database that he can customize without affecting your front-end database. Open *a09b1Cards* and save it as **a09b1Cards_LastFirst**. Create a navigation form using the Vertical Forms, Left template and drag the Bowman Cards, Donruss Cards, Fleer Cards, and Topps Cards reports into the form. Save the form as **Cards**, and set it so it opens each time the database is opened. Split the database, and save the back-end database with the default name. Save the database as **a09b1CardsKeith_LastFirst**. Close the database, reopen the *a09b1Cards_LastFirst* database in exclusive mode, and add a password of **eXploring!2016** to the database. This way, Keith cannot accidentally open your database. Close the database and exit Access. Based on your instructor's directions, submit the following:

> a09b1Cards_LastFirst
> a09b1CardsKeith_LastFirst
> a09b1Cards_LastFirst_be

Event Planning

You are the general manager of a large hotel chain. You recently moved all data for the company's event planning to an Access database. However, as the database size has increased, the database has become slower, so you have decided to use the built-in Access utilities to improve performance. You have also decided to add a password to improve security. Open *a09b2Hotel* and save it as **a09b2Hotel_LastFirst**. To improve the performance, you will run the Performance Analyzer tool, selecting all objects, and implement all four of the recommendations and ideas the program displays. When implementing the suggestion to create an MDE file, use the name **a09b2HotelExecutable_LastFirst**. You will also run the Table Analyzer tool on the Location table and accept the suggested change to the table. After you have implemented these changes, add a password of **eXploring!2016** to the database. Close the database and exit Access. Based on your instructor's directions, submit a09b2Hotel_LastFirst.

Capstone Exercise

Your company handles room registration, speaker coordination, and other functions for national conferences that are held at your campus throughout the year. The Sales Department mails schedules to speakers and building coordinators. The speaker database was modified by unauthorized personnel, and you will reverse the changes. For example, all of the relationships were deleted; they should be re-created. You have been asked to analyze the database, fix the relationships, and make the database more secure to avoid this situation in the future. The database tables may already be normalized; however, you will examine the tables to verify.

Restore Database Relationships

You have noticed the existing database has problems with relationships. You will open the database and create the relationships between the tables to make sure data is consistent in the database.

a. Open *a09c1NatConf* and save the database as **a09c1NatConf_LastFirst**.

b. Open each table in the database and look for normalization errors.

c. Open the Relationships window. Notice there are currently no relationships.

d. Add the Speakers, SessionSpeaker, Sessions, and Rooms tables to the Relationships window. Restore relationships by dragging the primary key from the primary table onto the foreign key of a related table.

e. Set the options to **Enforce Referential Integrity** and **Cascade Update Related Fields** for each relationship you create.

f. Save the changes and close the Relationships window.

Analyze Database Performance

It is important to verify that the database performs properly when it is used in a production environment. You will run the Performance Analyzer tool and take note of the recommendations, suggestions, and ideas in the analysis results.

a. Open the Performance Analyzer dialog box, click the **All Object Types tab**, click **Select All**, and then click **OK**.

b. Verify that the first item on the list (an idea) suggests creating an MDE file (which is called ACCDE in Access 2016). You will create an ACCDE file later.

c. Verify the third item on the list (an idea) suggests you change the data type of RoomID in the Sessions table from Short Text to **Long Integer**. You decide not to make this change.

d. Close the Performance Analyzer.

Split the Database

You have decided to split the database to allow the multiple database users to customize their individual front-end databases; the back end (the tables) remains safe and secure.

a. Split the database, accepting the default back-end name **a09c1NatConf_LastFirst_be**. The front-end copy of the database remains open.

b. Look for the linked tables in the front-end copy of the database.

Create a Navigation Form

You will create a navigation form that displays a new form and the three reports in the database. You will also set the database to open the navigation form whenever the database is opened.

a. Create a new form based on the Speakers table using the Form tool.

b. Save the form as **Add or Edit Speakers**.

c. Create a navigation form based on the Horizontal Tabs template.

d. Drag the new **Add or Edit Speakers form** to the first tab position.

e. Drag the reports to fill the next three tab positions.

f. Switch to Form view and test the navigation form. Save the navigation form with the default name and close it.

g. Set the database to open the navigation form when the database opens.

h. Test the navigation form by closing and then reopening the database.

Encrypt the Database with a Password and Create an ACCDE File

You will encrypt the front-end database with a password. In addition, you will convert the front-end database to the ACCDE file format.

a. Close the database. Reopen the database in exclusive mode.

b. Display the Set Database Password dialog box.

c. Type the database password **eXploring!2016** in both dialog boxes, and click **OK**.

d. Close and reopen the database to test the password.

e. Save the database as an Access Database Executable. Save the file with the name **a09c1NatConfExecutable_LastFirst**.

f. Close the database and exit Access. Based on your instructor's directions, submit the following:

a09c1NatConf_LastFirst
a09c1NatConf_LastFirst_be
a09c1NatConfExecutable_LastFirst

Using Macros and SQL in Access

LEARNING OUTCOME: You will create and use macros and SQL to manage data within a database.

OBJECTIVES & SKILLS: After you read this chapter, you will be able to:

CASE STUDY | Retirement Plan Contributions

Terry Jackson, owner of Sunshine Therapy Club, offers a 401(k) retirement plan to all full-time employees. Employees can contribute between 1% and 15% of their salaries to 401(k) accounts and receive a tax deduction on their federal tax returns. For employees who have been with the company for at least one year, the company will match the employees' contributions up to 5% of their salaries.

You have been asked to verify the accuracy of the Sunshine employee data and the employee contributions, ensuring that they fall within the plan guidelines. For example, only employees who have worked for the company for at least one year are eligible for the company match. Terry would also like to receive a weekly report that shows the detailed contributions per employee and the company matching contributions.

You decide to use macros and data macros to automate tasks in the database and to verify the eligibility of employees in the 401(k) plan. You will also construct several SQL statements and use an SQL statement as the record source for a report.

CHAPTER

10

Advanced Techniques

Syda Productions/
Shutterstock

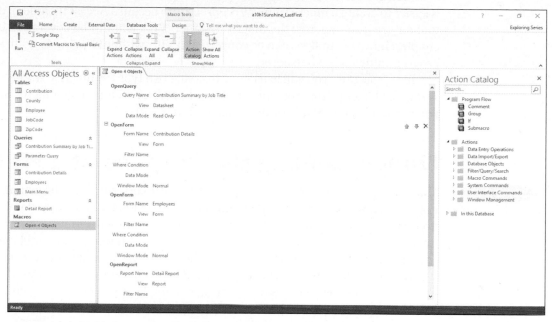

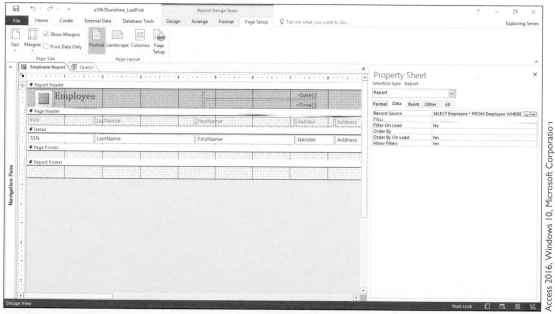

Access 2016, Windows 10, Microsoft Corporation

FIGURE 10.1 Retirement Plan Contributions Database

CASE STUDY | Retirement Plan Contributions

Starting File	File to be Submitted
a10h1Sunshine	a10h3Sunshine_LastFirst

Macro Design

Access provides developers with a variety of built-in tools to create tables, queries, forms, and reports. However, sometimes a developer needs to have more control over how the objects in a database behave individually or in relation to other objects. This type of functionality can be accomplished through programming code. Access provides two methods of programming—creating macros and creating procedures using Microsoft Visual Basic® for Applications (VBA). VBA is a programming language that works with Access and enables you to create macros or small procedures that run in the application. A *macro* is a series of actions that can be programmed to automate tasks. In general, it is easier to create a macro than a VBA procedure because Access includes a development tool for creating macros, the Macro Designer. VBA will not be covered in detail in this chapter; however, macros can be converted to VBA without having to write any complex programming code whatsoever.

In this section, you will learn how to create two types of macros: stand-alone macros and embedded macros. You will also learn how Access can create macros automatically when you add command buttons to forms and reports.

Understanding the Purpose of a Macro

STEP 1 ≫ Macros can be used to automate repetitive tasks or perform a specific action. You can use macros to group a series of commands and instructions into a single database object to accomplish repetitive or routine tasks simply by executing the macro. For example, if you import the same Excel workbook data into Access each week, you could create a macro to help you accomplish this task readily. Alternatively, you might want to add a button to a form to run the same report each week. Access creates macros automatically when you add certain controls to forms or reports, for example, if you create a command button in a form to open a report or print a customer order. The macro associated with the button executes when the button is clicked.

Access supports two categories of macros: stand-alone macros and embedded macros. A *stand-alone macro* is a database object that you create and use independently of other controls or objects. Stand-alone macros display as objects in the Navigation Pane. Figure 10.2 shows four stand-alone macros.

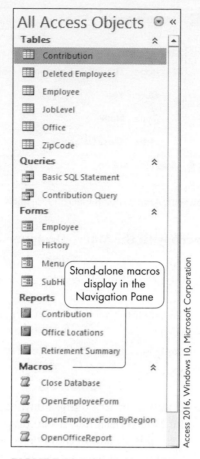

FIGURE 10.2 Stand-Alone Macros

Access 2016, Windows 10, Microsoft Corporation

An ***embedded macro*** is a macro that executes when an event attached to a control or object occurs. An ***event*** occurs when a user enters, edits, or deletes data; events also occur when users open, use, and close forms and reports.

On Close is an example of an event attached to an object. Whenever you close a form or a report, the On Close event is triggered and Access executes the steps stored in the macro if there is one attached to the On Close event.

Creating a Stand-Alone Macro

STEP 2 ❯❯ A stand-alone macro displays as an object in the Navigation Pane and can be run independently of other objects. You use the Macro Designer to create a stand-alone macro.

The ***Macro Designer*** was developed to make it easier to create or modify macros, and to add or delete actions from macros. When you begin to design a macro, you add actions that will list the tasks that you want the macro to perform. For example, you may want to add a MessageBox action to the macro to display a message to users when the macro runs. When there are multiple actions in a macro, Access executes the actions in the order in which they display.

After adding an action to the macro, specify the arguments you want for the action. An ***argument*** is a variable, constant, or expression that is used to produce the output for an action. For example, the MessageBox action contains four arguments, one of which is required. To see a short description of each argument, point to the argument box, and Access displays a short explanation for it. The MessageBox action contains the arguments *Message*, *Beep*, *Type*, and *Title*, as shown in Figure 10.3.

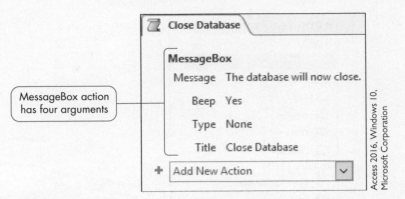

FIGURE 10.3 Macro Action with Arguments in Macro Designer

To add actions to a macro with the Macro Designer, complete one of the following steps:

- Click the Add New Action arrow, and choose the action you want to add to the macro.
- Type the action name directly into the Add New Action box; Access autocompletes the action name as you type.
- Locate an action in the Action Catalog, and click and drag (or double-click it) to add it to the macro.

You can also create an action by dragging a database object from the Navigation Pane to an empty row in the Macro Designer. If you drag a table, query, form, or report to the Macro Designer, Access adds an action that opens the table, query, form, or report. If you drag a macro to the Macro Designer, Access adds an action that runs the macro. Figure 10.4 shows the results of dragging the Employee form from the Navigation Pane into a new macro.

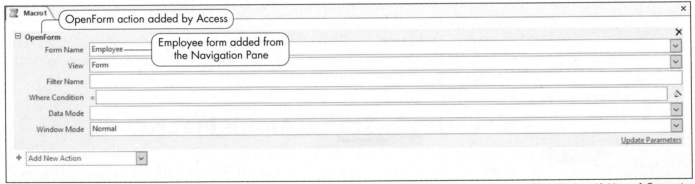

FIGURE 10.4 Drag the Employee Form into a Macro

To create a stand-alone macro using the Macro Designer, complete the following steps:

1. Click the Create tab.
2. Click Macro in the Macros & Code group. The Macro Designer is displayed, as shown in Figure 10.1 (top image). In this figure, the Navigation Pane is on the left, the macro-building area is in the middle, and the Action Catalog is on the right. The Action Catalog can be used as a reference as you design a macro.
3. Locate an action in the Action Catalog, and double-click it (or click and drag it) to add it to the macro.
4. Specify the arguments you want for the action you added to the macro.
5. Add actions and arguments to the actions to continue to build the macro.
6. Click Save when you finish building the macro.
7. Type a descriptive name for the macro. The macro name will display in the Navigation Pane, as shown in Figure 10.2.

It is always a good practice to test a macro to determine if it produces the expected results. Double-click the macro name in the Navigation Pane to run and test a stand-alone macro.

Using the Macro Designer to Edit a Macro

STEP 3 ▶▶ Once you have created a stand-alone macro and have determined that it works correctly, you might decide to modify, add, or delete actions. For example, you can edit an existing macro by adding an action to open the Employee form, as shown in Figure 10.4.

To edit a stand-alone macro using the Macro Designer, complete the following steps:

1. Right-click the macro name in the Navigation Pane.
2. Select Design View from the shortcut menu.
3. Modify, add, or delete macro actions, then save and close the macro.

Attaching an Embedded Macro to an Event

An embedded macro is attached to an event of a control on a form or report, or to an event of the form or report itself. After Update is an example of an event attached to a control. The After Update event is triggered each time you enter or update data into a field on a form. You can attach an embedded macro to the After Update event and evaluate the data entered in the field to verify that it falls within a set of parameters. In the Sunshine database, for example, if a user enters a 401(k) contribution in a form, a macro can verify that the amount is equal to or less than 15% of an employee's salary.

Create an Embedded Macro with the Command Button Wizard

STEP 4 ▶▶ You can use the Command Button Wizard to create an embedded macro automatically. After the wizard is finished, an embedded macro is inserted into the On Click event property of the button you add to a form or report.

To create an embedded macro using the Command Button Wizard, complete the following steps:

1. Right-click the form or report in the Navigation Pane.
2. Select Design View from the shortcut menu.
3. Click the Button control in the Controls group on the Design tab, and click in the form (or report) to place the button. The Command Button Wizard will launch, as shown in Figure 10.5.
4. Select a category from the Categories list, and select the desired action from the Actions list, as shown in Figure 10.6. Click Next.
5. Continue to step through the wizard, and select the option to display text or an image on the command button, as shown in Figure 10.7. If the Text option is selected, type the desired text to display on the button, and click Next.
6. Type the name for the button as it will be referenced in Access, as shown in Figure 10.8, and then click Finish.

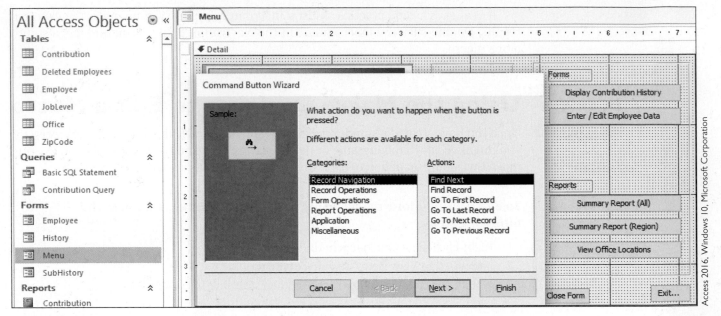

FIGURE 10.5 Command Button Wizard

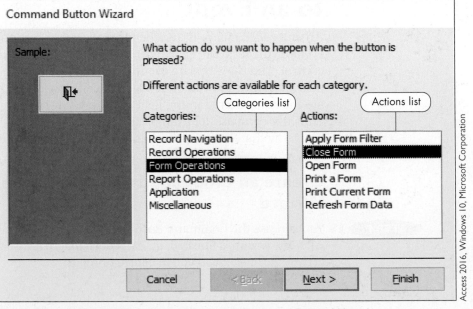

FIGURE 10.6 Select a Category and Action in Command Button Wizard

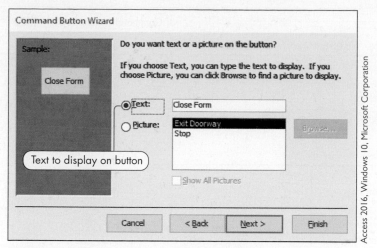

FIGURE 10.7 Select Text or a Picture to Display on Command Button

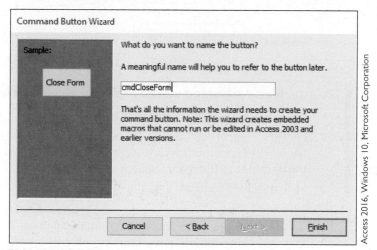

FIGURE 10.8 Type the Button Name and Finish the Wizard

Create an Embedded Macro with an Event Property

STEP 5 >> You can also add a macro to an existing control manually by clicking the ellipsis [...] in the event box of the control or object in the Property Sheet. When you add a macro to an event (such as the After Update event of a control or the On Click event of a button), Access embeds a macro in the object or control. The Event tab in the object's Property Sheet also enables you to open and edit the embedded macro. Figure 10.9 shows how an embedded macro displays in the Property Sheet for a control.

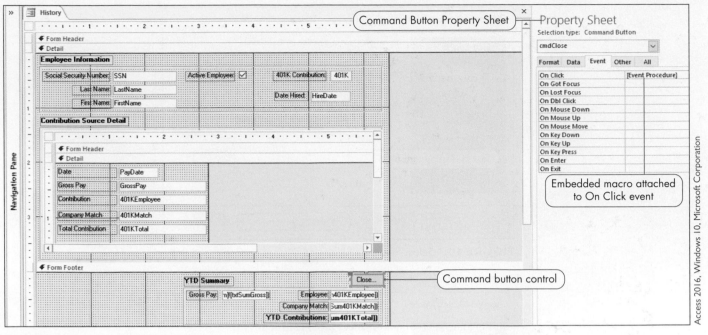

FIGURE 10.9 Embedded Macro

To attach an embedded macro to an event, complete the following steps:

1. Open the object in Design view and open the Property Sheet.
2. Click the control you want to add the macro to, and click in the desired event property box on the Event tab. When you click in an event property box, the ellipsis displays on the right side of the box, as shown in Figure 10.10.
3. Click the ellipsis, ensure that Macro Builder is selected, and then click OK.

The Macro Designer opens, and you can add actions using the same methods you used for the stand-alone macro. For example, you can create a macro to compute employee 401(k) contributions. The macro can display a message after the 401(k) contribution is selected, informing the employee (or the user) the amount that will be deducted each paycheck (by displaying the 401K Contribution Percent multiplied by the weekly Salary).

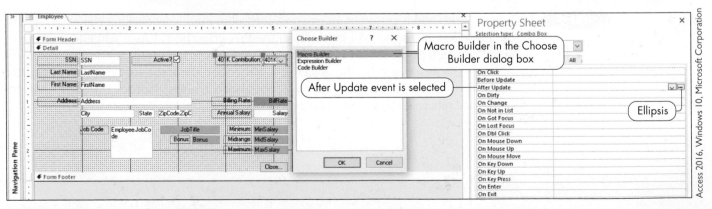

FIGURE 10.10 Create an Embedded Macro

TIP: EDITING AN EMBEDDED MACRO

To edit an embedded macro, open the form or report in Design view. Next, open the Property Sheet, and then click the event property that contains the embedded macro. Click the ellipsis, and Access opens the Macro Designer and displays the actions associated with the macro. Modify the embedded macro, click Save, and then close when finished. The macro remains embedded in the object.

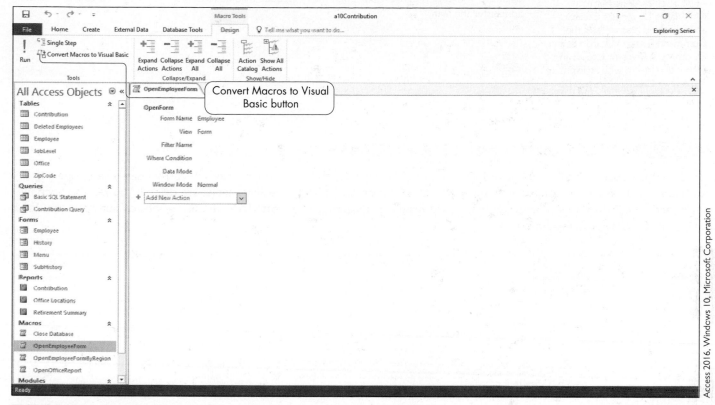

FIGURE 10.11 Convert a Macro to VBA

Quick Concepts

1. What is the difference between a stand-alone and an embedded macro? **p. 635**

2. How would you edit a stand-alone macro? **p. 637**

3. What is the advantage of using the Command Button Wizard to create an embedded macro? **p. 637**

Skills covered: Understand How a Macro Automates Tasks in a Database • Create a Stand-Alone Macro with the Macro Designer • Edit a Stand-Alone Macro with Macro Designer • Create an Embedded Macro Using the Command Button Wizard • Format a Command Button • Create an Embedded Macro with an Event Property • Create a Message Box

1 Macro Design

You were hired to manage the 401(k) plan at Sunshine Therapy Club. After you examine the design of the database, you decide to use stand-alone and embedded macros to display the forms and reports used to administer the plan.

STEP 1 » UNDERSTAND THE PURPOSE OF A MACRO

Because this is your first time working with the Sunshine Therapy Club database, you examine the current database by opening each table in Datasheet view. Next, you will open the Relationships window to see which tables are related. You will also open the forms and reports that are used frequently and determine that a macro can be created to open several objects automatically. Refer to Figure 10.12 as you complete Step 1.

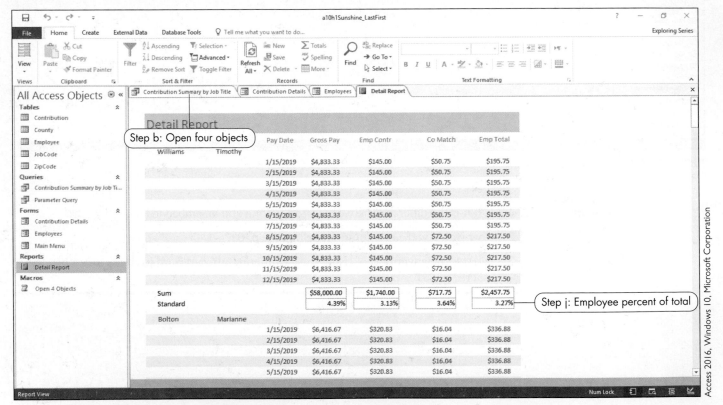

FIGURE 10.12 Sunshine Database Objects Open

a. Open *a10h1Sunshine* and save it as **a10h1Sunshine_LastFirst**.

> **TROUBLESHOOTING:** If you make any major mistakes in this exercise, you can close the file, open *a10h1Sunshine* and then start this exercise over.

b. Open the Employee table in Datasheet view, and examine the records. Open the Contribution table, and examine the records. Open the remaining tables, and examine the records. Close all tables.

You examine the data in each table to get acquainted with the database. The Contribution table contains the 401(k) contributions for each employee. The Employee table contains personal information for each employee.

c. Click the **Database Tools tab**, and click **Relationships** in the Relationships group to open the Relationships window.

You examine the table relationships to help you understand the data entry rules of the database. The Employee table contains a unique Social Security number (SSN) for each employee. The Contribution table contains an SSN field, but multiple contributions can be entered for each SSN.

d. Close the Relationships window. Open the Employee table, and add your data as a new record to the table. Type the following data when you enter your record:

SSN	**999-99-9999** (do not type the dashes)
LastName	**Your last name**
FirstName	**Your first name**
Gender	**Your gender**
Other fields	**The same data as Amanda Smith's record**

e. Close the Employee table.

f. Open the Contribution Summary by Job Title query and review the contributions by job title.

You will use this information to track the employee and employer contributions summarized by job title.

g. Open the Contribution Details form and scroll to the bottom of the data. Add three new entries using the following data:

SSN	PayDate	GrossPay	EmployeeContribution	CompanyMatch
999-99-9999	10/15/2019	$4,583.33	$458.33	$0.00
999-99-9999	11/15/2019	$4,583.33	$458.33	$0.00
999-99-9999	12/15/2019	$4,583.33	$458.33	$0.00

h. Open the Employees form. Advance to your record by clicking **Last record** in the Navigation bar. Change the **HireDate** to today's date. Close all open objects.

The HireDate will be used later to calculate the length of employment.

i. Open the Detail Report from the Navigation Pane. Locate your record (the last record of the report).

j. Compare your database with Figure 10.12. Close the report.

You would like to easily open the four objects that are used every day. You create a stand-alone macro to automatically open the four objects used in Step 1. Refer to Figure 10.13 as you complete Step 2.

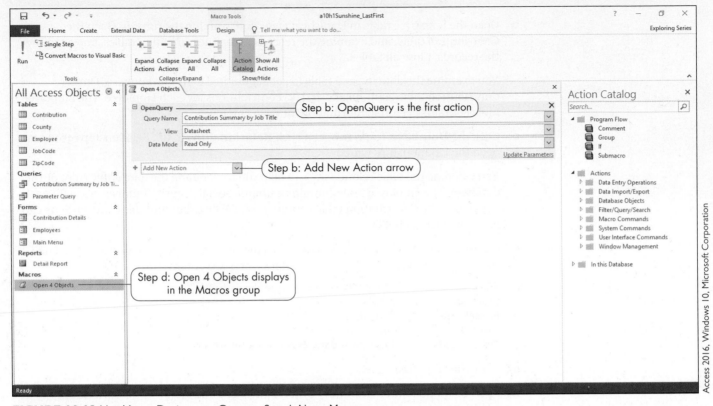

FIGURE 10.13 Use Macro Designer to Create a Stand-Alone Macro

a. Click the **Create tab**, and click **Macro** in the Macros & Code group.

The Macro Designer opens.

b. Click the **Add New Action arrow**, scroll down, and then select **OpenQuery** from the list of options.

The OpenQuery arguments are displayed. The OpenQuery action will open a query automatically.

c. Click the arrow at the end of each box, and select the following arguments:

Query Name	Contribution Summary by Job Title
View	Datasheet
Data Mode	Read Only

d. Save the macro as **Open 4 Objects**. Close the macro.

The Open 4 Objects macro now displays in the Macros Group in the Navigation Pane.

e. Double-click the **Open 4 Objects macro** to run it.

Only one object, the Contribution Summary by Job Title query, opens.

f. Close the query.

You created and tested a stand-alone macro in the previous step. Because the macro works correctly so far, you decide to edit the macro and add the other three objects. All four objects will open when you run the Open 4 Objects macro. Refer to Figure 10.14 as you complete Step 3.

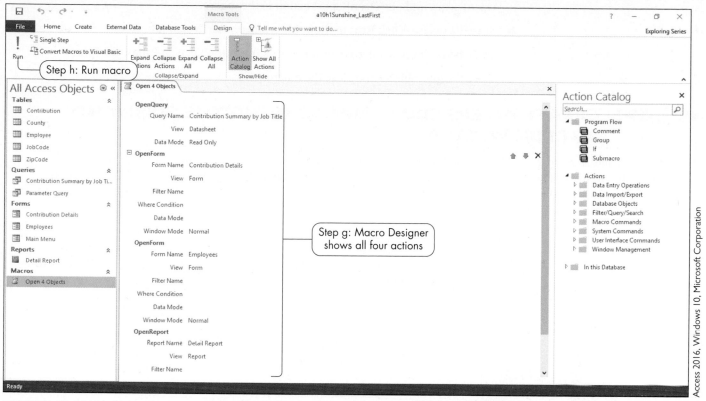

FIGURE 10.14 Use Macro Designer to Edit a Stand-Alone Macro

a. Right-click the **Open 4 Objects macro** in the Navigation Pane, and select **Design View**.

The Macro Designer opens.

b. Click in the **Add New Action box**, and type **OpenForm**.

You can type any action into the Add New Action box or select an action from the list. When you type an action, AutoComplete is enabled so you only have to type the first few letters of the action. The OpenForm arguments are displayed.

c. Select the following arguments:

Form Name	**Contribution Details**
View	**Form**
Window Mode	**Normal**

The remaining arguments are left blank.

d. Click in the **Add New Action box**, and type **OpenForm**.

The OpenForm arguments are displayed for the second form.

e. Select the following arguments:

Form Name	**Employees**
View	**Form**
Window Mode	**Normal**

The remaining arguments are left blank.

f. Click the **Add New Action arrow**, and then click **OpenReport**.

The OpenReport arguments are displayed for the report.

g. Select the following arguments:

Report Name	Detail Report
View	Report
Window Mode	Normal

The remaining arguments are left blank. You have added an OpenQuery, two OpenForms, and one OpenReport action to the macro.

h. Save the macro. Click **Run** in the Tools group on the Design tab.

The Open 4 Objects macro runs and opens the four objects one after the other.

i. Close the four objects and close the macro.

STEP 4 ›› CREATE AN EMBEDDED MACRO USING THE COMMAND BUTTON WIZARD

You created a stand-alone macro. Next, you will create an embedded macro attached to a control on a form. You will add a command button to the main menu with an embedded macro; the macro will open the Parameter Query when the button is clicked. The Parameter Query will prompt the user to enter a minimum salary and then display employees who earn at least that amount. Refer to Figure 10.15 as you complete Step 4.

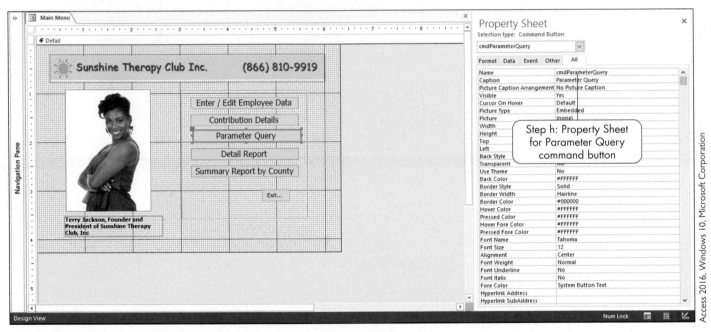

FIGURE 10.15 Create an Embedded Macro Using the Command Button Wizard

a. Double-click **Parameter Query** in the Navigation Pane. When prompted, type **70000**, and press **Enter**. Close the query.

The query displayed 10 employees who earn at least $70,000.00.

b. Right-click the **Main Menu form** in the Navigation Pane, and select **Design View** from the shortcut menu.

The Main Menu opens in Design view.

c. Click the **Button control** in the Controls group on the Design tab, and click in the space between the Contribution Details and Detail Report buttons.

The Command Button Wizard opens.

d. Select **Miscellaneous** from the Categories list, and select **Run Query** from the Actions list. Click **Next**.

e. Click **Parameter Query**, and click **Next**.

f. Select the **Text option**, and type **Parameter Query** as the display text. Click **Next**.

g. Type **cmdParameterQuery** as the name for the button. Click **Finish**.

h. Ensure that the **Property Sheet** is displayed from the Tools group on the Design tab with the button selected. Click the **Format tab** in the Property Sheet, set the button width to **2.25** and the height to **.25**. Click the **Font Size arrow**, and select **12**. Leave the Property Sheet open. Click and drag the **Parameter Query button** so that its left edge is aligned with the left edge of the buttons above and below it.

i. Switch to Form view, and click **Parameter Query**.

The query opens and prompts for the minimum salary amount.

j. Type **70000**, and press **Enter**.

The query results display all the employees with a salary of at least $70,000.

k. Close the query, and switch to the Design view of the Main Menu form. Click the **Parameter Query**, and ensure that Event tab is selected in the Property Sheet.

The embedded macro displays in the On Click property box.

l. Click the **ellipsis** ⬚ on the right side of the On Click property box. The Macro Designer opens and enables you to make modifications to the embedded macro. There are no modifications needed at this time. Close the Macro Designer.

m. Save and close the Main Menu form.

STEP 5 ›› **CREATE AN EMBEDDED MACRO USING AN EVENT PROPERTY**

Terry asks you to display a message to the employees each time they run the Detail Report. She wants to remind them to send the report to her every Friday. Refer to Figure 10.16 as you complete Step 5.

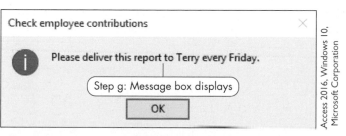

FIGURE 10.16 Message Displays When the Report Opens

a. Right-click **Detail Report** in the Navigation Pane, and select **Design View** from the shortcut menu.

The Detail Report opens in Design view.

b. Ensure that the Property Sheet is displayed. Ensure that the Event tab is selected on the Property Sheet.

c. Click the **ellipsis** on the right side of the On Open property box. The Macro Builder is selected by default. Click **OK**.

The Macro Designer opens and enables you to create an embedded macro.

d. Click the **Add New Action arrow** in the Add New Action box, scroll down, and then click **MessageBox**.

The MessageBox arguments are displayed.

e. Type **Please deliver this report to Terry every Friday.** (include the period) in the Message box.

f. Verify that *Yes* is in the Beep box. Select **Information** in the Type box. Type **Check employee contributions** in the Title box.

g. Save and close the macro. With the report in Design view, click the **View arrow**, and click **Print Preview** in the Views group to test the macro.

A message displays immediately, reminding users to send the report to Terry every Friday.

h. Click **OK**, close Print Preview, and then save and close the report.

i. Keep the database open if you plan to continue with the next Hands-On Exercise. If not, close the database and exit Access.

Data Macros

A data macro performs a series of actions when a table event occurs or whenever a named data macro is executed. Two main types of data macros exist—event-driven data macros and named data macros. Event-driven data macros are triggered by table events; named data macros can be run from anywhere in the database. Table events occur when users enter, edit, and delete table data. *Data macros* associate programming logic with tables; they also enable organizations to apply business logic to databases. Business logic describes the policies and procedures established by an organization. For example, you may want a macro to compare the values in two different fields when data is entered and perform an action as a result. When a form is based on a table that contains a data macro, the form contains the same logic and the same results of the data macro as the table.

Data macros, like stand-alone macros and embedded macros, use the Macro Designer. The actions available in the Macro Designer are different for data macros than for stand-alone or embedded macros; however, the user interface is the same for each macro type.

In this section, you will learn data validation techniques using data macros. You will learn how to create event-driven data macros and named data macros.

Identifying When to Use a Data Macro

STEP 1 ›› You can use data macros to validate and ensure the accuracy of data in a table. In a previous chapter, you learned how to use a validation rule to apply business logic to a single field in a table. However, when business logic requires the comparison of two or more fields, you need to use a data macro. For example, in the Sunshine database, you can compare an employee's hire date with today's date. If the employee has been with the firm for at least one year, then he or she is eligible for an employer match on the 401(k) contribution; otherwise, no employer match is available. To automate this type of business logic, a data macro is required.

Data macros can only be associated with table events; however, as stated earlier, a form that is based on a table that contains a data macro inherits the logic of the table. After you practice adding a few data macros, you will begin to see the power they add to a database.

Creating an Event-Driven Data Macro

STEP 2 ›› Table events occur naturally as users enter, edit, and delete table data. Event-driven data macros, such as After Delete or Before Change, can be programmed to run before or after a table event occurs.

> **To attach a data macro to a table event, complete the following steps:**
>
> 1. Open the table that will contain the data macro in Design view.
> 2. Click Create Data Macros in the Field, Record & Table Events group on the Design tab, as shown in Figure 10.17.
> 3. Click the event to which you want to attach the macro. For example, to create a data macro that runs before a record is saved, click Before Change.
> 4. Add macro actions using the Macro Designer. If a macro was previously created for this event, Access displays the existing macro actions.
> 5. Save and close the macro.

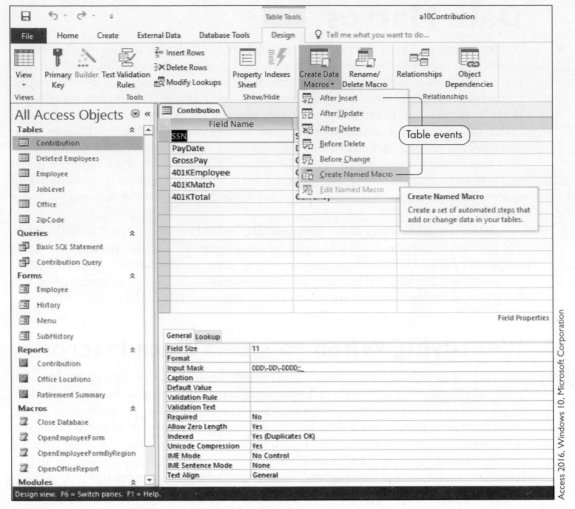

FIGURE 10.17 Data Macro Events

Test and Modify a Data Macro

STEP 3 ❭❭ In order to test the effect of a data macro, open the table to which the macro was added, and then add, delete, or update a record in order to trigger the macro. For example, if you attached a macro to the Before Change event, open the table, modify the data, and then advance to the next record to save the changes and to trigger the Before Change event. The data macro will run and execute the actions you created.

Creating a Named Data Macro

STEP 4 ❭❭ In addition to creating data macros that are triggered by events, Access enables you to create named data macros. You can access these macros from anywhere in the database, including running them from within another macro.

To create a named data macro, complete the following steps:

1. Ensure that the table is in Design view, click Create Data Macros in the Field, Record & Table Events group, and select Create Named Macro from the list (see Figure 10.18). The Macro Designer displays so you can create the macro logic (see Figure 10.19).
2. Save the macro with a descriptive name, such as DataMacro-Email. Figure 10.20 shows a data macro attached to the After Update event of the Employee table. The macro sends an email to the database administrator each time a record in the Employee table is updated.

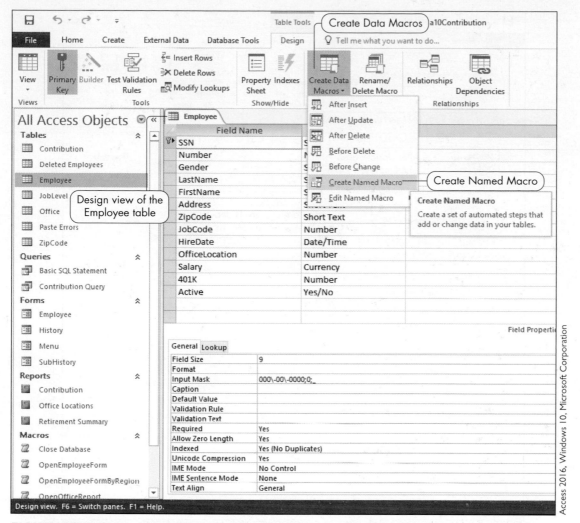

FIGURE 10.18 Create a Named Data Macro

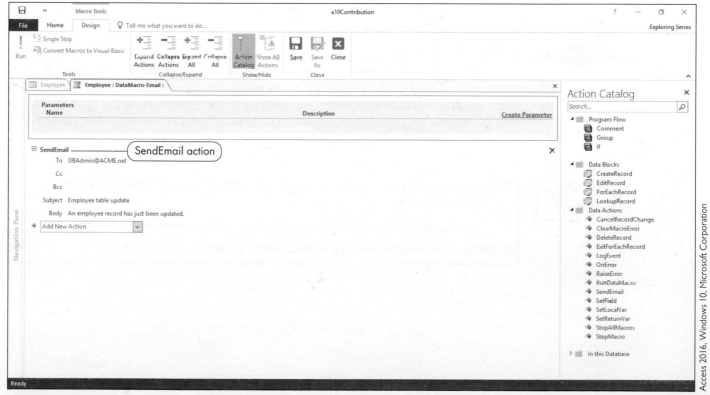

FIGURE 10.19 Named Data Macro Design

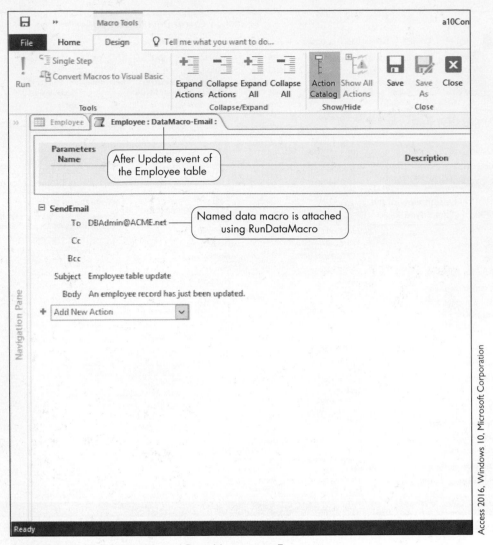

FIGURE 10.20 Attach a Named Data Macro to an Event

Attach a Named Data Macro to a Form

STEP 5 ❯❯ A named data macro can also be attached to an event in a form that is dependent on an underlying table. For example, you can associate a named data macro with an event property, such as After Update, in an employees form that is dependent on an employees table. You can run a named data macro from within another macro using the RunDataMacro action. Add the RunDataMacro action in the Macro Designer and select the named data macro using the Macro Name arrow.

Quick Concepts

4. How does a data macro differ from other macros that you create using the Macro Designer? *p. 649*

5. Give a specific reason as to why you would use a named data macro. *p. 652*

6. When does an event-driven data macro run? *p. 649*

2 Data Macros

You decide to demonstrate the power of data macros to Terry. You will show her how data macros help reduce data entry errors by validating data before it is added to a table. Although data macros are only created from within tables, you will demonstrate that named data macros can also be used with other objects in the database. You will create a named data macro in a table to send an email, and then attach the same named data macro to a form.

STEP 1 ›› IDENTIFY WHEN TO USE A DATA MACRO

You will identify an opportunity to create a data macro in the Employee table. Refer to Figure 10.21 as you complete Step 1.

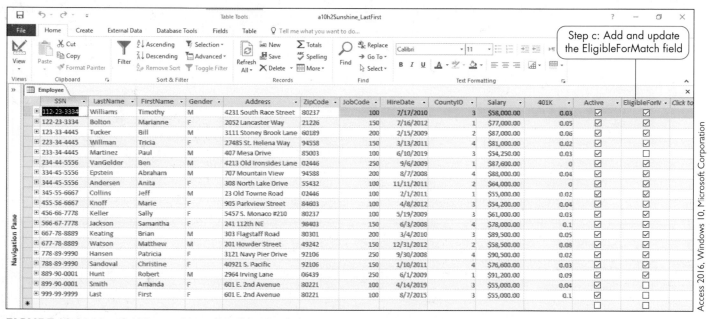

FIGURE 10.21 Identify When to Use a Data Macro

a. Open *a10h1Sunshine_LastFirst* if you closed it at the end of Hands-On Exercise 1, and save it as **a10h2Sunshine_LastFirst**, changing h1 to h2.

b. Open the Employee table in Design view.

c. Add a new field, **EligibleForMatch**, with data type **Yes/No**, to the end of the table. Save the table.

   You will use the new field to indicate which employees are eligible for the company 401(k) matching contribution.

d. Switch to Datasheet view.

e. Click in the **EligibleForMatch check box** in Record 1, for Timothy Williams. Because his HireDate is 7/17/2010, you indicate that he is eligible for the company match. Continue to update the first 10 records to indicate whether or not each employee is eligible for the company match. If an employee has been employed for at least one year, click to select the **EligibleForMatch check box**.

> **TROUBLESHOOTING:** Ensure that your own record contains today's date as the date of hire. As you have only joined the organization today, you will not be eligible for the company match.

STEP 2 ›› CREATE A BEFORE CHANGE DATA MACRO

The EligibleForMatch field can be updated automatically by a data macro based on the HireDate because the same eligibility rule applies to all employees. To eliminate the possibility of data entry errors, you will use the Before Change data macro to update the eligibility of an employee automatically. Refer to Figure 10.22 as you complete Step 2.

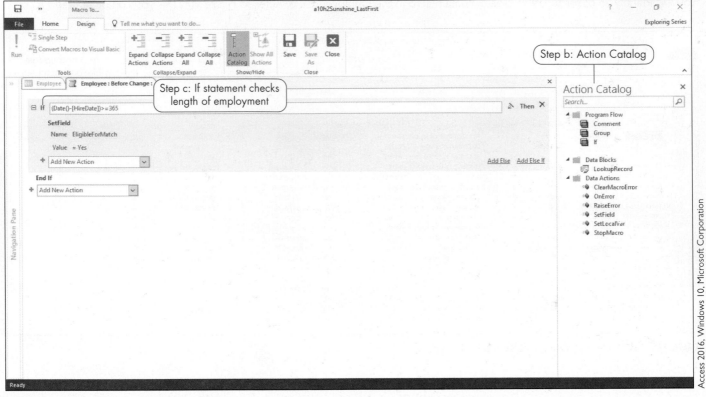

FIGURE 10.22 Before Change Data Macro

a. Switch to Design view. Click **Create Data Macros** in the Field, Record & Table Events group on the Design tab, and click **Before Change**.

The Macro Designer displays.

b. Drag the **If statement** from the Program Flow folder in the Action Catalog to the Add New Action box in the Macro.

The structure of the If statement is added to the macro.

c. Type **(Date()-[HireDate])>=365** in the Conditional expression box.

The expression determines if the employee has been employed at least one year (365 days) by subtracting the employee's hire date from today's date and then evaluating that difference to determine if it is greater than or equal to 365. If true, the macro will set the value of the EligibleForMatch field to Yes.

d. Select **SetField** from the Add New Action arrow within the If action.

The SetField arguments are added to the macro.

e. Type **el** in the **Name** box (and Access displays *EligibleForMatch*, the field name it predicts you are looking for). Press **Tab** to accept the EligibleForMatch field.

f. Type **yes** in the Value box.

Access checks the EligibleForMatch check box if the length of employment expression evaluates to true.

g. Save and close the macro. Save the Employee table.

STEP 3 ⟩⟩ TEST AND MODIFY A DATA MACRO

You decide to test the Before Change macro using the rest of the employee records (11–19). You will change one field in each record in order to trigger the Before Change event and verify the macro correctly updates the EligibleForMatch check box. You will also add an extra condition to the If statement in the macro that will update the check box if the employee is not eligible for the match. Refer to Figure 10.23 as you complete Step 3.

FIGURE 10.23 Data Macro with Else Statement Added

a. Switch to Datasheet view.

To test the accuracy of the data macro, you will retype the 401(k) contributions for records 11 through 19 in order to trigger the Before Change event. The macro will automatically select the EligibleForMatch check box for the appropriate records. Later, when new records are added to the table, the macro will run each time a record is entered.

b. Type **0.03** in the **401K column** of record 11 (Sally Keller). Click in the **401K column** of row 12.

Because employee Sally Keller was hired on 5/19/2009, she is eligible for the 401(k) match. The data macro checks the check box.

c. Type **0.1** in the **401K column** of record 12 (Samantha Jackson). Click in the **401K column** of row 13.

Because employee Samantha Jackson was hired on 6/3/2008, she is eligible for the 401(k) match. The data macro checks the check box.

d. Repeat the process for the remaining records.

You wonder if the macro will deselect an incorrectly checked EligibleForMatch check box. You decide to test the data macro for this condition.

e. Click the **EligibleForMatch check box** for your record to select it, and press ↓ to trigger the macro.

You realize that the check box remains checked even though you are not yet eligible for the company match. You decide to modify the data macro to update the check box if the employee is not eligible for the match.

f. Switch to Design view. Click **Create Data Macros** in the Field, Record & Table Events group on the Table Tools Design tab, and click **Before Change**.

The Macro Designer displays the If statement you set up earlier.

g. Click in the **If action**, and then click the **Add Else hyperlink** to add the Else statement.

You will add another SetField statement to deselect the EligibleForMatch check box if employees are employed for less than one year.

h. Type **s** in the Add New Action box; Access displays the *SetField* action. Press **Tab** to accept the SetField action.

i. Type **el** in the Name box; Access displays the *EligibleForMatch* action. Press **Tab** to accept EligibleForMatch.

j. Type **no** in the Value box.

The data macro will deselect the EligibleForMatch check box if the length of employment expression evaluates to false, that is, the length of employment is less than one year. Access attempts to add the Now function when you type *no*. Press **Esc**.

k. Save the macro. Close the macro. Save the Employee table.

l. Switch to Datasheet view, locate your record, and then change your proposed 401(k) contribution to **0.05**. Press ↓ to save your change.

The check box is unchecked by the data macro because you are not eligible for the match.

Terry wants to be notified when any changes are made to the Employee table. You decide to create a named data macro that will send an email whenever a change is made to the Employee table. Refer to Figure 10.24 as you complete Step 4.

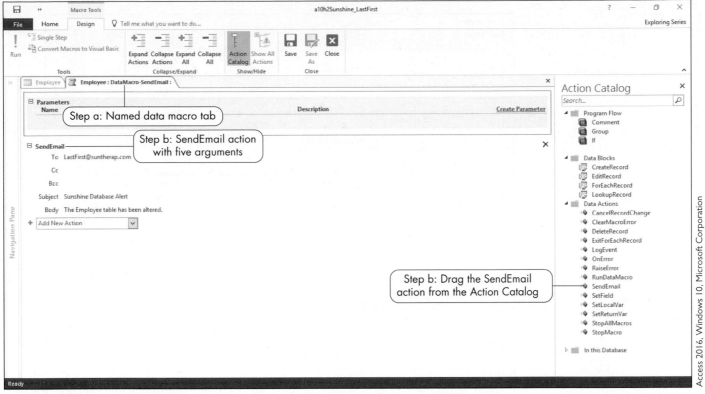

FIGURE 10.24 Create a Named Data Macro

a. Switch to Design view. Click **Create Data Macros** in the Field, Record & Table Events group on the Table Tools Design tab, and click **Create Named Macro**.

The Macro Designer displays.

b. Drag the **SendEmail action** from the Data Actions folder in the Action Catalog to the Add New Action box.

The SendEmail action and its five arguments are added to the macro.

c. Type your email address in the To argument box. Skip the Cc and Bcc arguments.

> **TROUBLESHOOTING:** Your instructor may provide you with an alternate email address to complete this step.

d. Type **Sunshine Database Alert** in the Subject argument box.

e. Type **The Employee table has been altered.** (include the period) in the Body argument box.

f. Save the macro as **DataMacro-SendEmail**. Close the macro.

g. Save the Employee table. Close the table.

You will attach the named data macro to a form event because many updates to the Employee table will be done through the Employees form. You decide to use the After Update event as the trigger for the send email macro. Refer to Figure 10.25 as you complete Step 5.

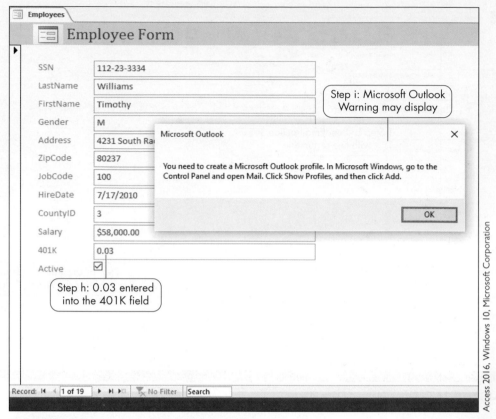

FIGURE 10.25 Test a SendEmail Named Data Macro

a. Open the Employees form in Design view.

b. Click **After Update** on the Event tab of the Property Sheet.

The ellipsis displays on the right side of the After Update property box.

c. Click the **ellipsis**, ensure that **Macro Builder** is selected, and then click **OK**.

The Macro Designer displays.

d. Click the **Add New Action arrow**, scroll down, and then select the **RunDataMacro action** from the list.

e. Select **Employee.DataMacro-SendEmail** using the Macro Name arrow.

f. Save and close the macro.

g. Save the Employees form, and switch to Form view.

h. Retype the existing 401(k) amount in the 401K field of the first record (Timothy Williams).

i. Press **Tab** two times to advance to the second employee.

As soon as you move to the second employee, the After Update event is triggered and the SendEmail macro is activated. Access attempts to send an email using the parameters you typed in Step 4.

> **TROUBLESHOOTING:** If an email client is not set up on the computer you are using, you may have to cancel this step and stop the macro. When your computer is correctly configured to send the email, the macro will run as expected.

j. Click **OK** if you receive the warning message shown in Figure 10.25. Click **OK** again, and click **Stop All Macros**.

If the warning message was not received as shown in Figure 10.25, click **Allow**. Check your email after a few minutes to see if you received the Sunshine Database Alert message.

k. Save and close the form.

l. Keep the database open if you plan to continue with the next Hands-On Exercise. If not, close the database and exit Access.

Structured Query Language

Until now, whenever you wanted to ask a question about the data in a database, you created a query. The query Design view enables you to select the tables you want to include and select the required fields from those tables. You can also add criteria and sorting in the query design grid. Whenever you create a query, you create a Structured Query Language (SQL) statement simultaneously. Access stores the SQL statement in the background.

In this section, you will learn the basics of SQL, the correlation between Design view and SQL view, and how to use an SQL statement in forms and reports.

Understanding the Fundamentals of SQL

STEP 1 ⟩⟩ *Structured Query Language (SQL)* is the industry-standard language for defining, manipulating, and retrieving the data in a database. SQL was developed at IBM in the early 1970s. Since then, Microsoft has developed its own version of SQL for Microsoft Access. All of the queries you created so far in this textbook were created using the built-in query tools; however, they could have been created using SQL.

When you learn SQL, you are learning the data retrieval and data manipulation language of all the industry-leading databases—SQL Server, Oracle, and SAP Sybase, to name a few. If you learn SQL in Access, your skills will be useful if you work in other database environments. You can use SQL to create a new query or to modify an existing query.

Figure 10.26 shows a basic query that was created in Design view. This query extracts all records from the Contribution table for the employee with SSN 456667778. Figure 10.27 shows the results in Datasheet view; the results contain 12 records. You can switch to SQL view to examine the statements generated by any query you create. To switch to SQL view, click the View arrow, and then select SQL View (see Figure 10.27).

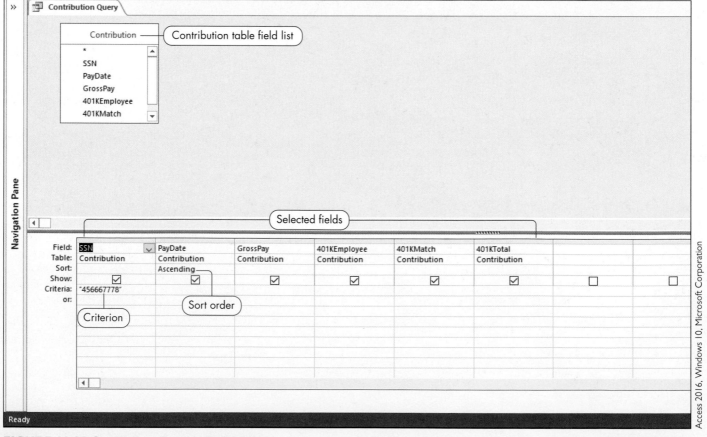

FIGURE 10.26 Contribution Query in Design View

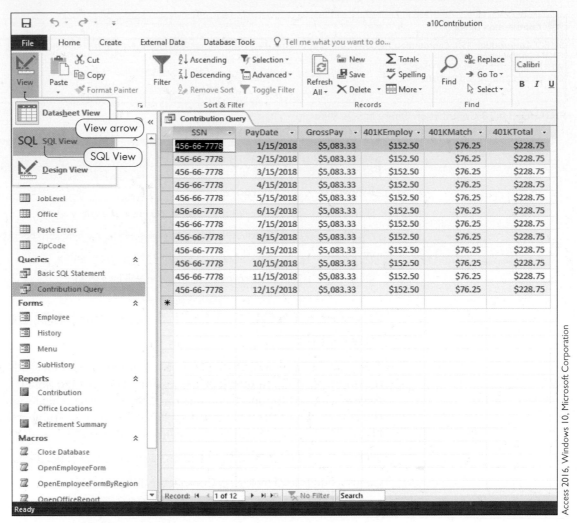

FIGURE 10.27 Contribution Query in Datasheet View

> **TIP: SQL VIEW**
> When you are working with queries in Access, you can switch to SQL view using three methods. You can click the View arrow and select SQL View from the list of options, you can right-click the query tab and select SQL View from the shortcut menu, or, from the open query, you can click the SQL icon at the bottom right of the Access window.

Interpreting an SQL SELECT Statement

STEP 2 ⟫ Similar to a select query, an **SQL SELECT statement** is used to retrieve data from tables in a database. Figure 10.28 shows the equivalent SQL SELECT statement of the Contribution query created earlier in Design view (shown in Figure 10.26). The words shown in UPPERCASE are SQL keywords. An **SQL keyword** defines the purpose and the structure of an SQL statement. Learning how to construct an SQL SELECT statement takes time because SQL lacks the graphical user interface found in Design view. To use SQL, you will first learn the four basic keywords found in a typical SQL SELECT statement—SELECT, FROM, WHERE, and ORDER BY. Table 10.1 lists the four basic keywords of an SQL SELECT statement, along with their purposes. Notice the correlation between the SQL keywords and the parameters found in Design view.

```
SELECT Contribution.SSN, Contribution.PayDate, Contribution.GrossPay, Contribution.[401KEmployee], Contribution.[401KMatch], Contribution.[401KTotal]
FROM Contribution
WHERE (((Contribution.SSN)="456667778"))
ORDER BY Contribution.PayDate;
```

FIGURE 10.28 Contribution Query in SQL View

Access 2016, Windows 10, Microsoft Corporation

TABLE 10.1	Four Basic Keywords of an SQL SELECT Statement and Their Purposes
Keyword	**Purpose**
SELECT	Specifies the fields to include in the query
FROM	Specifies the table or tables where the fields can be found
WHERE	Sets the criteria for the rows in the results
ORDER BY	Determines how the rows will be sorted

Pearson Education, Inc.

Dissect an SQL SELECT Statement: SELECT and FROM Keywords

The **SELECT keyword** instructs Access to return the specific fields from one or more tables (or queries). When a query or expression containing a SELECT statement is executed, Access searches the specified table (or tables), extracts the designated data, and displays the results. The **FROM keyword** specifies the table (or tables) that will be searched. In Figure 10.28, the SQL statement begins as follows:

SELECT Contribution.SSN, Contribution.PayDate, Contribution.GrossPay,

Contribution.[401KEmployee], Contribution.[401KMatch],

Contribution.[401KTotal]

FROM Contribution

In the statement above, field names are listed after the SELECT statement separated by commas. If fields from different tables have the same name, the table name prefix followed by a dot is required. In the above example, *Contribution.* displays before each field name because the same field names appear in other tables in the database. Some field names, such as 401KEmployee, 401KMatch, and 401KTotal, are enclosed by brackets [ ] when a field name has a leading numeric character. In the above example, the FROM command is instructing Access to pull data from the Contribution table.

If all fields in a table are required for a query, you can use the asterisk character (*) to select all of the fields in a table. For example, the following SELECT statement returns all fields and records from the Contribution table and displays the results in a datasheet:

SELECT *

FROM Contribution;

Dissect an SQL Statement: WHERE Keyword

After you select the tables and fields using SELECT and FROM, you can then filter the resulting records using the WHERE keyword. The **WHERE keyword** specifies the criteria that records must match to be included in the results. If your query does not include the WHERE keyword, the query will return all records from the table(s). In Figure 10.28, the SQL statement contains the following clause:

WHERE (((Contribution.SSN)="456667778"))

In this example, the WHERE clause specifies that only records with SSN equal to 456667778 will display in the results. Social Security numbers are generally stored in databases as text values rather than numeric, as they are not used in arithmetic calculations. Because in this example, the SSN field is a text field, the quotes are required around the SSN criterion.

Dissect an SQL Statement: ORDER BY Keyword

Typically, you want the query results to be arranged in a particular order. The ***ORDER BY keyword*** is used to sort the records by a certain field in either ascending or descending order. The ORDER BY clause must be added to the end of an SQL statement after the WHERE clause. In Figure 10.28, the SQL statement contains the following clause:

ORDER BY Contribution.PayDate;

In the statement above, the ORDER BY clause sorts the records in ascending order by PayDate. The ORDER BY sort order is ascending by default, so it is not necessary to specify when the records are to be sorted in ascending order. However, to sort in descending order, add DESC to the end of the ORDER BY clause. To sort the above records beginning with the most recent pay date, the statement would become as follows:

ORDER BY Contribution.PayDate DESC;

Learn Advanced SQL Statements

The easiest way to learn more advanced SQL statements is to create Access queries in Design view and then view the SQL statement in SQL view. Although some statements might seem complex at first, the more you work with SQL, the easier it will become to understand SQL statements. You will begin to recognize that each SQL statement contains a shared syntax. For example, most SQL statements begin with SELECT and end with a semicolon (;).

Action queries can also be translated into SQL statements. Update queries, append queries, make table queries, and delete queries each have their equivalent SQL keywords and syntax. For example, suppose you wanted to add all the records in Figure 10.27 to a new table named Archive. To do this, you would create a Make Table query. The equivalent SQL statement would be:

SELECT Contribution.SSN, Contribution.PayDate, Contribution.GrossPay,

Contribution.[401KEmployee], Contribution.[401KMatch],

Contribution.[401KTotal] INTO Archive

FROM Contribution

WHERE (((Contribution.SSN)="456667778"))

ORDER BY Contribution.PayDate;

Using an SQL SELECT Statement as a Record Source

When you create a form or a report in Access, the first step is to select a record source, such as a table or a query, in the Navigation Pane. The next step is to click the Create tab and select the Form tool, Report tool, or another tool so that Access can create the new object. Once the record source is selected and the form or report has been created, you can identify it in the Property Sheet of the database object. A sample report based on the Contribution table is shown in Figure 10.29.

Contribution

Contribution

3:56:11 PM

SSN	PayDate	GrossPay	401KEmployee	401KMatch	401KTotal
112-23-3334	1/15/2018	$4,833.33	$435.00	$152.25	$587.25
122-23-3334	1/15/2018	$6,416.67	$320.83	$16.04	$336.88
123-33-4445	1/15/2018	$7,250.00	$435.00	$217.50	$652.50
223-34-4445	1/15/2018	$6,750.00	$135.00	$27.00	$162.00
233-34-4445	1/15/2018	$4,520.83	$135.63	$6.78	$142.41
234-44-5556	1/15/2018	$7,300.00	$0.00	$0.00	$0.00
334-45-5556	1/15/2018	$7,333.33	$293.33	$146.67	$440.00
344-45-5556	1/15/2018	$5,333.33	$0.00	$0.00	$0.00
345-55-6667	1/15/2018	$4,583.33	$91.67	$18.33	$110.00
455-56-6667	1/15/2018	$4,516.67	$180.67	$9.03	$189.70
456-66-7778	1/15/2018	$5,083.33	$152.50	$76.25	$228.75
566-67-7778	1/15/2018	$6,500.00	$650.00	$325.00	$975.00
667-78-8889	1/15/2018	$7,458.33	$372.92	$130.52	$503.44
677-78-8889	1/15/2018	$4,875.00	$390.00	$0.00	$390.00
778-89-9990	1/15/2018	$7,541.67	$150.83	$75.42	$226.25
788-89-9990	1/15/2018	$6,383.33	$191.50	$67.03	$258.53

FIGURE 10.29 Contribution Report Created with Contribution Table

Create an SQL Record Source for a Report

STEP 3 Based on the information you learned about SQL in this section, you should be able to create an SQL statement as the record source for a report. You know that the basic structure of an SQL statement is as follows:

```
SELECT field names
FROM table name
WHERE specified criteria must be met
ORDER BY field name;
```

The sample Contribution report, as shown in Figure 10.29, contains all of the records from the Contribution table; therefore, no WHERE clause is required. The records are not sorted in a different order than the SSN order found in the Contribution table, so no ORDER BY clause is needed. Based on this information, the SQL statement for the record source of the Contribution report is as follows:

```
SELECT *
FROM Contribution;
```

Add an SQL Record Source to a Report

Now that you know the SQL record source for the Contribution report, you can replace the existing record source (the Contribution table) with the SQL statement.

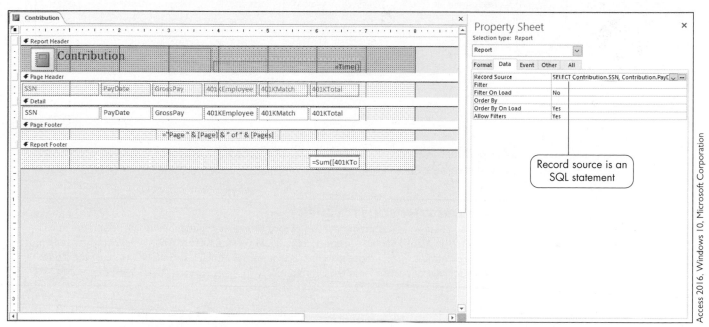

FIGURE 10.30 Contribution Report with SQL Record Source

Copy an SQL Statement from SQL View

The query discussed earlier, shown in Figure 10.26, contains SSN criteria and is sorted by PayDate. When you switch the query to SQL view, as shown in Figure 10.28, the SQL statement is displayed. Because the SQL statement is in text format, you can copy the statement and paste it into the record source of a report. For example, in the sample Contribution report, you can copy and then paste the SQL statement from the Contribution query into the Record Source property box (as shown in Figure 10.30). View the report in Print Preview, as shown in Figure 10.31.

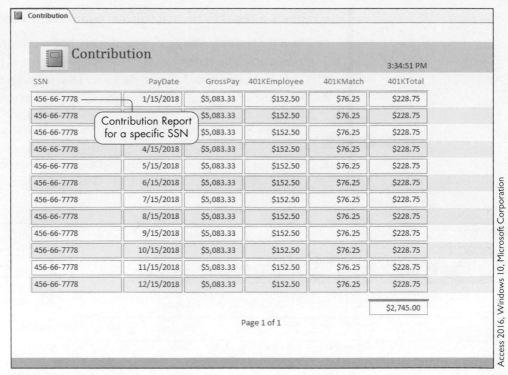

FIGURE 10.31 Contribution Report with Modified SQL Record Source

---

TIP: A LENGTHY SQL STATEMENT

When you paste an SQL statement into a record source, it might appear that the statement will not fit into the record source's property box. However, the Record Source property can hold most SQL statements, including those statements that are very long. Use Shift+F2 to open the Zoom window to view or paste a lengthy SQL statement.

Quick Concepts

7. What is the purpose of Structured Query Language (SQL)? *p. 660*

8. What is the purpose of the SQL SELECT statement? *p. 661*

9. Why would you use an SQL statement as a record source for a report? *p. 663*

Hands-On Exercises

Watch the Video for this Hands-On Exercise!

MyITLab® HOE3 Training

Skills covered: Create a Simple Query with SQL Statements • View the Equivalent SQL Statement in a Query • Create an SQL SELECT Statement as a Record Source

3 Structured Query Language

SQL will only be used in the Sunshine database in special circumstances. You suggest to Terry that you use an SQL statement for the record source of two reports. You explain that an SQL statement can be used in place of a table or query record source.

STEP 1 » **UNDERSTAND THE FUNDAMENTALS OF SQL**

You want a query that will display employees who are social workers, and you have decided to try creating it in SQL before making any changes to the Sunshine objects. You begin to create a new query, and then switch to SQL view, where you can practice writing an SQL statement. Refer to Figure 10.32 as you complete Step 1.

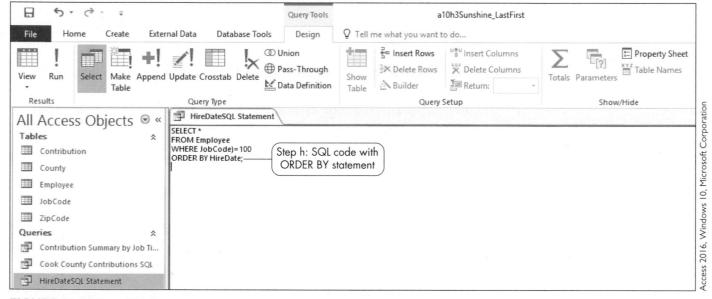

FIGURE 10.32 Basic SQL Statement

a. Open *a10h2Sunshine_LastFirst* if you closed it at the end of Hands-On Exercise 2, and save it as **a10h3Sunshine_LastFirst**, changing h2 to h3.

b. Click the **Create tab**, and click **Query Design** in the Queries group.

   The Show Table dialog box displays.

c. Close the Show Table dialog box without adding any tables.

   You will create a query using SQL statements rather than the usual query design interface.

d. Click **SQL** in the Results group.

   The abbreviated SELECT statement displays in the SQL window.

e. Move the insertion point after *SELECT* and before the semicolon (;). Type * and press **Enter**. Type **FROM Employee** to complete the SQL statement in the SQL window, and click **Run** in the Results group.

   The records for all 19 employees are displayed in the results. All fields from the Employee table also display.

f. Click the **View arrow** in the Views group, and select **SQL View**.

The current SQL statement displays in the SQL window.

g. Move the insertion point before the existing semicolon (;), revise the SQL statement to read as shown below (you only need to type the bold text), and then click **Run**.

SELECT *

FROM Employee

WHERE JobCode = 100;

You added a WHERE clause to extract only the employees who are social workers (JobCode = 100). Only eight employees are displayed in the results.

h. Click the **View arrow**, and select **SQL View**. Move the insertion point before the semicolon (;), revise the SQL statement to read as shown below (you only need to type the bold text), and then click **Run**.

SELECT *

FROM Employee

WHERE JobCode = 100

ORDER BY HireDate;

The same eight employees are displayed in the results, except now they display in HireDate order.

i. Save the query as **HireDateSQL Statement**. Click the **View arrow**, and select **Design View** to view the equivalent SQL statement in Design view. Close the query.

STEP 2 ›› CREATE A QUERY AND VIEW THE EQUIVALENT SQL STATEMENT

You want to create a query that will show all of the 401(k) contributions for Cook County employees. You want to see the equivalent SQL statement after you create the query in Design view first. Refer to Figure 10.33 as you complete Step 2.

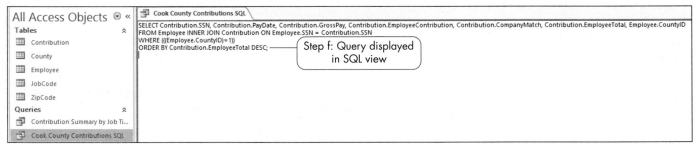

FIGURE 10.33 SQL Statement to Extract Cook County Contributions

a. Click the **Create tab**, and click **Query Design** in the Queries group.

The Show Table dialog box displays.

b. Add the Contribution and Employee tables to the Query design using the Show Table dialog box, and close the Show Table dialog box.

c. Add all the fields from the Contribution table to the query design grid. Add the CountyID field from the Employee table. Run the query.

All the fields of all 219 contributions are displayed in the results. You will add the criterion for Cook County.

d. Switch to Design view, and type **1** in the **CountyID** criteria row. Run the query.

> The numeral 1 is the Cook County ID and is used as the criterion for the search. Forty-eight contributions now display in the results.

e. Switch to Design view, and select **Descending** from the EmployeeTotal sort row. Run the query.

> The same 48 contributions are now displayed in descending EmployeeTotal order.

f. Switch to SQL view to see the equivalent SQL statement.

> You learned how to create a query in Design view first and viewed the equivalent SQL statement in SQL view.

g. Save the query as **Cook County Contributions SQL**. Close the query.

STEP 3 » USE AN SQL SELECT STATEMENT AS A RECORD SOURCE

Terry asks you to create an employee report sorted by the JobCode field. You decide to create the report based on the Employee table using the Report tool. You will then replace the Employee table record source with an SQL statement. Refer to Figure 10.34 as you complete Step 3.

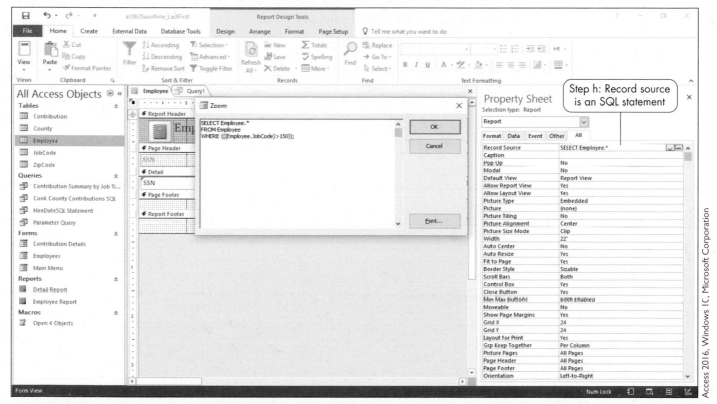

FIGURE 10.34 Report with an SQL Record Source

a. Click the **Employee table**, click the **Create tab**, and then click **Report** in the Reports group.

> Access creates a new tabular layout report.

b. Switch to Design view, ensure that the Property Sheet is open, select **Report** in the Selection type box, and then verify that the Record Source on the Data tab for the new report reads *Employee*. Close the Property Sheet.

c. Click the **Create tab**, and click **Query Design** in the Queries group.

> The Show Table dialog box displays.

d. Add the Employee table to the query design using the Show Table dialog box. Close the Show Table dialog box.

e. Add the * field from the Employee table to the query design grid. Run the query.

Nineteen employees are displayed in the results.

f. Switch to Design view, and add the JobCode field to the second column of the query design grid. Click the **Show box** for JobCode to deselect it, and type **>150** in the JobCode Criteria row. Run the query.

Six employees that match the criterion are displayed in the results.

g. Switch to SQL view, then select and press **Ctrl+C** to copy the statement in the SQL window.

h. Click the **Employee tab**, and open the Property Sheet from the Design tab. Delete the existing Record Source, and press **Ctrl+V** to paste the SQL statement you copied into the box. Press **Shift+F2**, and compare your statement with Figure 10.34.

i. Close the Zoom dialog box, and open the report in Print Preview to test the new record source.

The report does not fit onto one page; however, you can leave the report as is.

j. Save the report as **Employee Report** and close it.

k. Close the query without saving it.

l. Close the database and exit Access. Based on your instructor's directions, submit a10h3Sunshine_LastFirst.

Chapter Objectives Review

After reading this chapter, you have accomplished the following objectives:

1. Understand the purpose of a macro.

- A macro is an Access object that enables you to execute an action or series of actions. You can use macros to group a series of commands and instructions into a single database object to accomplish repetitive or routine tasks. A macro can be set to run automatically based on the status of a button, a form, or a report.

2. Create a stand-alone macro.

- A stand-alone macro displays as an object in the Navigation Pane and can be run independently of other objects. You use the Macro Designer to create a stand-alone macro. The Macro Designer is a tool in Access that makes it easier to create and edit macros. To run a stand-alone macro, double-click the macro name in the Navigation Pane.

3. Use the Macro Designer to edit a macro.

- Once you have created a stand-alone macro and determined that it works correctly, you might decide to modify, add, or delete actions. You can use the Macro Designer to edit macros in Design view. The user interface simplifies the tasks of adding actions and parameters to pre-existing macros.

4. Attach an embedded macro to an event.

- Embedded macros are attached to an event of a control on a form or report, or to an event of the form or report object itself. They can only be run from within the object.
- Create an embedded macro with the Command Button Wizard: You can add a control that automatically creates an embedded macro by using the Command Button tool to launch a wizard that prompts you through the steps. A command button can be placed on a report that will print the report, close it, or close the database automatically.
- Create an embedded macro with an event property: You can attach an embedded macro to an event by clicking the ellipsis in the Property Sheet of a specific control and associating the macro name with it.

5. Identify when to use a data macro.

- Data macros are only used with table events. You might add a data macro to a table to verify that a customer has no outstanding invoices before placing a new order, to keep track of any changes made to a specific table, or to send a confirmation email when a contributor makes a donation. A form based on a table that contains a data macro inherits the logic of the table.

6. Create an event-driven data macro.

- Event-driven data macros are triggered when a table event, such as After Delete or Before Change, occurs.
- Test and modify a data macro: To attach a data macro to a table event, open the table you want to add the data

macro to (in Design view) and click Create Data Macros in the Field, Record & Table Events group on the Design tab; to modify a data macro, reopen the macro and edit as needed.

7. Create a named data macro.

- You can access named data macros from anywhere in the database. You can run the named data macro from inside another macro using the RunDataMacro action.
- Attach a named data macro to a form: A named data macro can be run from within a form; for example, after a record is updated in a form, a macro that sends an email can be executed.

8. Understand the fundamentals of SQL.

- Structured Query Language (SQL) is the industry-standard language for defining, manipulating, and retrieving the data in a database. In fact, all Access queries use an SQL SELECT statement—behind the scenes—to extract data from tables.

9. Interpret an SQL SELECT statement.

- When you view an SQL SELECT statement in SQL view, the words shown in uppercase are SQL keywords. An SQL keyword defines the purpose and the structure of an SQL statement. The four basic keywords found in a typical SQL SELECT statement are SELECT, FROM, WHERE, and ORDER BY.
- Dissect an SQL SELECT statement: SELECT and FROM keywords: The SELECT keyword instructs Access to return the specific fields from one or more tables (or queries). The FROM keyword specifies the table (or tables) that will be searched.
- Dissect an SQL statement: WHERE keyword: The WHERE keyword specifies the criteria that records must match to be included in the results.
- Dissect an SQL statement: ORDER BY keyword: The ORDER BY keyword is used to sort the records by a certain field in either ascending or descending order.
- Learn advanced SQL statements: The easiest way to learn more advanced SQL statements is to create Access queries in Design view and then view the SQL statement in SQL view.

10. Use an SQL SELECT statement as a record source.

- Once a query is created using Design view, the SQL statements can be viewed by switching to SQL view. A correlation exists between each SQL statement and a query parameter.
- Create an SQL record source for a report: Once you know the basic structure of an SQL statement, you can use the SQL statement to create a record source that can be used as the basis for a report (or a form) rather than a table or a query.

- Add an SQL record source to a report: You can create a form or report without creating a new query because the record source is contained in the object. It is also easier to transfer a report (or a form) to another database because the record source is contained in the object. You can construct the record source of a report at run time using VBA (based on user input).

- Copy an SQL statement from SQL view: Locate the Record Source property of the form or report and either type an SQL statement into the property box or copy and paste a statement from the SQL view window.

Key Terms Matching

Match the key terms with their definitions. Write the key term letter by the appropriate numbered definition.

a. Argument
b. Data macro
c. Embedded macro
d. Event
e. FROM keyword
f. Macro
g. Macro Designer
h. ORDER BY keyword

i. SELECT keyword
j. SQL keyword
k. SQL SELECT statement
l. Stand-alone macro
m. Structured Query Language (SQL)
n. WHERE keyword

1. _____ A series of actions that can be programmed to automate tasks. **p. 634**

2. _____ A database object that you create and use independently of other controls or objects. **p. 634**

3. _____ Something that occurs when a user enters, edits, or deletes data; also occurs when a user opens, uses, or closes a form or report. **p. 635**

4. _____ A macro that executes when an event attached to a control or object occurs. **p. 635**

5. _____ A user interface that enables you to create and edit macros. **p. 635**

6. _____ A variable, constant, or expression that is needed to produce the output for an action. **p. 673**

7. _____ The industry-standard language for defining, manipulating, and retrieving the data in a database. **p. 660**

8. _____ A keyword that defines the purpose and the structure of an SQL statement. **p. 661**

9. _____ A block of text that is used to retrieve data from the tables in a database. **p. 661**

10. _____ The keyword that specifies the table (or tables) that will be searched. **p. 662**

11. _____ The keyword that instructs Access to return the specific fields from one or more tables. **p. 662**

12. _____ The keyword that is used to sort the records by a certain field in either ascending or descending order. **p. 663**

13. _____ The keyword that specifies the criteria that records must match to be included in the results. **p. 662**

14. _____ A macro that executes a series of actions when a table event occurs. **p. 649**

Multiple Choice

1. Which statement about macros is *true*?

(a) Embedded macros display in the Navigation Pane.

(b) Macros cannot be used to examine table data.

(c) The Macro Designer is the only way to automate tasks in Access.

(d) Stand-alone macros display in the Navigation Pane.

2. Which feature automatically creates an embedded macro?

(a) Macro Designer

(b) Command Button Wizard

(c) Report Wizard

(d) Form Wizard

3. Which statement is *true* about stand-alone macros?

(a) Stand-alone macros are created with the Macro Designer.

(b) Stand-alone macros exist outside the database.

(c) Stand-alone macros contain VBA code.

(d) Stand-alone macros can only be used with table data.

4. Which of these is a variable, constant, or expression that is needed to produce the output for a macro action?

(a) Command

(b) Statement

(c) Argument

(d) Event

5. Which statement is *false* for a named data macro?

(a) It must be created in a table.

(b) It cannot be attached to an event.

(c) It can be modified using the Macro Designer.

(d) It can be referenced using RunDataMacro.

6. Which event is triggered before a record is changed?

(a) Before Update

(b) On Close

(c) Before Delete

(d) After Insert

7. Which statement is *true* about SQL?

(a) It was originally invented to create formatted reports.

(b) When you create a query, SQL is created automatically.

(c) SELECT statements sort data from tables.

(d) SQL code can only be created using a special developer's interface.

8. Which SQL keyword returns a subset of the table records based on criteria?

(a) SELECT

(b) FROM

(c) WHERE

(d) ORDER BY

9. Which character separates field names in an SQL statement?

(a) >

(b) :

(c) "

(d) ,

10. Which of the following is a valid record source for a report?

(a) A data macro

(b) A SELECT statement

(c) A stand-alone macro

(d) A named data macro

Practice Exercises

1 Advertising Specialists, Inc.

Advertising Specialists, Inc., is a leading advertising agency with offices in Atlanta, Chicago, Miami, and Boston. The company asked you to create a new form named Chicago Employees that only contains employees in Chicago. You have also been asked to create a menu that users can use to open the three reports and one form. First, you will create a macro that opens the Switchboard Manager (a feature that enables you to create a menu system to navigate among objects in your database). However, you will then decide to use the Form Design to create a menu from scratch instead. Refer to Figure 10.35 as you complete this exercise.

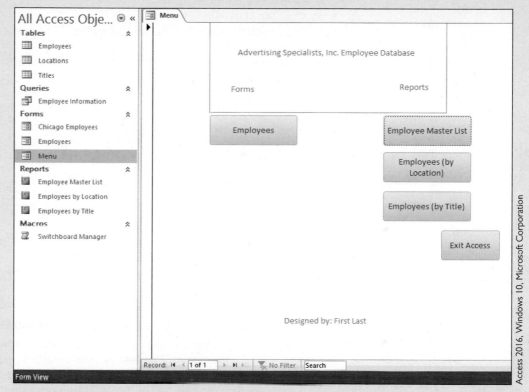

FIGURE 10.35 Menu Created with Command Buttons

a. Open *a10p1Advertise* and save it as **a10p1Advertise_LastFirst**.

b. Open the Employees table, and add yourself as a new record. Type **88888** as your EmployeeID. Type your last name, first name, and gender. Use the same values as the previous record (Marder) to complete the remaining fields. Close the table.

c. Open the Employees form in Design view. Click the **File tab**, click **Save As**, click **Save Object As**, and then click **Save As**. Type **Chicago Employees** in the Save As dialog box, and click **OK**. You will create a form that displays only Chicago employees.

d. Ensure that the Property Sheet is open, click the **Data tab**, and then click in the **Record Source property box**. Press **Shift+F2** to see a zoom view of the record source property.

e. Type **Select * From Employees Where LocationID="L03";** in the Record Source property to replace the existing Employees table with an SQL statement as the record source. Include the ending semicolon (;).

f. Click **OK**, and save the form. Switch to Form view. Advance through all the records to verify that only Chicago (L03) employees are showing. Close the form.

g. Open the **Employee Master List report** in Design view. Ensure that the Property Sheet is open, and note that the record source is the Employee Information query.

h. Open the **Employee Information query**, and switch to SQL view.

i. Copy the entire SQL statement from the query window, including the ending semicolon (;). Paste the SQL statement into the Record Source property box of the Employee Master List report, replacing Employee Information.

j. Switch to Report view of the Employee Master List report. Save and close the report, and then close the query.

k. Add the Switchboard Manager to the database by creating a macro as follows:
  - Click the **Create tab**, and then click **Macro**.
  - Enter **RunMenuCommand** in the Add New Action box. Press **Enter**.
  - Enter **SwitchboardManager** in the Command box.
  - Save the macro as **Switchboard Manager**.
  - Close the Macro Designer.
  - Right-click the macro in the Navigation Pane, and select **Design View** from the shortcut menu.
  - Type **MessageBox** in the Add New Action box. Press **Enter**.
  - Type **Please close the macro window.** (include the period) in the Message box. Press **Enter**.
  - Type **Close the Macro** in the Title box. Save and close the macro.

l. Double-click the **Switchboard Manager macro** in the Navigation Pane. The Switchboard Manager launches, but you decide not to create a switchboard. When the warning message displays, click **No** to close the dialog box. In the message box, click **OK**.

You decide to use the Form Design tool instead to create a menu from scratch. While the Switchboard Manager is an option for creating a menu system, creating a menu from scratch to navigate around the database offers an opportunity for total customization and control over your design.

m. Click the **Create tab**, and click **Form Design** in the Forms group.

n. Add the following labels, using Figure 10.35 as a guide:
  - A title label: **Advertising Specialists, Inc., Employee Database**
  - A subtitle label: **Forms**
  - A subtitle label: **Reports**

o. Use the Command Button Wizard to add the following buttons, using Figure 10.35 as a guide:
  - A button to open the Employees form. Set the text to display on the button as **Employees** and name the button **cmdEmployees**. Adjust the button position and size as shown.
  - A button to open the Employee Master List report. Set the text to display on the button as **Employee Master List** and name the button **cmdMasterEmployee**. Adjust the button position and size as shown.
  - A button to open the Employees by Location report. Set the text to display on the button as **Employees (by Location)** and name the button **cmdEmployeesLocation**. Adjust the button position and size as shown.
  - A button to open the Employees by Title report. Set the text to display on the button as **Employees (by Title)** and name the button **cmdEmployeesTitle**. Adjust the button position and size as shown.

p. Add the following button, using Figure 10.35 as a guide:
  - A button to quit the application. Set the text to display on the button as **Exit Access** and name the button **cmdExitAccess**. Adjust the button position and size as shown.

q. Add the following design elements, using Figure 10.35 as a guide:
  - A rectangle surrounding the title and the subtitle labels
  - A label at the bottom of the report: **Designed by: *your name***

r. Save the form with the name **Menu**.

s. View the Menu form in Form view. Click each button to test the functionality. Click the **Exit Access button** to test it; if Access closes, then your testing is complete.

t. Ensure that the database and Access are closed. Based on your instructor's directions, submit a10p1Advertise_LastFirst.

2 Reliable Insurance, Inc.

Reliable Insurance, Inc., has decided to raise the salary of any employee with a good performance rating by 5%. You will create a data macro to help implement this new policy. The company also creates a spreadsheet containing all employees from location L01 (Atlanta). The spreadsheet is faxed to the corporate office each month. The office manager would like to automate this process with a macro. Refer to Figure 10.36 as you complete this exercise.

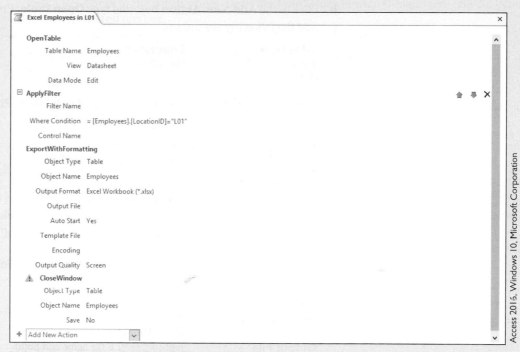

FIGURE 10.36 Macro to Export Data to Excel

a. Open *a10p2Reliable* and save it as **a10p2Reliable_LastFirst**.

b. Open the Employees table, and add yourself as a new record. Type **88888** as your EmployeeID. Type your last name, first name, and gender. Type **L01** for your location. Use the same values as the previous record (Marder) to complete the remaining fields.

c. Switch to Design view, and add a new field under the Salary field, named **SalaryAdjusted**, with data type **Currency**. Save the table.

d. Click **Create Data Macros** in the Field, Record & Table Events group on the Design tab, and click **Before Change**. The Macro Designer opens. Complete the following steps:

- Drag the **If statement** from the Program Flow folder in the Action Catalog to the Add New Action box in the macro.
- Type **[Performance]="Good"** in the Conditional expression box.
- Select **SetField** from the Add New Action arrow within the If action.
- Type **SalaryAdjusted** in the Name box.
- Type **[Salary]*1.05** in the Value box.
- Save and close the data macro.
- Click **Create Data Macros** in the Field, Record & Table Events group on the Design tab, and click **Before Change**. The Macro Designer reopens so that you can modify the macro.
- Click in the **If action**, and click the **Add Else hyperlink**.
- Select **SetField** using the Add New Action arrow.
- Type **SalaryAdjusted** in the Name box.
- Type **[Salary]** in the Value box.
- Save and close the data macro. Save the table.

Mid-Level Exercises

1 Northwind Exporters

MyITLab®
Grader

Northwind Exporters provides specialty foods to businesses around the world. You have been asked to filter the Orders form so that each employee can see only his or her orders. You will also filter a report using an SQL statement. Refer to Figure 10.37 as you complete this exercise.

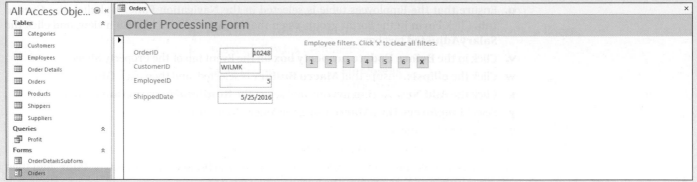

FIGURE 10.37 Filtering with an Embedded Macro

Access 2016, Windows 10, Microsoft Corporation

a. Open *a10m1Exporters* and save it as **a10m1Exporters_LastFirst**.

b. Open the Employees table and note that nine employees are shown. Close the table.

c. Open the Orders form. Advance through the orders using the Navigation bar at the bottom of the form. Notice that the EmployeeID value changes as you move to each order. Switch to Design view.

d. Add the first button to the form, as shown in Figure 10.37. Click **Cancel** when the Command Button Wizard displays. Open the Property Sheet. Set the caption of the command button to **1**. Set the size of the button to **.25"** high and **.25"** wide.

   You are planning to create an embedded macro to filter the order records for Employee ID 1 when the command button is clicked.

e. Ensure that the new 1 button is selected, and in the Property Sheet, click in the **On Click property box** on the Event tab. Click the **ellipsis**, and with Macro Builder selected, click **OK**.

f. Type **ApplyFilter** in the Add New Action box. Type **[EmployeeID]=1** in the Where Condition box. Save and close the macro.

g. Switch to Form view and notice the total orders (50), as indicated in the Navigation bar at the bottom of the form. Click **1**, and notice the total orders (4) for EmployeeID 1 in the Navigation bar. Advance through the orders, and verify the EmployeeID is 1 for each order.

h. Switch to Design view, copy the **1 button**, paste it to the right of button 1, and then set **2** as the caption. In the Property Sheet, with button 2 selected, click in the **On Click property box**, and then click the **ellipsis**. Modify the Where Condition box so it reads **2** instead of *1*. Test the new button in Form view.

i. Add buttons 3 to 6 using the same method as in Step h.

DISCOVER

j. Create a seventh button with the caption **X** to remove the filters so that all of the orders will display in the form. (*Hint:* Locate the appropriate action in the Add New Action list.) Test each new button in Form view when finished and save the form.

k. Switch to Design view. Select the seven buttons. Click **Align** in the Sizing & Ordering group on the Arrange tab to align the tops of the seven buttons. Increase the horizontal spacing between the buttons so that about two dots of space remain between them. Save and close the form.

l. Open the Customers report and take note of the range of countries represented.

m. Switch to Design view. Ensure that the Property Sheet is open, select the report, and then, on the Data tab, click the **Record Source property**. Type **SELECT * FROM Customers WHERE Country = [Enter a country];** in the record source in place of the Customers table.

n. Save the report. Switch to Print Preview, and type **USA** in the Enter Parameter Value dialog box. Click **OK**, and close the report.

o. Close the database and exit Access. Based on your instructor's directions, submit a10m1Exporters_LastFirst.

2 Payroll Service, Inc.

ANALYSIS CASE

Payroll Service, Inc., provides payroll services to midsized businesses in Massachusetts, Illinois, Colorado, and California. You have been assigned to help the company set up business logic rules using macros and data macros. Your first task is to set the default number of exemptions an employee can claim (based on marital status). You begin by setting single employees to claim only one exemption. You will also create a macro that will email the current list of employees to the main office. The main office needs the list in HTML format. Finally, you will create an SQL record source for a report.

a. Open *a10m2Salaries* and save it as **a10m2Salaries_LastFirst**.

b. Open the Employee table in Design view. Click **Create Data Macros** in the Field, Record & Table Events group, and click **Before Change**.

c. Drag the **If statement** from the Program Flow folder in the Action Catalog to the Add New Action box in the macro.

- Type **[MaritalStatus]="single"** in the If action box.
- Select **SetField** from the Add New Action arrow.
- Type **Exemptions** in the Name box.
- Type **1** in the Value box.
- Save and close the data macro.
- Save the table.

d. Switch to Datasheet view. In the first record, type **2** in the Exemptions field. Press ↓ to move to the second row to trigger the Before Change event and the data macro. The number *2* changes to *1*. Repeat the test on the second record. Close the table.

e. Click the **Create tab**, and click **Macro** in the Macros & Code group to open the Macro Designer.

f. Click in the **Add New Action box**, and type **EmailDatabaseObject**. Press **Enter**.

g. Add the following arguments:

Object Type	**Table**
Object Name	**Employee**
Output Format	**HTML (*.htm; *.html)**
To	*Your email address*
Cc	*(blank)*
Bcc	*(blank)*
Subject	Email Employee Table
Message Text	The Employee table is attached in HTML format.
Edit Message	No
Template File	*(blank)*

h. Save the macro with the name **Email Table**. Close the macro.

i. Double-click the **Email Table macro**. The macro runs and attempts to send the Employee table as an attachment. Click **OK** if you receive the Microsoft Outlook warning message, as shown in Figure 10.25. Click **OK** again, and click **Stop All Macros**.

If the warning message was not received, click **Allow**. Check your email after a few minutes to see if you received the Email Employee Table message.

DISCOVER

j. Open the Salaries by Gender report in Design view. Open the Property Sheet and verify the Record Source property contains *Employee*. Determine from the database which job code refers to which job title. Note the job code for Associate Consultant and the data type for this field.

k. Type an SQL statement into the Record Source property. The report should include all records from the Employee table except Associate Consultants. Switch to Print Preview, and verify the report contains 10 records with the overall average salary of $79,650.00. Save the report. Close the report.

l. Close the database and exit Access. Based on your instructor's directions, submit a10m2Salaries_LastFirst.

3 New Castle County Technical Services

RUNNING CASE

New Castle County Technical Services (NCCTS) provides technical support for a number of companies in the greater New Castle County, Delaware area. Now that you have completed Chapter 9, you are ready to work with macros and SQL.

a. Open the database *a09m3NCCTS_LastFirst* and save it as **a10m3NCCTS_LastFirst**. Close the NCCTS Navigation Form that opens automatically.

> **TROUBLESHOOTING:** If you did not complete the Chapter 9 case, return to Chapter 9, complete the case, and then return to this exercise.

b. Open the Archived Calls table in Datasheet view, observe the data, and then switch to Design view.

c. Add a new field named **Satisfied** to the last position in the table with a data type of Yes/No. Save the table.

d. Create a data macro attached to the Before Change event.

e. Use the SetField Action to populate the Satisfied field in the table. The Satisfied value will be set to Yes if the CustomerSatisfaction field contains a value of 3 or more. Otherwise, the Satisfied field will be set to No.

f. Save the macro. Close the macro. Save the table.

g. Switch to Datasheet view. For CallID 001, retype the Customer Satisfaction value as **5**, the next as **3**, the next as **2**, and the next as **1**. Modify the value for CallID 005 from 5 to **4** and click in the next record. Observe that the Satisfied field updates automatically as the values are entered. Close the table.

h. Open the Customer Information form, observe the data, and switch to Design view. Add an **Open Calls by Customer** button to the top-right corner of the form at the 0" mark on the vertical ruler and the 8.25" mark on the horizontal ruler, with a height of 0.5" and a width of 1.7".

i. Set the button to open the Calls by Customer report and name the button **cmdOpenCalls**.

j. Save the form, switch to Form view and click the **Open Calls by Customer** button to ensure that the report opens. Close the report and the form.

k. Open the Calls by Customer report in Design view. Open the Property Sheet, and click the **Record Source property box**. Right-click in the property box, and from the shortcut menu, click **Zoom**.

l. Add a WHERE clause to the end of the existing SQL statement that selects records from the Calls table with a customer satisfaction rating of 3 or more.

m. Test the report in Print Preview, ensure that all Customer Satisfaction values are 3 and above, and save and close the report.

n. Close the database and exit Access. Based on your instructor's directions, submit: a10m3NCCTS_LastFirst

Beyond the Classroom

Meetings

GENERAL CASE

You want to determine how many of the new employees in your database will attend orientation meetings on specific dates. You decide to create a command button to run a macro from a form that will display query results with meeting attendees. Open *a10b1Meetings* and save it as **a10b1Meetings_LastFirst**. In the New Employees Data Entry form, create a command button that will open the Orientation Meeting query. Place the button at the 5" mark on the horizontal ruler, aligned with the top of the SSN control. Set the caption of the button as **Run Orientation Meeting** and name the button **cmdOrientation**. Set the width of the button to **1.75"**. Test the button in Form view. When prompted, enter the meeting date of **11/5/2018**. Close the query. Save and close the form. Close the database and exit Access. Based on your instructor's directions, submit a10b1Meetings_LastFirst.

Troubleshoot: Fix a Macro

DISASTER RECOVERY

Open *a10b2Bonus* database and save it as **a10b2Bonus_LastFirst**. A macro named Macro—Open Objects was created to open the Employees table, the Employees Form, and the Employees Report. The macro is not working properly; the third object does not display at all, and the first two objects are read-only—you want them to open in edit mode. Analyze the macro, diagnose the problems, and then fix the problems. Save and run the macro to ensure that it works properly. Based on your instructor's directions, submit a10b2Bonus_LastFirst.

Capstone Exercise

You are employed at Specialty Foods, Ltd., a small international gourmet foods distributor. The company asked you to modify the database and improve the reliability of the data entry process. You decide to create a few macros and add a menu for the common forms and reports. You will also modify the record source of one of the reports.

Database File Setup

a. Open *a10c1Specialty* and save it as **a10c1Specialty_LastFirst**.

Create an Event-Driven Data Macro

A new field, ExpectedShipDate, was recently added to the Orders table. You will populate this new field when a new order is added using a data macro.

a. Open the Orders table in Datasheet view, observe the data, and then switch to Design view.

b. Create a data macro attached to the Before Change event.

c. Use the SetField Action to populate the ExpectedShipDate in the table. The ExpectedShipDate will always be 10 days after the OrderDate.

d. Save the macro. Close the macro. Save the table.

Test the Data Macro

You will change a value in the first record, and then move to the second record to trigger the macro.

a. Switch to Datasheet view of the Orders table.

b. Retype the OrderDate in the first record (Order No 10248), and press ↓. The macro will be triggered and automatically fill in the ExpectedShipDate with a date 10 days after the OrderDate.

c. Repeat the test on the second and third records (10249 and 10250). Close the table.

Create a Menu Form

You will create a menu form using Form Design view. Add three command buttons for the three forms in the database, and then add three command buttons for the three reports in the database.

a. Open the Main Menu form in Design view.

b. Add three buttons below the Forms label that will open the three forms in the database: Enter Customers, Enter Employees, and Enter Suppliers (in that order). Set the first one at the **2"** mark on the vertical ruler and the **1"** mark on the horizontal ruler. Set the height of the button to **0.5"** and the width to **1"**. The first button should have the caption

Enter Customers with the button named as **cmdEnterCustomers**.

c. Repeat the same procedure for Enter Employees and Enter Suppliers, setting each button immediately below the one before it.

d. Add three buttons below the Reports label that will print preview the three reports in the database: Employees, Orders, and Products (in that order). Set the first one at the **2"** mark on the vertical ruler and the **4"** mark on the horizontal ruler. Set the height of the button to **0.5"** and the width to **1"**. The first button should have the caption **Employees** with the button named as **cmdEmployees**.

e. Repeat the same procedure for Orders and Products, setting each button immediately below the one before it.

f. Save the form, switch to Form view, and then test the buttons. Close all objects except the Main Menu form.

g. Switch to Design view, add an **Exit button** that exits Access to the top-right corner of the form, at the **0"** mark on the vertical ruler and the **5"** mark on the horizontal ruler, with a height of **0.5"** and a width of **1"**. Name the button **cmdExit**.

h. Apply the **Slice theme** to the Main Menu form only. Save the form, switch to Form view, and then test the Exit button. Reopen the database.

Add an SQL Statement as a Record Source

You want to modify the records in the Employees report. You will modify the record source so that only employees with a Sales Representative position display in the report.

a. Open the Employees report in Design view. Open the Property Sheet, and click the **Record Source property box**.

b. Type an SQL statement into the Record Source property of the report. The statement should select all fields (*) for employees with the Sales Representative title. Save the report.

c. Test the report in Print Preview, and close the report.

d. Close the database and exit Access. Based on your instructor's directions, submit a10c1Specialty_LastFirst.

Access Introductory Capstone Exercise (Chs. 1–4)

You were recently hired by your local college to help with registering all transfer students. The college's Transfer Counseling Department is a one-stop location for transfer students to come with questions. They have been working with Excel spreadsheets generated by the Information Technology department, but they are hoping to do more with an Access database. They have had a number of problems, including employees putting information in the wrong fields, inputting information in the wrong format, and creating incorrect formulas. They are also hoping for more consistent ways of finding information, as well as being able to generate reports. Your tasks include importing an existing Excel worksheet as a table into your Access database; modifying the table; creating a relationship between two tables; creating queries with calculated fields, functions, and totals; creating a form for input; creating a report; and backing up the database.

Set Up the Database File and Import an Excel Worksheet

To start, you have been provided with a database the Information Technology department created. The database has one table and one form. You will be importing an Excel spreadsheet into a table and creating a primary key.

a. Open *aApp_Cap1_College* and save the database as **aApp_Cap1_College_LastFirst**.

b. Import the *aApp_Cap1_Transfer* Excel workbook into a new table named **Transfer Schools**. While importing the data, ensure that **StudentID** has a data type of **Short Text**, and select **StudentID** as the primary key.

Modify a Table

Now that you have imported the data from the spreadsheet, you will modify the field properties in the Transfer Schools table and demonstrate sorting.

a. Open the Transfer Schools table in Design view.

b. Set the StudentID field size to **10**.

c. Remove the @ symbol from the StudentID format property.

d. Change the AdmittingSchool field size to **75**.

e. Change the RegistrationFee and TuitionDue fields to have **0** decimal places.

f. Switch to Datasheet view. Resize the AdmittingSchool column by double-clicking on the border between AdmittingSchool and AdmissionDate.

g. Sort the Transfer Schools table on the CreditsTransferred field in ascending order.

h. Save and close the table.

Create Relationships

Now that the table is imported and modified, you will create a relationship between the Transfer Schools and Transfer Students tables.

a. Add the Transfer Schools and Transfer Students tables to the Relationships window.

b. Create a one-to-one relationship between the StudentID field in the Transfer Students table and the StudentID field in the Transfer Schools table. Enforce referential integrity between the two tables and cascade updates.

c. Save the changes and close the Relationships window.

Modify Data in a Form

You will demonstrate changing information in a form.

a. Open the Transfer Students Data Entry form.

b. Change the major for *Cornelius Kavanagh* to **Elementary Education**. Close the form.

Create a Query

Rey Rivera, a counselor in the center, would like your assistance in helping him find certain information. You will create a query for him and demonstrate how he can change information.

a. Create a new query using Design view. This query will access fields from both the Transfer Schools and Transfer Students tables. From the Transfer Students table, add the FirstName, LastName, Major, Class, and GPA fields. From the Transfer Schools table, add the AdmissionDate, TuitionDue, CreditsEarned, and CreditsTransferred fields.

b. Save the query as **Transfer Credits**.

c. Set the criteria in the AdmissionDate field to **8/1/2018**. Run the query (19 records will display).

d. Type **$1500** in the TuitionDue field for Diana Sullivan and type **3.51** as the GPA for Audrey Owen.

e. Save and close the query.

Create Calculated Fields

Now that you have created the query, you will create a second query for Rey that will calculate the number of credits students lost upon transfer, the tuition payments for which they will be responsible (assuming three payments per semester), and the due date of the first payment.

a. Create a copy of the Transfer Credits query. Name the copy **Transfer Credit Calculations**. Open the new query in Design view.

b. Remove the criteria from the AdmissionDate field.

c. Create a calculated field in the first empty field cell of the query named **LostCredits** that subtracts CreditsTransferred from CreditsEarned.

d. Create another calculated field named **TuitionPayments** that determines tuition paid in three installments. Using the Pmt function, replace the rate argument with **0.025/3**, the num_periods argument with **3**, and the present_value argument with the student's tuition payment. Use **0** for the future_value and type arguments. Ensure that the payment appears as a positive number.

e. Format the TuitionPayments calculated field as **Currency**.

f. Create another calculated field named **FirstPayment** after the TuitionPayments field. To calculate the due date, add **30** to their AdmissionDate. Run the query and verify that the three calculated fields have valid data.

g. Add a total row to the datasheet. Sum the TuitionDue column and average the TuitionPayment column. Save and close the query.

Create a Totals Query

Cala Hajjar, the director of the center, needs to summarize information about the transfer students for the 2018–2019 academic year to present to the College's Board of Trustees. You will create a totals query for her to summarize the number of transfer students, average number of credits earned and transferred, and total tuition earned by transfer institution.

a. Create a new query in Design view. Add the Transfer Schools table.

b. Add the AdmittingSchool, StudentID, CreditsEarned, CreditsTransferred, and TuitionDue fields.

c. Sort the query by AdmittingSchool in ascending order.

d. Show the Total row. Group by AdmittingSchool and show the count of StudentID, the average of CreditsEarned, the average of CreditsTransferred, and the sum of TuitionDue.

e. Format both average fields as **Standard**.

f. Change the caption for the StudentID field to **NumStudents**, the caption for the CreditsEarned average to **AvgCreditsEarned**, the caption for the CreditsTransferred average to **AvgCredits Transferred**, and the caption for the sum of TuitionDue to **TotalTuition**.

g. Run the query.

h. Save the query as **Transfer Summary**.

i. Close the query.

Create a Form

Hideo Sasaki, the department's administrative assistant, will handle data entry. He has asked you to simplify the way he inputs information into the new table. You will create a form based on the new Transfer Schools table.

a. Create a Split Form using the Transfer Schools table as the source.

b. Change the height of the AdmittingSchool field to be approximately half the current height.

c. Remove the layout from all the labels and fields. Shrink each field so it is approximately as large as it needs to be.

d. Click record **123455** in the bottom half of the split form. Make sure all values are still visible in the top half of the form. If not, adjust the controls so all values are visible.

e. Move the CreditsTransferred field so it is to the right of the CreditsEarned field on the same row.

f. Change the format of the TuitionDue field so the font size is **18** and the font color is **Red** (last row, second column in the Standard Colors section). Resize the field if necessary so the entire value displays.

g. Change the fill color of the StudentID field to be **Yellow** (last row, fourth column in the Standard Colors section).

h. Save the form as **Transfer Schools Form**. Save and close the form.

Create a Report

Cala is hoping you can create a more print-friendly version of the query you created earlier for her to distribute to the Board of Trustees. You will create a report based on the Transfer Credit Calculations query.

a. Create a report using the Report Wizard. Add the **Class**, **FirstName**, **LastName**, **Major**, **GPA**, and **LostCredits** fields from the Transfer Credit Calculations query. Do not add any grouping or sorting. Ensure that the report is in Landscape orientation.

b. Save the report as **Transfer Students Report** and view the report in Layout view.

Format a Report

Now that you have included the fields Cala has asked for, you will work to format the report to make the information more obvious.

a. Apply the **Wisp theme** (last row, first column) to this object only.

b. Group the report by the Class field. Sort the records within each group by LastName then by FirstName, both in ascending order.

c. Change the font size of the Class field to **16**.

d. Adjust the text boxes so the values for the Major field are completely visible.

e. Switch to Print Preview mode and verify that the report is only one page wide (Note: It may be a number of pages long).

f. Export the results as a PDF document using the file name **aApp_Cap1_Transfer_LastFirst**.

g. Save and close the report.

Close and Submit the Database

a. Create a backup of the database. Accept the default name for the backup.

b. Close all database objects and exit Access. Based on your instructor's directions, submit the following:

aApp_Cap1_College_LastFirst

aApp_Cap1_College_LastFirst_*CurrentDate*

aApp_Cap1_Transfer_LastFirst

In this project, you will add fields to a table and set data validation rules. You will also import a text file into a database, design advanced queries, and create a Navigation form. Additionally, you will use SQL to modify a record source and create an embedded macro to automate opening a report.

Database File Setup

a. Start Access. Open the file named *aApp_Cap2_Drivers*, and save it as **aApp_Cap2_Drivers_LastFirst**.

Import a Text File into the Database and Modify the Table

a. Create a table in the database by importing the delimited text file named *aApp_Cap2_Insurance_Text.txt*. Use the first row of the file as field names, use **InsuranceID** as the primary key, and then name the table **InsuranceCos_Text**. Accept all other default options.

b. Create a new field in the Agency Info table after *InsPhone* named **Web site** with the **Hyperlink data type**. Save the table. In Datasheet view, add the website **http://William_Smith.com** to the William Smith record (Record 1).

c. Create a new field in the Agency Info table after *Web site* named **AgentPhoto** with the **Attachment data type**. Save the table. In Datasheet view for Record 1 (William Smith), add the picture file named *aApp_Cap2_WmSmith.jpg* to the AgentPhoto field.

d. Set the validation rule of the InsuranceCo field to accept the values **AS**, **NAT**, or **SF** only. Set the validation text to read **Please enter AS, NAT, or SF.** (include the period).

e. Make InsuranceCo a lookup field in the Agency Info table. Set the lookup to get values from the InsuranceID field in the InsuranceCos_Text table. Accept the default label and save the table. In Datasheet view, click in any InsuranceCo cell and click the arrow to view the options. Close the table.

Create Queries to Analyze, Update, and Delete Records

a. Create a new query using Design view. From the Insurance table, add the DriverID, AutoType, TagID, and TagExpiration fields (in that order). Save the query as **Missing Tag Dates**.

b. Use Design view to set the criteria in the TagExpiration field to find null values. Run the query (two records will display). Save and close the query.

c. Create a new query using Design view. From the Drivers table, add the Class field. Change the query type to **Update** and set the criteria to update drivers whose class is *Minor* to **Junior**. Run the query (eight records will update). Save the query as **Driver Class_Update**, and close the query. View the updates in the Drivers table, and close the table.

d. Create a new query using Design view. From the Drivers table, add the Class field. Save the query as **Driver Class_Delete**.

e. Change the query type to **Delete**, and set the criteria to delete drivers whose class is **Special**. Run the query (one record will be deleted). Save and close the query. View the changes in the Drivers table, and close the table.

Create a Query to Prompt for Data

a. Create a new query using Design view. From the Insurance table, add the DriverID, AutoType, AutoYear, and TagID fields (in that order). Save the query as **Auto Year_Parameter**.

b. Set the criteria in the Auto Year field to display the prompt as **Enter the auto year:** and run the query. In the prompt, enter **2007**, and click **OK** to view the results (two records). Close the query.

Use the Performance Analyzer

a. Use the Analyze Performance tool to analyze the Drivers table. Note the idea to change the data type of the Weight field from Short Text to Long Integer. Close the Performance Analyzer dialog box. In the Drivers table, set the data type of the Weight field to **Number (Long Integer)**, and save and close the table.

Create a Navigation Form

a. Create a Navigation form based on the Vertical Tabs, Left template. Drag and drop the Drivers form onto the first tab of the form. Drop the Insurance form onto the second tab.

b. Drag and drop the Drivers report onto the third tab of the Navigation form. View the form in Form view, click each of the tabs, and then save the form as **Navigator**. Close the form.

Add an SQL Statement as a Record Source and Create an Embedded Macro

a. Open the Drivers report in Design view. Modify the record source of the report using a SQL statement to select all Drivers records with a Class of **Adult**. Print Preview the report (eight records will display). Save and close the report.

b. Open the Drivers form in Design view, click to add a command button at the intersection of the 6-inch mark on the horizontal ruler and the 3-inch mark on the vertical ruler.

c. Set the command button to open the report named Drivers. Use the default picture as the button. Set the name and the caption properties of the button in the Property Sheet to **Open Drivers Report**. Save the form. View the form in Form view, and click the command button.

d. Close all database objects, close the database, and exit Access. Based on your instructor's directions, submit aApp_Cap2_Drivers_LastFirst.

Microsoft Office 2016 Specialist Access

Online Appendix materials can be found in the Student Resources located at www.pearsonhighered.com/exploring.

MOS Obj Number	Objective Text	Exploring Chapter	Exploring Section
1.0 Create and Manage a Database			
1.1 Create and Modify Databases			
1.1.1	create a blank desktop database	**Chapter 1**, Introduction to Access	Creating a Database
1.1.2	create a database from a template	**Chapter 1**, Introduction to Access	Creating a Database
1.1.3	create a database by using import objects or data from other sources	**Chapter 2**, Tables and Queries in Relational Databases	Sharing Data
1.1.4	delete database objects	**Chapter 4**, Creating and Using Professional Forms and Reports	Form Basics, Hands-On Exercise
1.2 Manage Relationships and Keys			
1.2.1	create and modify relationships	**Chapter 2**, Tables and Queries in Relational Databases	Establishing Table Relationships
1.2.2	set the primary key	**Chapter 2**, Tables and Queries in Relational Databases	Creating and Modifying Tables and Working with Data
1.2.3	enforce referential integrity	**Chapter 2**, Tables and Queries in Relational Databases	Establishing Table Relationships
1.2.4	set foreign keys	**Chapter 2**, Tables and Queries in Relational Databases	Establishing Table Relationships
1.2.5	view relationships	**Chapter 2**, Tables and Queries in Relational Databases	Establishing Table Relationships
1.3 Navigate through a Database			
1.3.1	navigate specific records	**Chapter 1**, Introduction to Access	Recognize Database Object Types
1.3.2	create and modify a navigation form	**Chapter 4**, Creating and Using Professional Forms and Reports	Creating Forms Using Form Tools
1.3.3	set a form as the startup option	**Chapter 9**, Analyzing and Improving Database Performance	Controlling Navigation
1.3.4	display objects in the Navigation Pane	**Chapter 1**, Introduction to Access	Recognizing Database Object Types
1.3.5	change views of objects	**Chapter 1**, Introduction to Access	Recognizing Database Object Types
1.4 Protect and Maintain Databases			
1.4.1	compact a database	**Chapter 1**, Introduction to Access	Using Database Utilities
1.4.2	repair a database	**Chapter 1**, Introduction to Access	Using Database Utilities
1.4.3	back up a database	**Chapter 1**, Introduction to Access	Using Database Utilities
1.4.4	split a database	**Chapter 1**, Introduction to Access	Using Database Utilities
1.4.5	encrypt a database with a password	**Chapter 1**, Introduction to Access	Using Database Utilities
1.4.6	recover data from backup	Online Appendix	Online Appendix

MOS Obj Number	Objective Text	Exploring Chapter	Exploring Section
1.5 **Print and Export Data**			
1.5.1	print reports	**Chapter 4**, Creating and Using Professional Forms and Reports	Using Report Views
1.5.2	print records	**Chapter 4**, Creating and Using Professional Forms and Reports	Creating Forms Using Form Tools
1.5.3	save a databases as a template	**Chapter 1**, Introduction to Access	Creating a Database
1.5.4	export objects to alternative formats	**Chapter 8**, Exchanging Data Between Access and Other Applications	Exporting Data to Excel
2.0 **Build Tables**			
2.1 **Create Tables**			
2.1.1	create a table	**Chapter 2**, Tables and Queries in Relational Databases	Creating and Modifying Tables, Working with Data
2.1.2	import data into tables	**Chapter 2**, Tables and Queries in Relational Databases	Sharing Data
2.1.3	create linked tables from external sources	**Chapter 2**, Tables and Queries in Relational Databases	Sharing Data
2.1.4	import tables from other databases	**Chapter 2**, Tables and Queries in Relational Databases	Sharing Data
2.1.5	create a table from a template with application parts	**Chapter 2**, Tables and Queries in Relational Databases	Creating a Database
2.2 **Manage Tables**			
2.2.1	hide fields in tables	**Chapter 2**, Tables and Queries in Relational Databases	Creating and Modifying Tables and Working with Data
2.2.2	add total rows	**Chapter 2**, Tables and Queries in Relational Databases	Designing a Table
2.2.3	add table descriptions	**Chapter 1**, Introduction to Access	Recognizing Database Object Types
2.2.4	rename tables	**Chapter 1**, Introduction to Access	Recognizing Database Object Types
2.3 **Manage Records in Tables**			
2.3.1	update records	**Chapter 1**, Introduction to Access	Modifying Data in Table Datasheet View
2.3.2	add records	**Chapter 1**, Introduction to Access	Adding Records to a Table
2.3.3	delete records	**Chapter 1**, Introduction to Access	Deleting Records from a Table
2.3.4	append records from external data	**Chapter 8**, Exchanging Data Between Access and Other Applications	Importing an Excel Spreadsheet
2.3.5	find and replace data	**Chapter 1**, Introduction to Access	Working with Filters
2.3.6	sort records	**Chapter 1**, Introduction to Access	Performing Sorts
2.3.7	filter records	**Chapter 1**, Introduction to Access	Working with Filters
2.4 **Create and Modify Fields**			
2.4.1	add fields to tables	**Chapter 2**, Tables and Queries in Relational Databases	Creating and Modifying Tables and Working with Data
2.4.2	add validation rules to fields	**Chapter 2**, Tables and Queries in Relational Databases	Creating and Modifying Tables and Working with Data
2.4.3	change field captions	**Chapter 2**, Tables and Queries in Relational Databases	Creating and Modifying Tables and Working with Data

MOS Obj Number	Objective Text	Exploring Chapter	Exploring Section
2.4.4	change field sizes	**Chapter 2**, Tables and Queries in Relational Databases	Creating and Modifying Tables and Working with Data
2.4.5	change field data types	**Chapter 2**, Tables and Queries in Relational Databases	Creating and Modifying Tables and Working with Data
2.4.6	configure fields to auto-increment	**Chapter 2**, Tables and Queries in Relational Databases	Creating and Modifying Tables and Working with Data
2.4.7	set default values	**Chapter 2**, Tables and Queries in Relational Databases	Creating and Modifying Tables and Working with Data
2.4.8	using input masks	**Chapter 2**, Tables and Queries in Relational Databases	Creating and Modifying Tables and Working with Data
2.4.9	delete fields	**Chapter 2**, Tables and Queries in Relational Databases	Creating and Modifying Tables and Working with Data

3.0   Create Queries

3.1   Create a Query

MOS Obj Number	Objective Text	Exploring Chapter	Exploring Section
3.1.1	run a query	**Chapter 2**, Tables and Queries in Relational Databases	Running, Copying, and Modifying a Query
3.1.2	create a crosstab query	**Chapter 6**, Moving Beyond the Select Query	Summarizing Data with a Crosstab Query
3.1.3	create a parameter query	**Chapter 5**, Reducing Errors and Extracting Better Information	Customizing Output Based on User Input
3.1.4	create an action query	**Chapter 6**, Moving Beyond the Select Query	Determining When to Use an Action Query
3.1.5	create a multi-table query	**Chapter 2**, Tables and Queries in Relational Databases	Creating a Multitable Query
3.1.6	save a query	**Chapter 2**, Tables and Queries in Relational Databases	Creating a Multitable Query

3.2   Modify a Query

MOS Obj Number	Objective Text	Exploring Chapter	Exploring Section
3.2.1	rename a query	**Chapter 2**, Tables and Queries in Relational Databases	Running, Copying, and Modifying a Query
3.2.2	add fields	**Chapter 2**, Tables and Queries in Relational Databases	Creating and Modifying Tables and Working with Data
3.2.3	remove fields	**Chapter 2**, Tables and Queries in Relational Databases	Creating and Modifying Tables and Working with Data
3.2.4	hide fields	**Chapter 2**, Tables and Queries in Relational Databases	Creating and Modifying Tables and Working with Data
3.2.5	sort data within queries	**Chapter 2**, Tables and Queries in Relational Databases	Understanding Query Sort Order
3.2.6	format fields within queries	**Chapter 2**, Tables and Queries in Relational Databases	Creating and Modifying Tables and Working with Data

3.3   Create Calculated Fields and Grouping within Queries

MOS Obj Number	Objective Text	Exploring Chapter	Exploring Section
3.3.1	add calculated fields	**Chapter 2**, Tables and Queries in Relational Databases	Modifying a Multitable Query
3.3.2	set filtering criteria	**Chapter 2**, Tables and Queries in Relational Databases	Specifying Query Criteria for Different Data Types
3.3.3	group and summarize data	**Chapter 2**, Tables and Queries in Relational Databases	Specifying Query Criteria for Different Data Types
3.3.4	group data by using comparison operators	**Chapter 2**, Tables and Queries in Relational Databases	Specifying Query Criteria for Different Data Types
3.3.5	group data by using arithmetic and logical operators	**Chapter 2**, Tables and Queries in Relational Databases	Specifying Query Criteria for Different Data Types

MOS Obj Number	Objective Text	Exploring Chapter	Exploring Section
4.0 Create Forms			
4.1 Create a Form			
4.1.1	create a form	**Chapter 4**, Creating and Using Professional Forms and Reports	Creating Forms Using Form Tools
4.1.2	create a form from a template with application parts	**Chapter 4**, Creating and Using Professional Forms and Reports	Creating Forms Using Form Tools
4.1.3	save a form	**Chapter 4**, Creating and Using Professional Forms and Reports	Creating Forms Using Form Tools
4.2 Configure Form Controls			
4.2.1	move form controls	**Chapter 4**, Creating and Using Professional Forms and Reports	Form Basics, Hands-On Exercise
4.2.2	add form controls	**Chapter 4**, Creating and Using Professional Forms and Reports	Modifying Forms
4.2.3	modify data sources	**Chapter 4**, Creating and Using Professional Forms and Reports	Creating Forms Using Form Tools
4.2.4	remove form controls	**Chapter 4**, Creating and Using Professional Forms and Reports	Creating Forms Using Form Tools
4.2.5	set form control properties	**Chapter 4**, Creating and Using Professional Forms and Reports	Creating Forms Using Form Tools
4.2.6	manage labels	**Chapter 4**, Creating and Using Professional Forms and Reports	Modifying Forms
4.2.7	add sub-forms	**Chapter 4**, Creating and Using Professional Forms and Reports	Creating Forms Using Form Tools
4.3 Format a Form			
4.3.1	modify tab order	**Chapter 7**, Advanced Forms and Reports	Setting the Tab Order
4.3.2	configure print settings	**Chapter 4**, Creating and Using Professional Forms and Reports	Creating Forms Using Form Tools
4.3.3	sort records by form field	**Chapter 4**, Creating and Using Professional Forms and Reports	Sorting Records in a Form
4.3.4	apply a theme	**Chapter 4**, Creating and Using Professional Forms and Reports	Modifying Forms
4.3.5	control form positioning	Online Appendix	Online Appendix
4.3.6	insert backgrounds	**Chapter 4**, Creating and Using Professional Forms and Reports	Working with a Form Layout
4.3.7	insert headers and footers	**Chapter 4**, Creating and Using Professional Forms and Reports	Modifying Forms
4.3.8	insert images	**Chapter 4**, Creating and Using Professional Forms and Reports	Working with a Form Layout
5.0 Create Reports			
5.1 Create a Report			
5.1.1	create a report based on the query or table	**Chapter 4**, Creating and Using Professional Forms and Reports	Creating Reports Using Report Tools
5.1.2	create a report in Design view	**Chapter 4**, Creating and Using Professional Forms and Reports	Creating Reports Using Report Tools
5.1.3	create a report by using a wizard	**Chapter 4**, Creating and Using Professional Forms and Reports	Creating Reports Using Report Tools

MOS Obj Number	Objective Text	Exploring Chapter	Exploring Section
5.2 Configure Report Controls			
5.2.1	group and sort fields	**Chapter 4**, Creating and Using Professional Forms and Reports	Creating Reports Using Report Tools
5.2.2	modify data sources	**Chapter 10**, Advanced Techniques	Using an SQL SELECT Statement as a Record Source
5.2.3	add report controls	**Chapter 4**, Creating and Using Professional Forms and Reports	Modifying a Report
5.2.4	add and modify labels	**Chapter 4**, Creating and Using Professional Forms and Reports	Modifying a Report
5.3 Format a Report			
5.3.1	format a report into multiple columns	**Chapter 4**, Creating and Using Professional Forms and Reports	Modifying a Report
5.3.2	add calculated fields	**Chapter 4**, Creating and Using Professional Forms and Reports	Creating Reports Using Report Tools
5.3.3	control report positioning	**Chapter 4**, Creating and Using Professional Forms and Reports	Modifying a Report
5.3.4	format report elements	**Chapter 4**, Creating and Using Professional Forms and Reports	Modifying a Report
5.3.5	change report orientation	**Chapter 4**, Creating and Using Professional Forms and Reports	Modifying a Report
5.3.6	insert header and footer information	**Chapter 4**, Creating and Using Professional Forms and Reports	Modifying a Report
5.3.7	insert images	**Chapter 4**, Creating and Using Professional Forms and Reports	Modifying a Report
5.3.8	apply a theme	**Chapter 4**, Creating and Using Professional Forms and Reports	Modifying a Report

Glossary

Access A relational database management system in which you can record and link data, query databases, and create forms and reports.

Access Database Executable (ACCDE) A type of database file that prohibits users from making design and name changes to forms or reports within the database, and prohibits users from creating new forms and reports.

Action query A query that adds, updates, or deletes data in a database.

Add-in A custom program or additional command that extends the functionality of a Microsoft Office program.

Aggregate function A calculation performed on an entire column of data that returns a single value. Includes functions such as Sum, Avg, and Count.

AND condition A condition in a query, returns only records that meet all criteria.

Anomaly An error or inconsistency that occurs when you add, edit, and delete data.

Append query A query that selects records from one or more tables (the source) and adds them to an existing table (the destination).

Application part A feature that enables you to add a set of common Access components to an existing database, such as a table, a form, and a report for a related task.

Argument A positional reference contained within parentheses in a function such as a variable, constant, or expression, required to complete a function and produce output.

Attachment control A control that enables you to manage attached files in forms and reports.

Attachment field A field used to attach multiple files of various formats to an individual record; attached files can be launched from Access.

AutoNumber A number that automatically increments each time a record is added.

Back Up Database A utility that creates a duplicate copy of the entire database to protect from loss or damage.

Back-end database A database that contains the tables of the database.

Backstage view A component of Office that provides a concise collection of commands related to an open file.

Bound control Any control that is connected to a field in a table or query.

Calculated control A control that displays the result of an expression in a form or report.

Calculated field A field that displays the result of an expression rather than data stored in a field.

Caption property A property that is used to create a more understandable label than a field name that displays in the top row in Datasheet view and in forms and reports.

Cascade Delete Related Records When the primary key value is deleted in a primary table, Access will automatically delete all records in related tables that contain values that match the primary key.

Cascade Update Related Fields An option that directs Access to automatically change all foreign key values in a related table when the primary key value is modified in a primary table.

Clipboard An area of memory reserved to temporarily hold selections that have been cut or copied and allows you to paste the selections.

Cloud storage A technology used to store files and to work with programs that are stored in a central location on the Internet.

Column heading The field name's values that are displayed at the top of a crosstab query.

Combo Box control A control that provides a menu displaying a list of options from which the user can choose a single value.

Command A button or area within a group that you click to perform tasks.

Compact and Repair Database A utility that reduces the size of a database and fixes any errors that may exist in the file.

Comparison Operator An operator such as greater than (>), less than (<), greater than or equal to (>=), and less than or equal to (<=), etc. used to limit query results that meet these criteria.

Composite key A primary key that is made up of two or more fields.

Constant A value that does not change.

Contextual tab A tab that contains a group of commands related to the selected object.

Control A text box, button, label, or other object you use to add, edit, and display the data in a form or report.

Copy A command used to duplicate a selection from the original location and place a copy in the Office Clipboard.

Criteria row A row in Query Design view that determines which records will be selected.

Crosstab query A query that summarizes a data source into a grid (datasheet) of rows and columns.

CSV text file A file that uses a comma to separate one column from the next column, enabling the receiving software to distinguish one set of field values from the next.

Custom web app A feature which enables users to create a database that you can build and then use and share with others through the Web.

Cut A command used to remove a selection from the original location and place it in the Office Clipboard.

Data macro A macro that is triggered by table events. A data macro executes a series of actions when a table event occurs.

Data redundancy The unnecessary storing of duplicate data in two or more tables.

Data type Determines the type of data that can be entered and the operations that can be performed on that data.

Data validation A set of constraints or rules that help control data entered into a field.

Database A collection of data organized as meaningful information that can be accessed, managed, stored, queried, sorted, and reported.

Database Documenter A tool that creates a report containing detailed information for each selected object.

Database Management System (DBMS) A software system that provides the tools needed to create, maintain, and use a database.

Database Splitter A utility that enables you to convert a database into two files: a back-end database that contains the tables and a front-end database that contains the queries, forms and reports.

Datasheet view A grid containing fields (columns) and records (rows) used to view, add, edit, and delete records.

Date function A function that calculates the current date.

DatePart function A function that examines a date and displays a portion of the date.

Default value A way to specify what value that is automatically entered into a field when a new record is added to a table.

Delete query A query that selects and remove records from a table automatically.

Design view A view which gives users a detailed view of the table's structure and is used to create and modify a table's design by specifying the fields it will contain, the fields' data types, and their associated properties.

Detail section The section of the form or report where data is displayed.

Dialog box A box that provides access to more precise, but less frequently used, commands.

Dialog Box Launcher A button that when clicked opens a corresponding dialog box.

Embedded macro A macro that executes when an event attached to a control or object occurs, such as the On Click event of a command button or the On Close event of a form.

Encryption The process of altering digital information using an algorithm to make it unreadable to anyone except those who possess the key (or secret code).

Enhanced ScreenTip A small message box that displays when you place the pointer over a command button. The purpose of the command, short descriptive text, or a keyboard shortcut if applicable will display in the box.

Event An event occurs when a user enters, edits, or deletes data; events also occur when users open, use, or close forms and reports.

Excel An application that makes it easy to organize records, financial transactions, and business information in the form of worksheets.

Expression A combination of elements that produce a value.

Expression Builder An Access tool that helps you create more complicated expressions.

Field The smallest data element contained in a table, such as first name, last name, address, and phone number.

Field property A characteristic of a field that determines how it will look and behave.

Filter A feature which allows users to specify conditions to display only those records that meet those conditions.

Filter By Form A more versatile method of selecting data, enabling users to display records based on multiple criteria.

Find duplicates query A query that helps you identify repeated values in a table.

Find unmatched query A query that compares records in two related tables, and then displays the records found in one table, but not the other.

First normal form (1NF) A criterion satisfied when a table contains no repeating groups or repeating columns.

Fixed-length text file A file that allocates a certain number of characters for each field.

Footer Information that displays at the bottom of a document page.

Foreign key A field in a related table that is the primary key of another table.

Form A database object that is used to add data into or edit data in a table.

Form footer A section that displays one time at the bottom of a form.

Form header A section that displays one time at the top of the form.

Form tool A tool used to create data entry forms for customers, employees, products, and other tables.

Form view A view that provides a simplified user interface primarily used for data entry; does not allow you to make changes to the layout.

Format Painter A feature that enables you to quickly and easily copy all formatting from one area to another in Word, PowerPoint, and Excel.

FROM keyword A keyword that specifies the table (or tables) that will be searched in an SQL SELECT statement.

Front-end database A database that contains the queries, forms, and reports of the database.

Function A predefined computation that simplifies creating a complex calculation and produces a result based on inputs known as arguments.

Functional dependency A condition that occurs when the value of one field is determined by the value of another.

Gallery An area in Word which provides additional text styles. In Excel, the gallery provides a choice of chart styles, and in Power Point, the gallery provides transitions.

Group A subset of a tab that organizes similar tasks together.

Group footer A section that appears one time for each unique value in the grouping, below the group.

Group header A section that appears one time for each unique value in the grouping, above the group.

Grouping A method of summarizing data by the values of a field.

Header An area with one or more lines of information at the top of each page.

Hyperlink A data type that enables you to quickly link to any file on your computer or to a webpage on the Internet.

IIf function A function that evaluates an expression and displays one value when the expression is true and another value when the expression is false.

Importing A process that enables you to copy external data into your database without linking it to its source file.

Index A setting for a field that reduces the time it takes to run queries and reports.

Input mask A setting that restricts the data being input into a field by specifying the exact format of the data entry.

Input Mask Wizard A tool used to generate data restrictions (an input mask) for a field.

IsNull function A function that checks whether a field has no value.

Label Wizard A feature that enables you to easily create mailing labels, name tags, and other specialized tags.

Landscape orientation A document layout when a page is wider than it is tall.

Layout control A tool that provides guides to help keep controls aligned horizontally and vertically and give your form a uniform appearance.

Layout view A view that enables users to make changes to a layout while viewing the data in the form or report.

Linking A process that enables you to connect to a table or spreadsheet without having to import the data into your database.

Live Preview An Office feature that provides a preview of the results of a selection when you point to an option in a list or gallery. Using Live Preview, you can experiment with settings before making a final choice.

Lookup field A way to provide the user with a predefined list of values to choose from in a menu.

Lookup Wizard A tool that helps you create a menu of predefined values (lookup field) by asking you questions and using your answers to create the options list.

Macro A stored series of commands that carry out an action; often used to automate simple tasks.

Macro Designer A user interface that enables you to create and edit macros.

Make table query A query that selects records from one or more tables and uses them to create a new table.

Margin The area of blank space that displays to the left, right, top, and bottom of a document or worksheet.

Microsoft Office A productivity software suite including a set of software applications, each one specializing in a particular type of output.

Mini toolbar A toolbar that provides access to the most common formatting selections, such as adding bold or italic, or changing font type or color. Unlike the Quick Access Toolbar, the Mini toolbar is not customizable.

Module An advanced object written using the VBA (Visual Basic for Applications) programming language.

Multiple Items form A form that displays multiple records in a tabular layout similar to a table's Datasheet view, with more customization options than a datasheet.

Multitable query Results contain fields from two or more tables, enabling you to take advantage of the relationships that have been set in your database.

Navigation form A tabbed menu that ties the objects in the database together so that the database is easy to use.

Navigation Pane An Access interface element that organizes and lists the objects in an Access database.

Non-key field Any field that is not part of the primary key.

Normal forms The rules to optimize and fix potential repetition issues in a database.

Normalization The process of efficiently organizing data so that the same data is not stored in more than one table, and that related data is stored together.

Null The term Access uses to describe a blank field value.

Object (Access) A component created and used to make the database function (such as a table, query, form, or report).

One-to-many relationship When the primary key value in the primary table can match many of the foreign key values in the related table.

OneDrive Microsoft's cloud storage system. Saving files to OneDrive enables them to sync across all Windows devices and to be accessible from any Internet-connected device.

OR condition In a query, returns records meeting any of the specified criteria.

ORDER BY keyword A keyword that is used to sort the records by a certain field in either ascending or descending order in an SQL SELECT statement.

Order of operations A rule that controls the sequence in which arithmetic operations are performed. Also called the *order of precedence*.

Page footer A section that displays at the bottom of each page in a form or report.

Page header A section that displays at the top of each page in a form or report.

Parameter query A query where the user provides the criterion at run time.

Paste A command used to place a cut or copied selection into another location.

Performance Analyzer A tool that evaluates a database and then makes recommendations for optimizing the database.

Picture A graphic file that is retrieved from storage media or the Internet and placed in an Office project.

Pmt function A function that calculates the periodic loan payment given a fixed rate, number of periods (also known as term), and the present value of the loan (the principal).

Portable Document Format (PDF) A file format type created by Adobe Systems in 1993 for document exchange, independent of software application and operating system environment.

Portrait orientation A document layout when a page is taller than it is wide.

PowerPoint An application that enables you to create dynamic presentations to inform groups and persuade audiences.

Primary key The field (or combination of fields) that uniquely identifies each record in a table.

Print Preview A view that enables you to see exactly what the report will look like when it is printed.

Property Sheet The location where you change settings such as number format and number of decimal places.

Query A question about the data stored in a database answers provided in a datasheet.

Quick Access Toolbar A toolbar located at the top-left corner of any Office application window, this provides fast access to commonly executed tasks such as saving a file and undoing recent actions.

Read-only form A form that enables users to view but not change data.

Record A group of related fields representing one entity, such as data for one person, place, event, or concept.

Record source The table or query that supplies the records for a form or report.

Referential Integrity Rules in a database that are used to preserve relationships between tables when records are changed.

Relationship A connection between two tables using a common field.

Report A database document that outputs meaningful, professional-looking, formatted information from underlying tables or queries.

Report footer A section that displays one time at the bottom of a report.

Report header A section that displays one time at the top of the report.

Report tool A tool used to instantly create a tabular report based on the table or query currently selected.

Report view A view that enables you to determine what a printed report will look like in a continuous onscreen page layout.

Report Wizard A feature that prompts you for input and then uses your answers to generate a customized report.

Ribbon The command center of Office applications. It is the long bar located just beneath the title bar, containing tabs, groups, and commands.

Rich Text Format (RTF) A file format that enables documents created in one software application to be opened with a different software application.

Round function A function that returns a number rounded to a specific number of decimal places.

Row heading The field values displayed along the left side of a crosstab query.

Second normal form (2NF) A criterion satisfied when a table that meets 1NF criteria and all non-key fields are functionally dependent on the entire primary key.

Section A part of a form or report that can be manipulated separately from other parts of a form or report.

Section bar A bar that marks the top boundary of a section.

SELECT keyword A keyword that determines which fields will be included in the results of an SQL SELECT statement.

Selection Filter A method of selecting that displays only the records that match a criterion you select.

Shortcut menu A menu that provides choices related to the selection or area at which you right-click.

Simple Query Wizard Provides a step-by-step guide to help you through the query design process.

Smart Lookup A feature that provides information about tasks or commands in Office, and can also be used to search for general information on a topic such as *President George Washington*.

Sort A feature which lists records in a specific sequence.

Split form A form that combines two views of the same record source—one section is displayed in a stacked layout and the other section is displayed in a tabular layout.

SQL keyword A keyword that defines the purpose and structure of an SQL statement.

SQL SELECT statement A statement that is used to retrieve data from the tables in a database.

Stacked layout A layout that displays fields in a vertical column.

Stand-alone macro A macro that can be used independently of other controls or objects.

Status bar A bar located at the bottom of the program window that contains information relative to the open file. It also includes tools for changing the view of the file and for changing the zoom size of onscreen file contents.

Structured Query Language (SQL) The industry-standard language for defining, manipulating, and retrieving the data in a database.

Subform One form contained within another form.

Tab Located on the Ribbon, each tab is designed to appear much like a tab on a file folder, with the active tab highlighted.

Tab order The sequential advancing in a form from one field or control to the next when you press Tab.

Table The location where all data is stored in a database; organizes data into columns and rows.

Table Analyzer A tool that evaluates the tables in a database and normalizes them for you.

Tabular layout A layout that displays fields horizontally.

***Tell me what you want to do* box** Located to the right of the last tab, this box enables you to search for help and information about a command or task you want to perform and also presents you with a shortcut directly to that command.

Template (Access) A predefined database that includes professionally designed tables, forms, reports, and other objects that you can use to jumpstart the creation of your database.

Template A predesigned file that incorporates formatting elements, such as a theme and layouts, and may include content that can be modified.

Text file A common file format for exchanging data between two computer systems.

Theme A collection of design choices that includes colors, fonts, and special effects used to give a consistent look to a document, workbook, presentation, or database form or report.

Third normal form (3NF) A criterion satisfied when a table meets 2NF criteria and no transitive dependencies exist.

Title bar The long bar at the top of each window that displays the name of the folder, file, or program displayed in the open window and the application in which you are working.

Toggle commands A button that acts somewhat like light switches that you can turn on and off. You select the command to turn it on, then select it again to turn it off.

Total row A method to display aggregate function results as the last row in Datasheet view of a table or query.

Totals query A way to display aggregate data when a query is run.

Transitive dependency A condition that occurs when the value of one non-key field is functionally dependent on the value of another non-key field.

Unbound control Any control not tied to a specific field.

Uniform Resource Locator (URL) The location of a website or webpage on the Internet.

Update query An action query that changes the data values in one or more fields for all records that meet specific criteria.

Validation rule A setting that limits the data values a user can enter into a field.

Validation text A setting that provides a custom error message to the user when incorrect data is entered.

View The various ways a file can appear on the screen.

WHERE keyword A keyword that specifies the criteria that records must match to be included in the results of an SQL SELECT statement.

Wildcard A special character that can represent one or more characters in the criterion of a query.

Word An application that can produce all sorts of documents, including memos, newsletters, forms, tables, and brochures.

XML Paper Specification (XPS) A file format developed by Microsoft and designed to display a printed page on screen identically on any computer platform.

Zoom slider A feature that displays at the far right side of the status bar. It is used to increase or decrease the magnification of the file.

Index

A

Access
- connecting to external files, 497–507
- importing Excel spreadsheet to, 547–549
- importing text file into, 551–553

Access 2016, 4
- Database Tools tab, 78
- defined, 70
- External Data tab, 77–78
- fields, 74
- form, 75
- Form tools, 270–279
- macro object, 77
- module object, 77
- primary key, 74
- record, 74
- report, 76
- tables, 74
- template, 113

Access database
- linking to, 540–542

Access Database Executable (ACCDE), 73
- compatibility issues, 603
- creating, 602–603
- defined, 602

action queries, 392–393
- benefits of, 393
- defined, 392
- icons, 403
- saving and reusing, 403
- testing of, 393
- using, 392–393

adding
- attachment control to form, 505–506
- attachment control to report, 506–507
- attachment field, 502–503
- calculated control, 467–469
- default field value, 334–335
- emphasis to forms/report, 464–465
- fields, 280–281
- field to report, 305–306
- hyperlink field in design view, 499
- index, 585
- page break control, 469–470
- page break to group footer, 478
- password, 600–602
- records to desktop database, 116–117
- records to table, 86–88
- SQL record source to a report, 664–665
- subform, 275–276
- text or images to form/report, 465–467
- totals to footer, 477–478
- validation rule with validation text, 336–337

add-ins, installing, 17–18
advanced controls, 463–470
advanced functions
- using, 355–369
advanced select queries
- data analysis using, 352–369
advanced SQL statements, 663
aggregate functions, 243–249
- creating, 244–249
- and datasheets, 243–244
- defined, 243
AND condition, 180
anomaly, 608
append query, 392
- adding records to a table with an, 397–400
- creating select query before running, 398
- defined, 397
- run an, 399–400
- set append to fields in an, 398–399
application part
- databases, 117–118
arguments, 635
- falsepart, 360–363
- truepart, 360–363
attachment control, 504
- adding, 504–507
- adding to form, 505–506
- adding to report, 506–507
attachment field, 501
- adding, 502–503
- creating, 501–502
- editing, 502–503
- removing, 504
AutoNumber data types, 146

B

back-end database, 589
backgrounds
- forms, 285
Backstage view, 42–44
- customizing application options, 43
Back Up Database utility, 89–90
blank desktop database, 114
bound control, 463
built-in analysis and design tools, 580–591
- Database Documenter, 581–583
- Database Splitter, 589–591
- Performance Analyzer, 583–585
- Table Analyzer, 586–589
built-in functions, 234–237

C

calculated control, 464
- adding, 467–469
calculated field/result
- common errors, 223–224
- defined, 218
- queries, 218–222
- totals query, 248–249
- verifying, 225
Caption property, 148
Cascade Delete Related Records, 162
Cascade Update Related Fields, 162
checking spelling and grammar, 32–34
Clipboard, 30–32
cloud storage, 5
column heading, 412
column widths
- in forms, 280
- in reports, 306
combo box
- converting text box to, 448–449
- customizing, 449–451
Combo Box control, 448
Command Button Wizard
- creating embedded macro with, 637–639
commands
- defined, 10
- toggle, 27
Compact and Repair Database utility, 90–91
comparison operators, 180
composite key, 612
constant
- defined, 218
contextual tabs, 9
control(s)
- bound, 463
- calculated, 464
- defined, 272, 463
- forms, 282–283
- Layout view, 274
- page break, 469–470
- reports, 307
- unbound, 463
converting
- RTF to Word format, 521
- select query to update query, 394–395
- text box to combo box, 448–449
copying
- queries, 182–183
- text, 31

rerunning, 397
testing, 395–396
updating data with, 393–397
verifying, 397
usability testing, 271
user input
customizing output based
on, 352–355

validation rule
adding with validation text, 336–337
validation text
adding validation rule with, 336–337

values
in date range, 181
viewing
XPS, 527

Web app databases, 118–119
WHERE keyword, 662–663
wildcards, 179
Word
converting RTF to, 521
exporting data to, 521–524
exporting queries to, 523
exporting tables and queries to, 523

modifying RTF to, 523–524
selecting record source, 522
Word 2016, 4

XML Paper Specification (XPS)
defined, 525
exporting data to, 525–527
viewing, 527

Z

Zoom slider, 44